MOON HANDBOOKS®
NEW ORLEANS

© ANDREW COLLINS

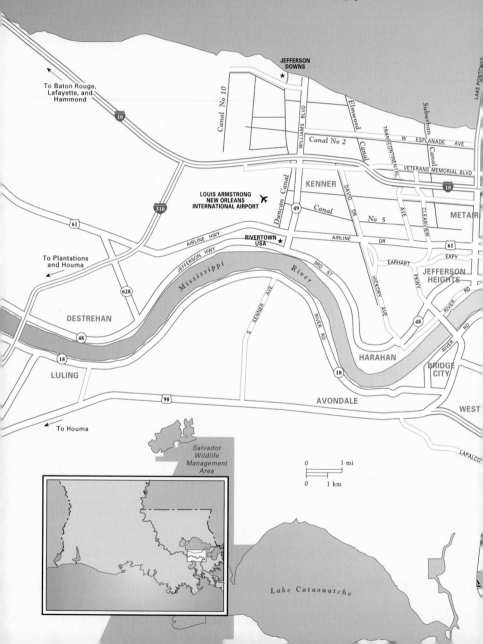

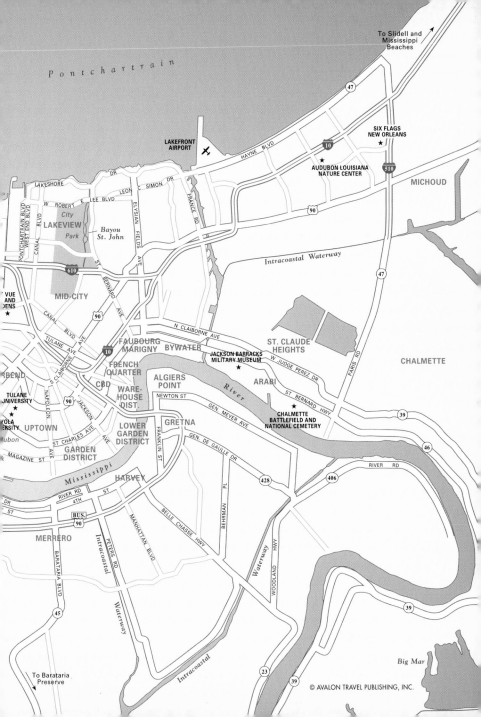

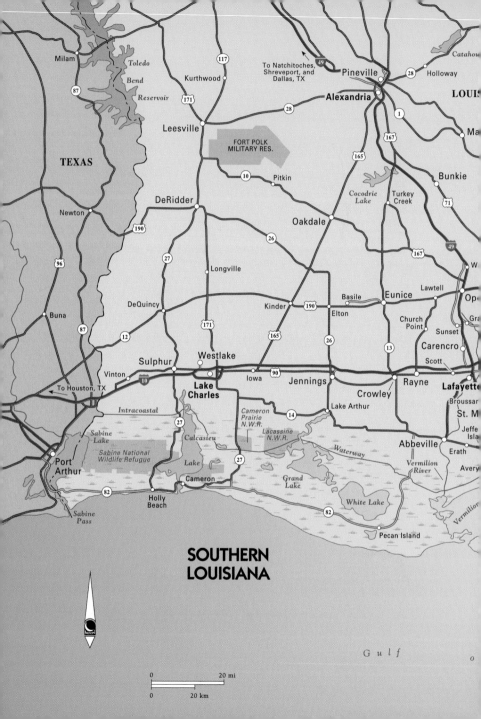

SOUTHERN
LOUISIANA

Deer Park

To Natchez, MS

To Jackson, MS

MISSISSIPPI

Mississippi River

15

Gloster

24

24 48

51

55

Bogue Chitto

98

Woodville

24

Angola

Tunica

Clinton

Kentwood

Tangipahoa

25

21

1

Jackson

67

Greensburg

Roseland

Franklinton

Bogalusa

St. Francisville

19

Amite

16

Amite

River

Folsom

Bush

To Hattiesburg, MS and Birmingham, AL

Morganza

New Roads

Independence

51

Abita Springs

Picayune

190

Denham Springs

Livingston

190

Hammond

Covington

41

59

Maringouin

12

Ponchatoula

Madisonville

Lacombe

10

Baton Rouge

1

61

Prairieville

22

Manchac

Mandeville

190

Slidell

10

Plaquemine

Gonzales

Sorrento

Lake Maurepas

55

Reserve

Metairie

Lake Pontchartrain

To Gulfport, MS and Mobile, AL

Lake Borgne

New Iberia

Lake Fausse Pointe State Park

White Castle

Burnside

Donaldsonville

Gramercy

61

10

Kenner

NEW ORLEANS

Lake Borgne

18

Lutcher

Boutte

Harahan

Gretna

Shell Beach

Jeanerette

90 182

Napoleonville

Lac Des Allemands

Luling

Westwego

Harvey

Lake Verret

Thibodaux

Des Allemands

Lake Salvador

Crown Point

Delacroix

Franklin

1

90

Barataria

39

Patterson

Morgan City

Lockport

Larose

Waterway

23

Breton Sound

Lower Atchafalaya River

Intracoastal

Houma

Bayou Terrebonne

Cut Off

Barataria Bay

Atchafalaya Bay

Chauvin

Bayou Lafourche

Leeville

Grand Isle

Cocodrie

Terrebonne Bay

Port Fourchon

M e x i c o

LAKE PONTCHARTRAIN CAUSEWAY (TOLL)

GREATER NEW ORLEANS MAPS

METAIRIE, KENNER, AND THE AIRPORT
Food 220–221

MID-CITY
Sights 102–103
Food 216–217

GREATER NEW ORLEANS
Accommodations 172–173

FRENCH QUARTER AND FAUBOURG MARIGNY
Sights 54–55
Entertainment 112–113
Accommodations 152–153
Food 186–187

CENTRAL BUSINESS AND WAREHOUSE DISTRICTS
Sights 84–85
Entertainment 130–131
Accommodations 160–161
Food 202–203

GARDEN DISTRICT AND UPTOWN
Sights 90–91
Garden District Accommodations 168–169
Garden District Food 208–209
Uptown and Riverbend Food 211

Lake Pontchartrain

LAKE PONTCHARTRAIN CAUSEWAY (TOLL)

METAIRIE

KENNER

JEFFERSON HEIGHTS

MID-CITY

LAKEVIEW

GARDEN DISTRICT

UPTOWN

RIVERBEND

City Park

Audubon Park

Mississippi River

LEON C. SIMON DR

FRANCE RD

ELYSIAN FIELDS AVE

N CLAIBORNE AVE

NEWTON ST

BEHRMAN PL

ST. BERNARD AVE

CANAL BLVD

PONTCHARTRAIN BLVD

WEST END BLVD

CANAL AVE

TULANE AVE

JACKSON AVE

ST. CHARLES AVE

MAGAZINE ST

NAPOLEON AVE

LEAKE AVE

RIVER RD

4TH ST

LABARRE DR

BONNABEL BLVD

METAIRIE RD

W ESPLANADE AVE

VETERANS MEMORIAL BLVD

CLEARVIEW PKWY

EXPY

EARHART

TRANSCONTINENTAL

AVE

61

DAVID DR

AIRLINE DR

WILLIAMS BLVD

3RD ST

HICKORY AVE

RIVER RD

S KENNER AVE

RIVER RD

48

541

90

10

610

49

BUS 90

0   1 mi
0   1 km

© AVALON TRAVEL PUBLISHING, INC.

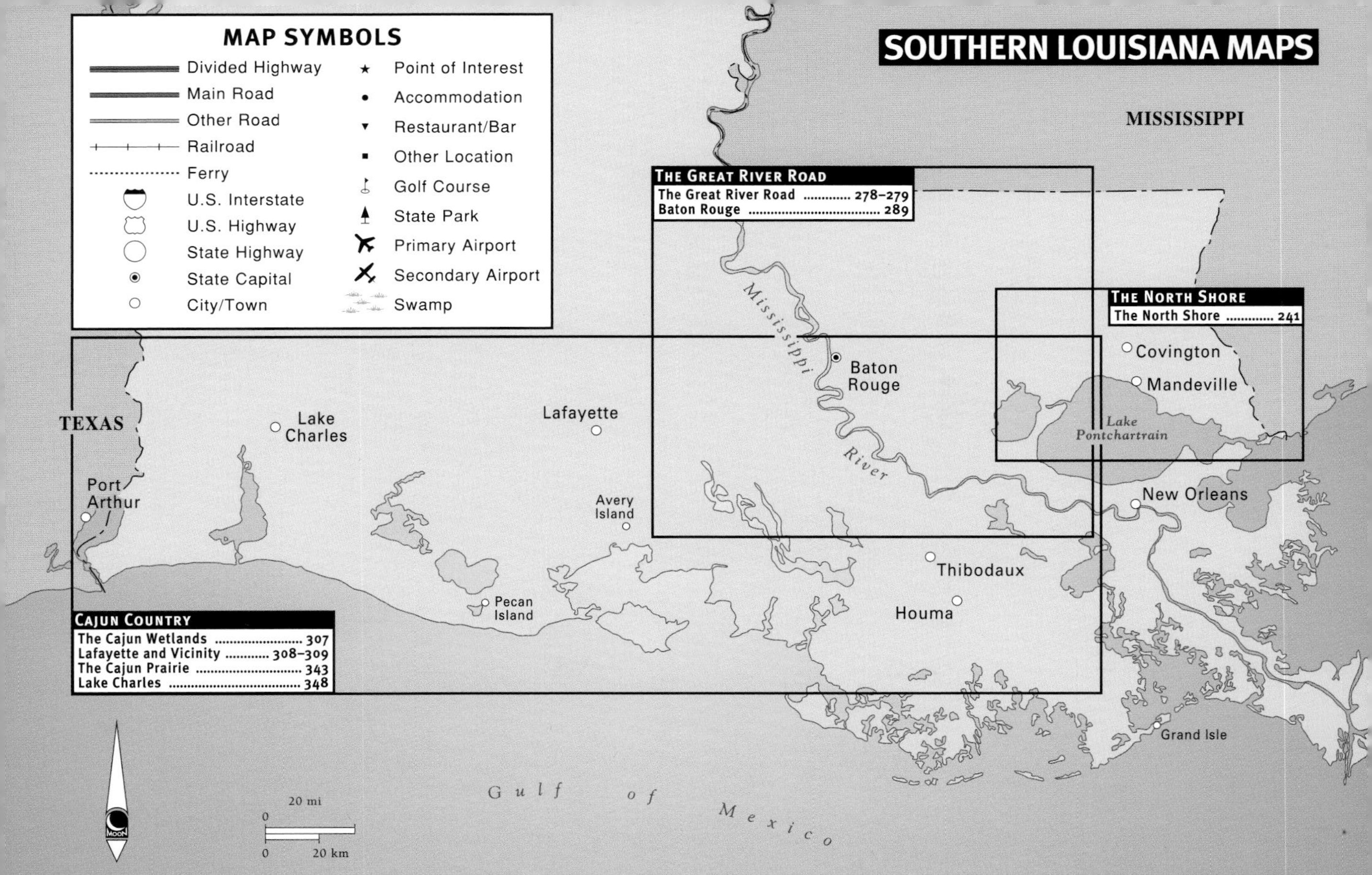

SOUTHERN LOUISIANA MAPS

MAP SYMBOLS

Divided Highway	★	Point of Interest
Main Road	●	Accommodation
Other Road	▼	Restaurant/Bar
Railroad	■	Other Location
Ferry	⛳	Golf Course
U.S. Interstate	▲	State Park
U.S. Highway	✈	Primary Airport
State Highway	✕	Secondary Airport
State Capital	◉	Swamp
City/Town	○	

MISSISSIPPI

Covington
Mandeville
Lake Pontchartrain
New Orleans
Grand Isle

Baton Rouge

Mississippi River

Thibodaux
Houma

Lafayette

Avery Island

Pecan Island

Lake Charles

Gulf of Mexico

TEXAS

Port Arthur

0   20 mi
0   20 km

© AVALON TRAVEL PUBLISHING, INC.

sunset over Lake Pontchartrain

© ANDREW COLLINS

MOON HANDBOOKS®

NEW ORLEANS

INCLUDING CAJUN COUNTRY AND THE RIVER ROAD PLANTATIONS

FIRST EDITION

ANDREW COLLINS

AVALON
TRAVEL

Contents

Introduction

No other city inspires such adoration from outsiders. They offer fervent hallelujahs in its cathedrals of cool jazz, and flirt with go-cup martyrdom on Bourbon Street. They pray to the gods of Creole cuisine in sleek bistros and raffish dives alike. Come join the ranks of the faithful. You just may find salvation in the debauched charms of this sultry subtropical metropolis on the Mississippi.

On the Road

Here's the lowdown on how to crash the never-ending party in the Big Easy without losing your head . . . or emptying your bank account.

Sights

Follow the path of the Voodoo Queen through the city of the dead. Tour Italianate mansions in the Garden District. Bask in the French Quarter's saucy yet genteel charms. New Orleans was made for wandering.

Entertainment

The first and last words in New Orleans entertainment are "Mardi Gras." But the festivities continue year-round—walk along Bourbon Street any night of the week to see for yourself. This is also one of the world's premier music venues, with jazz, blues, rockabilly, soul, and zydeco . . . all yours for the listening.

Accommodations 144

*Whether you want to spend your nights in
a Gothic Victorian manse, a historic bed-
and-breakfast, or a luxurious postmodern
tower, it's easier than ever to find a great
place to stay in New Orleans.*

Food 178

*Po'boys, gumbo, and étouffée, oh my!
Culinary epiphanies are not unusual in New
Orleans—some visitors experience two or
three. Food is more than a major attraction
here: it's the city's raison d'être.*

Shopping

Eighteenth-century French antiques, oil paintings, thousand-dollar Mardi Gras masks . . . the wares on display are as exotic as the city itself.

The North Shore

Separated from New Orleans by enormous Lake Pontchartrain, the vintage towns of the North Shore are abundant with funky historic districts, affordable boutiques and eateries, and forests dense with towering pines. They also make a convenient base for exploring the rest of Louisiana.

The Great River Road

Louisiana's near-mythic past lingers on in these charming old-world towns, where Spanish moss hangs from 200-year-old oaks, plantation homes rise like enormous Greek Revival wedding cakes, and fields of sugarcane seem to go on forever.

Cajun Country

Acadiana may be just a few hours' drive, but it's worlds away from city life in New Orleans. This is where people play boneshaking zydeco for the sheer joy of it, and everything from the jambalaya to the gumbo is served up hot and spicy.

ABOUT THE AUTHOR
Andrew Collins

© SUSAN CROSS

Travel writer Andrew Collins spends most of his life on the road, driving back and forth across North America, logging about 40,000 miles annually. He has visited more than 1,750 of the nation's 3,145 counties, and has spent more than 2,000 nights residing in hotel rooms, slumming with friends, or crashing with various relatives—he is always most appreciative of his hosts' kind generosity. Of the several places he's always wanted to live, New Orleans has thus far eluded him, but he visits as often as possible and enjoyed spending the better part of six months in southern Louisiana researching this book.

Andrew presently lives in Santa Fe, New Mexico. In recent years, he's also lived in Manhattan, Brooklyn, Connecticut's Litchfield Hills, and New Hampshire's Lake Sunapee region, and he's spent extended periods in Atlanta, Boston, San Francisco, and Rhode Island, as well as overseas in London and Amsterdam. He grew up in Connecticut, where he graduated from Wesleyan University in 1991.

He has contributed to more than 125 travel books as both writer and editor, authoring *Moon Handbooks Rhode Island* and *Moon Handbooks Connecticut*. Andrew's travel column, "Out of Town," appears in dozens of gay and lesbian newspapers throughout North America; he also writes regularly for several magazines, including *Travel + Leisure, Frommer's Budget Travel,* and *Sunset.*

On those rare occasions when he's not on the road, Andrew can be found browsing the goods at farmers' markets and gourmet food stores, or putting them to use in his kitchen. He also enjoys a variety of outdoors activities, including jogging, kayaking, and hiking, and follows professional baseball with a disturbing degree of fanaticism. A confessed pop-culture junkie, he scans online newspapers and newswires every day in search of odd trivia and amusing gossip about has-been celebrities. After finishing one of his guidebooks, he's been known to watch late-night sitcoms and cooking shows for hours on end, until fading blissfully into a trance-like stupor. Such is the life of the professional traveler . . .

Introduction

If you want to experience the real New Orleans, you'll find that perspective is everything. There is a part of the city that exists mainly for the amusement of tourists. Take the larger-than life outrageousness, even wantonness, that is Mardi Gras. Parade marchers dressed in everything from pink afro wigs to papier mâché lion's masks to grass hula skirts gyrate, samba, and cartwheel down St. Charles Avenue. In the French Quarter, automobile traffic is suspended and revelers crowd the streets, begging onlookers to toss them trinkets from the balconies above. You can see every costume and accessory imaginable: feather boas, chiffon togas, Indian headdresses, Easter bunny suits, leather chaps . . . and *everybody* is draped in strings of brightly colored beads. Around the Quarter, at least,

acts of licentious and drunken exhibitionism are the norm. This is the Mardi Gras most visitors expect. And it shouldn't be missed.

However, even during this massive celebration, which virtually shuts down the city's downtown, it's possible to witness a simpler slice of genuine New Orleans—to see locals just being themselves, relaxing with friends and family, and watching a good show. Move away from the frenetic French Quarter and head toward Uptown, a few blocks beyond the Central Business District. Arrive a bit before the start of one of the parades that rumbles down St. Charles Avenue in the days before Fat Tuesday. Instead of glassy-eyed tourists hollering and flashing each other, you're likely to see parents hoisting their toddlers into makeshift wooden seats bolted to the

Jackson Square,
French Quarter

tops of six-foot-tall stepladders, the better to catch the doubloons, beads, and other trinkets coming their way. If you didn't know any better, you might think you'd stumbled upon a small-town homecoming parade, not a libertine fracas whose highlights are immortalized each year in *Girls Gone Wild* videos.

It's true anywhere, but especially in a city as celebrated as New Orleans: If you make a point of checking out the less touristy parts of the city, you can come away with an entirely different sense of both the place and its inhabitants. But don't think the off-the-beaten-path experience is any more authentic than, or somehow superior to, the one you get hanging out in the touristy neighborhoods. New Orleans is a tourist-driven place—the city defines itself in large part by the zany circus it puts on every day of the year for outsiders. Thumb your nose all you want at the leisure-suit Larrys boarding swamp-tour boats and the rowdy college kids trawling the 24-hour daiquiri bars. They're as much a part of this city's identity as the lifelong locals who steer clear of the French Quarter year-round.

Bourbon Street may be the grand concourse of decadence, but it's exhilarating, too. Walk up and down this booze-soaked pedestrian mall and you will hear music. Maybe it's the sounds of a brass band emanating from a swanky jazz club. That's what you hear with your left ear, anyway. Your right ear catches some truly awful karaoke streaming out of a sports bar where convention-eers branded with "Hello, my name is" stickers gather to slurp down $2 hurricanes. Even with all that noise, both ears still pick up the sugary crooning of a guy singing Jimmy Buffett covers at another club. Wherever you walk along Bourbon Street, you're likely to hear sounds that clash like plaid slacks, a striped blazer, and a polka-dot necktie. From block to block, the specific sounds change, but the cacophony remains constant. Such a racket would be annoying, even infuriating, anywhere else. But it's all part of the music of New Orleans—this is why you came. You may not want to spend too much time stumbling along Bourbon Street, but to skip it entirely . . . well, you may as well not come at all.

Food is just as integral to understanding New Orleans. Many visitors experience one, maybe even two or three culinary epiphanies here. You may first *get* the whole New Orleans food scene while dining someplace fancy, perhaps one of the dozen or so restaurants around town that have been serving food since the Coolidge administration. That's all well and good, but you don't have to pray in the cathedrals to be touched by the city's culinary gods. Gustatory greatness is more often achieved by noshing on something relatively simple.

What's amazing about New Orleans is that you can saunter into a relatively uncelebrated tavern like Coops, on Decatur Street, sit down at the bar, order an Abita Turbo Dog brown ale, and an oyster po'boy. Expecting nothing more than humble sustenance, you bite into it, and taste those tender, fresh, slightly briny, lightly battered oysters enveloped within a pod of feathery French bread. And you declare, to nobody in particular, that this is not only the best oyster po'boy you've ever tasted, it's the best sandwich, period. It doesn't matter if nobody agrees with you. You have tracked down the holy grail of fried oysters, and nobody can take that away from you.

If you've never been to New Orleans, open your mind to all of the experiences the Big Easy sends your way. Ride on the vintage St. Charles Streetcar line, or spend a night in a massive four-poster bed at an 1820s Creole cottage. Offer fervent hallelujahs in the cathedrals of cool jazz. Flirt with go-cup martyrdom on Bourbon Street. Bite into a po'boy. Surrender to the debauched charms of this sultry subtropical metropolis on the Mississippi. These are the sights, sounds, and tastes that will tell you that you're in a city that's absolutely without peer.

New Orleans's Legacy

The strongest influence on the growth of this city may, arguably, be French, but no one nationality represents a decisive majority here, and, in fact, New Orleans's most historic neighborhood, the French Quarter, is more Spanish Colonial in appearance than French.

The city's distinctive style of cuisine and music, the pervasive infatuation with things carnal and pleasurable, the Gothic literary traditions, and the longstanding practice of voodoo-tinged Catholicism are legacies contributed not only by the French and Spanish settlers who occupied New Orleans throughout the 18th century, and by the Choctaw Indians who preceded them, but by the vast numbers of Acadian refugees ("Cajuns"), slaves brought from West Africa, American frontiersmen and traders, German farmers, Irish and Italian laborers, Slavs, Creole refugees from Haiti, and, more recently, Vietnamese. All told, the flags of France, Spain, England, the Confederacy, the Union, and even, briefly, independent Louisiana have flown over New Orleans.

These various groups haven't just left their mark on a particular neighborhood during a specific period, they've migrated to New Orleans in significant enough numbers to have a pervasive and lasting influence. The cultural gumbo has resulted in some rather odd traditions that last to this day. Many street and neighborhood names are pronounced differently in New Orleans than anywhere else in the world, from Conti (con-tie) and Cadiz (kay-diz) Streets to the Michoud (mee-shoh) neighborhood. Sometimes French and Spanish names are pronounced roughly as the French and Spanish would pronounce them, and sometimes they're pronounced as virtually nobody else on the planet would pronounce them.

The cuisine unique to New Orleans, which by itself is the biggest reason many visitors travel to this city, borrows widely from myriad cultures. Ingredients and dishes like filé (a powder of dried sassafras leaves popularized by the Choctaw), jambalaya (a rice casserole very similar to Spanish paella), okra (a podlike vegetable introduced by African slaves), and crawfish (a small freshwater crustacean that's prevalent in local waters) are as common in New Orleans restaurants as hamburgers and apple pie in most U.S. cities.

> *Mardi Gras remains New Orleans's defining moment, and although variations on this pre-Lenten free-for-all are celebrated famously in a number of cities with deep Catholic roots, the Crescent City version has its own distinct vibe, complete with colorful parades, costumes, and indescribable mayhem and silliness.*

The city's irrepressibly buoyant music is also distinctly local. Jazz was invented here, a conglomeration of mostly African-American traditions that has rural counterparts elsewhere in southern Louisiana in the form of zydeco and Cajun music. Blues, rock, and even opera were also embraced in New Orleans long before they were in most of the rest of the country.

The growth of Bourbon Street in the French Quarter into a bona fide tourist strip (or trap, some might argue) has actually been a more recent occurrence, and New Orleanians themselves spend relatively little time darkening the doorways of these exuberant, hormonally charged bars. Move off the beaten tourist track in New Orleans, and you can find sublime restaurants and inviting music clubs in some of the most out-of-the-way places. You only have to wander as far as Faubourg Marigny, just beyond the Quarter, to find genuine locals' hangouts. You'll find even more in Uptown and Mid-City. There's no denying the fun of poking around the French Quarter, however, crowds or not.

In the same spirit, it can be every bit as enjoyable and exciting to visit New Orleans during one of its world-class celebrations, such as Mardi Gras and Jazz Fest, as during a relatively quiet time, like July or November, when you'll have more of the city to yourself. Mardi Gras remains New Orleans's defining moment, and although variations on this pre-Lenten free-for-all are celebrated famously in a number of cities with deep Catholic roots, the Crescent City version has its own distinct vibe, complete with colorful parades, costumes, and indescribable mayhem and silliness. Mardi Gras in this city should be experienced by everyone once, but try not to let your only visit to New Orleans be during this time, when it's hard to get a real sense of the city's less party-oriented charms.

What you may miss when you visit New Orleans during a peak period is its leisurely pace, easygoing good nature, and gently tarnished appearance. The city remains to this day vintage, worn-in, and even shabby in many places. It still has the veneer of a hybrid French-Spanish-Caribbean city caught in some kind of time warp, its stucco facades chipped and worn. Houses throughout the city often have elaborate wrought-iron or wooden balconies, some of them with a distinct sag in the middle—they make you wonder how, even if, they pass building inspections.

It's incredible just how many New Orleans buildings from the early 20th, 19th, and even late 18th centuries have been spared by the wrecking ball, a much higher percentage than any large city in North America. Some people cite poverty as a reason so many structures are still standing, that New Orleans lacked the financial resources to repave its historic neighborhoods with modern buildings. But even during its busts, New Orleans has always been a city with plenty of wealthy citizens, and even in the fanciest neighborhoods, old homes have been carefully preserved for decades. New Orleanians simply treasure their heritage, cultural, musical, culinary, and architectural. New Orleans has been writing and enforcing strict preservation codes and restoring both its grand and its modest structures for several generations. When most cities were plowing over huge tracts of historic structures and replacing them with dreary housing projects, impersonal skyscrapers, and banal civic plazas, New Orleans—for the most part—happily embraced its past.

The most significant exception to this rule is the Central Business District, which has a few dozen high-rise office buildings, but even many of these structures are architecturally distinguished and date to the early part of the 20th century. The CBD also has a large number of vintage townhouses, bank buildings, and other handsome structures, and there are stately, hulking brick industrial buildings in the adjacent Warehouse District. In Tremé and several other low-income parts of town, you'll find the same loathsome and inhumane housing projects found in many other cities, although many of these

have been or are slated to be taken down. But overall, even in the grittiest parts of the city, it's easy to find eloquent examples of raised cottages, shotgun houses, Creole bungalows, and Greek Revival, Italianate, gingerbread, Gothic, and even Second Empire and Queen Anne homes. Some of these could use a facelift, and many of them will be restored in years to come. Just as there's no shortage of great old buildings in New Orleans, there's no lack of spirited buyers to snap them up and refurbish them.

Imagine another major U.S. city where downtown skyscrapers could nestle up to a 100-block village with the scale and look of a 200-year-old Colonial Caribbean town. The French Quarter's density of settlement definitely keeps New Orleans feeling urban—were buildings farther apart and fronted by lawns, the city might feel more like a large, historic town, somewhat the way downtown Savannah and Charleston do. But when you're in New Orleans, you're able to sense the bustle, excitement—and also the filth and grime—of a pulsing metropolis as it might have existed during the mid-19th century. Recent-model cars and modern attire almost look peculiar in the French Quarter, Faubourg Marigny, and most of Uptown—that latter neighborhood claims some 11,000 historic buildings. New Orleanians even embrace the past as they travel about town each day, as countless commuters get to and from work via the three dozen 1920s streetcars that run up and down St. Charles Avenue, clanging cheerfully as they go.

Another aspect of life (well, afterlife, to be precise) in New Orleans that feels like a carryover from long ago is the manner in which residents inter their dead. They don't bury them. The 18th-century Spaniards solved the problem of caskets dislodging and floating to the surface after bad rainstorms by building aboveground cemeteries, and the many such graveyards throughout the city continue to be tourist attractions. Alas, many of them are in dicey neighborhoods, and you should not tour them on your own, even in broad daylight. The aboveground tombs often have ornate markings, carvings, and other artwork—they can justly be thought of as museums, although locally they're more commonly referred to as "cities of the dead." You can tour several of the most historic and intriguing cemeteries on guided walks.

Southern Louisiana

New Orleans may be the most visited of Louisiana cities, but the entire southern half of the state has a strong visitor following, especially the arc of towns extending from Houma to Lafayette, known as Cajun Country or Acadiana, and the twisting swath of villages fringing the Mississippi River between New Orleans and Baton Rouge, known as Plantation Country. Baton Rouge itself, although not a major tourist draw, does have a cluster of truly first-rate attractions, and just north of that, beautifully preserved St. Francisville is the quintessential antebellum Southern town, with dozens of fine old homes and a friendly, leisurely pace. The fastest-growing part of Louisiana, both in actual population and in apparent popularity, is the North Shore, a string of towns encircling Lake Pontchartrain, less than an hour's drive from New Orleans, and loaded with great shopping, dining, and outdoor activities.

The boot-shaped state of which New Orleans is the hub (although not the capital), Louisiana—ideally and culturally—is divided into two halves, the northern and southern sections. Residents are quick to point out that northwestern Louisiana, anchored by the city of Shreveport, shares as much or more in common with bordering eastern Texas and southwestern Arkansas as with the rest of the state. Similarly, northeastern Louisiana, anchored by the smaller city of Monroe, is a bit more like southeastern Arkansas and western Mississippi. Many residents of New Orleans hail from other parts of southern Louisiana, but comparatively few come from the northern half of the state. And interestingly, relatively few are from Acadiana—only about 1 percent of all New Orleanians claim to be of Cajun descent.

The entire state of Louisiana covers some 48,000 square miles, which is about the size of New York State. The southern end of the state,

the area covered in this book's side-trip chapters, encompasses a much smaller region, extending about 200 miles east to west along the I-10 corridor, and only about 75 miles north to south.

Southern Louisiana's shoreline is actually a long way south of the I-10 corridor, but much of the coastal region is unpopulated, except for oil derricks, fishing concerns, commercial ports, and otherwise pristine wilderness. The mouth of the Mississippi lies some 75 miles, as the crow flies— or about 100 miles if you follow the curve of the river—southeast of New Orleans, and you can drive alongside this snaking waterway for a good bit of that way, clear down to the small port city of Venice. But there's little to see or do along this drive, and even fewer facilities and accommodations. By the same token, much of St. Barnard Parish, immediately east of New Orleans, is delta and gulf inlets with no roads; the same is true for the lower 40 or 50 miles of Terrebonne Parish, which extends southwest of New Orleans.

While southern Louisiana covers a decent-size area, the navigable and visited areas are quite easily reached from New Orleans. It's just a little over two hours from New Orleans to Lafayette, for example, and another hour or so out as far west as Lake Charles. Most of the plantations along the River Road lie less than an hour from New Orleans, as does Baton Rouge. St. Francisville, the base for exploring the River Road north of Baton Rouge, is about an hour and 45 minutes from New Orleans. The North Shore towns of Slidell, Mandeville, and Hammond are all less than 45 minutes from New Orleans.

And the Big Easy is also relatively close to the Gulf Coast beach communities in Mississippi, Alabama, and the Florida panhandle. Many visitors are surprised to learn that it takes exactly as long to drive across Louisiana via I-10 from New Orleans to Lake Charles as it does to take I-10 from New Orleans through coastal Mississippi and Alabama to reach Pensacola, Florida. And, in fact, the cities along this journey—Biloxi, Gulfport, Mobile, and Pensacola itself—share much in common with New Orleans in terms of architecture, food, music, and culture.

The Land

Louisiana, especially the southern end of the state, is—in geological terms—brand-spanking new. It's largely made up of sediment deposited by the Mississippi River or left in the wake of the continuously shifting Gulf of Mexico shoreline. It's tied with Florida for having the second-lowest mean elevation of any state (about 100 feet, which trails only Delaware), and its highest point—535-foot "Mount" Driskill, up north near Grambling and Minden, is not very high at all.

In southern Louisiana, elevations are as low as 8 feet below sea level in New Orleans to perhaps 300 feet in a few slightly elevated areas north of Lake Pontchartrain. The soil around most of the southern parishes is sandy, except along the delta land that has been formed by Mississippi River sediment. The topography is mostly coastal marsh, alluvial plains, and grassy prairie. To get an idea of what the hillier northern part of the state looks lie, visit the North Shore area above Lake Pontchartrain, especially the upper towns nearest the Mississippi border, where you'll encounter dense longleaf and shortleaf pine forest and some gentle hills. The entire state sits along an extremely gradual slope, which drops, on average, a couple of feet per mile from north to south.

The Mississippi River has always played a vital role in the appearance, development, and economy of New Orleans and of the state as a whole. Through the northern two-thirds of the state, it runs crookedly and tortuously north–south and forms the border between Mississippi and Louisiana. At 31 degrees latitude, the Mississippi-Louisiana border jogs along a straight west–east line to the Pearl River, which then forms the state border going north–south to the Gulf of Mexico. From the point where the Mississippi River is no longer the state border, it winds in southeast through the lower third of the state, cutting directly through Baton Rouge and New Orleans. All along this route, the land for several miles on either side of the river lies in Louisiana and has been formed entirely by river sediment.

The portion of the Mississippi that flows

Seven Sisters Oak, Mandeville

© ANDREW COLLINS

through Louisiana is famous in large part because it's the mouth of the river and it figures so large in the history of New Orleans. But this stretch represents just a fraction of the entire river, whose source is Lake Itasca, in northern Minnesota. All told, it wends some 2,350 miles, bordering Minnesota, Wisconsin, Iowa, Illinois, Missouri, Kentucky, Arkansas, Tennessee, Mississippi, and—finally—Louisiana, before it empties into the Gulf of Mexico. At this final phase, in southern Louisiana, the mighty river and its many tributaries form a fan-shaped delta. All told, the Mississippi River is the definitive drain for about 40 percent of the United States, acting as the watershed basin for parts of 31 states and three Canadian provinces. Waterways as far east as New York and as far west as Montana eventually empty into this vast body of water. There are only four drainage basins larger than this one in the world: the Amazon, in South America, and the Congo and the Nile, in Africa. It's the world's third-longest river.

Louisiana's shoreline is incredibly jagged and comprises some 6.5 million wetland acres, more than 40 percent of the entire nation's marsh ecosystem. Unlike the considerably more stable gulf shorelines of Texas, Mississippi, Alabama, and Florida, Louisiana's coast is continuously shifting, the result of the evolving play between the gulf currents and the flow of the Mississippi and other tributaries. The current Mississippi Delta, which extends across the southern Louisiana shoreline, took some 6,000 years to form. Its largest tributary, the Atchafalaya River, flows into the western end of the delta, southeast of Lafayette and southwest of Houma. The Atchafalaya's delta will eventually fill in much of northern Atchafalaya Bay and come to resemble the fully formed Mississippi River delta.

In addition to the Mississippi and Atchafalaya, the state's other major rivers are the Red (which flows from northwest Louisiana through Shreveport before joining the Mississippi), the Ouachita (in northeastern Louisiana), the Sabine (which forms the border between Texas and Louisiana), and the Pearl (which flows through southeastern Louisiana, where it forms the border with Mississippi, and into the gulf). A bayou is

snowy egret

simply the Louisiana term for what the rest of the country might call a brook, but, in fact, many bayous in Louisiana are large enough that they'd be called rivers elsewhere in the country. The word derives from the Choctaw term for a river, *bayuk,* and some larger bayous include Teche (which flows through the Cajun Country through St. Martinville and Breaux Bridge), Vermilion (which flows through Lafayette), LaFourche (which runs through Houma), and Bouef (which passes near Opelousas in St. Landry Parish).

If you're not already feeling a little soggy from reading all this, keep in mind that Louisiana also contains some 150 natural lakes, including the nation's fourth-largest man-made lake, 186,000-acre Toledo Bend Reservoir, which forms much of the east-west border between Texas and Louisiana. Toledo Bend is a popular recreational area, especially with fishing enthusiasts and boaters. In the southern part of the state, many of these "lakes" are really salt- or brackish-water lagoons that were once bays or inlets of the gulf but were eventually somewhat or entirely sealed off by the

MUDDY WATERS

Contrary to popular belief, the muddiness of the Mississippi River, and many of the other rivers and bayous in the state, is not a sign of pollution or any other unhealthy condition. The rivers become muddy because the fast-moving current is constantly transporting natural and easily eroded bottom sediments. In fact, according to the most recent studies on the river, there are no serious problems at all with contamination and pollution.

An odd thing about the state's rivers is that many of them flow at a higher elevation than the flood plains that surround them. The sediment brought downriver and deposited in Louisiana has built up the riverbanks, forming natural levees. When the river runs high, as much as one third of the state, and at least half of southern Louisiana—including all of metropoiltan New Orleans—would be one massive pool of water were it not for the intricate system of manmade levees and spillways constructed all along the river and its tributaries.

southern part of the state is considered a semi-humid, subtropical zone—it almost never receives snow (and then only a dusting), and in New Orleans, when the temperature occasionally dips to freezing on the coldest winter evenings, locals bundle up as though they're about to run the Iditarod. The state's average rainfall is about 55 inches per year, but some of the southern parishes average closer to 70 inches of rain annually—compare that with about 35 inches of rain each year in Seattle, and just 15 inches or so in dry areas of the country like Los Angeles. Yes, you can expect to get rained on during a typical visit in New Orleans—it's rainy all year, with the highest totals in the summer and the lowest in October and November, but there are no bone-dry months here.

With a low atmospheric ceiling and high humidity, nighttime to daytime low and high temperatures don't usually span a great range. The mean temperature for the year is about 60 degrees in the southern part of the state, but New Orleans usually feels warmer, even if the temperature isn't necessarily higher, because it's less breezy and the considerable concrete in its roads and buildings tends to absorb and retain heat. Average high temperatures in New Orleans in summer are about 92 degrees, with nighttime lows averaging a still very hot 75 degrees. In winter, throughout December, January, and February, highs average a quite pleasant 65 degrees, with lows a manageable 48 degrees. Win-

formation of barrier beaches or delta ridges from the gulf and rivers. The largest and most famous of these is Lake Pontchartrain, which is traversed by the longest bridge in the world, the 23-plus-mile Lake Pontchartrain Causeway. Barataria Bay, south of New Orleans, is another example of this kind of lake, as is Lake Maurepas, just west of Lake Pontchartrain and connected to it by Bayou Manchac, and Lake Salvador, just southwest of New Orleans and fringed by Jean Lafitte National Historic Park and Preserve.

Like the famous river that flows into it, the Gulf of Mexico is no slouch when it comes to superlatives. It's the fifth-largest sea in the world, covering nearly 600,000 square miles.

CLIMATE

Southern Louisiana is jokingly called the northernmost coast of Central America, and not just because of its banana-republic politics—it also has a climate that's more similar to Costa Rica than to most of the United States. Almost all of the

© ANDREW COLLINS

alligator in brush along Pearl River

NEW ORLEANS CLIMATE

Month	Average High	Average Low	Average Rainfall
January	61	42	5.0
February	64	44	6.0
March	72	53	4.9
April	79	59	4.5
May	84	65	4.6
June	89	71	5.8
July	91	73	6.1
August	90	73	6.1
September	87	70	5.5
October	79	59	3.0
November	71	51	4.4
December	64	45	5.8

Note: Temperatures are in degrees Fahrenheit; rainfall in inches.

ter is a wonderful time to visit. Summer can be simply unbearable on the most humid days, even considering that virtually every public accommodation, restaurant, shop, and attraction in New Orleans and the rest of the state is air-conditioned. Especially in the touristy French Quarter, which can be littered with garbage along Bourbon and outside bars on weekend mornings, it can feel and smell positively foul to walk around on a summer day. Spring and fall are fairly genial times to visit southern Louisiana, keeping in mind that temperatures can easily reach into the 90s during warm spells but that they more typically average in the upper 70s in September and October, and again in April and May.

New Orleans itself averages about 110 days a year with completely sunny skies, and about the same number of days with rain. Otherwise, it's partly cloudy or partly sunny, depending on whether you're an optimist or a pessimist about weather.

History

Pre-European Louisiana

In northeastern Louisiana, not too far from the city of Monroe, archaeologists have identified a series of ancient ceremonial mounds that some in the scientific community believe are the earliest physical evidence of human settlement on the entire continent. More recent but still prehistoric mounds dot the landscape of the state, especially in the northern and eastern regions. These mounds were a fixture in the early Native American farming communities that proliferated in these parts for the two to three millennia prior to European settlement.

Louisiana's Hopewell indigenous tribes thrived in the Gulf South from about 200 B.C. until nearly A.D. 900, with Mississippian tribes succeeding them in the 1500s. Native Americans of the 1600s and 1700s, when Europeans first began exploring the region, comprised three distinct branches, each with its own culture and language: Caddoan, Muskogean, and Tunican. It was this last branch, which included the Chitimacha, Attakapa, and other tribes, that mostly inhabited what is now southern Louisiana, with Muskogean and Caddoan Indians living in the central and northwestern parts of the state, respectively.

The effect of French and then Spanish settlement on indigenous persons living in Louisiana was, as it was wherever Europeans explored the New World, devastating. Many tribes were annihilated by disease, others squarely routed out, enslaved, or massacred by settlers. Still, some Native Americans managed to hang on and thrive in Louisiana, many of their members intermarrying with African-Americans. Today there are Chitimacha, Houma, Tunica-Biloxi, Coushatta, and Choctaw settlements in the state. Many geographical names in Louisiana have indigenous origins, among them Bogalusa (which means "black water"), Opelousas ("black leg"), and Ponchatoula ("hanging hair").

Most people think of the French explorer René-Robert Cavelier, Sieur de La Salle, as the earliest European settler in the region, and he was the first to establish a permanent stronghold in the name of his own country, in 1682. But 140 years earlier, Spaniards led by explorer Hernando de Soto first visited what is now Louisiana. They didn't stay, but they did leave behind diseases that proved fatal to many of the indigenous persons they encountered.

La Salle entered Louisiana down the Mississippi River from the north and claimed for France all the land drained by not only this massive river but also its vast network of tributaries. This parcel covered some 830,000 square miles and ran from the Gulf of Mexico to Canada, and from the Rocky Mountains to Mississippi. He first termed the region Louisiana (well, technically, Louisiane, which is its name in French) after France's reigning monarch of that period, Louis XIV.

1700–1766

Louisiana's period of French rule was barely more than three generations—France would cede the territory to the Spanish in 1762, before occupying it again for a short period preceding the Louisiana Purchase. Neither the first nor second periods of French rule proved to be profitable for France, and on the whole, one could say that

the entire episode was a failure from a colonial perspective. On the flip side, the French occupation planted the seeds for the emergence of New Orleans as one of young America's most fascinating cities.

New Orleans was not the first settlement in Louisiana by the French, although explorer Pierre Le Moyne, Sieur d'Iberville, did establish a toehold near the city on March 3, 1699 (Mardi Gras day, coincidentally). That same year, the French built a permanent fort about 90 miles east in Biloxi (now Mississippi), and, three years later, another 60 miles east in Mobile (now Alabama). The first permanent French settlement to go up in what is now Louisiana, in 1714, was Natchitoches, a still-charming small city in northwestern Louisiana, about 300 miles northwest of New Orleans. By the late 1710s, however, France had already failed to invest substantially in its new settlement and, unable to fund a full-fledged colony, the monarchy transferred control of Louisiana to Antoine Crozat, a French financier of considerable acclaim.

Crozat was able to make little headway with Louisiana, and just five years later, control of Louisiana was shifted to Compagnie d'Occident, led by a wealthy Scotsman named John Law. It became quickly apparent to Law and other authorities, however, that the southern Mississippi was vulnerable to plays for control by the two key competing European powers in colonial America, Great Britain and Spain. To protect their interests, the French built a new fort in 1718 along the lower Mississippi, christening the settlement La Nouvelle-Orléans, after Philippe, Duc d'Orléans. A handful of settlements were added along the Mississippi River to the north, and in 1722 France named young New Orleans the territorial capital of Louisiana.

Nouvelle Orléans' beginnings were almost pathetically modest. The site, at a sharp bend of the Mississippi River more than 5 feet *below* sea level, was little more than bug- and alligator-infested swampland, which the city's earliest residents shored up with landfill and dams. Part of the settlement covered one of the few bumps of higher ground along the river's banks. The site was chosen in part because a bayou (now known as Bayou St. John) connected the Mississippi River at this point to Lake Pontchartrain, which itself emptied into the gulf. For eons, the area's Native Americans had used the bayou as a shortcut for getting from the river to the gulf without having to paddle all the way south, nearly another 100 miles, to where the Mississippi entered the gulf.

Today's French Quarter, also known as the Vieux Carré (literally, Old Square), for the first several decades, encompassed all of New Orleans. It was anchored by the Place d'Armes, which would later be renamed Jackson Square. The river's course in relation to the city has changed slightly since the city's founding—in the early days, Jackson Square faced the riverfront directly, whereas today a significant strip of land and levee acts as a barrier between it and the river.

Law can be credited with making the earliest effort to interest European settlers in Louisiana. His first successful campaign brought not Frenchmen but Germans to the new territory. Law would convince Germans to move to Louisiana as indentured workers, meaning they were bound to work for an established period, and once their service commitment was complete, they were granted freedom. Law's Occidental Company used all the usual trickery and false advertising common throughout Europe in those days to attract immigrants and investors: it promised vast riches, huge mining reserves, and easy agricultural opportunities, virtually none of which was accurate.

During Law's first few years heading up control of Louisiana, his company managed to convince some 7,000 mostly German and French residents to migrate to Louisiana. A significant percentage of these migrants died from disease or starvation, as the colonial authorities were in no position at all to feed, clothe, and house the arrivals. If you stayed in Louisiana during these early days, in all likelihood

Louisiana's period of French rule was barely more than three generations— France would cede the territory to the Spanish in 1762, before occupying it again for a short period preceding the Louisiana Purchase. But the French occupation planted the seeds for the emergence of New Orleans as one of young America's most fascinating cities.

you did so only because you hadn't the means to return to Europe. Word of the false promise of Louisiana spread quickly back to France, but authorities allowed Law and his company to administer the territory until 1731, when the French monarchy finally stepped in to resume control.

Law was responsible for first importing West African slaves to Louisiana. His Compagnie d'Occident also owned the French Compagnie du Senegal, which controlled all French slave trade. Over roughly a 10-year period, about 3,000 mostly Senegalese slaves were taken from their homeland to Louisiana. Slaves worked on the handful of early plantations, and also on the countless smaller subsistence farms that developed around southern Louisiana, most engaged in the production and export of indigo and tobacco.

Back in control of the colony from 1731 through 1762, France failed utterly to turn Louisiana into a profitable venture. Furthermore, its strategic importance diminished sharply as England developed an upper hand, during the French and Indian War, which had begun in 1754, toward controlling Canada. In 1762, France hatched a diplomatic scheme to help impel Spain to join it and rout the British: it secretly handed over the Louisiana Territory to Spain, in the Treaty of Fontainebleau. In fact, the territory stayed in the family, as France's King Louis XV simply transferred the land to his own cousin, Spain's King Charles III.

The move ended badly for both France and Spain. France lost the war with Britain in 1763 and lost control of Canada. And Spain ended up with a lemon. One might argue, of course, that France really didn't lose a colony so much as it rid itself of what had become an enormous and depressing financial burden. Furthermore, as part of the peace treaty between the joint powers of Spain and France with their victor, Great

Britain was awarded all of Louisiana east of the Mississippi River, which became known as West Florida. Spain kept a much larger tract, which included all of Louisiana west of the river, along with a critical little area along the lower Mississippi River called Ile d'Orleans, which included the city of New Orleans. France was free of any part of Louisiana.

1766–1803

The actual physical transfer of Louisiana, and especially New Orleans, to Spain was an unmitigated disaster fraught with rebellion, virtual martial law, and ugly acts of violence. It didn't help that the residents of New Orleans had no idea that they had become subjects of Spain until 1766, when the first Spanish governor, Antonio de Ulloa, arrived that March and, like a wicked stepmother, immediately instituted a strict rule upon the city's inhabitants.

Almost as immediately, there were insurgencies, and in 1768 the situation became particularly dire when locals actually drove Ulloa and his cronies clear out of town. Spain hired a tyrannical military man, General Alejandro O'Reilly, to beat down the rebellion, which he did, quite successfully, in August 1769. He managed to get Spain in firm control of New Orleans, a rule that would last until the United States orchestrated the Louisiana Purchase in 1803, for although France technically owned Louisiana at that time, Spaniards continued to govern the city's day-to-day affairs right through the end.

The Spanish, like the French, made every possible effort to boost the colony's population, sending plenty of Spaniards to Louisiana throughout their period of rule. From a cultural standpoint, Louisiana remained squarely French, as the colonists from France far outnumbered any newcomers. The only reason the appearance of the French Quarter today more closely resembles Spanish colonial than French colonial architecture is that two huge fires burned much of the city during the Spanish occupation, and many of the new buildings that went up were constructed by Spanish authorities. The first fire hit the Quarter in 1788, apparently started by

candles at a religious observation; some 850 buildings burned, and about 200 of those were again lost in a smaller fire in 1794. It's Spain's influence that resulted in the wrought-iron balconies, shaded courtyards, and other features that typify French Quarter architecture.

Ironically, the majority of the newcomers to Louisiana during the Spanish period were actually French, or French-speaking, refugees. The most famous group were the Acadians, who had been cruelly expelled from the Maritime Provinces of Canada following the British victory. The French immigrants living in Acadian Canada were typically rounded up and forced onto ships—some were sent back to France, and others were reluctantly taken in by certain British colonies in what is now the United States. Many died in passage, or of poverty encountered where they landed. Spain, looking to boost the population of the Louisiana colony, enthusiastically welcomed the Acadians, who arrived in two major waves, the first in 1765 and an even larger one in 1784. Most of them settled in the marshes and swamplands of south-central and southwestern Louisiana. In Louisiana, the name Acadian gradually morphed into Cajun, as we all know it today, and Lafayette, Louisiana, became the hub of Cajun settlements.

A lesser-known group of refugees that also came to New Orleans and Louisiana in great numbers from 1791 through 1803 were white French settlers and some free people of color from the French colony of Saint-Domingue (now Haiti), who fled the island during the violent black revolution of the 1790s.

Louisiana's makeup changed a bit during the American Revolution, as Spain worked in concert with the American colonists to undermine their rivals, the British. They sent supplies and munitions to the colonists, and in 1779, after formally declaring war on Britain, their Louisiana militia captured all of the British settlements of West Florida. This included all of the Gulf Coast region between the Mississippi River and the Perdido River, which today forms the east-west state border between Alabama and Florida. Per the terms of the Treaty of Paris in 1783, Spain's assistance was, at the war's conclusion, rewarded with a chunk of land that included all of both East Florida (today's Florida) and West Florida (which today includes Alabama, Mississippi, and the nine Louisiana parishes east and north of the Mississippi River, now sometimes referred to as the Florida parishes).

With the young United States now in control of all the land east of the Mississippi River (except for East and West Florida), New Orleans and the entire Louisiana Territory grew dramatically in strategic importance. New Orleans became the seaport serving America's interior, as important rivers throughout Ohio, Kentucky, and Tennessee all fed to the Mississippi.

In yet another secret treaty, however, Spain in 1800 decided to transfer all of the Louisiana Territory, including New Orleans, back to France. The actual residents of New Orleans never even knew they were residents of a French colony for the three years they were back under the country's rule, as in 1803, the United States bought Louisiana from France for a mere $15 million. Even by the standards of that day, $15 million was a paltry sum for such an enormous parcel of land—approximately one-third of the land that now makes up the present-day continental United States. Because Spain still possessed East and West Florida, the nine Louisiana parishes east and north of the Mississippi River remained in Spanish hands until 1810, when the American residents of West Florida declared their independence and asked to be annexed by the United States.

1804–1865

Upon purchasing Louisiana from France, the United States immediately split the territory in two at the 33rd parallel, which today forms the northern border of Louisiana. All land south of that point became known as the Territory of Orleans and, confusingly, all land to the north became known as the Territory of Louisiana.

America named William C. C. Claiborne governor of the Orleans territory, which he ruled from the territorial capital, New Orleans. He endured a difficult period, attempting to introduce the American democratic political system to a people entirely unused to self-determined government. In 1790, some 10,000 new refugees from Saint-Domingue moved into New Orleans, doubling the population but adding further chaos to the city. In many respects, it's this final wave of French-speaking people from Haiti—white colonists of French descent and free people of color (*gens de couleur libres*)—that ultimately established the French-Caribbean character that exists to this day in New Orleans.

For a time, New Orleans deviated from rural Louisiana in its relative tolerance of racial diversity—the *gens de couleur libres* were, in many cases, well educated and quite able to forge good livings as builders, designers, artisans, and chefs. It's these early Creole immigrants who are in a large way responsible for the intricate and fanciful Creole cottages and other buildings still found throughout the city and southern Louisiana, and it's these same immigrants who helped to develop New Orleans's inimitable Creole cuisine, which blended the traditions of France, Spain, the Caribbean, Africa, and even the American frontier and Native Americans.

There was considerable intermingling in this early New Orleans society, as wealthy Europeans and Creoles commonly had mistresses, some who were *gens de couleur libres,* quadroons (one-fourth black), octoroons (one-eighth black), or some other mix of Anglo, Latin, African, and Native American descent. It's largely for this reason that the term Creole, when applied to people, is rather confusing. The name was first applied to upper-crust French settlers born in Louisiana but descended from mostly wealthy European families, as the very word derives from the Spanish *criollo,* a term that described persons born in the colonies rather than born in Europe or, for that matter, Africa. These days, just about any New Orleanian or Louisianan who can claim some direct combination of French, Spanish, Caribbean, and African blood can justly consider him- or herself a Creole, the exception being the descendents of the original French-Canadian refugees from Acadia, known as Cajuns.

The United States accepted the Territory of Orleans as the state of Louisiana on April 30, 1812—it thereby became the 18th state of the union, preceded only by Vermont, Kentucky,

JEAN LAFITTE AND LOUISIANA'S PIRATES

Piracy and its slightly more acceptable cousin, privateering, have been a part of southern Louisiana lore since the time of the region's settlement. This infamous and often ruthless practice developed in the Gulf of Mexico in the 16th century, when high-seas thieves began targeting Spanish galleons loaded with silver and gold and headed for that country's colonies in the New World. During times of war, European nations legitimized piracy, authorizing the crews of these renegade vessels to stop and seize the ships of opposing nations.

Louisiana developed into a hotbed of piracy because of its geography and topography: The state's irregular, marshy shoreline was punctuated with hundreds of hidden, protected coves, which made perfect havens for pirates. They could elude authorities, smuggle and hide their spoils, and build and repair ships in secret. During the 19th century, the most infamous of these bodies of water was Barataria Bay, a massive body of water just east of present-day Grand Isle; its northern edge lies about 40 miles due south of New Orleans, as the crow flies. The bay sits at the north-central tip of the Gulf of Mexico, about 500 miles north of Mexico's Yucatán Peninsula, 650 miles northwest of Cuba, 450 miles west of Florida's Gulf Coast, and 450 miles east of Texas's Gulf Coast. Strategically, no location offered better access to so many lucrative colonial shipping routes.

In this bay, the infamous Baratarians established a colony of illicit doings that included warehouses and docks. Pirate ships returned here with their bounties, and then auctioned them to visitors from New Orleans. Sometimes, they hauled their goods directly to New Orleans, where they found a vast and eager market. Everything from precious metals to foods, spices, and rum to African slaves were sold by the Baratarians, who were led during the height of their success by the Lafitte brothers, Jean and Pierre.

Unofficially, and even officially for time, authorities in New Orleans turned a blind eye to Jean Lafitte and his operations, unwilling to shut off the constant stream of valuable and heavily discounted goods into the city. It was not until Lafitte's disregard for the law became too flagrant that Governor William Claiborne finally ordered his arrest, offering a $500 reward for his capture.

Tennessee, and Ohio, following the original 13 states. The political system, with Claiborne as governor and New Orleans the capital, continued largely as it had from the time of the Louisiana Purchase.

America wasted no time in exploiting its new purchase, as thousands of entrepreneurial-minded settlers flocked to the busy port city during the first decade following the Louisiana Purchase. They were not welcomed in the French Quarter at all, and in fact the original Creoles would have nothing to do with American settlers for many decades. Some of these upstarts immediately starting amassing great riches in shipping and trade enterprises, building lavish homes in the American Quarter, which is now the Central Business District. Canal Street divided the two enclaves, and the median down this street came to be considered New Orleans's "neutral ground."

Today, the city's residents refer to any street median as neutral ground.

By the early 1800s, a century's worth of immigrants from all walks of life had contributed to one of the most racially, culturally, and economically diverse populations in the nation. Freed prisoners from France, Haitian refugees, slaves, European indentured servants, American frontiersmen, Spanish Canary Islanders, nuns, military men, and others now formed New Orleans's population and that of many of the communities upriver.

Britain and the United States had remained hostile to one another since the Revolution, and shortly after Louisiana became a state, the two nations entered into the War of 1812, which would last three years. By 1814, New Orleans figured heavily in the campaign, as the faltering British decided to go after several key ports along

In 1814, a fleet of American military ships descended upon the Baratarians' headquarters, seizing eight schooners, some 40 houses, nearly 100 men, and countless spoils. Jean Lafitte and the other leaders of the group heard of the impending attack before its onset and successfully hid from authorities before making their escape.

The War of 1812 was in full swing at this point, and late in 1814, the British launched plans to ascend the Mississippi River and attack New Orleans. Lafitte's exploits were legendary across the high seas at this point, and the British decided to approach him with an offer, figuring that he'd happily jump at the opportunity to exact his revenge against U.S. authorities. Lafitte was offered $30,000 and a captainship in the British Navy if he would join in their attack on the Americans.

Lafitte declined. Whether out of some deep loyalty to the United States or, more likely, because he believed he stood to gain more by aligning himself with the U.S. government, he tipped off Governor Claiborne about the impending British attack. He then volunteered his own considerable militia and fleet to defend New Orleans against the British—if Claiborne would agree to drop all charges against Jean and Pierre Lafitte and their fellow Baratarians.

Claiborne relayed the offer to Gen. Andrew Jackson, who had arrived to lead the defense of New Orleans against the British, and Jackson accepted without hesitation. In January 1815, during the Battle of New Orleans, Jean Lafitte and his cohorts performed admirably, greatly assisting American forces in turning back the British attack. Claiborne and Jackson kept their word, and U.S. authorities left the Baratarians alone from that point on.

The final fate of the Lafitte brothers is unrecorded. All that is known is that several years later, they moved their operations to Galveston Bay in Texas, but few additional details can be confirmed. In 1819, the U.S. Congress passed a law declaring piracy a crime punishable by death, and the government finally began pursuing and prosecuting pirates more vigorously. These circumstances may have helped to curtail the Lafittes' operations. Whatever became of the dashing buccaneer, his legacy—and tales concerning his exploits—live on.

the Gulf Coast and the Mississippi River in an effort to cut off the supply and trade system serving the interior United States. New Orleans, defended by Major General Andrew Jackson, was attacked by the British on January 8, 1815 — several days after British and American leaders had signed a peace treaty ending the War of 1812. Still, many believe that the British would not have formally ratified the treaty had they been able to pull off that final battle. Andrew Jackson's victory in the Battle of New Orleans helped to propel his political career, and in 1828 he was elected the seventh president of the United States.

The year 1812 was significant in New Orleans for another reason—it received the first steamboat, aptly called the *New Orleans,* ever to navigate the Mississippi River system; the boat steamed all the way from Pittsburgh via the Ohio River. Steamboats would greatly alter the nature

of commerce in New Orleans, as up until 1812 trade had been conducted by small vessels propelled chiefly by the river current, meaning that they could not return upstream once they arrived in New Orleans. In many cases, the boats were simply scrapped once they arrived.

Robert Livingston and inventor Robert Fulton were given a monopoly on the steamboat business for the first few years, but the two abandoned their stronghold in the face of outraged legal challenges, and the number of steamboats arriving and departing New Orleans grew rapidly; by the mid-1840s, more than 1,000 different steamboats were calling on New Orleans each year. Steamboats left New Orleans for the Midwest and the East Coast carrying tobacco, cotton, sugarcane, and many other goods. New Orleans also became a major trade port with the Caribbean islands, from which it imported fruit, tobacco, rum, and—illegally, after their importation was banned in 1808—slaves.

Louisiana's population stood at about 150,000 by 1820, having increased greatly since statehood with the arrival of settlers from other parts of the United States, who moved here to pursue new land and to far. The population grew to 350,000 by 1840, and to 700,000 by 1860, the start of the Civil War. During this period, the state become a U.S. superpower owing to its phenomenal agricultural growth, chiefly in cotton and sugarcane. Both small farms and massive plantations grew these crops, utilizing largely slave labor. Cotton was grown just about everywhere in the state, but somewhat less in the swampy southern regions, where sugarcane thrived in the warmer and wetter climate. In fact, sugarcane was always a more lucrative crop than cotton. The state also became a major rice grower—the crop was first planted in the southern and Mississippi River areas to feed slaves, but it proved profitable and was developed into a valuable commercial crop by the end of the 19th century.

With the outlying areas seeing huge growth in agriculture, the region's key port and gateway, New Orleans, grew by leaps and bounds. By 1820, it had already become the largest city in the South with a population of about 27,500, surpassing Charleston. After New York City, it was America's leading immigrant port of entry from 1830 until the Civil War, as immigrants headed to the interior Ohio and Mississippi River valleys by way of the city. It also ranked only second in the United States, again behind New York City, in its volume of commercial traffic, which increased tenfold from 1815 to 1840, from $20 million to $200 million. During several of these years, New Orleans actually exceeded New York City in wealth. Cotton, tobacco, grain, and meats were shipped down the Mississippi through New Orleans from the agricultural interior, and huge quantities of manufactured goods, sugar, and coffee were sent back upriver to settlers and other ports via the Gulf of Mexico.

By the 1850s, New Orleans had grown to become the fourth-largest city in the United States, and a leading cultural hub. Visitors from other parts of the country were struck by the

© ANDREW COLLINS

statue of Andrew Jackson, who led the Battle of New Orleans

city's distinctly Spanish architecture and Parisian ambience—it was a city of high fashion, opera and theater, lavish dining, and sophisticated parties. Already by this time, the city was beginning to celebrate Mardi Gras with parties and simple parades.

The hot and humid summers proved to be breeding grounds for yellow fever and other subtropical maladies, and although many residents died from the disease during these years, the city's population still grew to a staggering 170,000 by 1860.

The dynamic changed in the middle of the 19th century with the construction of railroads and canals, which made it possible for Midwestern states to move their products to the Eastern United States more quickly and cheaply than by way of New Orleans and the gulf. The city continued to prosper as a shipper of cotton and sugarcane. Louisiana relied heavily on slave labor to ensure the profitability of its agricultural markets, and New Orleans prospered hugely in this ignominious trade. Had the Midwestern states remained as dependent on New Orleans for trade as they were in the early part of the century, it's quite possible the state would not have sided with the South in favor of secession during the Civil War, but by 1860, Louisiana's interests were completely in step with the rest of the South's.

As the state capital, New Orleans enjoyed significant economic and political advantages that alienated it from the rest of Louisiana. After years of debate about this issue, the legislation finally resolved to relocate the capital to Baton Rouge, about 60 miles upriver, in 1849, where it has remained to this day the state political seat, excepting a 20-year period during and following the Civil War.

When South Carolina seceded from the Union in December 1860, following the election of Republican Abraham Lincoln, who sought to curb the spread of slavery, it set off a flurry of similar withdrawals among other southern states, with Louisiana seceding on January 26, 1861, the sixth to do so. It then joined in the effort toward war in becoming a member of the Confederate States of America.

Although much of the fighting took place in the coastal and mid-Atlantic states, New Orleans and Louisiana were vulnerable to Union attack for exactly the same reason they were attacked by the British during the War of 1812. If the Union army could capture and control the Mississippi River, it could cut off supply lines between the Confederacy and any states west of the river, and it could enjoy a continuous supply line to the interior Midwest. Precipitating just such an attack, the Confederates built fortifications along the river south of New Orleans.

In April 1862, Captain David G. Farragut led a flotilla of Union Navy ships to the mouth of the Mississippi, where it proceeded north toward New Orleans. He made it with little trouble, shelling and ultimately disabling the Confederate fortification and sailing rather easily to capture the South's largest city. Immediately, New Orleans was named the Union capital of all territory held by the Federal army in Louisiana, which soon included Baton Rouge, taken by Farragut's troops shortly after. The Confederate state government removed west about 60 miles to Opelousas, and

then scrambled nearly another 200 miles northwest to Shreveport, where it remained until war's end.

A corrupt northern fat cat, Union Major General Benjamin F. Butler, assumed control of New Orleans and Federally occupied Louisiana, running things a bit like the Spanish had—he was hated by all, including more than a few Union troops, and eventually was removed from office. By war's end the state itself stood politically divided, the Mississippi River Valley (including New Orleans and Baton Rouge) in Union control, and the western and northern regions still under Confederate control.

1865–1900

The period immediately following the Civil War, known as Reconstruction, was a grim one, and its policies that attempted to create an integrated society of whites and free blacks actually backfired, although it's much easier to criticize these measures with more than 140 years of hindsight.

President Lincoln signed the Proclamation of Amnesty and Reconstruction into law in December 1863, and so even before the war had ended, a civil government was established in those parts of Louisiana held by Union troops. When the war ended, this civil government assumed control of the state. Early on, it seemed as though little had changed for blacks, even though slavery had been formally abolished by this civil government. A number of the former Confederate leaders of prewar Louisiana held office in this new civil government, which immediately passed the infamous Black Codes. These edicts placed enormous restrictions on the rights and freedoms of the state's African-Americans, who were also denied the right to vote.

These conditions led to an extreme seesaw of power between the Republican and (largely ex-Confederate) Democratic sides of the government, which would bitterly divide Louisianans and precipitate tragic violence for the rest of the 19th century and well into the 20th. Blacks struck back against the government in New Orleans, first by rioting violently in 1866 until finally the federal government stepped in to impose order. These same issues, revolts, and riots flared up in other Southern states, and Congress responded by

DEAL OF THE CENTURY

By 1876, the divide between Republican and Democratic voters had narrowed, not only in Louisiana but all over the country. The U.S. presidential election at the time, with Republican Rutherford B. Hayes pitted against Democrat Samuel Tilden, makes the Bush-Gore debacle of 2000 look relatively mild.

In three states—Louisiana, South Carolina, and Florida—both parties claimed victory in the state gubernatorial elections, and thus the electoral votes due either Hayes or Tilden. In order to win the presidency, Hayes needed the electoral votes of all three states.

The lawmakers struck a rather sleazy but sly compromise. If the Democrats from all three states agreed to hand over the electoral votes to make Hayes the president, the Republicans would cede the three gubernatorial elections to the Dems. Louisiana elected Governor Francis R. T. Nicholls (a Republican would not occupy the governor's office again until 1980). This deal effectively ended Reconstruction in Louisiana—although Hayes was a Republican, he withdrew federal troops from New Orleans in appreciation of those much-needed final electoral votes.

drafting the Reconstruction Acts in 1867 and 1868, which President Andrew Johnson vetoed, but which passed with a two-thirds majority nonetheless. And so, formally, began the period of Reconstruction in the American South.

Reconstruction dictated that the 10 ex-Confederate states that had been returned to the Union would lose their rights to self-govern, and the federal military would instead step in to govern, until these states rewrote their constitutions with laws and language that Congress deemed acceptable. In effect, Louisiana was no longer a state until it submitted to the wishes of the federal government. The federally controlled state government then drafted a new constitution in March 1868, which wholly deferred to the sentiments of Congress: Adult males of all races were granted the right to vote—excepting fully declared ex-Confederates, who actually had their voting rights revoked—and blacks were assured

full civil rights. Interestingly, when the new constitution was presented to Louisiana citizens, voters approved it overwhelmingly. The majority of those who registered to vote that year were, in fact, black; whites, discouraged and disgusted by the process, largely stayed away from the polls.

Pro-Union white Southerners (called scalawags by their detractors), opportunity-seeking whites from the North (called carpetbaggers and hated even more by their detractors), and former slaves held the clear majority of political seats in Louisiana (and many other Southern states) during the eight years of Reconstruction. Among these Republican officeholders were Louisiana's first elected black governor, P.B.S. Pinchback; the first black U.S. Senator, Blanche K. Bruce; as well as black members of U.S. Congress and black holders of just about every state political post.

In the meantime, the most ardent opponents of Reconstruction, including quite a few prominent ex-Confederate leaders, went to extreme lengths to sabotage, tear down, and otherwise render ineffective the state's Republican leadership. From this effort came the development of such anti-black groups as the Ku Klux Klan (in northern Louisiana), the Knights of the White Camellia (in southern Louisiana), and the especially terror-driven White League. These and other groups, sometimes systematically and sometimes randomly, intimidated, beat, and many times lynched blacks and more than a few white sympathizers. The White League took credit for the assassination of several Republican elected officials. Some 3,500 members of the White League actually attempted to overthrow the state government during what came to be known as the Battle of Liberty Place, in New Orleans in 1874. During a fierce riot, they took over the city hall, statehouse, and state arsenal until federal troops arrived to restore order. For the next four years, the troops remained in New Orleans, overseeing the city's—and the state's—order.

Over the course of Reconstruction the voting situation in Louisiana grew increasingly volatile, as whites intimidated or threatened blacks to keep them from voting, and rallied voter support among anti-Republican whites. More and more officials and congressmen sympathetic to the South gained office, and they in turn pardoned and restored voting rights to many of the ex-Confederates.

White Democrats were swift in removing from blacks any rights they had gained during Reconstruction, and then some. In 1898, the state constitution was rewritten. Without expressly denying suffrage to blacks, it required poll taxes, literacy, and property ownership in order to vote, which disqualified most of the state's black voters.

While Reconstruction had a profoundly negative effect on the plight of blacks, a few strides were made during the 19th century. Many blacks ended up returning to work at a subsistence level on the farms where they once had been slaves, but some headway was made in education and social relief. The federal government established the Freedmen's Bureau, which helped to fund public schools for blacks throughout the South and issued other forms of assistance and economic relief.

The economy of the rural South faltered greatly following the Civil War, and various depressions, labor problems, and episodes of social unrest conspired to put many large and small farm owners out of business. For much of the 19th century, a large portion of southern farms were run by sharecroppers, whereby the owners of the land—many of them northerners who had bought failed farms—gave tenants equipment and materials to farm the land and live on a fairly basic level. The workers were also entitled to a small cut of the crop yield. Farm production in Louisiana began to increase under this system, but it was still far lower than before the Civil War, and even with bounteous crops, many farmers could not make ends meet.

New Orleans, whose economy had been devastated by the war, gradually staged an economic comeback over the course of the next half-century. The renewed growth in cotton and cane trafficking helped to jumpstart the city's shipping and trade economy, and the mouth of the Mississippi River was deepened and made accessible to much larger ships, many of which sailed from ports much farther away than in earlier times. Railroads were built across much of Louisiana, and in 1914, the opening of the Panama Canal brought new trade to New Orleans by way of Latin America. The city's population stood at 290,000 by 1900, with the state population up to about 1.4 million.

1900–World War II

Louisiana's economy began to diversify throughout the early 20th century, much more so than in most other agrarian southern states. Significant sources of oil were discovered in the northwestern part of the state, and natural gas sources were developed all over Louisiana. In 1938, huge oil deposits were discovered off the coast, and a massive oil-drilling industry grew up in southern Louisiana, especially in the towns southeast of Lafayette and southwest of Houma. Salt and sulfur mining also grew into a big contributor to the economy, chiefly in the southern belt extending from Lake Charles to southeast of Lafayette.

The farming economy continued to suffer through the early 1900s, however, and a severe recession took hold throughout the 1920s. The growing anguish and desperation among rural farmers helped to promote the ascendancy of one of the most notorious and controversial political figures in American history, Huey P. Long, a colorful, no-nonsense straight talker whose fervently populist manner played well with poor farmers and laborers. Long declared war on big corporations, especially Standard Oil, and took up the cause of small businesses and the common man. His actions early in his political career squarely favored those he claimed to want to help. Long was elected governor in 1928 and then U.S. senator in 1930, although he kept the governor's seat until 1932, when a handpicked successor took office. Still, he pretty much called the shots in state politics right up until his death. Long was assassinated in 1935 by Dr. Carl Weiss, the son-in-law of one of his political arch-enemies.

Long was instrumental in developing state public assistance and public works programs across Louisiana during the Great Depression, but he was also infamous for his nepotism and corruption, routinely buying off colleagues and tampering with the political process. The "Kingfish" ran the state like a fiefdom, and he actually ended up preventing federal funds from reaching the state during his last few years in office as a U.S. senator. Long may have died in 1935, but his brother, Earl K. Long, succeeded him as governor, as did his son, Russell Long. Until the early '60s, anti- and pro-Long factions continued to dominate Democratic party politics and therefore, because Dems controlled just about everything in Louisiana, state politics.

World War II boosted the Louisiana economy, with its need for mineral and oil resources. It was during this period that Louisiana developed the massive refineries and chemical plants still found along much of the Mississippi River and all

through the lower third of the state (especially Lake Charles and Baton Rouge), and it was also during the 1940s that the state's population demographic changed so that more Louisianans lived in cities than in rural areas.

At the same time, many rural citizens, especially blacks fed up with the state's segregation and racial mistreatment, left the South to seek factory jobs in Chicago, Oakland, and other northern and western cities. Other Louisianans moved to southeastern Texas, where jobs at refineries, factories, and shipyards in Beaumont, Orange, and Port Arthur abounded.

Government and Economy

The city of New Orleans is governed by a mayor and a city council of seven members, two of them elected at-large, and five elected from districts of roughly equal population. New Orleans is a predominantly Democratic, politically left-of-center city, generally quite progressive on social issues. The state on the whole, however, tends to be more conservative on social issues, and the proportion of Democrats to Republicans is closer.

New Orleans, as with the rest of Louisiana, has experienced quite a few booms and busts since World War II. The city is today the largest port in the United States, and it's second in the world only to Rotterdam in its value of foreign commerce and waterborne commerce. About 5,000 ships dock at New Orleans each year, a figure dwarfed only by the number of barges, which stands at about 50,000 annually. The state continues to rely heavily on such natural resources as salt, agricultural products, sulfur, petroleum, and natural gas, and many of the ships transporting these goods leave by way of New Orleans.

The intense trade presence has spawned an important commercial byproduct: banking. The CBD is one of the nation's leading centers of finance, with more than 50 commercial banks. During the strongest oil years of recent times, from the early 1970s through the early 1980s, the city's banks and other industries raked in plenty of money financing offshore oil production. Since the mid-1980s, however, a nation-

wide slump in oil prices has cost New Orleans and, even more acutely, Lafayette countless jobs. Nevertheless, the oil and natural gas industries continue to play vital roles in both the city's and the state's economy—the state contains just under 10 percent of the nation's known oil reserves, and it's the country's third-largest producer of petroleum (it's also the nation's third-largest refiner). And that's not even considering the possibility of additional oil reserves farther out at sea in the gulf. The state also produces more than 25 percent of the nation's natural gas. Salt and sulfur mining also contribute significantly to the state's coffers.

Other key industries for Louisiana include petrochemical production, where it ranks second in the nation (much of the chemicals and byproducts produced in the state are related to petroleum production); shipbuilding (Avondale Shipyards, just outside New Orleans, is the largest industrial employer in Louisiana); timber and forestry; commercial fishing (the state catches about 25 percent of all the seafood landed in the United States); and aerospace and aviation (Martin Marietta employs about 2,500 workers in metro New Orleans, where a plant builds the external fuel tanks for NASA's space shuttle program).

Farming, though diminished considerably over the past century, still represents a significant chunk of the state economy, although it has relatively little direct effect on New Orleans. Louisiana has about 23,000 farms, more than 2,000 of them with more than a thousand acres. Crops vary greatly, depending on terrain and climate. In the southeastern parishes, some citrus is grown, while northern parishes up near the Arkansas border are known for their timber production. Louisiana's nutrient-rich alluvial soil and plentiful rainfall make it the perfect state for many other crops, but the leaders are soybeans (the state's top crop, grown all over), cotton (mostly in the northeastern part of the state), sugarcane (predominantly in the Cajun Country parishes of St. Mary, Assumption, LaFourche, and Iberia), rice (produced mostly in the southwestern part of the state, especially Jefferson Davis and Acadia Parishes—New Iberia's Konrico Company is the oldest rice mill in America), and corn (grown in virtually every parish). Other popular crops include wheat, sorghum, sweet potatoes, strawberries, blueberries, peaches, and hot peppers. Sugarcane is a particularly important crop, and Steen's Syrup Mill in Abbeville, southwest of Lafayette, is the world's largest syrup plant. The massive Domino sugar refinery outside New Orleans is the largest such refinery in the nation. Louisiana also produces more shallots than any other U.S. state.

What has saved New Orleans's and Louisiana's economy in recent decades is tourism, which even following the lean months right after the terrorist attacks of September 11, 2001, continues to score high numbers. (It has been estimated that the decline in visitors following September 11 cost the state $200 million.) But one way or

What has saved New Orleans's and Louisiana's economy in recent decades is tourism, which continues to score high numbers. One way or another, New Orleans always seems to find a way to attract visitors.

another, New Orleans always seems to find a way to attract visitors. If convention trade falters, leisure travelers pick up the slack, and vice versa. Throughout the 1990s the city hosted so many business conventions and major festivals and events that, by 1996, their growth outpaced the number of hotel rooms available. Dozens of accommodations opened over the next five years, and now there's actually a bit of a glut of hotel rooms in town, which translates to strong competition and a buyer's market for visitors. But this is a temporary condition for New Orleans—tourism growth will be strong here for the foreseeable future.

Tourism has been an important source of revenue for New Orleans and the rest of southern Louisiana for centuries, but its prominence has grown dramatically during the past fifty years. Nearly 100,000 Louisianans work in the state's tourism industry, and travelers spend more than $5 billion during their visits to the state each year. A glamorous byproduct of tourism is the local film industry. The state has an aggressive film and video office that entices moviemakers to shoot in the state. In 2002 alone, the movies *The Runaway Jury* (based on a John Grisham novel, starring Dustin Hoffman and Gene Hackman, and filmed throughout metro New Orleans) and *Unchain My Heart* (about the life of Ray Charles, and filmed extensively in New Orleans and Hammond) brought in an estimated $50 million in revenue for the state, and those are just two of several major pictures shot in Louisiana recently.

INTRODUCTION

The People

Metro New Orleans covers a considerable area, some 360 square miles (about 160 of those square miles over water). The city itself is in Orleans Parish, but the metro area also encompasses Jefferson (home to Kenner and Metairie), St. Bernard (home to Chalmette), and St. Tammany (on the North Shore) Parishes. About 485,000 people live within the city limits, and the metro population is nearly triple that, about 1.33 million. The city can feel a lot more crowded, however, given that some 7 million tourists and conventioneers visit each year.

New Orleans's population actually declined slightly between 1990 and 2000, by about 2.5 percent. As of 2000, it ranked 31st in the nation in population, not far behind Tucson, Oklahoma City, and Portland, Oregon, and not far ahead of Las Vegas and Cleveland. New Orleans's metro population ranks 35th in the nation, and increased by 4 percent between 1990 and 2000; it's not far behind metro Charlotte or Las Vegas, and it's not far ahead of Salt Lake City, Austin, or Greensboro–Winston-Salem.

About 67 percent of New Orleans's residents identify as black or African-American, followed by 28 percent as white, and 2 percent as Asian. Only four U.S. cities with populations greater than 100,000 have a higher percentage of black residents (Detroit; Gary, Indiana; Birmingham, Alabama; and Jackson, Mississippi). About 33 percent of all Louisianans identify as black or African-American, the second-highest percentage in the nation, trailing only Mississippi. Only 3 percent of New Orleanians identify as being Hispanic or Latino, a relatively low number compared to most large U.S. cities. Statewide, a full 16 percent of Louisianans identify as being of French or French-Canadian extraction.

About 35 percent of all residents of New Orleans work in management, professional, and related occupations, 25 percent in sales and office jobs, and 22 percent in the service industry. About 25 percent of all New Orleans families live below the poverty level.

Of the roughly 69,000 households in Orleans Parish (home to New Orleans) headed by two people, 1,768 (2.5 percent) of them are headed

Mardi Gras

© ANDREW COLLINS

by same-sex partners. Of major U.S. metropolitan areas, New Orleans ranks eighth in this category, trailing only San Francisco, Miami–Fort Lauderdale, Austin, Seattle, Springfield (Massachusetts), Albuquerque, and Atlanta.

The state population, as of 2002, stood at 4,482,646, which ranked it 24nd in the nation, about the same as Alabama, a little behind Minnesota and Colorado, and a little ahead of South Carolina and Kentucky. It is, however, one of the slower-growing states in the country, ranking 40th in population increase between 1990 and 2000. The 5.9 percent growth during this period was the slowest of any state in the South. It's probably safe to assume that part of the reason for Louisiana's low growth rate was the loss of workers in the state's faltering oil industry.

Elsewhere in Louisiana, the largest cities are Baton Rouge (227,000), Shreveport (200,000), Metairie (146,000), Lafayette (110,000), Lake Charles (72,000), Kenner (70,000), Bossier City (56,000), Monroe (53,000), and Alexandria (46,000).

Of Louisiana's parishes, the fastest-growing between 1990 and 2000 were Ascension (32 percent), St. Tammany (32 percent), and Livingston (31 percent). Livingston and Ascension Parishes are adjoining and comprise the suburbs east and southeast of Baton Rouge, and St. Tammany Parish, which is also suburban, is along the fast-growing north shore of New Orleans. Two of the other four parishes with at least 15 percent growth (Tangipahoa and West Feliciana) are also suburbs of the Baton Rouge and New Orleans metroplexes; the other two are Lafayette Parish, which reflects a renewed growth in and around the city of Lafayette related to high-tech and other industries, and Allen Parish, a largely rural area northwest of Lafayette and northeast of Lake Charles.

On the Road

Louisiana and New Orleans are year-round destinations. Keep special events and festivals in mind when you plan your visit—Mardi Gras is the best known but by no means the only big party thrown in this city. Even during the dreaded hot and humid summer months, New Orleans remains fairly popular with convention travel and also throws several popular festivals. And with kids out of school at this time, family road trips throughout the southern half of the state are commonplace. Most attractions remain open year-round, although some reduce their hours or days in winter.

Weather-wise, early spring and late fall are wonderful for visiting the state, and early spring is also the ideal time to take a swamp tour and see the state in its full splendor. Magnolia trees and flower beds come to life beginning in early March and stay colorful all through summer. Winters in southern Louisiana are temperate and mild, and this is a great time to enjoy the charms of New Orleans.

WHAT TO PACK

Packing for a trip to Louisiana is like planning for any other trip in the southeastern United States, or to any city or town with a warm and wet climate and some water access. If you're visiting only New Orleans, you can pack as you might for any warm-weather city—it gets hot and humid from April through October, so stick with light clothing constructed of breathable fabrics at these times. Only a handful of high-end restaurants in New Orleans require jackets, ties, or dresses, but even in summer, it's customary to wear nice

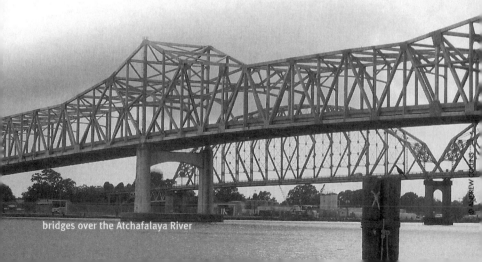

bridges over the Atchafalaya River

jeans or slacks, sandals or loafers, and a collared shirt at any reasonably nice restaurant. This is a touristy place, and especially when the weather is hot, you can get away with casual attire, but printed T-shirts, cutoff shorts, and flip-flops are frowned upon at most of the nicer establishments in New Orleans, including some of the dressier hotel lobbies and lounges. That sort of attire is just fine at inexpensive, casual restaurants and bars. The temperature rarely falls below freezing in Louisiana, but in winter it can get nippy, so you should pack a light winter jacket and gloves if you're coming in January or February. But don't overdo it on the warm clothing, as you can also see highs in the 60s and 70s on many winter days.

If you're planning to spend time exploring southern Louisiana outside the cities, casual dress is even more the norm, and formal attire unheard of. There are a few things you should plan to bring with you if you're planning to go on a swamp tour, hiking or fishing trip, or any other outdoorsy exploration. It can rain frequently just about any time of year in Louisiana, so definitely pack a travel umbrella, a waterproof jacket, hat, and shoes, and a small waterproof travel bag (to carry a camera, for instance).

In few parts of the state are you very far from almost any kind of household, clothing, food, or travel supply—distances in southern Louisiana between gas stations, grocery stores, and department stores are usually fairly short, the exceptions being very small towns in rural parts of the state.

SIGHTSEEING TOURS

For a variety of reasons, southern Louisiana is rife with tour operators, and these can be a great resource, whether to explore a place that's difficult to find or enjoy on your own, or to get a more detailed history of what you're seeing. In some cases, it's actually less expensive to visit an attraction or a series of them on a group tour than on your own. Many of these excursions last the better part of a day and involve a large group and a bus ride, but many other options involve low-key strolls through the Garden District and some of New Orleans's most famous cemeteries.

Tour operators in New Orleans typically take credit cards, but some of the smaller operations do not, especially those companies giving walking tours. Always confirm the payment options before you show up. Many tour operators require or strongly recommend reservations, but again, there are plenty of exceptions to this rule.

Even if you're not a big fan of tour excursions, there are certain places in Louisiana, and particularly New Orleans, where it's helpful to visit as part of an organized group with a knowledgeable leader. Cemeteries are an obvious one—they can be in dicey or even downright unsafe areas, and as fascinating as they are aesthetically, with their mausoleums and aboveground graves, they're best appreciated when described by an expert guide. Certain historic neighborhoods with notable architecture but few formal attractions or homes open to the public—such as New Orleans's Garden District—are also best explored as part of a tour.

The vast and ravishingly beautiful swamps and marshes throughout the region are also best visited on a tour, for logistical reasons if nothing else. An outsider would have little luck navigating these complex waterways. But guides can also point out the flora and fauna around you, and also find the best spots to see alligators, egrets, nutria, and other creatures of Louisiana swamps up close.

Many of the region's bus tours, which lead through the Plantation Country along the Mississippi River between New Orleans and Baton Rouge, are just as well avoided if you're the kind of person who loves hopping into the car and motoring about on your own, exploring scenic highways and byways. Most of the sites visited on these tours are open to the public anyway, and you can just as easily show up on your own for a tour, traveling at your own speed. If you don't wish to rent a car, however, these tours provide a convenient way to see at least one and possibly several plantations without having to worry about directions, logistics, and car-rental drop-offs. They're especially handy if you're only visiting New Orleans for a short time, and there is the added advantage of hearing about the towns and historic sites that line the river on the drive from New Orleans out to the plantations.

One of the best general tour companies in the city is the ubiquitous but highly reliable **Gray Line** (504/569-1401 or 800/535-7786, www.gray lineneworleans.com), which offers a wonderful variety of tours. One of the newest is the Louisiana Purchase walking tour of the French Quarter, which was begun in 2003 to commemorate that 1803 fire sale orchestrated by James Monroe and Robert R. Livingston. One of the more unusual Gray Line excursions is the Southern Comfort Cocktail Tour, a two-hour ramble through the Quarter in which strollers are regaled with stories of the Big Easy's colorful restaurants and taverns, along with the famous cocktails invented at them. Southern Comfort itself was created back in 1874 by M. W. Heron at a bar in the French Quarter. All Gray Line tours leave from the little lighthouse-style Gray Line booth at the foot of Toulouse Street by the river.

Another reliable company with a wide range of trips is **New Orleans Tours** (504/592-0560), which offers a variety of general excursions, from the Essential City Tour (good for an overview) to the New Orleans Voodoo Experience (corny, but a lot of folks love this one). It also gives bus tours out to the plantations on River Road.

Blue Dog Seafood Tours (800/875-4287, www.bluedogtours.com) offers the ultimate tour for fish lovers. These boat rides take visitors through the swamps, where you'll see the crew hoist gill and hoop nets for fish, traps for crawfish, and even box traps for wild boar. The narrative

© ANDREW COLLINS

alligators on log in Honey Island Swamp

also details how various residents of southern Louisiana—Cajuns, Isleños, Indians and escaped slaves, and Croatians and Vietnamese—historically eked out a living on fishing. The tour ends with a lavish feast of Louisiana seafood. Transportation to and from your hotel in New Orleans can be arranged for $15 per person; the tour and dinner cost $75 per person.

Cemetery tours are a favorite in New Orleans; they're usually entertaining but in some cases sensational, with mystical tales concerning voodoo and ghosts. If you'd prefer a straightforward graveyard tour that still has plenty of color and historical insights, try **Save Our Cemeteries** (504/525-3377 or 888/721-7493, www.saveour cemeteries.com), a nonprofit organization that preserves and protects some 31 of the city's burial grounds. It offers outstanding tours of both Lafayette Cemetery No. 1 and St. Louis Cemetery No. 1. These are well-done walks with excellent guides. The Lafayette tours are given on Mon., Wed., Fri., and Sat. at 10:30 A.M. and cost $6; the St. Louis tours are given only on Sun. mornings at 10 A.M. and cost $12.

Strongly recommended are the informative walks given by **Historic New Orleans Tours** (504/947-2120, www.tourneworleans.com). These tours are given daily at 11 A.M. and 1:45 P.M., departing from the **Garden District Book Shop** (at The Rink, Washington Ave. and Prytania St.). The tours last about two hours, and the cost is $14. (The same company also does French Quarter, Haunted, and Cemetery Voodoo tours.)

One of the more interesting ways to appreciate New Orleans's two favorite attractions is via the **John James Audubon** (504/586-8777, www .aquariumzoocruise.com), a riverboat that plies the Mississippi between the Aquarium of the Americas, at the foot of Canal Street, and the Audubon Zoo, at Audubon Park. The boat has daily departures from the Aquarium to the zoo at 10 A.M., noon, 2 P.M., and 4 P.M.; departures from the zoo are 11 A.M., 1 P.M., 3 P.M., and 5 P.M. There are few more enjoyable ways to appreciate the city skyline than from this lazy boat ride. The fare is $17 round-trip, and combination packages are available that include aquarium and zoo admission at a discounted rate.

Some of the other cruise boats offering excursions in New Orleans are also discussed in the Arts and Nightlife chapter, as these operators offer evening dinner and jazz cruises. **New Orleans Paddlewheels** (Poydras St. Wharf, 504/529-4567 or 800/445-4109, www.new orleanspaddlewheels.com) has several types of river excursions aboard the **Riverboat Cajun Queen,** built in the late 1980s as an exact replica of a late-19th-century vessel that sailed along the Atlantic and Gulf coasts, and on the

Paddlewheeler _Creole Queen,_ a 1983 boat based on an 1850s luxury paddlewheeler. Trips include Dixieland jazz cruises (with dinner included), hour-long river tours, and trips out to Chalmette battlefield, site of the Battle of New Orleans.

The **Steamboat _Natchez_** (Toulouse St. Wharf, behind Jackson Brewery, 504/586-8777) offers daily cruises with live jazz along the river at lunchtime, during the afternoon, and in the evening.

Tips for Travelers

STUDENTS

New Orleans is one of the all-time destinations among college-age travelers, with the rest of the southern part of the state, especially Cajun Country, also quite popular. It helps that the area has so many colleges and universities. New Orleans is home to Dillard University, Louisiana State University Medical Center, Loyola University, Tulane, the University of New Orleans, and Xavier University. Other colleges and universities found throughout the southern part of the state include Louisiana State University (Baton Rouge), McNeese State University (Lake Charles), Nicholls State University (Thibodaux), Southeastern Louisiana University (Hammond), Southern University (in Baton Rouge, it's the largest predominantly African-American university in the United States), and University of Louisiana (Lafayette), which also has a branch up in Monroe, in the northeast part of the state.

Within New Orleans, the restaurants, clubs, and shops along Frenchmen Street in Faubourg Marigny, Decatur Street in the French Quarter, all through the Warehouse District, Magazine Street all through Uptown and the Upper and Lower Garden Districts, and Maple Street Uptown all have a decidedly collegiate and youthful vibe. Bourbon Street is truly age-varied, but you're more likely to see conventioneers and yuppies parading along here more than you are college students.

STA Travel (www.counciltravel.com) is the definitive resource for student-age travelers—its website is a font of information on student deals all around the world. There are two STA travel agencies in the state: **STA Tulane University** (100 University Center, off St. Charles Avenue, Uptown, New Orleans, 504/865-5673) and **STA Louisiana State University** (LSU Union, Suite 143, Raphael Semmes Rd., Baton Rouge, 225/578-0840).

There's one youth hostel in New Orleans, the only one in the state, **Marquette House** (2249 Carondelet St., 504/523-3014, http://hometown.aol.com/hineworlns/myhomepage/index.html), which is in the Lower Garden District. It's part of **Hostelling International—American Youth Hostels** (202/783-6161, www.hiayh.org), which is a useful general resource for learning about hostels throughout the United States.

Many Louisiana museums and attractions offer student discounts; always bring your university or school I.D. card with you and ask even if such reduced prices or admissions aren't posted.

GAY AND LESBIAN TRAVELERS

New Orleans is something of a bastion of gay-friendliness in perhaps the most socially conservative and gay-hostile part of the nation, the Gulf South. Louisiana as a whole, along with its nearest states, Texas, Arkansas, Mississippi, and Alabama, offers no legal protection against discrimination on the basis of sexual orientation, and attitudes of many people living in smaller towns throughout the state are less than welcoming toward gays and lesbians.

New Orleans, on the other hand, has gay newspapers, a busy nightlife district that rubs right up against the more mainstream nightlife district in the French Quarter, a gay bookstore, and numerous lesbian and gay organizations and gay-owned businesses. Locals tend to be rather blasé about the sight of two women or two men walking hand-in-hand in the Big Easy, especially in the Quarter, Faubourg Marigny, and Uptown, which tend to have the highest lesbian and gay populations. Tourists, however, sometimes from less tolerant places, have been known to react less comfortably. And rarely, but occasionally, New Orleans has been the site of gay-related attacks and crimes, or more often fights or arguments along Bourbon Street, where drunken revelers sometimes lose their cool, and where the city's straight and gay nightclub rows collide (at St. Ann Street, to be precise).

> *New Orleans is something of a bastion of gay-friendliness in perhaps the most socially conservative and gay-hostile part of the nation, the Gulf South. Locals tend to be rather blasé about the sight of two women or two men walking hand-in-hand in the Big Easy.*

According to Census 2000, Orleans Parish (home to New Orleans) ranked 11th in the United States in counties by percentage of same-sex couples (defined as households headed by unmarried same-sex partners). New Orleans also ranked 25th among incorporated places with the highest actual number of same-sex couples, with a total of 1,768 of them. These stats don't pertain to single persons, and they're also dependent on couples voluntarily identifying themselves as gay. But both figures give a sense of how popular New Orleans is among gays and lesbians.

Statewide, New Orleans has by far the highest percentage of same-sex couples among the state's incorporated places, with several neighboring towns trailing just behind. Outside the immediate region, Baton Rouge ranked second in the southern part of the state, followed by the towns of Bogalusa, Hammond, New Iberia, and Houma. Quite a few gay people also live in Lafayette and Lake Charles, which with Baton Rouge contain the other gay nightlife options in the state.

Two annual events, Mardi Gras in the late winter and the Southern Decadence Celebration over Labor Day weekend, draw the greatest numbers of gay and lesbian visitors to New Orleans, but the city is always popular, and many of the B&Bs and hotels—especially in Faubourg Marigny—are gay-owned.

For information on nightlife and the scene throughout Louisiana and the Gulf South, consult the free biweekly *Ambush Magazine* (504/522-8049, www .ambushmag.com). The same publication also has a website just for gay goings-on during Mardi Gras, www.gaymardigras.com. Another publication with lots of information on the community is *Eclipse* (877/966-3342, www.eclipse-mag.com).

TRAVELERS WITH CHILDREN

Louisiana is an excellent, if not quite stellar, destination for families and travelers with children. The only real drawback is that the most-visited destination in the state, New Orleans, is more geared toward adults than children. This is not to say that kids won't enjoy touring some of the city's attractions, or that you won't find family-friendly hotels, inns, and restaurants. But do keep in mind that many of the city's smaller, high-end inns and fancier hotels tend to frown on children as guests, as do some of the rowdier or more sophisticated restaurants and bars.

But the New Orleans metro region has some outstanding attractions for kids, such as the Audubon Institute's facilities (which include the Audubon Zoo & Gardens, the Insectarium, the Aquarium of the Americas, the Entergy IMAX Theatre, and the Louisiana Nature Center), Rivertown U.S.A., Storyland at City Park, the New Orleans Historic Voodoo Museum, Musee Conti's Wax Museum, and—of course—the

Louisiana Children's Museum, right in the New Orleans CBD. Many of the excursions offered through the city and region, such as swamp tours, riverboat rides, and haunted house and voodoo tours, are a big hit with kids, especially teenagers.

Elsewhere in the state, the Konrico and Tabasco factory tours in New Iberia, and virtually all of the major attractions in Lafayette and Baton Rouge, such as Vermilionville and the U.S.S. *Kidd*, have a strong following with younger ones. In general, the plantations along the Great River Road tend to be more popular with adults, but Laura Plantation gives a lively tour that can be great fun for kids.

Many chain hotels and other accommodations throughout Louisiana allow kids to stay in their parents' rooms free or at a discount, and many restaurants in the state have kids' menus. Some of the Cajun restaurants with live music, such as Mulate's outside Lafayette and in New Orleans, are real family affairs. Fear not if you're headed to a seafood house with finicky kids who aren't wild about fish or clams—it's the very rare restaurant that doesn't offer a few chicken, burger, or grilled cheese options. Many museums and other attractions offer greatly reduced admission.

SENIOR CITIZENS

New Orleans has a strong following among senior travelers, but much of the surrounding region is even more popular with this demographic, in part because the city has a reputation—deserved or not—for crime, nightlife, and overall rowdiness. In fact, New Orleans is as hospitable as any city toward travelers 50, 60, or older, but the wild nightlife scene around the Quarter can be off-putting to some. Many persons seeking a more relaxed and slower-paced New Orleans experience prefer to stay in the Garden District, especially at one of the several hotels and inns along St. Charles Avenue. Quite a few retirees winter in the North Shore's St. Tammany and Tangipahoa Parishes, and also in the Lafayette and Lake Charles areas.

Louisiana is a family-friendly state, and with the growth in multigenerational travel—grandparents traveling with grandkids, or several generations of families vacationing together—the state's most family-oriented areas, such as Cajun Country and the North Shore, have become popular for these travelers.

Depending on the attraction or hotel, you may qualify for age-related discounts—the thresholds can range from 50 to 65. It can also help if you're a member of the **American Association of Retired Persons (AARP)** (800/424-3410, www.aarp.org). For a nominal annual membership fee, you'll receive all sorts of travel discounts as well as a newsletter that often touches on travel issues. **Elderhostel** (877/426-8056, www.elderhostel.org) organizes a wide variety of educationally oriented tours and vacations geared toward 55-and-over individuals or couples of whom one member is that age.

TRAVELERS WITH DISABILITIES

Louisiana is on par with other states as far as conforming to the guidelines set by the Americans with Disabilities Act (ADA). Within new hotels, larger and recently built restaurants, and most major attractions, you can expect to find wheelchair-accessible restrooms, entrance ramps, and other fixtures. But Louisiana has many hole-in-the-wall cafés, historic house-museums with narrow staircases or uneven thresholds, tiny B&Bs, and other buildings that are not easily accessible to persons using wheelchairs. If you're traveling with a guide animal, always call ahead and even consider getting written or faxed permission to bring one with you to a particular hotel or restaurant; though it's the rare instance in Louisiana that you won't be permitted to arrive with a guide dog.

A useful resource is the **Society for the Advancement of Travel for the Handicapped** (212/447-7284, www.sath.org).

MONEY
Banks, ATMs, and Credit Cards
Banks are plentiful throughout New Orleans and southern Louisiana, although fewer and farther

between in the handful of rural areas, including some of the smaller villages in the Cajun Country. The French Quarter is also lacking actual banks, although businesses with ATMs (automated teller machines)—including bars, hotel lobbies, souvenir shops, and convenience stores—abound. Just keep in mind that many of these places charge a high usage fee, as much as $3 to $5 per transaction, whereas actual bank ATMs usually only charge $1 to $2. Most banks in New Orleans are adjacent to the French Quarter in the CBD, and most are open weekdays from 9 A.M. until anywhere between 3 and 5 P.M., and on Saturdays 9 A.M. until noon.

Most ATMs are available 24 hours a day and accept a wide range of bank cards (typically Cirrus and/or Plus, for example) and credit cards. Crime is a legitimate, although somewhat overblown, concern in New Orleans, but you should exercise discretion—especially if you're alone—when using ATMs late at night, particularly in the CBD, which can be desolate at times. Walk away and choose a different machine if you see anybody lurking nearby or actually loitering inside the vestibule in which the machine is located, and never leave your car unlocked and running while you step out to use the machine.

Credit cards and bank cards are acceptable

A GUIDE TO LOUISIANA PRONUNCIATIONS

How do you pronounce "New Orleans"? It's sometimes heard as "N'AW-luhns" in movies and TV commercials, but New Orleanians most definitely do not pronounce it this way, and you shouldn't either—it sounds disrespectful, as though you're making fun of locals. The more conventional incorrect pronunciation is NOO or-LEENS. Say it this way and you'll be marked as an outsider (probably a northerner), but at least you won't be accused of being a jerk. Locals pronounce the city's name in a handful of relatively similar ways, the simplest and most common being "noo OHR-lins," or thereabouts. You don't have to say it with a big, silly drawl or with delicious emphasis, like you're a damsel in a Tennessee Williams play. Just say it quickly and casually. You might hear some locals, especially those with aristocratic tendencies, pronounce it "noo OHR-lee-ahns."

Having settled that, we move on to the rest of the rivers, lakes, towns, and streets of New Orleans and Louisiana. Pronouncing these place-names can be extremely tricky for outsiders. "Correct" pronunciation isn't really the point here—according to your French teacher, Chartres Street, in New Orleans' French Quarter, would be pronounced "shart." But the correct local pronunciation is "CHAR-ters" or "CHART-uz."

If you're the sort of traveler who would rather not sound like an outsider, or at least you'd prefer to sound like a veteran traveler, keep the charts of Louisiana place-name pronunciations on the pages that follow handy, and do your best to learn the major ones. Locals won't generally torment you for pronouncing words as an outsider, and in many cases there are two or more commonly accepted (though often hotly debated) ways to pronounce the same word, especially taking into consideration one's accent—Louisiana has several regional accents. However, if you can say things in a manner that's relatively local-sounding, even if you have a Yankee or international accent, you may be taken a little more seriously by the Louisianan you're addressing.

The pronunciation keys on the following pages are approximate and most definitely imperfect, again owing to the many regional nuances among locals, sometimes having grown up on the same block but still favoring one pronunciation over another. Syllables set in boldface are stressed (as in "CHAR-ters").

If a common street or place name is not listed, assume it's pronounced more or less the way it is elsewhere in the United States (for example, St. Louis Street, in the French Quarter, is pronounced here the way the Missouri city is, "saynt LOO-iss," not the way the French would).

forms of payment at virtually all gas stations and hotels, many inns and B&Bs (but definitely not some of the very small ones, which will take traveler's checks and sometimes personal checks), most restaurants (the exceptions tend to be inexpensive places, small cafés, diners, and the like), and most shops (again, the exception tends to be small, independent stores).

Currency

Louisiana receives relatively few international visitors directly from their countries of origin, but Louis Armstrong New Orleans International Airport does have direct flights from Canada and Honduras. The airport and the city itself do have currency exchange booths and services; at the airport, there's a branch of **Whitney National Bank,** in the ticket lobby next to the U.S. post office, that has a foreign-currency exchange. The ticket lobby also has a **Mutual of Omaha Business Center,** which has currency exchange services. Foreign currency is not accepted anywhere in New Orleans.

Currency exchange rates may change during the lifetime of this book, but here are a few very approximate samples from some major English-speaking nations: 1 British pound equals about US$1.72, $1 Canadian equals about US$0.77; $1 Australian equals about US$0.72; $1 New Zealand equals about US$0.64; and 1 Euro equals about US$1.20.

Costs

Depending whether you travel mostly in New Orleans or out to the outlying towns and cities, the cost of travel in Louisiana can be as expensive as some of the most costly U.S. cities, such as Boston or New York City, or as inexpensive as many average-priced destinations. Compared with other parts of the United States, most of Louisiana is either average or even a bit less expensive.

New Orleans, especially during the spring and fall high seasons, has some very expensive hotels, with rooms at top properties easily exceeding $300 nightly. However, the city also has a huge number of mid-priced and budget motels and inns, where rates often fall well below $100 nightly, even during busy times. During Mardi Gras, Jazz Fest, and when major conventions are in town, it can be tough to find a room in the city for under $150, and upscale business hotels will sometimes double their standard rates. On the positive side, because New Orleans has so many hotel rooms, many properties offer deep discounts during the slower summer months or at other periods when tourism is a bit slow.

Elsewhere in southern Louisiana, budget chain motels typically charge from $35 to $60 nightly, and midprice to upscale chain properties usually charge from $60 to $100, with some high-end hotels in Lafayette and Baton Rouge charging a bit more. Rates at inns and B&B outside New Orleans vary greatly according to how luxurious they are, but usually start as low as $50 for something basic to over $200 for a fancy suite at a plantation or high-end property.

It's fairly easy to eat well in New Orleans without spending a bundle. The city is famous for its exclusive, high-end restaurants, such as Commander's Palace, Emeril's, and Brennan's. But even the ultra-popular high-end eateries charge a bit less than comparable restaurants in San Francisco and New York. And many of the fanciest restaurants offer prix-fixe set meals, which can save you money. Ordering á la carte at one of the very top New Orleans restaurants, with appetizer, entrée, dessert, wine or a couple of cocktails, and tax and tips will set you back around $100 per person, but you can get an equally good meal for about half that at many other upscale eateries around town. And for just $15 to $25 per person, you can enjoy a full meal at the Gumbo Shop, Praline Connection, Mulate's, Mother's, or any number of other casual restaurants serving first-rate Cajun, Creole, soul, or home-style cooking. Elsewhere in southern Louisiana, prices at lower-end restaurants are the same or slightly less than in New Orleans, and at high-end restaurants usually 10 to 20 percent less. The one exception can be the North Shore suburbs, like Covington and Mandeville, which have some excellent but expensive high-end eateries that charge every bit as much as similar restaurants in New Orleans.

Shopping in Louisiana is not markedly more or less expensive than in other parts of the United

States, although you'll find some very pricey upscale boutiques and galleries in New Orleans and along the North Shore. Gas stations in Louisiana charge about the same as neighboring states.

Sales Tax

The Louisiana state sales tax is 4 percent. It's the only state in the nation that offers tax-free shopping to international visitors (see the *Shopping* chapter for details). In addition, municipalities come up with many additional local taxes, most prominently car-rental and hotel taxes. In New Orleans, for example, the hotel tax is a whopping 13 percent, and the car-rental tax is 12 percent.

Tipping

In the tipping-oriented United States, it's typical to leave a 15 to 20 tip on a restaurant check, but in larger cities, people tip slightly higher. In New Orleans you might want to edge toward 20 percent, obviously factoring in the level of service you receive. You might round up your change or leave as much as $1 when ordering a drink at a bar or a cup of espresso at a coffeehouse (some coffeehouses and cafés have tip jars on their counters and appreciate, but don't necessarily expect, you to drop a little change in); if you're ordering multiple drinks, tip more along the lines of 15 percent for the total bill. At nightclubs, the theater, or other places with a coat check, tip $1 per coat or bag.

Tip taxi drivers 15 to 20 percent, as well as hairstylists. At hotels, tip your parking valet $1 or $2 each time they retrieve your car; tip bellhops 50 cents to $1 per bag, and leave $1 or $2 per day for hotel housecleaning staff in your room. If the concierge performs any special tasks for you, tip $5 to $10. Room-service gratuities are typically built into the total bill, so leaving an additional tip is unnecessary and should only be done at your discretion; tip the local pizza or other food delivery person who brings dinner to your hotel room $2 or $3 depending on the total bill. At small inns and B&Bs, it's customary to leave somewhat more than this for cleaning and other staff. You may find an envelope left in your room especially for the purpose of tipping the staff. There seems to be no consensus about what to leave at small properties like this, but aim for a minimum of $2 or $3 per day, and anywhere from $5 to $10 per day if you received a great deal of personal service and attention (such as help with sightseeing and restaurant reservations) or you stayed in an especially big and luxurious suite that required a great deal of cleaning. At small B&Bs that are cleaned and serviced by the owners themselves, it is not necessary or even appropriate to leave a tip.

If you use the services of an individual tour guide, consider tipping 10 to 15 percent of the total cost. The practice varies greatly on package tours, but drivers and guides generally expect to receive anywhere from $2 to $10 per person per day, unless gratuities have already been included in the price of the tour.

BUSINESS HOURS

Most restaurants in urban and suburban parts of the state serve lunch from 11 A.M. or noon until 2 or 3 P.M. and dinner from 5 or 6 P.M. until 10 P.M. In New Orleans, there are a handful of eateries open 24 hours and many others serving food until midnight. In the French Quarter, many bars stay open and serve alcohol 24 hours a day; elsewhere in the city, bars are more commonly open until between 2 and 4 A.M. Elsewhere in the state, bars generally close at 2 A.M., and it's rare to find restaurants (except some fast-food chains) serving food past 10 or 11 at night. In some of the more rural parts of the state, especially the southwestern sections, expect lunch to end by 2 P.M. and dinner by 9 P.M. The post office is usually open 8 A.M.–5 P.M. on weekdays and also on Saturday mornings.

There's no reliable rule on typical shop hours, except that they seem to be getting gradually longer, to the point that major chain shops and stores in big shopping malls often stay open from 9 or 10 A.M. until 9 or 10 P.M., typically with shorter hours on Sundays. Local, independently operated boutiques and shops often don't open till late morning (especially in resort areas), and they often close by 5 or 6 P.M.; these same shops may not open at all on Sundays or even on Mondays

NEW ORLEANS PLACE NAMES

Burgundy (street): bur-GUN-dee	Melpomene (street): MEL-po-MEEN
Cadiz (street): KAY-diz	Metairie (suburb): MED-uh-ree
Calliope (street): call-ee-OPE	Michoud (street/neighborhood): MEE-shoh
Carondelet (street): care-OHN-deh-LET	Milan (street): MYE-lan
Chalmette (suburb): SHALL-mett	Pontchartrain (lake): PONCH-uh-train
Chartres (street): CHART-ers	Prytania (street): prih-TAN-ya
Clio (street): CLYE-o	Socrates (street): SO-crates
Conti (street): CON-tie	Tchoupitoulas (street): chop-ah-TOO-lehs
Decatur (street): de-KAY-dur	Terpsichore (street): TERP-sih-core
Iberville (street): IBB-bur-ville	Toulouse (street): too-LOOS
Loyola (school): lye-O-luh	Tulane (street/school): TOO-lane
Marigny (street/neighborhood): MAH-rah-nee	Vieux Carré (neighborhood): VYOO ka-RAY

or Tuesdays. In some densely populated areas you'll be able to find 24-hour full-service grocery stores, and 24-hour gas stations and convenience stores are found in several parts of the state, especially near highway exits of major interstate highways. Because shop hours vary so greatly, it's especially important to phone ahead if you're concerned about any one particular business being open when you arrive.

Louisiana is pretty quiet on Sundays and Mondays outside of New Orleans; in fact, it's a good strategy to plan your visit to be in New Orleans on those days and, especially if you're not much for crowds and nightlife, in another part of the state on Fridays and Saturdays. In many towns, even places that are quite touristy, like New Iberia or Covington, you'll find nary a shop open on Main Street on Sunday.

Many restaurants are dark on Mondays or Sundays or both, especially for dinner (as some of these serve Sunday brunch). Major attractions are often closed Monday and to a lesser extent on Sunday.

TIME ZONE

As with Mississippi, Alabama, Arkansas, and Texas, Louisiana falls entirely within the Central Standard Time (CST) zone. Chicago is in the same zone, Los Angeles two hours behind, Denver an hour behind, and New York and Atlanta an hour ahead. The Canadian Maritimes are two hours ahead; London, England, is six hours ahead; and Israel is eight hours ahead.

Remember that hours behind and ahead are affected by the fact that Louisiana, like most but not all American states and Canadian Provinces, observes Central Daylight Time (CDT): on the last Sunday in October, clocks are set back one hour through the first Sunday in April, when they are set back ahead an hour.

TOURIST INFORMATION

The state of Louisiana is broken down into numerous tourism regions. Usually each parish (like a county) has its own tourist board, and then certain cities (New Orleans, Lafayette, Baton Rouge) have their own offices of tourism. Each office has its own brochures and staff. It's wise to work directly with these offices when planning a trip to a specific area within the state—contact information for these offices is given in the appropriate chapters throughout the book. In many cases, the towns that make up a particular section of this book fall into more than one tourism region, so you may want to call two or three local offices to best plan out your itinerary and cull advice on upcoming events and attractions.

The statewide information bureau is the **Louisiana Office of Tourism** (1051 N. 3rd St., Room 327, Baton Rouge, LA 70802, 225/346-1857 or 888/225-4003, www.louisianatravel.com), which can send you a free Louisiana travel planner.

There are also 10 visitor welcome centers located throughout the state, some of which are unstaffed. These include locations at the Cabildo building on Jackson Square, in New Orleans, and in the State Capitol building in Baton Rouge. Other welcome centers serving the southern portion of the state include one at Kentwood, right off I-55 as you enter the state from Mississippi; one in Slidell, right off I-10 as you enter the state from the Mississippi coast; one in Pearl River, right off I-59 as you enter the state from Mississippi; one in St. Francisville, along U.S. 61 as you enter the state coming down from Natchez, Mississippi; and one in Vinton, right off I-10 as you enter the state from Texas. These all contain an array of brochures and range from quite helpful to not very—they're nice in a pinch or for basic questions, but you're always better off phoning ahead and obtaining local brochures and advice from the extremely useful regional and local tourist boards.

There are also visitor information kiosks in several spots at **Louis Armstrong New Orleans International Airport;** all visitor information employees at the airport are bilingual or multilingual.

Getting There and Around

GETTING THERE

New Orleans's airport is well-served by most major airlines and has direct flights to most of the nation's largest cities. It's centrally located, usually not terribly expensive, and pleasant to fly in and out of, so if you're coming for a short period or from a long distance, flying here makes plenty of sense. New Orleans also has direct Amtrak train service and Greyhound bus service from many big cities, but these modes of transport are often quite time-consuming and, especially in the case of trains, not always less expensive than flying.

Airports

Louis Armstrong New Orleans International Airport (900 Airline Hwy., off I-10, Kenner, 504/464-2650, www.flymsy.com) is a massive facility serving the entire Gulf South with service on about two dozen airlines. It's easy to find direct flights from most major U.S. cities (more than 35 in all) and also to such international cities as San Pedro Sala, Honduras, and Toronto, Canada. The airport is 15 miles west of downtown New Orleans.

Sample direct-flying times to New Orleans from major cities: Atlanta, 90 minutes; Chicago, 2 hours and 15 minutes; Los Angeles, 4 hours; Miami, 2 hours; and New York City, 3 hours.

New Orleans International Airport received a $850 million makeover between 1998 and 2001, which helped it accommodate a number of additional flights by Southwest Airlines, Midway, and Air Canada. All sorts of new food concessions have been added, including a huge Vieux Carré–inspired food court. Air traffic to New Orleans has increased by 32 percent since 1993.

In southern Louisiana, commercial service is also available to Baton Rouge, Lafayette, and Lake Charles. **Lafayette Regional Airport** (200 Terminal Dr., off U.S. 90, 2 miles southeast of downtown, 337/266-4400, www.lftairport.com) is served by American, Continental, Delta, and Northwest, with frequent direct flights to Atlanta, Dallas, Houston, and Memphis; it has on-site Avis, Budget, Enterprise, Hertz, and National car-rental agencies. **Baton Rouge Metropolitan Airport** (9430 Jackie Cochran Dr., 8 miles north of downtown off I-110, 225/355-0333, www.flybtr.com) is served by the same carriers and to the same four key cities as Lafayette Airport; there are Avis, Budget, Enterprise, and National car-rental agencies at the airport. **Lake Charles Regional Airport** (500 Airport Blvd., off Hwy. 385, about 10 miles south of downtown, 337/477-6051, www.flylakecharles.com) is served by Continental, with direct service to Houston; car-rental agencies here include Avis, Budget, Hertz, and National.

Generally, it's more expensive to fly to one of the smaller regional airports than to New Orleans. Airfares can change dramatically based on all sorts of factors, but to give an idea, as of this writing, the

PRONOUNCING LOUSIANA PLACE NAMES

Amite: AY-meet	Shreveport: SHREEV-port
Bossier City: BOH-zher CIT-ee	Tangipahoa: TAN-jah-puh-ho
Breaux Bridge: BROH bridge	Thibodaux: TIB-uh-doe
Calcasieu: CAL-cuh-shoo	Vacherie: VAH-shuh-ree
Carencro: CAIR-en-CROW	Atchafalaya: (swamp/river) UH-cha-fuh-lye-uh
Cloutierville: CLOO-chee-vill	Bayou Teche: (bayou) BYE-ew TESH
Houma: HOAM-uh	Bogue Chitto: (river) boe-guh CHEE-tuh
Lafayette: LAFF-ee-ette	Bonnet Carré: (spillway) BONN-ett CAIR-ee
Lafourche: la-FOOSH	Borgne (lake): BORN
Iowa: EYE-o-way	Fontainebleau (park): FOWN-ten-BLOO
Jeanerette: JENN-urh-ette	Manchac (bayou): MAN-shack
Monroe: MUN-roe	Maurepas (lake): MOOR-uh-paw
Natchitoches: NACK-ih-tish	Ouchita (river): WAW-shuh-taw
Opelousas: AH-puh-loo-suss	Sabine (river): suh-BEAN
Plaquemines: PLACK-ih-mens	Tchefuncte (river): CHUH-funk-tuh
Ponchatoula: PONCH-uh-tool-uh	

lowest sample airfares from New Orleans to several major cities were: Atlanta ($160), Chicago ($200), Houston ($140), Los Angeles ($275), New York ($140), and Toronto ($350). For the sake of comparison, those same flights from Baton Rouge would have been Atlanta ($200), Chicago ($275), Houston ($180), Los Angeles ($330), New York ($215), and Toronto ($440).

An alternative airport that's worth considering if you ever have trouble scoring a flight to New Orleans, or fares are especially high there because of a special event (like Mardi Gras or Jazz Fest), is **Jackson International Airport** (601/939-5631, www.jmaa.com) in Jackson, Mississippi, a three-hour drive north of the city. It's a fairly large airport serviced by nine airlines, with direct service to Atlanta, Baltimore/Washington, Charlotte, Chicago, Cincinnati, Dallas, Houston, Memphis, and Orlando. A bit smaller but slightly closer to New Orleans (a little under three hours away) is **Mobile Regional Airport** (800/357-5373, www.mobairport.com), which has direct service to Atlanta, Charlotte, Dallas, Houston, Memphis, and Orlando.

Transportation to and from the Airport

Getting from New Orleans International Airport to the French Quarter, a 15-mile trip that takes 25 to 35 minutes depending on traffic (which can be horrendous at peak travel times), is a relatively costly proposition. There are cabs, which you can pick up at the taxi stand outside baggage claim, that charge a fixed rate of $28 for one or two passengers and $12 per person thereafter. It makes very good sense if you're alone to offer to split the ride with another single person standing near you. Similarly, there's an airport limo service that started at the beginning of 2003. This costs $35 for one or two passengers and $10 per person (up to eight passengers capacity). You'll generally wait 10 to 20 minutes at the terminal's limo desk for this service, while cabs are usually there waiting for passengers outside the baggage claim.

For just $10 per person, you can take the **Airport Shuttle** (504/592-0555), which departs from New Orleans International Airport every 10 minutes and drops passengers at any downtown, CBD, or Garden District hotel.

For just $1.50, you can catch the **RTA bus** (504/242-2600, www.regionaltransit.org) from the airport to the northern edge of the CBD; it stops at Tulane Avenue near Elks Place, just a couple of blocks down from the Superdome and a couple of blocks uptown from Canal Street. If you don't have tons of luggage to cart around, it's a convenient and inexpensive option. The hotels along Canal Street and elsewhere in the upper half of the CBD are less than a 10-minute walk from the stop, but you'd be looking at a 1-mile stroll down to the Warehouse District and Jackson Square, and a considerably longer walk to the Garden District or Faubourg Marigny. You could walk from this bus stop a few blocks down Canal and pick up the St. Charles Streetcar, but you're looking at a lot of effort to save a few bucks, when you consider the economy of taking the Airport Shuttle.

If you're taking a cab someplace other than downtown New Orleans (meaning the CBD or French Quarter), you'll pay from $1.70 to $2.50 per mile (you can attempt to negotiate a better fare). For trips to Orleans, Jefferson, and Kenner Parishes, cabs charge $2.50 for the first one-sixth mile and 20 cents for each additional one-sixth mile and 40 seconds on the clock. There's also a flat charge of $1 per additional passenger. In St. Charles Parish, which comprises the towns west of Kenner and the airport, cabs charge $1.70 for the first one-fifth mile and 20 cents for each additional one-fifth mile or 40 seconds on the clock. Drivers must provide air-conditioning (and cannot charge for it), cannot refuse passengers for very short trips, and cannot charge for a "normal" amount of luggage.

Cruise Ships

New Orleans's popularity as a cruise-ship destination and as a point of embarkation, has risen steadily over the past two decades. Many people like leaving from New Orleans because it's such an enjoyable place to spend two or three days before or after the cruise. It's also a convenient debarkation point for cruises in the Western Caribbean—these typically call at Cozumel/Cancun, Jamaica, the Cayman Islands, and sometimes Key West. And when Cuba inevitably is opened up to U.S. tourism, ships from New Orleans will no doubt sail to Havana.

Cruise lines that regularly sail from New Orleans, typically leaving at the cruise terminal near the Hilton at Canal Street, include the youthful and budget-oriented **Carnival Cruise Line** (888/CARNIVAL, www.carnival.com). Carnival operates the M.S. *Inspiration,* which has offered seven-day Western Caribbean cruises out of New Orleans since 2000. Carnival also operates the massive *Conquest,* which offers seven-day Western Caribbean cruises; this 3,000-passenger ship, one of the largest to sail from New Orleans, began service early in 2003. A smaller Carnival option is the *Holiday,* which offers four- and five-day cruises down to Cozumel and Playa del Carmen, Mexico, near Cancun.

Slightly more upscale than Carnival and appealing to a slightly more mature demographic, Royal Caribbean Cruise Line (800/398-9819, www.royalcaribbean.com) offers five- to 10-night cruises to Grand Cayman, Key West, and Cozumel during the winter and spring on the 2,500-passenger *Grandeur of the Seas.*

A small cruise line with very small ships that mostly ply America's rivers and canals, **American Canadian Caribbean Line** (800/556-7450, www.accl-smallships.com) runs the *Niagara Prince,* which holds just 84 passengers, out of New Orleans on 15-day sails up the Mississippi and along smaller rivers to Chicago (offered in summer) and 12-day sails up the Mississippi and Tennessee Rivers to Nashville (offered during fall foliage season). Similarly intimate is the R/B *River Explorer* (888/456-2206, www.riverbarge.com), a 198-passenger vessel that plies the Mississippi, Cumberland, Missouri, and Ohio Rivers, the Atchafalaya Basin, and the Gulf Intracoastal Waterway, offering trips lasting from four to 10 days.

The only cruise line based in New Orleans is a distinctly American and rather unusual one: the **Delta Queen Steamboat Company** (800/543-1949, www.deltaqueen.com). This line includes three modern paddlewheel steamboats, which call New Orleans their home port but sail the entire river system of the central United States. Cruises from New Orleans can run as far as Pittsburgh and Minneapolis, and include such ports as St. Louis, Cincinnati, Louisville, Nashville, Chattanooga, Memphis, and Galveston. These luxurious, beautifully crafted boats have the feel of a lavish Victorian grand hotel, and even if you don't sail on one, it's great fun to watch them plying the Mississippi River. The *Delta Queen* itself is the oldest in the fleet, having been built in 1927 at a cost of about $1 million; the 285-foot vessel holds up to

174 passengers. The *Mississippi Queen* holds 414 passengers and was launched in 1976; it holds the world's largest calliope, which you can hear from a great distance. Finally, the **American Queen,** the largest steamboat ever built, commenced service in January 2003 and can carry 436 passengers.

Interstate Train Service

Amtrak (800/872-7245, www.amtrak.com) trains run across southern Louisiana, with stops (going east to west) in Slidell, New Orleans, Hammond, Baton Rouge (via a Greyhound bus connection), Schriever (near Houma and Thibodaux), Lafayette, New Iberia, and Lake Charles. This is a fairly hassle-free way to get to the region from Atlanta, Memphis, Houston, Pensacola, and a number of other big cities.

Three trains serve southern Louisiana, all of them including New Orleans as a stop. The *City of New Orleans* originates in Chicago and terminates in New Orleans; it also stops on the North Shore in Hammond. Other big cities along this route include Jackson, Mississippi; Memphis; and Centralia, Illinois. The train runs daily; southbound it leaves Chicago 8 P.M., reaches Memphis the following day around 6:30 A.M., and arrives in New Orleans at about 3:45 P.M. Northbound, it departs New Orleans at 1:55 P.M., hits Memphis at 10 P.M., and arrives in Chicago the next morning at 9 A.M.

The *Crescent* runs between New York City and New Orleans, with major stops that include Philadelphia, Washington, Charlottesville, Charlotte, Atlanta, and Birmingham. It also stops in Slidell. It leaves New York City daily at 2:50 P.M., stops in Atlanta the next morning at 9 A.M., and reaches New Orleans at 7:50 P.M.; northbound, it leaves New Orleans at 7:20 A.M., stops in Atlanta at 7:35 P.M., and reaches New York City the next day at 1:50 P.M.

The *Sunset Limited* is an east–west train that runs between Orlando, Florida, and Los Angeles, California, stopping in New Orleans as well as Schriever, New Iberia, Lafayette, and Lake Charles. Other big cities along this route include Jacksonville, Pensacola, Mobile, Gulfport, Houston, San Antonio, El Paso, Tucson, and Palm Springs. Westbound trains depart Orlando on Tuesdays, Thursdays, and Sundays at 1:45 P.M., stopping in New Orleans at 9:20 A.M. the following day (Wednesdays, Fridays, and Mondays), reaching El Paso at 3:10 P.M. the following day, and arriving in Los Angeles at 6:40 A.M. the day after that. Eastbound trains leave Los Angeles on Sundays, Wednesdays, and Fridays at 10:30 P.M., stopping in El Paso the next day at 3:30 P.M., reaching New Orleans the following day (Tuesdays, Fridays, and Sundays) at 8:30 P.M., and arriving in Orlando the next day at 8:45 P.M.

Taking the train isn't necessarily cheaper than flying, but it can be a relaxing and fascinating way to see the countryside. Amtrak offers a number of promotions and special passes; the latter can allow you to stop and overnight in cities served by Amtrak, making this a surprisingly practical way to visit several parts of the country on one affordable ticket. For example, the **North America Rail Pass,** which costs about $675 for peak travel periods (June 1 through October 15) and $475 for off-peak (the rest of the year), entitles the bearer to 30 days worth of unlimited rides and stopovers throughout the United States and Canada. There are rental-car agencies at Amtrak stations in most big cities.

International (non-U.S. or Canadian citizens) travelers qualify for a variety of national and regional unlimited passes (some for 15 days, others for 30). The cost for the National Rail Pass is $550 peak and $385 for 30 days.

Amtrak also offers a number of special rail deals, offered weekly and available online. Some of these discounts are substantial. They typically apply to travel two to six weeks in advance of the online postings, but sometimes they're good for travel several months in advance.

Interstate Bus Service

If it's been a while since you traveled by bus, be prepared for a surprise: many improvements have been made, movies are shown, and the rides are quite comfortable (and far less expensive than Amtrak).

Greyhound (800/229-9424) is the definitive interstate bus provider for Louisiana, with frequent and flexible service connecting to all neighboring states and throughout the country.

In southern Louisiana, Greyhound stops at dozens of cities and towns, the major ones being Baton Rouge, Crowley, De Ridder, Franklin, Gonzales, Hammond, Houma, La Place, Lafayette, Lake Charles, Mandeville, Morgan City, New Iberia, New Orleans, Opelousas, Ponchatoula, Raceland, Slidell, St. Francisville, and Thibodaux. There's almost no decent-sized community covered in this chapter that can't be reached from New Orleans via Greyhound. As opposed to Amtrak, Greyhound buses have multiple daily runs between New Orleans and many neighboring states. Travel times can be significantly longer (although not always), but fares are generally much cheaper.

Typical travel times on Greyhound from major cities around the United States to New Orleans: Atlanta, 10 to 12 hours; Austin, 10 to 12 hours; Chicago, 19 to 23 hours; Dallas, 12 to 14 hours; Denver, 30 to 34 hours; Houston, 7 to 9 hours; Little Rock, 12 to 15 hours; Los Angeles, 40 to 44 hours; Memphis, 7 to 10 hours; Nashville, 12 to 16 hours; Orlando, 14 to 17 hours; Pensacola, 4 to 6 hours; St. Louis, 16 to 17 hours; and Washington, D.C., 23 to 27 hours.

Greyhound offers the **Discovery Pass,** which can be purchased in increments of from 4 to 60 days, allowing unlimited stopovers throughout the duration of the pass. Different types and prices of passes are available to U.S., Canadian, and international travelers, but to give an idea, the Domestic Ameripass (for U.S. citizens) ranges from 7 to 60 days and costs from $183 to $519, and the International Ameripass (for international travelers) ranges from 4 to 60 days and costs from $128 to $479.

DRIVING

Southern Louisiana is at most points about 300 miles across; from the southernmost town covered in this book (Houma) to the northernmost (Kentwood), it's only about 120 miles by car. Because either interstate or limited-access highways run in relatively straight lines among the key destinations in southern Louisiana, and these roads typically have speed limits of 65 to 70 mph, the region is relatively easy to get around.

It's not difficult to cross southern Louisiana in one afternoon.

Metro New Orleans (meaning the South Shore towns, below Lake Pontchartrain) is about 20 miles across and 10 north to south. Traffic can be as difficult here, as in typically large U.S. cities (it's not markedly worse or better than average), but under average circumstances, it's fairly easy to get from one end of New Orleans to the other in 30 to 40 minutes. Downtown New Orleans is at the geographic center of metropolitan New Orleans, meaning that from here to any other point, it's usually not more than a 20- to 30-minute driving, barring traffic problems.

A car is your best tool for exploring southern Louisiana. If you're visiting only New Orleans, the pluses and minuses related to using a car about balance each other out. Against using a car, consider the following: Traffic can be frightful, many streets are one-way, street parking is scarce, garage and hotel parking is expensive, the central neighborhoods are walkable, cabs are easy to come by if not always completely reliable, and public transportation is decent, especially from the French Quarter to the most popular of the city's outlying neighborhoods, Uptown and Mid-City.

The pros for using a car: rental cars are generally a bit less expensive than elsewhere in the country, there's ample and sometimes free parking in some outlying neighborhoods, a car is handier than public transportation for exploring Uptown and Mid-City, a car is unquestionably useful if planning any side trips from the city, New Orleanians are relatively easygoing drivers (at least compared with drivers in many other big cities),and one day's rental car is often cheaper when shared among two or more people than shuttle or taxi transportation from the airport to downtown.

Again, if you're having trouble deciding whether to use a car or not, the most significant factor is probably this: are you planning to stay within the city limits the entire time, or do you expect to take some trips to other parts of the state? If you're only planning one or two days outside the city, you can always rent a car in downtown New Orleans for a day or two and then enjoy life without it the rest of your stay.

DRIVING DISTANCES FROM NEW ORLEANS

The Acadian Peninsula, New Brunswick, Canada	2,114 miles	Mobile, Alabama	143 miles
Anchorage, Alaska	4,451 miles	Nashville, Tennessee	530 miles
Atlanta, Georgia	470 miles	Natchitoches, Louisiana	274 miles
Baton Rouge, Louisiana	81 miles	Natchez, Mississippi	176 miles
Chicago, Illinois	929 miles	New York, New York	1,309 miles
Dallas, Texas	521 miles	Orleans, California	2,610 miles
Denver, Colorado	1,398 miles	Pensacola, Florida	200 miles
Gulfport, Mississippi	76 miles	Phoenix, Arizona	1,528 miles
Houma, Louisiana	58 miles	St. Louis, Missouri	678 miles
Houston, Texas	347 miles	San Antonio, Texas	544 miles
Jackson, Mississippi	186 miles	Shreveport, Louisiana	338 miles
Lake Charles, Louisiana	205 miles		
Little Rock, Arkansas	444 miles		
Los Angeles, California	1,900 miles		
Louisiana, Missouri	757 miles		
Memphis, Tennessee	394 miles		
Minneapolis, Minnesota	1,290 miles		
Mexico City, Mexico	1,292 miles		
Miami, Florida	863 miles		

Six places that share New Orleans's approximate latitude: Tallahassee, Florida; Austin, Texas; Chongqing, China; Lhasa, Tibet; Kuwait City, Kuwait; Cairo, Egypt.

Six places that share New Orleans's approximate longitude: the Galápagos Islands, Ecuador; Guatemala City, Guatemala; Mérida, Mexico; Memphis, Tennessee; St. Louis, Missouri; Thunder Bay, Ontario.

ON THE ROAD

If you're visiting New Orleans from another part of the South, and you're staying long enough that it's worth driving for eight hours or so, consider that the following cities all fall roughly within a 550-mile drive of the Big Easy: Atlanta, Houston, Dallas, Jackson, Little Rock, Memphis, Mobile, Nashville, Pensacola, and San Antonio. Within this perimeter, if you're traveling as a group of two or more, and you're staying in Louisiana for more than five days, it's probably most economical to drive, even if you rent a car from home as an alternative to logging extra miles and wear-and-tear on your own car.

For general information on commuting, road closings and construction, getting to and from Louisiana, and getting around the state, contact the **Louisiana Department of Transportation and Development** (Room 301, Box 94245, Baton Rouge, LA 70804, 225/379-1100). Its website, www.dotd.state.la.us, offers extensive information on numerous publications, traveler resources and road conditions, licenses and permits, and upcoming roadwork and projects.

An excellent resource for online transportation information in the state is www.apta.com/links/state_local/la.cfm, which has links to countless sites.

Road Names and Labels

Conversationally, Louisianans tend to call most numbered roads "Highway," as in, "take Highway 61 to Baton Rouge," or "follow Highway 25 to Folsom." This is true both for U.S. and state highways. In this book, interstate highways are indicated with an "I" before the number (e.g., I-10, I-510, etc.), all U.S. highways are referred to with a "U.S." before the number (U.S. 90, U.S. 61, etc.), and all other numbered state and local roads are referred to with a "Hwy." before the number (Hwy. 1, Hwy. 14, etc.).

Scenic Drives

Southern Louisiana has a good many scenic drives. Alas, there are also plenty of major routes that make for lousy sightseeing and suffer from heavy congestion.

Of interstate highways, I-10 is a convenient if rather dull highway that runs from the southwestern end of the state, near Lake Charles, due east to the southeastern part of the state, near Slidell, where it joins with I-59 and I-12. At Baton Rouge, I-10 curves down and loops through New Orleans before curving back up again to Slidell; I-12 runs due east from Baton Rouge to Slidell, bypassing New Orleans. Lafayette is located along I-10, midway between Lake Charles and Baton Rouge. Coming from the northwest, I-49 leads down from Shreveport, meeting with I-10 in Lafayette; eventually, plans are for I-49 to continue south from Lafayette, loop through Cajun Country (roughly following the course of present-day U.S. 90), and rejoin I-10 just west of New Orleans. Much of the work on this interstate has been completed, and so the route's present incarnation (U.S. 90) is mostly a fast limited-access four-lane highway with a 70 mph speed limit. Last, I-55 enters the state just north of Hammond from Mississippi, joining I-12 and then, just went of New Orleans, I-10.

All of the interstate drives in Louisiana are flat, straight, and at times monotonous, but each has some interesting aspects. A significant stretch of I-10 west of Baton Rouge and east of Lafayette passes through the Atchafalaya swamp basin, and along here the highway is completely elevated above the swamp, built along tall piers. It's rather unlike any other stretches of interstate in this country, and it's quite interesting the first time you drive it. There's not a great deal of variation along this drive, however, and the novelty does wear off after you've driven it a few times. People who have grown up in southern Louisiana would think you're just plain crazy for finding this drive interesting even the first time you try it. Similarly, a long portion of I-10 between Sorrento (east of Baton Rouge) and Kenner (west of New Orleans) also rides high along stilts through swampland, and the same is true for parts of U.S. 90 down near Houma.

Because Louisiana is basically flat, roads rarely curve or rise or offer expansive views, but many of them are novel because they pass alongside hulking levees or over swamps or other bodies of water. You have to search a bit to see the beauty in some of these drives. One that immediately comes to mind is the Great River Road, actually a series of numbered highways that hugs both banks of the Mississippi River from just outside New Orleans through Baton Rouge and up into Mississippi. Visitors are sometimes surprised to realize that you cannot generally see the actual river along this drive, as the road sits well below the levee; however, there are many spots where you can pull over or even drive atop the levee and catch a nice view, and many bridges and free ferry crossings are set along this road.

You cannot generally see the actual river driving along the Great River Road. What you will see is a surreal clash of the old and the new: rural villages, massive power plants and refineries, and sprawling 19th-century plantation estates sit side by side throughout this region.

What you will see is a surreal clash of the old and the new: rural villages, massive power plants and refineries, and sprawling 19th-century plantation estates sit side by side throughout this region.

U.S. 190, from Slidell west through the North Shore towns above New Orleans and then paralleling I-12 to Baton Rouge and cutting across the Cajun Prairies through Opelousas, Eunice, and Kinder, is culturally fascinating, offering varied glimpses of southern Louisiana life. You pass everything from pristine wildlife preserves to upscale bedroom communities to rural Cajun towns on this route. From the Cajun town of New Iberia, Highway 14 is an interesting drive west through Abbeville and eventually on to Lake Charles. At the Texas border south of Port Arthur, Highway 82 hugs much of the barely developed gulf shoreline in the southwest corner of the state before cutting northeast to join

Highway 14 at Abbeville. From Lafayette, Highway 182 offers a more interesting alternative to U.S. 90 as it cuts through the heart of Cajun Country, entering New Iberia and Franklin, then crossing the Atchafalaya River in Morgan City and continuing down to Houma.

Highway 1, near Houma at the small city of Raceland, can be traced either north through Thibodaux and eventually up to where it becomes part of the Great River Road and cuts up into Baton Rouge and then New Roads, or south through the sparsely populated towns leading to Grand Isle on the Gulf of Mexico. From New Roads, north of Baton Rouge, Highway 10 makes for a picturesque drive through rolling pine groves east through the Florida parishes to Bogalusa, at the Mississippi border. The pine-studded North Shore is, in fact, an entire network of lovely country drives beneath massive canopies of shade trees; Highways 25, 21, 41, 22, and 16 all make for engaging road trips. Crossing the 23-plus-mile Lake Pontchartrain Causeway, the world's longest bridge, can also be fascinating if you've never done it before; after the third or fourth time, however, this drive starts to feel a bit dull, and you can imagine how boring it must be for the thousands of commuters who cross the causeway twice a day. Finally, if you follow U.S. 90 east out of New Orleans, the very road on which actress Jayne Mansfield was killed in a car accident in the late '60s, you'll pass through some still pristine bayou and swampland, along the north shore of Lake Borgne (an arm of the Gulf of Mexico), and eventually continue into coastal Mississippi.

The worst roads for driving in southern Louisiana are generally the U.S. highways, which had been the main thoroughfares before the interstate system was built, mostly following World War II. On these roads, you're apt to encounter long and bleak traffic-choked stretches of strip malls, fast-food restaurants, and auto-repair shops. Ugly and slow-moving roads around metro New Orleans include U.S. 61 (a.k.a. Airline Highway, and it's awful pretty much the whole way from New Orleans to Baton Rouge), Veteran's Memorial Boulevard (in Metairie and Kenner), Esplanade Avenues (in Metairie and Kenner),

U.S. Bus. 90 (from Westwego along the West Bank to Algiers Point), U.S. 90 through Lafayette, and U.S. 190 through Baton Rouge.

U.S. 190 above the Lake Pontchartrain Causeway, north of Mandeville to downtown Covington, is a short and not entirely unpleasant bit of road, dominated by shopping centers—it is mainly notable, though, for its unbelievably dense and slow traffic, particularly heading southbound on weekday mornings and northbound in the late afternoons. This is a situation where two towns have grown rapidly, and because they're surrounded and also intersected by large tracts of swamp and marshland, there's no simple way to built new and bigger roads. This phenomenon hasn't taken rout in too many other parts of the region yet, but as southern Louisiana grows, the problem will start popping up elsewhere.

Speed Limits and Driving Laws

Speed limits along the interstates are generally 70 mph, but they drop a bit to 65 or 60 mph along those spans of elevated roadway passing over the swamps and bayous, and they drop further to 50 or 55 mph through congested areas, such as New Orleans and Baton Rouge. Other limited-access highways tend to range from 55 to 70 mph, depending on congestion. As in most states, however, officers typically don't pull over offenders who keep with 5 to 8 mph of the posted limit. The two-lane state and U.S. highways all through the region generally have speed limits of 55 mph along narrow rural stretches, and 65 mph in wider spots. These roads, especially in rural areas, are sometimes very heavily patrolled by police, and it's highly unsafe to speed on these—they're narrow with virtually no shoulder, and can be bumpy. You're most likely to encounter speed traps when entering villages or approaching major intersections along these highways; reductions in the speed limit are typically well-marked and preceded by "Speed Zone Ahead" or "Reduced Speed Ahead" signs. The wise driver will heed these warnings.

In New Orleans as elsewhere throughout Louisiana, a right turn after coming to a complete stop at a red light is permitted, except where posted. Pedestrians crossing the street onto which you're turning have right of way, and at several congested intersections in New Orleans, right turns on red are prohibited (and signed accordingly). Following the same rules, left turns at red lights are permitted *only if* you're turning from a one-way street left onto another one-way street.

Parking

Parking in New Orleans is a gamble—keep as few of your belongings in your car as possible if parking on the street or in an unattended lot. If you can't remove everything and/or don't have a car alarm and/or are deeply concerned, just pay the $15–30 per night most hotels and commercial lots charge. At some properties you'll pay less, at some smaller inns you may have free parking, but many, especially in the Quarter or near it, have no parking at all. There's really no consistent rule, and you should investigate this when booking a hotel room, as the added daily price can add up.

Downtown in New Orleans you'll find a fair amount of meter parking, but this is primarily short-term, costing 25 cents per 12-minute interval, usually with a maximum of one or two hours in one space. Note that at rush hour (7–9 A.M. and 4–6 P.M.), many of the main streets downtown are no-parking zones. Finding street parking in the Quarter is extremely difficult, especially in the Lower Quarter. And in the Upper Quarter, most of the street parking is restricted for residents with permits. In Faubourg Marigny, it's fairly easy to find a spot on the street, and it's not too bad in most of the Garden District and Uptown, although you'll find meters along Magazine and some of the more commercial stretches of St. Charles.

The parking lot next to Jackson Brewery charges $15 per day; it puts you very close to several hotels and virtually anything in the Quarter, and it's a well-lighted and fairly conspicuous place, making it a less likely target of crime. There are a few other lots right near it. However, during busy times of year, these lots fill up fast, especially if it's a weekend. Also, there are no in-and-out privileges.

Outside the Quarter and CBD, you can often find street parking (metered and otherwise, but beware streets that restrict overnight parking to cars with resident permits), and some shops and eateries Uptown and in other parts of the city have lots or dedicated spaces. As in most major cities, parking safety is an issue here; New Orleans is a tourist town, and visitors are traditionally seen as good targets. The unattended parking lots around the CBD can seem like a bargain, but remember that the owners of the lots bear no legal liability for stolen, damaged, or lost cars and other belongings.

One smart parking option, especially if you're staying for a few days or more, is to park at one of the long-term lots out by the airport (they run as low as $5 per day) and take a cab, bus, or shuttle into the city. You really can get by easily without a car in New Orleans, so it makes sense just to park it somewhere safe and out-of-the-way. The airport lots are fenced in and secure, too.

Obviously, you should not park in a designated handicap-parking spot unless you have the proper placard to hang from your rearview mirror; to obtain an official handicapped placard for your rental car, call 504/483-4610. Call 504/826-1900 for general questions about parking in New Orleans, 504/826-1880 for questions about parking tickets and violations, and 504/565-7450 (the Claiborne Auto Pound at 400 N. Claiborne Ave.) if you've been towed. If you've parked in a rush-hour no-parking zone, blocking a driveway, by yellow fire-lane rectangles, within 20 feet of a corner or crosswalk, within 15 feet of a fire hydrant, or in a street-cleaning, loading, or service zone, you will be ticketed and possibly towed. They're quite vigilant about this in New Orleans. Parking in the neutral ground (median) is prohibited, although you'll sometimes see locals do it.

Taxis

In New Orleans, taxis charge a flat rate from the airport to downtown. Rates within the city are $2.50 to start, plus $1 per mile thereafter. Keep in mind that cabs charge a flat rate of $3 per person *or* the meter rate, whichever is higher, during certain peak-visitor events, such as Mardi Gras and Jazz Fest. You don't hail cabs on the street in New Orleans or anywhere else in Louisiana, but you will often find them waiting at major intersections near Bourbon Street and other nightlife-heavy areas in the Quarter, near hotels (most hotel doormen can easily call or hail you a cab), and near casinos or other attractions. This is the sort of city where it's easy to lose track of time, especially if you're bar-hopping, so it's always a smart idea to have the name and number of at least a couple of cab companies.

Cab drivers have a good but not stellar reputation in New Orleans. They're generally trustworthy and friendly, but a high percentage of passengers are from out of town, and so it's not uncommon—as is true in many touristy cities—for cab drivers to pad the bill slightly by taking you on a circuitous route. This doesn't happen often, but to minimize the likelihood of being victimized by this sort of ploy, do your best to act as though you know where you're going (ideally, know the quickest route ahead of time and specify that way) and speak up if you're concerned about why a driver is taking you an unusual way. There's no need to be paranoid—if the driver explains that traffic or construction blocked the more conventional route, you can probably believe her or him. Jot down the driver's badge ID number, which is posted in all cabs, when you get into any cab, and report any driver who fails to perform satisfactorily. A number of gypsy cabs operate in New Orleans. These are private, generally unlicensed cabs that roam the city looking to pick up passengers. You have no guarantees as to service, safety, and reliability when using gypsy cabs, so it's best to avoid them entirely and use taxis operated by licensed and established cab companies instead.

Reliable cab companies in New Orleans include **Crescent City** (504/822-3600), **Checker-Yellow** (504/486-9967), and **United Cabs Co.** (504/522-9771). Other cities and larger towns throughout the region all have at least one local cab company.

Car Rentals

Just about all the major car-rental agencies are represented at New Orleans International Airport, including Alamo, Avis, Budget, Dollar, Enterprise, Hertz, and National.

Rates for car rentals in New Orleans typical start around $30 per day for economy cars but can easily rise to $40 or more per day during busy times, when conventions are in town, and so on. Weekly rates begin at about $150 per week for an economy car, and $190 for a mid-size car.

MASS TRANSIT

For visitors, using mass transit in rural areas, or even in smaller cities throughout the region, probably doesn't make sense compared with using your own or a rented car. Baton Rouge is the one place outside New Orleans where you could conceivably get by on the transit system, the **Capital Transportation Corporation (CTC)** (225/389-8282, www.ctctransit.com). But if you're just visiting Baton Rouge for a day or two, this option isn't especially practical, as you'd spend a good bit of time learning the routes and waiting for connections.

Most attractions in southern Louisiana's other decent-size city, Lafayette, are in outlying areas, so using the **Lafayette Transit System** (337/291-8570, www.lafayettelinc.net/lts) makes even less sense.

No communities in southern Louisiana have commuter rail, subways, or light rail.

In New Orleans, however, mass transit, in the form of buses and streetcars, can be extremely useful.

Buses and Streetcars

New Orleans is served by an extensive network of buses and streetcars operated by the **New Orleans Regional Transit Authority** (504/242-2600, www.regionaltransit.org). The number for the New Orleans Transit Police is 504/827-7920. The fare is $1.25 plus 25 cents per transfer; express buses cost $1.50. You must pay with exact change (depositing coins or inserting $1 bills into the fare box at the front of the bus or streetcar) or a VisiTour or TransPass (a monthly pass that costs $55 per month) upon boarding the bus. Neither food nor drink are permitted on buses or streetcars, nor are smoking or playing a stereo without headphones. Because they're historic, the St. Charles Streetcars are exempt from ADA (Americans with Disabilities Act) compliance, and passengers with disabilities may have trouble boarding. But all other RTA buses and streetcars are equipped to accommodate persons with disabilities. Additionally, the RTA provides vans with lifts and curb-to-curb taxi service for those unable to use buses or streetcars because of a disability; call 504/827-7433 for further information.

The famous, historic **St. Charles Streetcar** runs 24 hours a day along St. Charles Avenue, from Claiborne Avenue to Canal Street—it's a wonderful, scenic, atmospheric way to get between the CBD and Uptown. The fare is $1.25, plus 25 cents per transfer. The St. Charles line has been in operation, amazingly, since 1835, and the cars used today date to the 1920s. The St. Charles line began as the main railroad line connecting the city of New Orleans with the resort community of Carrolton, which is today part of the city. At its peak in service, New Orleans's streetcar service spanned some 200 miles. The 35 olive-green electric cars are originals, dating to the early 1920s, when they were built by the Perley Thomas Company, and they're much more than a tourist attraction: thousands

of New Orleanians commute to work on these trains each day.

New Orleans also has a fleet of streetcar-style buses that run the perimeter of the French Quarter—it's called the Vieux Carré Shuttle. The fare is the same as for the St. Charles Streetcar, and these buses run from 5 A.M. until about 7:15 P.M.

The **Riverfront Streetcar** runs the rather short but scenic 1.9-mile route along the riverfront; it operates weekdays 6 A.M.–midnight and weekends 8 A.M.– midnight. These modern red streetcars were built by New Orleans metal- and woodworkers. The fare for this line is $1.50, plus 25 cents per transfer.

At press time, crews were busy at work reintroducing streetcar service up and down Canal Street. After a 35-year hiatus, service is expected to return by the middle of 2004. Service will extend from the foot of Canal, by the ferry terminal for Algiers Point, all the way up to City Park Avenue; a spur line will connect from there along North Carrollton Avenue out to Esplanade Avenue, by the New Orleans Museum of Art.

Useful bus routes include the **Magazine Line** (bus number 11), which runs 24 hours along

St. Charles Streetcar, Garden District

© ANDREW COLLINS

the 6-mile stretch of galleries, shops, and restaurants from the Warehouse District through Uptown; the **Esplanade Line** (bus number 48), which runs from 4 A.M. to 1 A.M. and passes from the edge of the French Quarter (at Rampart and Esplanade) north along historic Esplanade Ridge and into City Park; and the **Canal Street Line** (buses number 40, 41, 42, and 43), which runs up to Lakeshore Drive, on Lake Pontchartrain.

If you're going to be using public transportation a lot, it's worthwhile to buy a **VisiTour pass,** which is sold by the Regional Transit Authority (RTA, 504/248-3900). The pass entitles the bearer to unlimited use of all streetcars and buses and costs $5 for a one-day pass and $12 for a three-day pass. You can buy these passes from the concierge or front desk of many hotels, or call the RTA Rideline (504/248-3900) for the name of a ticket outlet near you. There are RTA VisiTour kiosks in the Riverwalk shops and the Jackson Brewery shops, too.

Ferries

You can get from the CBD (at the foot of Canal Street) to the West Bank (at Algiers Point) via the frequently running ferry that operates from 6 A.M. until midnight. The ride is free for pedestrians and $1 per automobile.

Elsewhere along the Mississippi River, there are either inexpensive (usually up to $1 for cars and 50 cents for pedestrians, with fares collected only for westbound service) ferry crossings at many points up and down the river and in a few other parts of southern Louisiana. You can view a full list of crossings, with times and fares, at the **Louisiana Department of Transportation and Development** website, www.dotd.state.la.us/operations/ferry.shtml. There are 13 ferry crossings on the Mississippi River, with others across the Ouachita, Atchafalaya, and Calcasieu Rivers, as well as across Bayou Boeuf. These rides are typically quite short, and reservations are not taken. The ferries cross frequently, usually from early morning till well into the evening.

ON THE ROAD

Health and Safety

CRIME

As in any part of the country that is densely populated, concerns about crime and traffic are germane to planning a trip to southern Louisiana, and especially to New Orleans. The city has a reputation for crime, some of it deserved, some exaggerated. Since the mid-'90s, the city's crime rate has fallen, and the New Orleans Police Department, once the subject of scandals and internal investigations, has greatly cleaned up.

One improvement in safety in recent years has been the establishment of a fleet of Hospitality Rangers, employees of the Downtown Development District whom you can spot by their yellow polo shirts and straw hats. You can ask these folks for directions, visitor maps, restaurant ideas, and other tourist advice. They work with the New Orleans Police Department to report any suspicious goings-on, broken streetlights, and other urban problems. You can also ask a ranger to escort you to your hotel or your car.

A particular concern about crime in New Orleans is that it does happen far too often in parts of the city where tourists are likely to venture. Murders of tourists are rare, but both muggings and car-jackings, while infrequent, do happen from time to time. There are a few common-sense steps you can take to minimize your likelihood of being targeted, the first being to pay attention to your surroundings and walk along well-lighted and well-traveled streets. Do not venture into dark and mostly residential areas, and never go into cemeteries after dark. Travel in groups when possible. Take cabs to parts of town with which you're unfamiliar. Don't display valuables and jewelry conspicuously, and leave all but necessary items at home. If you do visit with a laptop computer, camera, jewelry, or any type of expensive or irreplaceable item, stay at a hotel with in-room safes or store your belongings in the hotel safe.

You want to strike a balance between alert and paranoid—don't cower and fret and worry so much about crime that you end up having a bad time. Looking scared and nervous may actually increase your odds of being a victim anyway, as many criminals prey on visitors who look disoriented or uneasy about their surroundings. The most frequent targets of muggings and other crimes in New Orleans are inebriated tourists, and these, unfortunately, are easy to find in the French Quarter late at night. The simplest way to keep safe is to avoid drinking yourself into an extreme stupor.

If you're anticipating a night of revelry, try at least to venture out as part of a group. Have the name and address of your hotel written down someplace safe, but never write your hotel room number down somewhere that a thief or pickpocket could get it. If you show up at your hotel having forgotten your room number, a lobby employee can always remind you. Also be sure to carry with you the name and number of at least one or two cab companies. If you have a cellular phone, carry it with you when wandering around New Orleans or just about anywhere unfamiliar to you—phones can come in extremely handy in an emergency.

Every bit of advice here should be heeded even more carefully if you're a woman, especially if traveling alone.

HOSPITALS AND HEALTH CARE

In all but a few rural parts of southern Louisiana, you're never terribly far from a hospital. In New Orleans, the best and most conveniently located facility is **Charity Hospital and Medical Center of Tulane** (CBD, 1532 Tulane Ave., 504/903-3000, http://gcrc.tulane.edu). Elsewhere in the southern half of the state, major facilities include **Baton Rouge General Medical Center** (8595 Picardy Ave., Suite 100, Baton Rouge, 225/763-4900, www.generalhealth.org), **Lafayette General Medical Center** (1214 Coolidge St., Lafayette, 337/289-7991, www.lafayettegeneral.com), **St. Tammany Parish Hospital** (1202 S. Tyler St., Covington, 985/898-4000, www.stph.org), and **Terrebonne General Medical Center** (8166 Main St., Houma, 985/873-4616, www.tgmc.com).

Pharmacies

You'll find pharmacies, many of them open until 9 or 10 P.M., throughout metro New Orleans and most of the southern half of the state, the only exceptions being the more rural towns in Cajun Country. The leading chains in Louisiana are **Rite Aid** (www.riteaid.com) and **Walgreens** (www.walgreens.com). Pharmacies open 24 hours include **Rite Aid—Houma** (1214 Grand Caillou Rd., Houma, 985/873-3612), **Rite Aid—Baton Rouge (2159 Staring La., 225/766-6210), Rite Aid—Lafayette** (4710 Johnson St., 337/988-7284), **Rite Aid—Garden District New Orleans** (3401 St. Charles Ave., 504/896-4575), **Walgreens—Hammond** (1910 W. Thomas St., Hammond, 985/345-1602), **Walgreens—Lake Charles** (2636 Ryan St., 337/433-0686), **Walgreens—Lower Garden District New Orleans (1810 St. Charles Ave., 504/561-8331), Walgreens—Mandeville** (2880 U.S. 190, 985/624-3912), and **Walgreens—Slidell** (1260 Front St., 985/641-5555).

WATER SAFETY

Always supervise children and exercise caution when boating, swimming, or fishing. Common sense applies—use life vests and/or other flotation devices, avoid swimming in areas that don't have lifeguards (which is the case at many of the state's swimming holes), and observe local regulations concerning boating, sailing, and fishing.

Motion sickness can be a serious, and sometimes unexpected, problem for passengers of boats. If you're at all concerned about this, or you've had bouts with seasickness in the past, consider taking Dramamine, Bonine, or another over-the-counter drug before setting sail; you may want to consult with a physician before your trip, if you're interested in the Transderm Scop patch, which slowly releases medication into your system to prevent seasickness but is not without potential side effects. In general, try to avoid sailing on an empty stomach or too little sleep, keep your eyes on the horizon and avoid reading or focusing intently on anything that's small or moving with the rock of the boat, stick as close as possible to the center of a ship, and

WEST NILE VIRUS

Louisiana has been battling mosquito-borne epidemics since the founding of New Orleans. Throughout the 19th century, yellow fever and (less frequent) cholera epidemics claimed the lives of hundreds, sometimes thousands, of the state's residents, most of them New Orleanians. When the link was finally made between mosquitoes and yellow fever in the late 1800s, the spread of this deadly disease was finally curtailed, largely by investing great sums of money in controlling the city's mosquito population.

Since 1999, however, a new mosquito-borne illness, one that's capable of causing encephalitis and other conditions lethal to humans, has become a major threat in the United States, and especially in sultry and swampy Louisiana. The West Nile virus has struck several times in parts of the state with extensive marshland, such as St. Tammany Parish, on the north shore of Lake Pontchartrain and just 50 miles north of New Orleans. Of the 25 Louisiana residents who died from the virus in 2002, four lived in this area.

The simplest and most obvious precautions you can take against the West Nile virus are using insect repellant and wearing long-sleeved shirts and long pants when visiting areas where mosquitoes are common. From spring through fall, mosquitoes pervade Louisiana, and given the sheer numbers of these pests and the number of times most Louisianans are bitten by them, the actual rate of West Nile virus infection in human beings is very, very low—and the possibility of dying is, despite sensational media reports, even lower. Most of those who perished from the disease were frail or elderly, and when you consider the West Nile mortality rate in the greater scheme of things, it appears to be less of a threat than plenty of other diseases and activities most of us aren't the least bit nervous about, from shoveling snow to catching the common flu.

What worries authorities most is that there's no West Nile vaccine for humans (there is one for horses, interestingly), and there's no concrete way to spread its prevention, as long as there are mosquitoes and birds, which also carry the virus, flying around freely. So the potential for a more deadly outbreak certainly exists. But as of this time, you probably shouldn't worry much about contracting the disease. And for what it's worth, New Orleans, St. Tammany Parish, and other communities in Louisiana have amazingly extensive programs and funding in place to battle mosquito infestations.

Another, perhaps slight, comfort is that most people who contract West Nile Virus never actually develop noticeable symptoms; they recover without ever knowing they've had it. About 20 percent of those who contract the virus develop nonspecific flu symptoms (fever, headaches, muscle weakness, body aches), and about 1 percent of all victims develop serious illness. The frail or very elderly aren't actually more likely to become seriously ill from West Nile Virus, but they are less likely to be able to recover from a serious onset of the disease. If you develop a mild case of the disease, the symptoms will generally disappear in a few days, as they might if you had an ordinary case of the flu.

The most frightening and lethal form of the virus, West Nile encephalitis, is an inflammation or infection of the brain, with symptoms that include flu-like sensations as well as neck stiffness, confusion and disorientation, tremors, convulsions, and in the most severe cases paralysis or coma. If you develop any serious or persistent symptoms, especially after having been in contact with mosquitoes, you should consult a physician as soon as possible.

consider staying above deck (if weather permits), as breathing fresh air often helps.

If you're canoeing or even just taking a swamp tour in southern Louisiana, you should be alert about the wildlife around you. Flooding is also a danger; if you have any doubt about whether the water level is too high, consult with locals or check with one of the many canoe-rental outfitters in the region. Do not go boating on a bayou or river that has risen above its normal banks, which happens rather frequently following heavy rains. You could easily end up getting lost or caught on underbrush in a false channel or where water has rushed onto a flood plain.

Snakes often hang in the branches of trees in the swamps and over bayous. Every now and then, you hear of a snake falling right into a canoe or a swamp-tour boat. If you're especially nervous, take a swamp tour in a covered boat—many of them have roofs. Trees overhead also sometimes have wasps' nests in them. In general, don't linger too much beneath dense canopies of tree branches, and certainly try not to jostle branches above you. Alligators are not a serious safety threat to boaters—just give them a wide berth and consider yourself lucky if you're able to get close enough for a picture.

WILDLIFE ENCOUNTERS

Louisiana is a wonderful state for any visitor hoping to see wildlife up close, whether on swamp tours, canoe and boating expeditions, hikes, or country drives. In general, the dangers associated with such encounters are minimal.

There are plenty of animals that can hurt you—alligators and poisonous snakes being the most obvious. Louisiana has some 40 varieties of snake, of which six are poisonous and one, the water moccasin (a.k.a. the cottonmouth), is rather common in swamps, both on the ground and in tree branches overhead. Cottonmouths are one of the few snakes out there that can bite underwater.

In the category of things any idiot should already know: Never feed alligators, challenge or agitate them, or swim in places commonly inhabited by them, especially at dusk or at night, when they most love to hunt.

Their bite can be deadly, and they're not terribly shy, so it's up to you to back off when you come near one of these dark tan, brown, or black creatures that tend to coil and sit near stream and river borders, and on logs and stumps in the water.

Coral snakes are quite secretive. They're rarely found south of Lake Pontchartrain, near marshes and swamps, or in coastal areas—they're a greater threat in the northern part of the state, but are sometimes found in Lake Charles and the higher parts of the Florida Parishes. Copperheads are more common but also tend toward forested areas and high ground; they're problematic chiefly because they camouflage themselves well and can easily be missed in a pile of leaves or on a log, as they tend to lie motionless. Pygmy rattlesnakes like grassy pinelands and dry coastal areas but are rarely found in the Mississippi River Valley or in marshes. Eastern diamondback rattlesnakes are somewhat common in the upland areas within the North Shore, include St. Tammany, Washington, and Tangipahoa Parishes; they prefer open pinelands. The final variety of poisonous snake in the state is the timber or canebrake rattlesnake, which prefers the eastern and northern sections of the state and is especially at home in hardwood forests.

Snakes are particularly worrisome after a storm, when waterways sometimes spill over and displace wildlife; snakes can wind up in storm drains, under piles of debris, and even in homes. The **Louisiana Department of Wildlife and Fisheries** has an excellent website, found at www.wlf.state.la.us, describing each of the state's snakes with pictures. It's worthwhile to take a look and learn what some of the common ones look like before spending a lot of time exploring.

If you're ever bitten by a water moccasin or any other snake, do not attempt to treat the bite yourself—go to the nearest hospital. And traumatized though you may be, try hard to remember what the snake looked like, as identification can be critical to correct treatment.

Alligators are great fun to watch up close, but they can cause serious bodily harm, and under no circumstances should you approach one. They can also easily be mistaken on the banks of rivers or lakes for logs, as they tend to sit up in the brush and sun themselves in warm weather. Be certain of what you're stepping on as you walk near the edge of a waterway. In general, make a bit of noise when wandering around places inhabited by snakes and alligators, as these creatures are not inherently aggressive toward humans and will generally scurry away or retreat if approached by people. In the category of things any idiot should already know: Never feed alligators, challenge or agitate them, or swim in places commonly inhabited by them, especially at dusk or at night, when they most love to hunt.

Your safest course of action is simply to go with knowledgeable locals, especially if boating, hiking, or touring swamps for the first time.

The animals most likely to make you miserable during a trip to Louisiana are mosquitoes, which just adore the often-still waters of the state's bayous and swamps. Bring plenty of insect repellant with you when pursing any kind of outdoor activity from March through October or even November. West Nile virus, which struck Louisiana more severely than most states since the late '90s, can be fatal, but the odds of contracting it are quite low. Other insects that can be problematic, especially in areas popular for swamp tours and hiking, include bees, wasps, stinging caterpillars, ticks, and fire ants. In late summer and fall, so-called lovebugs (which are a species of fly often seen flying as mated pairs) can be a nuisance during picnics and outdoor gatherings, and they muck up windshields and bumpers.

Dangerous mammals are not a major issue in southern Louisiana. The state does have coyotes, black bears, red wolves, bobcats, foxes, and many other mammals that are more likely a threat to small pets than to humans. Rabies occurs rarely in Louisiana—there are typically fewer than a dozen reported cases of animals being infected with rabies each year, and usually it's skunks and bats.

A final thing to watch for is poison ivy (and oak or sumac), common in many Louisiana state parks and preserves. Learn to identify the plants and to avoid them.

TRAVEL INSURANCE

Purchasing travel insurance makes sense if you've invested a great deal in a trip with prepaid accommodations, airfare, and other services, especially if you have any reason to be concerned about your ability to make the trip—perhaps impending medical concerns (check, however, the fine print regarding preexisting conditions). It's a good idea to purchase insurance from a major provider, such as **Access America** (800/346-9265, www.etravelprotection.com) or **Travel Guard International** (800/826-1300, www.travelguard.com). Typically these policies can cover unexpected occurrences such as trip cancellations, interruptions, and delays, as well as medical expenses incurred during your travels.

Communication and Media

PHONES

Southern Louisiana uses a few area codes. For New Orleans and the region immediately surrounding it, the area code is 504; much of the area surrounding New Orleans, including the North Shore and the eastern parts of the Cajun Country (such as Houma) uses 985; Baton Rouge and the rest of south central Louisiana uses 225, and southwestern Louisiana and Lafayette use 337.

Outside your local calling region, you need to first dial 1 and the area code. For directory assistance, dial 1, the area code, and 555-1212—the charge for directory assistance calls is typically 50 to 75 cents.

Note that in this book, where available, the local telephone number always precedes any toll-free number. Toll-free numbers have area codes of 800, 866, 877, or 888.

Pay phones generally charge 50 cents for local calls; if you're calling collect or using a calling card, there's a 25-cent surcharge. Most hotels charge anywhere from a 50-cent to $1.50 surcharge for local calls, toll-free calls, or just about any other kind of call placed from their phones; however, a number of smaller inns and also budget- to mid-price chains (Motel 6, Comfort Inn, Hampton Inn, Super 8, and so on) offer free local and toll-free charges. Long-distance rates can be outrageous at many hotels, and it's generally a good idea to use a calling card or buy a prepaid one. The latter are available at many convenience stores and gas stations, and at a wide range of prices. If you're a member of Costco, Sam's Club, or another wholesale discount store, consider buying one of the prepaid Sprint, MCI, or AT&T phone cards sold at these stores—often you can find cards that end up costing just 2 or 3 cents per minute.

Cellular Phones

Cell phones are part of life in the United States, and relatively few frequent travelers go anywhere without them. If you're a subscriber on one of the nation's major networks, such as Sprint PCS, Verizon, or AT&T, you'll find full coverage throughout most of southern Louisiana, with only a handful of rural areas being exceptions. Even in rural areas, you should have no trouble receiving the more expensive "roaming" service.

It's legal to jabber away on your cell phone while driving, but it's not a good idea, especially if you're unfamiliar with where you're going and driving on local surface roads. When possible, try to pull off to the side of the road to talk on the phone; if traveling on a multilane highway, try to stay in the right or center lane and drive defensively if you must talk on your cell phone. And even if you're not speaking on your phone, be alert to drivers around you who are. Some states and cities in the United States have banned cell phone use while driving. You can, legally, circumvent this ban by purchasing a hands-free attachment, which allows you to talk on your cell phone while driving without having actually to hold the phone.

It's polite to turn off your phone, or turn its ringer volume to "off" or vibrate, when in restaurants, hotel lobbies, shops, and other confined spaces; do not talk on your cell phone in libraries or fancy restaurants, and avoid doing so in general when you're in shops or even fast-food or casual venues. If you must do so, try to keep the call short and speak quietly.

INTERNET SERVICES AND COMPUTERS

There are an increasing number of public places in New Orleans and Baton Rouge where you can check the Internet—even some airport payphones now provide this service. The best and most convenient place to check email and surf the Web is the public library; there's one in virtually every Louisiana town, although only those in larger communities tend to have public computers. Libraries at Louisiana's several universities and colleges are also open to the public, but their policies vary regarding computer use; some only allow computer access to students, faculty, and staff. Libraries generally allow you to use their computers for short periods, ranging from 15 minutes to an hour.

A handful of cafés around the state have pay Internet stations, as does **Kinko's,** which has branches in Baton Rouge, Covington, Lafayette, Lake Charles, Metairie, and New Orleans (Uptown and in the CBD); it's open 24 hours a day in most locations, and quite late elsewhere. Kinko's is an excellent traveler's business and work resource, as it's also a place to make copies, buy some office supplies, use Federal Express and other shipping services, and rent time on computers (whether to surf the Internet, print out copies, scan photos, etc.).

If you're traveling with your laptop computer and looking to go online from your hotel, keep a few things in mind. First, check with your Internet service provider (ISP) about access outside your local area; if it's a local provider, you'll most likely have to call long distance. Some ISPs issue toll-free numbers or have local access numbers in other regions. Major U.S. ISPs (such as Earthlink and America Online) have several local access numbers throughout southern Louisiana; if you subscribe to one of these providers, you'll probably be able to access the Internet via local call in every major town and city in southern Louisiana, but there are some exceptions.

These days it's easy to plug your laptop computer into the phone jack at virtually any motel or hotel, whether they have dedicated data ports or not. It's a good idea to bring your own phone cord and cord coupler, which enables you to extend an existing hotel-room phone cord on the chance that it's very short or inconveniently located. Additionally, some of the major mid-priced and upscale hotel chains and an increasing number of inns and B&Bs now offer high-speed Internet service—often for a daily noon-to-noon fee (usually $8 to $10), you'll enjoy unlimited high-speed access, but in other cases it's free. This service generally works on any recent-model laptop with either a USB port or an Ethernet port (cables are typically provided in the hotel rooms), or through a card slot in your computer. Several cellular-phone providers offer wireless Web service, or Wi-Fi, among them Sprint PCS. National Wi-Fi carriers such as Wayport offer service at several New Orleans business hotels.

If logging on using your laptop is important to you, ask about phone policies before booking a room at a B&B or small inn. It's usually not an issue if you have a phone in your room, but in smaller places in rural areas, more than one guest room may be sharing a line, which means that you won't be able to log on for long periods without inconveniencing fellow guests. Some inns have only a common phone, and innkeepers are often very accommodating of guests who wish to log onto the Internet using their laptops if it's just a brief call, but if you're planning to be online a great deal, it's best to avoid staying at properties that don't offer in-room phones.

MAIL SERVICES

Right in the French Quarter, **Royal Mail Service** (828 Royal St., 504/522-8523) can pack and ship most any gift, artwork, or other items you've picked up during your travels. They're also a pickup point for FedEx and UPS. New Orleans's main branch of the **U.S. Post Office** (701 Loyola Ave., just west of Poydras Street in the CBD, 504/589-1714) is a clean and efficient facility with the longest opening hours of any post office in the state. It's open weekdays 7 A.M.–8 P.M., Sat. 8 A.M.–5 P.M., and Sun. noon–5 P.M. There are other branches with more limited hours in the French Quarter at 1022 Iberville St. (closed weekends), in the CBD at the World Trade Center at the foot of Canal Street, and on Lafayette Square just off St. Charles Avenue.

MEDIA

Louisiana has about 20 daily newspapers, and many more that run less frequently. The major daily for New Orleans, and widely read across the state, is the *Times-Picayune* (www.neworleans.net), which comes out daily. Other popular daily papers in southern Louisiana include Baton Rouge's *The Advocate* (www.theadvocate.com),

Hammond's *Daily Star* (www.hammondstar .com), Houma's *The Courier* (www.houma today.com), Lafayette's *The Advertiser* (www .theadvertiser.com), *Lake Charles American Press* (www.americanpress.com), and New Iberia's *Daily Iberian* (www.iberianet.com).

Louisiana has about 30 TV stations, with major network or PBS affiliates in Baton Rouge, New Orleans, and Lafayette, plus a couple in Lake Charles.

New Orleans Magazine (www.neworleans magazine.com) is a useful and well-produced monthly four-color glossy, with excellent din-ing, arts, and events coverage. *Louisiana Life* (www.neworleans.com/lalife) comes out quar-terly and has a wide variety of features on what to see and do across the state, with a focus on food, history, art, and music. An excellent re-source for metro New Orleans arts, dining, shopping, clubbing, and similar such diver-sions is the decidedly left-of-center *Gambit Weekly* alternative newsweekly (www.be-stofneworleans.com). The free Baton Rouge monthly *Country Roads* (www.countryroads mag.com) has useful information on towns along the Mississippi River.

Sights

In truth, New Orleans is not a city rife with museums and attractions. But it's a wonderful place to explore, whether your interests lie in history, architecture, people-watching, shopping, or eating. In that sense, its neighborhoods, especially the oldest and most colorful, are living and working museums. And best of all, there's no admission fee for exploring them, and they're open 24/7, especially the French Quarter.

Still, you'll find a nice range of indoor attractions, from an excellent and underrated art museum to a slew of engaging house-museums set about the city. The city's top attractions tend to be its neighborhoods, from the French Quarter to the Garden District. You can get a peek inside some of the most intriguing houses by seeing them on guided tours.

Plenty of visitors, even those who come for just the weekend, make a trip out of the city to do one or two things (and sometimes both): take a swamp tour, or visit some of the magnificent plantations flanking the Mississippi River

between New Orleans and Baton Rouge. For these trips, you can go one of two routes: Either book a trip through one of the many tour operators in the city, or rent a car and drive on your own to the plantations or the departure point for the swamp tours. If you're going on your own, see the side trip chapters in this book: Swamp tours are well-covered in the North Shore, Cajun Country, and River Road chapters, and plantations houses are covered in the Cajun Country and River Road chapters. It's not especially practical to visit the Cajun Country as a day trip from New Orleans—the drive takes two to

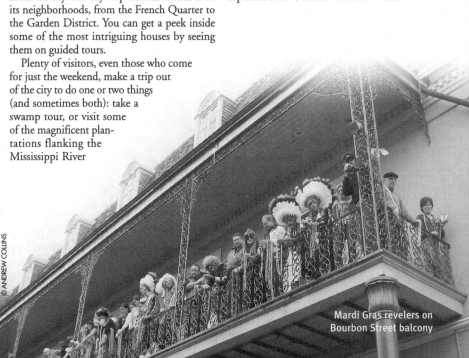

© ANDREW COLLINS

Mardi Gras revelers on
Bourbon Street balcony

FRENCH QUARTER AND FAUBOURG MARIGNY SIGHTS

KERLEREC ST.

ORLEANS ST.

ST. ANN ST.

MARAIS ST.

TREME ST.

CLAUDE AVE.

BARRACKS ST.

GOV.

NICHOLLS ST.

ROBERTSON

VILLERE

LAFITTE ST.

N. PRIEUR ST.

N. DERBIGNY ST.

CLAIBORNE AVE.

10

TREME

Louis Armstrong Park

★ NEW ORLEANS JAZZ NATIONAL HISTORIC PARK

URSULINES AVE.

PHILIP ST.

BURGUNDY ST.

DUMAINE ST.

★ VOODOO SPIRITUAL TEMPLE

ST. ANN ST.

ORLEANS AVE.

ST. PETER ST.

NEW ORLEANS HISTORIC VOODOO MUSEUM

CORNSTALK HOTEL ●

MADAME JOHN'S LEGACY ★

ST. LOUIS CEMETERY NO 2

FRENCH QUARTER

LOUISIANA OFFICE OF TOURISM

S. ROBERTSON ST.

S. VILLERE ST.

LA SALLE

TREME ST.

CROZAT ST.

BASIN ST.

N. RAMPART ST.

ST. LOUIS CEMETERY NO 1

TOULOUSE ST.

LOUIS ST.

MADISON AVE.

PRESBYTERE ★

ST. LOUIS CATHEDRAL ★

1850 HOUSE

PRESERVATION HALL ★

THE ARSENAL ★

★ MUSEE CONTI-THE WAX MUSEUM

HISTORIC NEW ORLEANS COLLECTION ★

THE CABILDO ★

JACKSON SQ

PONTALBA APARTMENTS

WILKINSON ST.

HERMANN-GRIMA HOUSE ★

SAENGER THEATRE ★

BIENVILLE ST.

IBERVILLE ST.

CONTI ST.

NEW ORLEANS PHARMACY MUSEUM ★

JACKSON BREWERY ★

CLEVELAND AVE.

CHARTIY HOSPITAL

S. LIBERTY ST.

SARATOGA ST.

ELK PL.

GERMAINE CAZENAVE WELLS MARDI GRAS MUSEUM ★

WILLIAMS RESEARCH CENTER ★

TULANE AVE.

MEDICAL CENTER OF TULANE

RITZ-CARLTON ●

DAUPHINE ST.

BOURBON ST.

ROYAL ST.

CHARTRES ST.

EXCHANGE ALY.

JEAN LAFITTE NATIONAL HISTORICAL PARK AND PRESERVE ★

TOULOUSE STREET WHARF

UNIVERSITY PL.

CANAL ST.

MOON WALK ★

GRAVIER ST.

COMMON ST.

N. FRONT BLVD.

Levee

PERIDIO ST.

CBD

UNION ST.

N. PETERS ST.

CLAY ST.

AUDUBON INSECTARIUM ★

Woldenberg Riverfront Park

LOYOLA AVE.

O'KEEFE AVE.

ST. CHARLES AVE.

BARONNE ST.

CAMP ST.

MAGAZINE ST.

SHOPS AT CANAL PLACE ★

POYDRAS ST.

NATCHEZ ST.

AUDUBON AQUARIUM OF THE AMERICAS ★

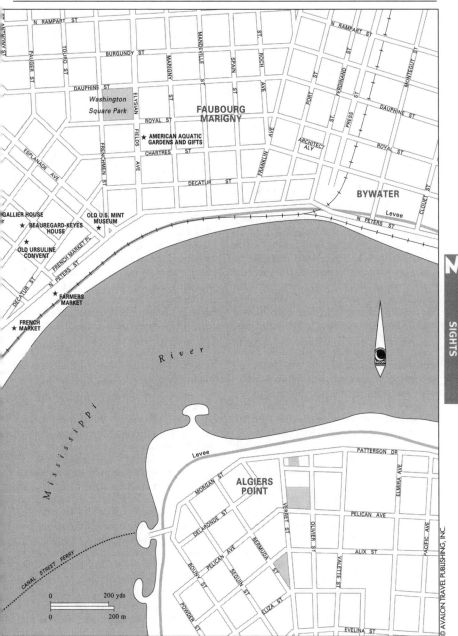

© AVALON TRAVEL PUBLISHING, INC.

three hours each way. But you can easily visit the North Shore or River Road regions as day trips.

If you do opt to go it on your own, you may save money, especially if there are three or four of you sharing a rental car. Guided bus tours charge by the person, so one or two people may find it cheaper or similar in cost to book a tour, especially when you factor in the cost of gas and admission to the plantations and swamp tours, which are generally included in the tour fee.

There are always tradeoffs between making your own daytrip and going with a guided tour. On any guided tour you're likely to be spending the trip with a fair number of other travelers, which can be good or bad depending on whether you're especially social. The tour buses draw heavily from among conventioneers, as well as travelers who have booked package tours to New Orleans. If you're a particularly independent-spirited person, you might not enjoy this experience. On the other hand, some of the guides and drivers who lead these tours give excellent narration throughout the tour, and some of them are quite funny to boot. (Though you can also end up with a guide who tells awful, corny jokes and tries to an annoying degree to get everybody on the tour to chit-chat and participate.) Still, consider a tour if you prefer a carefree vacation: You don't have to study road maps, think about where you're going, or worry about picking up and returning rental cars and so on. Several of the city's best tour operators are described later in this chapter.

Within the city of New Orleans, it's quite easy to get around most of the key neighborhoods using a combination of walking, public streetcars and buses, and the occasional cab. If you're staying in the French Quarter or CBD/Warehouse District, you can easily hoof it to just about any attraction within either of these neighborhoods as well as in Faubourg Marigny. It's possible to walk to at least the Lower Garden District from the French Quarter and actually quite easy from the Warehouse District, but not all that many people do. You have to walk beneath the massive U.S. 90 bridge, and for several blocks there, it's a less-than-charming stroll. It's easy and certainly more scenic just to take the St. Charles Avenue streetcar into the Garden District.

The Garden District and Lower Garden District are at the lower end of Uptown, a long and winding neighborhood that extends for several miles west of the CBD. It's a fairly safe area, as safe as the Quarter or other well-visited neighborhoods, but distances are great, and you need to be in good walking shape to visit the entire Uptown district on foot. One practical idea is to take the streetcar to the Garden District and walk through it to reach Magazine Street. Walk uptown along Magazine as far as you feel like, taking in the many blocks of cool antiques and other shops, and using public buses when your legs need a break. Once you get to Audubon Park, walk over to St. Charles Street, which runs parallel to Magazine, and take the streetcar back to the CBD.

Mid-City, an area that has grown in popularity with visitors, can be visited from the French Quarter quite easily by bus. Just take Bus 48 up Esplanade Avenue, the road that divides the French Quarter with the next neighborhood downriver, Faubourg Marigny. Mid-City contains City Park, site of the New Orleans Museum of Art and the New Orleans Botanical Gardens.

Across the Mississippi from the French Quarter is the West Bank, which includes a small chunk of land, Algiers Point, that's actually considered part of New Orleans proper but is mostly a series of suburbs. Algiers Point has the famous Blaine Kern's Mardi Gras World museum and a few streets of interesting old houses—you can easily explore this neighborhood by taking the free (to pedestrians) ferry that runs all throughout the daytime and into the early evening between the foot of Canal Street and Algiers Point. A free shuttle bus on the West Bank takes any guests interested to Blaine Kern's Mardi Gras World.

At the risk of generalizing, the rest of New Orleans proper holds relatively little interest for visitors, and parts of the city are either unsafe, industrial, or simply not pleasant to explore. There are also a handful of shopping centers and attractions in the suburbs immediately outside New Orleans, such as Metairie, Gretna, and Harahan. It's not practical to explore these communities unless you have a car, although you can get to some of the key points in these cities using public buses. It takes some time getting to know the bus schedule, however, and few tourists use them for such long trips—the fact is, few tourists, with or without private cars, spend much time exploring the close-in suburbs.

Hours and Admission

Hours at many smaller attractions can be very complicated and can change frequently throughout the year. For this reason, an attraction's hours are listed only when they're fairly straightforward and reliable; in all other cases the hours are listed as either "limited" or "seasonal." In these cases, you should phone ahead to ensure that the place will be open on the day that interests you.

Don't be put off by limited hours, though—in most cases, if you phone a week or two ahead and ask to see one of these smaller attractions by appointment, you'll be encouraged to set up a private visit. Most of these smaller establishments are operated by volunteers and supported by bequests and gifts; they typically charge a nominal entrance fee or perhaps request a donation.

Those attractions with a fairly steady flow of visitors offer the same hours you might expect of most local businesses and shops: 9 A.M. to 5 P.M., from five to seven days a week (Sundays, Mondays, and Tuesdays are the most common days when attractions are closed; even some of the most prominent plantation museums do close on Monday). In many cases, hours are reduced on Sundays. In summer you'll notice that some of these attractions stay open a bit later, and in winter some of them close at 4 P.M. or don't open until 10 or 11 A.M.

The admission given for each attraction in this book is for adults. At the vast majority of the attractions in the state, very young children are admitted free; grade-school kids, college students, and senior citizens very often receive discounts of 25 to 50 percent. Some places also give discounts to holders of AAA cards or military IDs—it's always a good idea to ask about discounts before paying.

Whatever these general rules of thumb, and whatever hours and admission are listed in this book, remember that hours (and other policies) may change with no notice. It's highly advisable that you phone ahead before visiting any attraction in Louisiana.

For additional information on attractions in New Orleans, get a copy of the official *New Orleans Visitor's Guide* from the **New Orleans Metropolitan Convention and Visitors Bureau** (504/566-5011 or 800/672-6124, www.neworleanscvb.com). For the 411 on attractions across the state, obtain a free copy of the *Louisiana Tour Guide and Official Louisiana Highway Map* from the state tourist board (225/342-8100 or 800/473-7829). You can also order the guide, book hotel rooms, and find Web links to many museums and attractions at the state website, www.louisianatravel.com.

ORIENTATION AND DIRECTIONS

New Orleanians rarely refer to compass directions when talking about how to get around the city or where something is. Part of the reason for this is that the city is bound on one side by the highly irregular Mississippi River, which, depending on which part of it you're facing, forms either the western, southern, or eastern border. Main roads tend to run parallel or perpendicular to the river, and since the river's direction changes, this means that New Orleans's street grid also changes its axis in different places. It can get very confusing trying to think in terms of east and west and north and south.

More often, the terms "lakeside" (meaning toward Lake Pontchartrain, and typically in a northerly direction) and "riverside" (meaning toward Mississippi, and typically in a southerly direction) are used when referring to streets that run perpendicular to the river. For example, somebody might tell you to drive up Esplanade

> *New Orleanians rarely refer to compass directions when talking about how to get around. The city is bound on one side by the highly irregular Mississippi River, which, depending on which part of it you're facing, forms either the western, southern, or eastern border.*

Avenue toward the lake. The terms "upriver" or "uptown" are used generally to refer to westerly directions, and the terms "downriver" or "downtown" are used for easterly directions. Canal Street, which people think of as running north-south, because it eventually connects the river to the lake, actually runs east-southeast toward the river. Looking across Jackson Square from mid-block on Decatur Street directly toward St. Louis Cathedral, you're actually looking due northwest, not north, as one tends to think.

A little more confusion: "Uptown" is both an adjective describing the direction opposite "downtown" and also the name of a neighborhood itself. So, you can be headed "uptown" but not actually be going as far as Uptown the neighborhood, which is technically defined as the blocks between Louisiana Avenue and Lowerline Street. However, many New Orleanians simply call anything upriver from the CBD and Pontchartrain Expressway (that big elevated highway that runs along the side of the CBD

and crosses over the Mississippi River to the West Bank) Uptown.

Got all that?

Don't worry too much if you don't. Just make sure you have a map of the city with you at all times, as this is one place where such a document is absolutely indispensable whether you're walking, driving, taking public transportation, or even using cabs. New Orleans is very much a collection of neighborhoods, and people refer specifically to neighborhood names as much as or even more than they refer to street names or various coordinates.

A good starting point for orienting yourself before wandering the city's streets is the **Preservation Resource Center** (923 Tchoupitoulas St., 504/581-7032, www.prcno.org), in the Warehouse District. Here you can read helpful thumbnails that describe each of the city's neighborhoods and pick up a free map describing each. The center also has detailed information on the various types of architecture that define New Orleans.

The French Quarter

Known also as the Vieux Carré (French for "Old Quarter" and pronounced "voh-cair-ee" in these parts), the French Quarter comprised the entire city of New Orleans during its first century or so, and it has always been the great hub of activity and social life, especially for Creoles. When Americans began moving into New Orleans to stake their fortunes in the early 1800s, the descendants of French and to a lesser extent Spanish settlers shunned them bitterly. The adjacent Central Business District (CBD) grew up at that time as the so-called American Quarter, extending well into what is now the present-day Garden District.

The French Quarter's enduring architecture, much of it from the late 18th century and clearly influenced by the ruling Spaniards of that time, has long been appreciated by preservationists. This was one of the first neighborhoods in America where concerned locals began preserving old buildings and passing local laws that prohibited the alteration or razing of historic structures and

the construction of buildings not in character with the rest of the neighborhood.

What also helped preserve the Quarter, at least throughout much of the 20th century, was its lack of prosperity. Especially following World War II, the neighborhood took a turn for the worst during the 1950s and '60s, and especially the Lower Quarter came to be thought of as something of a slum. A mix of hippies, gays, artists, antiques dealers, underprivileged families, a very few remaining descendents of early Creole families, and quite a few multigenerational Italian families (the most common of the neighborhood's immigrants during the early 20th century) lived here, and tourists visited some of the key nightspots, restaurants, and historic hotels nearest the riverfront and Canal Street but largely avoided the rest of it.

By about the mid- to late 1970s, preservation-minded locals began to promote the restoration of those sections of the Quarter that had

intersection of Barracks and Decatur Streets, French Quarter

fallen on hard times, and the city began talking up the neighborhood more aggressively as a unique urban destination. Fancier hotels, inns, and restaurants opened, and Bourbon Street nightlife thrived, especially as New Orleans became increasingly notable as a business-convention destination.

The French Quarter's rise in popularity has been almost meteoric since the late 1980s, a phenomenon that has had the rather familiar effect of raising the entire district's standard of living, but also pushing out many of the less economically solvent residents into less expensive—and less desirable—areas. Real-estate prices for French Quarter buildings, both residential and commercial spaces, have skyrocketed, but even in the early 2000s, the cost of living along the most desirable blocks of the French Quarter is a fraction of what it is in prominent neighborhoods in other big U.S. cities. Of course, costs are relative to income, and New Orleans salaries are generally lower than in many places.

The gentrification trend in the French Quarter has spilled over downriver into neighboring Faubourg Marigny since the mid- to late 1990s, and even more recently up Esplanade Avenue toward Mid-City. Nevertheless, those blocks nearest the Marigny and also farthest from the river, up near North Rampart Street, tend to be the quietest, especially at night. You should regard your surroundings carefully wherever you wander in the French Quarter, but especially in these sections, where it's best to move about in groups or use cabs late at night.

Officially, the Quarter extends downriver from Canal Street to Esplanade Avenue, and lakeside (in the direction of Lake Pontchartrain) from the Mississippi River to Rampart Street. A dozen streets run parallel to Canal and Esplanade between them, and six streets run parallel to Rampart down to the river. On the riverside edges of the Quarter, North and South Peters Streets run at a slight angle to the rest of the Quarter, roughly parallel to the bend in the river. All told, the French Quarter comprises 98 blocks, and there is not one single block that lacks architectural treasures and a rich history.

Most visitors focus on Decatur, Chartres, Royal, and Bourbon Streets—the main thoroughfares running roughly parallel to and extending from the river, and on the Lower Quarter, meaning the blocks between Canal Street and about St. Ann Street, which marks the downriver border of Jackson Square. In this roughly 30-block quadrant you'll find the lion's share of the French Quarter's hotels, restaurants, bars, shops, and tourist attractions, and you'll also find the most intense crowds.

If you walk along the streets parallel to Bourbon but farther toward the lake, you'll still find a smattering of hotels, restaurants, and bars, but few shops or attractions per se. But you'll see some wonderful old buildings, many of them private residences, especially on Dumaine and Burgundy Streets. Rampart is a real hit-or-miss street. The side of Rampart away from the Quarter is not especially charming and, in fact, forms the border of the fabled Storyville (a red-light district during the early 20th century) and Tremé, a mostly poor and predominantly African-American district characterized by several immense housing projects. This side of Rampart also forms one border of Armstrong Park, which does have some interesting features. The Quarter side of Rampart has a hodgepodge of buildings, including some of the city's divier gay bars and also a couple of superb jazz clubs, Donna's and the Funky Butt.

The main cross streets of the Lower Quarter are, from Canal to Jackson Square, Iberville, Bienville, Conti, St. Louis, Toulouse, St. Peter, Orleans (a half street that runs only from Royal to Rampart), and St. Ann Streets. Again, these streets are nearly choked with shops, restaurants, and other businesses catering primarily to tourists, which is not to say that they're lacking in appeal—you just have to wade through the crowds and overlook some of the cheesier and more commercial shops and restaurants that qualify more as tourist traps than bona fide points of interest.

Some of the finest antiques shops are along this stretch of Royal Street and the blocks just off it, where such establishments have thrived for more than a century, and you'll also find some excellent restaurants in these parts. Once you get beyond St. Ann and into the Upper Quarter, and wander the blocks between it and Esplanade (these being Dumaine, St. Philip, Ur-

French Quarter skyline

sulines, Governor Nicholls, and Barracks Streets), you'll find not only some superb examples of 19th-century residential architecture but also some of the city's true hotel and restaurant gems, many of them less touristy than those in the Lower Quarter. The section of the Upper Quarter nearest the river has the most commercial activity, especially at Decatur and North Peters Streets, where you'll find the famous French Market and quite a few shops and bars of interest. The Upper Quarter stretches of Royal and Chartres have some neat old hotels and a few eateries, but Bourbon, Dauphine, and Burgundy are mostly residential in the Upper Quarter.

It's difficult to capture the French Quarter's exact collective vibe—that changes from block to block. Architecturally, it feels like a cross between the Spanish and French cities of the Caribbean (such as Havana, the old part of San Juan, and Port-au-Prince, Haiti), Spain itself, and France. Little of the French Quarter bears any resemblance at all to even the historic residential neighborhoods found in other U.S. cities. Buildings tend to be painted in pastel colors and have frilly wooden or wrought-iron balconies with elaborate grillwork. Most of the oldest buildings in the neighborhood date to the late 1700s, when New Orleans was under Spanish control, as the previous French-style buildings that dominated prior to that time were mostly burned during one or both of the huge fires that engulfed the Quarter during this period, one in 1788 and a smaller one in 1794. This accounts for the distinctly Spanish look of many buildings.

But early Creoles (the term originally used to describe French colonists who had fled Haiti's black revolutions of the early 1800s) settled in and greatly determined the architectural and cultural flavor of the French Quarter as we know it. What you see today, at least in terms of architecture and layout, closely resembles the French Quarter of the 19th century.

Around Jackson Square

Jackson Square anchors the French Quarter and is a good place to begin your explorations. Originally known as the Place d'Armes (and then the Plaza de Armas, under Spanish rule), Jackson Square was renamed in honor of the seventh U.S. president, Andrew Jackson, who led the United States to victory during the Battle of New Orleans. A statue of Jackson, said to be the first equestrian statue ever erected to depict a horse balanced on its hindquarters, anchors the square and ranks among the city's favorite photo-ops (especially if you capture the image with St. Louis Cathedral in the background). The 14-foot-tall bronze was cast by artist Clark Mills in 1856 (at a then-astronomical cost of $30,000), the year that Baroness Micaela Almonester de Pontalba successfully lobbied city officials to transform Place d'Armes from a military parade ground into a civilized public garden. Note the inscription on the statue, which may seem unlikely on a statue in the South: "The Union Must and Shall Be Preserved." This was commissioned by Union Civil War General Benjamin Butler, the detested and brutal autocrat who ruled New Orleans with an iron fist during his short tenure there following the Union capture of the city midway through the war.

Jackson Square is a wonderful place to sit and read a newspaper, eat a muffaletta or a snack from one of the nearby cafés, and take in this earliest-laid-out section of New Orleans. Across Decatur Street from the square is a plaque marking the original riverfront—the Mississippi River nearly lapped at the edge of Jackson Square during the 18th century, before the course of the river shifted a bit south, and levees were constructed to protect the Quarter from flooding. Along the sidewalks that fringe Jackson Square on all sides (three of them are pedestrian ways with no motor vehicles), you'll find an eccentric bunch of mimes, artists, fortune readers, buskers, and other entertainers. And lined up along Decatur Street at the riverside of the square are horse-drawn carriages awaiting tourists booking excursions through the Quarter. (On that note, be careful of these carriages as they clip-clop through the neighborhood, especially if you're driving, and beware the messes they occasionally leave behind if you're on foot.)

St. Louis Cathedral, Jackson Square

M

SIGHTS

The north (lakeside) end of the square is dominated by **St. Louis Cathedral** (615 Père Antoine Alley, 504/525-9585, www.saintlouis cathedral.org, free tours 9 A.M.–5 P.M. Mon.–Sat., 1:30–5 P.M. Sun.), one of the most magnificent cathedrals in the United States. The current building was constructed in 1794 in the Spanish style, with two round spires rising from the facade, and then virtually rebuilt and remodeled in 1849, but simpler churches have stood on this site beginning with the arrival of Bienville in 1719— that first wooden structure was quickly dispatched by the forces of nature, when a hurricane swept through in 1723. During the 1849 remodel, huge steeples were added to the two symmetrical round towers, and the building has received additional restorations over the years. The cathedral was designated a minor basilica in 1964 by Pope Paul VI. Mass is said daily, and there's a gift shop, open 9 A.M.–6 P.M. daily.

The next four buildings—the Cabildo, the Arsenal, the Presbytère, and 1850 House—are part of the Louisiana State Museum system, as are the U.S. Mint and Madame John's Legacy in the Lower Quarter. Each charges a separate admission

fee; buy tickets to two or more buildings, and you get a 20 percent discount.

On the upriver side of the cathedral stands **The Cabildo** (701 Chartres St., 504/568-6968 or 800/568-6968, http://lsm.crt.state.la.us/site/ cabex.htm, open 9 A.M.–5 P.M. Tues.–Sun., admission $5), the building in which the formal transfer of Louisiana to the United States took place, following the Louisiana Purchase. The Spanish first constructed the Cabildo as their seat of government in the 1770s, but it and its replacement were destroyed during both city fires. The current structure, made of brick and stucco and built in the Spanish style with Moorish influences, was erected in 1794, serving again as the Spanish Administrative body, then as the Maison de Ville (Town Hall) during the very brief time the French reclaimed New Orleans. It would serve as the state supreme court headquarters for much of the 19th and early 20th centuries, and it was actually the site where the landmark *Plessy v. Ferguson* decision (which legalized segregation) was handed down. Many prominent visitors have been officially received in the Cabildo, from statesmen Henry Clay and the Marquis de

The Cabildo, Jackson Square

Lafayette to such distinguished figures of the arts as Mark Twain and Sarah Bernhardt. The building looks more French than Spanish today, because the original flat-tile roof was replaced with a Second Empire mansard roof in the late 1840s. The Cabildo became part of the Louisiana State Museum in 1911, but it suffered a devastating fire in 1988. Following an exhaustive restoration, the building reopened in 1994, and it now contains a comprehensive and fascinating exhibit tracing the history of New Orleans over the past 200 years, with the focus falling especially on the early period. The exhibits are grouped into 10 chronological sections, beginning with the region's Native Americans and ending with Reconstruction. Various stages in between include Colonial Louisiana, the Louisiana Purchase, and several exhibits relating to different aspects of antebellum Louisiana life, such as "Death and Mourning" and "Urban Life." Each section uses maps, photographs and drawings, historical documents, and informative narrative signs to describe the period and theme.

Adjacent to the Cabildo on the riverside of the building, the Greek Revival **Arsenal** (600 St. Peter St., 504/568-6968 or 800/568-6968, http://lsm.crt.state.la.us/site/arsenal.htm, open 9 A.M.–5 P.M. Tues.–Sun., admission $5) was constructed in 1839 and became part of the state museum complex in 1915. It also was badly damaged during the Cabildo fire of 1988, and also carefully restored. Both permanent and rotating exhibits are installed in the first and second floors of the building; among the former, "Louisiana and the Mighty Mississippi" explores how flatboats, ferries, steamboats, and keel boats helped New Orleans grow into one of the world's great river ports during the 19th century. And the related exhibit "Freshly Brewed: The Coffee Trade and the Port of New Orleans" examines the economic importance of the city's coffee trade.

Built in 1797 as a home for the priests of St. Louis Cathedral and standing just on the downriver side of it, the two-story **Presbytère on Jackson Square** (751 Chartres St., 504/568-6968 or 800/568-6968, http://lsm.crt.state.la.us/site/presbex.htm, open 9 A.M.–5 P.M. Tues.–Sun., admission $5) bears a structural resemblance to the

Cabildo. It was never used for its intended purpose, as its financier, Don Andres Almonester (a Spaniard of considerable means who also funded the Cabildo and St. Louis Cathedral), died before it was completed. The new U.S. government eventually completed it and used it to house the Louisiana state courts during the 19th century.

Like the Cabildo, it became part of the Louisiana State Museum in 1911. It houses a colorful permanent exhibit on the history of Mardi Gras both in the city and Louisiana in general. Videos and audiotapes and a wide array of artifacts detail how Louisianans have celebrated Carnival over the years, and how this event has grown to become one of the most popular festivals in the world.

Baroness Micaela Almonster de Pontalba commissioned the two compounds of row houses flanking Jackson Square in 1849 (the lower building, on St. Ann) and 1851 (the upper building, on St. Peter), and they continue to bear her name as the **Pontalba Apartments.** She hired three different prominent architects, including James Gallier (who built many of the Quarter's most distinguished structures), but had a rocky relationship with them all. Samuel Stewart ultimately finished the construction, but the Baroness closely supervised the process. Pontalba, in fact, completely renovated the entire property that surrounded the cathedral, convincing local authorities to change the name of what had been the Place d'Armes to Jackson Square (in honor of General Andrew Jackson, the victor of the Battle of New Orleans), and she came up with the idea of running two sets of row houses alongside it. She had inherited the land from her father, Don Almonester, the man who had financed the Cabildo, Presbytère, and St. Louis Cathedral following the devastating fire of 1788.

Each row of buildings, when it first opened, contained 16 separate houses on the upper levels and a series of shops on the lower levels. Her plan to build the Pontalba buildings and renovate the square and its existing buildings could be called one of the earliest examples of urban renewal, for the Quarter had fallen on hard times by the time she stepped in. For a period, her plan worked, but following the Civil War and

Pontalba Apartments

well into the early 1900s, Jackson Square and the neighborhood immediately around it began to deteriorate, and the Pontalba Apartments functioned as rather unfashionable tenements.

In 1921, one of the early champions of preserving the Quarter, William Ratcliffe Irby, purchased the Lower Pontalba Building from direct heirs of the Baroness for $68,000, whereupon he willed the entire property to the Louisiana State Museum. Eventually, the city purchased the upper building, on St. Peter Street. A full and badly needed reconstruction of the buildings was undertaken through the aid of the WPA (Works Progress Administration) throughout the 1930s, and the grand old townhouses were subdivided into smaller apartments.

No. 523 was restored in 1955 by the museum, to serve as an example of a fine New Orleans townhouse of the 1850s. Most of the furnishings therein were donated to the museum but are authentic to the exact period. Today the **1850 House** (523 St. Ann St., on Jackson Square, 504/568-6968 or 800/568-6968, http://lsm.crt.state.la.us/site/1850ex.htm, open 9 A.M.–5 P.M. Tues.–Sun., admission $3) is a small but popular museum that also has an excellent book and gift shop. The actual apartment occupies the two floors above the shop. Visitors can stand at edges of the doorways and peer into the rooms, gaining a sense of an 1850s row house owned by a family of somewhat considerable means. Some basic household goods are also displayed up close, such as a circa-1850 chamber pot—this is about as close as you'll ever want to get to one of those. Plaques on the third floor detail the lives of the home's inhabitants from 1850 to 1861. You leave the apartment via an exterior staircase that passes alongside the service quarters, through which windows allow viewing. These rooms include a ground-floor kitchen, which is actually more interesting than what you'll find on the upper floors, as examples of period-furnished Victorian living and sleeping quarters are quite easy to find in Louisiana (in museums, private homes, and inns), but Victorian kitchens are a good bit harder to come by.

As you emerge from Jackson Square facing the river, make a right turn and stroll a block, looking across Decatur Street at the regal **Jackson Brewery** (600 Decatur St., 504/566-7245, www.jacksonbrewery.com) building, once the largest independent brewery in the South. German architect Dietrich Einsiedel designed the fanciful structure, with its imposing central tower, in 1891. The brewery closed in 1970s, and the four-story building, with expansive views of the river, has been restored and refitted with shops, restaurants, and loft apartments.

A couple of blocks further upriver (toward Canal Street) along Decatur, you'll reach the main office of **Jean Lafitte National Historical Park and Preserve** (419 Decatur St., 504/589-3882 for recorded information, 504/589-2133 for live assistance, www.nps.gov/jela, open 9 A.M.–5 P.M. daily, admission free), which was established in 1978 to preserve a variety of natural and historic resources and properties throughout the Mississippi River Valley. The park actually has six distinct units, this one and two others in metro New Orleans (Chalmette Battlefield just east of the city, and Barataria Preserve on the West Bank) and three in the Cajun Country that deal with the history and culture of Cajun immigration; these latter sites are in Thibodaux, Lafayette, and Eunice. A seventh unit, the New Orleans Jazz National Historic Park, is being developed in Louis Armstrong Park, just opposite the north end of the Quarter. The center's best feature are its one-hour, 1-mile walking tours, given each morning at 9:30. These tours are limited to just 25 persons and fill up quickly at busy times; availability is on a first-come, first-served basis. You pick up a free pass on the morning of the tour. Other special programs and lectures are held at different times of year, and exhibits in the visitor center also rotate and focus on different aspects of New Orleans and Louisiana culture.

On a small grassy island along Decatur Street across from the park visitor center, note the dignified statue of the man who first plotted New Orleans at the site of the present-day French Quarter, Jean Baptiste Le Moyne de Bienville, brother of the explorer Pierre Le Moyne, Sieur d'Iberville. Jean Baptiste's decision in 1699 to establish a fortification on this miserable swampy spot raised the skepticism of many, but, of course, New Orleans has flourished to become one of the world's most charming (yet still swampiest and at times miserably hottest) cities.

The French Market Area

Turn back toward Jackson Square and stroll past it along the riverside of Decatur, past a newsstand and an elevated walkway that leads to the riverfront, to reach one of the city's most famous attractions, the **French Market** (Decatur and North Peters Streets), whose stalls run for several blocks, from St. Ann to Barracks Streets. Legend has it that this site stood as a Choctaw trading post long before the Spanish established an early market here in 1791. Parts of the current structure date to 1813. Originally, the stalls contained only a meat market, but subsequent structures were added all along North Peters Street throughout the 19th century, housing markets of fresh produce, flowers, spices, and other goods. Coffee stands were opened at opposite ends of the stalls, and one still remains to this day, the delightful **Cafe du Monde,** which serves cafe au lait and powdered beignets (French-style fried doughnuts) 24 hours a day. Many of the market's stalls still sell produce, meat, and other New Orleans foods, and these are also open 24 hours.

The part of the market nearest Jackson Square holds actual retail shops and a few eateries, some selling African and Latin American crafts and handiworks, others with souvenirs, candies, and other local goods. There's also a small shaded seating area, **Latrobe Waterworks Park,** with slate walkways, a fountain, and many benches and chirping birds—it's a peaceful spot to

> *French Market Seafood carries a tantalizing range of meats packed ready for your suitcase, including alligator jerky, oysters, and crabs. Rounding out this already enormous selection are big jars of Zatarain's crab boil, Creole mustard, freshly made pralines, raw honey, Zapp's potato chips, and just about anything else you can think of.*

SIGHTS

munch on some of the edibles you may have picked up at the **Farmers Market** section of the French Market.

The Farmers Market, an indoor market building, is oodles of fun for any food lover—it's a virtual eating shrine, and many of the foods here are bottled or packaged to be taken home or shipped just about anywhere in the world. Highlights include umpteen thousand types of bottled hot sauce, including several obnoxious novelty varieties, but also all the genuine Louisiana-made ones. Other goods include a wide array of imported teas, pecans dusted with all kinds of flavored sugars and seasonings (cinnamon, Amaretto, bourbon, maple sugar), Louisiana packaged foods and condiments (Tony Chechere's Creole Gumbo, for instance), many of the local spices and herbs used for Creole and Cajun cooking, sugarcane, cookbooks, ready-to-eat foods (you can get freshly ground alligator sausage in a bun), and sno-balls (those sweet frozen treats similar to Italian ice). All manner of produce is sold here, including mirlitons, Asian pears, persimmons, and eggplant. French Market Seafood (www.frenchmarketseafood.com) carries a tantalizing range of meats packed ready for your suitcase, including alligator jerky, oysters, and crabs. And rounding out this already enormous selection of delicious foods are big jars of Zatarain's crab boil, Creole mustard, freshly made pralines, raw honey, Zapp's potato chips, and just about anything else you can think of.

The lower half of the French Market, where it becomes more of an open-air bazaar (still covered much of the way) consists of a sprawling and slightly cheesy (not in the dairy sense of the word) **Flea Market,** not so much filled with secondhand treasures and garage-sale items as it is with T-shirts, beads, and other goodies typical of what you'll find in souvenir shops around the Quarter. It's not terribly exciting, but nothing much here costs much. On weekends, however, things become a little more interesting as a section of outdoor tables are set up next to the indoor section, and here you can find African masks, crafts, drums, and more one-of-a-kind pieces. Another weekend (Fri.–Sun.) feature of this end of the market shed is the **Artists Market,** which features works of dozens of mostly local sculptors,

painters, potters, and photographers. It's an affordable place, generally, to buy a genuine Louisiana-made work of art.

At the entrance to the French Market, along the median between North Peters and Decatur Streets, note the striking 13-foot-tall gilt statue of Joan of Arc seated atop a stately horse. The original was designed in France in 1889 by Paris sculptor Emmanual Fremiet; this 1972 version, made from a cast of the original, was given to the city of New Orleans from the people of France and placed originally in the CBD outside the old convention center, which was razed and replaced with the controversial Harrah's casino. The casino developers agreed to refurbish and rededicate the statue outside the French Market as part of a deal to build their facility.

The Lower Quarter

Decatur Street from Jackson Square through the Lower Quarter (to Esplanade) is a colorful stretch for strolling, less touristy than much of the neighborhood but still very much the domain of shops, eateries, and other commercial establishments. It's a funky stretch, sort of a holdover from the 1960s and '70s, when the Quarter became something of a hippie haven—you'll find some tattoo parlors, very divey bars, a few good restaurants (including Tujague's and Sbisa, both of which have been serving Creole food for more than a century), Central Grocery (a remarkable Italian-food store that's also home to the famed muffaletta sandwich), and some knickknack shops selling everything from toys to T-shirts to antiques (though not the fancy stuff found on Royal and Chartres Streets).

About three blocks down toward Esplanade Avenue along Decatur, make a left turn onto Ursulines Avenue, and then a right onto Chartres, stopping at the **Old Ursuline Convent** (1100 Chartres St., 504/529-3040, www.accesscom.net/ursuline, complex tours 10 A.M.–3 P.M. on the hour Tues.–Fri., 11:15 A.M., 1 P.M., and 2 P.M. Sat.–Sun., admission $5), which is believed to be the oldest extant building in the Mississippi Valley. The convent is part of a large ecclesiastic complex called the **Archbishop Antoine Blanc Memorial,** comprising the convent, the adjacent Herb and Old Rose Gar-

Decatur Street and courtyard outside the Old U.S. Mint Museum, French Quarter

dens, St. Mary's Church, and several related out-buildings. It's all owned by the Catholic Archdiocese of New Orleans, and named for the first arch-bishop of New Orleans, Antoine Blanc, who held this post from 1850 to 1860; before that, he was the city's fourth bishop, from 1835 to 1850. During Blanc's administration, the St. Louis Cathedral was rebuilt to approximately its present incarnation, and nearly 50 Catholic parishes were opened all throughout Louisiana.

King Louis XV of France established the Old Ursuline Convent in 1745 to house the Ursu-line nuns who first came to New Orleans in the late 1720s, making them the first nuns to estab-lish a permanent foothold in what is now the United States. This convent was their second home, completed in 1752; they moved to a new space at 4580 Dauphine St. in 1824, and then to their present Uptown home, at 2635 State St., in 1912. In those early decades, the convent housed everybody from orphans of French settlers of the Natchez Massacre to wounded British soldiers to exiled Acadians (Cajuns, as they're known now) to the city's destitute masses. During the early 1800s, the nuns conducted a school for the education of daughters of wealthy Louisiana

plantation owners—Baroness Pontalba was among the young ladies educated here. The Ur-suline Academy still functions today at the Con-vent's State Street locale and is the oldest continuously operated school for women in the United States.

The nuns and families of men engaged in the Battle of New Orleans in 1815 prayed for a mir-acle before the statue of *Our Lady Of Prompt Succor.* The Americans won that battle, and today a solemn mass is conducted here each year to give thanks for these answered prayers, and a mosaic at the convent, created in 1997, depicts scenes from the battle. Perhaps more of a miracle is that the convent, along with the neighboring Royal Hospital and Royal Barracks, survived both of the French Quarter fires of the late 1700s.

The nuns could not afford to remain in the convent by the 1820s, as New Orleans had be-come by then a fantastically wealthy merchant port, and the real estate of the blocks around Jack-son Square had become precious and expensive. They moved, and their convent was turned for a time into a Catholic boys school, then a temporary meeting place for the Louisiana State Legislature, and then the home of the Archbishop of New

Orleans. It was converted into a presbytère in 1899, after the purchase of a new archbishopric. The old convent is attached to **St. Mary's Church,** which Antoine Blanc had built in 1845 as a chapel for the archbishopric.

Opposite the convent, across Chartres Street, the **Beauregard-Keyes House** (1113 Chartres St., 504/523-7257, guided tours 10 A.M.–3 P.M. on the hour Mon.–Sat., admission $5) has a layered history. The handsome 1820s mansion was the home, following the Civil War, of the Confederate general P.G.T. Beauregard. It then become the home of novelist Frances Parkinson Keyes (pronounced "kize"). It's one of relatively few classic raised cottages in the French Quarter—the entrance and main floor are one level above the street. The house had a number of owners over the years, and by the mid-'20s was nearly slated for demolition before a group of women aware that Beauregard had lived here after the Civil War began a campaign to save it. In 1944, Frances Parkinson Keyes took possession of the house, and it was she who hired a firm to carefully restore it. She lived here until 1969, and one of her novels, *Madame Castel's Lodge,* actually portrayed Beauregard. In addition to that book, she wrote several of her 50-odd books here, including *Dinner at Antoine's, The Chess Players,* and *Blue Camellia.*

One of the lead attractions here is the formal garden, laid out by the wife of Switzerland's consul to New Orleans, who owned the house in the 1830s. You can see the formal parterre garden through brick "windows" with iron grills at the corner of Chartres and Ursulines Streets. And, of course, a stroll through it is included in any of the guided house tours, which depart every hour on the hour. Roses, day-lilies, crape myrtle, azaleas, sweet olive trees, irises, magnolia trees, and evergreen shrubs mix and bloom in one of the Quarter's loveliest gardens.

Follow Chartres Street two blocks to Barracks Street, turning right and following this a block, crossing Decatur Street, where a walkway leads into the main entrance of the **Old U.S. Mint Museum** (400 Esplanade Ave., 504/568-6968, http://lsm.crt.state.la.us/site/mintex.htm, open 9 A.M.–5 P.M. Tues.–Sun., admission $5, 20 percent discount when visiting multiple Louisiana State Museum buildings), another component of the Louisiana State Museum. This grand neoclassical building with a granite facade (the structure itself is composed of stucco and Mississippi River mud brick) was constructed in 1836 at a cost of about $185,000 at the behest of U.S. president Andrew Jackson, who hoped it would financially jumpstart the exploration of the nation's western frontier. Especially in contrast to the rest of the French Quarter, it's a building of massive proportions (the walls on the ground floor are three feet thick) and stature.

It is the only building in the country to have functioned as both a U.S. and a Confederate mint. It also housed Confederate troops for a time during the Civil War, but with the Union occupation, the mint was shut down until Reconstruction, at which time it resumed service as a U.S. mint. During the Civil War it was also the site of a controversial punishment of Confederate loyalist William Mumford. Shortly after Union forces took possession of the city, troops erected the U.S. Stars and Stripes flag over the Mint building. In an act that some people defended more as vandalism than treason, Mumford and a few friends stole the flag and dragged it through the city's mud- and manure-caked streets. For this act, Mumford was sentenced to death, and although a number of influential New Orleanians petitioned on his behalf following his trial, Mumford was hanged two months later from just below the Mint's flagstaff.

In 1909 the Mint was decommissioned, and in 1981 it was added to the state museum system. Today it contains a fascinating variety of exhibits that make it perhaps the most engaging of the several excellent facilities within the state museum collection. The building's history as a mint is chronicled on the first floor, and New Orleans's legacy as the birthplace of jazz is detailed on the second floor, as is a display of Newcomb pottery and crafts. A state historical center and archive occupies the third floor.

On the first floor, you can see the room in which coins and currency were actually minted. Many of the artifacts on display here come from other U.S. mints, such as the ones in Denver and Philadelphia—there's an 1868 coin press, historic photos, and other period materials and documents, plus several minted coins from the 1800s. There's also a small display dedicated to the building's architect, William Strickland, who trained under famous Greek Revival architect Benjamin Latrobe and who also designed the Tennessee State Capitol, as well as the mints in Charlotte and Philadelphia.

The jazz rooms on the second floor are filled with vintage photos and depictions of the city's early music legends, including such pioneers of the music form as Buddy Bolden, Jack Laine, John Robichaux, and Jelly Roll Morton (who lived not too far from here at 1443 Frenchmen St., just above Faubourg Marigny). Exhibits trace the city's history and the emergence of quadroon balls, minstrels, funeral marches, brass bands, opera, and ragtime, all of which precipitated and to different degrees influenced the modern jazz movement.

Materials also discuss the contribution to jazz of Congo Square, which was designed in 1817 as an assembly space for slaves, running along Rampart Street between St. Ann and St. Peter Streets. This place for funerals, worship, and other community gatherings inspired a brand of music that drew on the participants' African and West Indies heritage. It ceased to be by the 1850s, but today Congo Square is appropriately a neighborhood with several great jazz clubs. Another bearer of the jazz legend that's discussed is the New Orleans funeral as it pertains to musical celebrations of the African-American community. There's also a large tribute to Louis Armstrong, who grew up here. Among the more interesting artifacts is a handwritten letter composed by a young and admiring jazz enthusiast to legendary New Orleans pianist Armand Hug—the letter was written by Harry Connick Jr.

A nice element of the jazz exhibit is that you hear some of the earliest jazz tunes piped in the whole time that you're touring the rooms. Also on the second floor are three huge and colorful murals depicting New Orleans's fabled Storyville red-light district, which was one of the city's cultivators of jazz, and an exhibition hall where rotating shows are mounted.

From here you can make a brief detour into Faubourg Marigny, or stroll up tree-shaded Esplanade Avenue a few blocks, making a left onto Royal Street.

Royal Street

Fittingly, Royal Street is one of the finest addresses in New Orleans, and also one of the most distinguished streets for antiques shops and art galleries in the United States. Many businesses are members of the Royal Street Guild, a century-old collective of especially long-running and reputable shops, restaurants, and hotels. Rue Royale was christened by the French in the 18th century, and it served as New Orleans's "Main Street" for the city's first couple of centuries.

From Esplanade Avenue, which is how you'll be approaching the street if you're coming from the Mint, Royal Street begins as mostly a lane of distinguished residences. On your left (the riverside of the street) a couple of blocks in, you'll come to the **Gallier House** (1118-1132 Royal St., 504/525-5661, www.gnofn.org/~hggh, open 10 A.M.–4 P.M. Mon.–Fri., last tour leaves at 3:30 P.M., admission $6), part of a museum that also includes the Hermann-Grima House, on St. Louis Street—a combined $10 ticket gets you admission into both house-museums. The former home of famed New Orleans architect James Gallier, who designed the house in 1857, it's filled with exquisite furnishings from the 19th century, plus elaborate faux-marble and faux-bois (wood painted very carefully to resemble a more precious type of wood). The two-story cement facade is noted for its ornate balustrade balcony and slender, finely crafted columns. The tour includes a look at the carefully restored slave quarters and a finely maintained garden, which sparkles with fountains and slate walks.

Continue down Royal a couple of blocks. You'll pass the small and historic **Cornstalk Hotel** (915 Royal St.) on your right—it's fronted by an elaborate and much-photographed cast-iron fence, which dates to the 1840s and has an eye-catching motif of cornstalks choked with the vines of morning-glory blossoms.

At the end of the block, make a left onto Dumaine and walk down to No. 632, the site

MARIE LAVEAU:
VOODOO QUEEN OF NEW ORLEANS

Voodoo experienced its heyday in New Orleans in the 19th century. While most voodoo books and paraphernalia available in the French Quarter today are purchased by curious tourists, there's no question that some still take the practice very seriously.

Misconceptions about voodoo abound, and are often encouraged by its depiction in popular culture. Voodoo is based on the worship of spirits, called Loa, and a belief system that emphasizes spirituality, compassion, and treating others well. While there's nothing inherently negative about voodoo, its practice does allow its followers to perform rites intended to bring calamity upon their enemies. These traditions, such as piercing miniature effigies with sharp pins or burning black candles, are the most familiar among outsiders.

The origins of voodoo as a religious practice are indistinct. Voodoo rituals are based on a variety of African religious traditions, which were brought to the United States by West African slaves. In 18th-century New Orleans, where slaves were kept by French and Spanish residents, voodoo began to incorporate some of the beliefs and rituals of Catholicism as well.

Marie Laveau (circa 1804–1881) is the historical figure most connected with South Louisiana's rich voodoo tradition. A young and beautiful woman of French, African, and Native American extraction, she was New Orleans's high priestess of voodoo from roughly 1830 onward. She had numerous children, and at least one daughter continued to practice for many years after her mother's death, fuelling rumors that the original Marie Laveau lived into the early 20th century. Her grave in St. Louis Cemetery No. 1, on Basin Street, is still a site of pilgrimage for voodoo practitioners.

Laveau combined the understanding ear of a psychologist with the showmanship of a preacher to become one of the city's most vaunted spiritual figures. As a young woman, Laveau practiced as a hairstylist in New Orleans, a position that afforded her the opportunity to work inside some of the city's most prominent homes, and earn the confidence of its most prominent women. As she soaked up the gossip of the day, she also dispensed both practical and spiritual advice to her clients, no doubt sprinkling her words with healthy doses of voodoo mysticism and lore. Word of Laveau's talents as a voodoo priestess spread rapidly, and soon she was staging ceremonies in the small yard of her St. Ann Street home. Her most notorious ceremony, held annually in a swamp cabin along Bayou St. John on June 23 (St. John's Eve), became the stuff of legend.

Laveau was the most famous priestess to captivate New Orleans's residents, but she wasn't the last. Throughout the centuries, a number of women and even some men have carried on the tradition of the voodoo priestess. According to legend, believers can invoke her powers by visiting her grave, marking the tomb with three "X's" (a gris-gris, or charm), scratching the ground three times with their feet, knocking three times on the grave, and making a wish. Many people in New Orleans continue to celebrate St. John's Eve, and believe that on this night, the spirit of the Voodoo Queen makes herself known.

of another Louisiana State Museum house, **Madame John's Legacy** (632 Dumaine St., 504/568-6968 or 800/568-6968, http://lsm.crt .state.la.us/madam.htm, open 9 A.M.–5 P.M. Tues.–Sun., admission $3, 20 percent discount when visiting multiple Louisiana State Museum buildings). It's a fine example of a Louisiana French Colonial (or Creole) home from the late 18th century. Madame John's house was built to replace a home lost in the great fire of 1788. It survived the next, smaller fire of 1794 and is today one of just a few remaining pre-1800s buildings in the Quarter. The historic complex, which fronts Dumaine Street, comprises three buildings: a main house, a two-story garçonniere (living quarters, what we might call "crash pads" today, built by Creole families for younger men so that their assorted nighttime activities wouldn't disrupt the other family members), and a kitchen with cook's living quarters.

Typical of houses built in the late 1700s in New Orleans, Madame John's has a high double-pitched roof, and the main floor is one level above the street (to protect the living areas in the event of flooding). On the street-level floor is the preserved brick basement that functioned as a work area and storehouse. Tours are self-guided, and the only interior on the property open to the public is the main house, which now serves as an art gallery displaying the work of some of the state's most prominent, largely self-taught folk artists. There's also an exhibit in the ground-floor basement area that traces the history of the house and its various occupants. Madame John was, in fact, not a real person but a character in a George Washington Cable story called *Tite Poulette,* an 1873 tale that dealt with a familiar theme of the author, persons of mixed racial heritage who could pass for Caucasian. Cable, who was white, wrote sympathetically in favor of racial integration, much to the disgust of the majority of New Orleans's post–Civil War residents, living in the hostile and ugly times of Reconstruction. Cable ultimately moved to Northampton, Massachusetts. In a magazine article from the 1880s, this very house on Dumaine Street was identified by a local writer as the setting for *Tite Poulette,*

and thenceforth locals referred to it as Madame John's Legacy. The house was donated by its last occupant, Mrs. Stella Hirsch Lemann, to the Louisiana State Museum in 1947.

Walk back up Dumaine, crossing Royal Street, to reach the **New Orleans Historic Voodoo Museum** (724 Dumaine St., 504/523-7685, open 10 A.M.–8 P.M. daily, admission $7), where guided tours are given by historians versed in the city's rich voodoo lore. You're even greeted by a high priestess as you enter. The museum can arrange graveyard, vampire, and ghost tours. As you might guess, these excursions, highlighted by stories that are both amusing and scary, offer high entertainment value. But at the same time, the museum gives a very good overview of a practive still shrouded in secrecy and mystery and taken very seriously by its practitioners. Though the subject matter may be a tad on the ominous side, exhibits are neither gory nor frightening, and kids definitely enjoy this place.

The focus is on Marie Laveau, the anointed high priestess of voodoo who lived in New Orleans from the 1790s until her death in 1881. Laveau's father was a successful white planter, her mother a mulatto, so that Laveau herself was considered a quadroon. Laveau earned a living as a hairstylist for the Vieux Carré's wealthiest matrons, and in this capacity she developed her reputation as a leading voodoo priestess. During the museum tour you'll see her charmed wishing stump—touch it, and you're said to receive magical blessings. The museum contains ritual art and artifacts from Africa and Haiti, the two places from which New Orleans's distinctive brand of voodoo practice originated. You can arrange for private consultations and healing seminars with museum staff. Whatever your personal take on voodoo or other religions, keep in mind that many people practice voodoo with serious and solemn conviction, and this is not merely a sideshow, despite the emphasis on colorful stories and lore.

Return to Royal Street, and wander along this charming lane for several blocks before reaching one of the city's most underrated attractions, the **Historic New Orleans Collection** (533 Royal St., 504/523-4662, www.hnoc.org, open by tour only 10 A.M.–4:30 P.M. Tues.–Sat.), which is not only a vast repository of historical documents, but also a collection of restored buildings. General L. Kemper Williams and his wife, Leila, established this research facility in 1966, having long been avid collectors of important artifacts and memorabilia pertaining to the city's history. The museum occupies a series of buildings in the heart of the Quarter, including the 1792 Merieult House (which was built following the first of the city's fires and survived the second), a gracious house with Greek Revival architectural details. It contains the Williams Gallery and the museum shop, on the first floor, and the Louisiana History Galleries on the second level. Each gallery is dedicated to a specific period of the state's history (the French Colonial years, the Spanish Colonial years, Battle of New Orleans, etc.) and includes relevant maps, early editions of books, authentic furniture, and artwork illustrating that era. You can also admire art by nearly 50 New Orleans artists who have painted in the city over the past 200 years in the Laura Simon Nelson Collection. There are always one or two rotating exhibitions presented in the History Galleries. And the Monroe-Green Collection contains works by prominent Low Country artist William Aiken Walker, whose landscape, portrait, and still-life paintings of the 19th-century Atlantic and Gulf South offer great insights into its people and customs.

As you enter the complex's courtyard, you'll see the 1794 Counting House, another Spanish Colonial–style building that was given Greek Revival accents, and a second floor, in the 1830s. That and some other historic buildings all opening onto the central courtyard hold administrative offices, but the Williams Residence, an 1880s townhouse that the museum founders occupied until the death of L. Kemper in 1971, can also be toured—it's a room-by-room survey of how an upscale early-20th-century city home would have been furnished, a refreshing counterpoint to the majority of historic house-museums in New Orleans, which re-create the look of 19th or 18th centuries. That said, the Williams Residence does contain quite a few antiques, as a fine home of the early 20th century would. Watercolors by promi-

nent local artist Boyd Cruise decorate many of the rooms. The Williamses were inveterate collectors of many things, among them vintage maps of New Orleans and the Louisiana Territory, and you can glimpse several of these in the study. The Williams Residence can be visited by tour only, with tours given Tues.–Sat. at 10 A.M., 11 A.M., 2 P.M., and 3 P.M. Tours cost $4. Guided tours are available of the History Galleries; these are given at the same times as the house tours and also cost $4.

A short walk over from the main campus of buildings, the **Williams Research Center** (410 Chartres St., 504/598-7171, www.hnoc.org, open 10 A.M.–4:30 P.M. Tues.–Sat., admission free) is an additional facility within the Historic New Orleans Collection, a library of documents, manuscripts, and photos on the history of the city. The research center often has a changing exhibit or two open to the public, along with a permanent exhibit titled "Louisiana: Its Sites and Citizens," which explores the evolving daily life of the state's people over the years. Its research facilities are otherwise open only to scholars and others working on projects related to the Gulf South.

A block downriver from the Williams Research Center is a small but fascinating attraction that looks almost like another posh boutique on a tony stretch of Chartres Street, the **New Orleans Pharmacy Museum** (514 Chartres St., 504/565-8027, www.pharmacymuseum.org, open 10 A.M.–5 P.M. Tues.–Sun., admission $2). It occupies a genuine apothecary shop from the 1820s; the original owner, Louis J. Dufilho Jr., was actually the first licensed pharmacist in the nation, having earned his certification in 1816. New Orleans, with its devastating outbreaks of yellow fever throughout the 19th century, became one of the nation's leading centers of medicine largely out of necessity; Louisiana was the first state to pass a law certifying pharmacists. Displays give a sense of what a pharmacy of that period looked like, including rows of 1850s hand-carved mahogany cabinets filled with everything from established drugs to "gris-gris" voodoo potions, and also tells the story of Louisiana's development in medicine and health care. The various blood-letting equipment is particularly eye-opening—did you know that barber shops were one of the earliest practitioners of leeching blood, and that those cheerful red-and-white poles that stand outside barbers to this day actually were used to indicate to the customers that blood-letting was available inside? Out back in a courtyard you can examine a garden of medicinal herbs, and find out which plants are still known to cure what ails you. Also on display is an 1855 Italian marble soda fountain. This is quite an extensive facility, the two floors of this stately townhouse crammed with curious objects and informative displays.

Canal Street and the Riverfront

Follow Chartres Street a few blocks to Canal, the wide thoroughfare that separates the French Quarter from the Central Business District; it's also the terminus for the St. Charles Avenue streetcar as well as the place where you can soon pick up the new streetcar that will run up Canal to Mid-City, before turning onto Carollton Avenue and continuing all the way to City Park. In the early part of the 20th century, streetcars ran all over New Orleans, and all of them (with one exception, the Napoleon Avenue line) either began or terminated here.

Canal Street's appearance offers a marked contrast to the Quarter. It's lined with massive buildings, including a few high-rise chain hotels, and it's anchored by a long median, called a "neutral ground" in New Orleans, because back when this street separated the French Quarter from the American Quarter (as the CBD was then known), the median was considered to be the home turf of neither district. The French despised the American upstarts, who had flocked here to make their fortunes following the Louisiana Purchase, and the Americans thought the French archaic and strangely insular, and they furthermore held Catholics in low regard and believed the French Quarter to be a den of pirates, sailors, free people of color, and others they considered beneath their stations in life.

Because of that broad neutral ground, Canal is one of the widest streets in America, spanning about 175 feet from one side to the other. The street was so-named for the shallow canal—really a ditch—that ran here along the western ramparts of the original city down to the river. As it developed into the neutral ground between the American and French quarters over the course of the 19th century, Canal gradually became the city's most prominent merchant thoroughfare, a department store–lined spine from which cross streets packed with smaller shops radiated. In the WPA *New Orleans City Guide* of 1938, the neighborhood's chronologists give the following description of the area's commerce:

The tendency of certain business activities to concentrate in one section of the city, although not quite so pronounced as it once was, is to be noted in the side streets in the vicinity of Canal. Most of the fur dealers are still to be found along North Peters and Decatur Sts. Royal St. has become one of antique shops which, resembling the bazaars of the Orient, line the street on both sides for blocks and pour out their strange and beautiful wares on the sidewalk. Coffee roasters and packers are to be found, for the most part, along Magazine and Tchoupitoulas Streets from Canal to Howard Ave. Farther uptown, Poydras St. from Camp to the river is the wholesale fruit, produce, and poultry center, while the principal meat packers are found near Magazine and Julia Sts. The section between Camp St. and the river, and Canal St. and Jackson Ave., contains most of the wholesale jobbing houses and many of the manufacturing plants. Carondelet St. has always been the street of the cotton brokers and bankers.

Little of what's noted here from the Depression years holds true today, except that Royal still has dozens of fine antiques shops, and Carondelet and the rest of the CBD blocks off it have developed into one of the South's leading centers of finance and banking. Otherwise, districts for fur, coffee, and food have disappeared or dissipated. The section bounded by Camp, the river, Canal, and Jackson, described as a manufacturing district in this passage, is in part, at least between Canal and the Crescent City Connection Bridge (to the West Bank), still abounding with old warehouse and factory buildings. But nowadays, this area known as the Warehouse District pulses with trendy clubs, new hotels, art galleries, a few museums, and the city's massive convention center. It is still, however, along the riverfront, the site of New Orleans's commercial port.

Note that street names change as you cross from the French Quarter into the CBD. North Peters becomes Tchoupitoulas (although South Peters Street runs through the CBD parallel to Tchoupitoulas, a block closer to the river), Decatur becomes Magazine, Chartres becomes Camp, Royal becomes St. Charles, Bourbon becomes Carondelet, Dauphine becomes Baronne, and Burgundy becomes University. Rampart continues from the Quarter into the CBD, but changes from North Rampart (in the Quarter) to South Rampart once it crosses Canal. This rule holds true for all New Orleans streets, with Canal acting as the dividing point between "north" and "south" streets.

If you turn right up Canal from Chartres Street, you'll mostly be passing storefronts occupied by tatty souvenir shops and fast-food restaurants, along with the lobby entrances to several hotels. The street used to feel a bit dodgy as you moved away from the river, but the opening in 2000 of the **Ritz-Carlton** (921 Canal St.) inside what had been the Kress and Maison Blanche department store gentrified things considerably. On the opposite side of Canal, technically in the CBD, stands one of the South's true grandes dames, the **Fairmont New Orleans** (123 Baronne St.), which following a $51 million restoration in the late '90s looks every bit as regal as it did when it opened in 1893.

Still a bit farther up Canal are two of the city's most popular venues for concerts and plays, the **State Palace Theatre** (1108 Canal St., 504/482-7112 or 504/522-4435, www.statepalace.com) and, just around the corner, the **Saenger Theatre** (143 N. Rampart St., 504/524-2490, www.saengertheatre.com).

Were you to follow Canal Street toward the lake, it would take you more than 3 miles into Mid-City and eventually up to the cemeteries west

of City Park; there a right turn onto City Park Avenue followed by a quick left onto Canal Boulevard leads you clear to Lakeshore Boulevard and the curving shoreline of Lake Pontchartrain.

Back at the corner of Chartres and Canal, turn left and continue a block past Decatur until you reach the **Custom House,** which was constructed in the elaborate Egyptian Revival style as a courthouse in 1848, on the site of the old Fort St. Louis. During the 18th century, the fort had stood guard on what had then been the levee along the east bank of the Mississippi, whose banks are now found another 500 yards or so away down Canal Street. Between the city's founding in 1718 and the early 20th century, when the modern system of flood control and levees was built to rein in and control the Mississippi, the river shifted considerably; in other parts of the state, it made entire shortcuts and new arms and bends in the marshy terrain, forever altering its course and the landscape around it.

General P.G.T. Beauregard, who would figure prominently as a Confederate military leader during the Civil War, supervised the construction of this elegant and slightly intimidating structure, which takes up the entire block bounded by Decatur, Canal, North Peters, and Iberville Street. It was not actually completed by the time of the war. Beauregard, in fact, would never have the chance to see it through, and to add insult to injury, the hated Union general Benjamin Butler used the Decatur side of the building as his administrative headquarters. The not-yet-completed upper floors served as a prison for Confederate soldiers, among them the martyred citizen William Mumford, who spent a couple of months here before his hanging at the U.S. Mint. When this granite structure was finally completed well after the end of the war, the price tag stood at about $5 million.

The stately 30,000-square-foot building is slated to become home of the **Audubon Insectarium** (Canal and Decatur Sts., www.audubon institute.org/insect) in fall 2004. Plans call for it to contain the largest free-standing collection of insects in the United States, some 900,000 species. If just the thought of that makes your skin crawl, consider that visitors will have the opportunity to touch all kinds of live creatures, although many others will be presented through displays from a safe distance. As they did with the zoo and aquarium, the Audubon Institute intends to dispel the many preconceived notions humans have about animals—of course, the insect world has an especially serious image problem. As you might guess, the museum café will have an insect-themed appearance—although it will not actually serve anything with bugs. But at the museum's own bug-cooking demonstration "café", visitors will learn how many people around the world routinely snack on ants, grasshoppers, and other insects as an excellent, and some say delicious, source of protein. Less harrowing for squeamish visitors will be the massive butterfly room, where those fluttering, colorful insects will fly freely about a Japanese-style garden.

At the corner of South Peters Street, a block closer to the river, note the **Shops at Canal Place** (333 Canal St., 504/522-9200, www.theshopsatcanalplace.com, shops open 10 A.M.–6 P.M. Mon.–Sat., noon–6 P.M. Sun.), a fancy compound of retail shops, an art-house movie theater, and the Wyndham Canal Place hotel.

From the Shops at Canal Place, walk another block to the foot of Canal Street, where you'll find one of the most popular attractions in the city, the **Audubon Aquarium of the Americas** (1 Canal St., 504/581-4629, www.auduboninstitute.org, open 9:30 A.M.–7 P.M. daily, admission $14), which overlooks the Mississippi River. This stunning, contemporary building provides a glimpse of several important aquatic habits, including the Amazon rain forest, Mississippi River, a Caribbean reef, and the Gulf of Mexico (which, appropriately in this state, includes a replica of an offshore oil rig). Special tanks highlight certain species, such as sea otters, penguins, sea horses, jellyfish, and sharks—there's also a shark touch pool, where you can actually lay a hand on one of the gentler baby sharks. Try to be there for the shark feedings (Tues., Thurs., and Sat. at 1 P.M.) or penguin feedings (daily at 11 A.M. and 4 P.M.).

The last ticket is sold an hour before closing. Consider buying a combination ticket to the aquarium and Audubon Zoo ($18), the aquarium and the IMAX Theatre ($18), or all three

($25). Parking (with a ticket validated either when you enter the aquarium or IMAX Theatre) is available for $3 for up to four hours, $9 for four–five hours, and $10 for 6–10 hours.

The Aquarium is also home to the **Entergy IMAX Theatre** (504/581-4629), which shows documentaries and other action-packed features (many of them in 3-D) on a screen that rises nearly six stories. Admission is $8 ($13.50 for a double feature), and combination tickets with the zoo and aquarium are available.

As you leave the aquarium or theater and face the river, you'll be standing at the edge of lovely **Woldenberg Riverfront Park,** a 14-acre redbrick promenade that extends along the riverfront from here to behind Jackson Brewery. It is actually along this stretch that Le Moyne, Sieur de Bienville, established the site of New Orleans in 1718. Crape myrtle and magnolia trees provide shade over the numerous park benches, affording romantic views out over the paddlewheelers docked along the riverfront. Like much of the river, this was an industrial eyesore of warehouses and wharves before being converted to this charming urban park. The one quay that remains in use, **Toulouse Street Wharf,** is the home for the palatial excursion riverboat, *The Natchez,* from which calliope music plays on evenings before it departs for cruises along the river. Fringing the park is **Moon Walk,** a wooden boardwalk that extends along the riverfront, and indeed, it's a fine place on a warm evening to sit and admire the moon reflecting on the river. It was named, however, for the New Orleans mayor who had it constructed in the 1970s, Moon Landrieu (father of U.S. Senator Mary Landrieu).

Within the park, note the stunning *Monument to the Immigrant* statue, of Carrara white marble, created by noted New Orleans artist Franco Alessandrini; it commemorates New Orleans's role as one of the nation's most prolific immigrant ports throughout the 19th century and before that under the flags of France and Spain. Woldenberg Park has a few other sculptures of distinction, among them Robert Schoen's *Old Man River,* an 18-foot tribute to the Mississippi River carved out of some 17 tons of Carrara marble; and *Ocean Song,* a series of eight 10-foot-tall pyramids.

Walk the length of Woldenberg Park, then cut over to Jackson Square along the pathway that crosses beside Jackson Brewery. Head north up St. Peter Street, past Chartres and Royal Streets, making a right onto Bourbon. Here you'll come to the ramshackle-looking **Lafitte's Blacksmith Shop** (corner of Bourbon and St. Philip Streets), a lively neighborhood bar that occupies one of the few remaining buildings in New Orleans that survived both of the major late-18th-century French Quarter fires. It's believed to have been built in the late 1760s or early 1770s.

Armstrong Park

From Lafitte's Blacksmith Shop, assuming you have not stopped for too long to enjoy a few cocktails, continue up St. Philip Street to Rampart Street, across from which stands **Armstrong Park,** the main entrance of which is at the corner of Rampart and St. Ann Streets. Long considered the most dangerous tract of land close to the French Quarter, the park is now slated to undergo an ambitious $8 million transformation, in which it will become **New Orleans Jazz National Historic Park** (www.nps.gov/neor). Currently, the visitor center for the park is located at the other end of the Quarter, by the French Market, at 916 North Peters St.; call 504/589-4841 for further information.

The development of this new attraction will help not only the park but also the lakeside blocks of the French Quarter, including North Rampart Street, which can be spotty. The overhaul will include the renovation of five historic buildings and landscaping of many acres of parkland. The park is opposite the site of historic Congo Square, where slaves of African descent regularly celebrated their music traditions with drumming and dancing gatherings during the early 19th century. When the park project is complete, there will be a jazz resource library and visitor center near the park's entrance. It's a fitting renovation for the nearest bit of greenery to the French Quarter, a part that tourists have been warned away from for decades because of the neighbor-

STORYVILLE

J ust above the French Quarter, along Basin Street, which parallels Rampart Street one block over, is a still-dicey neighborhood that has been infamous for well over a century, Storyville. It was, from 1897 until 1917, the only officially sanctioned and legal red-light district in the country. For nearly 200 years, prostitution had thrived along streets all over New Orleans, a city that had more than its share of sailors, traders, laborers, and others seeking company during long spells away from home.

City politicos for years debated the best way to deal with this social fact of life, figuring that if they couldn't root out prostitutes and bordellos, they might as well sanction them—and tax them. It was city alderman Sidney Story who, in 1897, came up with the bright idea to create a legal red light district, and after him the neighborhood was named.

By all accounts, the system worked wonderfully well. Potential customers could peruse a directory, the *Blue Book,* containing names of brothels and prostitutes, along with prices and the various services available, and photos of many of the women. The city's illegitimate music movement, jazz, flourished in the city's legitimate sex district, as many bordellos hired jazz musicians (including Jelly Roll Morton and King Oliver) to entertain. At its peak, the neighborhood licensed some 750 ladies of the evening. And prostitution continued to be a big, albeit illegal business, in Storyville well into the 1960s, more than four decades after the red-light district was made illegal again.

You can get some sense of the neighborhood's history by watching the Louis Malle movie *Pretty Baby,* released in 1978 and starring a young Brooke Shields.

hood's crime problems. The new national park facilities are slated to open in the next two years.

As you might expect, Armstrong Park does contain a splendid statue of Louis "Satchmo" Armstrong, the native New Orleanian who defined jazz as much as any musician. Another attraction within the park is the **Mahalia Jackson Theatre of the Performing Arts** (parking inside the park gates, Orleans Avenue entrance), which hosts performances sponsored by the New Orleans Ballet Association and the New Orleans Opera Association. The park is named for the world-famous gospel singer Mahalia Jackson, who was born in New Orleans in 1911, although she came into her own as a professional musician in Chicago in the 1930s and died in that city in 1972.

Near Armstrong Park is arguably the most famous and most intriguing of all of New Orleans's so-called cities of the dead, **St. Louis Cemetery No. 1** (bound by Basin, Conti, Tremé, and St. Louis Streets), which has been the final resting place for many New Orleanians since the late 18th century. The burial ground was established in 1789 and set outside what was then the city border, above Rampart Street, the theory being that proximity to the deceased was in part responsible for the rampant yellow fever and cholera outbreaks of this period. It would be many decades later that the medical establishment proved that mosquitoes carried yellow fever, and that it could not be spread from one person—living or dead—to another.

There are about 700 tombs in this cemetery, interring many thousands of persons, as most of these above-ground structures are owned by families or groups and designed to hold more than one set of remains. The tombs can be quite elaborate and are constructed typically of brick, but covered in cement or stucco. Some of the oldest ones are today little more than crumbled ruins. Bodies were buried aboveground because New Orleans sits below sea level and has a high water table—the earliest attempts to bury the dead in the city failed during floods, as the caskets simply floated to the surface. St. Louis Cemetery is in a dicey part of the city, and you shouldn't just wander over on your own, even during the day, although efforts have been made in recent years to rid this district of crime. It's much wiser to visit via a guided tour. Among the best are those offered through **Save Our Cemeteries** (504/525-3377 or 888/721-7493, www.saveourcemeteries.com), which gives hour-long excursions through St. Louis Cemetery No. 1 on Sunday mornings at 10 A.M. They depart from the Royal Blend Coffee Shop at 621 Royal St., and reservations are not necessary. The cost (actually a suggested donation) is $12. Save Our Cemeteries also gives tours of Lafayette Cemetery, in Uptown.

Just opposite Armstrong Park at the site of what was Congo Square is the **VooDoo Spiritual Temple** (828 N. Rampart St., 504/522-9627, www.voodoospiritualtemple.org), which offers voodoo services, consultations, rituals, tours, and lectures. Priestess Miriam runs this center of voodoo worship and healing, which also sells handcrafted voodoo dolls, gris-gris and mojo bags, blessed candles, aroma oils, talismans, and books and CDs related to voodoo.

Bourbon Street

Leaving the park or the VooDoo Spiritual Temple, walk along Rampart Street to St. Peter, making a left and continuing three blocks across Bourbon Street to **Preservation Hall** (726 St. Peter St., 504/522-2841), which since 1961 has been one of the most popular and respected places to hear true New Orleans jazz. The band and the venue were formed expressly to keep the legacy of the city's distinctive style of jazz music alive for generations to come, and many of Preservation Hall's early members were musicians who came of age during the early part of the 20th century, when this originally controversial style of music began to hit its stride. It's a charming, informal place, with seating on vintage wooden benches and folding chairs and a good bit of standing room—attending a concert here is like watching an informal jam session in a community center in some rural town in Louisiana.

Visitors who have watched the Preservation Hall band perform in more formal concert venues around the world (they tour more than 100 days annually) are sometimes surprised by just how laid-back and warm (and small) their

© ANDREW COLLINS

Victorian houses along Esplanade Avenue, French Quarter

home performance space is. The exterior of the 1750s house, which later housed a cobbler shop and then a grocery, with a second-floor galley running the length of the facade, is pleasantly decrepit stucco—it almost looks abandoned by day. From the hall you can stroll along a carriageway, its wall hung with vintage jazz posters and concert bills, out to the landscaped courtyard for a breath of fresh air.

Return back up St. Peter Street a half block to the city's most extreme thoroughfare, **Bourbon Street,** which is either hated or loved by those who experience it—just about everybody seems to have a strong view regarding this unabashedly touristy row of nightclubs and drinking halls. Interestingly, although it's arguably the most recognizable street in New Orleans today, Bourbon was no more popular or important than the Quarter's other streets prior to its development into a nightlife sector. Bourbon Street is hardly mentioned in the WPA's exhaustively comprehensive *New Orleans City Guide,* written in 1938.

The street was named for France's royal dynasty, the Bourbons, in 1722, when the Quarter (which at that time was the entire city) was laid out. For the next 200 years, Bourbon was a pleas-

ant street to live and shop on, but it was never anywhere near as prestigious as Royal Street, which runs parallel a block closer to the river, or Chartres Street. It wasn't until the early part of the 1930s that, especially along the section nearest Canal, Bourbon Street began to develop more commercial cachet, as a handful of prominent shops and department stores opened along the first few blocks of Bourbon. Its fame, or infamy, really, came about following World War II, during the 1950s, a straitlaced decade for much of the country. At this time, a handful of strip clubs began to prosper along Bourbon, becoming a top draw for visiting tourists.

It has evolved today into a more eclectic entertainment district, still with a handful of strip bars, but now with places known for music and other types of entertainment, and you'll also find a handful of prominent hotels and restaurants on or just off Bourbon. Since the late '90s, the 100 and 200 blocks of Bourbon have seen a renaissance—this area, where there had been department stores for many decades, had become dark and ominous at night, when shops were closed. Visitors walking over from the CBD were often told to enter the Quarter down along Royal or Chartres Street and then walk up to Bourbon along Bienville or Conti Streets, but these days it's safer and quite customary to approach Bourbon directly from Canal.

The blocks from Iberville to St. Ann Streets are cordoned off during the evenings into a pedestrian mall—automobiles would find it impossible to drive along here anyway, as the streets fill with revelers, mostly visiting from out of town, who wander from bar to bar, go-cups (a.k.a. "geaux" cups) in hand. It's perfectly legal to saunter about the Quarter with an open container (as long as it's not made of glass), and many of the establishments here, especially along Bourbon, are open 24 hours. At St. Ann Street, the portion of Bourbon closed to vehicle traffic at night ends. This cross street also marks the point at which Bourbon becomes a gay entertainment district for roughly a block or so, and it's where you'll find a handful of the city's most popular gay and lesbian discos.

Two blocks later, at St. Philip Street, Bourbon begins to take on the residential character the rest of the street possessed during its early decades. From St. Philip the next four blocks to the Quarter's boundary, Esplanade Avenue, Bourbon is surprisingly peaceful, even on weekend evenings, and it's a fine spot for admiring 19th-century homes.

If you've just entered Bourbon Street from Preservation Hall, as this chapter's walking tour suggests, you'll be standing at its junction with St. Peter Street. A right turn leads a block to the gay bars around the corner of St. Ann Street and then, a block or two further, to Lafitte's Blacksmith Shop. Make a left turn onto Bourbon, and after two blocks you'll come to St. Louis Street. Make a right, and you'll soon be standing before another of the Quarter's best house-museums, the **Hermann-Grima House** (820 St. Louis St., 504/525-5661, www.gnofn.org/~hggh, open 10 A.M.–4 P.M. Mon.–Fri., with the last tour leaving at 3:30 P.M. Admission $6; $10 for combined ticket with Gallier House). The Hermann-Grima is a steep-roofed Federal-style mansion of the sort you'd more often see in Savannah or other old cities of British origin than New Orleans. Creole cooking demonstrations are held here on Thursdays, October through May—the Her-

mann-Grima House contains the only functional outdoor kitchen in the French Quarter, a holdover from its antebellum days (the house dates to 1831). Another unusual feature is the Quarter's only horse stable, adjacent to the charming courtyard garden. The house is run by the same people who operate the Gallier House, on Royal Street. The two house-museums have developed several self-guided tours, including **The African American Experience in 19th-Century New Orleans,** which interprets the lives of both enslaved and free persons of color and how they lived, coped, and ultimately thrived in New Orleans in the 1830s through the 1860s.

As you leave the Hermann-Grima House, turn left, continuing up St. Louis Street away from Bourbon, and make a left onto Dauphine, and then a block later, a right onto Conti (pronounced "con-tie") Street. This leads to the **Musee Conti–The Wax Museum** (917 Conti St., 504/581-1993 or 800/233-5405, www.get-waxed.com, open 10 A.M.–5 p.m. Mon.–Sat., noon–5 P.M. Sun., admission $7), which is completely cheesy, but fun for the kids and kitsch-seekers. The museum was established in 1963 and uses more than 150 life-size and realistically wrought figures to depict the city's history through a series of themed vignettes (kids especially seem to enjoy the eerie Haunted Dungeon).

At this point you could either return down Conti a block and a half to Bourbon Street, making a right and continuing along to Bienville Street, or you could take Dauphine over a block to Bienville Street and turn left—the latter route is a bit more relaxed, especially nice if you're one of those people who does not take easily to the crassness of Bourbon Street. Either way, make a point of stopping along Bienville Street (just in from Bourbon, in the direction away from the river) by the **Germaine Cazenave Wells Mardi Gras Museum** (813 Bienville St., 504/523-5433, www.arnauds.com/museum.html, Open 11 A.M.–10 P.M. Mon.–Fri., 6–10 P.M. Sat., and 10 A.M.–10 P.M. Sun., admission free), which is located at the fabled restaurant Arnaud's, a favorite gathering place in New Orleans since World War I. The restaurant's owners opened the museum in the early 1980s as a tribute to

Ms. Wells, who served as the queen of some 22 Mardi Gras balls from the late 1930s through the late 1960s. On display are many of Wells's ball costumes, plus other Mardi Gras Royal Court attire. Wells was the daughter of Count Arnaud and Lady Irma Wells, who founded the restaurant in 1918. Displays of the gowns are augmented by photos of the many balls where they were worn.

Back on Bourbon, note the small **New Orleans Musical Legends Park** (311 Bourbon St.), which opened in 2003 and already includes a statue of jazz clarinetist Pete Fountain and trumpet great Al Hirt. Additional statues, busts, and plaques will be added over the years, as notable jazz musicians are inducted.

From here, at the intersection of Bienville and Bourbon, you're just a couple of blocks from Canal, or you can walk back in the other direction along Bourbon or one of the parallel streets, such as Dauphine and Royal, to reach Faubourg Marigny.

FAUBOURG MARIGNY

The neighborhood immediately downriver from the Quarter—across tree-shaded Esplanade Avenue—is Faubourg Marigny, a neighborhood sometimes credited as America's first suburb; it was settled during the first decade of the 19th century as a result of the Quarter's overcrowding, and in many respects, it continues to function as an extension of the Quarter.

Faubourg Marigny was originally a plantation, established in the early 18th century—it's named for the last owner of the plantation, Bernard Xavier Phillippe de Marigny de Mandeville, a profoundly wealthy French aristocrat who lived from 1785 to 1868. The enterprising de Marigny, realizing that the French Quarter had outgrown its boundaries, began subdividing his plantation as early as 1805, selling off quadrants to Creoles, immigrants, and free men of color. The neighborhood was soon completely cut up into short square blocks, and it thrived, at first as its own incorporated city and then as part of New Orleans, for many decades.

Like the French Quarter, the neighborhood's fortunes waned following World War II, when it became popular to move away from inner-city boroughs and into the true suburbs—places like Metairie and Kenner. The Marigny fell into a complete state of disrepair and poverty, despite being named a National Historic District in 1974.

As real estate prices rose in the French Quarter in the late 1980s, savvy buyers—among them many artists, spirited professionals, and gays and lesbians—swooped in and snapped up the neighborhood's many charming cottages and houses. Before about 1995, there were still bargains to be had in Faubourg Marigny; this is certainly not the case any longer, but the neighborhood still has lower real estate costs than many other historic, centrally located residential districts in other big U.S. cities.

There are really no formal attractions in Faubourg Marigny. A chief activity is simply strolling about admiring old houses, the bulk of which are Creole and French West Indies–style cottages and larger Greek Revival homes, many of them painted in a riot of bright colors, and with intricate gingerbread, Gothic, and other Victorian details. Most of Faubourg Marigny is residential, but you'll find a handful of eateries and bars scattered throughout the district, especially along Royal Street, and you can also amble along one super-hip commercial strip, Frenchmen Street, which is lined with cool music clubs, dark and shadowy Gen-X bars, funky ethnic restaurants, and affordable cafés. Although it's nowhere near as touristy as the French Quarter, Frenchmen Street's reputation has grown exponentially since the mid-'90s, and it can feel as crowded along here on a weekend evening as it does along some of the Quarter's busier streets.

The neighborhood is bound by Esplanade Avenue, St. Claude Avenue, Press Street, and the Mississippi River, and from the Quarter it's most easily approached via Decatur Street. After crossing Esplanade, make a left onto Frenchmen, and this leads just a block or two to the little clutch of bars and cafés. From here, you're in a position to take a nice little residential tour of the neighborhood, keeping in mind that the Marigny is best known for its modest 19th-century cottages, not the grand high-style mansions more typical of the Garden District and even the Quarter. A

© ANDREW COLLINS

Creole cottage in Faubourg Marigny

pleasant loop is to walk downriver from Frenchmen Street along Chartres Street, crossing Elysian Fields Avenue, another wide street with a neutral ground, like Esplanade and Canal. A railroad extended clear along Elysian Fields Avenue from the 1830s through the 1950s, connecting downtown New Orleans and the Mississippi River with a resort area on Lake Pontchartrain (and also with ferry service across the lake to the cooler North Shore communities of Mandeville and Covington). Marigny was originally plotted as and named Elysian Fields after Paris's Champs Elysée (which, in French, means Elysian Fields).

Continue on Chartres for seven blocks to Press Street. Here turn left and walk up a block, returning to Frenchmen Street via Royal Street. Back at Elysian Fields, make a brief detour toward the river (taking a left from Royal) and stroll down a half block to visit **American Aquatic Gardens and Gifts** (621 Elysian Fields, 504/944-0410, www.pondsandfountains.com, open 9 A.M.–5 P.M. daily, admission free), a sprawling emporium with artfully arranged ponds, fountains, sculptures, terra-cotta, and plantings—it's worth strolling through even if you're not planning to buy anything.

Back on Royal, cross Elysian Fields Avenue, and as you approach Frenchmen, you'll see lovely **Washington Square Park** on your right, a delightful patch of tree-shaded lawns with park benches, surrounded by a wrought-iron fence. At Frenchmen, you can start a short tour of an especially charming part of the neighborhood: Continue upriver (west) along Royal, turn right up Touro Street, then left onto Dauphine, then left onto Pauger, and then left onto Kerlerec Street. Two blocks later, bear left onto Chartres Street, which will lead you back in less than a block to Frenchmen, where you began this walking tour. This little jumble of turns takes you through a section where the neighborhood's houses have been restored with particular flourish.

The two most common architectural types you'll see along this tour are Creole cottages and shotgun houses. A Creole cottage typically has a four-room floor plan and a steeply angled roof, while a shotgun house is a long one-room-wide structure with a continuous gable roof that extends the length of the house. Some suggest that shotgun houses are the distant offspring of African "long houses." Creole cottages share some of the characteristics of the lacy little bungalows found

© ANDREW COLLINS

a house along Royal Street, Bywater District

throughout the French West Indies and other parts of the Caribbean, and, indeed, their popularity was heightened by the influx of Haitian refugees in New Orleans in the early 1800s. Creole cottages, in the United States anyway, are pretty much unique to New Orleans, while shotgun houses are found all through the South, especially in rural areas. However, New Orleans's shotgun houses are far more colorful, often characterized by frilly gingerbread detail, rich woodwork, and bands of colorful paint. Indeed, most U.S. architectural forms found in New Orleans represent the most florid styles within the genre.

If you like Faubourg Marigny, consider staying at one of its many lovely B&Bs and inns—this is an excellent base for exploring the city while avoiding the herds of tourists. Most of the inns here are highly charming and also less

pricey than comparable properties a few blocks over in the Quarter. Do keep in mind that the Marigny has a number of unlicensed inns, which should be avoided. You can find out which of the city's licensed B&Bs are in Faubourg Marigny by checking with the Professional Innkeepers Association of New Orleans (PIANO), whose website is www.bbnola.com.

The next neighborhood downriver from Faubourg Marigny is **Bywater,** which is also bound by Pratt, the river, and St. Claude, with its downriver boundary being the canal. Bywater has greatly cleaned itself up since the early 1990s, and as Faubourg Marigny has become prohibitively exhibit for some, many homebuyers have moved farther downriver into this up-and-coming district, which also has a number of fine 19th-century homes, many in need of some TLC.

Central Business and Warehouse Districts

For at least a century following the U.S. purchase of Louisiana in 1805, American newcomers and the more established citizens of French descent maintained frosty and sometimes overtly hostile relations. Americans first settled in the neighborhood just upriver (technically southwest) of the French Quarter, now known as the Central Business District (referred to conversationally as the CBD). It was known then as the American Quarter, and the median running down Canal Street, which divides the two districts, gave rise to the term "neutral ground," which still today is what New Orleanians call any grassy median dividing opposing lanes of traffic on a wide street.

Although the CBD started out as a residential district, it was from the start a center of commerce, as the earliest residents were chiefly merchants and entrepreneurs keen on taking advantage of New Orleans's strategic location and America's recent acquisition of the territory.

Today the CBD is almost entirely without residential architecture, although some New Orleanians live in apartment buildings or, more recently, have moved into lofts and condos fashioned out of the old industrial structures in the section of the CBD nearest the river, the Warehouse District. Just about every building in New Orleans taller than six or seven stories is in the CBD, and some of the tallest structures rise to more than 40 stories (One Shell Plaza is the tallest, at exactly 50 stories) and can be seen from as far away as the lakefront, the airport, and the Mandeville Causeway along Lake Pontchartrain. It's not a terribly interesting neighborhood to look at, any more than any other financial district dominated by office towers, but in recent years, several high-caliber hotels have opened in the CBD, and with them came some first-rate restaurants, helping to make the area more popular with visitors.

This tour begins along St. Charles Avenue at Lafayette Square and continues mostly along the streets near the river, in the Warehouse District, before ending at the foot of Canal Street, where you can catch the ferry across the river to Algiers Point.

If you're starting out from the French Quarter, follow Royal Street out of the Quarter to Canal and continue across Canal to St. Charles Avenue (which Royal becomes, once it enters the CBD). Follow St. Charles in the direction of uptown for several blocks, perhaps pausing briefly to admire the 1920s skyscraper at 333 St. Charles, which was built as the city's Masonic Temple but now is home to the trendy Hotel Monaco.

On your left soon after you cross wide Poydras Street you'll come to lovely and green **Lafayette Square** (bound by St. Charles Avenue, Camp Street, and North and South Maestri Place), which was laid out in early 19th century as the American Quarter's version of the Place d'Armes (now Jackson Square). It was originally called Place Gravier but was rechristened in honor of the Marquis de Lafayette, who visited the city in 1825. Today the shaded and landscaped park with ample park-bench seating continues to be a pleasant place to relax or read a newspaper.

St. Charles Avenue itself is unremarkable as it runs through the CBD, lined with old and new office towers and hotels. It really doesn't begin to take form as a place to admire old homes and beautifully landscaped yards until you're well out of the CBD, in the Garden District. One building worth noting, however, is **Gallier Hall** (545 St. Charles Ave., 504/565-7457, free tours by appointment 9 A.M.–5 P.M. Mon.–Fri.), a hulking white Greek Revival building named for its architect, James Gallier, who designed the structure in 1850. Used as a special-events facility today, and as a spot where the city mayor greets members of the royal courts of Mardi Gras krewes (St. Charles Avenue is the main route for such parades), the building served as New Orleans City Hall from the late 19th through late 20th centuries. It's a stunning structure with massive Ionic columns.

Continue uptown along St. Charles Avenue, detouring briefly down Girod Street (a left turn),

SIGHTS

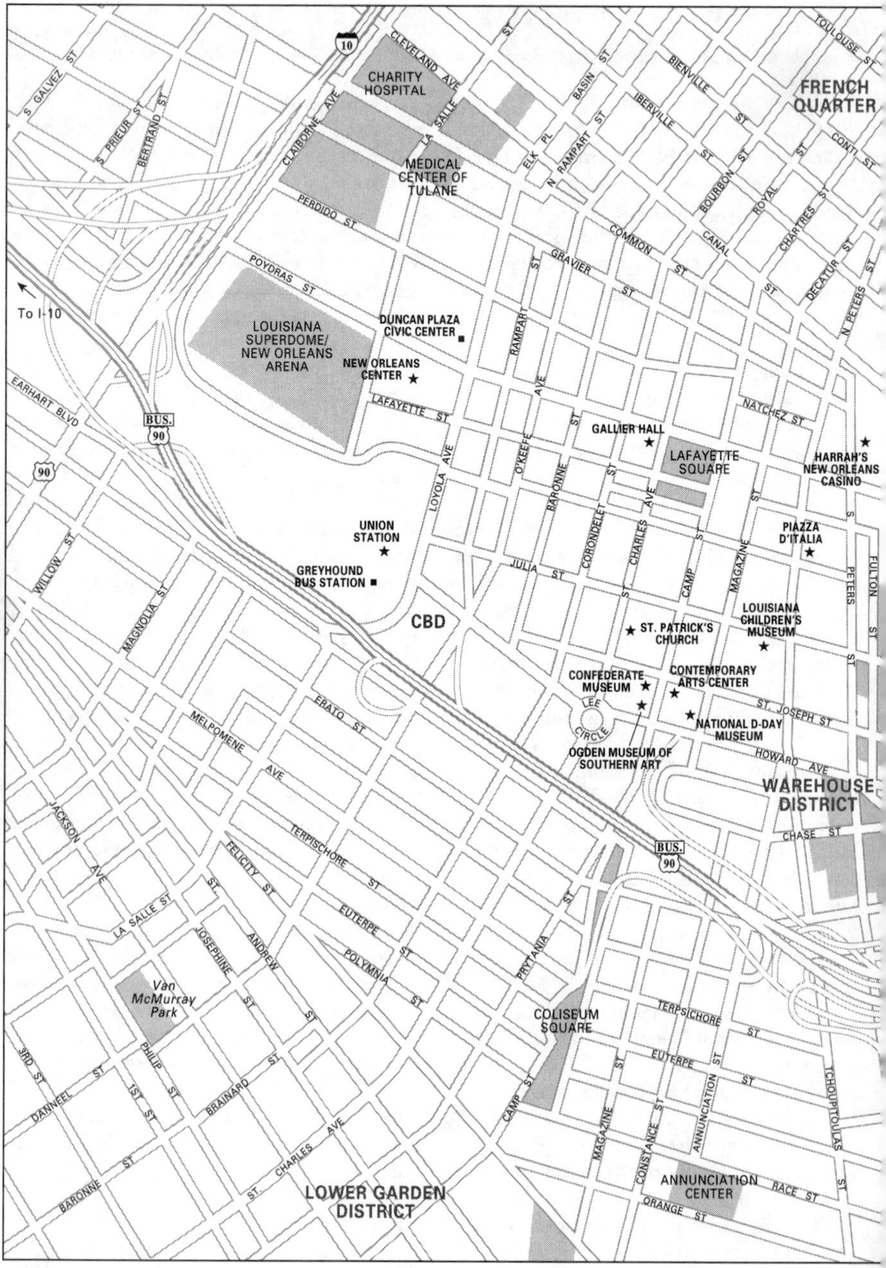

CHARITY HOSPITAL
MEDICAL CENTER OF TULANE
FRENCH QUARTER
LOUISIANA SUPERDOME/ NEW ORLEANS ARENA
DUNCAN PLAZA CIVIC CENTER
NEW ORLEANS CENTER
To I-10
GALLIER HALL
LAFAYETTE SQUARE
HARRAH'S NEW ORLEANS CASINO
UNION STATION
GREYHOUND BUS STATION
PIAZZA D'ITALIA
CBD
ST. PATRICK'S CHURCH
LOUISIANA CHILDREN'S MUSEUM
CONFEDERATE MUSEUM
CONTEMPORARY ARTS CENTER
LEE CIRCLE
NATIONAL D-DAY MUSEUM
OGDEN MUSEUM OF SOUTHERN ART
WAREHOUSE DISTRICT
Van McMurray Park
COLISEUM SQUARE
ANNUNCIATION CENTER
LOWER GARDEN DISTRICT
10
BUS. 90
90
S GALVEZ ST
S PRIEUR ST
BERTRAND ST
CLAIBORNE AVE
CLEVELAND AVE
LA SALLE
ELK PL
BASIN ST
N RAMPART ST
BIENVILLE
IBERVILLE
BOURBON ST
ROYAL
CHARTRES ST
DECATUR ST
N PETERS
TOULOUSE ST
CONTI ST
CANAL ST
COMMON ST
GRAVIER ST
PERDIDO ST
POYDRAS ST
LAFAYETTE ST
NATCHEZ ST
RAMPART ST
O'KEEFE AVE
LOYOLA AVE
BARONNE ST
CORONDELET ST
CHARLES AVE
CAMP ST
MAGAZINE ST
PETERS ST
FULTON ST
JULIA ST
EARHART BLVD
WILLOW ST
MAGNOLIA ST
ERATO ST
MELPOMENE AVE
ST. JOSEPH ST
HOWARD AVE
CHASE ST
JACKSON AVE
TERPISCHORE ST
FELICITY ST
EUTERPE ST
POLYMNIA ST
LA SALLE ST
JOSEPHINE ST
ANDREW ST
PRYTANIA ST
TERPSICHORE ST
EUTERPE ST
ANNUNCIATION ST
TCHOUPITOULAS ST
3RD ST
DANNEEL ST
PHILIP ST
1ST ST
BRAINARD ST
CAMP ST
MAGAZINE ST
CONSTANCE ST
ST. CHARLES AVE
BARONNE ST
RACE ST
ORANGE ST

SIGHTS

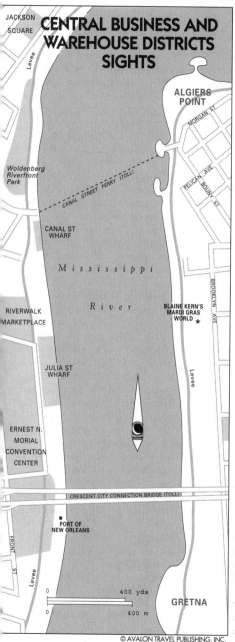

CENTRAL BUSINESS AND WAREHOUSE DISTRICTS SIGHTS

JACKSON SQUARE

Levee

ALGIERS POINT

MORGAN ST

Woldenberg Riverfront Park

CANAL STREET FERRY (TOLL)

PELICAN AVE

BOURY ST

CANAL ST WHARF

Mississippi

BROOKLYN AVE

River

RIVERWALK MARKETPLACE

BLAINE KERN'S MARDI GRAS WORLD ★

JULIA ST WHARF

Levee

MOON

ERNEST N. MORIAL CONVENTION CENTER

CRESCENT CITY CONNECTION BRIDGE (TOLL)

FRONT ST

PORT OF NEW ORLEANS

Levee

0   400 yds
0   400 m

GRETNA

© AVALON TRAVEL PUBLISHING, INC.

and then making a right onto Camp, another of Gallier's creations, **St. [ ] Church** (724 Camp St., 504/525-441[ ], first place of worship built in the Americ[ ] Quarter, completed in 1838. The lavishly or[ ]nate interior is known for its high vaulted ceilings and fine stained glass.

Back on St. Charles, continue as you were for a couple of blocks until you reach **Lee Circle,** formerly known as Tivoli Place, and now the hub for a small arts and museum district that has grown up on the streets just downriver from here since the mid-'90s. This is the one regal traffic circle in downtown New Orleans, and it imparts a slightly formal, urban air—a hint of Paris or London. Rising high over the traffic circle, which is a stop on the St. Charles streetcar line, stands a magnificent bronze statue of Robert E. Lee, the Confederate Civil War general; it sits atop a graceful marble column, the entire memorial rising 60 feet over the circle. It acts as a gateway to the Garden District and Uptown.

Exit the circle via Howard Avenue, heading toward the river (a left if you're approaching it from St. Charles Avenue coming from Lafayette Square), and then make your first left onto Camp Street, which also marks the boundary of the Warehouse District, generally said to be enclosed by Camp Street and the river, from the Crescent City Connection Bridge to Poydras Street. Here on the corner, on your left, is the **Ogden Museum of Southern Art** (925 Camp St., 504/539-9600, www.ogdenmuseum.org, Tues.–Sat. 9:30 A.M.–5:30 P.M.; $10), moved from a temporary space into a spectacular new building in August 2003, containing the largest collection of artwork from the American South in the United States. Much of the Ogden is an artful new construction, but it also incorporates portions of the old Howard Memorial Library, designed in the Richardsonian Romanesque style by native Louisianan architect H. H. Richardson, for whom that building style is named.

The complex includes the main building, which is a contemporary, five-story structure, along with the restored Patrick F. Taylor Library and the Clementine Hunter Education Wing, named for the famous Louisiana folk artist who

tation in Cloutierville produced some 4,000 career. This is as com- art as you'll find, with entury to the present, ates as well as Washing- type of media are rep- 3,000 items. Art of the Southern United States has been somewhat over-looked historically, but has recently come strongly into its own. Some of the key artists represented here are noted Mississippi watercolorist Walter Anderson, 19th-century South Carolina por-traitist Thomas Sully, New Orleanian abstract expressionist George Dunbar, Depression-era photographer Walker Evans, and legendary folk artist (and country preacher) Howard Finster.

Right next door, inside the elegant Confederate Memorial Hall (ca. 1891), the **Confederate Museum** (929 Camp St., 504/523-4522, www.confederatemuseum.com, open 10 A.M.–4 P.M. Mon.–Sat., admission $5) holds the second-largest assemblage of Southern Civil War memorabilia in the country, including some 125 battle flags, uniforms, weapons, and medical instruments, as well as the personal items of Robert E. Lee, P.G.T. Beauregard, Braxton Bragg, Confederate President Jefferson Davis, and other important Confederate figures during the war. As this war was the first ever recorded extensively through photographs, the museum has become especially known for its more than 500 tintypes, daguerreotypes, and other early photographic images. It is the oldest continuously operating museum in the state, having opened in 1891 in this Romanesque structure designed by another of the city's, and the South's, most distinguished architects, Thomas O. Sully (no relation to artist Thomas Sully, mentioned earlier). Continue down Camp to the corner of St. Joseph Street, and you can begin to sense the Warehouse District's artful gentrification, which is embodied by the **Contemporary Arts Center** (900 Camp St., 504/523-1216, www.cacno.org, gallery open 11 A.M.–5 P.M. Tues.–Sun., admission $5, free on Thursdays). A dramatic former warehouse with a redbrick facade and ranks of tall windows has been converted into this performing arts center with about 10,000 square feet of gallery space, in

which rotating exhibits are given throughout the year. The facility is behind the Lee Circle YMCA, just a block in from Lee Circle. CAC began in 1976 as a means to foster innovative, and often provocative, arts in New Orleans, and to that end, you can catch everything from bold photography and mixed-media installations to performances in modern dance, independent filmmaking, and edgy theater. Ticket prices for performances vary, but usually cost $10 to $15, and it's slightly cheaper if you buy tickets in advance rather than at the door. Performance times vary; some are given during the day, many at night. The excellent Cyber Bar & Cafe @ the CAC offers free Internet access to café customers; tea, beer, wine, and cocktails (this is New Orleans, after all) are available.

Turn right onto St. Joseph from Camp Street and continue a block, making a right onto Magazine, which leads to another of the city's more recent attractions. One of the nation's most exalted popular historians, the late Dr. Stephen Ambrose, founded the **National D-Day Museum** (945 Magazine St., 504/527-6012, www.ddaymuseum.org, open 9 A.M.–5 P.M. daily, admission $10) here in 1991. The museum opened to the public on June 6, 2000—the 56th anniversary of the amphibious World War II invasion. This is the only museum in the United States dedicated to this event, which involved more than a million Americans. It may seem like a random location for such a museum, but the Andrew Higgins factory, which now houses the museum, built ships during World War II, including some of the very vehicles that transported infantrymen to Normandy, an event that ultimately liberated Europe from Axis control. Ambrose lived in New Orleans until his death in 2002, and was a professor at the University of New Orleans. He is best known for such riveting World War II histories as *The Good Fight*, *The Wild Blue* (about B-24 fighter pilots), and *D-Day: June 6, 1944*.

Backtrack along Magazine Street, crossing St. Joseph, and continue a block to Julia Street, which today is lined with art galleries, loft offices, and apartments. It's also home to the **Louisiana Children's Museum** (420 Julia St., 504/523-1357, www.lcm.org, open 9:30 A.M.–4:30 P.M. Tues.–Sat., noon–4:30 P.M. Sun., in summer, also

9:30 A.M.–4:30 P.M. Mon., admission $6). New Orleans has become discernibly more kid-friendly over the years, and this enormous touch-friendly cache of interactive exhibits provides one of the better experiences for young ones. Many of the exhibits re-create grown-up activities or everyday errands on a kids' scale—there's a play grocery store, a miniature Port of New Orleans where youngsters can pretend to pilot a tugboat on the Mississippi and learn where all those bales of cotton and crates of sugar end up. Opportunities for children to deliver the news on a closed-circuit TV, play house inside a Cajun cottage, and experiment with different musical instruments reveal the extensive breadth of offerings. The target age for most of these exhibits is toddler up to about 12 or so, while a science lab that puts a fun spin on physics especially ignites the imaginations of the older kids. Visitors under 16 must be accompanied by an adult.

At this writing, the famous Tabasco hot-sauce company, based on Avery Island in the Cajun Country near Lafayette, was creating a **Tabasco-themed museum and country store** set inside a pair of adjoining Victorian row houses on Julia Street at the corner of St. Charles. The complex will be similar in look and feel to the country store and visitor center on Avery Island—very touristy, in all likelihood, but plenty of fun if you're a hot-sauce aficionado and you're not able to make it out to the real factory.

Follow Julia down toward the riverfront, passing Emeril's, the famous restaurant of TV chef Emeril Lagasse, and making a right turn onto South Peters Street. As you walk from this point toward the massive Crescent City Connection Bridge, which arches high over the neighborhood, the Warehouse District's wine bars and art galleries give way to gritty machine shops, commercial bakeries, and other vestiges of the neighborhood's industrial past. Still, the architecture is interesting clear to the bridge, and along South Peters you can see that some of these old buildings have been converted to apartments and modern offices.

Turn left down Diamond Street, which leads to New Orleans's own city-within-a-city, the **Ernest N. Morial Convention Center** (900 Convention Center Blvd., off Lower Poydras St., 504/582-3023, www.mccno.com), which has been a catalyst in reviving the neighborhood. The year it opened, it was the setting for the 1984 World's Fair; at this writing, the massive facility was about to receive a $455 million, 524,000-square-foot expansion, which will add to the already million-plus square feet of exhibition space. This move is being paid for with yet another room and restaurant tax increase; with the change in local tax law in 2002, hotel taxes were driven up to 13 percent. The sprawling skylighted convention center stretches out along the Mississippi River and below the Crescent City Connection Bridge, clear into the Lower Garden District.

Fronting the river outside the convention center is another behemoth, the **Port of New Orleans** (www.portno.com), which includes the huge cruise-ship terminal from which Carnival, Royal Caribbean Cruise Lines, Norwegian Cruise Line, the Delta Queen Steamboat Company, and RiverBarge Excursions launch ships all through the Mississippi River system and the Caribbean. This is principally an industrial port, however, and one of the world's leading hubs of international trade. It's the only deepwater port in the nation served by six major freight rail lines, and it leads the nation in market share for the import of plywood, steel, natural rubber, and—appropriate given the city's love of the stuff—coffee. About 2,400 ships come and go annually from and to the American Midwest via the river system, as well as Latin America, Europe, Asia, and Africa. Additionally, some 6,000 ships pass by the port facility each year on their way up or down the Mississippi. One final claim to fame: the facility encompasses the longest continuous wharf in the world, running some 2 miles from Henry Clay Avenue along the river to Milan Street; at any given time, up to 15 ships can tie up at the Port of New Orleans. Outside the port building is the dazzling contemporary sculpture *Mother River*, a 30-foot-tall work set inside a fountain that's meant as a tribute to the nearby Mississippi.

From the convention center, cut inland a block to Fulton Street, and make a right, following this interesting row of vintage warehouses for several blocks to Poydras Street, onto which a left turn leads a block (just beyond South Peters Street) to **Piazza D'Italia** (300 block on the west side of Poydras), a modern, outdoor park created in the style of a Romanesque square. It was laid out by renowned postmodern architect Charles Moore in 1978 to honor the contributions of New Orleans's thriving Italian community. A building facing Piazza D'Italia was converted into the 285-room Loews New Orleans hotel in 2003, which helped to restore the original piazza into a public park.

Across Poydras from the Piazza, **Harrah's New Orleans Casino** (512 South Peters St., 800/VIP-JAZZ, www.harrahs.com/our_casinos/nor) opened in a massive space along Canal Street in fall 1999. Its reception has been mixed at best, and many locals and visitors avoid the place entirely. The facility has free parking (with proof of playing), a 24-hour buffet, live entertainment, about 100 gaming tables, and some 2,500 slot machines. As of this writing, local star chef John Besh has been wooed by Harrah's to open a restaurant here—it'll specialize in steaks and seafood.

Another example of the city's once grungy and industrial downtown waterfront being turned into a popular attraction for visitors is **Riverwalk** (foot of Poydras Street, extending along river to the Morial Convention Center, 504/522-1555, www.riverwalkmarketplace.com), which is connected to the New Orleans Hilton Riverside hotel. You reach it from the casino simply by walking a block down Poydras. The long, snaking building with great river views holds about 140 shops (a mix of chains and local stores), a large food court, and four sit-down restaurants. Parking is available at the Hilton garage, the World Trade Center garage, and along Convention Center Boulevard; it costs just $3 for up to four hours of parking at any of these facilities if you spend more than $10 at any Riverwalk store and have your parking ticket validated.

Leave Riverwalk the way you came in, then make an immediate right off Poydras onto Convention Center Boulevard to reach Canal Street and the ferry for Algiers Point. Or, if you have a car parked near here, you might want to finish this tour by heading up Poydras about a dozen

blocks to the massive, 52-acre **Louisiana Superdome/New Orleans Arena** (1500 Poydras St., 504/529-8830, www.superdome.com), home to NFL's New Orleans Saints, Tulane football, college football's Sugar Bowl, and other key gridiron events as well as major concerts and some of the city's most popular annual events (including the New Orleans Home and Garden Show and the Essence Music Festival).

The gargantuan arena is the largest stadium with a roof in the world, holding some 72,000 fans for football (usually only about 20,000 for concerts, although seating was expanded to 87,500 for a Rolling Stones concert in 1981, setting a record for attendance at an indoor music concert). The roof alone covers some 10 acres and rises to a height of about 273 feet (nearly as tall as a 30-story building). The city commissioned construction of the dome in 1966, back when domed stadiums were all the rage, especially in places with excessively cold or hot climates and plenty of wet weather. Sultry, swampy New Orleans seemed like a perfect fit, and of course the huge Astrodome in similarly hot and humid Houston had been a huge success when it opened a few years earlier. Construction wasn't actually begun on the Superdome until 1971, and the facility didn't open until four years later. Tours of the facility were given until the early 2000s but have been suspended indefinitely, so your only chance of seeing this pleasure dome is attending one of the many events here.

Adjacent to the Superdome complex, on the south side, is the **New Orleans Centre** (1400 Poydras St., 504/568-0000), one of the city's more upscale shopping malls. It has about 60 shops, including Macy's and Lord & Taylor.

Just off Poydras, Loyola Avenue leads west a couple of blocks to the main branch of the U.S. Post Office and to the **Union Station** (Loyola Avenue and Earhart Boulevard) passenger terminal, a rather bland facility opened in the 1950s.

ALGIERS POINT

From the foot of Canal Street, you can catch the passenger and auto ferry making frequent trips all day long across the Mississippi River to Algiers

Point, on the West Bank but still part of the city proper. The mostly residential neighborhood with a vast cache of notable, if generally modest, 19th- and early-20th-century residences, has a handful of pleasant parks, a few B&Bs, pubs, and eateries, and a smattering of shops. Although it's easy to get to Algiers Point via the ferry, or by driving over the Crescent City Connection Bridge, this neighborhood has always felt and continues to feel distinct from the rest of the city, owing to that mile-wide boundary line separating it from the French Quarter and CBD, also known as the Mississippi River.

The little ferry service has been sending boats back and forth across the river since 1827, despite various bureaucratic efforts to eliminate it. Always the influential and very active Algiers Point Neighborhood Association has fought hard to keep the boat running, as such a cut in service could effectively wipe out the neighborhood's vibrancy. Service is offered daily from 6 A.M. until midnight, and there's no charge for foot passengers (cars pay just $1 for round-trip passage).

The top reason visitors venture across the river to Algiers Point is to visit **Blaine Kern's Mardi Gras World** (233 Newton St., Algiers, 504/361-7821, www.mardigrasworld.com, open 9:30 A.M.–4:30 P.M. (last tour) daily, admission $13.50), the largest builder of parade floats anywhere. Mardi Gras may take place over a relatively short period late each winter, but this place hums with activity every day of the year. From 9:30 A.M. through 4:30 P.M., free shuttle buses to and from the museum greet passengers at the Algiers Point ferry terminal. On the tour you'll see a video on the history of the city's Mardi Gras celebration.

The Garden District and Uptown

Technically, Uptown is really the area between Claiborne Avenue and Tchoupitoulas Street, running from Louisiana Avenue for nearly 40 blocks out to Lowerline Street, a few blocks beyond Audubon Park. But loosely speaking, any point upriver of the Crescent City Connection Bridge along or between St. Charles Avenue and Magazine Street could be considered Uptown, at least in relation to the Quarter and CBD. For the purposes of this book, the area has been broken down into the Lower Garden District, the Upper Garden District, Magazine Street, Audubon Park, and Tulane and Loyola Universities, which have adjacent campuses on the other side of St. Charles Avenue from Audubon Park. Once you get beyond Lowerline, you're really in Carrollton, which was formed in early 1800s as its own little distinct town but was eventually absorbed by New Orleans. The section where St. Charles Avenue meets with Carrollton Avenue, at the bend in the river, is known appropriately as Riverbend.

Uptown and the Garden District are remarkably diverse, and best known for picturesque residential architecture and a slower and more relaxed pace than in the French Quarter and certainly the corporate CBD. The architecture is more traditionally American in this area, rich in the Greek Revival and Victorian styles typical of well-to-do Southern residential building, but it has also been strongly influenced by the city's French, Spanish, and West Indian roots.

A car is fine for exploring the Garden District and Uptown, as street parking is pretty easy to find all along St. Charles, many of the residential side streets, and along Magazine Street (although there it's mostly metered). However, the best way to truly experience the surroundings and get a sense of the vibe is to walk, so if you are using a car, try to park it in one or more central locales and hoof it from there.

Since St. Charles is one-way (toward Canal Street) in the CBD, if you're driving from the direction of Canal Street, take Carondelet Street, which runs parallel to St. Charles, several blocks toward Uptown, then left onto Howard Street, and right onto Lee Circle, bearing right onto St. Charles. Or take Magazine Street, which is one-way toward Uptown from Canal and through the Warehouse District, beneath the Crescent City Connection Bridge, and into the Lower Garden District. Magazine continues one-way

SIGHTS

CARROLLTON
To Mid-City
and I-10

DUBLIN ST
S. CARROLLTON AVE
OAK ST
LOWERLINE ST
WILLOW ST
CALHOUN ST

S. GALVEZ ST
S ROMAN ST

RIVERBEND
FRERET ST
MAPLE ST
HAMPSON ST
ST. CHARLES AVE

NEWCOMB
COLLEGE

AUDUBON BLVD

TULANE
UNIVERSITY

URSULINE CHAPEL
AND MUSEUM
★
URSULINE
ACADEMY

NAPOLEON AVE
CADIZ ST

UNIVERSITY

STATE ST
MAGNOLIA ST

LOYOLA
UNIVERSITY

FRERET ST

JEFFERSON AVE
UPPERLINE ST

S LIBERTY ST
S SARATOGA ST

BROADWAY ST
WALNUT ST
PRYTANIA ST
COLISEUM ST
CAMP ST

ARABELLA ST

BARONNE ST

AUDUBON PARK
GOLF COURSE

Audubon

Park

UPTOWN

JOSEPH ST

ST. CHARLES AVE

COLISEUM ST
PRYTANIA ST

CADIZ ST

AUDUBON ZOO
& GARDENS
★

CALHOUN ST
WEBSTER ST

MAGAZINE ST

ELEONORE ST

JEFFERSON AVE

CAMP ST

BORDEAUX ST

NAPOLEON AVE

Avenger
Park

CHILDRENS
HOSPITAL

TCHOUPITOULAS ST

VALMONT ST

DUFOSSAT ST

UPPERLINE ST

LEAKE AVE

Levee

0   0.25 mi

0   0.25 km

LABAUVE DR
Levee

KLEIN ST

LOUISIANA PKWY

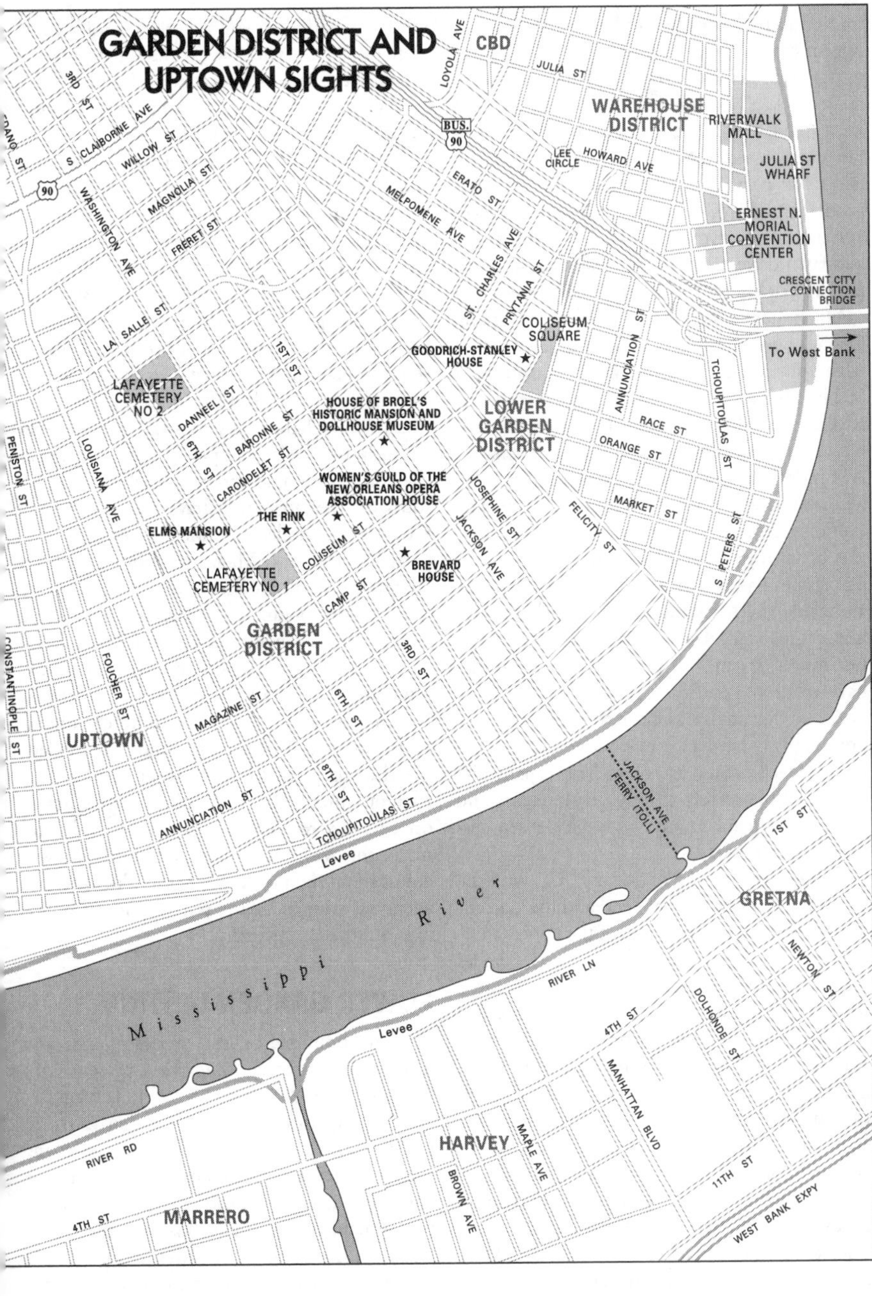

GARDEN DISTRICT AND UPTOWN SIGHTS

CBD

WAREHOUSE DISTRICT

RIVERWALK MALL

JULIA ST WHARF

ERNEST N. MORIAL CONVENTION CENTER

CRESCENT CITY CONNECTION BRIDGE

To West Bank

LOWER GARDEN DISTRICT

COLISEUM SQUARE

GOODRICH-STANLEY HOUSE ★

HOUSE OF BROEL'S HISTORIC MANSION AND DOLLHOUSE MUSEUM ★

WOMEN'S GUILD OF THE NEW ORLEANS OPERA ASSOCIATION HOUSE ★

THE RINK ★

ELMS MANSION ★

LAFAYETTE CEMETERY NO 1

LAFAYETTE CEMETERY NO 2

BREVARD HOUSE ★

GARDEN DISTRICT

UPTOWN

GRETNA

HARVEY

MARRERO

Mississippi River

Levee

Levee

JACKSON AVE FERRY (TOLL)

Streets and labels:
LOYOLA AVE, JULIA ST, LEE CIRCLE, HOWARD AVE, ERATO ST, MELPOMENE AVE, ST CHARLES AVE, PRYTANIA ST, ANNUNCIATION ST, RACE ST, ORANGE ST, MARKET ST, TCHOUPITOULAS ST, S PETERS ST, FELICITY ST, JOSEPHINE ST, JACKSON AVE, CAMP ST, COLISEUM ST, 1ST ST, BARONNE ST, CARONDELET ST, DANNEEL ST, 6TH ST, LA SALLE ST, LOUISIANA AVE, FRERET ST, MAGNOLIA ST, WILLOW ST, S CLAIBORNE AVE, WASHINGTON AVE, 3RD ST, PENISTON ST, CONSTANTINOPLE ST, FOUCHER ST, MAGAZINE ST, ANNUNCIATION ST, TCHOUPITOULAS ST, 6TH ST, 8TH ST, 3RD ST, RIVER LN, 4TH ST, MANHATTAN BLVD, DOLHONDE ST, NEWTON ST, 1ST ST, MAPLE AVE, BROWN AVE, RIVER RD, 4TH ST, 11TH ST, WEST BANK EXPY

BUS. 90

90

SIGHTS

© AVALON TRAVEL PUBLISHING, INC.

for about 10 blocks before becoming two-way once it crosses Felicity Street.

Magazine is a narrow two-lane street with dense pockets of commercial activity, so although it's a fascinating road to drive on, traffic does not move speedily. St. Charles is also only two lanes, but it's wider and divided by the neutral ground (median), on which the streetcar passes, and it has less commercial activity, so it tends to be a faster drive. Be aware, however, that streetcars have the right of way—be extremely careful not to block them when making a left turn from St. Charles onto a cross street. Wait on St. Charles with your left-hand turn signal on, and don't pull into the median until you're sure there are no streetcars coming and there's no oncoming traffic coming along the opposing lane of St. Charles. If you do sit in the median blocking the tracks while waiting for an opening in the opposing traffic, you're sure to hear the trolley driver clang the bells angrily at you. You can also take Tchoupitoulas, which parallels Magazine nearly alongside the Mississippi River, through Uptown. This is a mostly industrial stretch without much charm, but parts of Tchoupitoulas have begun to gentrify.

All of this advice aside, remember that you don't actually need a car to explore this area, despite the fact that it does cover a large expanse. It's quite feasible to rely chiefly on streetcars and buses to get in and around both the Garden District and Uptown.

Uptown is shaped like a broad "U," with the CBD at the lower (eastern) end and the Carrollton/Riverbend neighborhood at the upper (western) end. The main thoroughfares are St. Charles Avenue and Magazine Street, which run more or less parallel, extending in a southwesterly and then westerly and then northwesterly direction from the CBD to Carrollton. Magazine Street and St. Charles each run about 4.5 miles through the Garden District and Uptown. At their nearest points, they're just three blocks apart, at the very eastern end of Uptown, but they diverge slightly as they move westward, and at some points, like out near Audubon Park, it's about three-quarters of a mile from St. Charles to Magazine. Scores of cross streets connect Magazine

and St. Charles, so you can always walk easily from one to the other. St. Charles is served by the famous St. Charles streetcar, and Magazine Street by several buses, making it easy to go the length of either street from the CBD.

More than just a convenient and affordable mode of public transportation, the **St. Charles Avenue streetcar** is itself very much an attraction—it's the oldest continuously operating streetcar line in the world, having first clanged and banged down the avenue in 1835. The streetcar is a charming way to travel throughout Uptown, but to see the whole neighborhood, it makes sense to take the bus along Magazine one way through Uptown, and the streetcar the other. Because St. Charles runs one-way toward Canal Street in the CBD, you pick up the streetcar at the corner of Canal and St. Charles to go Uptown, but the cars actually travel west through the CBD along parallel Carondelet Street.

St. Charles and Magazine differ greatly in character, and the blocks between them also vary quite a bit in appearance, history, and architecture as you wend through the Uptown District. Magazine is New Orleans's original shopping thoroughfare—the name means "shop" in French. St. Charles Avenue is lined with hotels, restaurants, grand residences, and a handful of modern midrise apartments in the Lower Garden District, but into the Upper Garden District it takes on a mostly residential appearance, and it remains this way until you get well into Uptown, around Audubon Park, where the lakeside of the avenue is fringed by the stately campus buildings of Loyola University.

LOWER GARDEN DISTRICT

The area bounded by St. Charles Avenue and Tchoupitoulas Street, and the Crescent City Connection Bridge (Bus.U.S. 90) to Jackson Avenue, comprises the Lower Garden District, which for a time just a nice way of describing the less-fancy area between the CBD and the true (Upper) Garden District. It is not so much the domain of ritzy mansions as is the Upper Garden District, but the area's handsome old cottages, townhouses, and apartments have been touched increasingly by the wand of gentrification in recent years. In fact, the Lower Garden District has some of the finest examples of Greek Revival, Edwardian, and Queen Anne residential architecture in the city.

Along St. Charles Avenue, you'll find several hotels and restaurants, most of them moderately priced; parallel Prytania Street, a block south toward the river, has some of the same feel. The neighborhood also has several mostly generic-looking apartment buildings and hotels, which is another trait that distinguishes it from the more quaintly historic Garden District. One of the best spots for admiring architecture is Coliseum Square, which runs from Camp Street for four blocks between Melpomene Avenue and Race Street. Keep in mind that New Orleanians pronounce Melpomene, Terpsichore, Euterpe, and so on—the names of nine parallel streets from Coliseum Square nearly to Lee Circle—not the way they're pronounced when referring to the nine muses of classical Greek mythology, but rather "mel-puh-mean," "terp-sih-kore," and such.

The neighborhood stands on what had been part of the plantation of city founder Jean Baptiste Le Moyne de Bienville. It was divided into smaller plantations through the latter part of the 18th century, and then subdivided into small city lots in the early 19th century. A developer and city planner named Bartheleme Lafon was hired to create the new neighborhood. Lafon, a fan of Greek classics, envisioned a grand district of fountains, tree-lined canals, parks, and open-air markets, and he named the nine streets extending from Place du Tivoli (known today as Lee Circle) and Coliseum Square after the nine muses. He laid out Coliseum Square with plans to house a great coliseum, and Annunciation Square to be anchored by a massive cathedral. Prytania Street was laid out lengthwise through the district as the main thoroughfare.

The neighborhood developed not quite according to Lafon's plans. Many large homes were constructed throughout the new blocks, especially around Coliseum Square, but the coliseum and cathedral never came to fruition, and the Lower Garden District has never developed the cachet of the adjacent Upper Garden District,

where the city's wealthiest 19th-century Americans built their immense homes. By the late 1800s, quite a few smaller and simpler houses and cottages had been built throughout the district, many with fanciful Victorian trim, and Magazine Street had taken hold as one of the city's best destinations for shopping.

The Lower Garden District's fortunes waxed and waned through the early 20th century, and then plummeted as much as just about any New Orleans neighborhood following World War II. Huge swaths of neighborhood nearest the river were cleared to make way for a commercial railroad depot and later for the infamous St. Thomas housing project (it has since been razed). The massive Crescent City Connection Bridge was built over the Mississippi near the border between the CBD and the Lower Garden District (today, for all practical purposes, it *is* the border). This project not only took out more houses, it effectively cut the neighborhood off from the CBD, creating a vast no-man's-land of asphalt beneath the wide bridge. A second bridge across the river was proposed for where the ferry now runs cars back and forth between the foot of Jackson Avenue and the West Bank town of Gretna, but locals helped to keep that bridge from ever being built.

In the early 1970s, concerned residents, worried that the already frail and disjointed Lower Garden District would crumble even further into a state of decay, banded together to form the **Coliseum Square Association** (www.coliseum-square.org), which successfully fought off that second bridge proposal and also got the neighborhood listed on the National Register of Historic Places. The association gives an annual tour of homes each April—this is a terrific way to learn more about the neighborhood's wonderful architecture.

If you're exploring the area yourself, either drive to **Coliseum Square** and park near it, or take the St. Charles Avenue streetcar to around Melpomene or Euterpe Street and walk toward the river two blocks to reach the square. The blocks around the square, and also along St. Charles and Prytania, have the most attractive and interesting homes. There are no formal attractions or museums in this neighborhood, as most are private residences. Do note in particular the **Goodrich-Stanley House** (1729 Coliseum St.), a marvelously restored Creole cottage in which the famous African explorer Henry Morton Stanley (as in Stanley and Livingstone) lived as a young man.

To reach the Garden District from here, walk or drive in the direction of Uptown along Prytania Street or St. Charles Avenue, which are the two safest and most appealing ways to get there from the Coliseum Square area.

GARDEN DISTRICT

The Garden District is at once emblematic of New Orleans high society and of trendy urban living today—it's the home of novelist Anne Rice, edgy Nine Inch Nails singer Trent Reznor, football greats Archie and son Peyton Manning, and the cast of MTV's *Real World* in 2000. But pop culture aside, this is the New Orleans neighborhood where American aristocrats built their monuments of wealth during the prosperous boom times of the mid-19th century—by about 1900, most of the Garden District had been developed. The neighborhood's splendid homes line streets shrouded by towering live oaks, flowering magnolia trees, and graceful palms. The gardens surrounding these properties sometimes outshine the homes themselves.

Like the Lower Garden District, this entire neighborhood is protected as a National His-

---

ANNE RICE: NEW ORLEANS'S QUEEN OF THE DAMNED

Author Anne Rice, New Orleans's most famous and visible resident, lives in a stately 1857 Greek Revival and Italianate mansion at 1239 1st Street in the Garden District. Rice was born on October 4, 1941 in the city's Mercy Hospital (with the given name of Howard Allen O'Brien—unusual for a baby girl). She lived in New Orleans for the first 16 years of her childhood. A job transfer took her family to Richardson, Texas, where she completed high school and began dating fellow journalism student Stan Rice.

They married a couple of years later, and in 1961 the young couple moved to San Francisco's funky Haight-Ashbury District. Both studied creative writing at San Francisco State University, with Anne publishing her first short story, "October 4, 1948," in 1965. A year later she gave birth to a daughter, Michele. Stan began to receive considerable acclaim for his poetry, and when the Rices moved across San Francisco Bay to Berkeley in 1969, Anne wrote her first treatment of what would become her most famous work, *Interview with the Vampire*, in short-story form.

Tragedy struck in 1972 when their daughter Michele succumbed to leukemia. But within a year, Anne had focused her grief into converting *Interview* into a full-length novel. It was completed in 1973, and accepted by Knopf, the prestigious imprint of Random House, for publication in 1976. The film rights were sold to Paramount; but it would be 18 years later before the film, starring Tom Cruise, Brad Pitt, Kirsten Dunst, Stephen Rea, and Antonio Banderas, was completed and released. Most of the film was shot in southern Louisiana, includes several scenes in the Garden District, and specifically at Lafayette Cemetery No. 1.

The Rices continued to write prolifically throughout the 1970s and '80s, with Stan teaching and eventually chairing the Creative Writing department at San Francisco State University for many years. Anne Rice went on to produce such noted historical novels as *The Feast of All Saints* (1979) and *Cry to Heaven* (1982), but her greatest acclaim has come from building on *Interview* to develop seven more Gothic novels, *The Vampire Lestat* (1985), *The Queen of the Damned* (1988), *The Tale of the Body Thief* (1992), *Memnoch the Devil* (1995), *The Vampire Armand* (1998), *Blood and Gold* (2001), and *Blackwood Farm* (2002) and *Blood Canticle* (2003).

toric District. It began as part of Bienville's sprawling plantation and was converted to a series of smaller spreads during the mid- to late 18th centuries, before being further subdivided and sold to developers in the 1830s. It was laid out into quite large blocks, with the idea that it would appeal to "new" Americans of considerable means. The neighborhood thrived as an exclusive enclave of ostentatious mansions, most of which still stand today.

The best way to experience the Garden District is on an organized walking tour, several of which are offered by different companies. As with the Lower Garden District, there are few formal attractions open to the public here, but experienced guides can point out notable buildings and discuss their heritage and the often colorful stories behind them and their past and present owners. Strongly recommended are the informative walks given by **Historic New Orleans Tours** (504/947-2120, www.tourneworleans .com). These tours are given daily at 11 A.M. and 1:45 P.M., departing from the **Garden District Book Shop** (at The Rink, Washington Avenue and Prytania Street). The tours last about two hours and cost $14. (The same company also does French Quarter, Haunted, and Cemetery Voodoo tours.) **The Rink** (Washington Avenue at Prytania Street) was the South's first roller-skating rink, built in the 1880s and converted many years later into a row of boutiques and shops. The Garden District Book Shop is the

Together these nine works comprise *The Vampire Chronicles.* (*Queen of the Damned* followed *Interview* onto movie screens in 2002.)

Rice has also written a trilogy of novels that comprise *The Mayfair Witches* trilogy, and under pseudonyms A.N. Roquelaure and Anne Rampling has published several other works. Rice's own New Orleans home is the inspiration for Mayfair Manor, the home of the Mayfair Witches.

The Rice's second child, son Christopher, was born in 1979. (Christopher Rice wrote his first novel, *A Density of Souls,* in 2001. Like so many of his mother's works, it is set in New Orleans. The book received mixed reviews but has already earned the younger Rice a strong following. His second novel, *The Snow Garden,* was released in 2003.)

In 1989, Stan Rice retired from his SFSU job and the family relocated back to Anne's hometown, New Orleans. Rice has been a fixture in the Garden District ever since, having bought and restored St. Elizabeth's Orphanage (at 1314 Napoleon Ave.), a massive former boarding house and girls' orphanage built in 1865. She bought the 55,000-square-foot Second Empire building in 1993, and for several years it was open to the public for tours. Inside were books, furnishings, more than 800 dolls, and other collectibles amassed by the Rice family over the years. As of this writing, the building was for sale, with tours no longer offered.

Sadly, on December 9, 2002, Stan Rice passed away suddenly after a battle with brain cancer. He left behind an impressive legacy of poetry and painting. Immediately following his death, Anne left news of his passing and discussed her future plans on her fan telephone hotline (504/522-8634), and her website, www.annerice.com, which she updates regularly.

A recent note to her fans reads,

Hello to my readers, new and old. I am still charged with the energy of Blackwood Farm. I've decided Blackwood Farm is a state of mind. Be sure the entire gang will survive for another novel. And after that my entire career will take a huge and mysterious turn. My direction will be so strange that many may abandon me, but who knows?. . . . I send you my sincere love. Let me be your cultural bandit forever—Anne

most famous of these businesses, and an excellent place to pick up rare and out-of-print books on the city, as well as signed editions of Anne Rice novels.

Also very good are the guided walks given by **Gray Line** (504/569-1401 or 800/535-7786, www.graylineneworleans.com). These 2.5-hour tours leave daily at 10 A.M. and 1 P.M. from the French Quarter (you're first taken by bus from here to the Garden District) at the little Gray Line lighthouse kiosk behind Jackson Brewery. The cost is $18.

One of the more distinctive tours is of **Lafayette Cemetery No. 1** (Washington Avenue and Coliseum Street, open 7:30 A.M.–2:30 P.M. Mon.–Fri., 7:30 A.M.–noon Sat., admission free), which is one of relatively few "cities of the dead" in New Orleans that's relatively safe to explore, at least during the day. The guided tours offered by **Save Our Cemeteries** (504/525-3377 or 888/ 721-7493, www.saveourcemeteries.com), a non-profit organization that preserves the city's burial grounds, are definitely the best way to go, and these cost $6. The one-hour walks are held Mon., Wed., Fri., and Sat. at 10:30 A.M. Lafayette Cemetery No. 1 is especially popular with fans of Anne Rice's *The Vampire Chronicles* trilogy; it was featured in the movie *Interview with the Vampire*.

If you're exploring the area on your own, take the streetcar up St. Charles to Jackson Avenue, or drive and park anywhere in the neighborhood along Prytania or its side streets. The Garden District is bounded by St. Charles Avenue and Magazine Street, from Jackson Avenue for about a dozen blocks to Louisiana Avenue.

Right as you alight the streetcar at Jackson Avenue, you'll come to one small but noteworthy attraction, especially if you have an interest in miniatures. The **House of Broel's Historic Mansion and Dollhouse Museum** (2220 St. Charles Ave., 504/525-1000 or 800/827-4325, www .houseofbroel.com, open 10 A.M.–5 P.M. Mon.– Sat., admission $10) is set inside an imposing Victorian along the avenue. The first part of the house was built in the 1850s, and a major addition, which converted it to the immense three-story mansion that you see today, was added on in the 1890s. This is a fine tour not only to get a look

at the living quarters and furnishings of an exceptional Garden District residence, but also to admire the hundreds of dolls, miniatures, and other collectibles that fill the rooms.

At the other end of the district on St. Charles, note the **Elms Mansion** (3029 St. Charles Ave., 504/895-5493, www.elmsmansion.com), built by a railroad tycoon after the Civil War and notable for its Flemish oak carvings and original tapestries. Tours are available only to groups and by appointment, but it's worth stopping to admire this Italianate Victorian from the street.

The most distinctive and impressive Garden District homes are set mostly along Prytania Street (a block from St. Charles) and the blocks just off it along 1st, 2nd, and 3rd Streets. There are also some prominent structures along Jackson Avenue. Architecturally, the grandest mansions tend to be in the Greek Revival style, but you'll also see a number of Italianate Victorians and even some traditional raised Louisiana cottages, which are, in fact, much larger than what most of us think of when we hear the word "cottage."

Followers of Anne Rice should make a point of stopping in front of **Brevard House** (1239 1st St.), a hybrid Greek Revival and Italianate mansion with spectacular cast-iron balconies. Here the novelist lives; it's also where she and her husband raised their son, Christopher Rice, a novelist in his own right. Her husband, poet and artist Stan Rice, passed away in December 2002.

One of the only houses in the neighborhood that can be toured by the public, by advance appointment only, is the **Women's Guild of the New Orleans Opera Association House** (2504 Prytania, 504/899-1945, admission $5), which is furnished approximately as it looked when its last private owner, Nettie Seebold, passed away and willed the home to this organization. The circa-1865 home, also a mix of Italianate and Greek Revival styles, is filled with exquisite 18th- and 19th-century American furniture and artwork. It was built by noted New Orleans architect William A. Freret.

MAGAZINE STREET

New Orleans's original and enduring shopping street, Magazine Street (the name comes from the

French "magasin," which means "shop") follows the curve of the Mississippi River for about 6 miles from Canal Street through the CBD and then on through the Lower and Upper Garden Districts, Uptown, and on by Audubon Park. It's a shopping paradise, yet with very few chain or franchise businesses. Magazine is distinct because it embraces independent shops, restaurants, coffeehouses, and bars, and it's popular along different stretches with New Orleanians of every background, economic and social strata, age, and ethnicity. In some places it's collegiate and funky, others upscale and popular with the many professionals who reside in the residential blocks between Magazine and St. Charles Avenue. The stretch of Magazine through the Lower Garden District is famous for its antiques shops, but you can find secondhand clothiers and furniture stores of varying quality all along Magazine.

The street begins in the CBD, at Canal Street, just a few blocks down from St. Charles, and forms one of the main spines through the Warehouse District. Here it's lined with old warehouse buildings, galleries, and a few nightclubs, shops, and restaurants. Beyond the Crescent City Connection Bridge, under which Magazine passes, the street is for about 10 blocks a rather downcast and mostly residential stretch. It doesn't really pick up and become busy with activity until you cross Felicity Street, at which point begins one of the South's most impressive and famous clusters of antiques shops. The lower stretch, between here and the bridge, does have loads of potential, and more than a few developers and preservation-minded homebuyers have begun buying up the tired-looking but promising townhouses along here. In time, there's little question that Magazine's gentrification will extend unbroken from the Warehouse District clear through Uptown, as whatever sections look slightly seedy today are tomorrow's hot spots for B&Bs, restaurants, antiques shops, and galleries.

> *Magazine Street is distinct because it embraces independent shops, restaurants, coffeehouses, and bars, and it's popular along different stretches with New Orleanians of every background, economic and social strata, age, and ethnicity—in some places collegiate and funky, others upscale and popular.*

UPTOWN AND AUDUBON PARK

The city's favorite place for strolling, right near the campuses of Loyola and Tulane, is leafy **Audubon Park** (St. Charles Avenue at Walnut Street, 504/861-2537), a 340-acre spread with moss-draped oak trees, lush lawns with picnic areas, lagoons, and athletic facilities that include tennis courts, a golf course, and paved trails for jogging, in-line skating, and strolling. It's a wonderful spot for picnicking, strolling, and admiring the many impressive statues, many of them depicting animals and set within the park's zoo, and many created by WPA artists during the 1930s.

The park occupies what had been a plantation and also the estate of Jean Etienne De Boré, who developed a system of granulating sugar in 1794 that did for Louisiana's sugar business about what the cotton gin did for the state's cotton trade. The city bought the tract of land in 1871, naming it New City Park, and eventually Audubon Park in honor of artist and ornithologist John James Audubon, who lived for many years both in New Orleans and outside Baton Rouge up near St. Francisville. The park quickly became famous after hosting the World's Industrial and Cotton Exposition in 1884, a 100th-anniversary celebration of the first shipment of Louisiana cotton to a foreign port. At this festival, the park's grounds and buildings were lighted with electricity, just six years after Thomas Edison first began experimenting with electric light bulbs.

The upper part of the park, between Magazine Street and St. Charles Avenue, consists of the park's golf course, as well as the winding lagoon and many gardens and benches. Below Magazine Street, toward the river, lies the **Audubon Zoo & Gardens** (6500 Magazine St., 504/581-4629 or 800/774-7394, www.auduboninstitute.org, open 9:30 A.M.–5 P.M. (an hour later on summer weekends) daily, admission $10, $18 for zoo and aquarium combo ticket), which contains nearly 2,000 animals. It's a wonderful place to explore verdant, overgrown gardens rife with just about every species of flora known to Louisiana. If you're taking the St. Charles Avenue streetcar, get off at stop number 36 for the park and zoo. If coming by car, the zoo has plenty of parking.

A favorite attraction at the zoo is the Louisiana Swamp exhibit, the next best thing to taking a swamp tour, and even better in one respect: you're guaranteed to see the creatures of region's marshes and swamps up close and personal. The swamp exhibit is an actual re-creation of a Depression-era Cajun swamp settlement, complete with old bayou shacks and a trapper's cottage. In addition to learning about the animal life common to this environment, such as alligators and raccoons, you can see Spanish moss, cypress knees, and other flora common in the swamp.

Another exhibit that emphasizes both wildlife and its relationship to people and the environment is the Jaguar Jungle, which re-creates a Mayan rain forest and includes, in addition to the two dignified yet powerful jags themselves, storks, spider monkeys, and sloths. The display also features realistically rendered reproductions of stone carvings at famous Central American and Mexican archaeological sites, such as Chichén Itzá and Copán. In 2003, the jaguars mated successfully—a rare instance of such a thing in captivity. Other crowd-pleasers in other sections of the zoo include a pair of nearly 400-pound white tigers, an huge Indonesian komodo dragon, a few rather extroverted gorillas, and many monkeys. Kids love to ride the carousel (rides are $2), which features some 60 figures of endangered species.

Animal feedings are another big draw. These are scheduled all through the day in a variety of zoo venues; they can give you a list at the admissions desk. Among the animals that are quite engaging to watch at feed times are giraffes and gators. You can also watch them feed live insects to tropical birds.

The campuses of New Orleans's two most famous institutions of higher learning, Loyola University and Tulane University, sit adjacent to one another opposite the park. Loyola faces St. Charles Avenue just opposite Audubon Park, as does Tulane just a bit farther upriver, although much of its modern campus extends along the blocks farther toward the lake from St. Charles, off Freret and Broadway Streets. The presence of both schools has helped to infuse the businesses along Magazine Street and in the nearby Riverbend and Carrollton neighborhoods with a youthful, collegiate buzz.

Established by the Jesuit order in 1911, Catholic **Loyola University** (6363 St. Charles Ave., 504/865-3240 or 800/4-LOYOLA, www.loyno.edu) had been a Catholic prep school since 1904. Fronting St. Charles Avenue are the school's stately redbrick buildings with terracotta trim, built in the Tudor Gothic style. Loyola has an enrollment of 5,500 students, of whom 3,500 are undergraduates.

Tulane University (6823 St. Charles Ave., 504/865-5000, www.tulane.edu), a private nonsectarian research university that comprises 11 schools and colleges, began as the Medical College of Louisiana in 1834, its need brought about in part by the city's constant struggles to contain deadly yellow fever epidemics. In 1847 it became the University of Louisiana, a public university. A huge 1883 bequest by a wealthy New Orleanian named Paul Tulane allowed the university to expand into a much more comprehensive facility, and to be reorganized as a private university; it was renamed Tulane in honor of this financial gift. The campus covers some 110 acres of Uptown and includes more than 80 buildings.

Tulane ranks as one of the top schools in the South, with about 7,500 undergraduate students and another 5,000 enrollees in the graduate program. About a third of all students are from New Orleans, with most of the remainder hailing from all throughout North America; about 8 percent of the student body is from outside the United States. Notable divisions include the Tulane University School of Medicine, the second-oldest medical school in the Deep South, and the highly esteemed A. B. Freeman School of Business and the Tulane Law School.

The older Tulane buildings are set along or near St. Charles and include several Romanesque structures of considerable architectural acclaim. It's a pretty campus to walk through, although neither it nor Loyola contain any public attractions or museums of note.

Along State Street, a few blocks northeast of Tulane's campus, the **Ursuline Chapel and Museum** (2635 State St., 504/899-7374, www.ursulineneworleans.org), part of the Ursuline Convent, is home to a gilded statue, *Our Lady of Prompt Succor,* which commemorates a quite miraculous military victory, the Battle of New Orleans, which took place during the War of 1812. In fact, the war had already ended a couple of weeks prior to the battle, but news of the peace treaty had not yet reached either the advancing British troops or the American defenders, led by future President Andrew Jackson. At the time, the city looked exceeding vulnerable to attack, and New Orleanians solemnly prepared for the worst but hoped for the best. The more faithful among the citizens sat inside the Old Ursuline Convent on Chartres Street in the French Quarter and prayed to Our Lady of Prompt Succor all through the night of January 7, 1815, for a successful outcome to the battle slated for the following day. The parishioners struck a moral deal: if their American army successfully fended off the Brits, they would dedicate the city to her.

The American army of 4,000, never taken seriously by the arrogant but impressively trained British troops, who were fresh from victory against Napoléon in Europe, faced some 8,000 enemy military men. Amazingly, Jackson led his troops—a motley mix of former Haitian slaves, pirates, federal militia, and American frontier settlers—to a decisive victory during which just a handful of Americans lost their lives, versus some 2,000 dead or missing British troops.

The statue inside the chapel is a national shrine to this victory, and each year a special mass is held on January 7 during which Our Lady and her infant are honored during a splendid high mass.

The museum, which contains religious artifacts as well as correspondence between the convent and Thomas Jefferson, James Madison, and King Louis XV, may be toured by appointment; admission $1.50.

CARROLLTON

Carrollton is today just another Uptown neighborhood of New Orleans, but this charming residential district with a couple of hip spans of eateries (it's especially strong on Asian restaurants) and shopping began as its own little town, incorporating in 1843. In those early years, Carrollton was a summer resort, separated from the city of New Orleans by several miles of plantations and swampland. Located at a major bend in the Mississippi River, the town's popularity grew when a railroad line was built connecting it to New Orleans. Soon the place began to bustle with a racetrack, beer gardens, charming summer cottages, and a hotel. It served as the seat of Jefferson Parish for a time, before being swallowed up by the mother ship, New Orleans, in an 1874 annexation.

The Carrollton Historic District today preserves an eclectic collection of mostly Craftsman, Colonial Revival, Greek Revival, and Italianate bungalows and houses, many of them painted in bright shades, and most dating to the late 19th and early 20th centuries.

The southern end of South Carrollton Avenue, from St. Charles up to about Claiborne, is every bit as charming as St. Charles itself, with a grassy neutral ground that serves as the streetcar line, and huge oak trees draped with Spanish moss hanging over the street. The span of South Carrollton Avenue nearest St. Charles has a handful of good eating places. This subsection of Carrollton, known as **Riverbend,** also has a handful of funky clothing and gift boutiques, most of them along Dublin and Hampson Streets.

If you walk down **Maple Street** in the opposite direction from Carrollton Avenue, downriver, you'll also encounter a small and enchanting entertainment-retail district, with many 19th-century cottages now housing coffeehouses, bars, and shops. This section is just a few blocks from Tulane's campus, and it tends to be frequented by students from there and Loyola.

A final street worth exploring in Carrollton is the town's old main thoroughfare, **Oak Street,** which runs toward the river off Carrollton Avenue, about six blocks from St. Charles. This funky strip of buildings has been the latest in the area to gentrify.

Mid-City

Mid-City can mean pretty much any portion of New Orleans situated between I-10 and I-610, which form a triangle in the middle of the city, and also extending north toward the lake above I-610. This includes massive City Park, and the mostly residential blocks on either side of it, and it also takes in the interesting and up-and-coming neighborhood where Canal Street and Carrollton Avenue intersect, as well as Esplanade Ridge, the also up-and-coming neighborhood on either side of Esplanade Avenue from Rampart Street (at the edge of the French Quarter) to Bayou St. John and the southeast corner of City Park. Mid-City, therefore, covers a chunk of New Orleans that's much, much larger than the French Quarter or CBD and is even bigger in total area than Uptown. However, other than City Park and the few patches of gentrification mentioned above, it's not generally a part of town that holds much interest for visitors, although simply driving or biking around Mid-City you're likely to pass by some fascinating blocks of distinguished residential architecture, and to find some cool neighborhood restaurants and funky bars.

Mid-City is best explored by car, although most of the few key sites mentioned below can also be reached by city bus, and will soon be accessible via the new Canal Street streetcar line, due for completion in 2004.

It is *possible* to begin this tour by walking Esplanade Avenue from the French Quarter, but it's about a 2.5-mile stroll to reach the New Orleans Museum of Art in City Park, and the middle span of this walk, from Rampart Street to Claiborne Avenue, known as Faubourg Tremé, is downcast and dodgy. If you're the sort of person who doesn't stand out obviously as a tourist and you feel comfortable walking through what is in places a lower-income urban neighborhood, consider walking at least one way, ideally dur-

New Orleans Museum of Art

© ANDREW COLLINS

© ANDREW COLLINS

statue along Esplanade Avenue, Esplanade Ridge

ing the late morning or midday. Even the somewhat transitional stretch of Esplanade passes by some beautiful old Greek Revival and Italianate mansions, and the stroll up Esplanade's tree-shaded neutral ground affords a much better sense of the area's rich history than driving or even taking a slow-moving bus. Do not make this walk after dark, however.

As you head up Esplanade Avenue, in an area known historically as the **Esplanade Ridge** neighborhood, the first span of your walk, from Rampart Street to Claiborne, about six blocks, is the most severely dilapidated, although a number of buildings along this stretch have been restored in recent years, among them the impressive **Rathbone Inn B&B** (1227 Esplanade Ave.) and the **Hotel Storyville** (1261 Esplanade Ave.). You'll soon reach Claiborne Avenue, over which the elevated I-10 highway zooms.

Cross under the interstate and continue up Esplanade. Along this stretch, which is still very much in a state of flux (although definitely im-

proving), the avenue bears a considerable resemblance to St. Charles Avenue in Uptown. Indeed, just as the wealthiest Americans in the city built their mansions in the Garden District throughout the 19th century, quite a few wealthy Creole families erected stately homes along Esplanade.

Stop for a moment at the triangular sliver of a park where Miro Street crosses Esplanade, and Bayou Road branches off from Esplanade diagonally. Here stands the marble-and-cement *Goddess of History—Genius of Peace* statue, along with a couple of park benches. This is a particularly pretty spot along Esplanade Ridge. If you stroll up Bayou Road for a block, on your right you'll pass one of the loveliest B&Bs in all of Louisiana, the elegant House on Bayou Road, as well as the exceptional restaurant Indigo.

Back on Esplanade, just up and across the street from the statue at Miro Street, is the **Degas House** (2306 Esplanade Ave., 504/821-5009, www.degashouse.com), the only former residence of famed French Impressionist Edgar Degas that's open to the public. You can stay in one of the seven lavish guest rooms, some with fireplaces and Jacuzzis, or stroll (by appointment only) through the 1852 house in which the artist lived briefly from 1872 to 1873, while visiting relatives on his maternal side (his mother and grandmother were born in New Orleans). Tours include a walk through the house and the immediate neighborhood; they last about an hour, and a donation of $10 per person is suggested.

Continue up Esplanade about eight or nine more blocks, taking note of how the neighborhood continues to improve, the houses looking ever larger and more stately, and also more recently restored. Above Howard Avenue up until the edge of City Park, Esplanade Avenue is a lovely thoroughfare, and the cross blocks around Ponce de Leon and Maurepas Streets have become a bustling little restaurant row since the late '90s. There are several good spots here to grab a snack or a cup of coffee.

Just a few blocks east is the **Fairgrounds Race Track** (1751 Gentilly Blvd., 504/948-1285, www.fgno.com), the third-oldest thoroughbred-racing course in the nation. There's live racing

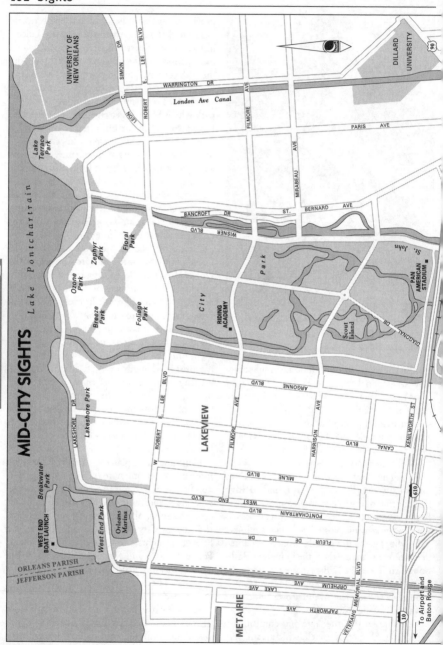

MID-CITY SIGHTS

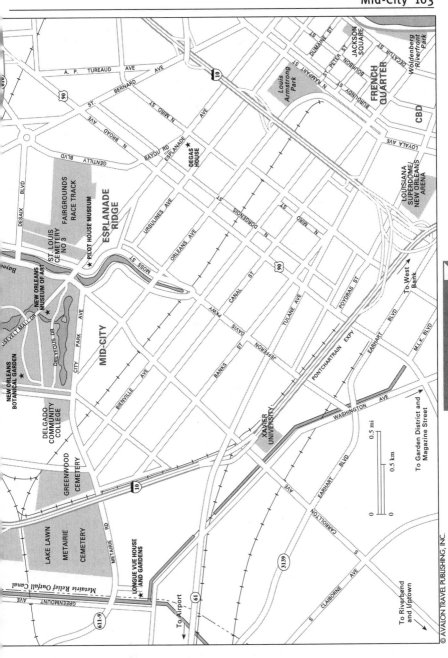

SIGHTS

© AVALON TRAVEL PUBLISHING, INC.

from Thanksgiving through March, and an off-track-betting parlor is open year-round, where you can wager on events elsewhere in the country.

Back on Esplanade, just up from the cluster of restaurants, you'll come to **St. Louis Cemetery No. 3** (Esplanade Avenue between Lada Court and Moss Street), which is one of the safer ones in the city for exploring during the day. Just pop inside the small office by the entrance gate to pick up a map, and wander this narrow "city of the dead," which abuts the racetrack in places. As is true for all cemeteries and even most parks in New Orleans, you should not enter this facility after dark, and it's wise to explore it with a friend or two.

Turn right out of the cemetery and follow Esplanade just 150 yards farther, making a left onto Moss Street, which curves alongside the east bank of Bayou St. John to reach one of the only surviving Colonial plantations in the South, the **Pitot House Museum** (1440 Moss St., 504/482-0312, open 10 A.M.–3 P.M. Wed.–Sat., admission $5, includes guided tour), which overlooks the lazy, slow-moving bayou. The house is named for early occupant James Pitot, who was the first mayor of New Orleans after it was incorporated.

Retrace your steps back along Moss Street to Esplanade, make a left, and continue across the bayou, which puts you at the southeast edge of the 1,500-acre **City Park** (1 Dreyfous Ave., 504/482-4888, www.neworleanscitypark.com). Larger than New York City's Central Park, City Park contains a wealth of outdoors activities. Facilities include Bayou Oak Golf Course, one of the largest tennis facilities in the South, 8 miles of lagoons ideal for fishing and canoeing or pedal-boating, an old-fashioned amusement park called Carousel Gardens, and a children's playground called **Storyland,** which features 26 larger-than-life sculptures, each based on a different fairy tale.

City Park sits on what had been, more than two centuries ago, a swampy oak forest, and it still contains the largest collection of mature live oaks in the world, some believed to date back to the 1400s or earlier. You can stop by the park's visitor center for a map and history of the entire compound, along with bits of information on some of the most famous oak trees, at the **Timken Center** (1 Dreyfous Ave., 504/483-9475), a Spanish Mission-style building that opened in 1913 as a gaming casino. It also contains public restrooms and a pleasant, casual restaurant.

The park's greatest cultural draw is the fabulous **New Orleans Museum of Art** (City Park, 1 Collins Diboll Circle, 504/488-2631, www.noma.org, open 10 A.M.–5 P.M. Tues.–Sun., admission $6), whose vast holdings (totaling some 40,000 objects) span many cultures and eras, from pre-Columbian and Native American to European Postimpressionist. The museum is justly known for its excellent rotating exhibits—in 2003 it celebrated the 200th anniversary of the Louisiana Purchase with an exhibition called "Jefferson's America and Napoleon's France." It's also an architectural marvel, consisting of an imposing Greek Revival building that dates to 1911, and a cleverly appended modern addition that was completed in 1993.

The permanent collection is as eclectic as it is extensive. The top (third) floor contains African, pre-Columbian, and Asiatic works in a rather compact network of smallish galleries. On the second floor you'll find the most extensive holdings—and you'll also gain a very clear sense of how the two wings of the museum fit together and co-exist and contrast architecturally. The newer wing contains the impressive Lupin Foundation Center for Decorative Arts, a fascinating array of glassworks and ceramics, mostly of the 19th and 20th centuries. The second floor of the original museum has a few rooms decorated with period 18th- and 19th-century furnishings, as well as a survey of European and American artists from the present dating back several hundred years. Included are several paintings by Degas, three priceless Imperial Easter eggs created by Peter Carl Fabergé, and works by such notables as Monet, Gauguin, Picasso, Braque, Modigliani, Matisse, Kandinsky, Marsden Hartley, O'Keeffe, Man Ray, and Diane Arbus. There aren't necessarily a great many "must-sees" at NOMA, but the museum does a nice job giving an overview of art through the ages, and it also provides extremely detailed background information on the paintings and furnishings.

© ANDREW COLLINS

view up Decatur Street

The museum's latest venture, completed in spring 2003, is the Sydney and Walda Besthoff Sculpture Garden, a five-acre run of gardens, magnolias, camellias, pines, and ancient live oak trees interspersed with 42 sculptures. Noted artists with works here include Henry Moore, George Rickey, Jacques Lipchitz, and George Segal. You traverse the grounds over bridges and footpaths that wind over lagoons and through gardens.

The **New Orleans Botanical Garden** (1 Palm Dr., City Park, 504/483-9386, www.new orleanscitypark.com/garden, open 10 A.M.– 4:30 P.M. Tues.–Sat., admission $5) opened as a project of the WPA in 1936, bringing together the unique visions of landscape designer William Wierdon, building architect Richard Koch, and artist Enrique Alferez, each of whom had a hand in the layout. The dozens of grand statues set throughout City Park were largely the work of Alferez, a local artist of immense talent who passed away in 1999 at the age of 98 after a career spanning seven decades, beginning in the 1930s. Many of his designs are reliefs of the female figure and garden benches, and most are surrounded by the park's lush landscaping. There are some 2,000 types of plants here, in-cluding several themed gardens (aquatics, ornamental trees and shrubs, perennials).

In 2002, the park reopened its Conservatory of the Two Sisters, the first stage of a massive overhaul that will eventually see the entire Botanical Garden rejuvenated. The conservatory includes the Living Fossils Wing, in which you can observe today's plants displayed alongside their fossil ancestors. In the Tropical Forest Room, a roaring waterfall forms the backdrop for one of the largest collections of exotic flora in the South.

From the intersection of Canal and Carrollton, you can follow gracious palm-shaded Carrollton Avenue west (upriver) for a little less than a mile through a neighborhood of mixed-income housing that contains a number of Victorian and early-20th-century houses and cottages in various states of refurbishment. This drive follows the path of the soon-to-be-completed Canal Street streetcar, so that eventually you'll be able to ride the cars from City Park all the way to the foot of Canal, between the French Quarter and the CBD.

The neighborhood around the intersection of Carrollton Avenue and Canal Street is an interesting one, with a mix of fairly ordinary workaday shops and fast-food restaurants, along with quite a few notable cafés, ethnic restaurants, and interesting old houses. The incomparable Italian pastry and ice-cream shop **Angelo Brocato's** makes for an especially enjoyable snack break. Like St. Charles Avenue, Esplanade Avenue, and to a certain extent Carrollton Avenue, upper Canal Street was a place during the late 19th century where quite a few wealthy New Orleanians built impressive homes, many of them immense wood-frame Italianates and Greek Revivals. On the nearby side streets are a mix of mostly smaller shotgun houses, Creole cottages, and gingerbread Victorians. The neighborhood is neither touristy nor overly polished—just a genuine slice of residential New Orleans, and a neighborhood that's racially and ethnically diverse.

From here you could turn down Canal Street back to the Quarter, or continue along Carrollton Avenue under the I-10 freeway overpass and

for another couple of miles to reach Carrollton. Or you could take Canal Street in the opposite direction of the Quarter, toward the lake, for nearly a mile, making a left onto City Park Avenue. This road takes you by New Orleans Country Club, Louisiana State Charity Cemetery, Metairie Cemetery, Greenwood Cemetery, and, right at the border between New Orleans and Metairie, the **Longue Vue House and Gardens** (7 Bamboo Rd., Old Metairie, 504/488-5488, www.longuevue.com, open 10 A.M.–4:30 P.M. Mon.–Sat., 1–5 P.M. Sun., admission $10), a lush and exotic 80-acre estate that once belonged to a cotton broker and now comprises a period-furnished Classical Revival manor house and spectacularly landscaped grounds. This is one of the most impressive attractions in the city, but many visitors never get here because it's slightly off the beaten path.

Eastern New Orleans and Chalmette

There are a handful of attractions elsewhere around New Orleans and the neighboring communities. It's best to explore these sites on their own, rather than as part of a linear tour, as distances between them are considerable, and the drives to and from these places are not especially intriguing.

One attraction that's of particular interest to outdoor lovers is the 85-acre **Audubon Louisiana Nature Center** (Joe Brown Memorial Park, Dwyer Road and Read Boulevard, 504/246-5672, www.auduboninstitute.org, open 9 A.M.–5 P.M. Tues.–Fri., 10 A.M.–5 P.M. Sat., and noon–5 P.M. Sun., admission $5), which makes a nice change of pace from the urbanity of downtown New Orleans. You reach it by heading east for about 10 miles on I-10, then heading south onto Read Boulevard at Exit 244 (it's about a 15-minute drive from the Quarter). The park is a couple of blocks south on your left. Here you'll find an extensive network of nature trails, a butterfly garden, and a kids-oriented discovery loft with hands-on learning stations that shed light on the flora and fauna (including flying squirrels, snakes, and other local critters) of the region. When

you're actually here wandering through the lush foliage and swamps, it's hard to imagine you're on the eastern edge of a major city. On Saturdays at 10:30 A.M. and 3 P.M., and on Sundays at 3 P.M., staff lead guided tours through the grounds. There's also a planetarium that offers shows four times each Saturday and Sunday afternoon; call 504/246-STAR for details.

The only one of the sites within the Jean Lafitte National Historical Park and Preserve that touch on Louisiana's military history, **Chalmette Battlefield and National Cemetery** (8606 St. Bernard Hwy., Chalmette, 504/281-0510, www.nps.gov/jela, open 9 A.M.–5 P.M. daily, admission free) commemorates the important victory by Andrew Jackson and his American troops during the Battle of New Orleans, in 1815. The battlefield lies just 6 miles southeast of downtown New Orleans and comprises a 1.5-mile tour road (with six interpretive placards set along it at pull-offs) through the scene of the action, Chalmette National Cemetery, and the 1833 Malus-Beauregard House. The latter had no role in the battle, of course, having been built 18 years after it, but it's a dashingly handsome Creole mansion with long, graceful verandas and stout columns. It looks like the anchor of one of those classic southern Louisiana plantations, but, in fact, the house had no ties to a farm. It was built as a residence and occupied by a number of wealthy merchants and prominent figures, the last private owner being Judge René Beauregard.

Again not closely related to the Battle of New Orleans itself, Chalmette National Cemetery was actually commissioned as a graveyard for Union soldiers felled during the Civil War, although veterans of subsequent wars—the Spanish-American War, World Wars I and II, and Vietnam—are also interred here. You can visit the graves of four men who fought in the War of 1812, one of whom actually participated in the Battle of New Orleans. There's also an obelisk, Chalmette Monument, that stands high over the battlefield. The monument was commissioned in 1840 shortly after former President Jackson returned to the scene of the battle to mark its 25th anniversary, but construction wasn't begun until 1855, and the monument was not completed for another 53 years.

In terms of understanding the battle itself, how it evolved, and why the British failed so miserably, the placards and exhibits inside the visitor center are most useful. The park extends down to the banks of the Mississippi, so you get a very clear sense of where the British came ashore and where the Americans awaited them. The Battle of New Orleans, fought on January 8, 1815, with most of the action in just two hours, was the last military conflict ever waged between U.S. and British troops.

Free talks on the battle are given daily at 11:15 A.M. and 2:45 P.M. Check for interpretive programs, videos, and performances, scheduled regularly throughout the year, and when in New Orleans, be sure to drop in on the headquarters of the Jean Lafitte National Historical Park and Preserve, in the French Quarter at 419 Decatur St. Here you'll find information on all of the park's six sites throughout southern Louisiana.

Almost as far east as Chalmette, the **Jackson Barracks Military Museum** (6400 St. Claude Ave., 504/278-8242, www.la.ngb.army.mil /jbmm.htm, open 7:30 A.M.–4 P.M. Mon.–Fri., 9 A.M.–3 P.M. Sat., admission free), about 3 miles east of downtown and only a mile from Chalmette Battlefield, explores the region's role in several military engagements dating back to the American Revolution. Weapons, artifacts, and historical documents are all shown, as well as memorabilia concerning wars of the past century.

Metairie and Kenner

Old Metairie nestles up against the New Orleans border and has some very upscale residential neighborhoods, despite being strangled on all sides by busy interstates and even busier Veterans Boulevard. It's a nice neighborhood for poking around, and a bike trail runs right through part of the area. It's also close to Longue Vue House and Gardens. To explore this area, take I-10 west from downtown to exit 231A, and make a left onto Metairie Road, passing by New Orleans Country Club on your left and Metairie Cemetery on your right. You'll pass signs for Longue Vue House and Gardens after about a half-mile. Continue straight across the canal, and Metairie Road winds through the Old Metairie section of town. If you venture off onto the cross streets, you'll pass through some elegant neighborhoods, many with fine old homes from the early 20th century. Metairie Road is also lined with good restaurants.

Just southeast of Armstrong International Airport, kids enjoy **Rivertown U.S.A.** (415 Williams Blvd., 504/468-7231, www.rivertownkenner.com, open 9 A.M.–5 P.M. Tues.–Sat., admission to each museum $3, $15 for all museums, $6 for combined ticket to the Space Station, Planetarium, and Observatory). This expansive educational and museum complex comprises the Daily Living Science Center, Space Station, Planetarium and Observatory, Wildlife and Fisheries, and Cannes

Brûlée Native American Center. There's also a Mardi Gras Museum, a Saints Hall of Fame, a toy train museum, and a children's castle. In short, you won't have trouble finding two or three museums or exhibits with appeal, no matter what your interests.

In the Mardi Gras Museum, a particular favorite of out-of-towners, you can board a simulated Mardi Gras float, watch artisans at work on floats and costumes, and take a look at a wide array of beads, posters, costumes, and collectibles related to both the city Mardi Gras parades held throughout the state as well as the rural Courir du Mardi Gras celebrations, which are held mostly in rural Cajun communities. Cannes Brûlée Native American Center hosts a wide range of music, crafts, storytelling, and history demonstrations and lectures; in a re-created bayou setting, you can learn about the folk traditions, foods, medicinal plants, and crafts of the Native American cultures indigenous to Louisiana. More than 700 varieties of regional wildlife are on display, both mounted in dioramas and alive in a 15,000-gallon aquarium. Other museums detail Kenner's history, toy trains, and NFL football's New Orleans Saints.

A highlight for many visitors is the Science Center, which comprises the Louis J. Roussel Laser Planetarium & River Max Theater, the Freeport McMoRan Observatory, and an interactive museum dedicated to the exploration of space and the development of scientific technology. Visitors can explore touch-friendly exhibits on meteorology, electricity, the human body, gravity, and world geography. The Planetarium has astronomy shows twice a day on Tuesdays and Fridays, and three times daily on Saturdays.

Rivertown is also home to the Rivertown Repertory Theatre, which presents a half-dozen professional musicals and plays throughout the year. You reach Rivertown by taking I-10 west to Exit 223, Williams Boulevard; head south on Williams for about 2.5 miles.

The West Bank

The West Bank comprises a stretch of suburbs and even a bit of New Orleans proper, including historic Algiers Point, although that section is covered above as a side trip via the free (for passengers) ferry from Canal Street in the CBD across the river. New Orleans city limits continue along the West Bank of the river for several miles, extending about 2 miles inland, all the way out to English Turn, a big inverted "C" of the Mississippi River, roughly across from the town of St. Bernard. It's not a part of the city many people explore, as it holds few formal attractions and is not exactly a hotbed of dining or entertainment, but there are a few reasons to wander across the river.

In keeping with New Orleans's ever-confusing orientation, the West Bank portion of New Orleans proper actually lies *east* across the river from downtown and the French Quarter, as the crow flies. With a serpentine river like the Mississippi, people refer to everything on one side as the West Bank and everything on the other as the East Bank (as the river *generally* flows in a north–south direction), but at many of its sharply curving points, the river can run east–west, west–east, and even south–north.

The West Bank is mostly a series of small but densely settled communities that include Gretna, Harvey, Marrero (which sits along the edges of Lake Cataouatche), and the even larger Lake Salvador. Farther west, as you follow U.S. 90, you'll pass through Westwego (one of the few Cajun settlements in metro New Orleans), and eventually out to the towns of Mimosa Park and Boutte, before U.S. 90 continues down into LaFourche Parish, the easternmost section covered in this book's Cajun Country side-trip chapter. You reach the West Bank from downtown New Orleans via the Pontchartrain Expressway, which rises over the Crescent City Connection Bridge; this is the final bridge over the Mississippi River before it empties into the Gulf more than 100 miles downstream, although there are a handful of car-ferry crossings farther downriver.

Swamp tours can be great fun, but if you want to experience the wetlands of southeastern

Louisiana at your own pace, and independent of a tour group, you should strongly consider spending a day at **Barataria Preserve** (6588 Barataria Blvd., or Hwy. 45, near Crown Point, Marrero, 504/589-2330, www.nps.com/jela, open 7 A.M.–7 P.M. daily during daylight savings time, 7 A.M.–5 P.M. the rest of the year, admission free), a division of the Jean Lafitte National Historical Park and Preserve.

Geologically speaking, the Mississippi Delta is still a newborn, having been formed with sediment and silt deposited at the mouth of the Mississippi some 5,000 years ago. It's been a gradual process, with the area now encompassed by New Orleans having been built up just about 2,500 years ago. The river continues to deposit sediment, and the delta continues to expand, as it does in the Atchafalaya basin. Here at Barataria Preserve, you have the chance to explore and learn about one of the world's most substantial delta ecosystems, a series of bayous, marshes, swamps, and woodlands that appear at first to be almost virginal and untouched by man. Indigenous tribes, however, began settling on the delta from almost the moment it was dry and large enough to support human life. As Europeans arrived, they settled here to fish and trap as the Native Americans had, and later immigrants have cultivated the land in different ways, most recently for oil drilling. This was also the domain of the notorious pirate for whom the park is named, Jean Lafitte, who declared himself the King of Barataria during his heyday toward the end of the 18th century.

Barataria Preserve is a haven for an amazing variety of plant life, which thrives in this subtropical climate. Depending on water salinity, elevation, soil type, and moisture, different species thrive. Along the natural ridges and levees, there's dense hardwood forest, along with towering live oaks, but the habitat changes to palmetto groves on the lower back slopes of the levees. Water covers most of the lower regions of the levees throughout much of the year, and so in these swamp areas you'll encounter bald cypress trees, and then treeless marshes beyond the swamps.

The preserve makes an ideal habitat for anybody interested in getting outside for hiking and canoeing; fishing is allowed as long as you've obtained a valid permit. The preserve contains 8 miles of hiking trails, 2.5 miles of which run across well-maintained boardwalk, allowing a close look at the swamp ecosystem and the many critters who live within. Just keep in mind that many of these animals are chiefly nocturnal, so you may not see much of them during the day. Animals that you may see during the day include gray squirrels, swamp rabbits, armadillos, and nutria, curious furry animals introduced from Argentina that have become something of a pest because of their vast quantities. Heron, ibis, and egrets fly freely through the swamp, and all sorts of scaly creatures, from turtles to frogs to snakes, slither and crawl about. Of course, as in any Louisiana swamp, you may very well encounter alligators, which like to sun along dry levees and river banks during warmer times of year; you may sometimes see them lying in shallow water, too, only their eyes and nostrils peering out above the water. There's no reason to be alarmed as long as you give them their space and avoid making any aggressive gestures; alligators are not at all interested in human visitors, and most of them are quite used to seeing canoes and people.

There are 9 miles of waterway dedicated exclusively to canoe use, on which no motorized craft is permitted. These are accessible at three separate canoe launches and afford a great chance to experience the terrain as the earliest humans to inhabit southeastern Louisiana would have, in total quiet. Just watch for snakes curled around the branches of overhanging trees—it's not a common problem, but snakes have been known to fall into boats passing beneath them. Another 20 miles of Barataria waterway is open to both motorized and nonmotorized boats, and there are several launches in the area for motorized craft. You can rent canoes just outside the preserve.

Barataria has picnic spots in several parts of the park, with restrooms both at the visitor center and at the parking area for the Pecan Grove and picnic tables.

The Visitor Center is open daily 9 A.M.–5 P.M.; trails and parking areas open at 7 A.M. and close at 7 P.M. during daylight savings time (roughly mid-April through mid-October) and 5 P.M. the rest of the year. Reservations are required for the Saturday morning canoe treks, the bird-watching excursions, the sunset strolls, and the moonlight canoe treks; call ahead for details on these engaging activities. Guided nature walks are given Sun.–Fri. at 1:30 P.M., and the 25-minute video *Jambalaya: A Delta Almanac* is presented throughout the day. Check for interpretive programs, videos, and performances scheduled throughout the year, and when in New Orleans, be sure to drop in on the headquarters of the Jean Lafitte National Historical Park and Preserve, in the French Quarter at 419 Decatur St. Here you'll find information on all of the park's six sites throughout southern Louisiana.

Entertainment

It's the reason plenty of visitors come to New Orleans: to be entertained. Usually, in this city, entertainment takes the form of watching a jazz, blues, or rock band captivate an audience in one of the city's seemingly endless array of lounges, bars, and live-music halls. Or it's attending Mardi Gras or Jazz Fest, two of the world's most exalted live-music events, or one of the many smaller festivals and parades held in the Crescent City throughout the year.

New Orleans's reputation as party central is well-deserved, but enjoying a night on the town can involve a wide range of activities that appeal to many tastes. There is, of course, the city's salacious side, evidenced by the significant num-

ber of strip clubs, adult bookstores, and the like. You'll also find a big (though not particularly successful) casino in the Central Business District. You'll find a wide range of mod lounges, old-world watering holes, festive gay bars, and stately hotel cocktail lounges in New Orleans, with the greatest concentration in the Quarter. But New Orleans, and all of southern Louisiana for that matter, truly stands out for its rollicking live-music scene: it's one of the world's premier venues for jazz, blues, rockabilly, soul, zydeco, and Cajun music, and the city's venues range from hole-in-the-wall dives to massive music halls. You'll find top-notch live music just about any night of the week.

© ANDREW COLLINS

Mardi Gras

FRENCH QUARTER AND FAUBOURG MARIGNY ENTERTAINMENT

To Ernie K-Doe's Mother-In-Law Lounge

To Sweet Lorraine's

Louis Armstrong Park

TREME

★ MAHALIA JACKSON THEATRE OF THE PERFORMING ARTS

ST. LOUIS CEMETERY NO 2

ST. LOUIS CEMETERY NO 1

DONNA'S

FUNKY BUTT AT CONGO SQUARE ▼

GOOD FRIENDS

735 NIGHTCLUB AND BAR ▼

LAFITTE'S BLACKSMITH SHOP ▼

CAFE LAFITTE IN EXILE ▼

BOURBON PUB/PARADE DISCO

▼ OZ

FRITZEL'S EUROPEAN JAZZ PUB ▼

FRENCH QUARTER

CAT'S MEOW ▼

GENNIFER FLOWERS' KELSTO CLUB ▼

PRESERVATION HALL ★

LE PETIT THEATRE DU VIEUX CARRE ★

CAJUN CABIN

DUNGEON BAR ▼

TUJAGU

JACKSON SQUARE

SAENGER THEATRE ★

BOMBAY CLUB ▼

SHIM-SHAM

CHARTIY HOSPITAL

FAMOUS DOOR ▼

NAPOLEON HOUSE CAFE

FLEUR DE LIS THÉÂTRE ★

▼ O'FLAHERTY'S

CRESCENT CITY BREWHOUSE ▼

STATE PALACE THEATRE ★

RHYTHMS ▼

CAN-CAN CAFE

ANDREW JAEGER'S HOUSE OF SEAFOOD

STEAMBOAT /NATCHEZ

MEDICAL CENTER OF TULANE

CAROUSEL BAR

LIVING ROOM ▼

HARD ROCK CAFE

LIBRARY LOUNGE/FRENCH QUARTER BAR

RED FISH GRILL ▼

KERRY IRISH PUB ▼

CBD

HOUSE OF BLUES ▼

COYOTE UGLY SALOON ▼

LOUNGE LIZARD

LANDMARK'S CANAL PLACE ★ ★

Woldenberg Riverfront Park

SOUTHERN REPERTORY THEATRE

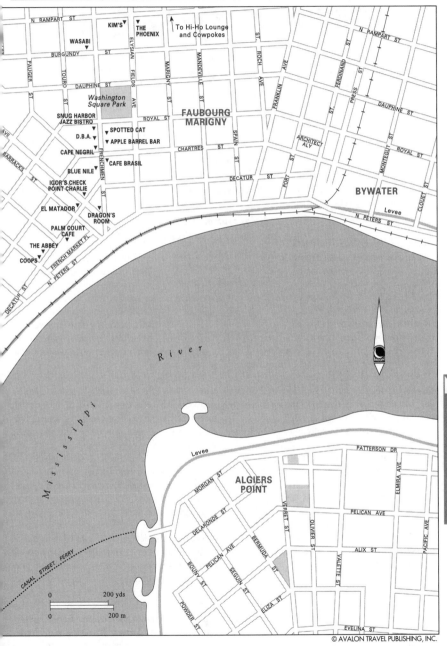

© AVALON TRAVEL PUBLISHING, INC.

Nightlife

The simplest way to partake of the city's nightlife is just to walk along Bourbon Street any evening. Inevitably, you'll hear the music simultaneously of two or more bars along this raucous stretch—it's a bit like being stuck between two radio stations. Bourbon is loud, occasionally obnoxious, and sometimes frightfully crowded. The street is closed to automobile traffic at night, except at the cross streets, where you do have to watch yourself. Most of the establishments along here stay open 24 hours, and you can carry your booze from bar to bar, as long as you're nursing a plastic "go-cup" and not a bottle or other glass container. This scenario contributes to what is very often a drunken scene, where the soles of your shoes stick to the booze (and whatever else) stuck to the pavement. Bourbon Street is not for everybody, but you should at least check it out once during your visit, ideally on a busy evening. It's a caricature of New Orleans, but at the same time, it captures the almost ferocious enthusiasm with which people in this city indulge in music, drinking, dancing, and socializing.

Bourbon Street is virtually ignored by locals and die-hard music fans, however, as this rollicking, touristy stretch of clubs doesn't necessarily book the best acts in town, and also brims with goofy strip joints, karaoke bars, and other giddy hangouts. You can find some genuinely excellent music spots in other parts of the French Quarter, and North Rampart Street, on the slightly dicey edge of the district, has some of the best improvisational jazz clubs in the country. You can always count on a good show at the city's longtime favorite music clubs, such as Tipitina's or the Palm Court. And the chain restaurant-club House of Blues, though every bit as touristy as Bourbon Street, can be counted on to present high-caliber bands.

You'll also find some great music acts at bars

People like to cut loose in this city, and to lose themselves in the revelry, and that can be, of course, great fun. But with so little structure and so few rules, a weekend in New Orleans can be a bit too liberating for some people.

and taverns in the hipster-infested Warehouse District, and at some of the hotel bars in the adjacent CBD. St. Charles Avenue and Magazine Street both have a handful of decent live-music venues Uptown, and in Faubourg Marigny, the trendy historic district just downriver from the Quarter, Frenchmen Street pulses with vibrant jazz, reggae, and rock venues. But just as you can find terrific food outside the tourist-oriented parts of the city, you can also find excellent music clubs in Mid-City, up near the lake, and in neighboring communities like Metairie and Kenner.

You don't survive for long in New Orleans as a musician unless you've really got what it takes to keep people tapping their toes and leaning in on the edge of their seat, meaning that any veteran band in this town—whether or not you as a visitor have heard of it—could hold its own anywhere in America.

Even in bars that don't have live music, you'll almost always find a kickin' jukebox, a DJ spinning danceable beats, or piped-in tunes with that unmistakable New Orleans–inspired sound. People in this city need music the way they need water and air. So you're going to hear great music everywhere; you don't have to settle in on a bar with a live band to enjoy yourself.

New Orleans has some of the great hotel lounges in the country. These include swanky spaces in grande dame properties—the sorts of bars with walk-in cigar humidors and waiters in tails. But more recently, a crop of edgy boutique hotels has grown up in New Orleans, and many of these places have fashionable cocktail bars where it can be fun to convene with a group of friends.

The city's more youthful types tend to favor divey, hole-in-the-wall lounges Uptown and in Faubourg Marigny, and also along bohemian Decatur Street in the Lower Quarter. You might detect a hint of self-consciousness or even attitude in some of these spots, especially if you're neither pierced nor tattooed (or if you're wearing tennis shoes and a rugby shirt). But at its core, New Orleans behaves like a genial small town, and even these sorts of places tend to welcome outsiders.

Among the strip clubs in the Quarter, the gay bars mostly in the Upper Quarter, and the thousands of tourists and conventioneers who descend upon New Orleans each week, the city has an obviously sexual vibe—it's not difficult to pick people up in New Orleans, whether you're gay, straight, or bi, whatever your age or style. It's a city where many bars stay open 24 hours and serve very stiff drinks. And there's a pretty hardcore drug scene at even some of the most tourist-friendly clubs around town.

People like to cut loose in this city, and to lose themselves in the revelry, and that can be, of course, great fun. But with so little structure and so few rules, a weekend in New Orleans can be a bit too liberating for some people. On the plus side, many bars and clubs are within walking distance of hotels and inns, and cabs are easy to find outside most major venues, so you don't have to drive anywhere to have a good time. Try, though, to set some limits for yourself before a big night on the town. And should the opportunity arise to pick somebody up at a bar, exercise common sense—tell somebody with you where you're going, introduce your new friend to somebody else you know, even somebody else you've just met. Never give a stranger the impression that you're alone, unaccounted for, or in any way vulnerable.

By the same token, avoid walking back to your hotel or inn alone from bars and clubs, even if you've only had a drink or two. It's prudent to take a cab even short distances if it's late and you're on your own. This isn't the menacing, crime-ridden city that some have made it out to be, but bad things do happen to visitors, sometimes in broad daylight, even in the heart of the French Quarter. And they're most likely to happen to visitors who have had a bit to drink and abandoned their common sense.

For the scoop on live music at local bars and clubs, check out the tourism publications found in just about every hotel, and also scan the listings of New Orleans's outstanding alternative newsweekly, *Gambit Weekly* (504/486-5900, www.bestofneworleans.com). The publication *OffBeat* (504/944-4300 or 877/944-4300, http://offbeat.com) is the best source in the state for learning about Louisiana's music scene, recordings by local artists, and where to catch live performances. The magazine's website is a font of great information. The *Times-Picayune* (800/925-0000, www.nola.com) comes out with a full calendar of nightly goings-on, plus festivals, art exhibits, and other timely events. It's in the *Lagniappe* section, which comes out Fridays. An excellent monthly glossy with great features and extensive listings on restaurants, sightseeing, and shopping is *New Orleans Magazine* (504/832-3555, www.neworleans.com).

Bars, clubs, and other nightlife venues are listed in their most appropriate categories (Dance Club, Neighborhood Hangouts, Live Music, etc.), but keep in mind that many of these places fit in multiple categories.

LIVE MUSIC
Rock and Blues

For catching rock (both hard-edged and down-home), jazz, zydeco, and blues, there may be no club in the city more acclaimed and also more festive than **Tipitina's** (501 Napoleon Ave., 504/895-8477), in Uptown. Purists may tell you that Tip's has lost its edge and no longer presents the best—or at least most distinctive—local acts, but anybody looking for an introduction to the city's eclectic music scene should head here. Entertainment varies greatly, but whoever's performing, you can probably dance to it.

Catch mostly top blues and funk acts at the **Howlin' Wolf** (828 South Peters St., 504/529-5844), a cavernous nightclub in the Warehouse District, not far from the convention center. This is one of the city's biggest and most prominent music venues, and it also books rocks, alternative, pop, R&B, and most every other style of band.

Mermaid Lounge (1100 Constance St., 504/524-4747) has long been known for some of the best alternative, punk, and indie rock in

THE MUSIC OF SOUTHERN LOUISIANA

Jazz was born in New Orleans, and the area between Lafayette and Lake Charles is famous for its Cajun and zydeco music, but just about every other style of music known to America has enjoyed a heyday in Louisiana, including blues, rock, gospel, and even opera, which took root here long before it did anywhere else in the country. In fact, the nation's first opera was performed in New Orleans in 1796.

Here's a rundown of some of the music genres you may not connect immediately to Louisiana but that have very deep roots here.

Rock and Roll, Pop, and Soul

Rock music was a natural outgrowth of blues, gospel, and country-western traditions, and some say it was born in New Orleans, where in the late 1940s a singer named Roy Brown sang a tune called "Good Rockin' Tonight," the first song that used "rock" as a term for this faster-paced, danceable variation on the blues. A book by music historian Robert Palmer called *Memphis Rock and New Orleans Roll* traces the development of rock music to these two cities along the Mississippi.

New Orleans's jazz traditions contributed the sassy roll to rock music, while Memphis contributed the harder-edged blues born in the Mississippi delta towns south of the city. The area between the two cities was rich with Pentecostal gospel sounds, which also influenced the development, ironically, of that devil music, rock'n'roll. New Orleans's brand of rock music is especially influenced by piano playing, keyboards, and even accordion, which suggests a link between rock and zydeco.

Maybe the most famous Louisiana rock legend is Fats Domino ("Walking to New Orleans"), who emerged from the New Orleans club scene. Local session musicians have long attracted the attention of big-city record producers, who sent stars like Little Richard to the Big Easy to make albums. Other rock, pop, and soul greats from the New Orleans area include Allen Toussaint, Percy Mayfield, the Dixie Cups, Ernie K-Doe, Irma Thomas, the Neville Brothers, Professor Longhair, Frankie Ford, Lee Dorsey, and Dr. John, many of whom recorded at the Cosimo Matassa music studio. More recently, New Orleans's music scene spawned the alternative pop-rock band Better Than Ezra, as well as the gangsta sounds of Master P and his empire of rappers, including his young son, Lil' Romeo (born in 1989).

Rock has been shaken up a bit with Louisiana influences, such as country and bluegrass, to form rockabilly music, made famous by the likes of Jimmy Clanton, Joe Clay, Floyd Kramer, Jerry Lee Lewis, Jim Reeves, Farron Young, Slim Whitman, and Hank Williams Sr. The term bandied about today for Cajun- and zydeco-tinged rock music is "swamp pop," and you'll hear it in the more current clubs all throughout Cajun Country.

Country and Bluegrass

Country music, and its close cousin bluegrass (or perhaps child is a better term, since this style was born out of old-time country music traditions), share certain similarities with Cajun and even zydeco, but their routes are distinctly Anglo-American (specifically Scots-Irish) rather than French, German, or African-American. Many of the first Anglo settlers in Louisiana, who began arriving in the early 1800s, hailed from Kentucky and neighboring states and brought with them traditions of fiddling and ballad-singing.

Early barn dances and jamborees gave country music a widespread following, and the *Louisiana Hayride,* broadcast out of Shreveport's Municipal Auditorium on KWKH, popularized the genre in the 1940s and '50s, introducing Americans to Hank Williams, Johnny Horton, Johnny Cash, and Elvis Presley. The rocking honky-tonk style of country music, though not unique to Louisiana, thrives throughout the state. Western swing, which bands like the Hackberry Ramblers perform today, mixes country music with Cajun, blues, jazz, and other genres in a distinctly Louisiana way.

The northern end of the state has especially strong country and bluegrass traditions, but you can find live performances at venues in New Orleans, as well as in the Florida Parishes, nine parishes that extend from Baton Rouge east along I-10 and then I-12 north of Lake Pontchartrain to the Mississippi border. Jerry Lee Lewis was born in Ferriday, and in Abita Springs, the *Piney Woods Opry* is a live radio-broadcast celebration of bluegrass. Former governor Jimmie Davis was one of the state's earliest country recording stars. Current country stars with Louisiana roots include Sammy Kershaw, Tim McGraw, Lonnie Wilson, Michael Rhodes, and the Whitstein Brothers.

Gospel

Gospel has deep roots in Louisiana, although it tends to be more often performed in the northern half of the state. Black gospel music, which has been celebrated in the state for many years, has its routes with the African slaves who first sung biblical songs and hymns known as "spirituals." Generally, these songs, which are performed in churches today, are performed a cappella, but other gospel music is accompanied by instruments and often has jazz, bluegrass, soul, and blues overtones. You can find performances not only at churches but at festivals and conventions. Some of the bigger music clubs in New Orleans, notably the House of Blues, feature gospel choirs from time to time.

Classical and Opera

Classical music and opera have been little influenced by Louisiana's other more homegrown music forms, but they've been appreciated in this region since the late 18th century, when the first opera ever performed in the United States debuted in New Orleans. An early American classical composer, Louis Moreau Gottschalk, was born in New Orleans, and incorporated African and Caribbean themes in his music. Classical concerts are held in just about every city in the state, and the Louisiana Sinfonietta, based in Baton Rouge and led by acclaimed composer Dino Constantinides, is especially well-regarded. Notable Louisianans who have earned acclaim in this genre included opera singer Shirley Verret and virtuoso pianist Van Cliburn, from Shreveport.

Resources

The publication *OffBeat* (http://offbeat.com) is the best source in the state for learning about Louisiana's music scene, recordings by local artists, and where to catch live performances.

Putumayo World Music (www.putumayo.com) has produced two excellent albums of Louisiana music, *Zydeco*, which focuses on that genre, and the broader *Louisiana Gumbo*, which includes great soul, R&B, and blues from throughout the state.

One great way to enjoy Louisiana music while visiting is on the radio. Favorites include KRVS-FM (88.7 in Lafayette, and 90.5 in Lake Charles), which specializes in zydeco and Cajun; WKJN-FM (103.3 in Baton Rouge), another Cajun favorite; and in New Orleans, WRNO-FM (99.5) for jazz, zydeco, and Cajun; WWNO-FM (89.9) for jazz; and WWOZ-FM (90.7, www.wwoz.org) for jazz, gospel, and zydeco.

You can learn more about the state's music scene from the state tourism office, or from the Louisiana Music Commission (www.louisianamusic.org), and the site www.cajunzydeco.net. Finally, the **William Ransom Hogan archive at Tulane University** (6801 Freret St., Jones Hall, Room 304, 504/865-5688) has a Web archive of New Orleans jazz at www.tulane.edu/~lmiller/jazzhome.html. You can stop by and visit the archive in person; it's open 8:30 A.M.–5 P.M. weekdays and 9 A.M.–5 P.M. Sat.

town. The trick is finding this near–falling down house on the edge of the Warehouse District, in the shadows of the Crescent City Connection Bridge; all that fist-pumping music, fortunately, drowns out the street traffic. Because the neighborhood is quite desolate, although not especially crime-ridden, you might want to take a cab.

Touristy though it is, the New Orleans outpost of the **Hard Rock Cafe** (418 North Peters St., 504/529-5617) can be counted on for some pretty good rock acts. Again, it's a major tourist haunt, often packed with conventioneers (it's just a block off Canal Street), but the **House of Blues** (225 Decatur St., 504/529-2624) does many things well, and it's a great place to watch some of New Orleans's best blues, rock, zydeco, and other pop bands. The restaurant serves good food, the decor is colorful and fun, and the Sunday gospel brunch is especially enjoyable.

The **Shim-Sham** (615 Toulouse St., 504/299-0666) is a divey, loud, and intimate rock and alternative music club in the heart of the Quarter. The crowd tends toward young (under 30) and riotous. Can be very fun depending on the band.

You can catch different types of music at the **Cat's Meow** (701 Bourbon St., 504/523-2788), from oldies to modern rock. Some nights there's karaoke. It can be a little cheesy, but the place has a loyal following.

A Faubourg mainstay, the **Blue Nile** (534 Frenchmen St., 504/948-BLUE) presents a broad mix of cool music, from jazz to world beat to Latin dance music to garage rock. With its plush lounge seating and tile floors, it's an elegant place to socialize and drink with friends early in the evening, and the music usually kicks off around 10 P.M.

A great Mid-City neighborhood hangout that was said to be a favorite of Earl K. Long and his political cronies, **Dixie Taverne** (3340 Canal St., 504/822-8268) hosted everyone from Liberace to Chuck Berry back in the day but presently books a wide variety of rock, metal, and alternative music. Sip a Dixie beer while you enjoy the show.

In Uptown, the **Maple Leaf Bar** (8316 Oak St., 504/866-9539) serves up some of the best blues in town.

Cajun and Zydeco

Right on Bourbon you can hear some great Cajun music at **Cajun Cabin** (503 Bourbon St., 504/529-4256), which has bands all week long. Another good stop for foot-stomping Cajun music is **Michaul's** (840 St. Charles Ave., 504/522-5517), which is also a restaurant serving decent Cajun fare.

Eclectic

Dos Jefes Uptown Cigar Bar (5535 Tchoupitoulas St., 504/891-8500) draws locals and students for live jazz and folk music. **O'Flaherty's** (514 Toulouse St., 504/529-1317) is a good place to catch live Irish music. **Mid-City Lanes Rock 'n' Bowl** (4133 S. Carrollton Ave., 504/482-3133) is practically a music (and bowling) institution, an offbeat place to catch live bands of all types; it's especially known for zydeco (on Thursdays), retro, and swing.

Along the Marigny's nightclub strip, **Cafe Brasil** (2100 Chartres St., 504/949-0851) is nothing really to look at—just a big room with high ceilings, colorfully painted walls (with art for sale hung on them), bare floors, and a large dance area. You come for the hoppin' often-Latin dance music, plus hip-hop, reggae, and other styles, depending on the night.

Catch salsa, meringue, and other Latin tunes at **Copa Cabana** (4609 Airline Hwy., 504/456-6089), a popular club out in Metairie.

In Uptown, drop by **Neutral Ground Coffeehouse** (5110 Danneel St., 504/891-3381) to catch live bluegrass performances. This atmospheric coffeehouse, said to be the oldest in the city, also has open-mic night on Sundays, and poetry readings on many nights.

Jazz

Since 1961, **Preservation Hall** (726 St. Peter St., 504/522-2841) has been one of the city's top places to hear true New Orleans jazz. The Preservation Hall Band formed originally with members of the city's long-standing jazz elite, pioneers in the field who by the 1960s were already 70 or 80 years old. Top musicians continue to join the Hall's ranks, performing in the low-key and surprisingly intimate concert hall much of the year, and touring cities all over the world for more than 100 days of the year. It's a must-attend for any jazz lover.

Fritzel's European Jazz Pub (733 Bourbon St., 504/561-0432) books some of the better jazz musicians along raucous Bourbon Street. This is a place to catch very traditional jazz. There's no cover, and just a one-drink minimum. Another spot along Bourbon with consistently good Dixieland jazz is the **Famous Door** (339 Bourbon St., 504/522-7626).

One of the most famous and delightful venues in the city for catching live jazz is the **Palm Court Cafe** (1204 Decatur St., 504/525-0200), in an elegant 19th-century building near the French Market with ceiling fans, an elegant mahogany bar, exposed-brick walls lined with photos of jazz greats, and a kitchen producing quite tasty Creole

THE BIRTH OF JAZZ AND BLUES

Jazz wasn't invented in one definitive instant—it evolved over perhaps 20 or 30 years during the early part of the 20th century, and in several parts of New Orleans's African-American community. The state has produced several jazz luminaries, among them Jelly Roll Morton, Doc Souchon, Sidney Bechet, King Oliver, and crooner Harry Connick Jr.

Jazz music typically uses both individual and collective improvisation, syncopation, and distinctive vocal effects, and it has its origins in European, African, and Caribbean traditional music. Commonly you'll hear blues vocalizing sung to jazz instrumental accompaniment. Many people trace jazz to a popular cornet player named Buddy Bolden, who performed regularly in New Orleans from the mid-1890s until about 1910. Through the 1910s and '20s, ragtime-style jazz and other music forms with a spontaneous, upbeat tempo began to attract a following, albeit an underground one, in New Orleans.

This thoroughly modern and iconoclastic style of music was not, initially, well-received by the mainstream, and in fact, hard as it is to believe now, it was shunned by organizers of Mardi Gras parades for years. During the early years, many people considered this music style to be scandalous and impudent—they criticized it at least as harshly as early critics of rock and roll denounced that music. Jazz was seen as a crude bastardization of more acceptable music styles. In 1901 the American Federation of Music spoke of efforts to "suppress and discourage the playing and publishing of such musical trash as ragtime"; the *Musical Courier* in 1899 referred to a "wave of vulgar filthy, and suggestive music which has inundated the land."

But over time, jazz would win the hearts of even the harshest naysayers, and today there's really no style of music for which the city is better regarded.

Blues music has its origins upriver a bit from New Orleans, about 300 miles north in the fruitful delta farming regions of northwestern Mississippi, especially the towns near Clarkdale. It's said that blues derives from the field hollers of cane and cotton workers in these parts. Eventually, the soulful vocals were joined with guitars, drums, and horns to become the modern form of blues celebrated today all through the South and especially in Louisiana. Huddie "Leadbelly" Ledbetter, who wrote such classics as "Goodnight Irene" and "Midnight Special," grew up in Shreveport, in the northwest corner of the state, and is often credited as the father of blues music.

Blues, along with New Orleans jazz, melded together in the 1950s to influence a new genre: rhythm and blues, or R&B. It is a distinctly commercial genre that was begun with the express intent of getting airplay on the radio and acclaim for its stars through record sales, and to that end it has always incorporated the catchiest and most accessible elements of the genres from which it borrows.

All around the state, and especially in Baton Rouge and New Orleans, clubs present live blues performers, and this often sorrowful, sometimes joyous, style of music also influences much of the jazz, rock, country-western, and gospel tunes heard elsewhere in the state.

ENTERTAINMENT

fare. Because seating is at tables over dinner, reservations are a must. Each night a different one of the city's top jazz bands performs.

Another wonderful place for truly exceptional music is **Pete Fountain's Jazz Club** (New Orleans Hilton, 3rd floor, 237 North Peters St., 504/525-6255), a show that can often book up early, so here, too, you should definitely call ahead to make a reservation (Fountain doesn't play every night, so call ahead to confirm when he's in town and performing). Pete Fountain is one of the legends of Dixieland jazz, having played with Al Hirt, the Dukes of Dixieland, and other top musicians of the genre. He first gained a national audience performing live on the Lawrence Walk show in the late '50s, and since then, he's been a guest on countless variety shows.

> *360° is one of the most memorable places to dance and have cocktails. Sometimes in New Orleans it's easy to forget you're in a true, modern city, but not when you're inside this 33rd-floor space—the world's largest revolving lounge, with panoramic views.*

Up on dodgy Rampart Street, mixed in with a handful of mostly divey gay bars, you'll find a pair of the French Quarter's hottest jazz venues, **Funky Butt at Congo Square** (714 N. Rampart St., 504/558-0872) and **Donna's** (800 N. Rampart St., 504/940-5442). The latter pulls in outstanding brass-band music, and also serves up delicious barbecued ribs. It's arguably the best place in town for modern jazz. Bilevel Funky Butt has live music on its second level, but you might just stop in for cocktails downstairs in the very sexy and inviting lounge. The whole place is flamboyantly decorated, and it's a favorite hangout of the Marsalis clan. It's so well-known for its music that people sometimes overlook the great food—the kitchen turns out very good Creole fare.

The aptly named **Snug Harbor Jazz Bistro** (626 Frenchmen St., 504/949-0696) is a cozy and classy spot in Faubourg Marigny where you can catch some of the city's top jazz acts and enjoy some pretty tasty food. Practically across the street is a far-less-famous jazz club that qualifies as one of the coolest little music finds in the city,

the **Spotted Cat** (623 Frenchmen St., 504/943-3887), a happily cramped and sweaty dance hall with a long happy hour, a nice selection of those designer martinis, and great live bands. There's jazz much of the time, usually with a danceable beat, plus rock, blues, bluegrass, salsa—you name it.

Uptown, the **Columns Hotel** (3811 St. Charles Ave., 504/522-0581), a splendid plantation-style mansion with ornate decor, presents exceptional New Orleans jazz in its lovely Victorian Lounge.

One of the cheesiest and most-likely-to-be-made-fun-of bars in town, the **Gennifer Flowers' Kelsto Club** (720 Bourbon St., 504/524-1111) showcases the "talent" of the woman infamous for alleging an affair with former President Bill Clinton. Customers are treated to a jazzy piano cabaret performance of silly songs that poke fun at a variety of subjects and contain a good bit of sexual innuendo.

Other excellent options for jazz include **Sweet Lorraine's** (1931 St. Claude Ave., 504/945-9654), a locals' favorite on a quiet, historic street on the edge of the Marigny. Open 24 hours, **Mo's Chalet** (3201 Houma Blvd., Metairie, 504/780-2961) is a favorite place to catch late-night jam sessions; there's jazz and blues here most evenings.

Soul and R&B

Andrew Jaeger's House of Seafood (622 Conti St., 504/522-4964) books some very good R&B acts, as does **Rhythms** (227 Bourbon St., 504/523-3800). The famed **Praline Connection** (907 South Peters St., 504/523-3973) presents a Sunday gospel brunch at its Warehouse District locale.

Ernie K-Doe's Mother-in-Law Lounge (1500 N. Claiborne Ave., 504/947-1078) was the haunt of one of New Orleans's most flamboyant musicians, Ernie "K-Doe" Kador, who passed away in 2001. K-Doe was noted for such R&B smash hits as "Mother-in-Law" and

"T'Ain't It the Truth," and his club in the Tremé neighborhood, a short cab ride from the Quarter (it's not generally safe to walk there), preserves his legacy by continuing to present first-rate R&B music by some of the city's legends. The jukebox has an impressive selection of classic tunes, also.

DANCE CLUBS

Among the high-energy haunts in the Quarter, the **Dungeon Bar** (738 Toulouse St., 504/523-5530) is a favorite place for popular dancing into the wee hours (it's open midnight to sunrise), as is tourist-filled **Utopia** (227 Bourbon St., 504/523-3800). **735 Nightclub and Bar** (735 Bourbon St., 504/581-6740) is a snazzy mixed gay/straight club where DJs spin everything from the latest trance and hip-hop to breakbeat and house. The place often hosts record-release parties.

The **Audubon Club** (1225 St. Charles Ave., 504/566-1717) is a favorite spot with college students and other young, well-dressed locals. It's a slick-looking bar, too, and it offers some great drink specials. **Ampersand** (1100 Tulane Ave., 504/587-3737) is a favorite spot for students and other young stylish things in the CBD. They have dancing some nights, hip-hop and reggae theme nights, plus Latin, international, R&B, and other good tunes you can dance to.

HIP LOUNGES

A beautiful space known for its designer martinis, the **Bombay Club** (830 Conti St., 504/586-0972) feels a bit like the library of an exclusive club. There's also a dining room serving quite good French-Asian bistro fare. A trendy spot across from House of Blues, the **Lounge Lizard** (200 Decatur St., 504/598-1500) is a bit less loud and frenetic but also presents a host of talented rock and blues bands most evenings.

An over-the-top, offbeat hangout with red velvet walls, ambient candlelight, and often campy bands, **El Matador** (504 Esplanade Ave., 504/569-8361) is especially renowned for its Saturday night flamenco dancing. You'll usually

find a pierced-and-tattooed bunch milling about the place. It's one of the few bona fide locals hangouts in the Quarter.

Metropolitan (310 Andrew Higgins Dr., 504/568-1702) is a swank lounge and dance club in the Warehouse District with a self-consciously hip crowd. One of the more scene-y options around town is the **Circle Bar** (1032 St. Charles Ave., 504/588-2616), with a retro decorative scheme and a cool crowd. It overlooks Lee Circle, near Hotel Le Cirque. A hot spot that opened in 2003 near Emeril's, the **Wine Loft** (752 Tchoupitoulas St., 504/561-0116) has handsome doormen, valet parking, and snazzy decor—it's nirvana for yuppies who like wine. Beware the attitude, but enjoy that big wine list (200 bottles, and 70 vintages available by the glass). The kitchen stays open late and serves up tasty little plates of creative finger foods (baked brie en croute, citrus-cured gravlax).

360° (World Trade Center, 33rd Floor, 2 Canal St., 504/522-9795) is one of the most memorable places to dance and have cocktails. Sometimes in New Orleans it's easy to forget you're in a true, modern city, but not when you're inside this 33rd-floor space—the world's largest revolving lounge and dance club, with panoramic views of the city and river. You pay for the view here—drinks are pricey.

GAY AND LESBIAN

New Orleans, especially the French Quarter and Faubourg Marigny, has one of the greatest concentrations of gay bars in the country. Most have a decidedly male following, but there is one lesbian bar in town. Most, also, are small and neighborhoody in feel, with either a very quiet or very cruisy ambience. The two most popular gay dance clubs sit opposite one another on Bourbon at the corner of St. Ann: The **Bourbon Pub/Parade Disco** (801 Bourbon St., 504/529-2107) and Oz (800 Bourbon St., 504/593-9491). The former has a slick dance floor upstairs and a typically packed video bar on the ground level, while **Oz** has dancing on the ground floor and more lounge-y spaces upstairs. Both have long wraparound balconies on the second floor, which are

Mardi Gras revelers on balcony of Oz

favorite perches from which to gaze at the throngs of revelers on Bourbon Street.

Just down Bourbon a block, **Cafe Lafitte in Exile** (901 Bourbon St., 504/522-8397) has been serving the gay community about as long as any bar in town. It draws more of a 30- to 50-something crowd, a bit more mature than at Oz and Bourbon Pub. Here, too, you can people-watch from an upper balcony. Other fun hangouts for gay folks include laid-back **Good Friends** (740 Dauphine St., 504/566-7191), which has a pool table and a low-attitude demeanor, and **MRB (Mississippi River Bottom)** (515 St. Philip St., 504/524-2558), just a block off Decatur Street, which is known for its leafy patio.

The Marigny also has several gay bars, the most popular being **Kim's** (940 Elysian Fields Ave., 504/944-4888), the city's premier (mostly) lesbian hangout, which is noted for its first-rate DJs. Across the street, **The Phoenix** (941 Elysian Fields Ave., 504/945-9264) is a dark and cruisy place popular with leather-and-Levi's types. For country-western two-stepping and line dancing, head to **Cowpokes** (2240 St. Claude Ave., 504/947-0505), the only such venue in New Orleans. It's in the Marigny. Although the club

welcomes everybody, it has a predominantly gay and lesbian following.

If you're out in Metairie, drop by **Angles** (2301 N. Causeway, 504/834-7979), the main gay and lesbian dance club and bar in those parts.

HOTEL BARS

Maybe the most famous hotel lounge in the city, the **Sazerac Bar & Grill** (123 Baronne St., 504/529-4733), at the grand Fairmont Hotel, is named for the noted drink, a concoction of rye whiskey and the local Peychaud's bitters. This is also a first-rate restaurant, serving creative New Orleans fare. The elegant Windsor Court Hotel presents live jazz trios in its classy **Le Salon Lounge** (300 Gravier St., 504/596-4773), which specializes in hard-to-find wines, champagnes, and specialty liquors. It's also the only smoke-free lounge in town. The hotel is home to the very clubby **Polo Lounge** (504/523-6000), a horse-y spot with oil paintings and polo photos and memorabilia.

The ultra-swank **Loft 523** (523 Gravier St., 504/200-6532) books cool jazz or tango bands in its intimate lounge with exposed-brick walls and

CASINOS IN THE BIG EASY

It's not exactly Las Vegas, and the Louisiana cities of Shreveport and Lake Charles are considerably more popular as gambling hubs, but metro New Orleans does have a pair of 24-hour gaming facilities.

The mother ship for gamblers here, **Harrah's New Orleans Casino** (512 South Peters St., 504/533-6000, www.harrahsneworleans.com) opened in the late '90s under a cloud of controversy. It's the largest gaming facility in the South, a massive facility with 2,900 slot machines and 125 gaming tables. A restaurant serves traditional American fare and isn't really worth the visit unless you happen already to be here gambling.

The metro area's second big gaming hall is **Treasure Chest Casino** (5000 Williams Blvd., Kenner, 504/443-8000, www.treasurechest-casino.com), which is actually a floating casino docked on Lake Pontchartrain and fairly near New Orleans International Airport. There's live entertainment here nightly, a poker room, and a buffet restaurant.

nice place to unwind, or perhaps play backgammon, after catching a show or concert at the nearby Saenger Theatre. A cart loaded with expensive chocolates circles the room, doling out sweets to go with the cocktails. The hotel's **French Quarter Bar** (504/524-1331) presents live jazz many evenings and serves a full menu of New Orleans fare. And in the regal lobby lounge, you can listen to live piano and soulful crooning in the evenings, and enjoy a sumptuous afternoon tea during the daytime.

At the Royal Sonesta Hotel, the **Can-Can Cafe** (300 Bourbon St., 504/586-0300) has long been acclaimed for its outstanding Dixieland jazz shows. Recline in a plush sofa at the **Living Room** (316 Chartres St., 504/581-1200), a supremely inviting lounge with book-lined shelves and game tables at the W New Orleans—French Quarter. Soak up the literary history and old-world ambience of the dignified Hotel Monteleone by having drinks in the colorful **Carousel Bar** (214 Royal St., 504/523-3341), in which an almost kitschy 1940s 24-seat bar—festooned with bright lights and garish decorations—slowly revolves around the center of the room.

mod, low-slung furniture. There's dancing to a DJ late into the evenings when live musicians aren't performing. At the similarly fabuous International House, **Loa Bar** (221 Camp St., 504/553-9550) feels both hip and vaguely spiritual ("Loa" refers to deities or divine spirits in voodoo tradition), with its tall Gothic church mirrors and the glow of hundreds of candles. Where some modern bars feel overdesigned and uncomfortable, Loa offers plenty of sumptuous sofa seating, and the staff is surprisingly relaxed and friendly.

The W New Orleans attracts a cool clientele to its **Whiskey Blue** (333 Poydras St., 504/525-9444) cocktail lounge with leather club chairs, banquette seating, and slick contemporary decor. Noted nightlife celeb Randy Gerber, husband of Cindy Crawford, runs this and a similar operation in New York City.

At Ritz-Carlton, the **Library Lounge** (921 Canal St., 504/524-1331) is a quite fabulous fireside lounge with a walk-in humidor and a list of fine wines, scotches, and aperitifs—it's a

RESTAURANT BARS

Many, even most, of the restaurants described in the Food chapter of this book also double as popular spots for cocktails, live music, and socializing, sometimes into the wee hours. The majority of them are better known for dining than for drinking. Here's a rundown of some of the best restaurants at which to hoist a mug (or, more likely, clink martini glasses):

Tujague's (823 Decatur St., 504/525-8676) is famous for its original cypress-wood bar and elegant French mirror, which was imported from Paris the year this classic Creole bar and tavern opened, 1856. The ancient café at the GB>Napoleon House Cafe (500 Chartres St., 504/524-9752) is a great place to soak up the Quarter's rich history—they also serve cheap and delicious food in here. Another nice place to nosh while drinking is the oyster bar at Ralph Brennan's **Red Fish Grill** (115 Bourbon St., 504/598-1200), a good place to begin a bar crawl along Bourbon Street.

Coops (1109 Decatur St., 504/525-9053) is a comfortably worn pub in the heart of the Quarter, near the French Market, with exemplary bar food—it draws a loyal bunch of locals and repeat tourists. **Crescent City Brewhouse** (527 Decatur St., 504/522-0571) has different types of live music most nights and is usually a lot of fun. Offbeat **Igor's Check Point Charlie** (501 Esplanade Ave., 504/949-7012, $4–12) is a music club, restaurant, pool place, and self-serve laundry—what more could you ask for? The crowd tends to be youthful and countercultural, and the live bands tend to be blues and jazz, along with a healthy dose of alternative rock. The dark, seductive ambience of the **Dragon's Room** (435 Esplanade Ave., 504/949-1750) seems vaguely reminiscent of an opium den; it's above Siam Cafe Thai restaurant, serves as the perfect setting for colorful cocktails and catching groovy lounge music.

On the ground floor of Adolfo's, in the Marigny, the dark and cozy Apple Barrel Bar (611 Frenchmen St., 504/948-3800) is happily low-keyed yet hip, nice for cocktails before heading out to the noisier music clubs along Frenchmen. Just up the street, **Wasabi** (900 Frenchmen St., 504/943-9433) is half trendy sushi bar, and half refreshingly untrendy neighborhood bar serving great Japanese beer. At the festive Jamaican restaurant **Cafe Negril** (606 Frenchmen St., 504/944-4744), drop by many evenings for live reggae music and ska bands.

Suits and powerbrokers hobnob at the tiny but popular bar in **Herbsaint** (701 St. Charles Ave., 504/524-4114), one of the CBD's hippest restaurants. It's less chaotic and intense than some of the other high-profile restaurant lounges in the neighborhood, such as **Cobalt** (333 St. Charles Ave., 504/565-5595), at the ultra-swank Hotel Monaco. At the other end of the spectrum, the Warehouse District's **Mulate's** (201 Julia St., 504/522-1492) is a giant, down-home Cajun dance hall with live bands and plenty of dancing. The laid-back **Ugly Dog Saloon & BBQ** (401 Andrew Higgins Dr., 504/569-8459, $4–10), which occupies a slightly ugly Warehouse District building, has terrific happy-hour deals, tasty barbecue, and a chatty staff. Stop by hip but easygoing **Sugar Magnolia**

(1910 Magazine St., 504/529-1110) to mingle with Garden District locals and employees from the neighborhood's several antiques shops. Uptown's **Clancy's** (6100 Annunciation St., 504/895-1111) is the quintessential feel-good neighborhood restaurant, with the quintessential feel-good neighborhood bar. **Igor's Buddha Belly Burger Bar** (4437 Magazine St., 504/891-6105) is similar in feel and concept to its sibling Check Point Charlie, although its relative proximity to Tulane and Loyola give it more of a collegiate ambience.

The bar at **Restaurant Indigo** (2285 Bayou Rd., 504/947-0123) captures the elegance of an old-world New Orleans supper club. Few people venture out of their way here solely to partake of the cocktail bar, making it a bit of a sleeper in this category (the restaurant is white-hot popular, tho, so the bar does tend to fill up with patrons waiting for tables on weekend evenings). Out in Metairie, 9-to-5ers like to relax after work at trendy **P.F. Chang's China Bistro** (Lakeside Shopping Center, 3301 Veterans Memorial Blvd., Metairie, 504/828-5288, $9–18).

SINGLES HAUNTS

All the rage of late, especially among under-30 tourists, is **Coyote Ugly Saloon** (225 N. Peters St., 504/561-0003), a hormonally charged pick-up joint named for the giddy movie about, aptly, a bunch of beautiful women tending bar at a hormonally charged pick-up joint (in New York City). **d.b.a.** (618 Frenchmen St., 504/942-3731), a hipster-infested hangout in Faubourg Marigny, is a good place to meet locals, hear live bands, and drink from a selection of about a zillion kinds of beer (plus many types of whisky and tequila). The crowd is young and laidback but with a touch of style. It's much like its counterpart, in New York City's artsy East Village.

Lucy's Retired Surfers Bar (701 Tchoupitoulas St., 504/523-8995; 5961 Magazine St., 504/895-0240) feels like frat-sorority party most evenings, especially weekends. It's known as one of the city's more popular meat markets, and it's also great place to suck down margaritas. A festive Aussie-inspired bar in the Warehouse District, **Vic's Kangaroo Cafe** (636 Tchoupitoulas St.,

Lafitte's Blacksmith Shop, French Quarter

504/524-4329) has live music throughout the week and serves up fairly traditional Down Under pub fare. It's on a quiet stretch of Tchoupitoulas, in a haggard old building, but it's quite festive inside. The crowd is young and raucous. Fun-loving locals mix it up with tourists at **Polynesian Joe's** (869 Magazine St., 504/525-9301), a giddy and kitschy South Seas–themed place with its own sandpit volleyball court. The kitchen prepares pretty decent Cajun and Creole, fare, too.

It's nothing special for food, but **Samuel's Oyster Bar & Grille** (1628 St. Charles Ave., 504/581-3777) is reliable drinks, has a good happy hour crowd (three-for-one drinks early on Wednesday evenings), and is a convenient option if you're staying at one of the several hotels on or near St. Charles in the Lower Garden District. The best seating is on the deck overlooking the street.

Mingle with University of New Orleans students and area locals well away from the tourist districts at **The Dock** (1926 West End Park, 504/284-3625), a festive lakefront bar with live rock and blues and great water views. It's a 15- to 20-minute drive north of the Quarter—take I-10 to West End Blvd., and follow this up toward the lake.

Handy to know about if you've got time to kill before a flight, **Vesper's Bar and Grill** (1414 Veteran's Memorial Blvd., Metairie, 504/833-0050) has a long weekdays happy hour (3–8 P.M.), which makes it a favorite of locals and travelers. There's also a long menu of burgers, pizzas, Cuban sandwiches, and other casual fare. There's live music many evenings, and it's also a popular placing for dancing late on weekends.

NEIGHBORHOOD HANGOUTS

In a touristy part of the Quarter but on a somewhat quiet block, **Kerry Irish Pub** (331 Decatur St., 504/527-5954) is cozy if not especially Irish-looking—it has live music many nights, brick floors, Tiffany hanging lamps, and dollar bills and other currency taped to the bar ceiling. Some music is Irish but other times you'll hear traditional folk performers. The highly atmospheric **Lafitte's Blacksmith Shop** (941 Bourbon St., 504/523-0066) occupies the oldest building in North America still used as a bar. It's a great place just to while away an evening, drawing a cool mix of locals and those tourists perseverant enough to wander beyond the busiest blocks of Bourbon.

A rough-and-tumble low-frills pub with a bizarre crowd of employees of other bars and restaurants, tattooed and pierced types, Goths, and other characters, **The Abbey** (1123 Decatur St., 504/523-7150) is a popular place to get drunk, nurse a hangover, and get drunk again— without necessarily ever leaving. Don't be afraid— it's really not as menacing as it sounds, or looks for that matter; just pop in, grab a bar stool, and take in the local color. On the edge of the Marigny, the low-keyed (okay, divey) **Hi-Ho Lounge** (2239 St. Claude Ave., 504/947-9344) is a neighborhood hangout that books some enjoyable rock and jazz bands minus the crowds and craziness of the Quarter.

A nice place to mix your appreciation of a good drink with your admiration of religious iconography, **St. Joe's** (5535 Magazine St., 504/899-3744) is a quintessential Uptown neighborhood bar with a twist: the place is filled with ancient wooden crosses, recovered church pews, votive candles, and other vestiges of Christianity. The vibe is funky and slightly irreverent, and there's a cool juke and a cheery patio out back. Another of the neighborhood's cool spots for mingling and hoisting a frosty mug of beer, **Le Bon Temps Rouler** (4801 Magazine St., 504/895-8117) draws in a full range of Uptowners, from college students to hipsters to music fans—there are live rock and blues bands some nights (usually no cover charge) and always a stellar jukebox. The place also turns out decent pub grub— quesadillas, chili cheeseburgers, wings, etc. Out by the campuses of Tulane and Loyola, **T.J. Quills** (7600 Maple St., 504/866-5205) is a favorite for inexpensive boozing, especially into the wee hours—it's a casual tavern where students stop off for a nightcap (or seven) on their way back from clubbing downtown.

A laid-back and decent enough Mexican restaurant, **Superior Grill** (3636 St. Charles Ave., 504/899-2400) becomes one of the hottest happy hours in town on Wednesdays. What's the big draw? Perhaps it's those three-for-one margaritas that keeps everybody smiling. You'll mostly find a locals bunch at the friendly **Half Moon Bar** (1125 St. Mary St., 504/522-0599),

near Coliseum Square in the Lower Garden District. It's a nice place to shoot a game of pool or have a beer after antiques-shopping or exploring this funky neighborhood.

A happy little dive with something of a hipster following and a truly age- and style-varied following, the **Red Eye Grill** (852 South Peters St., 504/593-9393) is just a zero-decor hangout that feels colorful only because it's filled each night with friendly and enthusiastic revelers. It's not quite a singles scene, but meeting people is certainly the focus for some patrons. The place also serves hefty burgers and other good pub fare.

The **Ernst Cafe** (600 South Peters St., 504/525-8544) has been a popular bar since the Warehouse District was, well, a warehouse district—the high-ceilinged corner bar opened in 1902. It occupies a handsome late-Victorian corner building with a long, curving wrought-iron balcony, and today it's mostly a place for after-work drinks and casual food. The location, near many hotels and the convention center, is a big draw.

RIVERBOAT TOURS

The 1,000-passenger *Creole Queen* **Paddle-wheeler** (27 Poydras St. Wharf, 504/529-4567 or 800/445-4109, www.neworleanspaddlewheels .com) offers Dixieland jazz dinner cruises nightly. Arrive at 7 P.M. for the two-hour excursion, which leaves port at 8 P.M. There are also two daytime cruises, at 10:30 A.M. and 2 P.M., respectively, which include lunch and a tour of Chalmette Battlefield, site of the Battle of New Orleans. This authentic, period-style paddlewheeler, powered by a massive 24-foot-diameter wheel, is decorated with Victorian-style furniture and a polished parquet dance floor. Fares range from $16–22 for daytime excursions (depending on whether you partake of the optional lunch) and $50 for dinner cruises.

The **Steamboat** *Natchez* (Toulouse St. Wharf, behind JacksonBrewery, 504/586-8777, www .steamboatnatchez.com) offers daily cruises with live jazz music along the river. The original *Natchez* was constructed in 1823 and served the important Mississippi River trade route between the cities of Natchez, Mississippi, and New Orleans. The present *Natchez,* which is 265 feet long and 44 feet wide, was constructed in 1975 and bears a close resemblance to the grand steamboats of the 19th century. However, today's boat is quite luxurious, and fully air-conditioned, for which the 1,600 passengers it accommodates are surely grateful. Fares range from $18–25 for daytime excursions (typically at lunchtime and during the afternoon), and $28–50 for evening cruises; the higher fares include lunch or dinner.

As hokey as it may seem to hop aboard one of these tourist ships, both the *Creole Queen* and the *Natchez* book first-rate Dixieland jazz bands, and these jaunts along the river afford spectacular views of the city's skyline. The food offered is generally good, if unspectacular (keep in mind that menus are designed for hundreds of passengers to dine at the same sitting.) Prime rib, Southern fried chicken, and catfish *louisiane* (with Cajun spices and a white-wine marinade) are typical.

Festivals and Events

If you're a fan of colorful, exciting festivals, there is—of course—no better time to visit New Orleans than during Mardi Gras and the Carnival season that leads up to it for several weeks. The wild goings-on during Mardi Gras in the New Orleans French Quarter have given the overall event a reputation for debauchery. Indeed, if you're seeking that kind of an experience, the Quarter on Fat Tuesday will not let you down.

But Mardi Gras elsewhere in the city, notably in Uptown along the St. Charles Avenue parade route, is much more family-oriented and tends to be dominated by locals, or at least by Louisianans. Furthermore, just about every community in the state throws memorable Mardi Gras parades, parties, and other events leading up to the big day, and these, too, cater to locals and families and have a more wholesome feel.

And Mardi Gras is just the tip of the iceberg. Year-round, New Orleans and Louisiana offer a full dance card of festivals and special events worth building a trip around. As you might guess, the majority of these events revolve around food, music and art, but you'll find celebrations of everything from the city's rich ethnic cultures to popular holidays with Big Easy slant. Events held in summer, when tourism slows, often appeal more to other Louisianans, and they can be great fun.

Especially for Mardi Gras and Jazz Fest, but also for some of the other popular events in town (weekends leading up to Christmas, July Fourth, the French Quarter Festival, and Southern Decadence), the city can fill up fast, so it's wise to book well ahead. And if you're not interested in these most popular events, you should avoid visiting when they're scheduled. The biggest events tend to dominate the city and draw some serious crowds.

JAZZ FEST

Officially called the **New Orleans Jazz & Heritage Festival** (504/522-4786, www.nojazzfest.com), this music fan's dream come true has been going strong since 1969 and has grown to be nearly as popular as Mardi Gras. The 12 stages buzzing with jazz musicians of every persuasion and sub-genre are the main reason to come, but it's also a time to attend music workshops and arts and crafts sales and demonstrations, and to sample an unbelievable array of great foods served at some 150 stalls. On Monday and Tuesday in the middle of Jazz Fest, you can attend the low-key MO Fest, a showcase for local up-and-coming musicians held at Woldenberg Park. Six acts perform each afternoon.

Jazz Fest organizers always work out deals with dozens of local hotels, so if you book ahead, as only a limited number of rooms are blocked at each property, you can secure a pretty good rate, ranging from $89 at some of the chain properties on the West Bank and in Metairie to $149 at lower-end downtown hotels (Hampton Inn, Courtyard Marriott), to well into the $200s for the upper-end business-oriented hotels in the Quarter and CBD. Just call the participating hotel that interests you (a full list is available at the festival website), and ask for the rate code NJF.

ENTERTAINMENT

MARDI GRAS

It's appropriate that New Orleans should have the most famous Mardi Gras—or Carnival—celebration in the United States. It was on Mardi Gras that explorer Pierre Le Moyne, Sieur d'Iberville, first encamped here along the Mississippi River. Well, to be exact, Le Moyne chose a spot about 60 miles downriver from today's New Orleans, but his visit marked its beginning.

Mardi Gras (French for "Fat Tuesday") is known in many parts of the world as Carnival, from the Italian for "taking away the meat" or "putting away the flesh." For some people, Mardi Gras is *the* time to visit New Orleans, but it's not for everyone; this rollicking celebration draws intense crowds. Though the parades are free, the city's hotels book up, and the costs of airfare and parking skyrocket—still, the people-watching, and the chance to catch beads and trinkets, can warrant the inconvenience.

You can have a great time, while saving money and avoiding crowds, by checking out Mardi Gras in a smaller Louisiana city. Lafayette, in the heart of Cajun Country, has probably the second-biggest Mardi Gras in the state, and Baton Rouge has a good one, as do the communities along the North Shore of Lake Pontchartrain, in St. Tammany and Tangipahoa Parishes.

Many of Louisiana's smaller rural communities hold *Courir de Mardi Gras* (literally, "the Running of the Mardi Gras"). This event dates back to the Cajun migration, with roots in medieval France. During Courir de Mardi Gras, groups on horseback, in carriages, and in pickup trucks race about the countryside, knocking on doors and "begging" for ingredients for a massive communal pot of gumbo. They sing, dance, or engage in shenanigans in their attempts to solicit chicken, rice, sausage, and onions. At the end of the day, celebrants gather for a gumbo feast and fais-do-do (Cajun dance party).

History and Customs

Mardi Gras's most famous events are parades and gala balls sponsored and hosted by private clubs, called krewes. The parades and ball have new theme each year, typically a historical or mythical event. A parade has a lead float, a king's float, then a couple of dozen more floats. About 65 krewes hold parades during the Carnival season.

The krewe's captain leads the procession on a float or on horseback, followed by that year's officers (kings, queens, and so on), followed by marching bands, motorcycle squads, teams of clowns, and other entertainers. A gala ball follows, during which the royal court and its officers, in flamboyant costume, are feted into the wee hours. The galas are private (and if you are invited, it's tuxedos or tails for men, floor-length gowns for women).

Those walking or riding the parade throw trinkets, bead necklaces, and doubloons (commemorative coins) to the spectators lining the route. It's said that during parade season, watchers are festooned with some 3 million plastic commemorative cups, 2 million gross beads, and well over 20 million doubloons.

Everybody ends up catching something during a Mardi Gras parade. Enhance your odds by screaming at the top of your lungs, wearing a costume, making eye contact, and having adorable kids by your side—that trick works so well, it's worth borrowing kids for the event. Along the main parade route you'll see hundreds of stepladders where people plop their young kids so they'll be able to see over the standing adults. The traditional call of parade watchers hoping to catch goodies and treats is "Throw me something, Mister," but you won't hear many people saying this anymore. Sometimes what you do hear is off-color and amusing.

In New Orleans, documentation exists of Mardi Gras parades first being held in 1837, but the krewes were not formed until 1857, when Krewe of Comus illuminated the city with its fiery torches. Comus started the tradition of pageant-style parades, with dancers and entertainers frolicking on the street alongside the floats and marchers.

Lafayette crowned its first king in 1897 and has been throwing the biggest Mardi Gras parades and balls outside New Orleans ever since. One nice thing is that the Southwest Louisiana Mardi Gras Association Pageant and Ball in Lafayette welcomes the public. Elsewhere, Mardi Gras balls are usually private, sometimes with ties to the debutante season.

The Rex Parade uses the Fatted Ox, or Boeuf Gras, as its symbol, to represent the last meat feast before Lent. Rex is the king of Mardi Gras, and he arrives in New Orleans by riverboat on Lundi Gras (Fat Monday), when there's a huge party at Spanish Plaza, on the Mississippi River. Admission is free, but you must wear a Mardi Gras mask.

You'll see three colors when watching Mardi Gras: purple, green, and gold. These hues represent justice, faith, and power, and were introduced to New Orleans Mardi Gras in 1872 by the first parade of Rex, which also gave Mardi Gras an official theme song, "If Ever I Cease to Love," from a burlesque play of that period.

King cakes, crumbly coffeecake-like confections iced in the colors of Mardi Gras, are sold at bakeries all over the city through Ash Wednesday. A small plastic baby is baked into each king cake, and the person whose piece of cake contains this trinket is responsible for providing next year's king cake.

Practicalities

Hotels book up a full year in advance, but many people cancel— you can often find reasonable rooms on a few weeks' notice.

For all practical purposes, Mardi Gras weekend extends from the Friday before Fat Tuesday through midnight on Fat Tuesday. As the clock tolls midnight on Tuesday, Mardi Gras comes to an abrupt end, and cleaning crews swarm the Quarter and the parade route, embarking on the Herculean task of removing debris, cups, and broken beads.

Mardi Gras season always kicks off on the same day, but the date of Fat Tuesday varies from year to year. Everything begins on January 6, the Twelfth Night Feast of the Epiphany. Fat Tuesday is the day before Lent, when Christians traditionally feast on meat before giving it up for 40 days. Thus, Mardi Gras always falls 46 days before Easter, and before the first day of Lent, Ash Wednesday. In 2004, it falls on February 24; in 2005 it's February 8; in 2006 it's February 28; and in 2007, it's February 20.

No official parades run through the French Quarter—the streets are simply too narrow. But there's plenty going on there, from smaller informal groups staging their own processions to spectators tossing beads off balconies to (often drunken) revelers on the streets below. The goings-on in the Quarter are not family-oriented, and partying, exhibitionism, and all-around debauchery are typical.

Parade routes are listed in the *New Orleans Times-Picayune*. Many hotels distribute free guides to guests, and a handful of magazines dedicated to Mardi Gras are available at city bookstores and newsstands.

ENTERTAINMENT

The rates come with certain restrictions, such as deposits or, in some cases, full prepayment, plus minimum-night stays that vary from property to property.

WINTER

Christmastime is simply huge in New Orleans, celebrated with great fanfare, as befits a city that loves to celebrate and clings dearly to long-held traditions. Many restaurants in town present special Reveillon dinner menus and there are jazz, gospel, choral, and just about every other kind of concert held throughout the month at a variety of clubs, but also right on Jackson Square in front of St. Louis Cathedral. Food lovers should check the website of *Louisiana Cookin'* magazine (www.louisianacookin.com), as that publication sponsors a series of free cooking demonstrations at Le Petit Theater (616 St. Peter St.), held almost daily at 3 P.M. throughout the month. Chefs from top restaurants around town come by and show how to prepare everything from duck and andouille chowder to bread pudding with whiskey sauce.

The plantations on the river road gussy up with Christmas decorations and throw a variety of events and concerts, there's caroling along the New Orleans riverfront many evenings, Chanukah is celebrated at Congregation Temple Sinai (6227 St. Charles Ave.), and huge bonfires are lit along the river in towns throughout southern Louisiana. One favorite tradition is the **Candlelight Tour of Historic Homes and Landmarks** (504/522-5730), held in mid-December and involving such attractions as the Old Ursuline Convent, the 1850 House museum, and the Gallier House. Also, from late November through January 5, City Park comes alive for the **Celebration in the Oaks** (504/483-9415), a fabulous holiday light show that draws more than a half-million visitors annually. You can drive through the park, walk the 2-mile route, or see it on a horse-drawn carriage ride. Sights include a life-size re-created Acadian village with live zydeco and Cajun music, and the park's Storyland playground is given holiday decorations. This trip through the largest live-oak forest in the world is not to be missed during the holidays. For a full list of

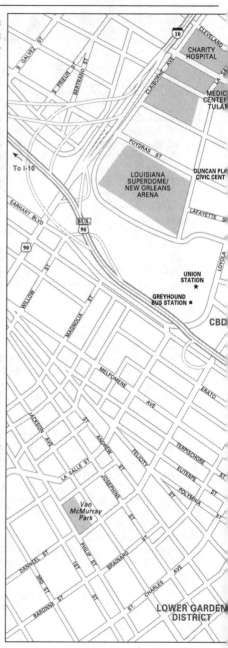

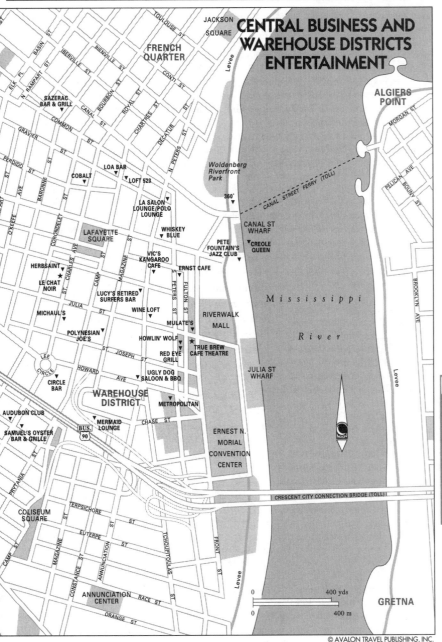

CENTRAL BUSINESS AND
WAREHOUSE DISTRICTS
ENTERTAINMENT

JACKSON SQUARE

FRENCH QUARTER

ALGIERS POINT

SAZERAC BAR & GRILL

LOA BAR

COBALT

LOFT 523

LA SALON LOUNGE/POLO LOUNGE

WHISKEY BLUE

LAFAYETTE SQUARE

VIC'S KANGAROO CAFE

ERNST CAFE

PETE FOUNTAIN'S JAZZ CLUB

CANAL ST WHARF

CREOLE QUEEN

HERBSAINT

LE CHAT NOIR

LUCY'S RETIRED SURFERS BAR

WINE LOFT

MICHAUL'S

MULATE'S

RIVERWALK MALL

Woldenberg Riverfront Park

360°

CANAL STREET FERRY (TOLL)

POLYNESIAN JOE'S

HOWLIN' WOLF

RED EYE GRILL

TRUE BREW CAFE THEATRE

Mississippi River

CIRCLE BAR

UGLY DOG SALOON & BBQ

JULIA ST WHARF

WAREHOUSE DISTRICT

METROPOLITAN

AUDUBON CLUB

MERMAID LOUNGE

SAMUEL'S OYSTER BAR & GRILLE

BUS. 90

CHASE ST

ERNEST N. MORIAL CONVENTION CENTER

CRESCENT CITY CONNECTION BRIDGE (TOLL)

COLISEUM SQUARE

TERPSICHORE

EUTERPE

ANNUNCIATION CENTER

RACE ST

ORANGE ST

GRETNA

0   400 yds
0   400 m

ENTERTAINMENT

© AVALON TRAVEL PUBLISHING, INC.

events and concerts held in the city, check the website: www.christmasneworleans.com.

On New Year's Eve, you can take a special Mississippi River cruise aboard the **Steamboat Natchez** (504/586-8777 or 800/233-BOAT, www.steamboatnatchez.com); it features dancing and great food, and it's a terrific vantage point for catching the **New Year's Eve Midnight Fireworks** held along the riverfront.

Devotees of the city's most famous literary luminary rush to the Big Easy in late March to attend the **Tennessee Williams/New Orleans Literary Festival,** www.tennesseewilliams.net, which celebrates the playwright who gave us such iconographic works as *A Streetcar Named Desire* and *The Glass Menagerie.* The five-day gathering is replete with writing classes helmed by experts and notables, celebrity interviews, panel discussions, stagings of Williams plays, a walking tour, poetry slams, and the always enjoyable Stanley and Stella Shouting Contest. Attendees in recent years have included George Plimpton, Dorothy Allison, Diane McWhorter, and Jim Grimsley.

Introduced to New Orleans during the 19th century by its many Sicilian immigrants, **St. Joseph's Day** is still celebrated with great élan in the city's Italian-American community. The observance of this feast on March 19 traces back to the Middle Ages, when people built altars to St. Joseph, who they believed had answered their prayers and delivered them from famine. Modern participants continue to celebrate by constructing elaborate and riotously colorful altars in their homes and churches. An altar is also displayed in the CBD at the International House hotel (see their website, www.ihhotel.com/stjosephsday.html for details). Public St. Joseph's Day festivities occur in the CBD's Piazza D'Italia, at 300 Poydras Street. Smaller celebrations take place in private homes—signs welcome friends and strangers alike in to view family altars and enjoy cakes,

> *Devotees of the city's most famous literary luminary rush to the Big Easy in late March to attend the Tennessee Williams/New Orleans Literary Festival, which celebrates the playwright who gave us such iconographic works as* **A Streetcar Named Desire** *and* The Glass Menagerie.

breads, and other foods. Be sure to take them up on their hospitality.

SPRING

Far less touristy than some of the big New Orleans events and quite fun, mid-April's **French Quarter Festival** (800/673-5725, www.french quarterfestival.com) presents a few hundred local musicians on more than a dozen stages around the Quarter. Some excellent bands attend, performing everything from blues to zydeco to gospel. There's a fireworks display on the Mississippi, and some 60 booths serve food and drinks. Art exhibits and children's activities round out the fun.

The nation's fifth-largest 10K road race, the **Crescent City Classic** (www.ccc10k.com) is held in New Orleans each April. About 18,000 athletes from some 20 nations run through the French Quarter, up Esplanade Avenue, and to City Park.

In May, fans of one of nature's most perfect little fruits (no, it's not a vegetable) head over to Chalmette's **Tomato Festival,** a great time to sample Creole tomatoes (which were first grown in Haiti and popularized here when the early French settlers fled to New Orleans in the early 1800s).

Late May is the perfect time for foodies and wine buffs to visit the Big Easy, for the **New Orleans Wine & Food Experience** (www.nowfe.com), a mouthwatering event where some 800 wines from more than 250 wineries are featured, along with food from about 100 of the city's top restaurants.

SUMMER

In early June, thousands pile into the Louisiana Superdome for the **Indoor Super Fair** (504/587-3800), an event geared especially toward families and kids. For about a week, the dome is filled with amusement rides, food booths, carnival games, and live music. $10 gets you a day's worth of unlimited rides—a pretty good deal, especially on weekends when the fair runs from noon till midnight (it runs 5 to 11 P.M. on weekdays). On June 8, the official World Ocean Day, the Audubon Aquarium celebrates **Ocean Fest** (www.auduboninstitute.org), a great time to learn about the oceans of the world through shows and exhibits, and also participate in a variety of kids' activities, from face-painting to arts and crafts.

Fourth of July celebrations are staged in several area towns (Hammond, Bogalusa, Slidell, Mandeville, Thibodaux), as well as New Orleans itself, with **Go 4th on the River** (www.go4thontheriver.com), an all-day extravaganza held at Woldenberg Park with live bands, cruises on vintage paddlewheel riverboats, and special events all along the riverfront, from the French Market to the Riverwalk shops. You can also ferry over to **Blaine Kern's 4th of July Party** (504/361-7821, www.mardigrasworld.com), held at the world-famous Mardi Gras float-making factory and museum, on the West Bank just across the river from the Quarter. There's barbecue and burgers, door prizes, and a spectacular fireworks show on the levee, which you can see from all around downtown. A bit mellower and more local in feel is Kenner's **Fourth of July Freedom Fest,** a fireworks and music party held at the grounds of the Treasure Chest Casino.

The **Essence Music Festival** (www.essence.com) presents the music of dozens of African-American musicians over three days and nights in early July. You can also attend about 15 different seminars and talks that touch on political, social, and religious issues, and you can browse Afro-centric crafts, art, books, souvenirs, and food at a festival market. A short drive southwest of New Orleans at St. Gertrude Catholic Church in Des Allemands, mid-July marks the **Louisiana Catfish Festival** (985/758-7542), a time to appreciate that favorite freshwater fish of the South. There are catfish-cooking demonstrations and competitions, and more frightening, catfish-eating contests, plus music, rides, and carnival games.

New Orleans celebrates the legacy of one of its most famous sons in early August with **Satchmo Summerfest,** www.satchmosummerfest.com, which includes live music by brass, swing, and early jazz bands. The mostly free festival also includes a jazz mass, local foods, and discussions and exhibits on Louis "Satchmo" Armstrong and his era.

FALL

Labor Day Weekend is the **Southern Decadence Celebration** (www.southerndecadence.com, 504/522-8049), a Mardi Gras–like gay and lesbian three-day festival held at venues throughout the Quarter and Faubourg Marigny, and including dance parties, drag shows, and a leather-gear block party. It's one of the wildest and most popular gay-and-lesbian celebrations in the country. In the middle of September, **Inter-Fest & Expo** (504/581-2860, www.inter-fest.org), held at Louis Armstrong Park, is a two-day celebration of the many ethnic cultures that make up New Orleans. Myriad styles of dance, song, films, art, and food are presented.

Fear not if you're skittish about severe weather: the **Southern Comfort Hurricane Festival** (504/522-5555) is about the famed Louisiana cocktail (nowadays typically made with rum, Southern Comfort, orange juice, and sweet-and-citrusy Hurricane mix) and watching live rock bands. The talent includes a mix of local and national music acts, usually some pretty big names. It's held at Riverfront Park, behind Audubon Park Zoo, in late September.

Across the river in early October, the **Gretna Heritage Festival** (www.gretnafest.com) features live music, events at the German Heritage Center, a German beer garden, rides and games, an arts-and-crafts show, and other fun activities. There's also a big flea market, the **Collector's Fest** (504/486-7691), held in downtown Gretna a week or so before. Around the same time, the Audubon Zoo hosts **Tony Chachere's Louisiana Swamp Festival** (800/774-7394, www.auduboninstitute.org). Arts and crafts are sold throughout the zoo, which also offers plenty of animal feedings and up-close animal activities, live Cajun and zydeco music, and the food of Louisiana's Cajun Country: boudin noir, cracklins, seafood po'boys, fried alligator, and so on.

In mid-October, the small suburb of Bridge City, just across the river from Harahan via the Huey P. Long Bridge, hosts the two-day **Gumbo Festival** (504/436-4712), which affords visitors the chance to sample many types of gumbo and other Cajun foods and to listen to Cajun music. To work off all that eating, there's a 5K run. Late in October, the Audubon Institute (www .auduboninstitute.org) sponsors kids-oriented Halloween-themed activities at its facilities— these include **Boo at the Zoo** (including a zoo "ghost" train and trick-or-treating) and the similarly ghoulish **Scarium at the Aquarium.**

The Performing Arts

Although New Orleans can claim one of the world's most dynamic live-music scenes, it's relatively less famous as a center of the performing arts. Still, you'll find a handful of very good theaters and performance halls in New Orleans and the towns surrounding it. There are only a few large-scale venues for formal concerts and theatrical performances, and, in fact, many big-name musicians favor comparatively small-time stages when their tour stops in this city. New Orleanians are loyal, knowledgeable, and excited about music, and performers appreciate the enthusiasm and enjoy playing a club that's small enough to encourage a close connection between the musicians and the fans.

There are a handful of mostly independent, fringe-style theaters in New Orleans, plus a few places where national touring companies perform Broadway hits and top-selling rock stars throw shows. Beyond that, it takes almost no planning and very little effort to find a place to catch a jamming live show in New Orleans, even on a Monday or Tuesday night. Just check the listings of some of the papers listed below to see who's on where, or simply stroll through the French Quarter. More than a dozen clubs along Bourbon Street have music bellowing from their doors every night of the week, and these places rarely charge a cover (although they will typically have a one- or two-drink minimum).

The colorful free entertainment paper *Gambit Weekly* (504/486-5900, www.bestofnewor-leans.com) is an indispensable resource for finding out what's playing around town. The publication *OffBeat* (504/944-4300 or 877/944-4300, http://offbeat.com) is the best source in the state for learning about Louisiana's music scene, recordings by local artists, and where to catch live performances. *Where Y'at Magazine* (504/891-0144, www.whereyat.net) is another good place for arts and nightlife listings, as is *Lagniappe* (504/826-3464, www.timespicayune.com), which is produced on Fridays by the *Times-Picuyane.*

For general information, listings, and calendars pertaining to the arts throughout New Orleans and Louisiana, contact the **Louisiana Division of the Arts** (P.O. Box 44247, Baton Rouge, LA 70804, 225/342-8180, www.crt.state.la.us/arts). The organization's main function is to write grants for people involved in the arts in Louisiana, but the website also has useful links to local groups involved in arts-in-education, dance, design arts, folklife, literature, music, theater, and visual arts and crafts. The site has a detailed calendar that lists arts events of all types throughout the state.

THEATER AND CONCERT VENUES

At Tulane, check out what's showing at **Dixon Hall** (Newcomb Pl. off Freret St., 504/865-5105, www.tulane.edu); it's usually a classical-music concert, or a student theater or dance production. Tulane also sponsors and hosts the annual **Shakespeare Festival** (www.neworleansshake-speare.com), a professional Actors Equity–affiliated organization that presents two Shakespeare works and usually one other work by a prominent playwright throughout June and July.

Bourbon Street got a new theater in 2003 with the opening of the **Fleur de Lis Théâter**

(317 Bourbon St., 504/328-2611), a modern 200-seat venue with a state-of-the-art light and sound system. The theater presents colorful revue-style cabaret productions each evening.

The **Jefferson Performing Arts Center** (1118 Clearview Pkwy., Metairie, 504/885-2000, www.jpas.org) hosts major Broadway-style shows and a variety of musical performances throughout the year.

In one of the CBD's few patches of greenery, **Lafayette Square** (off St. Charles Avenue), you can catch free concerts by some of the city's top bands every Wednesday evening at 5 P.M. Local bars and restaurants sell food and drinks, and area art galleries display some of their works for sale.

In Armstrong Park, the **Mahalia Jackson Theatre of the Performing Arts** (parking inside the park gates, Orleans Avenue entrance) hosts the main performances sponsored by the **New Orleans Ballet Association** (504/522-0996, www.nobadance.com), which books some of the world's most important ballet companies. The Theatre of the Performing Arts, named for New Orleans–born gospel singer Mahalia Jackson, is a popular venue for music concerts and festival events, as well as being home to performances by the **New Orleans Opera Association** (504/529-2278, www.neworleansopera.org), which is highly active in promoting New Orleans's illustrious opera legacy. In 2003, the organization commissioned a brand-new opera, *The Baroness,* which dramatizes the fascinating life of Baroness Micaela Almonester de Pontalba, for whom Jackson Square's famed Pontalba apartment buildings are named. The baroness married into the wealthy Pontalba family at age 15 and lived most of her life between New Orleans and Paris. Each year the association sponsors two to three classic works of opera as well.

Le Chat Noir (715 St. Charles Ave., 504/581-5812, www.cabaretlechatnoir.com) is an innovative bar-cabaret-theater that stages intriguing, independent-minded plays, musicals, jazz shows, and performance pieces, many of them tending toward the festive and occasionally outrageous. Main productions are staged in the swanky Cabaret Room, which is modeled after a 1940s nightclub, with candles glowing atop each table; note the dress code—no jeans or shorts are permitted. Bar Noir is a less dressy space, where you can sip cocktails and mingle with the city's theater types and arts glitterati.

Le Petit Theatre du Vieux Carré (616 St. Peter St., 504/522-5081, www.lepetittheatre.com) dates to 1916 and is the oldest community theater in the nation. It stages some popular Broadway-style shows, musical revues, and the like. The theater company began simply as some friends acting out plays in the living rooms of the earliest members, but soon the group began renting a space in the lower Pontalba Building. Growing popularity led the group to move into its current locale, a marvelous Spanish Colonial theater built in 1922. In addition to the main stage, a smaller venue mounts productions, and there's also a concert series.

At Loyola University, there's often something interesting going on at the **Nunemaker Auditorium** (Monroe Hall, 3rd floor, 504/861-5441), a small performance space where students of the school's College of Music often give recitals.

In Kenner, **Rivertown Repertory Theatre** (325 Minor St., 504/468-7221, www.rivertownkenner.com), part of the Rivertown Museum complex, presents dramas, comedies, and Broadway musicals from September through May.

Major traveling Broadway-style productions are staged frequently at the **Saenger Theatre** (143 N. Rampart St., 504/524-2490, www.saengertheatre.com), which also hosts big music concerts, comedy acts, and so on. Past performers have included Norah Jones, Margaret Cho, and Tori Amos. In summer, there's a Summer Classic Movie Series, which presents vintage (pre-1970) movies on the big screen. Around the corner, the **State Palace Theatre** (1108 Canal St., 504/482-7112 or 504/522-4435, www.statepalace.com) hosts the same types of events, including its own Classic Movie Series.

Southern Repertory Theatre (Shops at Canal Place, 365 Canal St., 504/835-6002, www.southernrep.com) occupies a handsome space on the 3rd floor of the luxury Shops at Canal

Place on the edge of the Quarter—this may seem like an odd theatrical location, but this mall also has a first-rate movie theater that books artsy, independent films. Southern Rep stages a half-dozen plays each year, most by noted Southern playwrights (Tennessee Williams, Lillian Hellman, Lorraine Hasberry, etc.) and local New Orleans writers.

The funky **True Brew Cafe Theatre** (200 Julia St., 504/945-6789) is a coffeehouse and bar that also stages a lot of one-man/woman shows, open-mic nights, comedy, and other innovative and thoughtful works.

CINEMAS

There are mega-movie complexes all through the suburban towns of Metairie, Kenner, and across the river on the West Bank, but New Orleans also has some venues right downtown. One of the most popular is **Landmark's Canal Place** (Shops at Canal Place, 333 Canal St., 504/581-5400), which specializes in art-house films but also shows a fair share of blockbusters. Another cool spot, not only for movies but for performance art, experimental music, poetry readings, and provocative art installations, is **Zeitgeist** (1724 Oretha Castle Haley Blvd.,

504/525-2767, www.zeitgeistinc.org), a non-profit arts center on the edge of the Lower Garden District (three blocks toward the lake from St. Charles Avenue up Euterpe Street). A throwback in this day of massive multiscreen cinemas is Uptown's **Prytania Theatre** (5339 Prytania St., 504/891-2787), an old-fashioned movie house that shows Hollywood blockbusters on its massive single screen, making it great fun for action flicks and movies with lots of special effects.

ARTS AND CRAFTS GALLERIES

Louisiana has a rich, multicultural tradition in the arts and crafts, and you'll find hundreds of outstanding galleries in New Orleans, with especially strong concentrations along Royal and Chartres Streets in the French Quarter, in the Warehouse District, and along Magazine Street in Uptown. Other communities with important commercial art galleries include Covington on the North Shore, Lafayette, and Lake Charles.

You'll find a full listing of notable art galleries and art museums on the website of the **Louisiana Division of the Arts,** www.crt.state.la.us, under the link for Visual Arts and Crafts.

The Great Outdoors

Excellent opportunities for hiking, biking, camping, boating, fishing, bird-watching, and golfing lie within a short drive of downtown New Orleans, and numerous swamp tours start from the North Shore of Lake Pontchartrain and in the Cajun Country west and southwest of New Orleans. The state's mild winters are ideal for outdoor activities, while summer can be oppressively hot. But there's really no time of year that you won't see people outside enjoying themselves.

AMUSEMENT PARKS

The old Jazzland theme park underwent a massive $20 million transformation, completed in

2003, en route to becoming **Six Flags New Orleans** (12301 Lake Forest Blvd., 504/253-8100, www.sixflags.com/parks/neworleans). This is the premier Gulf Coast venue for thrill rides and amusements. Highlights include five wild roller-coasters, plus a panoply of both adrenaline-rush and relaxing rides. The park also hosts several variety shows, including a Mardi Gras party held on Fridays and Saturdays all summer long. Hours vary greatly, so it's best to call, but typically the park opens at 10 A.M. and stays open until between 8 and 10 P.M. The park is open daily through most of the summer, and weekends in the fall and spring. All-day general-admission passes cost $32.99, and season passes just $69.99. Check the Six Flags website for special online discount deals.

BIKING

With narrow streets and concerns about theft, New Orleans is not an ideal city for biking, and you'll see relatively few cyclists here. However, most of Louisiana is excellent biking terrain, generally flat and in many areas quite scenic. The only real drawback is the relatively high amount of auto traffic and the many narrow roads. Throughout this book's chapters covering side-trips, you'll find listings of bike-rental shops and also advice about picturesque and scenic routes.

There are a few bike clubs in the region. The **New Orleans Bicycle Club** (www.gnofn.org/~nobc) and **Crescent City Cyclists** (http://home.gnofn.org/~cyclists) are geared toward racing but list a number of good cycling routes and bike shops on their websites, as well as articles on cycling. There's also a useful regional bike magazine, *Southern Cyclist* (www.southerncyclist.com), whose website usually has some articles on Louisiana.

BIRD-WATCHING

From yuppies to senior citizens, families to singles, every kind of Louisianan seems to be taking up bird-watching these days, especially those folks who live around the coast. As hobbies go, this is one of the least expensive and most educational. Best of all, birds are abundant in the state year-round, though of course the species you're likely to see depends often on the season; there are hundreds of species throughout Louisiana.

Much of the best birding is along the coast and around Lake Pontchartrain, quite close to New Orleans, and throughout the Cajun Country wetlands and bayous. Species commonly spotted in many parts of southern Louisiana include pelicans, great blue herons, great and snowy egrets, green-winged teals, mottled ducks, American widgeons, turkey vultures, red-shouldered (and other) hawks, American kestrels, least sandpipers,

> *Six Flags New Orleans is the premier Gulf Coast venue for thrill rides and amusements. Highlights include five wild roller-coasters, plus a panoply of both adrenaline-rush and relaxing rides.*

several types of gull, several types of tern, mourning doves, nighthawks, belted kingfishers, purple martins, blue jays, wrens, mockingbirds, robins, cardinals, sparrows, and meadowlarks.

South Louisiana's two **Audubon Society** chapters are useful contacts for learning about birding in Louisiana. The Orleans chapter's website, www.jjaudubon.net, contains a full South Louisiana Bird Guide, with detailed descriptions of 13 key birding areas (including New Orleans City Park) in and around greater New Orleans and the Cajun Country. There's also an extensive chart that lists the birds most prevalent in the Grand Isle and New Orleans areas—hundreds of birds are included, and you can click on bird names for a full page on that species with photos, descriptions, and tips on identification.

Popular spots for birding near New Orleans include the **Barataria Preserve Unit of Jean Lafitte National Historical Park and Preserve,** (6588 Barataria Blvd. /Hwy. 45, near Crown Point, Marrero, 504/589-2330, www.nps.com/jela), which contains nearly 10 miles of trails and lies just south of the city. The park's Bayou Coquille Trail is a pavement-and-boardwalk trail that is known for myriad wildlife sightings. About 4 miles east of I-510, along U.S. 90, 22,000-acre **Bayou Sauvage National Wildlife Refuge** (http://southeast-louisiana.fws.gov/bayousauvage.html) offers some excellent trails through marsh and hardwood forest, as well as a birding observation deck. At Tabasco Jungle Gardens, on Avery Island, you'll see one of the largest nesting areas for egrets anywhere in the country. In the North Shore town of Covington, an hour's drive north of New Orleans, you'll find the **Wild Bird Center** (808 N. U.S. 190, Suite F, 985/892-0585, www.wildbirdcenter.com/cov), a one-stop bird-watching shop with all sorts of books, binoculars, and related products.

GOLFING

There are a number of excellent courses near New Orleans, especially above Lake Pontchartrain on the North Shore. Many of the best public golf facilities are described in this book's side-trip chapters. If you live or play regularly in Louisiana, it makes sense to join the **Louisiana Golf Association** (1003 Hugh Wallis Rd., Suite G, Lafayette, LA 70508, 337/265-3938, www.lga golf.org). The association's website contains information on Louisiana clubs, upcoming local tournaments, and many additional resources.

The **Louisiana's Audubon Golf Trail** (866/AGT-IN-LA, www.audubontrail.com) leads duffers to seven of the top public facilities in the state. You can reserve tee times online at any of the Audubon courses, which include Olde Oaks Golf Club (in Shreveport and co-designed by PGA star Hal Sutton), Cypress Bend (in Many, near Toledo Bend Resevoir), Calvert Crossing (in Calhoun, just west of Monroe), Gray Plantation (in Lake Charles, and named one of the best new courses of 2000 by *Golf Digest*), Tamahka Trails (near Marksville), The Bluffs (near St. Francisville and co-designed by Arnold Palmer), and The Island (south of Baton Rouge on the west bank of the Mississippi River, near Plaquemine).

The PGA tour's **HP Classic** (504/831-4653, www.pgatour.com) takes place in late April or early May each year at **English Turn Golf and Country Club** (1 Clubhouse Dr., 10 miles southeast of the French Quarter on the West Bank, off Hwy. 406, 504/392-2200, www.englishturn.com), a semi-private club that is open to visitors by arrangement. Jack Nicklaus designed this world-class 18-hole course.

The **Tournament Players Club of Louisiana at Fairfield** (866/NOLA-TPC, www.tpc.com) is a $20 million course created for professional tournament play but open to the public. The course is slated to open in spring 2004. Famed golfing architect Pete Dye, with assistance from PGA touring professionals Steve Elkington and Kelly Gibson, designed the fabulous layout. The course sits along a 250-acre tract by Bayou Segnette State Park, a 20-minute drive from downtown New Orleans.

Audubon Park (www.auduboninstitute.org/park/tee.htm, 504/212-5290) has had a golf course since 1898, but this short par-62 course had languished in recent years. The course was completely overhauled in 2003, and is now looking better than ever. The 18-hole course is mostly par-3s, but there are four par-4 and two par-5 holes. At City Park, locals head to what many consider to be New Orleans's best links, **Bayou Oaks Golf Course** (1040 Filmore Ave., 504/483-9396, www.neworleanscitypark.com), a complex comprising four 18-hole, par-72 courses; there's also a lighted 100-tee driving range, a full pro shop and restaurant, and lessons. Few municipalities in this country have better public golf within city limits.

A semi-private course that's also quite popular is **Lakewood Country Club** (4801 General De-Gaulle Dr., 504/393-2610, www.lakewoodgolf.com), which has hosted numerous PGA tournaments and is kept in spectacular shape. It's a much more costly day of golf, but serious duffers love it. *Golf Digest* magazine has named semi-private **Eastover Country Club** (5690 Eastover Dr., 504/245-7347, www.eastovercc.com) the best place to play in the city. There are two 18-hole courses to choose from here. Across the river in Gretna you can play **Timberlane Country Club** (Timberlane Dr., 504/367-5010, www.timberlanecc.com), a semi-private course that's been innovatively cut through a stunning cypress swamp. Esteemed designer Robert Trent Jones Sr. designed the layout.

HEALTH CLUBS

A day pass for **Downtown Fitness Centers** (Canal Place, 333 Canal St., 504/525-2956; Sheraton Hotel, 500 Canal St., 504/525-2500; New Orleans Centre, 1400 Poydras St., 3rd floor, 504/569-9985) is $12, or $55 per week. These upscale fitness centers are outfitted with all the latest equipment. Another good option for visitors is expansive **Elmwood Fitness Center Downtown** (1 Shell Square, 701 Poydras St., 504/588-1600), which has massage, spinning and aerobics classes, and a juice bar. Day passes cost $10.

In Mid-City, **Climb-Max** (5304 Canal St., 504/486-7600) indoor climbing gym is a great place to work off those po'boys—the place has more than 5,000 vertical feet of textured walls and boulder surfaces. Full instruction is available.

Spas

Body Contours (220 Julia St., 504/454-3300), in the Warehouse District, offers four-hands, Swedish, and deep-tissue massage, plus hot-stone therapy, either on-site or in the privacy of your hotel room.

The environmentally sensitive **Earthsavers** (434 Chartres St., 504/581-4999; 5501 Magazine St., 504/899-8555; 3256 Severn Ave., Metairie, 504/885-5152) has earned a following for its all-natural exfoliants, moisturizers, and other skin-care products. The shop also offers spa services and aromatherapy.

If you have the sort of budget where you can still relax after forking over $100 for a 50-minute massage, then by all means head to the luxe spa at the **Ritz-Carlton** (921 Canal St., 504/524-1331), the city's most opulent facility. Warm-stone reflexology, hydrotherapy, facials, and Magnolia Sugar Scrubs (a body polish using the essence of magnolia and botanical extracts) are among the sybaritic offerings.

Hip celebs often call at **Belladonna Day Spa** (2900 Magazine St., 504/891-4393), an airy, modern bath-and-body shop that's also a topnotch unisex spa. Set inside a Victorian house, interior treatment rooms are soothing and minimalist, with a Japanese ambience. Bindi herbal body treatments, shiatsu, and manicures and pedicures are among the most popular services.

SPECTATOR SPORTS

With the huge tourism base and wealth of hotel rooms, New Orleans has become a favorite host for major professional sporting events, from football's Super Bowl (most recently held in the city's Superdome in 2002) to the NCAA's Men's Final Four (in 1982, 1987, 1993, and 2003). The 73,000-seat **Louisiana Superdome** (1500 Poydras St., 504/529-8830, www.superdome.com) was built in 1975 and is the largest stadium in the world with a roof. It's the home stadium of the National Football League's **New Orleans Saints** (504/731-1700, www.neworleanssaints.com). In

case you're wondering about the name, it's a reference to the popular jazz anthem "When the Saints Go Marching In"—but also, New Orleans was awarded the NFL franchise on November 1, 1966, All Saints' Day. The stadium is also home to one of the most beloved college football matches, the **Nokia Sugar Bowl** (504/525-8573, www .nokiasugarbowl.com), which is played in late December or early January each year between two of the nation's top collegiate teams. The Bowl has also hosted college football's national championship 17 times, including in 2000, when Florida State defeated Virginia Tech. It's nearly impossible to find a hotel room in New Orleans when this event comes to town, so plan well ahead if you wish to attend.

Next door, the **New Orleans Arena** (1501 Girod St., www.neworleansarena.com) opened in 1999 and has seating for 20,000. It's a popular concert venue as well as the place to watch the NBA basketball team **New Orleans Hornets** (504/525-HOOP or 866/444-HOOP, www.nba .com/hornets), which moved from Charlotte to New Orleans before the 2002 season. Before that, New Orleans had gone many years without an NBA team.

Some of the city's colleges have very good sports programs. **Tulane** and the **University of New Orleans** field Division I college football teams, and both have excellent baseball teams. UNO also excels in women's volleyball, and Tulane is a major force in women's basketball. For information on the athletic program at Tulane, visit the school's athletic program website, http://tulanegreenwave.ocsn.com. For UNO sporting-event information, check out www.unoprivateers.com.

Baseball fans come to watch the Minor League **New Orleans Zephyrs** (www.zephyrsbaseball .com), the Triple-A affiliate of the Major League Houston Astros. They play at 3,000-seat Zephyr Field (Airline Drive between Transcontinental and David Drives), in downtown Metairie. With a pool and Jacuzzi, weekly fireworks displays, and games with players just one level away from big-league baseball, the Zephyrs enjoy some of the highest attendance of any Triple-A team. They're members of the Pacific Coast League.

ENTERTAINMENT

FISHING CHARTERS

H ere in a part of the world where humans have reclaimed much of the land they live on from the Gulf, the Mississippi River, and its related bodies of water, fishing is not only hugely important to Louisiana's economy, it's one of the most popular sporting activities around. But before you go casting your line into the Mississippi, considering booking a fishing trip with one of the many expert charters around the area. These guys know where to look and what to look for, and they can provide all the licenses necessary, plus tackle and a knowledgable guide who can maneuver the state's maze of inland waterways. It's a great chance to hunt for redfish, trout, red snapper, and tuna. Many of these operators can clean and pack your catches at the end of the trip, and many area restaurants will cook and prepare your haul for you.

In Metairie, **Blue Water Booking** (124 E. Oakridge Park, 504/975-3474, www.bluewaterbooking.com) arranges both inland and offshore fishing excursions. It's one of the most reliable and respected fishing charters around, and it can customize any trip of just about any length year-round. **Captain Phil's Saltwater Guide Service** (4037 Hugo Dr., 504/348-3264) is another reliable outfitter for trips out to the Gulf; he sails out of Marrero, on the West Bank. **Griffin Fishing Charters** (800/741-1340, www.neworleansfishintours.com), out of the atmospheric fishing village of Lafitte, is another excellent charter company that provides both fresh- and saltwater adventures.

If you'd prefer cruising through the bayous and lakes for redfish and speckled trout, consider **Papa Joe's Cajun Wetland Service** (382 W. Meae Dr., Gretna, 504/392-4409, www.fishneworleans.com). Joe's has a great website on which he keeps a diary of who sails with him each day, along with a lively record (and pictures) of their successes.

Another popular option is **Captain Nick's Wildlife Safaris** (102 Arlington Dr., Luling, 504/361-3004 or 800/375-FISH, www.captnicks.com), which can customize a trip into the swamps or out onto the open waters of the Gulf. Nick's arranges cameras and fishing tackle. It's based out of Luling, on the edge of Plantation Country and a 25-mile drive southwest of New Orleans.

The area around Houma and coastal Terrebonne Parish has dozens of fishing marinas and charters, especially around the towns of Dulac and Cocodrie. The **Houma Area Convention and Visitors Bureau** (985/868-2732 or 800/688-2732, www.houmatourism.com) distributes a very useful free brochure on fishing in the area, listing charters and information on the most common species caught. In Chauvin, a 15-mile drive southeast of Houma, **Co Co Marina** (106 Pier 56, Chauvin, 504/594-6626 or 800/648-2626, www.rodnreel.com/cocomarina) provides fishing charters and also offers condo and boathouse-apartment rentals, modern and comfortable spots where you can stay before or after you set out for a day of casting a line.

Horseracing

Mid-City's **Fairgrounds Race Track** (1751 Gentilly Blvd., 504/948-1285, www.fgno.com), the third-oldest thoroughbred-racing course in the nation, offers live racing from Thanksgiving through March. An off-track-betting parlor is open year-round, so you can wager on events elsewhere in the country. Key events at the track include Louisiana Champions Day, the New Orleans Handicap, and the Louisiana Derby.

TAKING TO THE WATER

Louisiana has nearly 400 miles of coastline, but if you count the many inlets and rivers, the state's total shoreline is many thousands of miles. About 15 percent of the state's 51,000 square miles are covered by water. River sports (such as canoeing and kayaking and rafting) are popular along the waterways of Jean Lafitte National Historical Park's Barataria Preserve, the Tchefuncte and Bogue

boat launch on the Pearl River, near New Orleans

Chitto Rivers in St. Tammany Parish (on the North Shore), the Atchafalaya Swamp in Cajun Country, and the Calcasieu and Whiskey Chitto Rivers near Lake Charles. The Mississippi River is, somewhat surprisingly, not all that popular with recreational boaters, as it tends to be dominated by huge commercial freighters, and the extensive levee system separates it from the smaller and more interesting inlets and tributaries that are ideal for exploring by nonmotorized craft. You'll find aquatic outfitters and tour providers throughout the state; individual canoeing, kayaking, rafting, and tubing outfitters are listed in the regional side-trip chapters in this book. For information on boating safety and regulations throughout Louisiana, contact **Louisiana Department of Wildlife & Fisheries (LDWF)** (2000 Quail Dr., Baton Rouge, LA 70808, www.wlf.state.la.us). The website provides information on registration, boating classes and safety, and the like.

The website **Sportsmansresource.com** lists Louisiana boat-rental agencies, boating charters, and many other relevant resources.

There are a handful of marinas in metro New Orleans, including the **Municipal Yacht Harbor** (401 N. Roadway St., New Orleans, 504/288-1431), which is on Lake Pontchartrain up near

Breakwater Park. Out in Venice, a two-hour drive down Hwy. 23 along the Mississippi River, there's **Cypress Cove Marina** (226 Cypress Cove Rd., 504/534-9289 or 800/643-4190, www.rodnreel.com/cypresscove), which also has a small motel and restaurant. This may seem like a long way to go, but it's definitely a faster way to get by boat from New Orleans to the Gulf of Mexico than if you leave from New Orleans directly, either by way of the river or Lake Pontchartrain. From Cypress Cove it's just another 15 miles or so to the Gulf.

GENERAL RESOURCES

There are several excellent resources for learning more about the region's wealth of outdoor diversions. A good way to begin is by contacting the **Louisiana Department of Wildlife & Fisheries (LDWF)** (2000 Quail Dr., Baton Rouge, LA 70808, www.wlf.state.la.us). You can write to request brochures on the state parks and outdoor activities, or visit the useful website, which lists the phone numbers of the appropriate person or office for information on public boat ramps, song birds, hunting licenses, and the like. Another state department with an informative website, the

Mississippi River

Louisiana Department of Natural Resources (LaSalle Office Building, 617 N. 3rd St., Baton Rouge, LA 70802, 225/342-4500, www.dnr.state.la.us) can provide information on conservation, coastal restoration, and mineral resources throughout the state.

For the lowdown on each of Louisiana's 18 state parks, 16 state historic sites, and one state preservation area, contact the **Louisiana Office of State Parks** (Box 44426, Baton Rouge, LA 70804, 225/342-8111 or 888/677-1400, www.crt.state.la.us/crt/parks). The website has a helpful interactive map locating state parks—click on the park in question, and you'll learn the property's acreage, history, facilities, parking and usage fees, hours, and distinctive features.

Day-use fees are $2 per vehicle (for up to four people, 50 cents per person thereafter) at state parks and $2 per adult at state historic sites. The $30 annual pass entitles the bearer to free day admission to all of the parks and historic sites. The parks website also gives fees for day-use facilities (such as group pavilions and meeting areas), and for camping, group camping, overnight cabins and lodges, swimming pools, and rental boats. Fees are the same for residents and nonresidents.

A wonderful way to learn about Louisiana's outdoors and become involved with keeping them clean is to join the state chapter of the **Nature Conservancy** (P.O. Box 4125, Baton Rouge, LA 70821, 225/338-1040, http://nature.org). This highly respected and influential organization was founded in 1951, and the Louisiana chapter has been instrumental in preserving some 19 of the state's most precious natural settings. Some of the preserves are not open to the public, but six properties are, and you can generally visit them anytime during daylight hours. The properties open to visitors are Lafitte Woods Preserve (in Grand Isle), White Kitchen Preserve (in the Pearl River basin by Slidell, best visited via one of the area's swamp tours), Cypress Island (near Breaux Bridge on Lake Martin), Mary Ann Brown Preserve (30 miles north of Baton Rouge in the Tunica Hills), Abita Creek Flatwoods Preserve (in Abita Springs), and Lake Ramsay Preserve (near Covington). Preserves are open from an hour before dawn to an hour after sunset. Stay on marked trails, refrain from using bikes or vehicles (and from camping), and observe the conservancy's common-sense regulations concerning litter, bird-nesting sites, and so on.

Nature Conservancy properties are found all

around Louisiana, but those open to the public are mostly near New Orleans and Baton Rouge, in the southeastern part of the state. White Kitchen is a dramatic section of Honey Island Swamp that's a favorite for bird- and wildlife-watching—while swamp tours offer the best look at it, you can also explore it via a boardwalk that cuts right through the marsh. Lafitte Woods preserves the best tract of oak and hackberry forest on the Grand Isle barrier island, about a two-hour drive south of New Orleans; this favorite spot for observing migratory songbirds has several walking trails and a 300-foot-long boardwalk overlooking acres of estuary and tidal ponds. The 2,800-acre Cypress Island is a favorite nature retreat in Cajun Country—

it's famous for its rookery that hosts as many as 20,000 herons, egrets, and ibis each year.

An equally important conservation advocate and resource is the **Audubon Society,** which has two chapters in the state. The **Orleans Audubon Society** (504/834-BIRD or 877/834-BIRD, www.jjaudubon.net/ppdoas.htm), based in Metairie, serves the Greater New Orleans area and has a website with loads of information on birding throughout southeastern Louisiana. Based in the state capital, the **Baton Rouge Audubon Society** (www.braudubon.org) oversees the Peveto Woods Sanctuary, down along the southwest Louisiana coast south of Lake Charles. The 40-acre tract is one of the state's many exceptional birding areas.

Accommodations

After years of suffering through a hotel shortage, New Orleans saw unprecedented growth in its number of accommodations during the late '90s. Most of the new hotels opened in the Central Business District and the adjoining, and increasingly trendy, Warehouse District, and many are geared toward business travelers and conventioneers. But even leisure travelers should take note: the best and most competitively priced selection of accommodations in the city has shifted from the French Quarter to the CBD. Although the crush of hotel development has subsided, there are still several new properties in the can. The historic St. Charles Regency apartment build-

ing, at 1205 St. Charles Ave., is slated to become a luxurious 286-room hostelry by 2004. The upscale Loews chain is renovating a postmodern office tower in the Warehouse District—it will become a 282-room hotel in 2004. Trendy boutique hotels have caught on quickly in the Big Easy, and another is planned for the CBD's old Western Union Building—this property is expected to offer relatively low rates, under $100 nightly. The 105 compact rooms at what will be known as the Western Union Hotel are to contain flat-screen TVs and a Euro-Asian design scheme.

For proximity to everything New Orleans is famous for, however, the French Quarter re-

view toward French Quarter of old Maison Blanche department store, now the Ritz-Carlton

mains the hub of accommodations, with dozens of hotels in all shapes and sizes. There are not many chain properties, and none that could be called cookie-cutter hotels. For this reason, even though the French Quarter has few places that could be called hip or modish, it remains a popular choice among all kinds of New Orleans visitors, because it's easy to find rooms in this neighborhood that embody the history and charm of this city's rich French-Spanish history.

Outside the CBD and French Quarter, greater New Orleans has significant numbers of charming inns and B&Bs, mostly in the Garden District, Faubourg Marigny, and Mid-City, as well as significant concentrations of budget- and mid-priced chain hotels, mostly in eastern New Orleans and in neighboring Metairie and Kenner.

Many, many people book hotel rooms in New Orleans for Mardi Gras as much as a year ahead, but a good number of these folks cancel sometime during the year, with the great number of cancellations occurring within two months of the celebration.

An excellent resource for finding out more about the city's many fine smaller properties is **PIANO—Professional Innkeepers Association of New Orleans** (www.bbnola.com), which has about 50 member inns and B&Bs. The organization's website has a very useful online reservations and availability function that enables you to search for properties with rooms open, even at the last minute.

FINDING A ROOM

It's always a good idea to book your accommodations as far ahead as possible, and it's especially important that you do so when planning a stay at an inn or B&B, as such properties are fewer and farther between than motels and hotels, and they have fewer rooms. Southern Louisiana is famous for celebrations and festivals. Mardi Gras may be the most famous, but New Orleans also books up solid during Jazz Fest and throughout the year when conventions are in town. Lafayette and Baton Rouge book up less often, but can also be popular during festivals. Check the tourism websites—and this book—to learn when events are slated to occur throughout the state, so you can plan accordingly.

As for booking a hotel room for Mardi Gras, keep in mind that this festival culminates during the weekend, Monday, and Tuesday that precede Ash Wednesday, the date of which changes each year. Fat Tuesday falls on February 24 in 2004, February 8 in 2005, and February 28 in 2006, to give you an idea. But there are parades and related celebrations during the weeks from Christmas leading up to Mardi Gras, so it can sometimes be tough booking a room on weekends through early spring. Also, Mardi Gras is celebrated with great enthusiasm not just in New Orleans but in more or less every town in the state. During the apex of the celebration, expect rooms to be somewhat tough to score in Lafayette, Baton Rouge, and other towns and cities. Still, you can usually find a vacancy somewhere in these communities, even if booking a few days before Mardi Gras.

Folks have their different strategies for booking Mardi Gras rooms in New Orleans. First, keep in mind that the city will be nearly sold out Friday, Saturday, Sunday, Monday, and Tuesday nights of Mardi Gras week. The entire city clears out on Ash Wednesday, making it very easy to score rooms throughout the rest of the week and into the following week. However, the city is a mess the first few days after Fat Tuesday, so it might not be a wonderful time to visit. The week prior to Mardi Gras is fairly popular, but you can usually find hotel rooms without much difficulty during this time.

Many, many people book hotel rooms in New Orleans for Mardi Gras as much as a year ahead, but a good number of these folks cancel sometime during the year, with the great number of cancellations occurring within two months of the celebration. So don't get discouraged if you try reserving rooms several months out and find that all your favorite hotels are booked up—undoubtedly, some of these places will have rooms available closer to the date, and some will put you on a waiting list. The easiest and simplest way to book a Mardi Gras overnight is on one of the online travel sites, such as Orbitz or Expedia. Again, you may find almost nothing available if you check these sites four to six months before Mardi Gras, but be patient and check back often. Typically, you'll not only find more rooms available within a month or two of Mardi Gras, but you'll even find some reduced rates, as hotels with cancellations scramble to sell those last few rooms.

It's not a bad idea to check with some of the smaller inns and B&Bs in New Orleans, too. The very popular ones fill up quickly for Mardi Gras, but some perfectly nice ones often have availability right up to the big event. B&Bs and inns can be your best back-up plan when a convention lands in New Orleans and steals away all the rooms of chain hotels. Do keep in mind that during Mardi Gras and Jazz Fest, you can expect to pay 150 to 250 percent more for a room than during slower periods, and rooms can also be heavily marked up when big conventions are in town.

Now, here's the good news: it's easier than ever to get a good room in New Orleans. The hotel-building boom that's been going since the mid-'90s is projected to run until 2005. At the same time, both business and leisure travel have softened since the economy turned in the late '90s and terrorism concerns put a damper on big-city travel in 2001. This has left New Orleans with, for the first time in years, a frequent glut of unoccupied hotel rooms. Even the most recent Mardi Gras, in 2003, failed to fill up the city's hotel rooms completely. So for the foreseeable future, you can expect to find some pretty decent hotel bargains in New Orleans. Reliable online booking sites serve up good deals. If you have some favorite properties, check about packages that may include free meals, tickets to attractions, upgrades, or other perks. It should be a buyer's market though at least 2005.

WHAT IT WILL COST

There are two basic factors on which accommodations base their highest and lowest rates, both tied in closely to supply and demand. Price ranges indicated in this book reflect the highest rates, double-occupancy, during high season. Don't be put off if you see a hotel listed in the $150–250 range when you're seeking something under $100 nightly. There are hotels in New Orleans whose highest rates hover around $200 nightly but drop to as low as $70 during slow times. It's always a good idea to phone ahead or visit a property's website and ask about special packages and seasonal, weekday, or weekend discounts.

Expect to pay more during holidays or during a few exceptionally popular weekends (Mardi Gras, Christmastime, etc.), for suites or rooms that sleep more than two, and for rooms with amenities such as fireplaces, hot tubs, and decks. Expect to pay less (often as much as 50 percent less) off-season (especially summer in sultry New Orleans), during the week at leisure-oriented country inns and B&Bs (especially in the Cajun Country and near plantations, which are popular weekend destinations), during weekends for urban hotels and motels in business-oriented areas (such as Baton Rouge and, to some extent, Lafayette), and for rooms with fewer amenities (shared baths, twin beds, brick-wall views, no TVs, etc.).

Rates at New Orleans hotels don't change a whole lot from weekday to weekend, but there are some exceptions. You can occasionally get a romantic inn or B&B, the sort of place that books up heavily on weekends, to cut you a break on weekdays, especially Mondays or Tuesdays, and especially if it's off-season. It never hurts to explain when booking that you'd like to come during a quieter time and are curious whether the inn could offer any deals or specials on slower days of the week. Conversely, in the corporate-oriented Central Business District, some of the upscale chain hotels that cater to convention trade and business travelers will offer reduced rates on weekends, at least during the slower tourist season (meaning summer and the period between Thanksgiving and Christmas).

Accommodations in this book are grouped according to the following price categories: Under $50, $50–100, $100–150, $150–250, and over $250. These ranges are based on the cost of an establishment's standard room, double-occupancy, during high season, which generally means fall and spring in southern Louisiana.

CHOOSING AN ACCOMMODATION

Unless you have your hopes set on a specific property, or a hotel with very specific amenities, it probably makes more sense to choose the location where you'd like to stay before choosing the exact accommodation. The loveliest room in a neighborhood that you find inconvenient or too touristy isn't going to feel lovely. Remember that you can get a lot more bang for your buck by staying slightly off the beaten path.

No matter what it says in a property's brochure, remember that nothing at your hotel—breakfast, a pool, an exercise room, turn-down service, local phone calls—is truly free. These extras may be included in the rate, but this means that rates at properties with oodles of perks, amenities, and facilities are going to be higher than rates at properties without them. These extras are all well and good provided you're really going to take advantage of them, but think seriously about booking a room at a country inn that's renowned for its lavish full breakfasts or an upscale hotel whose business and conference facilities are extensive. Do you eat breakfast? Are you in town on business?

As the old real estate cliché goes, location is everything when it comes to finding the right place to stay—even if just for the night. Once you've established what you're willing to spend and what level of accommodation will suit you, think about where you plan to spend most of your visit. Are you looking to hide away with your mate in a romantic suite, rarely emerging until check-out? Or will you be spending as little time as possible in your room or even in the town where you're staying? Does a view matter? Being with walking distance of shops or New Orleans's legendary nightlife? To satisfy one of these needs, you may have to sacrifice another.

One major caveat before relying heavily on state- or regionally produced travel planners and brochures: The organizations that produce these publications are often funded by a hotel tax that is added onto your room rate. Other tourist boards are member-based. As long as a lodging pays its taxes or pays membership dues to a particular board of tourism, it may be entitled to be included in any literature published by the state and local tourist boards. This means that these brochures and publications often will not or cannot refuse a listing to even the seediest, dreariest, and most horrible establishment.

What does this mean in practice? Having anonymously inspected a great number of the properties listed in New Orleans and elsewhere in southern Louisiana, I can say that 10 to 20 percent of them are highly suspect, and several of them make the hotel in *The Shining* look like a Ritz-Carlton. You would think that some sort of ratings system would be in place to keep properties that are truly unsanitary, substandard, or unsafe from being recommended unconditionally by organizations aiming to promote tourism, but such are the mysterious ways of governmental bureaucracies.

This is not to suggest that establishments omitted from this book are substandard—there are simply too many hotels to review in this guide, and thus what you'll find is a representation of the most appealing properties in the region, in every price category. Especially in New Orleans, which has scores upon scores of hotels, motels, inns, and B&Bs, I had to select only a fraction of the places that I actually feel quite confident recommending. To that end, I tried to write about those places representing the greatest value, which is figured roughly by considering the rates, the location, the facilities, and the level of cleanliness and staff professionalism I encountered. A change in management can raise or lower the quality of a property almost overnight, but it's safe to say that at press time I'd have recommended every single property in this book to my mother (and that's saying a lot).

Inns and Bed-and-Breakfasts

To get a real feel for the area you're visiting, consider choosing a B&B or country inn over a larger chain property. It's sometimes believed that chains offer better rates, more consistent standards, better amenities for business travelers, and greater anonymity, but this is far from always—or even

LEGAL AND ILLEGAL BED-AND-BREAKFASTS

Some of the most charming rooms in the city are found in unlicensed or illegal B&Bs or guesthouses. Many of these "underground" establishments advertise heavily. Probably no harm will come to you simply for staying at one, and certainly plenty of travelers do it, so why even think twice before booking a room at such a property? There are a couple of reasons.

Letting out rooms to tourists has long been a tradition in New Orleans, and its origins are harmless enough. Owners of the many grand and historic houses in the French Quarter and other visitor-friendly neighborhoods simply rented a room or two, or even several, as a way to earn a little extra income. Many travelers enjoyed staying at these informal accommodations, saving a little moeny, getting to know the hosts, and living as though they were residents of New Orleans.

The problem is that the city of New Orleans requires B&Bs to be licensed, and yet it seems to make little effort to enforce this rule. So the upstanding innkeepers around town who did go through the hassle of getting approval to open an inn, and then paid the various fees, are at a competitive disadvantage to those who run properties illegally.

As a consumer, the main risk you face staying at an illegal B&B is that you have little or no recourse for remedying any disputes that arise with the owners, and you have no legal protection should you be injured. Illegal short-term rentals often fail to comply with fire and safety regulations; if they do so, it's on a voluntary basis, since nobody inspects them. They also rarely carry the proper commercial insurance that a licensed inn is required to have, which poses a liability risk to visitors.

Outside of protecting your own best interests, you're actually helping the city of New Orleans and its historic neighborhoods by choosing to patronize only licensed and legal B&Bs. Illegal vacation rentals don't contribute their share of taxes to the city—and worse, in a city with a high crime rate and a number of urban problems, they do little to foster community cooperation and neighborhood pride. Think of it this way: every illegal vacation rental is a building that should, per zoning laws, be resident-occupied. And when neighborhoodss like the Upper French Quarter and Faubourg Marigny are filled with transient vacation rentals, neighborhood stability is lost. It's in the best interest of these parts of town to have as many buildings occupied by residents, or by legitimate inns where the owners live on premises or have regular on-site staff.

The easiest way to ensure that the B&B you're interested in is licensed, legal, and up to proper standards is to choose one of the more than 40 properties that are members of **PIANO—the Professional Innkeepers Association of New Orleans** (www.bbnola.com), an organization that formed in 2000. PIANO has been lobbying the city to pass an ordinance that would come down hard on illegal inns and vacation rentals by making it a municipal criminal offense to advertise or solicit for customers. Actual renters or customers would not be affected, nor would the paper, website, or organization that ran the ad. As of this writing, the outcome of PIANO's effort had not been decided, but with so many excellent and reliable licensed inns in New Orleans, it's probably smartest to stick with these and avoid illegal B&Bs.

often—the case. Some smaller B&Bs, especially those that offer shared baths, have among the least-expensive rooms in Louisiana, and this rule holds especially true in New Orleans.

Furthermore, staying at a small historic property need not involve socializing with either your hosts or fellow guests, or placing phone calls and logging onto the Internet with your laptop from a common area. An increasing number of higher-end inns (this is less true of B&Bs in rural areas) have recognized the needs of business travelers and begun installing in-room direct-dial phones, data ports, cable TVs, VCRs, and even high-speed Internet access. If privacy is important to you, ask if any of the rooms have separate outdoor entrances. You might be surprised how many places do, often in carriage houses, former slave quarters, or other outbuildings set away from the main house.

All of this is not to suggest that more social and welcoming B&Bs and country inns are scarce—the kinds of places where guests compare notes on their finest antiquing conquests before a roaring evening fire, or conspire together to attack the area's most challenging hiking trails over a four-course full breakfast. The most successful innkeepers have learned to leave alone the independent travelers but gently direct the ones seeking local advice and connections, like hard-to-score dinner reservations and directions to secret fishing holes that you'll never find in brochures or even in this book. If it's your wish, a B&B can offer both camaraderie and a personal concierge—and these perks come with no extra charges.

In the broadest sense, B&Bs are smaller than country inns. At B&Bs there tend to be fewer than 10 rooms (sometimes only one or two), the owners often live on the premises, breakfasts tend to be intimate and social, common areas small and homey, and facilities and amenities minimal (rarely are there phones or TVs in guest rooms, or is there a restaurant or exercise room). At inns you may find anywhere from several to 100 rooms, a full staff of employees (the owners often live off-property), breakfasts served in dining rooms and often at your own private table, spacious and more formal common areas, and an array of facilities and amenities.

More often than not, breakfast at a country inn is continental, while breakfast at a B&B is full (with a hot entrée and often three or four courses). It's less of a rule, but country inns typically charge more than B&Bs and, although they're often less personable and quirky, they maintain a higher standard of luxury and offer a greater degree of privacy. These are general differences, and in many cases the lines between country inns and B&Bs blur considerably. Regardless of these distinctions, inns and B&Bs share many traits: usually they are historic or designed in a historic style, rooms typically vary in layout and are decorated individually in period style, and settings are often rural, scenic, or historic.

An excellent resource for finding out about great inns and B&Bs throughout New Orleans is **PIANO (Professional Innkeepers Association of New Orleans)** (www.bbnola.com), which lists more than 40 licensed properties throughout the city. A statewide organization that lists reliable places to stay in just about every parish is **Louisiana Bed & Breakfast** (225/346-1857, www.louisianabandb.com). It's always a good idea to choose inns that belong to professional organizations such as these, where only properties that are run to a certain standard are admitted.

Hotels and Motels

The majority of the state's hotels and motels are perfectly nice, and a few are downright homey and charming. However, most of the unacceptable accommodations in Louisiana, as is true just about everywhere in the country, are lower-end chain motels, many of them located off interstates or busy roads. There are exceptions, of course, as there are some truly awful B&Bs out there and some surprisingly unkempt and poorly run moderate to upscale hotels. You can increase your odds of picking a good property by keeping a few things in mind:

Look for *recent* stickers in lobby windows that indicate the hotel has been approved by AAA or the Mobil guides, and really check credentials of motels on busy roads within an earshot of a major highway (they're not only apt to be noisy, but they're more likely to be rendezvous points for any number of illicit activities). Motels that rent rooms by the hour are usually not very savory, and there are several of them in Louisiana.

At any property with which you're unfamiliar, ask to see the room before you check in, and if the front desk refuses or even hesitates, you can safely assume they're harboring secrets that shall be revealed to you only after you have left a credit-card imprint (like the postage-stamp-size guest towels are frayed and threadbare, and the air-conditioner is broken). If you see plants or personal effects on the sills of guestroom windows, or rusty cars in the parking lot, you have no doubt stumbled upon a residential hotel with facilities that are probably not up to the expectations of most travelers (this may sound like a joke, but a few of these places are listed in the brochures produced by tourist boards).

A few chains are consistently reputable or have especially good products in Louisiana, including most of the high-end ones. Of economical and moderately priced chains, best bets include Clarion, Comfort Inn/Comfort Suites, Courtyard by Marriott, Four Points, Hampton Inn, Hilton Garden Inn, Holiday Inn Express, Motel 6 (the best bare-bones chain in the state), and Quality Inn. There are some very nice Super 8 and EconoLodge motels in Louisiana, too, but these are less consistent in quality. Other economical and moderately priced chains that vary considerably in quality from property to property include Best Western, Budget Host, Days Inn, Ramada, and Travelodge. Independently operated budget motels are inherently no better or worse than chain properties—don't rule them out just because you've never heard of them. But do check them out ahead of time.

The French Quarter

Here in the city's activity heart you'll find the greatest density of hotels, many of them set inside adjoining rows of Victorian townhouses, and a smattering of B&Bs. You'll be steps from the most famous nightlife, dining, and shopping in the city. And because this is a historic district, you won't end up in some bland cookie-cutter convention hotel—most of these are in the Central Business District (CBD), on the fringes of the Quarter. With a couple of exceptions, it's generally not a good idea to pick a place right on Bourbon Street, even if you love to party; the rates are often disproportionately higher at these places, and you're almost certain to hear plenty of street noise. If revelry is a high priority, opt for something on a nearby street; nowhere in the French Quarter are you far from places to eat and play. In general, hotel rates are quite high in the French Quarter, although many good deals can be found if you shop around, and you can often get a better deal here than at some of the luxury convention-oriented hotels in the CBD. If you've never been to New Orleans, and especially if you're just staying for two or three nights, it makes sense to book a room in this neighborhood, but consider some of the outlying areas, too, especially if you're more comfortable in a smaller inn or B&B, of which there are few in the Quarter. Parking is tight in the Quarter; most properties offer valet or self garage parking for $20 to $25 nightly.

HOTELS AND MOTELS
$100–150
Easy access to the superb restaurant Stella is reason enough to stay at the family-run **Hotel Provincial** (1024 Chartres St., 504/581-4995 or 800/535-7922, www.hotelprovincial.com), a well-priced upscale inn with 93 cheery rooms decorated individually with Louisiana antiques and reproduction French period furnishings. Many rooms open onto a sunny courtyard with two swimming pools. Service is efficient and friendly. This complex of historic buildings includes a former 1830s military hospital.

A well-located and relatively affordable option right across from the Jackson Brewery building and next to Johnny's Po'boys, the **Historic French Market Inn** (501 Decatur St., 504/539-9000 or 888/538-5651, www.frenchmarketinn .com) contains 95 tastefully appointed rooms with floral bedspreads, brass beds, reproduction antiques, exposed-brick walls, and the usual slate of in-room amenities: TVs, phones with voice mail, irons and boards, hair dryers. In back, rooms lead out to one of the Quarter's trademark quaint courtyards, in this case anchored by a small pool. Continental breakfast isn't included, but it costs a mere $1.99, and there's a snug coffeehouse next to the tiny lobby.

Le Richelieu (1234 Chartres St., 504/529-2492 or 800/535-9653, www.lerichelieuhotel.com) books up fast because it's been one of the Quarter's most popular mid-priced hotels for many years. Indeed, standard one-bed rooms often rent for under $100 nightly. Rooms feel fairly typical of chain properties but with a bit more character, such as antique-style ceiling fans and reproduction antiques. The 86-room European-style property sits along a quiet stretch of Chartres Street in the Lower Quarter, an easy walk from Bourbon Street activity, the French Market, and Faubourg Marigny. There's a café serving light food throughout the day (along with room service), a cocktail bar, and a garden swimming pool. There's also free and secure self-parking.

Quirky, offbeat, and offering one of the better rates in the French Quarter, the family-run **Olivier House** (828 Toulouse St., 504/525-8456 or 866/525-9748, www.olivierhouse.com) is just off the hubbub of Bourbon Street, set inside a towering Greek Revival townhouse. Rooms and suites contain a mix of older and newer furnishings, and each has a different layout and decorative scheme; some are pet-friendly, and the whole property is well-suited to guests traveling with children. Suites have wet bars, kitchenettes, and some are split-level, with romantic upstairs sleeping lofts. A favorite room is the Garden Suite, whose downstairs flagstone living room has actual beds of flowers, a banana tree, and a spectacular gurgling fountain. There's free off-street parking (almost unheard of in this part of the Quarter), a pool, and free local phone calls, making this friendly, low-key property an excellent value.

$150–250

The **Bourbon Orleans** (717 Orleans St., 504/523-2222 or 800/WYNDHAM, www.wyndham.com) occupies most of a block at Bour-

bon and Orleans Streets, making it party central—several gay and straight nightclubs are but a stone's throw from the Bourbon Street entrance. It makes sense, therefore, to book a room facing one of the side streets and not Bourbon if you want to get any sleep at night—all rooms have good soundproofing, though. This is one of the best properties close to Bourbon Street, as many of them are overpriced and a bit chaotic with the swarms of crowds outside the door. This Wyndham Historic Hotel, which dates to 1817, has a professional staff and 216 large rooms with tall windows, long flowing drapes, floral-print bedspreads, Queen Anne reproduction antiques, marble bathrooms, and high-speed Internet access. There's no full-service restaurant, but Cafe Lafayette serves very good breakfasts.

The only accommodation right on Jackson Square, **Place D'Armes Hotel** (625 St. Ann St., 504/529-7142 or 800/366-2743, www.placedarmes.com) has a couple of other things going for it—for example, it's just a short walk from those heavenly beignets at Cafe du Monde. The property consists of nine adjacent 18th-century buildings, all carefully restored and containing a total of 83 rooms. Many of them overlook delightful courtyards shaded by crape myrtle and magnolia trees, or the colorful street life of Jackson Square; many of these have balconies. Some bargain-priced smaller rooms have no view but perfectly charming furnishings. Complimentary continental breakfast (including fresh-squeezed orange juice) is served in a small tile-floor café, but you're also welcome to dine in the courtyard or back in your room.

Part of the acclaimed Melrose Hotel Group, a collection of four intimate, luxury New Orleans accommodations, the **Hotel Royal** (1006 Royal St., 504/524-3900 or 800/776-3901, www.melrosegroup.com) occupies a marvelous 1827 Creole townhouse that was a private home until 1940s, then a Laundromat, and then a humdrum hotel until 2001, when it was completely refurbished. Although it's just a block off Bourbon Street, the hotel is in the Lower Quarter, down a few blocks from the more touristy and crowded areas. The 30 units have high ceilings and in many cases wrought-iron balconies and exposed

FRENCH QUARTER AND FAUBOURG MARIGNY ACCOMMODATIONS

RATHBONE INN

KERLEREC ST.

BARRACKS

MELROSE MANSION

ST. ANN ST.

ORLEANS ST.

N. PRIEUR ST.

LAFITTE ST.

ROBERTSON ST.

VILLERE ST.

TREME ST.

CLAUDE ST.

MARAIS ST.

GOV. NICHOLLS ST.

Louis Armstrong Park

TREME

10

CLAIBORNE AVE.

N. DERBIGNY ST.

URSULINES AVE.

PHILIP ST.

BURGUNDY ST.

FRENCH QUARTER

HOTEL ROYAL

CORNSTALK HOTEL

ST. LOUIS CEMETERY NO 2

ROBERTSON ST.

VILLERE ST.

LA SALLE ST.

TREME ST.

CROZAT ST.

BASIN ST.

ST. LOUIS CEMETERY NO 1

TOULOUSE ST.

ORLEANS ST.

ST. ANN ST.

DUMAINE

BOURBON ORLEANS

PLACE D'ARMES HOTEL

MADISON

ST. PETER ST.

OLIVIER HOUSE

LOUIS ST.

N. RAMPART ST.

CONTI ST.

BOURBON ST.

HOTEL MAISON DE VILLE

JACKSON SQUARE

WILKINSON ST.

CHARTIY HOSPITAL

CHATEAU LEMOYNE

IBERVILLE ST.

BIENVILLE ST.

ROYAL ST.

OMNI ROYAL ORLEANS

HISTORIC FRENCH MARKET INN

TULANE AVE.

SARATOGA ST.

S. LIBERTY ST.

ELK PL.

CLEVELAND AVE.

MAISON ORLEANS

DAUPHINE ST.

MEDICAL CENTER OF TULANE

UNIVERSITY PL.

RITZ-CARLTON

HOTEL MONTELEONE

CHARTRES ST.

EXCHANGE ALY.

W NEW ORLEANS–FRENCH QUARTER

BIENVILLE HOUSE HOTEL

N. FRONT BLVD.

CANAL ST.

COMMON ST.

PERDIDO ST.

CBD

GRAVIER ST.

LOYOLA AVE.

UNION ST.

O'KEEFE AVE.

BARONNE ST.

ST. CHARLES AVE.

CAMP ST.

MAGAZINE ST.

N. PETERS ST.

CLAY ST.

Woldenberg Riverfront Park

POYDRAS ST.

NATCHEZ ST.

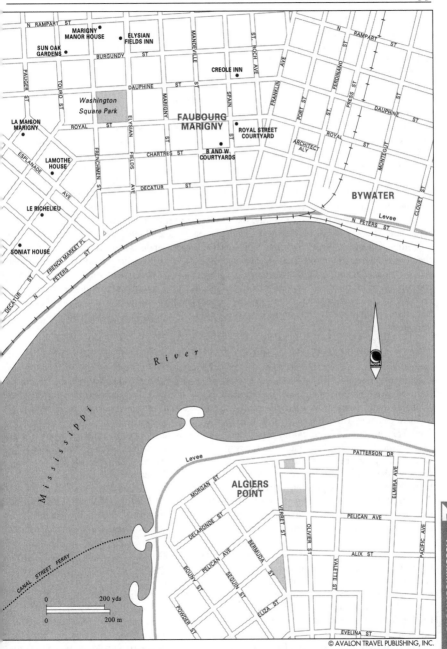

N
ACCOMMODATIONS

© AVALON TRAVEL PUBLISHING, INC.

brick; some look down over the romantic courtyard anchored by a fountain. The most exclusive rooms are the balcony suites, with wet bars and Jacuzzi tubs, but every room has individual climate control, coffeemakers, and irons and boards. A light continental breakfast is included.

The intimate **Bienville House Hotel** (320 Decatur St., 504/529-2345 or 800/535-9603, www.bienvillehouse.com) sits along Decatur Street, close to the River, Canal Street, and several good bars and eateries with a mellower ambience than those a few blocks up on Bourbon Street—that being said, you're not far from those either. By French Quarter standards, rooms here are large, airy, and looking especially dapper after a huge top-to-bottom overhaul recently. Bathrooms are attractive with white tile and upscale amenities. The best units offer sterling views of the river, but wherever you sleep, consider having coffee in the morning on one of the inviting rooftop sundecks; there's also a pool with a very civilized lanai surrounding it. The ground-floor restaurant, Gamay, serves some of the best contemporary Creole cooking in town.

The **Hotel Monteleone** (214 Royal St., 504/523-3341 or 800/535-9595, www.hotel-monteleone.com), famous for its immense red neon rooftop sign, is a favorite because of its rich history—this 1886 property hosted Tennessee Williams many times, as well as Eudora Welty, William Faulkner, Truman Capote, and Richard Ford. For this reason, it's one of only three hotels in the country that has been named a Literary Landmark by the Friends of Libraries USA. You can sense the hotel's distinguished history simply by walking through the gracious marble lobby. Another plus is the great location on Royal Street, steps from rowdy Bourbon Street action but safely away from the noise and commotion. Thanks to a massive renovation completed in 2003, the 573 rooms look better than ever, but keep in mind that many units are quite small and in some cases dark, and some look out at other hotel rooms (pricier rooms overlook the French Quarter or the Mississippi River, just a few blocks away). It's worth staying here if you can score a good deal—otherwise, some of the Monteleone's nearby competitors offer nicer, or at

least brighter, rooms at similar or better prices. Amenities include four restaurants and a wonderful rooftop pool (heated year-round) and fitness center.

With a prime spot in the Quarter, steps from dozens of great shops and restaurants, the **Omni Royal Orleans** (621 St. Louis St., 504/529-5333 or 800/THE-OMNI, www.omnihotels.com) has a devoted following but is less famous than some of its competitors and could even be called underrated. The lavish, rambling property contains 360 smartly furnished rooms with understatedly elegant decor, three phones, coffeemakers, and irons and boards; top rooms have balconies and whirlpool tubs, and just about all of them afford an impressive view of the Quarter. Public areas include a long, gracious marble lobby with tall arched windows and cushy chairs overlooking the colorful street life outside. It can get busy here, but the staff consistently keeps its cool and its humor. On the roof you'll find a fitness center and heated pool, along with a seasonal poolside café. There are a couple of natty bars on the ground floor, along with the hallowed Rib Room restaurant, a retro-hip favorite of carnivores.

Not your typical Holiday Inn, the **Chateau LeMoyne** (301 Dauphine St., 504/581-1303 or 800/465-4329, www.holiday-inn.com) occupies a row of 1940s townhouses, along with some vintage 19th-century structures built in the classic Creole style. It's been a hotel since 1971. Some rooms are in former slave quarters, and others contain such rich architectural details as cypress wood beams, exposed-brick walls, and lacy ironwork. Common areas include tree-shaded redbrick patios anchored by a pool. There's also a fitness center. There are 171 rooms with period reproductions and all the usual modern chain-hotel amenities you'd expect of a Holiday Inn.

Over $250

A bit of a departure from many W Hotels, which tend to be sleek and modern, **W New Orleans—French Quarter** (316 Chartres St., 504/581-1200 or 888/625-5144, www.starwood.com/whotels) occupies a stately old building with many rooms set around a magnificent courtyard. It captures the pizzazz and old-world charm of the

French Quarter, but in other respects, it's definitely a W Hotel: the 100 or so rooms have plush featherbeds with 250-thread-count linens, soft earth tones, framed black-and-white photos, TVs with high-speed Internet via infrared keyboards, VCRs, CD players, large work desks, two phones, Aveda bath products, and fully stocked minibars with microbrew beers and iced teas. In addition to all these creature comforts, the W employs perhaps the most attentive and helpful staff of any property in the French Quarter—they'll do just about anything you ask to make your stay memorable. Sip cocktails and nosh on snacks in the mod Living Room, or book a table for dinner at Bacco, a stellar restaurant serving contemporary New Orleans-meets-Italy cuisine. You won't find a more alluring, skillful balance between French Quarter charm and high-tech sophistication.

Celebs and business leaders favor the super-posh Hotel Maison de Ville, parts of which date to the 1700s. It's just off Bourbon Street, but once inside this cloistered property, you'd never know you're in the most raucous part of the city.

Celebs and business leaders favor the super-posh **Hotel Maison de Ville** (727 Toulouse St., 504/561-5858 or 800/634-1600, www.maisondeville.com), parts of which date to the 1700s (these are believed to be among the oldest extant buildings in the city). It's just off Bourbon Street, but once inside this cloistered property or one of the adjoining Audubon Cottages, you'd never know you're in the most raucous part of the city. There are 16 rooms set among two main buildings, one of them a former slave quarters, with a central courtyard and fountain. Additionally, on nearby Dauphine Street, there are seven private cottages. In every unit you'll find museum-quality antiques, four-poster beds, framed Audubon prints, and marble bathrooms; some have exposed brick walls and fireplaces. The exceptional Bistro at Maison de Ville is one of the top special-occasion restaurants in the French Quarter, specializing in creative contemporary Creole fare.

The French Quarter isn't really all that authentically French these days, but don't tell that to the staff and creative team behind the deluxe **Maison Orleans** (904 Iberville St., 504/670-

2900, www.maisonorleans.com), a 75-room boutique hotel run by the esteemed Ritz-Carlton chain that replicates the dignity and flair of a 19th-century Parisian town home. Rooms are decked in such stylish treasures as Louis XVI-inspired writing desks, brocade-upholstered wing chairs, and gilded mirrors. Guest have full use of the restaurants and other facilities of the much larger, adjacent Ritz-Carlton hotel.

In 2000, the Ritz-Carlton opened a larger property, the 452-room **Ritz-Carlton** (921 Canal St., 504/524-1331 or 800/241-3333, www.ritz-carlton.com), right on busy Canal Street, inside the massive Kress and Maison Blanche department store buildings, on the very edge of the Quarter. The glazed terra-cotta, twin-towered building has long been one of the city's architectural landmarks. This is the perfect choice for the ultimate vacation of pampering: the Ritz has a 20,000-square-foot state-of-the-art spa, a chic health club and gym, a clubby Library Lounge with a walk-in humidor, two other handsome bars, and a grand full-service restaurant, Victor's Grill, which serves nonpareil contemporary Continental cuisine. The well-trained staff tends to guests' every need, from free complimentary overnight shoeshines to nightly turndown service. Richly furnished rooms feel right out of old-world Paris, with 300-count Frette linens, goose-down pillows, Italian-marble baths, and floor-to-ceiling windows.

INNS AND BED-AND-BREAKFASTS
$100–150
The **Lamothe House** (621 Esplanade Ave., 504/947-1161or 888/696-9575, www.lamothehouse.com) is perfectly situated if you want to be near the French Quarter but in a quieter locale—and quick access to the city's hottest neighborhood, Faubourg Marigny. It's set along oak-lined Esplanade Avenue, the border

between the Quarter and Marigny, and it's an easy walk to clubs, restaurants, and shops in either neighborhood. Of course, at this cloistered Victorian inn you may simply want to curl up with your honey in your gracious hand-carved canopy bed, or lie on a chaise-longue in the lushly landscaped garden patio set around a small swimming pool. Rooms in this pretty-and-pink building contain such original architectural elements as intricately crafted ceiling medallions, marble-top nightstands, period artwork and wallpapers, and overstuffed Victorian couches. There's free off-street parking, and continental breakfast is included.

$150–250

An intimate, super-luxurious small hotel that isn't cheap but isn't unreasonably priced either, the **Soniat House** (1133 Chartres St., 504/522-0570 or 800/544-8808, www.soniathouse.com) sits on a quiet street close to the French Market and Faubourg Marigny. The hotel is set within an 1820s house built by one of New Orleans's most distinguished families. Rooms, overflowing with British, French, and Louisiana antiques, have such fancy extras as bath-side phones and extra reading pillows. You can relax in the elegant sitting room, with its well-stocked honor wine bar, or enjoy breakfast (which costs extra) either in your room or at a table by the lily pond in the courtyard.

The **Cornstalk** (915 Royal St., 504/523-1515) does things the old-fashioned way. It has no website, it accepts no online reservations, and there's no toll-free number. A dated and rather dreary sign greets guests out front, and guest bathrooms are small and not especially memorable. These might be a turnoff for some, but the place has a loyal following of repeat guests who appreciate the inn's informative staff, antiques-filled rooms with sweeping drapes and high ceilings, Oriental rugs, and in some cases fireplaces. This Victorian inn is fringed by an oft-photographed ornate cast-iron fence, which dates to the 1840s and has a distinctive cornstalk design—in fact, the hotel's yellow Italianate exterior has appeared in quite a few coffee-table books and movies. At the front of the house are a cheerful front garden, and upstairs a long balcony runs along the facade; both spots

are perfect for people-watching or sipping a drink while admiring the passersby on Royal Street. The Cornstalk's a quirky place, and with rates that often dip well below $150 during slower times, it can be a pretty good deal, too, especially considering the plum location.

It's not quite in the French Quarter, but if you can stand a 10-minute walk down Esplanade Avenue, the **Rathbone Inn** (1227 Esplanade Ave., 504/947-2100 or 800/947-2101, www.rathbone inn.com) can be a perfectly good base for exploring the area. It's also a short drive south of City Park and the eateries along Esplanade Ridge; the inn sits on the edge of historic Storyville, an area gradually undergoing an urban renaissance. The inn is set inside a lavish and expertly restored 1850 Greek Revival mansion. There are 12 rooms, each with not only a private bath but a kitchenette—some have balconies, and all have high ceilings and well-chosen antiques. A complimentary continental breakfast and afternoon wine-and-cheese reception are included, and the banana tree–shaded courtyard, with a Jacuzzi, makes a tranquil spot for whiling away an afternoon.

Over $250

A deluxe B&B on the border between the French Quarter and Faubourg Marigny, **Melrose Mansion** (937 Esplanade Ave., 504/944-2255 or 800/650-3323) occupies one of the most dramatic buildings on regal Esplanade Avenue, a Gothic Victorian 1880s mansion with tall French windows, fingerlace ironwork, tall pillared balconies and verandahs, and huge rooms, many of them full suites with sitting areas. The suites open onto grand balconies and have whirlpool tubs with separate showers, antique armoires, settees, and four-poster king-size beds. All rooms have marble bathrooms and gorgeous antiques and high-quality reproductions. Rates include nightly cocktails and hors d'oeuvres and full gourmet breakfasts. There's a heated pool and 24-hour concierge. It's not hard to see why the hotel is such a favorite with honeymooners, but keep in mind that the rates are high, and the service and amenities don't always quite live up—it's a good choice, however, if you can snag a reduced rate on the Internet or at a slower time.

ACCOMMODATIONS

Faubourg Marigny and Bywater

This trendy, on-the-up neighborhood just downriver from the Quarter has much of the bustle of its more famous neighbor, including some excellent restaurants and nightlife. Visitors unused to city living can be intimidated because it's a mostly residential neighborhood that can feel a tad quiet at night, and it does have a few rough patches. But this is also a real, historic New Orleans neighborhood, with a trove of stunning Creole cottages and Victorian treasures. There are no full-service hotels here, but you'll find oodles of cute inns and B&Bs. Prices here are about 75 to 90 percent of what you'd pay for comparable accommodations in the Quarter—the less central you are, the less pricey. In many cases, there's ample parking on the street, and some B&Bs have free off-street parking.

INNS AND BED-AND-BREAKFASTS

$50–100

One of the few pet-friendly inns in the city, the moderately priced **Royal Street Courtyard** (2446 Royal St., #3, 504/943-6818 or 888/846-4004, www.virtualcities.com/ons/la/n/lan97010.htm) occupies a rambling historic compound. Among the nine rooms, several have fully equipped kitchens, and all have at least a refrigerator, cable TV, and a phone. This gay-popular inn is especially known for its verdant tropical courtyard, punctuated with fish ponds, blooming flower gardens, and a secluded hot tub. The same owners operate the adjacent Ariana Inn, an 1850s Greek Revival mansion with 14 high-ceilinged rooms, all with private bath. Continental breakfast is included.

An affordable, charming B&B a few blocks downriver from Washington Park and about eight blocks from the Quarter, the **Creole Inn** (2471 Dauphine St., 504/948-3230, www.creoleinn.com) is run by a museum curator and former professor with a great knowledge of the neighborhood's, and the city's, history and architecture. There are five rooms, two of which

have two bedrooms and can accommodate up to four guests. Accommodations have high ceilings and hardwood floors, and a simple mix of antiques and rattan pieces, plus TVs with VCRs, cordless phones with voice mail, and private baths. There's a lounge where you can check email on a computer, and a secluded patio with a fountain. Continental breakfast is included. This friendly, easygoing hostelry is one of the better values of any inn within walking distance of the Quarter, but keep in mind that one night's deposit is required and will be forfeited if you cancel less than 60 days out.

$100–150

Just inside Faubourg Marigny, a few steps from Esplanade (which forms the border with the Quarter), **La Maison Marigny** (1421 Bourbon St., 504/948-3638 or 800/570-2014, www.lamaisonmarigny.com) blends the homey ambience of a small B&B with the creature comforts of a luxury hotel. Each room has cable TV, high-quality bedding, plush bath towels, multi-speed ceiling fans and central air and heating, and phones with data ports. Rooms have lavish dark-wood antique beds, handsome oak and mahogany furnishings, polished hardwood floors, attractive area rugs, and 12-foot ceilings—the place oozes with character without being over-decorated or frilly. There are just three guest rooms in this meticulously restored 1898 house, meaning that you're assured personalized service, but hosts Dewey Donihoo and John Ramsey also take care to respect guests' privacy. Breakfast is served in a sunny, foliage-choked courtyard.

If you really want to experience life in one of New Orleans's most charming and historic neighborhoods, an area that's well off the beaten tourist track but still just a short walk from the Quarter, consider a stay at the romantic **B and W Courtyards** (2425 Chartres St., 504/945-9418 or 800/585-5731, www.bandwcourtyards.com), an eight-room B&B set inside three 19th-century buildings with delightful connecting courtyards. This peaceful hideaway is a favorite with guests seeking privacy (it's not suitable for children), and innkeepers Rob Boyd and Kevin Wu are warm and enthusiastic hosts. Rooms are decked with fine antiques and fine linens, all with private bath, central air-conditioning and heat, and fresh flowers, and most of them open onto one of the courtyards. In the rear courtyard, you can soak in a Jacuzzi under the stars. There are a couple of nattily furnished long-term suites available.

A relative newcomer in the hip Marigny, **Elysian Fields Inn** (930 Elysian Fields Ave., New Orleans, 504/948-9420 or 866/948-9420, www.elysianfieldsinn.com) offers a lot of hotel for relatively reasonable rates. Accommodations in this striking 1860s Greek Revival mansion include eight guest rooms and a large suite with both a queen bed and a queen sleeper sofa. In-room amenities include Aveda bath products, Italian-marble bathrooms (most with whirlpool tubs), flat-screen TVs with VCR/DVD players, and central air/heat; the polished wood floors are fine Brazilian mahogany, and ceiling fans whirr from the 10- to 14-foot ceilings. The rooms are filled with sleek and sophisticated Mission-style antiques and neutral-tone linens, and some units have sleigh beds or four-poster beds; the unfussy aesthetic is a nice departure from some of the city's more clutter-filled B&Bs. Were this property a few blocks over in the French Quarter, rates would be another $100 per night. But Elysian Fields isn't far from the Quarter, and it's just a couple of safe blocks from the hip dining and nightlife along Frenchmen Street.

A small house-museum with stunning gardens and two guest suites, **Sun Oak Gardens** (2020 Burgundy St., 504/945-0322, www.sunoaknola.com) is a colorful and striking Greek Revival Creole cottage painted in four colors and designated a city landmark. Wide-plank heart-pine floors, antiques culled from throughout southern Louisiana, and a small maze of patios and flowering gardens make this a marvel of historic preservation and one of the most distinctive architectural treasures in Faubourg Marigny, a neighborhood rife with great buildings. Up a winding staircase you'll reach the dormer suite, a cozy room with a pitched ceiling, bathroom with clawfoot tub, antique half-tester bed, and a sleeper sofa (the room can accommodate four guests). The Garden Suite overlooks the courtyard and has an iron half-tester bed and a loft sleeping area. Both units share a full kitchen with a dining area. It's an ideal B&B for friends traveling together and planning to stay for several days or more.

Near the northern edge of this funky neighborhood, **Marigny Manor House** (2125 N. Rampart St., 504/943-7826 or 877/247-7599, www.marignymanorhouse.com) sits along a quiet stretch that may feel a tad out of the way if you're not used to big cities but offers a wonderful sampling of vintage 19th-century residential architecture typical of New Orleans. The offbeat bars and restaurants of Frenchmen Street are a short walk away. The tan Greek Revival house, meticulously restored, has four neatly furnished, reasonably priced rooms with designer fabrics, marble-top chests, four-poster beds, and Oriental rugs over hardwood floors. One room has a balcony overlooking the brick fern-and-flower-bedecked courtyard.

Central Business and Warehouse Districts

This is New Orleans's rather modern downtown, which still means that you'll find a lot of buildings from the early 20th century, and some even older, especially down closer to the river in the Warehouse District. And except for the artsy Warehouse District, with its high-ceilinged brick buildings with tall windows, many of which reveal galleries and restaurants, most of the CBD feels rather impersonal and corporate. The section nearest the French Quarter, from Canal to Poydras Streets, abounds with hotels, the most charming and distinctive of which are reviewed in this chapter. Many others—the Marriott, the Sheraton, the Inter-Continental, and a bunch of lower-end chain properties—are not included, partly because of space restrictions, but partly because they tend to court convention business, charge business rates, and offer little charm and personal service. They're often perfectly nice hotels with, in some cases, very fancy rooms, but you may end up paying $50 to $100 more per night for a room simply because it's inside a massive hotel with a huge staff and oodles of facilities that you'll never use.

A pleasant trend of late, however, has been an influx of smaller, more characterful boutique hotels opening inside early-20th-century office buildings—the Wyndham Whitney, the Monaco, the Drury Inn, and several others fit this description. You can find some elegant, imposing, grand, and occasionally economical hotels in the CBD, but you generally will not find a property that captures the jazzy personality or charming architecture of old-world New Orleans. Street parking is nonexistent to impossible in the CBD; most hotels offer garage or valet parking for $20 to $30 nightly. You can also find some lots, some staffed and some unstaffed, that charge anywhere from $5 to $20 per 24-hour period, but in these lots you typically will not have in/out privileges.

HOTELS AND MOTELS

$50–100

It's a cookie-cutter chain hotel that could just as easily be in central Dubuque as in the Central Business District, but the **Sleep Inn** (334 O'-Keefe Ave., 504/524-5400 or 877/424-6423, www.sleepinn.com) has 129 clean rooms and a safe if uninspired location in the heart of downtown (the Superdome is four blocks away). Parking costs about $20 a day, but otherwise, this is an easy-on-the-budget option with an outdoor pool and free continental breakfast.

About the only drawback about the well-run **Clarion Hotel New Orleans** (1300 Canal St., 504/299-9900 or 877/424-6423, www.clarion-hotel.com) is a somewhat drab setting along upper Canal Street, a few blocks north of the French Quarter. On the other hand, this is one of the few hotels in New Orleans in this price range from which you can easily walk to Bourbon Street, the Superdome, and the many restaurants and shops downtown. The hotel is set inside an attractive Victorian brick building, and it offers a number of amenities, including a full-service restaurant, room service, an exercise room, a pool, continental breakfast, and in-room microwaves, refrigerators, irons and boards, and hair dryers. Valet parking is $10 to $15 nightly (it's more expensive on weekends).

$100–150

A relatively new option in the historic Cotton Exchange building, the **Cotton Exchange Hotel** (231 Carondelet St., 504/962-0800 or 888/884-6126, www.cottonhotelneworleans.com) has just about 100 rooms, all with high ceilings, tall windows, and tasteful if ordinary furnishings; think neutral colors and striped wallpaper. There's a small rooftop pool and lanai, and rooms have WebTV, coffeemakers, phones with voice mail, and other amenities you'd expect of a business hotel. Frequent Internet specials can make this one an excellent value.

One of the better midrange chain hotels in the CBD, **Comfort Suites** (346 Baronne St., 504/524-1140 or 877/424-6423, www.comfortsuites.com) has only one drawback—its name is something of a misnomer. The rooms are not truly suites, though each features a half-partitioned sitting area with a desk and small

ACCOMMODATIONS

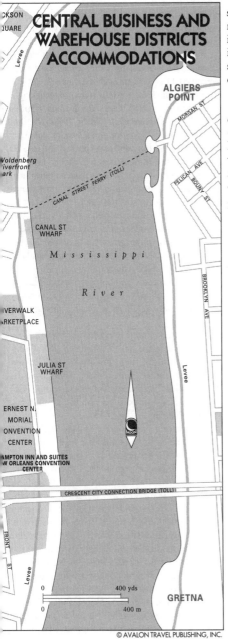

CENTRAL BUSINESS AND WAREHOUSE DISTRICTS ACCOMMODATIONS

ALGIERS POINT

MORGAN ST

PELICAN AVE

BOUNY ST

Woldenberg Riverfront Park

CANAL STREET FERRY (TOLL)

CANAL ST WHARF

M i s s i s s i p p i

R i v e r

BROOKLYN AVE

RIVERWALK MARKETPLACE

JULIA ST WHARF

Levee

ERNEST N. MORIAL CONVENTION CENTER

HAMPTON INN AND SUITES NEW ORLEANS CONVENTION CENTER

CRESCENT CITY CONNECTION BRIDGE (TOLL)

FRONT ST

Levee

0   400 yds

0   400 m

GRETNA

© AVALON TRAVEL PUBLISHING, INC.

sofa; some do have whirlpool tubs. Windows of many rooms are sealed shut and frosted, making it a bit dreary and stuffy in here. There's nothing special about this hotel, but rooms this size—with refrigerators, coffeemakers, and microwaves—at these rates are hard to find just a 10-minute walk from the Quarter.

Part of a popular Midwest-based chain, the only Louisiana locale of the **Drury Inn & Suites** (820 Poydras St., 504/529-7800 or 800/DRURY INN, www.druryinn.com) offers one of the best values in the CBD. This 156-unit hotel, with a mix of standard rooms and two-room suites, occupies a handsome 10-story 1917 building (formerly the Cumberland Telephone Building) five blocks from both the French Quarter and the Superdome. High ceilings and tall windows bathe the rooms in sunlight; each has a marble-accented bathroom, free high-speed Internet access, and pleasant contemporary—if generic—furnishings. You can relax in the rooftop pool and hot tub, and you get discount admission to a health club across the street. Many of the building's original details, such as the ornamental lobby staircase and Waterford crystal chandeliers, have been carefully preserved. An expansive and hot continental breakfast is included in the rates, which often dip below $100 nightly, especially on weekends.

A cool, reasonably priced hotel in the slick Warehouse District, the **Ambassador New Orleans** (535 Tchoupitoulas St., 504/527-5271 or 888/527-5271, http://clients.neworleans.com/ambassador) is situated within three neighboring redbrick warehouses that date to the 1850s. The look and feel blends the new and old. Ceiling timbers, steel beams, worn stucco, and brick are left exposed, and the 163 rooms have large writing desks, in-room safes, tall windows, hardwood floors, and wrought-iron four-poster beds. There's a full-service restaurant that provides room service, and a warm and inviting lounge.

The **Hampton Inn and Suites New Orleans Convention Center** (1201 Convention Center Blvd., 504/566-9990 or 800/HAMPTON) differs a bit from the usual modern chain properties—it's set inside a five-story redbrick building from the early 1900s that once contained a cotton mill. There's a shaded park beside the hotel, and the convention center, casino, Riverwalk shops, and Warehouse District are all close by. There are 288 guest rooms, many of them suites, some with mini-kitchens, Jacuzzi tubs, and separate bedrooms. High ceilings with tall windows keep things light and bright. A coin laundry, concierge, business center, pool, and fitness room round out the amenities.

There aren't many hotels in New Orleans that offer better views of the Carnival parade route than **Hotel Le Cirque** (936 St. Charles Ave., 504/962-0900 or 800/684-9525, www.hotellecirque.com), which towers over Lee Circle. Like the W hotels and the International House, this is a hotel for hipsters, with mod furnishings, monochromatic color schemes, and a trendy eatery, Lee Circle Restaurant. But here, rates typically hover around $100 nightly and often dip well below that during slower times. This former YMCA has been handsomely retrofitted, but a simple design and smallish rooms help keep the prices down. As you might guess, this is a favorite address of artists, younger travelers, and others with a yen for style and a desire to save money.

$150–250

With a handy location near the French Quarter and along the streetcar line to the Garden District, the **Royal St. Charles Hotel** (135 St. Charles Ave., 504/587-1641 or 800/205-7131, www.royalsaintcharleshotel.com) makes sense if you're seeking a central location and stylish, understated accommodations. Original art fills the 143 contemporary rooms, which also hold bathrobes, minibars, custom-made lightwood furniture, in-room safes, and in-room faxes and modems. The hotel is part of a minichain called New Orleans Boutique Hotels, which also runs the Queen & Crescent Hotel (in the CBD) and the Garden District Hotel.

Intimate and hidden away on a narrow CBD street, the classy **Omni Royal Crescent** (535 Gravier St., 504/527-0006 or 800/THE-OMNI, www.omnihotels.com) offers a low-key boutique-hotel ambience. The 98 rooms of this eight-story property have sturdy custom-made mattresses, imported bath amenities, terry robes,

honor bars, and soft lighting; some have whirlpool tubs, and several suites have floor-to-ceiling windows, VCRs, and CD players. There's a rooftop pool and adjacent gym, and on the ground floor you'll find the upscale and well-received Thai restaurant Benjarong.

One of the few long-term-stay properties right in downtown New Orleans, the **Embassy Suites Hotel New Orleans** (315 Julia St., 504/525-1993 or 800/EMBASSY, www.embassysuites.com) sits just steps from the trendy art galleries and eateries of the white-hot Warehouse District. This 16-story building with 372 rooms makes a plush nest, especially for guests planning to stay more than a few days—each suite has high-speed Internet, kitchenettes with mini-refrigerators and microwaves, work tables, and couches; the double suites sleep up to six guests, as they have sleeper sofas. Perks include complimentary full breakfast in the seven-story atrium lobby café, a 24-hour fitness center, and a lap pool and hot tub. This is a great neighborhood—safe but lively and not nearly as touristy as the Quarter, which is just a short walk away.

Site of the famous Rene Bistrot, the relatively new **Renaissance Pere Marquette** (817 Common St., 504/525-1111 or 888/236-2427, www.renaissancehotels.com) rises 18 stories over the CBD, with 275 smartly furnished rooms. CD players, dual-line cordless phones, hair dryers, irons and boards, 27-inch TVs, and complimentary morning papers are standard with every room. There's also an outdoor pool and gym.

One of the more creative hotel conversions in New Orleans in recent years, the **Wyndham Riverfront** (701 Convention Center Blvd., 504/524-8200 or 800/WYNDHAM, www.wyndham.com) is set inside a vintage tobacco warehouse a short walk from the casino, the Riverwalk mall, the galleries of the Warehouse District, and the Quarter. It's a convenient location, and the hotel has upscale, modern rooms with high-speed Internet, large windows, and warm furnishings in muted earth tones.

The **Renaissance Arts Hotel** (700 Tchoupitoulas St., 504/613-2330, or 888/236-2427, www.renaissancehotels.com) opened in summer 2003 in the artsy Warehouse District, on the edge of the CBD. This upscale 217-room hotel occupies a five-story former warehouse. A distinctly urban, sleek addition to the city, it even has its own first-floor art gallery. Rooms are airy and spacious, with tall windows. Yes, it's part of the Marriott chain, but the hotel has a boutique-y ambience, owing in part to the high staff-to-guest ratio and personal service. The in-house restaurant, run by acclaimed New Orleans restaurateur Rene Bajeux, has quickly become a neighborhood favorite for its creative French Creole cuisine.

New Orleans has seen an influx of longer-stay hotels in recent years, among them the new **Homewood Suites Downtown** (409 Baronne St., 504/581-5599 or 800/468-3571, www.home woodsuites.com), a 12-story building in the heart of the CBD. You'll find 30 two-bedroom suites and 136 one-bedroom units, all with full kitchens, breakfast tables, two cable TVs, two phones with data ports, irons and boards, complimentary continental breakfast, and evening cocktail and snack receptions Monday through Thursday. There's also an indoor pool, exercise room, guest laundry, 24-hour convenience store, and business center. It's a popular spot for business travelers, but families or leisure visitors staying for several days can make good use of this hotel, which often offers reduced prices on slower weekends.

Pet-friendly hotels have become more commonplace over the past few years, but it's rare to find an upscale property that actually rolls out the red carpet for dogs: the **Hotel Monaco** (333 St. Charles Ave., 504/561-0010 or 866/685-8359, www.monaco-neworleans.com), part of the San Francisco–based Kimpton boutique-hotel chain, greets four-legged friends with a "bone appetite package," which includes a pet bed and doggie treat. You can even arrange for a staff member to walk your dog. And if you don't have your own animal companion with you, request a complimentary goldfish in a bowl for your bedside. Of course, there's much more to the luxurious Monaco than pet-friendliness. The 250-room property occupies a 19-story 1920s building on St. Charles Avenue that once contained a Masonic temple. Decor is playful and imaginative, with African- and Caribbean-influenced color schemes, Italian-cotton linens, CD stereos, and cushy colorful sofas and wing chairs in each room. Suites have whirlpool tubs. Susan Spicer's Cobalt Restaurant occupies the ground floor—it's one of the best hotel eateries in the Big Easy, and that's saying a lot.

Set inside a vintage redbrick bank building near the bustling intersection of Poydras and St. Charles (an ideal locale for viewing Mardi Gras parades), **The Whitney** (610 Poydras St., 504/581-4222 or 800/WYNDHAM, www.wynd-ham.com) offers one of the better values among upscale hotels in the CBD—rates often dip below $150 nightly. This is partly because the hotel is relatively small (just 93 units) as CBD hotels go, and the rooms themselves are a bit small. Still, with earthy color schemes, plush linens, ergonomic chairs and work desks, high-speed Internet, and handsome marble bathrooms, the accommodations are completely comfortable. The restaurant 56 Degrees, set inside the elegant former bank lobby, serves commendable Asian-meets-Creole fare, offering three meals daily.

The stately **Lafayette Hotel** (600 St. Charles Ave., 504/539-9000 or 888/856-4706, www.the-lafayettehotel.com) is the most appealing and best-located of an empire of small, upscale boutique hotels set throughout New Orleans, all with elegant but in some cases staid decor and competent but unspectacular service. This hotel, inside a grand five-story 1916 building that served as a Navy barracks during World War II, sits beside attractive Lafayette Square and is right on the streetcar line. The 44 luxurious rooms are swathed in floor-to-ceiling drapes and designer fabrics. Also expect to find French doors opening onto small wrought-iron balconies, mahogany furniture, and British botanical prints—it's all very deluxe and proper. Suites have VCRs and whirlpool tubs. Some of the other properties that are part of the same company, New Orleans Fine Hotels—the French Market Inn, the Cotton Exchange, and Hotel Le Cirque—are also reviewed in this chapter, and check out the company web page (www.neworleansfinehotels.com) for details on the other lodging options, which include the Chateau Dupre (in the Quarter), the Holiday Inn Express (CBD), the Parc St. Charles (CBD), the Pelham Hotel (CBD), and the St. James (Warehouse District).

ACCOMMODATIONS

RECYCLE, RE-USE

New Orleans has long had a tendency to re-use and adapt old buildings in innovative ways. This is especially true of the city's hotels and inns, several of which were constructed for entirely different purposes. Here are a few properties with especially colorful histories:

Drury Inn & Suites (820 Poydras St., 504/529-7800 or 800/DRURYINN, www.drury inn.com). This mid-price chain inhabits the 1917 Cumberland Telephone Building and still contains the carefully preserved ornamental lobby staircase and Waterford crystal chandeliers that greeted past generations of phone company employees—a pre-dotcom example of office excess.

Hotel Monaco (333 St. Charles Ave., 504/561-0010 or 866/685-8359, www.monaco-new orleans.com). It's only right that visitors to the swanky Hotel Monaco feel like members of some exclusive club upon entering the property's luxe confines. Before it was converted into a hotel, this 19-story neo-Gothic wonder, built in 1926, housed the city's Masonic Temple. If only these walls could talk . . . .

International House (221 Camp St., 504/553-9550, www.ihhotel.com). Before opening to house a stylish hotel in 1998, this timelessly beautiful 1906 Beaux-Arts building served as one of New Orleans' leading institutions of high finance, the Louisiana Bank & Trust Co. In the 1940s the building earned its present name, International House, when it became headquarters for a newly formed nonprofit trade group whose aim was fostering world peace. It was the forerunner not only to the World Trade Center that presently stands at the foot of Canal Street, overlooking the Mississippi River, but to more than 300 additional world trade centers that have been established in cities all over the world. It's only appropriate, of course, that International House is today a favorite destination of dignitaries, financiers, and world travelers.

Ritz-Carlton (921 Canal St., 504/524-1331 or 800/241-3333, www.ritz-carlton.com). Lay your head where Liz Claiborne and Cuisinart once reigned; this deluxe hotel is in a former department store building that once housed Kress and the Maison Blanche, built back in the days when they knew how to build department stores (1910, to be exact). It's only appropriate, by the way, that Liz Claiborne still has a strong following among fashionable shoppers in New Orleans; she's a direct descendant of Louisiana's first governor, William C.C. Claiborne.

St. Vincent's Guest House (1507 Magazine St., 504/523-3411, www.stvincentguesthouse.com). An order of nuns known as the Daughters of Charity built this place as an orphanage during the Civil War–era yellow fever epidemic, and cared for several generations of children here. Look on the walls for photos of them in their flying-nun habits.

The Whitney (610 Poydras St., 504/581-4222 or 800/WYNDHAM, www.wyndham.com). Built in 1883, the Whitney was for many years one of New Orleans' most prestigious banking institutions. Now it's a 93-room boutique hotel, but you can still get a sense of the building's previous incarnation by exploring the ground-floor restaurant, 56 Degrees, which occupies the former bank lobby. Teller windows are still visible, flanking the kitchen. And the old safety-deposit vault is now a private dining room.

Over $250

In reader polls conducted by leading travel magazines, the 319-room **Windsor Court Hotel** (300 Gravier St., 504/523-6000 or 888/596-0955, www.windsorcourthotel.com) has been ranked among the top few hotels in the world. With that in mind, the Windsor Court has a lot to live up to, and in some ways it's hard to understand what all the fuss is about. Sure, this hotel that opened in the early 1980s contains a $10 million collection of British art that includes originals by Gainsborough and Reynolds. There's a high staff-to-guest ratio, and these employees know how to please guests. And the large rooms, most of them full suites, contain high-quality Euro-elegant furnishings and Italian-marble baths, giving them the feel and look of a posh English country home. But you'll pay dearly to stay here, and the aesthetic doesn't really capture the jazzy exuberance of New Orleans—the hotel feels as though it was airlifted from London or New York City and dropped down in the heart of the CBD. Some people love it, others find it stuffy. Amenities include one of the most lavish and formal restaurants in the city, a full health club, a pool, and a 24-hour concierge.

More contemporary and urbane in ambience than W's French Quarter property, the **W New Orleans** (333 Poydras St., 504/525-9444 or 888/625-5144, www.whotels.com) occupies a 23-story downtown skyscraper near the shops of Riverwalk, the art galleries of the Warehouse District, and New Orleans's white elephant of a casino. The hotel is a favorite with young business execs, owing to its state-of-the-art wiring and high-tech gadgetry (in-room high-speed Internet, CD players, VCRs, cordless dual-line speaker phones), as well as its sexy and sleek Zoe Bistrot restaurant and ultracool Whiskey Blue cocktail lounge. Rooms on the upper floors have exceptional river and city views. Aveda bath products, marble baths, and monochromatic black, gray, and white color schemes complete the oh-so-cool look and feel.

There's no better time to visit the **Fairmont New Orleans** (123 Baronne St., 504/529-7111 or 800/527-4727, www.fairmont.com), or at least walk through it, than during the Christmastime holidays, when the lobby is transformed—a long canopy of white "angel hair" hangs the length of the marble entryway, with shiny ornaments, trimmed trees, and poinsettias as far as you can see. The entire hotel was dramatically renovated in the late '90s at a cost of $51 million and now lives up to its old-world reputation—remaining one of the most fashionable addresses in the South since 1893. The hotel has 700 rooms with marble baths, down pillows, and other cushy amenities, plus a rooftop health club with tennis, a pool, and spa. The Sazerac Bar & Grill is another highlight of this property that fringes the Quarter along Canal Street—it's named for the Sazerac cocktail was invented in New Orleans in 1859. The only drawback can be flaws in the service—it's a big hotel with a big-hotel feel, and sometimes staff can be slow with requests.

New Orleans had nothing even vaguely resembling a hip, contemporary hotel before **International House** (221 Camp St., 504/553-9550, www.ihhotel.com) opened in 1998. Since then, a few other properties have taken a similarly enlightened approach to hospitality, but this beacon of beige, which occupies a 1906 beaux-arts building, remains the coolest address in town. The restrained decorating scheme of muted colors is not without whimsy: seven times each year the lobby is reborn to celebrate a particular festival or holiday that's dear to New Orleans, from All Souls'/All Saints' Day in early November to the voodoo-based St. John's Eve in late June. Each of the 119 light-filled rooms has a CD player and a selection of discs featuring the music of New Orleans luminaries, and neatly matted black-and-white photos of jazz greats line the walls. Other amenities include two-line speakerphones, with data ports, and bathrooms with Aveda spa products. Given the fashionable clientele it courts, it's no surprise that the hotel's Loa Bar is a favorite spot for well-coiffed, dressed-in-black sorts to rub elbows and mingle. And the restaurant, Lemon Grass, serves superb Pan-Asian fare.

The International House team, headed by owner Sean Cummings, also operates a more intimate and even more luxurious property nearby,

Loft 523 (523 Gravier St., 504/200-6523, www .loft523.com), which may just be the most edgy and distinctive boutique hotel in the South. Starting from its airy, minimalist lobby with white walls and earthy tones, Loft 523 deviates from the typically ornate style of many New Orleans properties. This place is new, sexy, and swank, with the emphasis squarely on contemporary urban design. The 16 SoHo loft–inspired rooms and two penthouse suites (with garden terraces)

have low-slung, mod furnishings, luxuriant Frette linens, and plenty of high-tech gadgetry (Sony five-speaker CD stereos, DVD surround-sound TVs, high-speed Internet, cordless phones). Each of the glass-and-limestone showers has double showerheads and Aveda bath products. The hotel occupies an 1880s dry-goods warehouse in the CBD, its high ceilings and tall windows helping to create the artsy mood. Room service is available from the International House hotel.

The Garden District and Uptown

There's a great variety of accommodations in this huge neighborhood that extends for several miles upriver from the CBD. Closest in, for about 20 blocks past the CBD, you'll find a mix of inns, B&Bs, and full-service motels and hotels, most of them along St. Charles Avenue and Prytania Street. These places generally cost 10 to 30 percent less than comparable accommodations in either the Quarter or the CBD. The plus is that the neighborhood, even where it's somewhat built up, has its own charm and a less chaotic pace than downtown or the Quarter; it's also an easy streetcar ride or fairly short cab ride from the CBD and Quarter. The disadvantage, to some, is that you can't walk to the Quarter or CBD from here, at least not easily, and the neighborhood feels less urban—it's not as all-night and rockin'. If you're coming to New Orleans for the frenetic nightlife and nonstop revelry, you may feel out of touch over here. If you'd prefer a little more peace and quiet but still want to be near great dining and shopping, or if you're here with a family, this area, generally known as the Lower Garden District, makes a lot of sense.

Farther into the Garden District and Uptown, there aren't any full-service hotels, but you'll find a significant number of inns and B&Bs, set anywhere on the blocks between St. Charles Avenue and Magazine Street. Some of these places can feel quite removed from the city, and sometimes that's in a good way—you might find yourself staying on a gracious tree-lined street sandwiched between fancy homes, or a short walk from Audubon Park or the funky and laid-back shop-

ping and dining along Magazine Street. Seasoned visitors to New Orleans, who've "been there and done that," often favor accommodations in this neighborhood over those in the more touristy or business-oriented neighborhoods downriver.

HOTELS AND MOTELS
Under $50
New Orleans's only youth hostel, the **Marquette House** (2253 Carondelet St., 504/523-3014, www.hiayh.org) is a quirky complex of 19th-century wood-frame buildings in the Garden District, a short walk from the St. Charles Avenue streetcar. The hostel has 155 beds and eight private rooms, and it has 24-hour access (a must, of course, in a city as wild as this one). There's fenced parking ($5/night), a laundry, a patio and picnic area, storage lockers, and a communal kitchen. Dorm rooms are separated by gender and include about 10 to 15 beds a room. Rates are about $15 to $25 per person, depending on the time of year and whether there's a big event in town. Reservations are absolutely essential if you're planning to come for Mardi Gras or Jazz Fest, and they're a good idea in summer, when many students are traveling to New Orleans. Tulane and Loyola are a short streetcar ride or long stroll away. The hostel does accept MasterCard and Visa.

$50–100
The family-owned **Avenue Garden Hotel** (1509 St. Charles Ave., 504/521-8000 or 800/379-5322, www.avenuegardenhotel.com) has just 23

rooms set in a restored 1890s building with gracious balconies and ample charm. It's within walking distance of the CBD and a 10-minute streetcar ride from the French Quarter. The rooms mix reproduction New Orleans–inspired antiques with such up-to-date amenities as CD radio/alarm clocks, hair dryers, irons and boards, and voice mail; suites have VCRs, microwaves, refrigerators, and sofa sleepers— accommodations are simple but comfortable, more than satisfactory considering the price.

> *The Garden District, even where it's somewhat built up, has its own charm and a less chaotic pace; it's also an easy streetcar ride or fairly short cab ride from the CBD and French Quarter.*

A great location close to the CBD and Garden District, and accommodations set inside historic 19th-century buildings, set the **Quality Inn & Suites St. Charles** (1319 St. Charles Ave., 504/522-0187 or 877/424-6423, www.qualityinn.com) apart from other midrange chain properties. The rooms themselves, as well as the level of service, are fairly standard, but this is a dependable option with a nice swimming pool.

The unabashedly low-tech but super-charming (and affordable) **St. Charles Guest House** (1748 Prytania St., 504/523-6556, www.stcharlesguesthouse.com) makes the perfect roost if you're looking to save a few bucks and don't mind rooms without TVs or phones. The staff is friendly and helpful, always willing to offer advice and directions to the many Europeans, students, artists, and other independent-spirited travelers who stay here. The modest pension has 30 guest rooms set among four adjoining historic buildings; the rock-bottom-priced units share bathrooms (these start at just $45 nightly for a single). There's a pool and courtyard out back shaded by banana trees, and continental breakfast is included.

$100–150
The spa facilities are the hallmark of the **Avenue Plaza Hotel & Spa** (2111 St. Charles Ave., 504/566-1212, www.avenueplazahotel.com), a 256-room hotel in the heart of the Garden District. There's also a fitness center, sauna, hot tubs, and aerobics classes at the spa. Otherwise, this is

a fairly standard chain-style hotel that's well-suited to longer stays, as rooms and suites have kitchenettes, king-size beds, and plenty of room to kick around in; the one-bedroom suites have a sitting and dining area separate from the sleeping room. A large pool and patio behind the hotel and a rooftop sundeck and Jacuzzi with nice downtown skyline views complete the picture. Service can be spotty, but as rates sometimes fall to around $100 nightly, it can be a decent value.

Anne Rice had a cow when the Popeyes and Copeland's restaurant magnate Al Copeland opened the art deco **Clarion Grand Boutique Hotel** (2001 St. Charles Ave., 504/558-9966 or 877/424-6423, www.clarionhotel.com), a 44-room low-rise property with a delightful and convenient location on St. Charles, smack in the middle of the Garden District. Some say Rice and Copeland just like to feud for the publicity. Who knows? The controversy notwithstanding, this is a great little hotel with fair rates and pretty good service compared with other midrange properties in New Orleans. It's also the only art deco hotel in the city. Try to get a unit with a balcony overlooking St. Charles (keeping in mind that traffic noise can be a bummer). Rooms have big windows that let in plenty of light, and all have refrigerators, microwaves, coffeemakers, safes, dual-line phones with voice mail, and bold, attractive furnishings. Copeland's Cheesecake Bistro provides room service, and continental breakfast is included in the rates.

A top-notch property Uptown, the 100-room **Hampton Inn Garden District** (3626 St. Charles Ave., 504/899-9990 or 800/HAMPTON, www.hamptoninn.com) occupies an attractive midrise building that's a short streetcar ride from Audubon Park, Tulane, and Loyola. It's a bit farther from the CBD and French Quarter than most of the other hotels on St. Charles, but that's a plus if you're seeking a quieter experience—this stretch of St. Charles is less developed and has fewer tall buildings. This Hampton Inn is above average as the chain

ACCOMMODATIONS

goes, with particularly bright and well-kept rooms; some suites have Jacuzzi tubs.

One of the Garden District's—and the city's—best little treasures, the **Prytania Park Hotel** (1525 Prytania St., 504/524-0427 or 888/498-7591, www.prytaniapark.com) has 62 warmly furnished rooms set in two buildings at the lower end of the neighborhood, an easy streetcar ride from the CBD (St. Charles Avenue is just a block away). The hotel has some great features, such as loft suites geared toward families, which have queen-size beds on the ground floor and sleeping areas in a loft up above. Another plus is the lobby store with snack foods. In every room you'll find refrigerators, microwaves, ceiling fans, and elegant reproduction antiques. The grounds are verdantly landscaped with cheery courtyards, and the staff is first-rate. If you don't mind giving up some of the facilities found at other hotels, such as a pool or restaurant, this is a terrific find.

INNS AND BED-AND-BREAKFASTS

$50–100

A reasonably priced option with plenty of character, the **Acadian Orleans Inn** (2041 Prytania St., 504/566-1411,www.acadianorleansinn .com) opened in fall 2002 on the edge of the Garden District. The least costly rooms are perfectly pleasant, though spare, with quilted bedspreads and simple furnishings; more lavish rooms have fancier beds and linens and a bit more space. All rooms have high-speed Internet, cable TV, and phones, and continental breakfast is included. It's a reliable option, and with just 19 guest rooms, it's more intimate and personal than one of the comparably priced chain properties nearby along St. Charles Avenue.

The **Green House Inn** (1212 Magazine St., 504/525-1333 or 800/966-1303, www.green inn.com) offers a change of pace from so many of New Orleans's richly urbane inns and B&Bs. The decorative scheme here is tropical and whimsical, from the pool out back shaped like a palm tree to the verdant and colorful landscaping. It's also one of the lower-priced properties in town, set in the Lower Garden District, an area

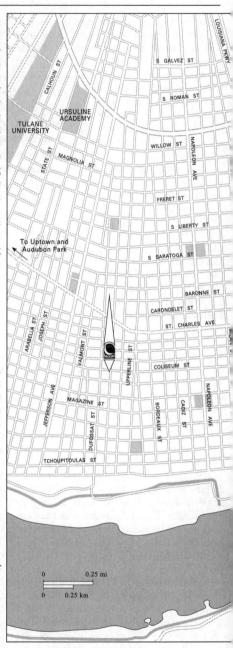

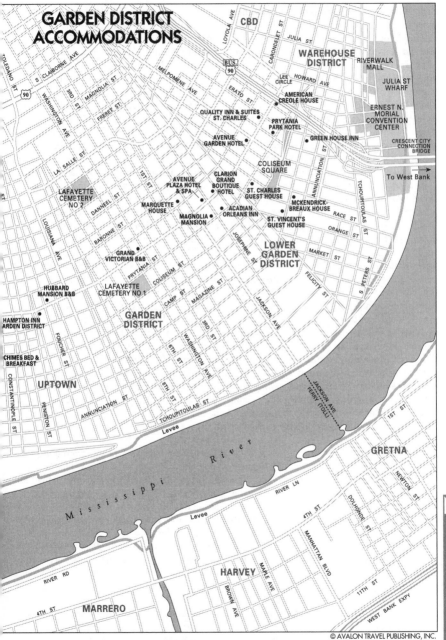

GARDEN DISTRICT ACCOMMODATIONS

© AVALON TRAVEL PUBLISHING, INC.

that continues to gentrify as new homeowners move in and fix up the many great old houses in this neighborhood. Discounts are offered to college and grad-school students, and to guests staying a week or longer. Rooms are well-outfitted with king-size beds, TVs with VCRs, mini-refrigerators, phones with modems, ceiling fans and central air, and CD/clock radios—the kinds of amenities you'd expect of a much pricier hotel. There's a small workout room, and a hot tub alongside the pool. The patio by the pool is clothing-optional. The Green House Inn has a loyal gay/lesbian following, but all are welcome.

Easy on the wallet and steps from great antiques shopping on lower Magazine Street, **St. Vincent's Guest House** (1507 Magazine St., 504/523-3411, www.stvincentguesthouse.com) occupies a three-story brick building that's actually a vestige of the Union occupation of New Orleans during the Civil War. It was during this period that officials commissioned construction of the building to serve as an orphanage. Today it's a moderately priced inn with a beautifully preserved exterior that includes a courtyard and pool and gracious wraparound balconies with delicate wrought-iron filigree. A common sitting room inside has electrical outlets and data ports for your laptop computer. Rooms themselves are simple if a bit frilly, with ceiling fans, white-wicker furniture, floral-print fabrics, and air-conditioning, phones, and TVs (but no cable). Full breakfast is included, and there's free parking.

$100–150

A longtime favorite set well Uptown, between the Garden District and Audubon Park (and within easy strolling distance of Magazine Street shopping and dining and the St. Charles Avenue streetcar), the **Chimes Bed & Breakfast** (1146 Constantinople St., 504/488-4640 or 800/729-4640, www.chimesbandb.com) has just five lovingly furnished rooms facing a lush courtyard. Each has private bath, a queen-size mahogany or iron bed, stained- and leaded-glass windows, refrigerator, French doors, high ceilings, phones with answering machines, and cable TV; some have fireplaces, and two have twin beds that can accommodate kids or additional guests. This is a

great base for exploring Uptown, a wonderful neighborhood that some visitors miss out on because they devote so much of their time to the French Quarter. The inn has a devoted repeat following and tends to book up early, so reserve as far ahead as possible. An expansive continental breakfast is included.

McKendrick-Breaux House (1474 Magazine St., 504/586-1700 or 888/570-1700, www.mckendrick-breaux.com) on the edge of Magazine Street's antiques row, in the up-and-coming Lower Garden District, nearly fell to the wrecking ball several years ago before preservation-minded owner Eddie Breaux turned it into a B&B. The three-story 1865 mansion, once part of a plantation, has been meticulously restored. Many rooms contain such architectural details as original ceiling medallions, clawfoot tubs, and plaster moldings. There are nine rooms and, unusual for New Orleans B&Bs, each can accommodate up to three guests, making this a great choice for friends traveling together or parents with one child. Three rooms open onto a foliage-filled courtyard; each has a private bath, high-thread-count linens, original artwork by area artists, free local phone calls and data ports, cable TV, central heat and air, and robes, hair dryers, and irons and boards. Considering the amenities and first-rate staff, this is one of the best deals in the city, with rates beginning at $135 nightly, which includes continental breakfast.

$150–250

The Garden District's fanciest accommodation is **Magnolia Mansion** (2127 Prytania St., 504/412-9500 or 888/222-9235, www.magnoliamansion.com), a stately 1850s wedding cake of a house designed by James H. Calrow, who also constructed Anne Rice's nearby home at 1239 1st St. The house served as the headquarters for the U.S. Red Cross from 1939 through 1954. It strikes a dashing figure from the street, with its 11 elaborate Corinthian columns and double-galleried veranda; moss-draped live-oak trees and magnolias tower over the grounds. There are nine rooms, which vary in price according to their size and amenities. All have TV with VCRs and high-speed Internet, and there's limited free parking (based on availability). Honeymooners and others celebrating special occasions favor this property for its over-the-top furnishings, such as floor-to-ceiling velvet drapes, mahogany four-poster beds, cast-iron clawfoot tubs, double Jacuzzis, and Toulouse Lautrec–inspired murals; the Vampire Suite contains a massive hand-carved bed that's a replica of the one used in the movie *Interview with the Vampire*.

There are just three units at the **American Creole House** (1124 St. Charles Ave., 504/522-7777 or 800/999-7891, www.creolehouse.com), but each is a full suite with both a queen bed and queen sleeper sofa, a separate living/dining area, and either a full kitchen or kitchenette. The Balcony Suite, which overlooks St. Charles Avenue, is a favorite. These suites are ideal for business travelers in town for a while, families, or others seeking plenty of room to spread out. The inn is just a couple of blocks upriver from Lee Circle, an easy stroll to the CBD and Warehouse District.

If you don't have the chance to visit the famed plantations along the River Road, you can at least get a sense of some of them with a stay at the **Grand Victorian B&B** (2727 St. Charles Ave., 504/895-1104 or 800/977-0008, www.gvbb.com). Each of the seven high-ceilinged rooms in this fanciful 1893 Victorian mansion are named for Louisiana plantation homes and contain the kinds of museum-like furniture you'd find at places like Oak Alley and Nottoway. Destrehan Room contains a dramatic 1850s Renaissance Revival highback bed, Evergreen a half-tester Eastlake Victorian bed—whatever room you choose, expect a big, oversized antique bed that you may not want to get out of each morning. The tall windows in the parlor overlook the clanging St. Charles Avenue streetcar, and continental breakfast is served in a sunny dining room or on the porte-cochere balcony.

The **Hubbard Mansion B&B** (3535 St. Charles Ave., 504/897-3535, www.hubbardmansion.com) may look like one of those grand Greek Revival mansions along the Mississippi River—in fact, it's a brand-new construction, based on a fine antebellum mansion on a bluff in Natchez, Mississippi. An advantage for some guests is that the place has the modern amenities and solid feel of a new building, complete with thick walls and central air-conditioning. Rooms overflow with authentic period (and some reproduction) antiques, such as massive crown-canopy beds with rich linens, mahogany armoires, and marble-top dressers. This is a romantic nest, and it's right along St. Charles, a short trolley ride from downtown and the Quarter.

Elsewhere in New Orleans

Within the city limits, there are two other areas worth considering for accommodations, Mid-City and New Orleans East. Keep in mind that these two sections are nothing alike and nowhere near each other. Mid-City comprises the blocks along or just off Esplanade Avenue north from the French Quarter to City Park, home to the art museum. In this area, you have about a dozen B&Bs and inns to choose from, most of them quite charming and stately. You can take the bus from here down Esplanade into the Quarter and Faubourg Marigny, but it's generally easiest if you have a car when staying up here—walking to the French Quarter can be managed in about 15 to 30 minutes, but it can require walking through some dodgy sections and is not recommended after dark. There's a burgeoning little district of eateries and shops just below City Park and near most of these inns, and the neighborhood itself is quite charming and getting more appealing every year.

New Orleans East is a soulless, semi-industrial area just off I-10 about 10 miles (a 15- to 20-minute drive) east of the French Quarter. You won't find inns over here, but there are quite a few midrange to budget chain properties, and it's very close to the Six Flags amusement park. Stay out here only if you have a car—and to save some money, as a chain motel/hotel in this area will cost 25 to 60 percent less than a comparable one in the CBD, and you won't have to pay for parking. If you plan on exploring Slidell or the

GREATER NEW ORLEANS ACCOMMODATIONS

To Mandeville and Covington

Lake

LAKE PONTCHARTRAIN CAUSEWAY (TOLL)

To Baton Rouge

JEFFERSON DOWNS

HILTON GARDEN INN

Canal No 10

WILLIAMS BLVD

Elmwood Canal

TRANSCONTINENTAL

Suburban Canal

DOUBLETREE NEW ORLEANS LAKESIDE

W ESPLANADE AVE

FAIRFIELD INN AIRPORT

Canal No 2

VETERANS MEMORIAL BLVD

Bonnabel Canal

BONNABEL BLVD

COMFORT SUITES KENNER

KENNER

Duncan Canal

DAVID DR

METAIRIE R

LOUIS ARMSTRONG NEW ORLEANS INTERNATIONAL AIRPORT

49

Canal

No 5

AVE

CLEARVIEW

METAIRIE

METAIRIE RD

METAIRIE EXPY

HILTON NEW ORLEANS AIRPORT

AIRLINE

DR

61

AIRLINE HWY

RIVERTOWN USA

EARHART

JEFFERSON HEIGHTS

To Plantations and Houma

JEFFERSON HWY

3RD ST

River

TOWNPLACE SUITES BY MARRIOTT

HICKORY AVE

RIVER RD

Mississippi River

S. KENNER AVE

RIVER RD

48

DESTREHAN

628

48

HARAHAN

BRIDGE CITY

541

LULING

18

90

AVONDALE

WESTWEGO

To Houma

LAPALCO BLVD

Salvador Wildlife Management Area

0   1 mi
0   1 km

MooN

Lake Cataouatche

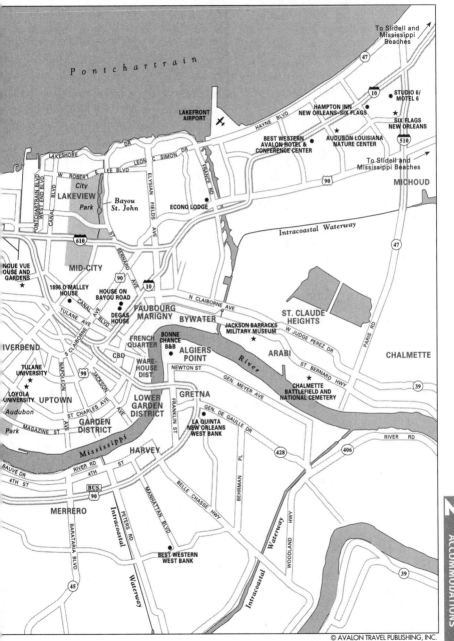

eastern North Shore, or coastal Mississippi, this is a very good base. Among the hotel cluster areas in metro New Orleans, however, it is probably the least charming overall.

HOTELS AND MOTELS

$50–100

One of the least expensive motels in metro New Orleans (well, at least of those that are clean and up to comfortable standards), this recently constructed **Econo Lodge** (4940 Chef Menteur Hwy., 504/940-5550 or 800/553-2666, www.econolodge.com) sits just down the road from Six Flags and a short drive from the city proper and, on the North Shore, Slidell. Amenities in the few-frills (but clean) rooms include coffeemakers, hair dryers, and irons and boards. You can often find rooms here for less than $50 nightly.

$100–150

If you're planning to spend a lot of time at the Six Flags New Orleans amusement park, consider the **Hampton Inn New Orleans—Six Flags** (12340 I-10 Service Rd., www.hamptoninn.com), a reliable modern property on the east side of the city. It offers easier access to Slidell and coastal Mississippi beaches than other New Orleans accommodations. A midrise hotel just off I-10, the **Best Western Avalon Hotel & Conference Center** (10100 I-10 Service Rd., New Orleans, 504/378-7000 or 888/819-5090, www.bestwestern.com) is a new, well-kept property near Six Flags and Bally's Lakefront Casino. The eight-story hotel has 175 rooms, an outdoor pool, complimentary continental breakfast, business services, and laundry service.

INNS AND BED-AND-BREAKFASTS

$100–150

Don't let the Irish name fool you, the **1896 O'-Malley House** (120 S. Pierce St., 504/488-5896 or 866/226-1896, www.1896omalleyhouse.com) isn't themed after the Emerald Isle. But it is named for one of the city's most prominent Irish citizens of the late 19th century, Dominick O'Malley,

a newspaper publisher credited with exposing the corruption of local politicos. Innkeepers Kevin Bourgeois and Tommy Crane own this gracious Colonial Revival mansion with original cypress-wood mantels, pocket doors, and other artful details. The house is located in an up-and-coming Mid-City neighborhood, close to the art museum and the restaurants of Esplanade Ridge. Each of the antiques-filled rooms has a private bath with granite counters, cable TV, phones with data ports, and all the other creature comforts you'd expect of a big-city accommodations; some units can accommodate three guests. An especially bounteous continental breakfast is included. Were this property in the Quarter or Garden District, rates would be at least $50 more per night, and yet the location is an advantage for guests seeking peacefulness and a friendly, neighborhood ambience. It's on the edge of an iffy but up-and-coming neighborhood, right by where Canal and Carrollton meet; you just need to be a little more adventuresome to stay here than in more central parts of town. Within a short walk are Angelo Brocato's and several other good restaurants. When the Canal streetcar gets going, the area is only going to get more interesting.

Appropriately near the New Orleans Art Museum in City Park, **Degas House** (2306 Esplanade Ave., 504/821-5009, www.degashouse.com) is not only an inn but a museum—it's the world's only home or studio that housed French Impressionist painter Edgar Degas that's open to the public. Degas lived in the house for about a year in 1872 while visiting his maternal relatives, who were successful New Orleans cotton merchants. The artist painted some 22 works while living here. The B&B contain nine rooms that vary considerably in size and luxury. All have full bath and hardwood floors with well-chosen antiques; some larger suites have private balconies and Jacuzzi tubs, and one can accommodate extra guests on a sleeper sofa; three units have fireplaces. Guests get a free tour of the museum portion of the house, which is hung with framed reproductions of many Degas works. All rooms have cable TV and phones with voice mail, and continental breakfast is included.

$150–250

There are few spots in New Orleans, let alone places to spend the night, where you can experience the city while feeling totally removed from the hustle, bustle, and crowds. The fabled bed-and-breakfast **House on Bayou Road** (2275 Bayou Rd., 504/945-0992 or 800/882-2968, www.houseonbayouraod.com) sits about midway between the French Quarter and City Park, along Esplanade Ridge. Although intimate, the place is run with the polish and grandeur of a small luxury hotel, a big reason that actors, musicians, and other notables like to stay here when in town. There's a full concierge service, ample off-street parking, full and filling Southern breakfasts—they'll even arrange for you to be picked up and delivered here by limo from the airport. The two-acre property is set back from the road and lush with herb and flower gardens, courtyard patios, and ponds. The main house, a former indigo plantation, dates to 1798 and contains three guest rooms and suites; there are four more rooms in a second building as well as a luxury Creole cottage. Units contain mostly 19th-century antiques, wet bars with complimentary sherry, some in-room Jacuzzis and fireplaces, and feather beds; the cottage has Audubon prints, a queen-size bed and sleeper sofa, a fireplace, VCR, CD player, and Jacuzzi, plus a private porch with rocking chairs. Guests can also take a dip in the pool or relax in the hot tub. Country living doesn't get much better than

House on Bayou Road

this, and the House on Bayon Road isn't even in the country. The property is a short drive from the Quarter, but there are also some great restaurants nearby in the Mid-City neighborhood, and best of all, next door the B&B runs its own outstanding restaurant, Indigo, helmed by acclaimed chef Kevin Vizard.

Metairie, Kenner, and the Airport

Like New Orleans East, these suburbs west of New Orleans make sense as a place to stay only if you have a car and are looking to save some money. Rates out here generally run 20 to 40 percent lower than in the CBD for comparable chain hotels. It's also helpful to stay out here if you need to be near the airport. Quite a few new and well-maintained chain hotels have opened in Kenner (site of the airport) and, to a lesser extent, Metairie; there's a lot of business out this way, so the area makes sense for corporate travelers. It's also where you'll find several all-suites hotels that specialize in long-term stays. Although built-up and in some cases a bit industrial, Metairie and Kenner are not unpleasant places, and they are close to scads of good restaurants and shopping centers. All the hotels out this way offer free parking to guests for the duration of their stays. Guests can often leave theirs car for a nominal charge (or even free of charge) after staying for at least one night. Lastly, this is a good base if you plan to spend only part of your time in New Orleans and the rest on the North Shore, visiting plantations along the River Road, or even if you're heading to Baton Rouge during the day.

ACCOMMODATIONS

HOTELS AND MOTELS

Under $50

If you have a car and plan on exploring not only New Orleans but the greater area, the **Studio 6** (12330 I-10 Service Rd., at Bullard Avenue, 504/240-9778 or 888/897-0202, www.motel6 .com) makes a great choice if you're staying more than a few days. All units have voice mail, fully equipped kitchens, and work areas, and there's a guest laundry. Pets are accepted. Rates start as low as $240 weekly (daily rates are available, but slightly more expensive). The hotel is right by the airport, near the intersection of I-10 and I-510. Less costly for simple one- or two-night stays is the nearly adjacent **Motel 6 New Orleans** (12330 I-10 Service Rd., at Bullard Ave., 504/240-2862 or 800/4-MOTEL-6, www .motel6.com), where rooms are smaller and don't have kitchens, but the rates are among the lowest in metro New Orleans.

$50–100

A relatively new and meticulously kept midprice business hotel 3 miles from the airport, the **Hilton Garden Inn** (4535 Williams Blvd., Kenner, 504/712-0504 or 800/774-1500, www .hilton.com) is right by the Treasure Chest Casino and the Pontchartrain Convention Center. It's not exactly a charming location, but it's convenient, and there are dozens of restaurants within a short drive. Interstate access is easy, and the price is right. Best of all, rooms have plenty of perks, such as microwaves, coffeemakers, refrigerators, voicemail and data ports, large work desks, and dual-line phones; suites have sleeper sofas in the sitting room, thus easily accommodating four guests. There's also a business center, pool, and gym.

The moderately priced **Comfort Suites Kenner** (2710 Idaho Ave., Kenner, 504/466-6066 or 877/424-6423, www.comfortsuites.com) is a relatively new building just off the interstate and very close to the airport. Rooms are spacious, all with wet bars, mini-refrigerators, two phones, and high-speed Internet. There are indoor and outdoor pools, a hot tub, and a gym, and continental breakfast is included. A very reliable property all-around.

Just north of the airport and close to Esplanade Mall, the **Fairfield Inn Airport** (1801 32nd St., Kenner, 504/443-9800 or 800/228-2800, www.fairfieldinn.com) has four floors of modern, well-kept rooms with work desks and good lamps, data ports, iron and boards, and—in some rooms—refrigerators. A pool, exercise room, and whirlpool are on-site, and Colonial Golf and Country Club is a short drive away, along with several restaurants.

$100–150

Of the several long-term-stay accommodations out near the airport, the **TownPlace Suites by Marriott** (5424 Citrus Blvd., Harahan, 504/818-2400 or 800/257-3000, www.townplace.com) offers among the most luxurious and pleasant accommodations. The compound of spacious, contemporary townhomes sits right off Clearview Parkway (U.S. 90), near the Huey P. Long Bridge that connects Harahan with the West Bank. The airport is 5 miles west, and downtown New Orleans is 10 miles east. Each of the 125 rooms has a fully equipped kitchen, and some have two bedrooms (all units can sleep up to four guests). There's a 24-hour gym, pets are welcome, continental breakfast is offered on weekdays, and there's a pool and barbecue area. The hotel is geared toward business travelers, but it also makes sense for families or friends traveling together and staying in town for an extended period. Rates are lowest if you rent by the week—they start as low as around $600 per week (or about $2,000 per month).

An upscale high-rise business hotel near Lake Pontchartrain, the **Doubletree New Orleans-Lakeside** (3838 N. Causeway Blvd., Metairie, 504/836-5253 or 800/222-TREE, www.double tree.com) offers plush accommodations for much less than you'll pay in New Orleans proper. It's right by the causeway leading across the lake to the tony North Shore suburbs, and it's close to several very good (and untouristy) Metairie restaurants. Many rooms look toward the lake, and others out at the New Orleans skyline, some 10 miles southeast. Some units have microwaves and mini-refrigerators, and guests can use the pool, fitness center, and extensive business facilities. There's a free courtesy shuttle to the airport, but this is one of the only hotels out this way that charge for parking.

Although the chain as a whole can be hit-or-miss in quality, the **Hilton New Orleans Airport** (901 Airline Dr., 504/469-5000 or 800/774-1500, www.hilton.com) is a lavish and well-run property practically a stone's throw from New Orleans International Airport. This is one of the priciest of the airport accommodations, but it does have its perks, including spacious rooms with marble-accented bathrooms, minibars, and such recreational amenities as a walking/jogging track, tennis court, pool, and fitness center. There is a charge for hotel parking.

The West Bank

The large area on the West Bank of the Mississippi River, across from New Orleans, includes an area called Algiers Point that actually falls within New Orleans city limits; here, too, are the close-in suburbs of Harvey, Gretna, and Marrero. There are a fair number of chain properties out this way, but it's not an especially convenient base for exploring the city, and only a handful of accommodations on the West Bank are included in this chapter. In general, you face the same pros and cons out here as you do by the airport or in New Orleans East; additionally, there's a toll charge for crossing the Mississippi River, and the West Bank suburbs feel quite removed from the city, even though some of them are actually a slightly shorter drive than from the airport into downtown New Orleans.

HOTELS AND MOTELS
$50–100
A great value if you don't mind being across the river, the 140-room **Best Western West Bank** (1700 Lapalco Blvd., Harvey, 504/366-5369 or 800/780-7234, www.bestwestern.com) is about a 20- to 25-minute drive from New Orleans proper. The advantage is in saving a few bucks on a room that would cost you twice as much in the city, and having free parking in a safe suburban area. There's a pool, hot tub, landscaped grounds, and a courtyard bar, guest laundry, continental breakfast, and weekly Cajun cookouts, and rooms have refrigerators. The Boomtown

Belle Casino and Oakwood Center shopping mall are within a short drive.

Adjacent to Oakwood Mall in Gretna, about a 10- to 15-minute drive south of the city, **La Quinta New Orleans West Bank** (50 Terry Pkwy., Gretna, 504/368-5600 or 800/531—5900, www.lq.com) is a dependable midrange option with on-site laundry and continental breakfast.

INNS AND BED-AND-BREAKFASTS
$100–150
One of the few inns on the West Bank, **Bonne Chance B&B** (621 Opelousas Ave., 504/367-0798, www.bonne-chance.com) is situated in historic Algiers Point and consists of a main Eastlake Victorian house dating from the 1880s and a small restored raised cottage next door. There are two guest suites in the main house and three in the cottage; each has plenty of room to spread out. The Angel Suite contains a surround-sound music system, TVs and VCRs both in the bedroom and sitting room, a steam-shower, and a whirlpool bathtub with marble trim. The suites in the cottage have full modern kitchens and are popular with guests staying for several days. Guests can relax in a pretty, shaded courtyard with a fountain and gazebo. It's just a few blocks' walk to the free passenger ferry that runs regularly back and forth across the Mississippi to downtown New Orleans. There are also a few pubs and cafés within walking distance.

Food

It's not especially unusual these days to say that a city's restaurants rank, collectively, among its top three or four attractions. With the culinary revolution that began in the 1980s and has continued unabated ever since, travelers increasingly spend as much time thinking about where they're going to eat during their vacation as they do planning their sightseeing. But food in New Orleans is more than a major attraction, it is—for more than a few visitors—the city's raison d'être. And this isn't a trend of the '90s or even '80s, unless you mean the 1880s. New Orleanians, and the travelers who adore this city, have been worshipping food as a virtual deity since at least the late 18th century, and in some circles before

that. Food in this city is *that* good, and dining out is a pastime granted the utmost importance.

Serious as New Orleanians are about food—and they'll talk about it, debate it, praise it, and dissect it for hours on end—they actual observe the ritual of dining with great warmth, humor, and ease, typically consuming considerable quantities of wine and liquor along the way.

New Orleans claims plenty of handsome dining rooms: old-world spaces with dim lighting, dark-wood paneling, and gilt mirrors; slick new restaurants with curvaceous banquettes, recessed mood lighting, and larger-than-life abstract art. People here like to eat surrounded by pretty things just as much as everybody else. However, few New Or-

© ANDREW COLLINS

leanians would ever forgive a restaurant's so-so cooking simply because it has a beautiful interior or first-class white-glove service. That's all well and good, but in this town, if you want your restaurant to survive, you worry about one and only one thing, and that's the food on the plate.

It then follows that New Orleans seems to have more divey and dilapidated restaurants serving heavenly food than any city in America. Just as people here won't support a fancy-looking eatery with mediocre cooking, they'll flock to some dumpy hole-in-the-wall on the worst crime-ridden block in the city if the place serves tasty food. The paint may be peeling, the floorboards may be slanted and cracked, the place may not even look sanitary. But the most catastrophic aesthetic miscues can be overlooked if the kitchen turns out a half-decent jambalaya or oyster-and-Brie soup.

It's not unusual, of course, for a raffish and run-down restaurant serving good food to become popular *because* it's such a dump—diehard food lovers like the idea that they've worked a little and perhaps even taken their lives into their own hands in order to taste the best of a particular dish or style of cuisine. But in New Orleans, this sort of thinking is taken to great extremes. One suspects that more than a few restaurateurs have intentionally neglected the appearance of their dining room, just to boost their approval rating with hipsters seeking out peculiar places to eat.

These rules apply to the city's quirkier, home-style restaurants, mostly neighborhood joints with modest aspirations, run by cooks who simply want to make good food and share it with people. For a restaurant to become truly respected and well-regarded, and ideally covered by the national food media, it generally does have to offer a charming ambience, fine service, and excellent food. The competition in New Orleans among destination restaurants—places that visitors make a special point of dining in—is fierce. Right off the bat, the city has about two dozen restaurants that have been famous for more than 50 years, and some of them for well over a century.

Then you have the chef celebs, like Emeril Lagasse, Susan Spicer, and virtually any member of the illustrious Brennan family. These highly regarded restaurateurs, along with many of their peers, each have at least two restaurants around town, and every time a name chef in New Orleans opens a new place, it garners immediate attention from the editors of glossy food and travel magazines. Finally, there are the so-called neighborhood restaurants, found mostly in Uptown and Mid-City, slightly off the tourist track. It's a bit of a myth that these places are little-publicized secrets that few tourists know about. Many of today's travelers rank dining out among their favorite activities when they visit a city, and they seek out those very neighborhood restaurants, especially in a place like New Orleans. First-time visitors may not know as much about places like Clancy's, Gabrielle, Feelings Cafe, and Uglesich's, but after their second and third trips to New Orleans, they're making regular forays to these and the many other superb neighborhood cafés around town.

Dress

Casual attire is the norm outside New Orleans, except at a few high-end spots in Baton Rouge. New Orleans can be dressy, which can be uncomfortable during the warmer months, and just plain annoying to many visitors who come here with casual duds expecting to have a gay old time. It seems to be more the old-time upper-crust local families, politicos, and business leaders who perpetuate the affection for formal dress at a handful of New Orleans's most upscale eateries. Or maybe it's all a plot hatched by the New Orleans clothing manufacturer Wemco, the largest producer of neckties in the world. In any case, if you don't like playing dress-up, don't—you'll find plenty of superb restaurants in town that don't require ties or jackets.

Restaurant Prices

Following the phone number of most restaurants included in this book, the average range of the cost of dinner entrées has been provided (e.g., $5–15). This is a general range that does not take into account the occasional high-priced special or unusual dish on a menu. For coffeehouses, gourmet markets, and some of the fast-food-oriented eateries in the book, no range has been given. And for restaurants where dinner is not served, the range of the cost of lunch entrées has been given.

Cuisines

TRADITIONAL CREOLE AND CAJUN

Creole cooking is the true ethnic cuisine of a city that has no single ethnicity, but by and large its influences are French and West African, owing to its having been prepared early on for French families by their African slaves. The bounty of fresh seafood in nearby waters led to Creole cuisine's reliance on fish and shellfish, and the city's Spanish, German, and later American influences also contribute to this distinctive cuisine that is found nowhere else in the world, although it bears some similarities to the Low Country cuisine of the Coastal Carolinas and Georgia. Traditionally, Creole cuisine has been wholly distinct from Cajun cooking, although both share French traditions and an emphasis on seafood. These days, the line between Creole and Cajun cooking has blended considerably, despite the fact that ardent supporters of both styles of cuisine insist the two are as different as night and day. The best Creole restaurants in New Orleans usually serve a few (or quite a few) dishes of Cajun origin, but most of southern Louisiana's Cajun restaurants, excepting some high-end nouvelle places, serve little in the way of the Creole cooking common to New Orleans.

Butter, cream, herbs, salt, and pepper are key components of Creole cuisine, the same being true to some extent for Cajun fare, although lard is used more often than butter and cream in the latter style. For both styles of cooking, the so-called holy culinary trinity of bell peppers, celery, and onions cooked in a roux of oil and flour is the foundation for countless dishes. Cajun cooking is often more spicy than Creole cuisine, although neither style uses truly hot seasoning as much as many visitors seem to imagine. Cooks in Louisiana use spices and chilies liberally, how-

The bounty of fresh seafood in nearby waters led to Creole cuisine's reliance on fish and shellfish, and the city's Spanish, German, and later American influences also contribute to this distinctive cuisine that is found nowhere else in the world.

ever, so if your tongue or digestive system is sensitive to this sort of thing, ask your server for advice on which dishes to avoid.

It's also often said that Creole cooking is "city" cuisine, while Cajun cooking is served mostly out in the country. In part for this reason, you won't find all that many true Cajun restaurants in New Orleans or even the towns around it—better to explore the Cajun parishes west and southwest of New Orleans to find these, especially around the cities of Houma, New Iberia, and Lafayette. Creole cuisine, on the other hand, is ubiquitous in New Orleans, and you can detect Creole influences at just about every kind of eatery in town, from Chinese restaurants to Italian trattorias to French bistros. Chefs are always finding inventive ways to sneak Creole recipes and ingredients into other styles of cuisine.

Most of the restaurants listed in this category throughout the chapter practice a fairly traditional form of Creole and, in some cases, Cajun cooking. The many establishments where you're likely to find contemporary cooking are listed under the heading "Creative and Contemporary." But the lines between old and new, traditional and innovative do blend easily.

CREATIVE AND CONTEMPORARY

Restaurants mentioned in this category serve a style of cuisine that has come to be called many things since nationally acclaimed chefs like California's Alice Waters and New Orleans's own Emeril Lagasse became household names among gourmet-cooking junkies: some call it New American or fusion, others eclectic, world-beat, or just plain contemporary. In this city, chefs will sometimes describe their cooking as "modern New Orleans" or "nouvelle Creole."

The city's truly famous institutions of dining, for the most part, still serve fairly traditional Creole cuisine, but the hottest and most-talked-about restaurants in the city fall under this "Creative and Contemporary" heading. Seemingly every month, one or two new places open, though a good many have not—despite sleek and arty dining rooms and fancy ingredients spun together in unusual and sometimes bizarre ways—lasted.

There's no set criteria for qualifying as a contemporary restaurant, and the styles of cuisine at these places vary considerably. But common denominators include relatively high prices ($20 and up for entrées) and menus that give lengthy and almost dramatic descriptions of each dish, its myriad accompaniments and contents, its style of preparation, and often the origins of key ingredients.

CASUAL COOKING

A mainstay of many restaurants around the French Quarter and other visitor-oriented neighborhoods around New Orleans, casual cooking could just as easily be called pub fare or bar food. These places serve food that's more substantial than short-order diner fare, and in an atmosphere where you do sit down at a table, order from a menu, and enjoy a full-service meal. But the food is simpler and typically less expensive than what you'll find in either traditional Creole restaurants or contemporary ones. In addition to bar-and-grill establishments, pizza parlors, low-frills seafood restaurants, brewpubs, and cafés serving more than just coffee and light snacks are included under this heading. In many cities, this style of food is little more than basic sustenance—but in New Orleans, even casual cooking is usually prepared with the freshest possible ingredients and the utmost culinary integrity. It doesn't matter who you are in this city, from a regular working Joe to a hotshot politician to the average tourist, you'll always be treated to high-quality cooking.

ETHNIC

For the most part, the restaurants included in this heading serve a specific national or ethnic cuisine, usually from an East Asian or Latin American country. But there are also listings within these headings for Middle Eastern, West African, and certain European styles of cuisine. If a place serves traditional Italian food, for instance, it's likely been listed here.

New Orleans doesn't have a widespread reputation for great ethnic fare, but that's really only because it's already so famous for its own distinctive local cuisine. This is, after all, one of the world's busiest ports, and the city has been a haven for immigrants from all over the globe for centuries. Some of the Vietnamese eateries in New Orleans rank among the best in the nation, and you can also find simply stellar sushi, dim sum, and Thai food. The proximity to Latin America has helped bring in a fine range of Mexican, Cuban, and pan-Latin restaurants. In fact, if you're visiting New Orleans for more than a couple of days and you love the cooking of a particular nation, it really makes sense to try it out here. You may reason that it's better to save ethnic dining for back home, at least if you come from an area with a similarly commendable selection of such restaurants, but many New Orleans Asian, Mexican, and Middle Eastern restaurants incorporate local ingredients (especially seafood) on their menus.

Alas, the French Quarter is extremely weak on ethnic food, for exactly the reason just mentioned—most tourists in New Orleans have no interest in eating Szechwan or Cuban fare. It's more the locals who dine in the city's ethnic restaurants, and so these tend to be in the most residential of the city's neighborhoods: Uptown, Mid-City, and out in the neighboring communities of Metairie, Kenner, and Gretna. The scene is changing, however, as a handful of good ethnic restaurants have opened in the Central Business District and Faubourg Marigny since the late '90s, and the trend seems to be headed into the Quarter.

QUICK BITES

Dining establishments that fall within this heading offer some of the most delightful and unusual "only in New Orleans" experiences you can find. It could be a greasy-spoon diner, a shack

M

FOOD

A CULINARY GLOSSARY

Louisiana is a state with its very own food vernacular, and many of the dishes, as well as the ingredients, that appear commonly on menus in New Orleans and elsewhere in the state are little-known in the rest of the world. The popularity of Cajun and Creole cooking has spread dramatically in recent years, so that many foodies living on other continents now know roughly what jambalaya and étoufée are. Still, there are quite a few terms out there that you may not be familiar with. Here follows a quick reference guide to some of the most popular Louisiana foods, along with, where relevant, a guide to pronouncing them.

Andouille (an-DEW-ee): A lean pork sausage that carries a bit of a kick; it's a staple of gumbo, red beans and rice, and many other dishes.

Bananas Foster: Invented at Brennan's restaurant, this rich dessert consists of bananas simmering in hot rum over vanilla ice cream.

Beignets (BEN-yay): Similar to fried dough, but without holes, these square French doughnuts are deep-fried and then served with a dusting of powdered sugar. To many fans, it's an act of blasphemy to eat beignets without a cup of café au lait.

Blackened (fish, chicken, etc.): This is a Cajun preparation, traditionally used on redfish but more recently applied to just about any kind of fish or meat, that involves coating the fillet with a heady pepper-thyme-onion-garlic seasoning blend and then flash-frying it in a very, very hot cast-iron pan.

Boil (as in "crawfish boil" or "crab boil"): A quintessential Cajun seafood dish, where shellfish is boiled in a spicy broth. It's a mess to eat, and therein lies the fun.

Boudin (boo-DHAN): A Cajun smoked sausage, often served with mustard, that consists of ground pork roast, pork liver, chopped onions, cayenne pepper, and other spices.

Café au lait (CAFF-ay oh LAY): A cup of roughly equal parts coffee and steamed milk. In Louisiana, coffee is typically laced with chicory (CHICK-ree), a spice made of ground

and roasted endive roots that adds just the tiniest edge.

Courtbouillon (COOH-boo-yahn): The Cajun version of cioppino, or a tomato-based bouillabaisse (seafood stew).

Cracklins: Not much of the food listed here could be called healthy, but cracklins are just plain awful for you. They taste good, though. Cracklins are just bits of pork fat, sliced up and sautéed in a skillet.

Étouffée (AY-too-FAY): From the French word meaning "to smother," étouffée is one of the most popular Cajun dishes, typically made with shrimp or crawfish and a vegetable- (often tomato-) based sauce. It's usually served over rice.

Filé (FEE-lay): Ground sassafras leaves; this spice introduced by the region's Choctaw Indians is a common ingredient in gumbo and other soups and stews.

Grillades (gree-LODS): Diced meat marinated in vinegar to produce a rich gravy; it's traditionally served with grits.

Gumbo: Of the many foods people associate with southern Louisiana, gumbo may be the most famous. This soup with African origins typically contains seafood mixed with spicy andouille sausage, and often a bit of okra and filé seasoning. Okra, which in the Bantu language is called *nkombo* (hence the derivation of the soup's name), is less a staple of gumbo served at contemporary Creole restaurants today, where newer and sometimes unexpected ingredients are sometimes substituted. Duck and andouille sausage has become a favorite gumbo combination in recent years, and crawfish, crab, and crawfish are often used. Some gumbo is served with a side of white rice, which many diners mix in with their soup. Gumbo has a muddy, brownish consistency and colors, and it should be thick and spicy but not necessarily all that hot. The dish has become something of a clichéd metaphor representing the many cultures that have made New Orleans and southern Louisiana the complex blend that it is today.

Jambalaya (jahm-buh-LYE-uh): The Cajun equivalent of Spanish paella, this rice casserole typically contains andouille or tasso plus a variety of seafood.

Macque choux (mock shoe): A popular side dish of corn scraped off the cob and smothered in tomatoes, bell peppers, onions, and a variety of spices.

Mirliton (MER-lee-ton): Known as a chayote or christophine in other parts of the world, this pear-shaped squash is commonly stuffed with seafood or meat and served the way stuffed peppers are.

Muffaletta (muff-uh-LETT-uh): Central Grocery serves the best take on these Italian cold-cut sandwiches filled with provolone, spiced ham, salami, and green-olive relish. Some restaurants serve them hot, but loyalists consider this to be a no-no.

Oysters Rockefeller: An original recipe of Antoine's, oysters Rockefeller are served baked on the half-shell and topped with a bit of spinach and an absinthe-flavored liqueur, such as Pernod.

Po'boy: The name for any sandwich made with French bread; common po'boys come filled with fried oysters, fried shrimp, andouille or other smoked sausages, roast beef, or meatballs. If you order a po'boy "dressed," it'll come with lettuce, tomatoes, pickles, and other dressings or condiments.

Praline (prah-LEEN): A sugary confection made with cream, butter, caramelized brown sugar, and pecans.

Red beans and rice: It is what it sounds like, but somehow this humble meal is elevated to a loftier status when served in Louisiana. Simmered in ham hocks and tasso or andouille sausage, the kidney beans and their gravy are served over white rice. Traditionally, Mondays are the favorite time for this dish, but there's really no time when a plate of red beans and rice doesn't hit the spot.

Remoulade (reh-moo-LAHD): A mayonnaise-based sauce flavored with mustard, capers, herbs, and/or horseradish and typically served with chilled shrimp or other meats.

Roux (rue): This is the base for many Cajun and Creole dishes: it's basically flour lightly browned in oil, which is then used to thicken just about anything.

Sazerac: A favorite cocktail, best sipped at the swell-egant Sazerac Bar in the Fairmont Hotel, consisting of rye whiskey, absinthe substitute, Peychaud's bitters, and sugar; the original recipe (from 1857) called for absinthe, but since that substance was banned in 1912, Pernod or the local Herbsaint typically pinch-hits.

Tasso: Another member of the Cajun/Creole sausage family, tasso is smoked beef or pork sausage used in many stews, pastas, and other dishes.

serving fried oysters, a fast-food restaurant (no national chains have been included), a pastry shop, a deli, or a hot-dog cart. The idea is that you get in and get out quickly, having, in many instances, devoured a memorable meal—maybe a soft-shell-crab po'boy, a burger slathered in blue cheese, or a cup of chestnut-flavored gelato. Some of these places are open 24 hours, others only for breakfast or lunch. Many of the best ones in New Orleans are found in out-of-the-way neighborhoods, or they feel a bit run-down inside; hey, that's part of the fun.

At these sorts of restaurants, you probably aren't going to end up doing your heart any big favors—many of them specialize in deep-fried, sugar-laden, or heavily salted grub. They're mostly inexpensive, however, and they serve the sort of food that'll fill you up. Best of all, these above any other kind of restaurant in New Orleans are the sorts of places where you're likely to rub elbows with the locals—to really see up close how New Orleanians live, or at least how they eat. And in this city, if you watch the locals eat, you're learning a great deal about how they live.

JAVA JOINTS

New Orleanians were frequenting coffeehouses as part of their daily routine long before Starbucks caught on and Seattle became the nation's de-facto caffeine capital. Starbucks outlets do appear all over the Cresecnt City, but the national chain has more sway with tourists than with locals, who tend to favor either indie options or local chains **C.C.'s** (www.ccscoffee.com) and **P.J.'s** (www.pjscoffee.com).

You'll find about a dozen branches of C.C.'s around town, including locations on Magazine Street and Louisiana Avenue Uptown, Royal Street in the Quarter, Poydras Street in the CBD, Esplanade Avenue in Mid-City, and in Metairie, Kenner, and other nearby burbs. There's a light selection of food served, including the usual muffins and pastries. Overall, C.C.'s seem to have cozier seating than most of its competitors.

There are P.J.'s locales on Camp and Magazine streets in the CBD, Frenchmen Street in Faubourg Marigny, Magazine and Streets Up-town, and also in Metairie, Kenner, and many suburbs (as well as at the airport). The large Maple Street coffeehouse has a nice patio. Some locations serve substantial café fare. Many folks think P.J.'s is the big winner when it comes to hot and iced teas.

Rue de la Course is a smaller, funkier, and somewhat more interesting local chain, with six locations around town, half Uptown, one in the Quarter, and one in the CBD.

As for the seemingly ever-popular **Starbucks** (www.starbucks.com), you'll find branches on Canal Street in the CBD, on Magazine and Maple streets Uptown, and in just about all the burbs.

PICNIC SUPPLIES AND GOURMET GOODS

The line between restaurant, grocery, and specialty food shop blurs considerably in New Orleans. The best wine store in the area, Martin Wine Cellar, also has one of the best delis. Central Grocery, in the French Quarter, is most famous for its hefty muffaletta sandwiches, but don't overlook the fact that it carries wonderful and hard-to-find imported groceries. Some of the leading restaurants in the city also have gift shops where you can buy gourmet food, plus the usual souvenir T-shirts and ball caps.

The farmer's market held inside the French Market is the most famous place to find gourmet edibles for sale in the city, but you can find a wide range of tasty local foods at just about any New Orleans grocery store, even a national chain.

If you love browsing market-fresh food, don't miss the **Crescent City Farmers Market** (www.crescentcityfarmersmarket.com), held three times a week at different locations around town and featuring a phenomenal roster of vendors and chefs. You'll find fresh oysters, soft-shell crabs, alligator, watermelons, blueberries, yams, Creole tomatoes, pecans, kumquats, orchids, fresh-cut flowers, pheasant, Creole cream cheese, Italian sugar cookies, sausages, maple syrup, red lentil balls, filé powder, and countless more delectables. It's held in the Warehouse District on Saturday mornings (8 A.M.–noon) at 700 Magazine St., Uptown at 200 Broadway St. (near Audubon Park at

Uptown Square) on Tuesday mornings (10 A.M.–1 P.M.), and in Mid-City at 3700 Orleans Ave. on Thursday afternoons (3–6 P.M., an hour later in summer). Farmers markets have been a part of life in New Orleans since the French and Spanish governments governed the city in the 18th century, and they remain just as vibrant to this day.

COOKING CLASSES

A great way to learn about the city's rich culinary heritage is to attend one of the many cooking demonstrations held throughout the city.

Gumbo's Creole/Cajun School of Cooking (714 St. Peter St., 504/525-3354) offers classes in a vintage French Quarter kitchen. Lunch and recipes are included. At the Riverwalk shopping center, **Creole Delicacies Gourmet Shop and Cookin' Cajun Cooking** (1 Poydras St., #116, Riverwalk, 504/586-8832 or 800/786-0941, www.cookincajun.com) is not only a cooking school but a first-rate shop for finding local ingredients and cookware. The two-hour classes cost $20 per person and include a full meal and a 10 percent discount in the gourmet shop. Finally, the **New Orleans School of Cooking** (524 St. Louis St., 504/525-2665 or 800/237-4841, www.neworleans schoolofcooking.com) offers both three-hour (daily at 10 A.M.) and two-hour (daily at 2 P.M.) courses, led by colorful chef Kevin Belton, that include a meal, recipes, and a great deal of lively storytelling. These cost $20 to $25 and are held daily. Both Creole and Cajun cooking are covered with these courses.

One of the more unusual settings for these demonstrations is Blaine Kern's Mardi Gras World museum, on the West Bank. Here at the **Mardi Gras School of Cooking** (233 Newton St., 504/362-5225, www.gumbos.net), you learn and have a chance to prepare a wide variety of Creole and Cajun dishes. The demo kitchens are set amid the huge Mardi Gras floats, which are being constructed at this facility year-round.

In December *Louisiana Cookin'* magazine (www.louisianacookin.com) sponsors a series of free cooking demonstrations at Le Petit Theater (616 St. Peter St.), held almost daily at 3 P.M. throughout the month. Chefs from top restaurants around town come and show how to prepare everything from duck and andouille chowder to bread pudding with whiskey sauce.

The French Quarter

TRADITIONAL CREOLE AND CAJUN

Among those few remaining New Orleans restaurants where men must wear a jacket in the evening and no patron may stroll in wearing shorts, **Galatoire's** (209 Bourbon St., 504/525-2021, $14–24), which opened in 1905 and has been run by the Galatoire family ever since, most deserves a visit, even if you have an aversion to dressing up. As much fun as the dining itself is watching the local politicos hobnob and broker deals, especially on Friday afternoons—the true regulars among Galatoire's many loyal patrons have been coming here for generations, often taking their seat at the same table. Despite its formal ambience and popularity among well-heeled locals, Galatoire's isn't all that expensive.

From the enormous menu you can try everything from lavish high-end dishes like grilled pompano with sautéed crabmeat meunière to broiled steaks and lamb chops béarnaise. But several chicken and seafood entrées weigh in around $15, including shrimp au vin and oysters Rockefeller. Crêpes suzette and banana bread pudding stand out among the rich desserts. The main dining room has always maintained a "no reservations" policy, although you can reserve a seat in the upstairs dining room, which was added after a major makeover in 1999.

It's probably not fair to describe **K-Paul's Louisiana Kitchen** (416 Chartres St., 504/524-7394, $27–39) as traditional, since much of the food at Paul Prudhomme's famous restaurant is prepared quite innovatively. The celeb chef, who was a kitchenhold name long before Emeril, was

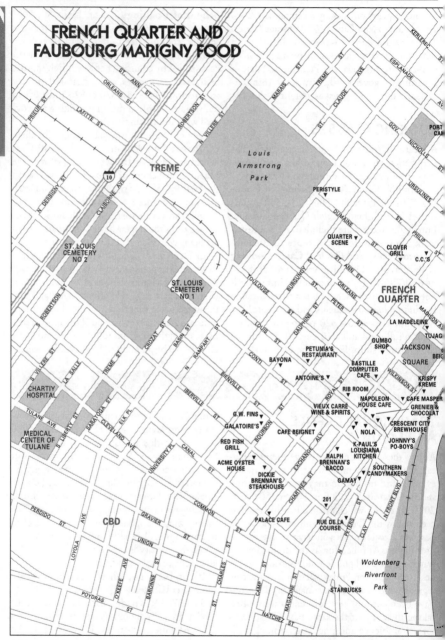

FRENCH QUARTER AND FAUBOURG MARIGNY FOOD

TREME

Louis Armstrong Park

ST. LOUIS CEMETERY NO 2

ST. LOUIS CEMETERY NO 1

PERISTYLE ▼

QUARTER SCENE ▼

CLOVER GRILL
C.C.'S ▼

FRENCH QUARTER

PORT CAI

NICHOLLS

URSULINES

PHILIP

MADISON AI

LA MADELEINE ▼

TUJAG

GUMBO SHOP ▼

PETUNIA'S RESTAURANT ▼

BAYONA ▼

JACKSON SQUARE

BEIC

BASTILLE COMPUTER CAFE ▼

ANTOINE'S ▼

RIB ROOM ▼

KRISPY KREME ▼

CAFE MASPER

NAPOLEON HOUSE CAFE ▼

GRENIER & CHOCOLAT

VIEUX CARRÉ WINE & SPIRITS ▼

G.W. FINS ▼

GALATOIRE'S ▼

CAFE BEIGNET ▼

NOLA ▼

CRESCENT CITY BREWHOUSE

RED FISH GRILL ▼

K-PAUL'S LOUISIANA KITCHEN ▼

JOHNNY'S PO-BOYS

ACME OYSTER HOUSE ▼

RALPH BRENNAN'S BACCO ▼

SOUTHERN CANDYMAKERS ▼

DICKIE BRENNAN'S STEAKHOUSE

GAMAY ▼

201 ▼

PALACE CAFE ▼

RUE DE LA COURSE ▼

CHARTIY HOSPITAL

MEDICAL CENTER OF TULANE

CBD

Woldenberg Riverfront Park

STARBUCKS ▼

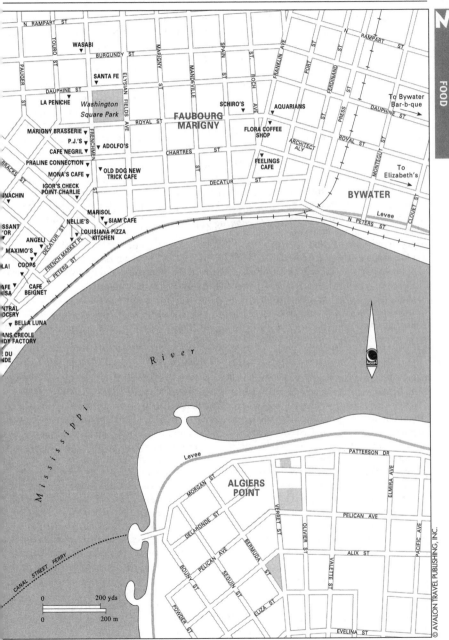

largely responsible for first popularizing Cajun cooking outside Louisiana, and this is still an excellent, although extremely pricey, place to sample such fare as turtle soup finished with hard-boiled eggs and dry sherry; bronzed swordfish with a sauce of roasted pecans, jalapeños, browned garlic butter, veal glaze, and lemon juice; or blackened stuffed pork chops with a mushroom zinfandel sauce. Sweet potato pecan pie and bread pudding with lemon sauce and chantilly cream are favorite sweet endings. The once-intimate dining room in this 1834 building took no reservations for many years, but a 1996 expansion added more seating, and nowadays you can reserve a table.

> *Celeb chef Paul Prudhomme, who was a kitchenhold name long before Emeril, was largely responsible for first popularizing Cajun cooking outside Louisiana.*

One of the true granddaddies of old-fashioned Creole cooking, **Antoine's** (713 St. Louis St., 504/581-4422, $21–39) opened its door in 1840 and hasn't missed a beat. Such dishes as oysters Thermidor (baked on the half-shell and served with bacon and tomato sauce) and avocado stuffed with shrimp ravigote (marinated peeled and boiled shrimp with a chilled sauce of Creole mustard, horseradish, mayonnaise, capers, and hardboiled eggs) were invented here. Be forewarned: the menu is in French, but the solicitous waitstaff will happily explain what's what. The list of options seems endless, with cheeses, sauces, salads, and side of vegetables all available á la carte along with crab omelets, chateaubriand for two, backfin lump crabmeat au gratin, broiled trout with crawfish and white wine, and so on. Deciding what to eat is only half the challenge—figuring out *where* to eat can also test your decision-making skills: there are 15 dining rooms, some for private parties but most open to the public. The Rex Room is decked in Mardi Gras photos, while the Japanese Room, which was opened a century ago but closed during World War II for four decades before a 1984 revival, is a study in Japanese decorative arts.

Tujague's (823 Decatur St., 504/525-8676, $15–22) is a neat old corner bar and tavern that's been around since 1856, making it the

second-oldest continuously operated restaurant in New Orleans. It sits opposite the French Market, and it serves many of the local Louisiana produce and seafood sold there. In fact, little on this menu varies from what diners might have ordered for lunch or dinner more than a century ago: beef brisket in Creole sauce, shrimp rémoulade, herb-and-greens gumbo, pecan sauce. In addition to the usual cocktails and wines, Tujague's serves its own microbrewed beer. Drinking here has quite a legacy, as the cypress-wood bar is original, and the handsome French mirror was shipped here from Paris the year the restaurant opened. Even if you don't come for a meal, at least stop in to chat with the other locals and tourists who frequent this hallowed institution.

Cafe Sbisa (1011 Decatur St., 504/522-5565, $14–25) is a dark and clubby space with the feel of a big-city brasserie—tile floors, mirrors, amber lighting, and well-dressed staff impart an air of informal elegance. In 1899, the Sbisa family opened this cheerful bistro inside an 1820s building near the French Market. It's an excellent place to try the New Orleans seafood classic courtbouillon (a bouillabaisse-like stew of gulf fish, shrimp, mussels, crabmeat, crab claws, and Creole seasonings), but neither will you go wrong with trout Eugene (topped with shrimp, crawfish tails, and crab fingers with herbed rice and asparagus) or honey-roasted chicken with three-cheese pasta and mustard greens. One of the favorite places to dine is on the second-floor balcony overlooking Decatur Street and the French Market. This longtime New Orleans standby has never lost its popularity, in part because prices are quite reasonable, especially considering the big quantities of food.

A dainty little restaurant that serves up prodigiously huge crepes, **Petunia's Restaurant** (817 St. Louis St., 504/522-6440; $11–23) occupies a pink three-story 1830s townhouse whose sunny (and also pink) dining rooms reveal the builder's masterful woodworking. You can get pastas, traditional Creole fare (a nice jambalaya, for in-

REVEILLON

December is a wonderful time to visit New Orleans for several reasons, not the least of which is the moderate weather. But for food-lovers, the big draw is Reveillon, an ancient Creole (and Catholic) celebratory feast dating to the 1830s, which originally was held on Christmas and New Year's Eves but now happens throughout the month of December and is celebrated by all walks of life, regardless of any particular religious affiliation. Still, for many people, the most special Reveillon dinners are held Christmas or New Year's Eve.

The Christmas meal was traditionally held following Midnight Mass at St. Louis Cathedral. Families would return home and spend time together sharing a fairly austere meal of egg dishes, sweetbreads, and a rum cake. This has historically been the more restrained of the two Reveillon meals, as the New Year's Eve feast has always consisted of elaborate desserts, plenty of whiskey and wine, and lots of laughing, singing, and dancing.

Dozens of restaurants in New Orleans offer Reveillon menus throughout the month of December. These are prix-fixe menus, usually four or five courses, and many establishments do offer Reveillon on Christmas or New Year's Eve, although you should reserve well ahead if you plan on attending on the eves or on Christmas or New Year's Day. Favorite venues for this celebration include Begue's, Dickie Brennan's Steakhouse, Galatoire's, Palace Cafe, Rene Bistrot, The Rib Room, Tujague's, Upperline, and Zoe Bistrot.

At traditional Tujague's, the choices are limited and the menu straightforward: shrimp remoulade, a soup of the day, boiled brisket of beef with horseradish sauce, braised lamb shanks in a Creole stew, banana-bread pudding, and chicory-laced coffee; the meal costs about $30 per person. More cutting-edge places around town have fancier and more unusual offers, such as Zoe Bistrot ($40 per person), where you might start with yellow-tomato bisque with grilled scallops and roasted garlic, followed by crab-and-fig salad with poached beets and roast grouper with sweet-potato cakes and a blood-orange butter sauce, finishing with chestnut mousse cake with sauce anglaise. Of course, most restaurants change their menu each year.

stance), and blackened fish, but the crepes are what sets this place apart from others around town. The St. Francis, filled with shrimp, crabmeat, ratatouille, and a creamy cheese sauce earns plenty of accolades. Save room for the St. Louis dessert flambé, with vanilla ice cream, bananas, cherries, and pecans afire. Breakfast is another of Petunia's specialties—consider eggs St. Louis (English muffins topped with grilled tomatoes, crabmeat, poached eggs, and homemade hollandaise sauce).

Even in the Quarter, it's rare to find a restaurant with as illustrious a history as the **Napoleon House Cafe** (500 Chartres St., 504/524-9752; bistro $12–24, café $4–7). Everything here—the tile floor, the scruffy plaster walls with peeling paint, the wobbly old wooden tables, and the eclectic prints, vintage photos, paintings, and chandeliers with orange light bulbs—contribute to the old-timey air. The front room is a bar where a light café menu is offered. Through the bar is a cozy dining room, and then a lush and characterful courtyard with partially covered seating. If alone, dine at the bar, read a book, chat with the friendly bartenders, eavesdrop, and try to grasp this room's 200-year-old history of entertaining New Orleanians. The building was first owned by New Orleans mayor Nicholas Girod, who offered the home as a residence to exiled Napoléon Bonaparte in 1821; supposedly, the Little Corporal was quite interested, but he died before he could ever move to New Orleans. You can try a wide range of foods in both of Napoleon House's dining areas: the café serves tapenade, feta, and goat cheese spread; boudin with Creole mustard, Corsican salad (red leaf lettuce, Kalamata olives, cherry tomatoes, toasted walnuts, red onion, gorgonzola, and raspberry vinaigrette), and the trademark house muffaletta, served hot with ham, Genoa salami, pastrami, Swiss cheese, provolone, and Italian olive salad. In the bistro, consider grilled salmon topped with citrus cream and served with Louisiana cane syrup glaze and sweet potato straw, or a delicious smoked rabbit with tasso jambalaya. There's an excellent wine list, too.

CREATIVE AND CONTEMPORARY

An eclectic, highly regarded restaurant on a quiet stretch of Dauphine, **Bayona** (430 Dauphine St., 504/525-4455, $14–21) fuses traditions, recipes, and ingredients from a handful of cultures all known for great food. Chef Susan Spicer, who was named best chef in the Southeast in 1993 by the prestigious James Beard Foundation, dreams up such imaginative combos as lamb loin with a goat cheese–zinfandel sauce, and seared ceviche with peppered fruit salsa and ancho-mango coulis. Desserts are no mere afterthought here—notable is crème brûlée with Chartreuse, star anise, and ginger; and toasted pecan roulade with caramel mousse and pecan syrup. There's a huge, commendable wine list. The setting, an 18th-century Creole cottage filled with trompe l'oeil murals of the Mediterranean countryside and a plant-filled courtyard, is the quintessence of romance.

Peristyle (1041 Dumaine St., 504/593-9535, $22–26) is the domain of one of the city's top chefs, Anne Kearney, who comes up with some wonderful French-influenced American recipes, such as a starter of grilled Louisiana quail salad with pancetta, watercress, spinach, Montasio cheese, and sherry vinaigrette; or a main dish of grilled marinated tuna steak with crispy potato cakes, pickled fennel relish, and a preserved lemon–chive fumet. It's in a vintage building on a quiet street at the edge of the Quarter, near slightly ominous Rampart Street, but the interior is elegant and soft, with terrazzo marble floors. This is chiefly a dinner restaurant, but lunch is served on Fridays.

The **Rib Room** (Omni Royal Orleans Hotel, 621 St. Louis St., 504/529-7046, $18–36), despite a dull name that conjures up visions of old-hat restaurants from yesteryear, may just be the best steakhouse in the city. The dining room is unabashedly retro, with its soaring ceilings with timber beams, an exposition kitchen under a curving brick archway, big comfortable leather chairs, huge arched windows overlooking Royal Street, and pepper mills the size of fire hydrants. The staff is both deft and fun-loving—many employees have been here for three or four decades. The food is heavenly and in some instances, such as the pan-seared foie gras with ginger-pear relish, visionary. There's a tender filet mignon whose preparation changes each week. Nouvelle foodies may scoff at this place, but it's a cool and hip dining venue almost in spite of its legacy. Red-meat lovers swear by the hefty cuts served up at **Dickie Brennan's Steakhouse** (716 Iberville St., 504/522-CHOP, $16–33), which is known for bacon-wrapped tournedos of beef served over smoked gouda and garlic-mashed potatoes. Steamed Maine lobsters, blackened prime rib, and the double-cut pork chop over smoked bacon–and–apple hash topped with grilled onion are also big draws. This is a clubby, upscale space, but (neat) casual attire is customary and the mood relaxed.

There aren't many restaurants on exuberant Bourbon Street worth going out of your way for, but Ralph Brennan's **Red Fish Grill** (115 Bourbon St., 504/598-1200, $16–28), set inside a former department store just a block into the Quarter from Canal, is an exception. This first block of Bourbon has revived in recent years; it was once dominated by department stores, and after closing time the stretch felt dark and ominous. This restaurant opened in 2000 and has helped to recharge the block. The cavernous main dining room reverberates with piped-in rock music, and huge redfish mobiles dangle overhead—this is no wallflower of a restaurant, but the noisy and festive ambience makes it fun for friends dining together, singles, and anybody heading out afterwards for a tour of Bourbon Street's nightlife. To one side is a spacious oyster bar with huge oyster half-shell sculptures; you can order from the main menu in here, too. The barbecued oysters are a great starter, served with a tangy blue-cheese dipping sauce, and the kitchen also turns out an amazingly delicious chocolate bread pudding. But few dishes here beat the hickory-grilled redfish served over crawfish and potatoes and topped with a lemon-butter sauce. Inside the swank W Hotel French Quarter, **Ralph Brennan's Bacco** (310 Chartres St., 504/522-2426, $10–25) offers stylish dining at unusually low prices. The dining room, with its recessed lighting, white napery, and natty patrons and staff, complements the informal but hip W Hotel and feels like the perfect place to see and be seen without feeling that you have to dress to the nines. The food is modern Italian, but quite a few dishes have notable Creole accents. Beef carpaccio with arugula, white truffle oil, and Parmigiano-Reggiano; and soft-shell crab with creamy crawfish risotto and sweet-and-spicy pepper jelly are fine choices. Bacco also offers a handful of $10 entrées, including crawfish–and–blood orange pene, and herb-roasted chicken.

One of the top restaurants to open in the Quarter in the past few years (in 2001, to be exact), **G.W. Fins** (808 Bienville St., 504/581-3467, $19–29) is a bit of a departure from most seafood-based New Orleans restaurants: although many local dishes are offered here, the kitchen serves fresh fish flown in from all over the world, from Alaskan halibut to Scottish salmon. The setting, a converted warehouse with lofty ceilings, warm woods, and cushy booths, is contemporary and upbeat—it feels more CBD than French Quarter. Specialties worth seeking out include wood-grilled escolar with eggplant ragout and tomato fondue, New Bedford sea scallops with mushroom risotto and mushroom butter, and sautéed mangrove snapper with daikon cakes and a lemongrass reduction. There's nothing overly convoluted or cutesy about the cooking, just fresh fish with modern ingredients presented with flair.

A dramatic space with red walls and very dim, sexy lighting, **201** (201 Decatur St., 504/561-0007, $17–26) occupies a pale-yellow Italianate building on Decatur. It's a fun and festive option for creative Louisiana cooking, and it's a little less famous, and thus less crowded, than many comparable restaurants in the Quarter. You might start with fried-green-tomato salad with lump crabmeat, arugula, and rémoulade, followed by pecan-crusted gulf fish of the day over roasted butternut squash risotto, baby beans, and sweet-pepper coulis.

Everybody knows about **NOLA** (534 St. Louis St., 504/522-6652, $18–33), Emeril Lagasse's restaurant in the French Quarter, although not everybody loves it. When you're a big fish in an even bigger sea, it's hard not to be noticed and also criticized. After all, Emeril isn't the only dazzling chef in New Orleans—he isn't even the only great one on his block. When all is said and done, however, NOLA delivers great cooking and a lively dining experience that pretty much lives up to its billing, and service is generally reliable. Just keep in mind that it can be hard to get a table, so book ahead, and expect a wait even when you show up on time for reservation. It's not a big restaurant, although there are a few seats at the bar, which can be useful if you're dining alone or coming in without a reservation. The restaurant typically sets aside a very limited number of tables for walk-ins. If you're hoping to nab one, you should plan to arrive a good half-hour before the restaurant opens at 6 P.M. The menu changes often, but some favorites include a stuffed chicken wings appetizer with a house-made dipping sauce, citrus-horseradish–crusted red drum roasted on a cedar plank and served with lemon butter sauce and a Creole tomato salad, and—as a finale—the NOLA buzz bomb, a dense flourless chocolate cake with bittersweet chocolate mousse and brandied apricots wrapped in chocolate ganache.

With a gorgeous bi-level interior inside the former Werlein's Music Store, the **Palace Cafe** (605 Canal St., 504/523-1661, $18–25) ranks among the most cosmopolitan-looking of the several outstanding Brennan-family restaurants in New Orleans. It can get touristy, as it's close to several convention hotels, but don't be put off by the location—the kitchen consistently prepares some of the best and most exciting New Orleans fare in the city, and the staff is highly personable and efficient. Signature dishes are many: there's an oyster pan roast poached in rosemary cream and topped with bread crumbs, crabmeat cheesecake baked in a pecan crust with wild mushrooms, panéed rabbit with tasso ham and Gruyère cheese over fettuccine with leeks and carrots, and catfish pecan meunière. It's all good, and every dish is presented with a great flourish. The restaurant serves a particularly enjoyable Sunday jazz brunch. Of the city's high-end (but not super-expensive) special-occasion restaurants, Palace Cafe leads the pack.

Most of the restaurants actually in or attached to the French Market are ordinary at best and not worth the bother. An exception, sort of hidden behind the main market building, is **Bella Luna** (914 N. Peters St., 504/529-1583, $17–28), a grand neoclassical space with Palladian windows affording spectacular views of the river. Here you might begin with beef carpaccio sprinkled with capers and olive oil, served with sun-dried tomato bruschetta and fresh-herb salad. Slow-roasted Schweinshaxe (pork hind shank) in an Abita beer sauce with house-made sauerkraut is a Continental nod; or consider over-roasted half-duckling with mashed potatoes and Grand Marnier orange sauce. This is classic Continental fare with few surprises, but it's always prepared competently and served by a well-trained, somewhat formal staff. Although jackets and ties aren't required here, you may want to dress a bit for this one.

It's right on busy Decatur Street, inside the Bienville House Hotel, but **Gamay** (320 Decatur St., 504/299-8800, $15–30) feels discreet, its entrance rather difficult to find and its reputation stellar but rather hushed. Gamay has a loyal following, including many die-hard locals and repeat visitors who don't want it to become overly touristy. The kitchen offers a modern—even, in some cases, daring—take on Creole cuisine. The barbecued shrimp with sweet potato mash on jalapeño-cheese biscuits is memorable, and the grilled buffalo rib eye with three-bean ragout and brandied Portobello-cream sauce makes a superb entrée.

In a city known, at least locally, for its many exceptional Italian restaurants, **Maximo's** (1117 Decatur St., 504/586-8883, $12–30) stands out for its fire-roasted meats, feathery-light and fresh handmade pastas, and deftly prepared sauces. Even a simple marinara sauce served with the starter of tender sautéed (not fried or breaded) calamari reaches ethereal heights. Part of the amusement here is dining in the rear room, which

has booths, tables, and a long bar looking directly into the open kitchen, where chefs are the live entertainment. It's great fun to watch and listen to the camaraderie, the sizzle, and the fresh steaks, chicken, sausage, and seafood cuts getting tossed onto the fiery grill. Jazz played over the sound system is a bit easier to hear in the front dining room, meaning that the rear dining room is well-suited to conversation.

Opened quietly in 2002, **Stella!** (1032 Chartres St., 504/587-0091, $16–29) has quickly become a Quarter favorite, in spite of (or perhaps because of) its discreet, slightly out-of-the-way location. Although it's set inside the Hotel Provincial, Stella! is a ways down Chartres Street from the busier half of the neighborhood—you sort of have to know about it to find it. Not everybody loves the silly name either, but the tribute to Stanley Kowalski can be forgiven, as the food is anything but silly. Once inside this dapper, clubby dining room, you'll be treated to truly creative fare, such as sublime seared Hudson Valley foie gras with quenelles of Granny Smith apples, toasted brioche, huckleberry jam, and a burgundy reduction; and an entrée of Creole spice–dusted grouper and cornmeal-crusted frogs' legs with seafood jambalaya risotto and lemon Tabasco honey butter. Some of these dishes may sound overwrought, but ingredients complement each other nicely.

CASUAL COOKING

Acme Oyster House (724 Iberville St., 504/522-5973; also 7306 Lakeshore Dr., 504/282-9200; $5–12) has since 1910 been a reliable option for fresh bivalves. Always packed with tourists, it can be crazy in here in this casual place with red-checked tablecloths, but it's worth braving the frenzy for very good po'boys, gumbo, and other straightforward fare. Is it oyster nirvana, as some people claim? No, in truth, it's not any better than a lot of oyster bars around town, but its rich history and convenient location make it a fun place. You can also get shrimp and soft-shell-crab po'boys, burgers, jambalaya, gumbo, and a first-rate oyster-artichoke bisque. **Johnny's Po-boys** (511 St. Louis St., 504/524-8129, $4–8), opened in 1950, is an unprepossessing little place

Louisiana Pizza Kitchen

po'boys here are as good—and as big—as any around town, and you don't have to battle with the lines typical of more popular places. So prodigious are these French-bread cargo ships that it's nearly impossible to put the thing down once you've managed to grasp it; there's too great a threat that its contents will drop unceremoniously to the table. Other home-style favorites include rabbit-and-smoked-sausage jambalaya, crab claws marinated in Italian vinaigrette, and fried alligator bits. There's a pool table in back, and dark-wood tables and exposed brick give the place a warm feel, as does the super-friendly and welcoming staff. Just one caveat—the cramped and unpleasant bathrooms, reached through the rear courtyard, leave much to be desired.

Cafe Maspero (601 Decatur St., 504/523-6250, $5–10) is more atmospheric and spacious than Johnny's—seating is under brick arched ceilings, at big wooden tables, or you can dine at the bar. The place is famous for its sandwiches, such as the roast beef and Swiss, the veggie muffaletta, and the smoked sausage. But New Orleans fare, from jambalaya to catfish platters, is similarly delicious. The strawberry daiquiris are so refreshing it's easy to forget the high alcohol content; these drinks are strong. Another place that's so touristy it's hard to believe it can really live up to the hype, the **Gumbo Shop** (630 St. Peter St., 504/525-1486, $7–16) does deliver the goods, from kicky shrimp Creole over rice to first-rate crawfish étouffée to a nicely prepared filet mignon with sautéed mushrooms. Of course, the gumbos really are terrific. The complete Creole dinners, at just $19, are a steal—you get an appetizer, vegetable, entrée, and dessert, with several choices in each category.

Crescent City Brewhouse (527 Decatur St., 504/522-0571, $8–20) occupies the first two floors of a white-brick building on Decatur. As brewpubs go, it serves surprisingly decent and varied food, but you come mostly to sample the various microbrews, which are prepared Bavarian-style, with simple, natural ingredients (just water, malt, hops, and yeast)—the light Weiss beer is a house favorite. Offerings from the menu include lemon chicken wings, fried calamari and caponata, shrimp po'boys with

with tables sheathed in red-checkered cloth and surrounded by bentwood chairs. It's only open till 4 each afternoon but fills up daily for breakfast and lunch. It's best-known for its namesake sandwiches, but you can also get platters of fried seafood. Classic po'boys include tuna, country-fried steak, and the Judge Bosetta (with ground beef, Italian and hot sausage, and Swiss cheese).

Nellie's (91 French Market, 504/568-1777, $4–10), by Louisiana Pizza Kitchen, is cheap, divey, and good, with oysters and similar-such food. It's right by the flea market at French Market—just a simple and casual place that does traditional New Orleans food right. The bloody Marys and margaritas are excellent, too. The owner of **Coops** (1109 Decatur St., 504/525-9053, $5–15) sought to create a space that's equal parts bar and restaurant, and indeed this untouristy and underrated hangout on raffish Decatur Street succeeds on both counts, offering the convivial spirit of a neighborhood pub and food that's pub-style but consistently high caliber. The oyster

fiery habanero ketchup, seared scallops with roasted pepper–and–vermouth cream, and raspberry roast duck.

An affordable and romantic eatery in the Lower Quarter, **Quarter Scene** (900 Dumaine St., 504/522-6533, $9–15) sits at a relatively peaceful corner just a block from Bourbon, inside a yellow wood-frame house with big bay windows facing both Dumaine and Dauphine Streets. The candlelit dining room is filled with local artwork. Tennessee Williams was a regular, and the restaurant has long had a strong following with the gay community. The food is straightforward and fairly traditional, mostly of the Cajun and Creole variety, including first-rate red beans and rice, pecan catfish, fried seafood platters with waffle fries, and shrimp omelets. Quarter Scene has no liquor license, but you're welcome to bring your own, and there's never a corkage fee.

A dark and divey corner tavern that's so popular for its hefty burgers that there's sometimes a line outside the door, **Port of Call** (838 Esplanade Ave., 504/523-0120, $6–14) serves the full range of traditional American comfort foods, including pizza, steaks, and huge baked potatoes topped with all kinds of goodies (they come with the burgers). The burgers, made with freshly ground beef and piled high with melted cheddar, really are that good.

You'd think there'd be more places to scarf down a big meal late after a night of drinking and dancing, but **Angeli** (1141 Decatur St., 504/566-0077, $6–14) is one of the only decent places in the Quarter that's open into the wee hours (24 hours on weekends, and till 4 A.M. the rest of the week). A wide range of munchies and light bites are offered, including pizzas, wraps, wings, waffles, designer coffees, all kind of beers, and addictive flatbread with sun-dried tomato pesto and parmesan cheese—pretty much any food you might crave late at night. Often, old black-and-white movies are shown against a rear wall of the dining room, which draws an eclectic crowd that's especially interesting (ravers, gays, club kids, yuppies, artists) the later you eat here. There's usually light jazz playing in the background, and the busy street-corner location allows for optimum people-watching.

Louisiana Pizza Kitchen (95 French Market Pl., 504/522-9500; also 615 S. Carrollton Ave., 504/866-8900; 2112 Belle Chasse Hwy. Gretna, 504/433-5800, pies $7–9, entreés $7–14) serves food throughout the day, which surprisingly few substantial eateries in the Quarter do (most are open for lunch and dinner but close in between, and several serve dinner only). It's right on the edge of the French Market, facing the U.S. Mint museum. The gray-brick room has walls decked with local art (for sale) and black-and-white checked floors—it's a vaguely art deco look. Pizzas are of the thin-crust variety baked with little grease, and toppings tend toward creative. The pizza topped with applewood-smoked bacon and chives with mozzarella cheese, sour cream, and Roma tomatoes is a classic. The crawfish pie is also great. Pita wraps, pastas, calzones, and hefty salads (try the one with blue cheese and roasted pecans) round out the menu.

ETHNIC

The French Quarter has precious few ethnic restaurants, but a new standout that's worth investigating is **Bennachin** (1212 Royal St., 504/522-1230, $8–14), one of the only West African eateries in the South (odd when you consider the region's, and especially Louisiana's, clear ties to West Africa through its many decades of importing slaves from Senegal). It's actually been in New Orleans for some time, but the restaurant, whose owner hails from Cameroon, moved from its original Mid-City locale to the Quarter in 2003, inside what had been a Turkish restaurant. Recommended dishes include stews of beef, ginger, peanuts, and spinach; a red bean soup that seems like an appropriate progenitor to New Orleans cuisine; and couscous with a tart yogurt sauce. There's always a daily lunch special for under $6.

QUICK BITES

People sometimes overlook the fact that **Central Grocery** (923 Decatur St., 504/523-1620) really is a grocery store, in this case carrying a mouthwatering array of fine imported Italian foods, many of them hard to find in the United States. But, of course, the place is most famous for being home of the incredibly delicious muffaletta sandwich, made with Italian bread coated in sesame seeds that's then stuffed with ham, salami, mortadella, provolone cheese, and a generous helping of olive salad (made of chopped green and Kalamata olives, carrots, capers, garlic, and olive oil). The restaurant claims to have invented this dish—skeptics are less sure, but there's little denying that Central Market makes one of the best, and they serve it cold, in contrast to many delis and restaurants around town. There are more than a few fans who simply cannot visit New Orleans without having at least one of these sandwiches, and ardent devotees have been known to have them shipped to far-flung corners of the globe. There's no dining room per se, just a counter in back with a few benches. A bag of Zapp's potato chips goes especially well with a muffaletta. As for the grocery section, you'll find imported oils and vinegars, fine cheeses, gourmet pastas, anchovies, nuts, and just about every other gourmet product you might find at a neighborhood grocery store in an Italian city.

Cafe Beignet (819 Decatur St., 504/522-9929; 1031 Decatur St., 504/522-6868; 334B Royal St., 504/524-5530, $3–8) is a minichain of touristy but reliable cafés around the Lower Quarter, good for coffee and teas, light sandwiches, and an impressive selection of pastries and sweets. There's nothing especially noteworthy about them, but they can be handy in a pinch, especially when the actual hallowed hall of beignets and coffee, Cafe du Monde, is too crowded. Two of these branches are roughly across the street from the French Market. The cult popularity of **Krispy Kreme** (620 Decatur St., ground floor of Jackson Brewery, 504/581-4680; also 825 Clearview Pkwy., Metairie, 504/779-9620) holds true even in the French Quarter, and even though the city's first branch of the fast-growing national chain opened a mere stone's throw from Cafe du Monde. Of course, some people find it silly that anyone would eat doughnuts at a franchise restaurant when you can get Krispy Kremes at gas stations and grocery stores all around the country.

But an addiction is an addiction, and some fans of these fried treasures simply must get their fix. The Big Easy is an appropriate setting for Krispy Kreme, as the original recipe for these soft and chewy doughnuts was purchased by the first Winston-Salem doughnut shop in the 1930s from a French chef in New Orleans.

Lucky Dogs, those little brown-and-red weiner-shaped hot dog carts in the French Quarter, are ideal for a quick snack—there's usually one along Decatur near Jackson Brewery.

It's late, you're hungry (maybe even a little tipsy), and you have a craving for greasy food. It's times like these when you'll count your lucky stars that a place like the **Clover Grill** (900 Bourbon St., 504/598-1010, $3–7) never closes and never stops frying up wonderfully fattening and gooey cheeseburgers, pecan waffles topped with bananas, vanilla malts, and bowls of grits swimming in melted butter. Part of the fun at this loud, dishy diner—where the menu is filled with jokes and the wisecracking staff is quick to make fun of customers—is enjoying the constant merriment. Three of the city's most popular gay bars lie within a block of the Clover Grill, and so drag queens and disco bunnies typically make up a chunk of the clientele.

Clover Grill

© ANDREW COLLINS

A source of delectable sweets, the **Croissant D'Or** (617 Ursulines Ave., 504/524-4663) is a classic French bakery that also serves light lunch fare, homemade soups, fresh salads, and good breakfasts. It's in the Lower Quarter, near the Old Ursuline Convent, and it makes a nice break from exploring the neighborhood's rich architecture. Although part of a Texas-based chain, the Jackson Square outpost of **La Madeleine** (547 St. Ann St., 504/568-0073; also 601 S. Carrollton Ave., 504/861-8662; 1327 St. Charles Ave., 504/410-8500; 3300 Severn Ave., Metairie, 504/456-1624; 4–7) feels so authentically New Orleans that many visitors think the chain originated here. This and the other locations around town serve up very good and reasonably priced French café food, such as French onion soup, crème brûlée, baguette sandwiches of several varieties, and pesto-pasta salads. You'll also find excellent coffee and such toothsome breakfast treats as ham Florentine crepes and custom omelets.

JAVA JOINTS

What began as a humble coffee stand to serve the customers and employees of the produce stalls in the French Market in 1862, **Cafe du Monde** (1039 Decatur St., 800/772-2927; also Riverwalk Marketplace, 1 Poydras St., 504/587-0841) has grown into one of the most legendary food operations in the country, included in coffee-table books, written about in newspapers and magazines, and discussed on television programs. Part of its mystique and popularity is that the place is open 24/7, except for Christmas, and that it serves so few foods (although it serves them all well). The mainstays are beignets (French-style fried doughnuts dusted with powdered sugar) and dark-roasted coffee laced with chicory and traditionally served "au lait" (a cup filled half with hot milk, half with coffee) but also available black. You can also order fresh-squeezed orange juice, white or chocolate milk, iced coffee (a recent innovation, having debuted in 1988), and sodas (an even more recent innovation, and some say an abomination). The cafe is mostly an open-air operation consisting of

Cafe du Monde

dozens of small marble tables surrounded by green vinyl chairs and covered with a tentlike roof. Waiters clad in white shirts with black bow ties and white-paper hats whisk about gracefully, delivering plates of beignets at breakneck speed. In cold weather, the area is warmed with heating lamps, but you can also grab one of the few tables in a small and fully enclosed dining area. There are now a handful of satellite locations of Cafe du Monde, mostly in area shopping malls, which keep shorter hours and definitely lack the ambience of the original.

The Quarter has a branch of the city's most famous coffeehouse chain, **C.C.'s**, at 941 Royal St., at the corner of Dumaine Street. It's a cozy spot, meaning that seating is a bit limited, but it's also warmly lighted and charmingly furnished, with several cushy armchairs. **Bastille Computer Cafe** (605 Toulouse St., 504/581-1150) is perfect when you need to log onto the net; it's in an old brick cottage in the heart of the Quarter. Here you can grab a coffee and rent a computer or use your own laptop to access the Web. Bastille has a full slate of CD burners, business services, and design, scanners, digital photo editing, and every other service you could possibly need—even computer lessons are available here.

PICNIC SUPPLIES AND GOURMET GOODS

Grenier & Chocolat (517 St. Louis St., 504/586-8880) carries imported Leonidas chocolates from Belgium, along with dozens of similarly rich and artful-looking candies. It's a tiny, exquisite little confectioner on a quiet street just off Decatur. For more than a century, **Evans Creole Candy Factory** (848 Decatur St., 504/522-7111 or 800/637-6675) has been crafting delicious pralines. Still today, you can watch the candy-makers working on a fresh batch of pralines through the big windows of this shop in the French Market, which is also an excellent source for hand-dipped chocolates, dark-chocolate turtles (Creole pecans topped with caramel and dipped in chocolate), chocolate-covered maraschino cherries, and other tempting sweets. **Southern Candymakers** (334 Decatur St., 504/523-5544), also in the French Market, is a full retail shop with pralines, marzipan, peanut brittle, fudge, and lots of other sweets that will do horrible things to your teeth but will make the rest of you quite happy. You can stop by for a free sample, too.

It's not a real chore finding alcohol in the French Quarter, but when it's your own bottle of wine, liquor, or beer that you're seeking, look no further than **Vieux Carré Wine & Spirits** (422 Chartres St., 504/568-WINE), which has an especially impressive selection of wines. The store will deliver purchase within the Quarter and CBD.

Faubourg Marigny and Bywater

TRADITIONAL CREOLE AND CAJUN

One of the city's definitive gay restaurants, **Feelings Cafe** (2600 Chartres St., 504/945-2222, $15–26) is set on a quiet street in a charmingly decrepit-looking old building several blocks past Frenchmen Street (it's a 10- to 20-minute walk from the Quarter). It's known best for its Sunday brunch (try the crab cakes with poached eggs and Hollandaise sauce) but serves first-rate Creole and Continental fare at every meal. Specialties include seafood-baked eggplant (a slice of fried eggplant topped with a combination of dirty rice, shrimp, crabmeat, and crawfish and covered with a rich seafood butter sauce), blue cheese steak, and Gulf fish *moutarde* (sautéed local fish with lemon butter, topped with Dijon mustard, Hollandaise, roasted almonds, and new potatoes). Peanut butter pie is the trademark dessert. The setting is a shabby-chic dining room with art (for sale on the walls), along with a shady patio and a piano bar. It's a real locals' favorite, worth venturing a bit off the beaten path.

For a sublime blend of soul and Creole cooking, drop by the **Praline Connection** (542 Frenchmen St., 504/943-3934; also 907 S. Peters St., 504/523-3973), famous for both its crawfish étouffée and its bread pudding. This is one of several great eateries, along with a number of hopping bars and music clubs, that you can find along ultra-hip Frenchmen Street. There are a few Praline Connections around town these days, but the original on Faubourg Marigny's Frenchmen Street tends to draw the greatest praise. In two simple dining rooms, the mostly African-American staff, clad in natty white shirts, black bow-ties, and black fedoras, move about efficiently with hot platters of red beans and rice, collard greens, bread pudding with caramel sauce, étouffée, smothered pork, and other hearty—and often quite spicy—renderings of both soul and Creole cooking. Local beers and wines are sold, and you can pick up the ingredients and seasonings here to prepare your own renditions of these foods back home. The Warehouse District branch is a full-on gospel and blues hall with live music and a fabulous brunch.

the Praline Connection, Faubourg Marigny

CREATIVE AND CONTEMPORARY

A positively charming and little-known gem occupying a romantic second-floor space along a historic and residential stretch of Royal, **Aquarians** (2601 Royal St., 504/944-7770, $13–22) is yet further proof of the emerging cachet of Faubourg Marigny as a hot neighborhood for dining. The tiny dining room has just about a dozen tables, and soft lighting, eclectic artwork, and laid-back but knowing service put everybody in a great mood. Dine on crab cakes with a zesty Creole mustard sauce, rare-seared tuna, and outstanding carrot cake. Although seafood is the main event here, steaks and pastas are also available. It's open late most evenings, and patrons are encouraged to linger over coffee after their meal, enjoying the view of rooftops of neighboring Creole cottages and shotgun houses.

Marigny Brasserie (640 Frenchmen St., 504/945-4472, $16–21) is a slick, modern space whose kitchen puts a contemporary spin on both Louisiana and French ingredients and recipes. The braised chicken with yellow rice and a caper-and-olive tapenade reflects the kitchen's simple

approach to fine, contemporary food. Several light salads are available, including a delicious tomato and Spanish tarragon plate with goat cheese. The stylish bar is a relaxing place to sip cocktails before heading to one of the nearby music clubs. A hip little spot with the look and feel of a postindustrial diner, healthful **Old Dog New Trick Cafe** (517 Frenchmen St., 504/943-6368, $5–11) is one of the city's best vegetarian restaurants, serving creative and flavorful meat-free fare. Try the slightly scary-sounding tofu-rama sandwich (broiled curried tofu with onions, mushrooms, and a ginger-peanut sauce), or the hearty polenta Medici, layered with black beans, red-and-green-pepper sauce, rosemary, goat cheese, and roasted veggies. Several pizzas are served, along with a wide range of vegetarian burgers and breakfast specialties.

A relative newcomer along Esplanade Avenue that's quickly garnered lots of attention, **Marisol** (437 Esplanade Ave., 504/943-1912, $17–26) presents a first-rate menu of Spanish-influenced edibles. Nosh on such dazzling starters as carpaccio of venison with slivered olives, pickled fennel, and pimento aioli, or house-made ricotta ravioli with lobster sauce, before moving on to pan-roasted guinea hen with pearl onions, yellow carrots, and house-made fettuccine. You can drop by for tapas happy hour on weekday early evenings. The wine list is first-rate, and there's a well-chosen selection of cheeses. In warm weather, dine on the romantic, lushly landscaped courtyard.

CASUAL COOKING

Despite the name, **Bywater Bar-b-que** (3162 Dauphine St., 504/944-4445, $5–12) is more than just a place to get tasty smoked ribs, pulled pork, and tangy barbecued chicken. This campy restaurant with a shrine to Barbie dolls and a "no-smoking" section that consists of a chair nailed upside down to the ceiling also serves pastas, grilled veggies, pizzas, and—at breakfast—eggs Benedict, huevos rancheros, and plenty of other yummy edibles. The diminutive restaurant is in the Bywater neighborhood, about a dozen blocks downriver from Frenchmen Street. It's definitely worth checking out if you're in these parts, and deserving of a special trip if you are a fan of barbecue. Way out on the east end of Bywater, easygoing **Elizabeth's** (601 Gallier St., 504/944-4810, under $6) requires an even longer journey from the Quarter, but it does serve exceptional breakfasts and lunch (it's not open for dinner). Owner-chef Heidi Trull comes up with all sorts of imaginative specials, and also manages to chat with many of her customers, some of whom travel here from the farthest reaches of the city. The Loula May breakfast po'boy is a local specialty—it comes served on fresh-baked French bread and spilling over with scrambled eggs, hot andouille sausage, and melted cheddar. Order cheese grits or a side of praline-flavored bacon to go with it. Lunch favorites include turkey club sandwiches, fried catfish po'boys, and sides of fresh-cut sweet-potato fries.

Restaurant Mandich (3200 St. Claude Ave., 504/947-9553, $11–20) is another great restaurant that's a little bit of an adventure to reach—a cab might be your best strategy, as the walk from the Quarter is too long and a bit shady. This family-owned, working-stiffs restaurant with dark-wood paneling and a low-frills ambience specializes in those two cuisines so often celebrated and blended in New Orleans: Creole and Italian fare. Pan-fried trout fillet in lemon-butter sauce topped with sautéed crabmeat is not only one of the best dishes served here, it's one of the best you'll taste in New Orleans. Also try the bordelaise oysters on the half-shell with garlic sauce.

During normal dining hours, **La Peniche** (1940 Dauphine St., 504/943-1460, $6–14) is nothing special—just a friendly, reasonably priced neighborhood café serving satisfying breakfast, lunch, and dinner fare—country-fried steak, pecan waffles smothered with peanut butter, good burgers, and coffee. At 3 in the morning, however, especially after you've just stumbled out of a bar or caught a case of the late-night munchies, La Peniche feels like paradise—the place is open 24 hours except for one 43-hour span from Tuesday at 2 P.M. till Thursday at 9 A.M. The dishy staff and colorful local following make it a fun place to eavesdrop or make new friends. On the border between the Marigny and the Quarter, **Igor's Check Point Charlie** (501 Esplanade Ave., 504/949-7012, $4–12) is equal parts music club, pool hall, self-service laundry, and restaurant. The food is probably the least compelling reason to go, but it's decent—burgers, sandwiches, and other comfort snacks. The crowd tends to be young and local, and the kitchen serves food late (the laundry is open 24 hours).

ETHNIC

Along elegant Esplanade Avenue, **Siam Cafe** (435 Esplanade Ave., 504/949-1750, $9–18) is a reliable option for Thai fare, and it's also known for a trendy lounge upstairs called the Dragon Room, where hipsters and yupsters hold court while sipping foofy cocktails. It's open late for dinner, and the seductive red lighting and Asian decorative pieces make it easy to lose yourself in here for a couple of hours. On the edge of Faubourg Marigny, just a few blocks up Frenchmen Street from the main cluster of bars and restaurants, **Wasabi** (900 Frenchmen St., 504/943-9433, $9–19) serves excellent sushi and a delicious grilled squid dish. The deep-fried jumbo soft-shell crab stir-fried with jalapeños, onions, and Asian spices is a real treat. Also try baby octopus salad, soft-shell crab rolls, or one of the many daily-changing specials. The dark and cozy space is actually half mellow-cool neighborhood bar and half Japanese restaurant.

Big portions of traditional Italian and Creole fare are heaped onto the plates at **Adolfo's** (611 Frenchmen St., 504/948-3800, $12–21), a longtime neighborhood standby that's especially strong on seafood dishes like crab-and-crawfish cannelloni and sautéed soft-shell crabs. There's usually a very nice rack of lamb on the menu, too, often paired with a rosemary-garlic sauce. It's a small place, and reservations are a must if you have four or more in your party. Downstairs, the Apple Barrel Bar is a dark and cozy spot to nurse a cocktail before or after dinner.

Very good Southwestern fare is presented at **Santa Fe** (801 Frenchmen St., 504/944-6854, $8–17), in a rambling old house in Washington Park. The chiles rellenos are great, as is the chicken Maximilian, which is breaded and then rolled around an Anaheim pepper and stuffed with chorizo and cheese. There's an inexpensive buffet brunch served on Fridays. Service is friendly and brisk, a rarity in the laid-back Marigny.

Mona's Cafe (504 Frenchmen St., 504/949-4115; also 4126 Magazine St., 504/894-9800; 3149 Calhoun St., 504/861-2124; 3901 Banks St., 504/482-7743; $5–12) serves great, cheap Middle Eastern food and is also a richly stocked Lebanese grocery. Start with some snacks, such as zaater bread (baked with ground thyme, oregano, sesame seeds, sumac, and olive oil), mixed hummus and foul (mashed fava beans with garlic, hot peppers, lemon, and olive oil), and spinach pie. Chicken kabobs, gyros, lamb chops, and grapeleaf platters rank among the several excellent entrées.

New Orleans architecture, music, and even food have been influenced by the Caribbean, but **Cafe Negril** (606 Frenchmen St., 504/944-4744, $10–15) is one of the only places in the metro area that serves an entirely West Indian menu. The space along the Frenchmen Street entertainment strip is bright and colorful (there's a larger-than-life Bob Marley mural on one wall), and the food is quite good and well-seasoned, with an emphasis on seafood (such as Jamaican jerk fish of the day). The ceviche starter is excellent, and regulars swear by the West Indies curried goat stew.

QUICK BITES

Set inside a strikingly restored historic building in the heart of the neighborhood, **Schiro's Community Cafe** (2483 Royal St., 504/944-6666, $4–10) serves many needs of locals—it's not only a restaurant serving three meals every day but Sunday, but also a small grocery store and Laundromat. Baked stuffed catfish, which is served on Fridays, is a specialty that even nonlocals will travel here for, but anytime it's a nice spot for sandwiches, burgers, and other munchies.

JAVA JOINTS

Sharing a corner with a couple of gay bars on the border between the Marigny and Bywater, **Flora Coffee Shop & Gallery** (2600 Royal St., 504/525-6724) is a cool little place with sidewalk seating, worn-in furnishings, big portions of coffee elixirs, and light snacks. It's a nice place to read a book or chat with locals. The local chain **P.J.'s** has a sunny storefront café at 524 Frenchmen St.

Central Business and Warehouse Districts

M

FOOD

CREATIVE AND CONTEMPORARY

A boisterous power-lunch room that's also a hit with the dinner crowd, trendy **Herbsaint** (701 St. Charles Ave., 504/524-4114, $17–24) sits along a nondescript stretch of St. Charles, its setting brightened by tall windows, soft-yellow walls, a tile floor, and a young and good-looking staff. Start with fried frogs' legs or a plate of herb gnocchi with wild mushrooms, sage, and roasted garlic. The Muscovy duck leg confit with dirty rice and citrus gastrique is a top main course. The wine selection is terrific; also offered are many cool cocktails (lime gin fizz, for instance) and wine-tasting flights of three vintages. **Restaurant Cuvée** (322 Magazine St., 504/587-9001, $18–28) has one of the finest wine lists in the South, plus A-one Creole cooking infused with contemporary French, Spanish, and other Mediterranean ingredients. Start with char-grilled local oysters served with Parmigiano-Reggiano and white-truffle oil, pause to enjoy a salad of pepper-crusted tuna carpaccio with fresh heart of palm and teardrop tomatoes, and then move on to a spectacular main dish of mustard-and-herb-crusted fillet of salmon with lump crabmeat, Brie orzo, and lemon confit. The lighting fixtures in this elegant dining room, with exposed brick walls, dark-wood trim, and white linens, are fashioned from wine bottles of prestigious vintages. It's an ideal locale for a special occasion but without the pretension that mars some of the CBD's top dining establishments.

Bayona chef-owner Susan Spicer, one of the city's top cooking personalities, is part owner of **Cobalt** (333 St. Charles Ave., 504/565-5595, $16–25), a white-hot restaurant inside the supercool Hotel Monaco, an easy stroll from the Quarter. The hip dining room, softly illuminated by indirect blue light, occupies the ground floor of the former Masonic temple on the St. Charles Avenue streetcar line. The mood is unfussy and lively, and Cobalt is as popular for cocktails as for dinner—you can combine your eating and drinking efforts by grabbing a seat at the oyster bar. The menu mixes Old South ingredients and recipes with modern accents; consider a starter of steamed barbecued mussels served alongside grilled jalapeño bread, followed by pepper jelly–crusted rack of lamb with rosemary cheddar grits, broccoli rabe, and a smashed grape–zinfandel sauce. A very agreeable option at the hip but affordable Hotel Le Cirque, **Lee Circle Restaurant** (3 Lee Circle, 504/962-0915, $14–26) is a bit more upscale than the hotel but won't necessarily break your bank account. And it delivers truly terrific and innovative nouvelle Creole fare, such as mirliton bisque with jumbo lump crabmeat and roast Abita Springs quail with foie gras stuffing and truffle cream. The setting is a cool, urbane dining room peopled with young, well-dressed types.

Restaurant August (301 Tchoupitoulas St. 504/299-9777, $18–32) is presided over by talented and charismatic chef John Besh, the Louisiana born-and-bred kitchen wizard who first made Artesia on the North Shore famous. He opened this Warehouse District restaurant in 2001, inside a handsome late-1800s Creole French building, and it's been tough to get a table here ever since. Besh presents uncomplicated yet richly nuanced contemporary American fare, with healthy doses of both local and Mediterranean ingredients. The light salad of lavender-grilled figs, Serrano ham, goat cheese, and arugula makes for one of the restaurant's most celebrated starters. You might follow with olive oil–poached halibut with artichokes, beets, and wilted greens, or an imaginative lasagna layered with rabbit, sweetbreads, and chunks of fresh lobster. Do save room for goat-milk cheesecake with rosemary-honey ice cream and a hint of bee pollen.

Rene Bistro (817 Common St., 504/412-2580, $15–22) is another of the stellar and relatively young hotel restaurants that's generating lots of buzz around the CBD. Chef René Bajeux is widely regarded as one of the top French cooks in the United States, having previously served as executive chef at the Windsor Court. His menu, which has few dishes more costly than $20, focuses on classic French bistro fare but with many creative twists—you won't go wrong with the sautéed skate served with an artichoke and green bean salad and topped with a caper emulsion. Sautéed foie gras with a white truffle flan and Reisling reduction has fans of goose liver swooning. There's live jazz many evenings, and the Sunday brunch ranks among the tastiest such affairs in the city.

The bigger and louder of Emeril Lagasse's acclaimed restaurants, **Emeril's** (800 Tchoupitoulas St., 504/528-9393, www.emerils.com) takes its hits from critics who complain about haughty service and high prices, but this is the domain of one of the world's most famous chefs, and it's always packed. All in all, if you can get a table here (book well ahead), go for it—Emeril didn't become famous for no reason. He's a great cook with a great kitchen staff, and the food here is more complex and imaginative than at NOLA, his French Quarter restaurant. Try citrus-and-tea-glazed duck with savory caramelized onion bread pudding and haricots verts, or grilled filet mignon with truffle-creamed potatoes, sautéed asparagus, crispy root vegetable chips, and a red-wine reduction. Desserts include a laudable Key lime pie with berry coulis as well as crepes filled with homemade mascarpone cheese and topped with orange sauce. The space is airy, high-ceilinged, and dramatic, the quintessence of Warehouse District chic.

Quirky **Eleven 79** (1179 Annunciation St., 504/299-1179, $11–20) has a strong local following for its Creole-inspired Italian fare. The grilled calamari with pecorino-cheese polenta is heavenly, and you won't go wrong either with oysters panne served with a white rémoulade. The diminutive, charming restaurant occupies a restored bungalow in the shadows of the Pontchartrain Expressway bridge, just on the edge of the Warehouse and Lower Garden Districts. An airy postmodern space drawing a stylish crowd, **Metro Bistro** (200 Magazine St., 504/529-1900, $17–26) sits just a few steps from an otherwise sleepy stretch of Magazine. The cuisine here is contemporary French with

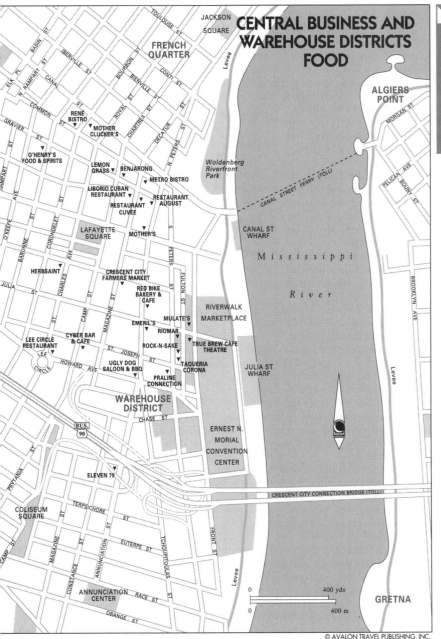

CENTRAL BUSINESS AND WAREHOUSE DISTRICTS FOOD

FOOD

FRENCH QUARTER

JACKSON SQUARE

ALGIERS POINT

RENÉ BISTRO

MOTHER CLUCKER'S

O'HENRY'S FOOD & SPIRITS

LEMON GRASS

BENJARONG

METRO BISTRO

LIBORIO CUBAN RESTAURANT

RESTAURANT CUVÉE

RESTAURANT AUGUST

Woldenberg Riverfront Park

CANAL STREET FERRY (TOLL)

CANAL ST WHARF

LAFAYETTE SQUARE

MOTHER'S

Mississippi

River

HERBSAINT

CRESCENT CITY FARMERS MARKET

RED BIKE BAKERY & CAFE

EMERIL'S

MULATE'S

RIOMAR

RIVERWALK MARKETPLACE

CYBER BAR & CAFE

LEE CIRCLE RESTAURANT

ROCK-N-SAKE

TRUE BREW CAFE THEATRE

UGLY DOG SALOON & BBQ

TAQUERIA CORONA

JULIA ST WHARF

PRALINE CONNECTION

WAREHOUSE DISTRICT

CHASE ST

BUS. 90

ERNEST N. MORIAL CONVENTION CENTER

ELEVEN 79

CRESCENT CITY CONNECTION BRIDGE (TOLL)

COLISEUM SQUARE

ANNUNCIATION CENTER

GRETNA

0   400 yds

0   400 m

© AVALON TRAVEL PUBLISHING, INC.

definite Louisiana influences. Steak au poivre crusted with peppercorns and pan-seared is served with a cognac-peppercorn sauce and aromatic rosemary pommes frites. Roasted Cornish hen on wilted greens with sweet potato purée and toasted Louisiana pecans is another fine dish. Voyeurs should ask for a seat overlooking the exhibition kitchen.

Although it can fill up with business travelers (it's two blocks from the convention center), bustling **RioMar** (800 South Peters St., 504/525-FISH, $14–22) maintains a warm and personal ambience, owing largely to the well-trained staff and welcoming dining room, set inside a vintage industrial building with a slate floor and barrel-vaulted archways. The specialty is seafood prepared Latin American style. You could make a small meal of the ceviche sampler, with four types of raw seafood each cured in a different Latin tradition: Spanish (with octopus and olive oil), Panamanian (with habanero peppers and lime), Ecuadorian (with shrimp, tomato, and citrus juice), and Peruvian (with tomatoes, onions, and cilantro). Entrée highlights include littleneck clams steamed with parsley and chorizo, and yellowfin tuna served rare and wrapped in Serrano ham with a chickpea purée and Romesco sauce. Pork chops and steaks are also served.

At the ultra-swank International House hotel, **Lemon Grass** (217 Camp St., 504/523-1200, $14–24) is a dark and sexy dining room with dark and sexy patrons. The food, which is generally excellent, is almost an afterthought for many of the hip diners who come here to see and be seen. Still, don't overlook such tempting starters as the spring roll of minced chicken, jicama, and wood ear mushrooms served with a light citrus sauce, or crab cakes serves with a wonton and sweet Creole mustard–chili coulis. Main courses include wok-smoked salmon steak with grilled vegetables, and Asian curry gulf shrimp over angel-hair pasta.

> *The slightly scandalous name of Mother Clucker's may seem gimmicky, but this really is a fine place to sample no-frills Southern-style chicken dishes, from fried tenders to spicy wings, plus baked macaroni 'n' cheese that'll make your mom jealous.*

CASUAL COOKING

The slightly scandalous name of **Mother Clucker's** (132 Carondelet St., 504/528-0099, $3–10) may seem gimmicky, but this really is a fine place to sample no-frills Southern-style chicken dishes, from fried tenders to spicy wings, plus baked macaroni 'n' cheese that'll make your mom jealous. The long list of sides includes addictive sweet-potato fries, and they turn out some nice desserts, too, including king cakes at Mardi Gras (it's just a block off the parade route). An inexpensive and inviting little spot on a charming street in the Warehouse District, **Red Bike Bakery & Cafe** (746 Tchoupitoulas St., 504/529-2453, $7–16) specializes in light and healthful cooking, not the sort of food you may expect in this city. The creatively topped pizzas are a favorite choice, as are the many excellent salads and sandwiches. There's live Latin music some evenings, when the place is quite popular as a bar.

Like the famous original outside Lafayette, **Mulate's** (201 Julia St., 504/522-1492, $13–19) serves up tasty Cajun fare alongside rollicking Cajun music. You'll often see big groups of people and families seated in this enormous dance hall and restaurant on the edge of the Warehouse District, a short walk from the casino and the Quarter. It can feel a little bus tour–isty in here, but if you're not able to make it out to the real Cajun Country, this is a nice opportunity to experience authentic music and food from the region. Specialties from the long, long menu include catfish Mulate (topped with crawfish étouffée), crabmeat au gratin, and—when you just can't make up your mind—Mulate's Cajun Seafood Platter, which includes stuffed crab, fried crawfish tails, butterflied shrimp, fried catfish, fried oysters, jambalaya, corn macque choux, and home-style fries.

ETHNIC

By many accounts, **Rock-n-Sake** (823 Fulton St., 504/581-7253, $15–22) serves some of the freshest and most interesting sushi in the South, including spicy crawfish rolls, giant clams, wasabi-infused tobiko, and baby soft-shell crab. Tofu teriyaki "steak," udon noodles with thinly sliced beef and onions, snow crab salad, barbecued eel over rice, and chicken katsu round out the menu. The dining room is noisy and vibrant, a bit like a nightclub (plenty of regulars come to sip sake martinis, melon balls, and other pretty cocktails), with Mardi Gras masks and large contemporary paintings covering the walls, and loud rock and pop music blasting in the background. The staff and the crowd tend to be young and in-the-know.

Check out **Liborio Cuban Restaurant** (321 Magazine St., 504/581-9680; also 7724 Maple St., 504/865-9600, $11–19) when the mood for hearty, authentic Cuban fare strikes. New Orleans has a long and close relationship with Cuba, or at least it did during the 18th and 19th centuries, and this casual Warehouse District restaurant does the island nation's robust cuisine justice. The kitchen serves up a terrific paella with shrimp, squid, and pork, as well as stuffed Cuban steaks, lobster-stuffed steak, hefty Cuban sandwiches, and caramel flan for dessert. A snazzy upscale space on the ground floor of the Omni Crescent Hotel, **Benjarong** (228 Camp St., 504/571-7500, $10–22) brings French- and Creole-inspired Thai cooking to the CBD; it's run by the owners of the esteemed Bangkok Cuisine, on South Carrollton in Mid-City.

QUICK BITES

The celeb photos lining the walls of **Mother's** (401 Poydras St., 504/523-9656, $4–12), a glorified cafeteria with brash lighting, Formica tables, and chatty servers, attests to its long-standing popularity—it opened in 1938, and still it draws a mix of downtown office workers, hungry tourists, and local politicos. The most famous dishes here are the roast beef or baked ham po'boys, but you can also get very good gumbo, jambalaya, étouffée, and other humble Creole and Cajun fare. It opens in the morning at 5 A.M., which is good to know if you happen to be returning back to your CBD hotel late after bar-hopping with hunger pangs. An easy-going down-home hangout in the Warehouse District, the **Ugly Dog Saloon & BBQ** (401 Andrew Higgins Dr., 504/569-8459, $4–10) can be counted on for cheap drinks (especially during the weekday happy hours), great crawfish boils on Sundays in late winter, and a nice range of barbecued favorites, such as pulled-pork sandwiches. Fancy it ain't.

JAVA JOINTS

The **Cyber Bar & Cafe** (900 Camp St., 504/523-0900), at the Contemporary Arts Center, is more than a convenient spot to check your email and surf the Web. The artsy, attractive place has all kinds of coffee drinks plus beer and wine, and it's an excellent spot for sandwiches, snacks, and desserts (baked fresh at several New Orleans bakeries). Attached to a funky theater and performance space, **True Brew Cafe** (200 Julia St., 504/524-8441) is most crowded before and after performances but makes a nice respite any time of day. Soups, salads, and sandwiches are offered, plus the usual array of baked goods and coffee drinks.

The Garden District and Uptown

TRADITIONAL CREOLE AND CAJUN

There are only so many of New Orleans's most vaunted institutions of fine dining that you can possibly try during any one visit—even if you have the time, you may not have the appetite. If you must put one place at the top of your list, make it **Commander's Palace** (1403 Washington Ave., 504/899-8221, $25–40), the flagship eatery in the famed Brennan family empire, and *the* place to try turtle soup, gulf fish seared in a cast-iron pan, and bread pudding soufflé—especially if you're uninitiated to such famous New Orleans foods. Lunch really isn't super-expensive (there's a wonderful three-course prix-fixe for about $30 at lunch, and $35 at dinner), making it a good time to test the waters. At dinner, consider the Creole-spiced filet mignon served over truffled buttermilk-mashed potatoes, caramelized onions, smoked mushrooms, and tasso marchands de vin. The weekend jazz brunches are the stuff of legend. Reservations, as far ahead as possible, are a must.

CREATIVE AND CONTEMPORARY

In an unassuming yellow clapboard house on the corner of Austerlitz and Magazine, **Kelsey's Restaurant** (3923 Magazine St., 504/897-6722, $19–25) prepares globally inspired Creole cuisine that's both fresh and uncomplicated. You might try lamb chops with a fig-mint reduction with potatoes au gratin and oven-roasted tomatoes, or grilled local gulf fish of the day served Provençal style with roasted artichokes and a vine-ripened tomato, capers, and a light butter sauce. Blackened sea scallop wontons with a sweet chili sauce makes a superb starter. The dining room is airy and casual, as unpretentious as the food.

Opened in 2001 to consistently enthusiastic reviews, **Sugar Magnolia** (1910 Magazine St., 504/529-1110, $12–20) offers a classy but relaxed neighborhood bistro experience, complete with a low-key but knowledgeable waitstaff, and a crowd of regulars that huddles around the bar each evening sipping martinis and wines by the glass. It's one of the first serious dining destinations to open along Lower Magazine Street, making it a favorite place for a meal to cap off a day of antiques shopping. The restaurant occupies a pair of carefully restored 19th-century buildings, with exposed-brick walls, wrought-iron balconies, and colorful contemporary artwork. From the moderately priced menu, consider oysters flash-fried in an iron skillet and served with garlic-lemon butter and a griddle-seared brioche, fried green tomatoes crowned with blackened shrimp rémoulade, a hickory-smoked half-pound burger with cheddar and applewood-smoked bacon, or cornmeal-dusted soft-shell crabs and crawfish with Hollandaise sauce and dirty rice.

Uptown has become such a great dining destination in recent years that what had been a discreet locals' hangout for many years, **Clancy's** (6100 Annunciation St., 504/895-1111, $16–27), has almost come to feel a tad touristy. No matter the increasing crowds—the staff works hard to fit everybody in and make both regulars and newcomers feel right at home. The loosely Creole-meets-Italian menu changes often but usually has a few reliable standbys, such as fried oysters with Brie, smoked soft-shell crab with lump crabmeat, and filet mignon with Stilton and a red-wine demi-glace. There are several dining areas in this rambling building, the quietest and most romantic being upstairs, the more convivial and social in the front room adjacent to the bar.

One of the first eateries to get tourists out of the French Quarter and up to Riverbend, **Brigtsen's** (723 Dante St., 504/861-7610, $19–26) occupies a lovely Victorian cottage with a warm, homey dining room with Victorian-style wallpaper and soft lighting. The restaurant is perhaps most famous for its amazingly good and ever-changing seafood platter, which on a typical night might include grilled drum fish with shrimp and corn macque choux sauce, crabmeat Thermidor, baked oysters Rockefeller, baked oyster with bacon and leeks, deviled crab, and eggplant caponata (all for a quite reasonable $25). Other commendable dishes include a starter of rabbit tenderloin on an andouille-Parmesan grits cake with spinach and Creole mustard, and braised venison on a potato pancake with roasted vegetables and apple cider pan gravy. Tuesday through Thursdays, come between 5:30 and 6:30 P.M. and you can enjoy a three-course dinner for just $16.95.

On bustling Oak Street, intimate **Jacques-Imo's Cafe** (8324 Oak St., 504/861-0886, $12–22) presents a mix of eclectic contemporary dishes and New Orleans standbys. Loyal fans can't rave enough about the ever-changing list of specials, which has featured smothered rabbit with onion-strewn grits, and country-fried venison chop with wild-mushroom pan gravy. The fried mirlitons with oysters and rich oyster-tasso hollandaise sauce are also commendable. Finish off your meal with energy-pumping coffee-bean crème brûlée. Reservations are available only for large groups, and the place fills up quickly. So expect quite a wait on most nights—pass the time at the charming bar.

One of the most convivial restaurants in the city, **Upperline** (1413 Upperline St., 504/891-9822, $18–25) is run by colorful owner JoAnn Clevenger, who loves to mingle with patrons and talk about her wonderful art and photography collection, which fills the restaurant's eclectically furnished dining rooms. Chef Ken Smith prepares Creole food with plenty of inventive twists and global spins: beef tournedos with Stilton, balsamic mushrooms, and thyme is one exceptional entrées, and grilled gulf shrimp with warm salad Niçoise and tapenade also scores high marks. One of the best ways to enjoy a meal here is to order the seven-course Taste of New Orleans dinner ($35), which includes duck étouffée, oyster stew, fried green tomatoes with shrimp rémoulade (a true Big Easy classic prepared to perfection here), andouille gumbo, spicy shrimp with jalapeño cornbread, roast duck with ginger-peach sauce, and warm bread pudding with toffee sauce. It's hard to say who will be angrier at you for indulging in such a meal: your doctor or your dentist.

In a cozy, lacy Uptown cottage on a narrow stretch of Magazine Street, **Martinique Bistro** (5908 Magazine St., 504/891-8495, $13–19) is a little gem of an eatery that woos diners with its sweetly romantic dining room and cloistered courtyard. Even if the food weren't wonderful, you could feel happy just spending a couple of hours here with a date. But the Caribbean-inspired French fare is outstanding—it's prepared by chef Hubert Sandot, who is, in fact, of both West Indies and French descent. Specialties include shrimp with sun-dried-mango curry, sesame-crusted salmon with sweet banana sauce, and jerk lamb shank braised in a sauce of Riesling and papaya. Many wines are sold by the half-bottle.

A high-ceilinged storefront restaurant along a lively stretch of Magazine, **Lilette** (3627 Magazine St., 504/895-1636, $17–23) is one of the neighborhood's more idiosyncratic and enjoyable restaurants, a setting equally suitable for a special occasion or a meal after or before shopping (both lunch and dinner are served). Unlike many or even most of the city's upscale contemporary dining establishments, Lilette's kitchen rarely attempts to improve upon Creole or Cajun cooking and instead borrows heavily from France and Northern Italy for inspiration. The grilled hanger steak with thin-cut fries and marrowed bordelaise sauce tastes fresh from a Paris bistro. More complex is the entrée of roasted Muscovy duck breast with cabbage, chorizo sausage, and black-olive sauce. **Dick and Jenny's** (4501 Tchoupitoulas St., 504/894-9880, $14–23) keeps regulars happy with its neighborhood feel, outgoing staff, and reasonably priced contemporary city fare. Grilled filet mignon with lobster and Brie is a dazzling main dish, and don't miss the crab cake served atop a fried green tomato. The only kicker is one you might expect of such a popular place: there's almost always a pretty long wait for a table (and reservations are not accepted).

Make the trek way Uptown to **Maple Street Cafe** (7623 Maple St., 504/314-9003, $13–19), a dapper neighborhood restaurant serving first-rate contemporary versions of Continental and Mediterranean cooking. A bountiful Greek salad makes a refreshing starter, while pepper-crusted sliced breast of duck drizzled with blueberry cognac sauce is typical of the main dishes, which change often. Oyster amandine is a favorite starter. The narrow two-tier dining room has tile floor and cream-colored walls. There's also dining in a small courtyard. A lovely pale-blue Riverbend café with marvelous cooking and convivial service, **Sara's** (724 Dublin St., 504/861-0565, $12–19) occupies one of the neighborhood's many delightful little cottages, on a row with several cheery shops. It's a source of delicious, offbeat cuisine that fuses Indian, Mediterranean, Thai, French, and Creole flavors. Jamaican-spiced lamb chops, pecan-crusted chicken with a citrus-ginger reduction, and *saag paneer* (house-made Indian farmer's cheese) with baby spinach and spices reflect the kitchen's deft handling of these varied cuisines. Cool off with a mango daiquiri.

Semolina (3226 Magazine St., 504/895-4260; also 5080 Pontchartrain Blvd., 504/486-5581; 137-139B Westbank Expwy., Gretna, 504/361-8293; 3501 W. Chateau Blvd., Kenner, 504/468-1047; Clearview Shopping Center, 4436 Veterans Memorial Blvd., Metairie, 504/486-5581; $8–18) is a burgeoning local chain of slick-looking upscale pasta restaurants. You'll find some fairly traditional Italian-style dishes here, but the menu spans the globe, offering such unusual fare as Thai curry shrimp over angel hair, a baked cake of macaroni-and-cheese (one of its most popular innovations), Greek-inspired gyro pasta served in a sour cream-tzatziki-feta sauce, and the more ubiquitous (in New Orleans, anyway) jambalaya pasta.

CASUAL COOKING

Okay, it's a fairly unabashed ripoff of a certain similar-sounding national chain, but **Copeland's Cheesecake Bistro** (2001 St. Charles Ave., 504/593-9955; also 4517 Veterans Memorial Blvd., Metairie, 504/887-3125, $7–17) does serve consistently tasty American food, and in big portions. You could spend an hour debating the virtues of the 40-some-odd varieties of cheesecake, from chocolate praline to cherries jubilee. Or maybe skip the specialty dessert for a scandalously rich white-chocolate bread pudding with Frangelico cream and almonds. Don't overlook the savory

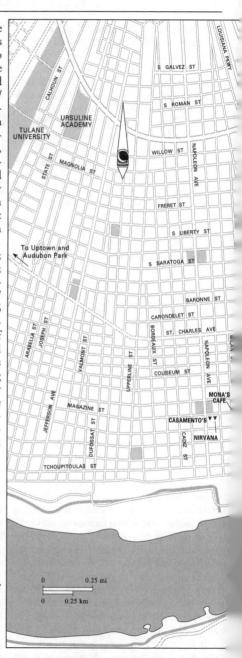

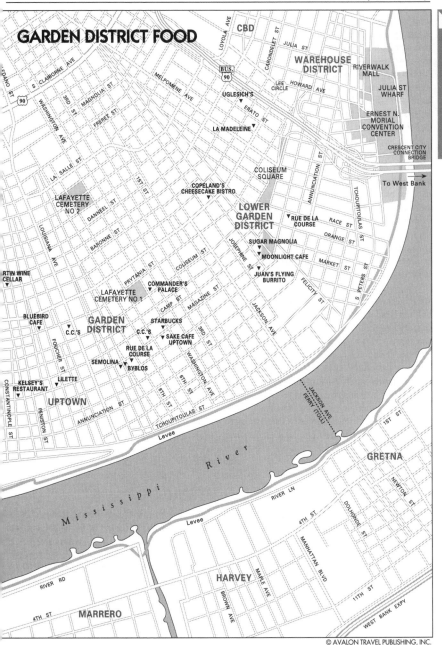

FOOD

GARDEN DISTRICT FOOD

CBD

LOYOLA AVE

CARONDELET ST

JULIA ST

WAREHOUSE
DISTRICT

RIVERWALK
MALL

BUS.
90

MELPOMENE AVE

LEE
CIRCLE

HOWARD AVE

JULIA ST
WHARF

UGLESICH'S ▼

ERATO ST

ERNEST N.
MORIAL
CONVENTION
CENTER

LA MADELEINE ▼

CRESCENT CITY
CONNECTION
BRIDGE

EDANO ST

90

S CLAIBORNE AVE

3RD ST

MAGNOLIA ST

FRERET ST

WASHINGTON AVE

LA SALLE ST

COLISEUM
SQUARE

ANNUNCIATION ST

To West Bank

LAFAYETTE
CEMETERY
NO 2

DANNEEL ST

1ST ST

COPELAND'S
CHEESECAKE BISTRO

LOWER
GARDEN
DISTRICT

RUE DE LA ▼
COURSE

RACE ST

LOUISIANA AVE

BARONNE ST

COLISEUM ST

JOSEPHINE ST

ORANGE ST

SUGAR MAGNOLIA ▼

MOONLIGHT CAFE

MARKET ST

TCHOUPITOULAS ST

RTIN WINE
CELLAR ▼

PRYTANIA ST

JUAN'S FLYING ▼
BURRITO

FELICITY ST

S PETERS ST

LAFAYETTE
CEMETERY NO 1

COMMANDER'S ▼
PALACE

CAMP ST

MAGAZINE ST

JACKSON AVE

BLUEBIRD
CAFE ▼

C.C.'S ▼

GARDEN
DISTRICT

STARBUCKS
▼

C.C.'S ▼

SAKE CAFE ▼
UPTOWN

3RD ST

FONCHER ST

RUE DE LA ▼
COURSE

WASHINGTON AVE

SEMOLINA ▼

BYBLOS ▼

6TH ST

CONSTANTINOPLE ST

KELSEY'S
RESTAURANT ▼

LILETTE ▼

UPTOWN

ANNUNCIATION ST

9TH ST

6TH ST

JACKSON AVE
FERRY (TOLL)

PENISTON ST

TCHOUPITOULAS ST

Levee

GRETNA

1ST ST

River

NEWTON ST

Mississippi

RIVER LN

4TH ST

DOLHONDE ST

MANHATTAN BLVD

Levee

11TH ST

RIVER RD

HARVEY

MAPLE AVE

WEST BANK EXPY

4TH ST

MARRERO

BROWN AVE

© AVALON TRAVEL PUBLISHING, INC.

stuff, too: there's blackened ahi tuna with wasabi vinaigrette, spicy tempura Chinese chicken with a chili garlic sauce, hot turkey French dip, and a host of pastas, salads, wraps, and burgers.

A casual Creole–soul food restaurant that may just serve the tastiest fried chicken in town, **Dunbar's** (4927 Freret St., 504/899-0734, $8–13) occupies a nondescript, almost downcast, white building in a plain Uptown neighborhood; there's nothing fancy about the setting, and this in part accounts for its friendly feel. That tasty fried chicken is always served as a special on Mondays, paired with red beans, salad, and cornbread, or as a Thursday blue plate, paired with mustard greens, candied yams, and cornbread, but you can also just order it as a regular platter with fries and garlic bread. Other mainstays include fried seafood platters, stuffed crabs, burgers, po'boys, and 8-ounce steaks.

Convenient to Audubon Park, the casual **Riverhouse Cafe** (5961 Magazine St., 504/894-0046, $6–13) is a great lunch or dinner spot for straightforward New Orleans–style pub fare, including fresh soft-shell crab po'boys, oyster platters, and smoked sausage. The burgers are among the best you'll taste Uptown, and the staff is very friendly. It's open late most nights.

So concerned about the freshness of its bivalves is **Casamento's** (4330 Magazine St., 504/895-9761, $6–14) that this famous yet surprisingly humble restaurant on mid-Magazine Street closes down from June through August, when oysters are out of season. Italian immigrant Joe Casamento opened the place in 1919, installing the trademark tile floors that give the restaurant its clean, distinctive look today. Casamento's stands out from other oyster bars in several ways: it makes its own sandwich bread, and it serves excellent homestyle Italian food, like spaghetti and meatballs. As for those oysters, you can order them fresh on the half-shell, in a stew, or on a loaf (basically a monstrous po'boy). The soft-shell crab platter is yet another commendable specialty.

A daft favorite of slackers, artists, and students, **Igor's Buddha Belly Burger Bar** (4437 Magazine St., 504/891-6105, $5–11) occupies a colorful space that includes both a dining room and a self-service laundry (just like Igor's Marigny hangout, Check Point Charlie). The half-pound burgers are seriously good, and on Mondays they serve free red beans and rice until they run out of the stuff. It's one of the better late-night options on Magazine.

Just an old-time burger and cocktail tavern with decent—not great—food but a warm ambience, **O'Henry's Food & Spirits** (634 S. Carrollton Ave., 504/866-9741; also 301 Baronne St., 504/522-5242; 710 Terry Pkwy., Gretna, 504/433-4111; 3020 Severn Ave., Metairie, 504/888-9383; 8859 Veterans Memorial Blvd., Metairie, $6–14) has a big menu with many types of deli-style sandwiches, plus a handful of Creole specialties. You can grab a table and enjoy the view over tree-lined Carrollton. The house specialty is a burger topped with pastrami and melted Swiss. The other locales, throughout greater New Orleans, are less atmospheric.

A favorite late-night destination for hungry, pizza-craving college students, **Reginelli's Pizzeria** (741 State St., 504/899-1144, $6–12) serves some of the best pies in New Orleans, along with massive calzones, focaccia sandwiches, and big salads. The Parthenon pizza, topped with garlic herb sauce, mozzarella, artichokes, roma tomatoes, onions, fresh mushrooms, and feta cheese, is a winner. **Moonlight Cafe** (1921 Sophie Wright Pl., 504/522-7313, $6–13) is a funky little retro tavern with simple wooden tables, alternative music, and a colorful crowd. The menu lists a seemingly endless variety of finger foods, such as burgers, babaganoush, charbroiled salmon kabobs, shrimp po'boys, gyros, and wraps. There's a great beer selection, too.

ETHNIC

Youthful and raffish **Juan's Flying Burrito** (2018 Magazine St., 504/569-0000, $4–8) has wooden booths, brick walls, and an artsy, alternative staff and crowd. Art covers the walls, and loud music fills this spot, one of the best quick bites along the lower stretch of Magazine, close to antiques shops. The fare is a mod take on Tex-Mex, with such filling fare as the Veggie Punk burrito (with potatoes, jalapeños, jack cheese, lettuce, and salsa) and shrimp tacos. You'll also find a nice range of beers and margaritas. **Taqueria Corona**

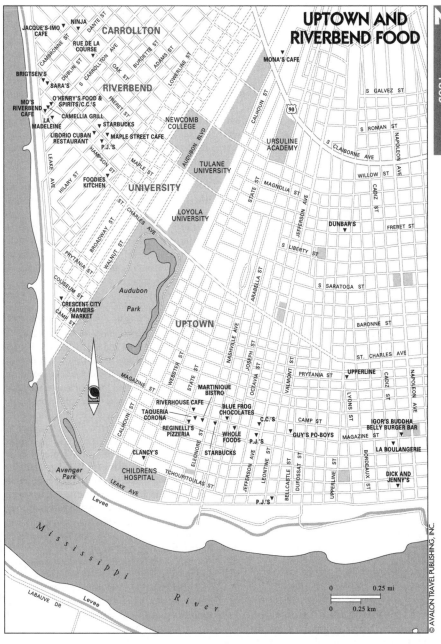

(5932 Magazine St., 504/897-3974; also 857 Fulton St., Warehouse District, 504/524-9805; 3535 Severn Ave., Metairie, 504/885-5088; and 1827 Hickory Ave., Harahan-River Ridge, 504/738-6722, $3–12) is a snug, homey Mexican joint low on ambience but big on flavor. These taquerias, with several locales around the city, serve serious regional Mexican fare, not just the usual Americanized Tex-Mex. You might start with the piquant black-bean soup with sour cream and cilantro, followed by *pollo asado* (a half-pound chicken breast marinated and charbroiled, served with pico de gallo). You could also just get a plate of tacos, which come in many varieties: chorizo, shrimp, tongue, fish, chicken, pork, ground beef, and cheese. Pitchers of sangria and margaritas are a bargain.

Some folks swear that the original **Byblos** (3218 Magazine St., 504/894-1233; also 1501 Metairie Rd., Metairie, 504/834-9773; 2020 Veterans Memorial Blvd., Metairie, 504/837-9777, $9–17), an excellent Middle Eastern restaurant in an Old Metairie shopping center, is better than the newer location on Magazine Street. Both are very nice, however, and the Magazine Street version is more atmospheric.

Ninja (8433 Oak St., 504/866-1119, $10–22), which occupies what looks a bit like a modern suburban house, serves outstanding Japanese fare and sushi—it's in Carrollton, along up-and-coming Oak Street. There's a high-ceilinged, open dining room on the second floor and a bar downstairs. Closer to town on the edge of the Garden District is another stellar Japanese restaurant, **Sake Cafe Uptown** (2830 Magazine St., 504/894-0033, $12–20). Yellowtail tartare with Russian caviar is a specialty.

New Orleans doesn't have a wealth of Indian restaurants, but **Nirvana** (4308 Magazine St., 504/894-9797, $9–17) definitely serves the needs of curry and naan fans. At lunch, there's a phenomenal $6.95 lunch buffet that has a justifiably fanatical following.

QUICK BITES

Uglesich's (1238 Baronne St., 504/523-8571, $5–14) is a tiny place with a near-fanatical following—it's a couple of blocks off St. Charles in a grimy industrial section of the Lower Garden District, where it's been serving food to a loyal clientele since the 1920s. You almost always have to wait in line for as long as an hour for a table, and even then you must order at the counter, take a number, and wait a while longer for your food (the restaurant is open only for lunch, and only on weekdays). The process of eating here is a labored one, but the servers keep the mood light, and there's no disputing the sensational home-style Creole food, such as oyster-and-Brie soup and crabmeat au gratin.

A humble late-night diner-esque restaurant where you're apt to see college students, blue-collar workers, and neighborhood hipsters all digging into filling breakfast fare and other stick-to-your-ribs foods, **Mo's Riverbend Cafe** (614 S. Carrollton Ave., 504/866-9301, under $6) keeps strange hours—it's open daily 9 P.M. to 2 P.M. Devotees swear by the fried chicken.

A superb choice if you're super-hungry for delicious, artery-choking comfort food, **Camellia Grill** (626 S. Carrollton Ave., 504/866-9573, $4–8) specializes in burgers—the house classic is called a Doc Brinker, and it comprises two burgers with melted Swiss on rye bread with sides of chili and slaw. A long list of pies, cakes, and ice cream treats are offered for dessert, and breakfast is also an enjoyable meal in this funky old house in the Riverbend section of Uptown. The seating is limited to stools set around a zigzag-shaped counter, and the place fills up quickly, so expect a wait. A loveable dive on a quiet Uptown street corner, **Guy's Po-Boys** (5257 Magazine St., 504/891-5025, under $6) offers daily-changing sandwich specials, great shrimp po'boys, and other comfort chow. The bare-bones decor somehow adds to the experience.

Do as many locals do and drop by **Bluebird Cafe** (3625 Prytania St., 504/895-7166, $3–9) for tasty no-frills breakfast fare, including spicy huevos rancheros and light-as-a-feather waffles.

Although it deserves ample praise for being the city's best wine shop, and one of its top gourmet grocery stores, **Martin Wine Cellar** (3827 Baronne St., 504/896—7380; also 714 Elmeer Ave., Metairie, 504/896-7350, $4–9) does one thing as well as any restaurant in the city: deli sandwiches. The food here is more typical of Sonoma's wine country than New Orleans—there are no crawfish or oysters on the menu, but you can get such toothsome sandwiches as the Green Giant (grilled pepper- and onion-flavored smoked sausage, lettuce, and tomatoes on French bread), plus zesty tomato-pesto salad. The list of sandwich options goes on and on, and they're served in fairly massive portions. You order your meal at the counter and then take a seat in the plant-filled glass-brick dining room amid the legions of yuppies and epicureans. Apart from the deli, there's a large wine and liquor store, plus shelves stocked with all sorts of imported and local savories and sweets. The second locale, just off Veterans Boulevard in Metairie, is a short drive from the west side of City Park.

JAVA JOINTS

Uptown has the greatest concentration of coffeehouses in the city, especially along Magazine Street, where you'll find several atmospheric branches of the local chains, **P.J.'s, C.C.'s,** and **Rue de la Course.** There's also a **Starbucks** along Magazine, if you must go with Seattle java. Strictly in terms of ambience, as all of these places have pretty good coffee and a variety of light snacks, the mid-Magazine branch of **Rue de la Course** (3128 Magazine St., 504/899-0242) is the most atmospheric and inviting of these places, especially if you're in the mood to read or peck away on your laptop. The dark and handsome old-world café has a large, high-ceilinged dining area cooled with old-fashioned ceiling fans. Tables have study lamps and many have access to electrical outlets. You can also dine at one of several tables along the busy sidewalk. Rue de la Course doesn't offer a tremendous amount in the way of food, just pastries and cakes, but the coffees and chai tea are top-notch.

PICNIC SUPPLIES AND GOURMET GOODS

This part of town being where most of the city's well-heeled professionals live, it's hardly surprising that it has some of New Orleans's largest and best-stocked gourmet grocery shops, including Martin Wine Cellar, which is described above, under Quick Bites. **La Boulangerie** (4526 Magazine St., 504/269-3777; also 625 St. Charles Ave., 504/569-1925), is a delightful storefront French bakery with great food. Here you can taste some of the lightest, flakiest croissants around, along with light sandwiches and delectable pastries. It opened a second location in the CBD in 2003.

Blue Frog Chocolates (5707 Magazine St., 504/269-5707) specializes in sensuous, wonderful imported European candies and truffles, including whimsical Italian flowers fashioned out of candy. It's in a dainty blue wood-frame house Uptown.

Foodies Kitchen (7457 St. Charles Ave., 504/865-9646; also 720 Veterans Memorial Blvd., Metairie, 504/837-9696) is your best bet if you're looking for a complete prepared meal and gourmet snacks on the side. It's perfect if your hotel room has full or partial kitchen facilities, or if you're headed somewhere for a picnic. Many fine wines, cheeses, breads, and sweets are also available. The Metairie location is a big fancy building on the impossibly busy Veterans Boulevard, but it has an eat-in café, which the Uptown version does not. The gourmet grocery chain **Whole Foods** (5600 Magazine St., 504/899-9119; 3135 Esplanade Ave., 504/943-1626) opened a massive branch along Magazine Street in 2002; it's fairly close to Audubon Park. The city's original location in Mid-City is rather cramped. There's also an in-store café serving creative sandwiches, salads, and the like.

Elsewhere in New Orleans

TRADITIONAL CREOLE AND CAJUN

On a modest Mid-City side street, **Christian's** (3835 Iberville St., 504/482-4924, $17–26) is set strikingly in a renovated Lutheran church, a salmon-colored Gothic wood-frame building with a tall and distinctive belfry. These days, visitors come to worship the old-school Creole cooking, prepared with a few nods to country French cuisine. There's a simple but flavorful starter of steamed mussels with shallots and white wine; top main dishes include braised sweetbreads with a sherry demiglaze, and shrimp-and-crab-stuffed eggplant. It's just around the corner from the fabulous dessert café Angelo Bracato's.

CREATIVE AND CONTEMPORARY

The dining complement to the fabulous House on Bayou Road B&B, **Restaurant Indigo** (2285 Bayou Rd., 504/947-0123, $24–30) occupies an 1860s building that has been a grocery store, reggae club, and pool hall over the years. You'd hardly know it, judging from the marvelously restored building's appearance today, with its high pressed-tin ceilings, finely crafted woodwork, and elegant metal sconces climbing the walls like grapevines. Indigo's noted chef, Kevin Vizard, mixes Creole, Mediterranean, and regional American ingredients in creating such sublime fare as crawfish gazpacho and roasted redfish stuffed with scallop mousseline and finished with melted leek and shrimp velouté. Sunday brunch—try the duck confit salad with pistachios, shaved onions, and roasted beets—is a favorite excuse for folks from all over the city to head out this way, perhaps before moving on to play around in City Park or visit the art museum.

Up close to the lakefront in the northwest corner of the city, **Wolfe's of New Orleans** (7227 Pontchartrain Blvd., 504/284-6004, $18–24) is worth the 15-minute drive from downtown to sample some of the more creative

contemporary New Orleans fare around. You might start with garlic-crusted oyster "nachos" with crispy shoestring mirliton, roasted sweet peppers, and salsa verde with pepperjack cheese. Notable among the entrées is oven-braised whole poussin with pancetta, roasted salsify, sautéed peashoots, oven-dried tomatoes, and Perigueux sauce (black truffles and cream). Talented owner Tom Wolfe worked as a sous-chef for Emeril Lagasse, and his experience shows. The setting is a cozy cottage warmed on cool nights by a fireplace. Another of the city's most esteemed chefs, Greg Sonnier, and his wife, Mary, run **Gabrielle** (3201 Esplanade Ave., 504/948-6233, $16–24), a low-key, intimate eatery (it has seating for just 40 people) presenting globally inspired Louisiana fare—the barbecue shrimp pie and crawfish enchiladas con queso rank among the favorite dishes. Sonnier earned his wings working for Paul Prudhomme at K-Paul's, and his menu definitely highlights the flavors of Cajun cooking, but Sonnier takes it to new and exciting levels.

Nearby is cozy **Cafe Degas** (3127 Esplanade Ave., 504/945-5635, $12–19), which serves such superb French cuisine as salade Niçoise, seafood brochette, and Cajun-style bouillabaisse. There's nothing overly trendy or complicated about Degas—the cooking is authentic and reminiscent of true French bistro fare. In warm weather you can enjoy a meal on the lush garden patio, which is the perfect place to end an afternoon of exploring Mid-City. Another of the bumper crop of fine restaurants along historic Esplanade Ridge is **Lola's** (3312 Esplanade Ave., 504/488-6946, $11–18). The small BYOB eatery takes no reservations and no credit cards—it's a small-scale operation whose owners focus on food above all else. And this Mediterranean-inspired cooking stands up to any in the city: consider fragrantly seasoned paella heaped with chorizo and shellfish, the refreshing chilled gazpacho, and the fresh ceviche. Nearly across the street, Whole Foods grocery has an exceptional selection of well-priced wines.

In Lakeview on the west side of City Park,

THE CELEBRATED CRAWFISH

Nicknamed "mud bugs" or "craw daddies," crawfish are easily the most celebrated of Louisiana's many varieties of seafood. These humble three- to four-inch freshwater crustaceans, found in swamps, bayous, and rivers, are worshipped with palpable fanaticism and served year-round at restaurants throughout the state, but especially in the Cajun Wetlands. They bear a strong resemblance to their much larger saltwater cousins, lobsters.

Louisiana is home to about 30 varieties of crawfish, better known as crayfish in other parts of the world. Two species, the white river crawfish and the red swamp crawfish, are harvested commercially. Live crawfish are first harvested around December; a good season lasts into mid-summer. Peak months are March through May. This is the best time to visit a restaurant in Acadiana for authentic crawfish boils.

For many outsiders, crawfish are an acquired taste, typically first encountered as ingredients in native Cajun fare like étouffée. Eating them boiled, by breaking their shells and extracting their tender and faintly sweet meat, takes a bit of effort and can be quite messy—it's all part of the fun. The crawfish are boiled live in a concoction of water, seasoning (Zatarain's makes the most famous brand), cayenne pepper, Tabasco or other hot sauce, lemon juice, olive oil, salt, and bay leaves. Among true devotees, this is by far the best way to eat crawfish.

You can also find crawfish served fried in po-boys or platters, in a thick bisque, in salads, and as "dressing" atop redfish, drum, snapper, and other local seafood. In fact, there really aren't too many savory dishes served in Cajun Country that *aren't* made with crawfish.

The earliest settlers in the Cajun Wetlands began eating and farming crawfish as early as the 18th century, with commercial crawfish farming taking hold in the 1940s. At first, fishing operations relied on the natural bounty of crawfish that flourished in the Atchafalaya Basin, but harvests often fell short of demand, which increased—and continues to increase—steadily every year. In the 1960s, Louisiana State University developed a system for successfully raising crawfish in manmade ponds. Water level is critical to crawfish farming, and these controlled ponds allow the manipulation of water levels, virtually guaranteeing successful harvests even during years when low rainfall in the Atchafalaya Basin lead to weak crawfish crops.

Many of those employed in crawfish fishing come from families that have been in this business for multiple generations. They fish with traps similar to lobster traps—these pillow-shaped wire containers have a pair of funnels that allow crawfish to wander in.

Most farmers raise crawfish using manmade ponds during periods when they're not engaged in other types of farming; it's an especially popular practice among rice farmers. It's usually possible to harvest more than 1,000 pounds of crawfish per acre, and most commercial ponds range between 20 and 40 acres.

Today, more than 90 percent of the crawfish farmed commercially in the United States come from Louisiana, where some 1,600 farmers and nearly 1,000 commercial fisherman produce the crop. In a good year, the combined annual yield of crawfish—both raised in farms and fished from natural wetlands—exceeds 100,000,000 pounds and has an impact on the state economy approaching $125,000,000.

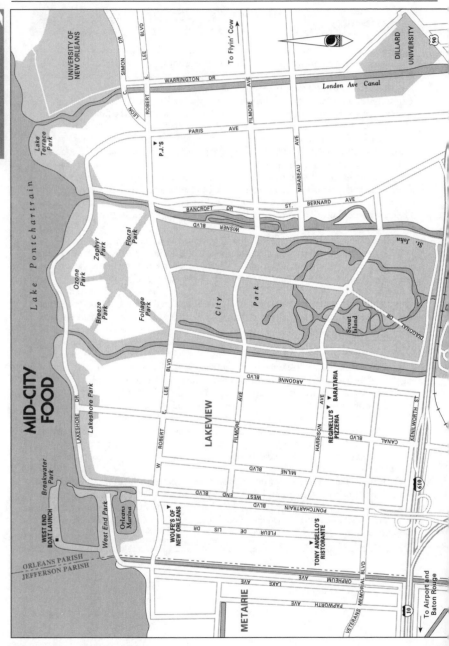

MID-CITY
FOOD

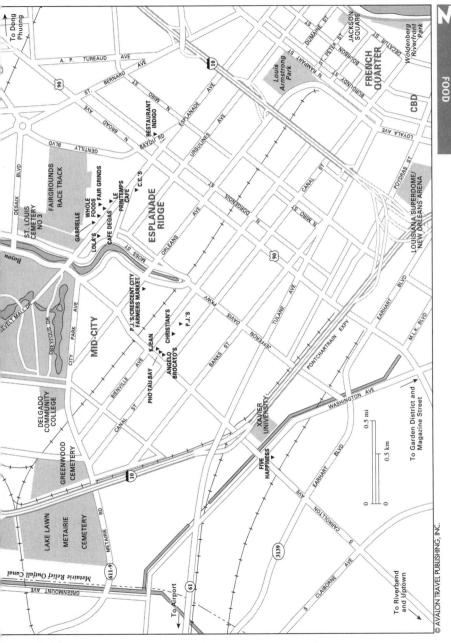

FOOD

© AVALON TRAVEL PUBLISHING, INC.

Barataria (900 Harrison Ave., 504/488-7474, $13–22) is famous for owning its own set of oyster beds and therefore bringing in some of the freshest bivalves around town (they're available raw, baked with Romano, Parmesan, and Asiago cheese, and served any number of other ways). But you can also try such classic Creole dishes as panéed veal with lump crabmeat in a lemon-butter sauce, and double-cut pork chops with jalapeño grits and a side of oyster dressing.

CASUAL COOKING

Around the corner from Angelo Bracato's, **Kjean** (236 N. Carrollton Ave., 504/488-7503, $4–10) seafood is a ragged little shanty serving no-nonsense food at low prices—it's perfect when you just want a quick bite. Just grab a number at the busy counter and order an oyster or shrimp po'boy. It's also a market, selling freshly caught fish, pig's feet, and a variety of raw and prepared foods. A handy option if you're up near the lakefront or University of New Orleans, **Flyin' Cow** (5219 Elysian Fields Ave., 504/288-8979, $3–8) serves up gyros platters, po'boys, buffalo wings, juicy burgers, milkshakes, and fresh cheesecake. It's a funky, student-infested spot that serves late on Friday and Saturday nights.

ETHNIC

You have to travel a bit to find **Tony Angello's Ristorante** (6262 Fleur de Lis Dr., 504/488-0888, $8–15), which is set inside a pedestrian-looking ranch house near the canal separating New Orleans from Metairie, up near the lakefront. But for home-style, red-sauce Italian fare, it's hard to think of a better place to enjoy a meal. The staff treats everybody like family. Despite its humble appearance, the restaurant attracts many prominent New Orleanians (Harry Connick Jr. is said to be a regular) for its filling and hearty cooking. The novelty dish that has really made Tony Angello's famous is the Feed Me platter—just utter these words, and you'll be served a vast sampling of house specialties, brought out one plate after the other. It's best to tackle this multicourse adventure with a friend or two.

Le Printemps Cafe (3125 Esplanade Ave., 504/945-1919, $8–14) is set inside a cute painted-lady house next to Cafe Degas and serves tasty French-Asian fare. You might start with smoked duck and roast marinated shrimp with a light balsamic sauce, followed by lamb chop sautéed with shallot-olive paste and garlic panko, served au jus. The staff is charming and eager to please. Fairly close to the chain motels and hotels in East New Orleans, and not too far from Six Flags amusement park, **Dong Phuong** (14207 Chef Menteur Hwy., 504/254-0214, $6–13) ranks among the city's better options for Chinese food. Why is it that all, or most, of the best Asian eateries in this city are out some ways from downtown? Anyway, this is a simple spot that serves excellent Asian food, including a house-specialty duck soup with bok choy and shiitake mushrooms that fans can't get enough of. Attached is a bakery selling Asian and French treats.

Close to the Metairie border and the campus of Xavier University (just off I-10 and Airline Highway), **Five Happiness** (3605 S. Carrollton Ave., 504/482-3935, $9–16) serves commendable Mandarin and Szechwan fare in a bright dining room festooned with Chinese artwork and decorations. Crispy whole fish available with a variety of sauces is a house favorite, with the type of creature varying according to what's fresh on any given day. The bird's nest of minced shrimp, dried black mushrooms, and water chestnuts enmeshed within a "sandwich" of iceberg lettuce leaves is as tasty as it is artful. Don't be put off by the neighboring fast-food restaurants and auto-repair shops—this is the real deal. A superb Vietnamese restaurant with branches in Metairie and Gretna, **Pho Tau Bay** (216 N. Carrollton Ave., 504/485-SOUP; also 3116 N. Arnoult Rd., Metairie, 504/780-1063; 113 Westbank Expressway, Gretna, 504/368-9846, $7–14) opened a Mid-City branch in a slick space right next to Angelo Brocato's in August 2003. Dive into crab-and-pork egg rolls, tofu with a hoisin-peanut sauce, shellfish wonton soups, and lemongrass beef. The food is freshly and expertly prepared, and the service friendly.

QUICK BITES

After a day of exploring City Park or a visit to Longue Vue House and Gardens, take a snack break detour at **Angelo Brocato's** (214 N. Carrollton Ave., 504/486-0078), an old-world bakery that's famous not only for its superb Italian pastries but for tantalizing house-made ice cream, Italian ice, and gelato in all kinds of tempting flavors, such as panna cotta, chestnut, and rum custard. The Mid-City hole in the wall, just off Canal Street and a few blocks south of City Park, also serves fabulous cannoli and cookies. It feels like something out of Brooklyn, and it's in the heart of a small cluster of eateries and shops with a neighborhoody feel.

JAVA JOINTS

A cheerful neighborhood coffeehouse near the Fair Grounds racetrack and just off Esplanade Avenue, the amusingly named **Fair Grinds** (3133 Ponce de Leon St., 504/948-3222) serves all the usual hot and iced coffee drinks, plus a variety of snacks. The homey space with racetrack collectibles, framed photography, and green walls is well-suited for working on your laptop or reading, as there are reading lamps on many tables and comfortable seating.

Metairie, Kenner, and the Airport

TRADITIONAL CREOLE AND CAJUN

Try to make a reservation a few days in advance for **Drago's** (3232 N. Arnoult Rd., Metairie, 504/888-9254, $11–35), a riotously popular restaurant with limited seating and parking. The emphasis here is on seafood, much of it prepared with a Louisiana slant. The lobster dishes are particularly noteworthy. Try lobster Marco (whole lobster stuffed with fresh sautéed shrimp and mushrooms in a light cream sauce over angel hair pasta). Apart from the usual seafood, blackened duck over linguini with oysters and cream is delicious. You can sit at the bar, which affords clear views of the grill guys charbroiling oysters (which many regulars eat a couple dozen of as a full meal), or dine in one of the noisy but festive dining rooms. The high volume of business has just one drawback: the waitstaff often seems harried and (understandably) frazzled.

CREATIVE AND CONTEMPORARY

One of a handful of South Shore suburban restaurants that actually merits making a special trip from downtown, **Vega Tapas** (2051 Metairie Rd., 504/836-2007, $5–13) is the classiest of several restaurants in a small strip in Old Metairie.

Tomato-red walls and high ceilings create an elegant but informal ambience for sampling tapas, most with a vaguely Mediterranean but always innovative spin: smoked salmon and avocado salad with a horseradish-tarragon dressing, eggplant napoleon layered with oven-dried tomatoes, house-made mozzarella, arugula, and sun-dried-tomato pesto; and sautéed sweetbreads and cremini mushrooms with prosciutto and a sherry beurre blanc. One of the few big-ticket restaurants out near the airport, **Le Parvenu** (509 Williams Blvd., Kenner, 504/471-0534, $14–24) draws even foodies who rarely leave downtown for creative and beautifully presented contemporary Creole fare. Try the sautéed snapper with herbed crabmeat and a lemon beurre blanc.

Out toward the airport in Harahan, **Zea Rotisserie and Brewery** (1655 Hickory Ave., Harahan, 504/738-0799; also Esplanade Mall, 4450 Veterans Memorial Blvd., Metairie, 504/780-9090) specializes, as the name suggests, in meaty fare served on a spit and handcrafted microbrewed beers. But the menu is really quite eclectic, offering a wide range of foods from all over the world, among them wood-grilled rainbow trout, sweet-pepper chicken wings, and spare ribs (available with hickory barbecue sauce or sweet-and-spicy Thai style). It's a cavernous place, usually echoing with chatter and lively conversation.

METAIRIE, KENNER, AND THE AIRPORT

KENNER

SUNSET BLVD

VINTAGE DR

E LOYOLA DR

CHATEAU BLVD

SAKE CAFE

C.C.'S

SEMOLINA

VINTAGE DR

WILLIAMS BLVD

LAKE TRAIL DR

POWER BLVD

WILSON DR

ACADEMY DR

BISSONET PLAZA

FOLSE DR

AVRON BLVD

BELLE DR

W ESPLANADE AVE

W ESPLANADE AVE

WILLOWDALE

GAMBINO'S

To Baton Rouge

10

VETERANS HWY

O'HENRY'S FOOD & SPIRITS

TAQUEROS TAQUERIA-CANTINA

KENNER

Lafreniere Park

UTICA ST

VINELAND DR

LOUIS ARMSTRONG NEW ORLEANS INTERNATIONAL AIRPORT

AIRPORT RD

49

ROOSEVELT BLVD

N ATLANTA ST

DAVID DR

AIRLINE PARK BLVD

LAFRENIERE ST

HARING RD

W METAIRIE AVE

To River Road Plantations

61

P.J.'S

WILLIAMS BLVD

LEE'S HAMBURGERS

GIOVANNI'S PO-BOYS

TRUDEAU DR

PIERCE AVE

AIRLINE DR

ELSIE AVE

61

LE PARVENU

48

JEFFERSON HWY/3RD ST

3154

DICKORY AVE

3139

RIVERTOWN

Mississippi River

HILLBILLY BAR-B-Q

RIVER RIDGE

P.J.'S

TAQUERIA CORONA

ZEA ROTISSERIE AND BREWERY

COFFEE COTTAGE

CITRUS BLVD

18

RIVER RD

SOUTH KENNER

CITRUS RD

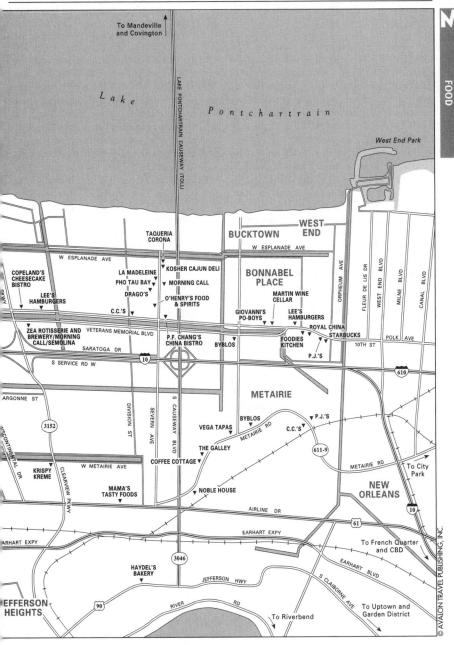

FOOD

CASUAL COOKING

The Galley (2535 Metairie Rd., Metairie, 504/832-0955, $7–16) is a casual and fun seafood shack with great food. Shrimp and crabmeat au gratin is a top pick, and several tasty sides are available (mac-and-cheese, sweet potato fries). More than a few fans of the genre swear that **Hillbilly Bar-B-Q** (208 Tullulah Ave., River Ridge, 504/738-1508, $4–11), on a side street near the Mississippi—a short drive southeast of the airport—has the best barbecue in metro New Orleans. The meats are smoked over Kentucky hickory after receiving a kicky dry-spice rub, and all the usual sides (slaw, beans, potato salad) are available.

If you have a hankering for a huge sandwich, head to **Giovanni's Po-Boys** (1325 Veterans Memorial Blvd., Metairie, 504/835-4558; also 2506 Airline Dr., Kenner, 504/469-1594, $3–8), which makes the best meatball-and-sausage po'boy in town. They also make very good hot muffalettas, as well as the rest of the usual array of po'boys. The ambience, or lack thereof, won't get this place on the cover of any interior design magazines—it's bare-bones and divey, set inside a drab little building on drab Veterans Boulevard.

© ANDREW COLLINS

Giovanni's Po-Boys

ETHNIC

The upscale and trendy Pan-Asian chain **P.F. Chang's China Bistro** (Lakeside Shopping Center, 3301 Veterans Memorial Blvd., Metairie, 504/828-5288, $9–18) has a branch out by the mall in Metairie. The always-packed restaurant is well-regarded for its big arty drinks and such creative fusion fare as pan-fried shrimp dumplings with chili-pepper soy sauce, orange-peel chicken with chili peppers, and scallops wok-fried with a light lemon sauce. *The* restaurant in greater New Orleans for authentic dim sum, **Royal China** (600 Veterans Memorial Blvd., Metairie, 504/831-9633, $8–15) is a rather ordinary-looking Chinese restaurant that presents a lavish and tasty assortment of about 50 of these creative small plates, including crab–and–cream cheese wontons, stir-fried squid in black-bean sauce, and sweet rice-flour crepes with red-bean paste and powdered sugar. There's a full menu of other, more expected Chinese dishes, too, but dim sum is the restaurant's raison d'être.

Noble House (2700 Metairie Rd., Metairie, 504/828-8484, $14–22) is a beautiful Asian bistro with rich polished hardwood floors, a gracious staff, and maybe the most elegant sushi bar in the New Orleans area. Indeed, the raw-fish specialties here are elaborate and delicious, including a maki roll packed with fresh snow crab, whitefish, and lime. The Chinese duck crepes with fresh orange and hoisin port sauce make a terrific starter, while red snapper served with artichoke hearts in green curry stars among the entrées. Another superb option for sushi is **Sake Cafe** (817 W. Esplanade Ave., Kenner, 504/468-8829, $11–20). Try the Kenner roll, a tempura-battered treat with crab stick, avocado, and whitefish. Deals on beer, sake, and sushi abound during the daily happy hour, held 3–6 P.M.

Taqueros Taqueria-Cantina (2723 Roosevelt Blvd., Kenner, 504/441-8888, $7–15) is an authentic Mexican restaurant with creative, often sophisticated fare and an attractive art-filled dining room (don't be put off by the unimpressive strip-mall setting or the restaurant's vaguely irritating name). Finish your meal with the treacly coconut cheesecake.

QUICK BITES

Kosher Cajun Deli (3519 Severn Ave., Metairie, 504/888-2010, $4–11) fits the bill when you're craving chopped liver, smoked fish, and other deli favorites. It's a basic deli lunchroom in a prosaic storefront near Causeway Boulevard. You'll also find a nice selection of gourmet prepared foods and groceries.

Drop by **Mama's Tasty Foods** (3901-A Airline Dr., Metairie, 504/833-8030, $4–10) for homestyle cooking that would make your own mama jealous. Trout po'boys, chicken gizzard on a stick, and side orders of shrimp-fried rice are among the more memorable choices from the long menu.

A mini-empire of burger joints that delights carnivores, **Lee's Hamburgers** (904 Veterans Memorial Blvd., Metairie, 504/836-6804; 4301 Veterans Memorial Blvd., Metairie, 504/885-0110; 2100 Airline Dr., Kenner, 504/472-0966; 103 Schlief Dr., Belle Chasse, 504/392-9922, $3–9) cooks up juicy patties smothered in several toppings. You can also get chili-cheese fries and, at some locales, more substantial fare like fried shrimp and grilled chicken platters. For fans of local fast food, this is a must.

JAVA JOINTS

Similar in concept to the French Quarter's Cafe du Monde, **Morning Call** (3325 Severn Ave., Metairie, 504/885-4068; also Clearview Shopping Center, 4436 Veteran's Memorial Blvd., Metairie, 504/779-5348) is open 24/7 and serves a short menu whose specialties include piping-hot cafe au lait and beignets. Unlike Cafe du Monde, it's never overrun with tourists, but by the same token, Morning Call doesn't have nearly as interesting a location—it's in a small shopping center across from Lakeside Shopping Center. The interior is quite elegant, though. Long mirrored marble counters line one side of the room; the other contains small wooden tables. Servers in white paper caps skirt about the room, delivering plates of food. Next door is the Lakeside Newsstand, which is also open 24 hours.

Coffee Cottage (2559 Metairie Rd., Metairie, 504/833-3513; also 5860 Citrus Blvd., Jefferson, 504/818-0051) is a cute wood-frame house in Old Metairie, known for its homey decor and terrific desserts, such as tiramisu, white-chocolate mousse cake, and Key lime pie. It's also a source of excellent creative sandwiches and salads,

the neon sign outside Morning Call restaurant

ranging from Creole chicken salad tossed with pecans and Creole mustard to honey ham–and–cheese focaccia sandwiches.

PICNIC SUPPLIES AND GOURMET GOODS

Haydel's Bakery (4037 Jefferson Hwy., Jefferson, 504/837-0190) has long been a favorite stop for desserts: Mardi Gras king cakes, pecan pies, white-chocolate bread pudding, almond croissants, and praline cheesecake. The trademark Cajun Kringle is a hallmark of this bakery: it's a ring-shaped pastry jammed with pecan filling. **Gambino's** (4821 Veterans Memorial Blvd., Metairie, 504/885-7500) is known for its huge six-layer Doberge cakes, which come in chocolate, lemon, or caramel. Cookies, king cakes, biscotti, and sublime pralines are also available.

The West Bank

CREATIVE AND CONTEMPORARY

Reason alone to trek out to Gretna, **Red Maple** (1036 Lafayette St., 504/367-0935, $12–21) is helmed by one of the city's rising culinary stars, Randy Barlow, who's worked in several top restaurants. The place began as a gruff working-class bar in the 1960s and gradually evolved into a simple restaurant, but these days it's become a serious dining operation with first-rate modern New Orleans fare. Steaks and seafood dominate the menu. In warm weather, grab a table on the garden patio.

ETHNIC

If you love real (not watered-down) Chinese food, consider making the trek across the river to **China Blossom** (1801 Stumpf Blvd., Suite 8, Gretna, 504/361-4598, $7–16), which despite being in a suburban shopping center has a pleasant, somewhat upscale interior—the service is accommodating and friendly, too. The cuisine here mixes traditional Asian ingredients and techniques with quite a few foods from Louisiana. You might begin with crawfish Na (a crepe filled with crawfish tails, minced pork, diced onions, and mushrooms), and then move on to marinated prawns grilled and served over glazed pecans, fried oysters, catfish in a ginger-and-garlic sauce, or sweet-and-sour pork. There's really not a bad dish on the menu. Another great

Gretna Asian restaurant is **9 Roses** (1100 Stephens St., 504/366-7665, $7–14), which features such delectable Vietnamese dishes as whole steamed fish with scallions, ginger, and a tangy soy sauce.

The West Bank, especially Gretna, is a good bet for Italian cooking, and **Tony Mandina's** (1915 Pratt St., Gretna, 504/362-2010, $8–14) does this genre justice. The menu strays from the traditional with a handful of exceptional locally influenced seafood dishes. Come for angel hair marinara, grilled lemon-pepper chicken, *strata del mare* (seafood layered with pasta, mozzarella, and red sauce), and eggplant Dominic Jude (battered eggplant medallions layered with shrimp and crabmeat and topped with shrimp Alfredo sauce). Past the racks of vino at **Antonio's Wine Cellar** (601 Terry Pkwy., Gretna, 504/361-1332, $8–16) you'll find a cozy dining room serving very good, very traditional Italian fare—it's lunch only on weekdays, dinner on Friday and Saturday nights. Free wine tastings are held here regularly, and, of course, you can buy your own bottle of wine to enjoy with your meal.

JAVA JOINTS

If you're over exploring Gretna and need a coffee break or a light lunch, consider **Common Grounds** (335 Huey P. Long Ave., 504/227-2200), which has rotating art exhibits and tasty food.

Shopping

It's not necessarily the main thing tourists do in New Orleans, but then again there are few visitors who leave without sampling the aisles of exotic produce and hard-to-find spices that fill the French Market, or browsing the antiques stores along Magazine Street, where you can buy the very quality and style of furnishings found in some of those grand plantation homes out on the River Road.

Shopping in New Orleans tends to be a byproduct of other popular aspects of the city's heritage—dining, music, art, historic preservation. The city doesn't have as important a fashion retail scene as most other major U.S. metropolises, nor is it teeming with chain stores. You'll find one or

two branches of all the big ones, but often in malls well away from the city's most interesting neighborhoods. Thankfully, key shopping areas like the French Quarter and Uptown's Magazine Street have largely resisted chain development and emphasize independently owned shops, many of them selling products you're likely to find only in New Orleans.

This chapter is organized by neighborhood, and within these sections by types of retail. Greater New Orleans has several large shopping centers and malls, which are listed individually within the neighborhood sections below. In each of these write-ups, a few key, representative stores are mentioned in passing; some notable shops at malls and shopping centers are described later in the section in greater detail within their

view up Royal Street

own appropriate subcategory (Clothing, Souvenirs and Gifts, etc.).

New Orleans has a vast array of food items for sale, from packaged candies and goodies to gourmet groceries to prepared foods and picnic supplies. Most of the places selling food are listed in the Food chapter of this book, rather than here, because they tend to sell ready-to-eat food as well. Many of the city's souvenir shops, too, carry New Orleans spices and sauces, pralines and other confections, and other gourmet gifts.

Most goods and retail products, as well as groceries, specialty foods, wine, souvenirs, and gifts, cost the same or less in New Orleans than in other big cities. You don't run a huge risk of being gouged, even when buying T-shirts and shot glasses or other silly gifts in even the most touristy shops. Competition is pretty fierce in the French Quarter, and sales tactics are rarely aggressive or sleazy. If you're shopping for antiques and art, however, do keep in mind that the stores along or near Royal and Chartres Streets have a reputation for carrying some of the most expensive furnishings in the South, and, some argue, at excessively marked-up prices. Magazine Street is considered a less pricey source of art and antiques, and even there you're not going to find any amazing bargains. It's almost always a seller's market when it comes to fine furnishings and antiques in New Orleans. True bargain hunters will have better luck heading to the North Shore town of Ponchatoula, an hour away, where it's said that more than a few New Orleans antiques dealers buy many of their wares in the first place.

Shops in the French Quarter tend to open late in the morning and close early in the evening, though souvenir-oriented shops usually stay open into the late evening hours. Many shops in the Quarter are open daily, with some—especially antiques stores and art galleries—closing one day a week, typically Monday or Sunday. The same

rules apply to Magazine Street and the Warehouse District. Otherwise, shops throughout New Orleans keep hours fairly typical of what you'll find in other big cities, opening at 9 or 10 A.M. and closing around 5 or 6 P.M., with some of the major retail chains open until 9 or 10 P.M. It's the rare shop in New Orleans that doesn't accept plastic, and many shops in the city's more visitor-friendly areas will ship your purchases back home. You may be surprised how easy it is to get even some perishable food items overnighted safely to just about anywhere, from muffaletta sandwiches at Central Grocery to the seafood and meats at the French Market.

Antiques Organizations and Publications

Whether you're a novice or an expert, your antiquing success will be enhanced if you consult a few publications before setting out. The country's leading resource is *Antiques and the Arts Weekly* (The Bee Publishing Co., Box 5503, Newtown, CT 06470, 203/426-3141), a mammoth 200-page feast of detailed auctions (with photos), museum and gallery exhibits, book reviews, antiques show calendars, shopping tips, and engaging features. Subscriptions are $67 annually. The paper has a fine website, www.antiquesandthearts.com, whose most helpful and unusual resource is an exhaustive list of antiquarian books and their authors. The paper's emphasis is somewhat on New England, where it is based, but there's plenty of information on shops and auctions in Louisiana, too.

Regionally, the *Antiques Gazette* (985/429-0575, www.theantiquesgazette.com), based in Hammond, is a terrific resource with hundreds of listings for shops through southern Louisiana and bordering states. A one-year subscription costs $16, but the paper is distributed free at many shops and tourism office centers.

The French Quarter

Royal Street is the most exclusive address for shopping in the French Quarter, known for upscale antiques and first-rate art galleries. Parallel Chartres Street has some of the same kinds of stores, as do the blocks connecting them. The ritzier shopping is in the Lower Quarter; once you venture past around St. Peter Street, you'll find funkier boutiques, such as mod clothiers, eccentric costume shops, edgy galleries, and places with a distinctly youthful vibe. Decatur Street is similarly offbeat when it comes to retail, and it's also a good area for finding cheesy T-shirts, Tabasco and other Louisiana food products, crawfish-embroidered everything, souvenir "go-cups" (the plastic mugs tourists carry around the Quarter filled with daiquiris and hurricanes), and every other imaginable trinket and souvenir. In such an irreverent and party-oriented city, it's not surprising that many of the souvenir shops emphasize sex, drinking, and off-color humor in their gifts, toys, cards, and novelties. Decatur Street also leads to the mother ship of New Orleans shopping, the French Market, which contains retail shops, a lively farmer's market, and a flea market.

MALLS AND SHOPPING CENTERS

Jackson Brewery (600 Decatur St., 504/566-7245, www.jacksonbrewery.com), also known as Jax Brewery, contains some 50 shops and eateries inside a dramatic 1891 former brewery nearly across from Jackson Square. From the upper floors, you can take in very nice views of the Mississippi River. You'll find a mix of interesting shops (the New Orleans School of Cooking) and touristy ones (such as Cajun Clothing Co., where you can pick up your very own crawfish-embroidered polo shirt), plus the city's only Virgin Megastore, and other chains like Chico's clothing and Krispy Kreme doughnuts. There's a small food court, and Pat O's on the River is a favorite spot for cocktails at sunset.

The posh **Gallery of Shops** (901 Canal St.,

Jackson Brewery building, French Quarter

LOUISIANA TAX-FREE SHOPPING

If you're visiting from another country, you're entitled to a refund of the state sales tax, and in certain cases, the local sales tax, on goods purchased in Louisiana. This policy, unique among the 50 states, was introduced as a way to help promote visitation by foreign travelers, and depending on how much shopping you do, you really can save a bit of money.

The refund is available to visitors who have a valid foreign passport *and* an airline or other international round-trip ticket of up to 90 days' duration. Canadians are the one exception to the passport rule; they may provide proof of residency by showing a driver's license or birth certificate. If you come from any other country, you must supply a passport. Resident aliens, foreign students, U.S. citizens living in other countries, and citizens with dual citizenship in the U.S. and another country are not eligible. The refund does not apply to services, hotel charges, car rentals, food and beverages, or personal goods bought for use while in Louisiana, and only purchases made at participating shops qualify.

To take advantage of this program, ask for a refund voucher at the shop where you make your purchase—any participating merchant will be able to provide you with this, once you show them your passport (or other ID, if Canadian). It's important to remember that you will not be given the refund at the time of purchase—this happens at the Louisiana Tax Free Shopping Refund Center at New Orleans International Airport. At the actual shop you'll pay the full price, including tax, for your purchase, and you'll be issued a voucher in the amount of the refund due you. You must present the voucher and all original receipts for every purchase to qualify for the refund.

Refunds under $500 are issued in cash; refunds over $500 are issued by check and mailed to your home. You can also mail in your vouchers and receipts to receive a refund. In this case, you must mail the original vouchers, copies of the receipts, your travel ticket, a copy of your passport, a statement explaining why you didn't collect the refund at the airport, and a statement explaining where the merchandise is presently located to **Louisiana Tax Free Shopping Refund Center** (Box 20125, New Orleans, LA 70141).

504/524-1331), at the new Ritz-Carlton hotel, contains such high-end boutiques as Solarté and Asiantiques. It's an appropriate setting, as the shops occupy the first floor of the former Maison Blanche department store. Farther down Canal, the **Shops at Canal Place** (333 Canal St., 504/522-9200, www.theshopsatcanalplace.com) is the fanciest full-scale mall in the immediate downtown area, with branches of such acclaimed emporia as Saks Fifth Ave., Coach, Kenneth Cole, Brooks Brothers, Gucci, Betsey Johnson, Laura Ashley, and Pottery Barn. There's also an excellent movie theater that specializes in indie and foreign films but also plays some blockbusters.

If you're a big fan of massive shopping malls, by the way, consider a trek to Metairie, which has one of the region's top such venues. The **Lakeside Shopping Center** (3301 Veterans Blvd., Metairie, 504/835-8000) contains more than 135 shops,

among them Coach, Nicole Miller, J. Crew, Restoration Hardware, and Williams-Sonoma. The anchors are Dillard's and JC Penney. There's also a trendy P.F. Chang's restaurant.

ART AND ANTIQUES

The mission of **RHINO Contemporary Craft Co.** (Shops at Canal Place, 310 Canal St., 504/523-7945; 927 Royal St., 504/569-8191) is to promote and sell the hand-crafted decorative arts, furniture, objets d'art, and clever creations of local talents. RHINO stands for "Right Here in New Orleans" and, indeed, that's where all the goods here come from. The famous "Blue Dog" artist George Rodrigue operates his **Rodrigeau Studio** (721 Royal St., 504/581-4244) in a warmly lighted space nearly behind St. Louis Cathedral. You can buy everything from original oil paintings to inexpensive Blue Dog gifts. The inspiration for these works is the owner's terrier, Tiffany, who passed away some years ago. **Gallery Nine-Forty** (940 Royal St., 504/558-0000) specializes in New Orleans–themed works, including many compositions related to Mardi Gras.

Look for original works by M. L. Snowden, Peter Max, LeRoy Neiman, Frederick Hart, and other notables of the contemporary art world at **Hanson Gallery** (229 Royal St., 504/524-8211). There are two branches of the world-famous **Martin-Lawrence Gallery** (433 Royal St., 504/299-9055) along Royal Street. The roster of star artists with works here is astounding: Picasso, Chagall, Warhol, Erté, and so on. Owned by one of the most respected artists in Louisiana, the eponymous **Michalopoulos Gallery** (617 Bienville St., 504/558-0505) carries dozens of James Michalopoulos's vibrant, architectural renderings, with their trademark skewed angles and impressionistic brushwork. Many of his works feature Creole houses or classic French Quarter townhouses. Sharon Stone, Bruce Willis, and Bonnie Raitt are among his most notable collectors. Michalopoulos co-owns the exceptional North Shore restaurant Etoile.

Bassetti Fine Art and Photographs (233 Chartres St., 504/529-9811) carries many fine works of Southern art photography. **Callan Fine Art** (240 Chartres St., 504/524-0025) has lovely 18th- and 19th-century Impressionist and other fine paintings, with the works of the French Barbizon movement a particular specialty. One unusual venue is **Stone + Press Gallery** (238 Chartres St., 504/561-8555), which specializes in artists of the first half of the 20th century who work in etching, lithography, and wood engraving, as well as mezzotints painted by many contemporary luminaries. It's one of only four galleries in the South that's a member of the International Fine Print Dealers Association. Photo giants like Ansel Adams, Edward Curtis, Elliott Erwit, Henri-Cartier Bresson, and Helmut Newton have works available at the prestigious **Gallery for Fine Photography** (322 Royal St., 504/568-1313).

A French Quarter fixture since 1938, **New Orleans Silversmiths** (600 Chartres St., 504/522-8333) handcrafts gold, platinum, and sterling silver and also carries many vintage pieces, as well as corkscrews, candlesticks, and other fine works. The Quarter's only gallery dedicated to studio glass, **Royal Cameo Glass** (636 Royal St., 504/522-7840) shows pieces created by some of the nation's leading artists in this medium. Browse through an amazing variety of folk and contemporary arts made throughout the state at **Crafty Louisianians** (523 Dumaine St., 504/528-3094), including wood carvings made by Houma Indians, zydeco instruments from Cajun Country, and paintings and other artwork in many media. Acclaimed artist Louis Sahuc sells his fine black-and-white images at **Photo Works New Orleans** (839 Chartres St., 504/593-9090)—there are beautiful shots of the city as well as other places Sahuc has traveled.

Since 1899, **Keil's Antiques** (325 Royal St., 504/522-4552) has been specializing in 18th- and 19th-century antiques from France and England, from marble mantels and magnificent crystal chandeliers to garnet chokers. Another of the most famous and expensive antiques shops in the Quarter is **Gerald D. Katz** (505 Royal St., 504/524-5050), a trove of both small and large furnishings culled from fine estates throughout Louisiana and the South. You might expect to find some first-rate French antiques in the Quarter, and indeed, the **French Antique Shop** (225 Royal St., 504/524-9861), which moved to New Orleans from Paris in 1939, has an extensive and impressive array of fine Gallic furnishings from the 18th and 19th centuries as well as some striking Asian vases and accessories. Specialties include gilt-leaf mirrors, salvaged mantels, dining-room tables, and bronze statuary. The tiny and terrific **Brass Monkey** (235 Royal St., 504/561-0688)

> *Since 1899, Keil's Antiques has been specializing in 18th- and 19th-century antiques from France and England, from marble mantels and magnificent crystal chandeliers to garnet chokers.*

SHOPPING

the flea market held outside French Market

carries a wonderfully odd assortment of antique collectibles, from Limoges boxes to ancient walking sticks to vintage medical paraphernalia—expect the unexpected.

The sleek showrooms of **Hurwitz Mintz** (227 Chartres St. and 211 Royal St., 504/568-9555; 1751 Airline Dr., Metairie; 504/378-1000), which has been a fixture in New Orleans since the 1920s, are something to behold; they occupy several large shop windows along prominent blocks of Chartres and Royal Streets. Inside the windows you'll find curvaceous and striking modern furniture arranged cleverly and colorfully. Hurwitz Mintz isn't an antiques shop, as it carries all the major lines of today's furniture makers, from Drexel-Heritage to Henredon, but it is a great place to find reproduction antiques, as well as striking postmodern and abstract sofas, beds, chairs, and tables that complement the antiques you may already own. Prices are surprisingly reasonable, especially given the prime locations in the Quarter.

SOUVENIRS AND GIFTS

Your best bet for souvenirs is simply to stroll the length of Decatur Street and pop inside a few shops, as there are many of them, and they're pretty similar. For more of the same, check out the stalls at the Flea Market at French Market building. A reliable stop for one-hour film developing, **French Quarter Camera** (809 Decatur St., 504/529-2974) also stocks a wide array of photographic equipment, from cameras and film to batteries, filters, and tripods.

The **Museum Shop at the Historic New Orleans Collection** (533 Royal St., 504/598-7147) sells all manner of Louisiana memorabilia and artifacts, many with a historical bent. You'll find a huge supply of regional books, plus tote bags, letter openers, commemorative minted coins, pens, and so on. The **Little Toy Shop Too** (513 St. Ann St., 504/523-1770) is a great store in the Pontalba Building filled with very cool things, including precious miniatures, collectibles, toy soldiers, and imported European toys, as well as games and gifts that aren't so fine and breakable, which you could actually entrust to the hands of playful kids.

Perhaps the best, or at least the silliest, of the quirky gift and novelty shops along Decatur, **Funrock'n** (Decatur and Gov. Nicholls Streets, 866/255-0491) carries bizarre and tacky knickknacks you probably never knew you needed: Elvis lamps, *Day of the Dead* lunchboxes, "Satan Was a Lesbian" refrigerator magnets, *The Scream* posters, iron-ons, cards, and other peculiarities.

Beautiful and, in some cases, very fine and expensive handmade pens as well as fine stationery, note cards, diaries, and related writers' tools are found at elegant **Scriptura** (328 Chartres St., 504/299-1234; 5423 Magazine St., 504/897-1555).

CLOTHING

A whimsical and offbeat clothier with two Quarter locations and another on Magazine, **Frock Candy** (520 St. Philip St., 504/566-1133; 830 Royal St., 504/566-9222; 3336 Magazine St., 504/891-9230) sells funky and reasonably priced women's club gear, makeup, T-shirts, and jewelry. It's a hit with local clubgoers. A favorite men's fashion shop, especially with the gay community and nightcrawlers who like to form-fitting, trendy wear, **Rab-Dab Clothing and Gifts** (508 St. Philip St., 504/529-3577) specializes in gym, swim, and club duds. With locations in the Quarter and Uptown, **Hemline** (609 Chartres St., 504/529-3566; 3025 Magazine St., 504/269-4005) is a favorite women's clothing boutique carrying Diesel, BCBG, Diane von Furstenberg, and other trendy labels. Search for top-of-the-line designerwear (DKNY, Prada, etc.) at **Prima Donna's Closet** (1218 St. Charles Ave., 504/525-3327; also 4409 Chastant St., Metairie, 504/885-3327); there's a plus-size shop adjacent at 1206 St. Charles.

You can shop for fun if slightly hokey Cajun clothing, complete with a crawfish logo, at **Perlis** (6070 Magazine St., 504/895-8661; Riverwalk, foot of Poydras Street, 504/581-6746; Jackson Brewery, Decatur Street, 504/523-6681).

BOOKS AND MUSIC

Across from the House of Blues music club, the **Louisiana Music Factory** (210 Decatur St., 504/586-1094) is a noted music shop with a great selection of jazz, Cajun, and zydeco music. You'll find both used and new CDs, plus books, videos, posters, and other music memorabilia. It does a brisk mail-order business. Although part of a chain, **Bookstar** (414 N. Peters St., 504/523-6411) feels like an indie shop because of its personal feel, expert staff, and outstanding selection of locally themed books dealing with Louisiana travel, food, history, music, and every other facet of the state. It also hosts some of the best book signings in town.

You can relax in an armchair while perusing the secondhand tomes at **Beckham's Bookshop** (228 Decatur St., 504/522-9875), a good source of rare and hard-to-find antiquarian titles. There's a strong collection of first editions. William Faulkner actually lived for several months at what is now **Faulkner House Books** (624 Pirate's Alley, behind St. Louis Cathedral, 504/524-2940). Here, in 1925, he wrote *Soldiers' Pay.* The store stocks rare first editions of his works, plus collections of his letters. It's also a fine source of contemporary fiction by both local and faraway authors. **Crescent City Books** (204 Chartres St., 504/524-4997) contains two floors of out-of-print and antiquarian titles. It's an exceptional source of local history and literature, scholarly books, and hard-to-find titles on philosophy, ancient history, and literary criticism—a real book lover's bookstore.

COSMETICS

Arguably the best among several wonderful perfumeries around town, **Hové** (824 Royal St., 504/525-7827) has been proffering high-quality imported and locally made fragrances, lotions, soaps, and bath oils since the 1930s. Outrageous **Fifi Mahony's** (934 Royal St., 504/525-4343) is your one-stop salon and makeup counter for that occasion when you're trying to make a statement. Pop in and browse the wigs that come in every

> *William Faulkner actually lived for several months at what is now Faulkner House Books. Here, in 1925, he wrote Soldiers' Pay. The store stocks rare first editions of his works, plus collections of his letters.*

SHOPPING

LOUISIANA FOOD FINDS

Some of your most memorable—and distinctive—purchases may be products you can nosh on. From New Orleans out through the Cajun Country, dozens of businesses specialize in manufacturing specialty foods and drinks. Here's a round-up of favorite Louisiana-made food products:

Abita Beer: Abita Springs, on the North Shore about an hour from New Orleans, first became famous for its crystalline artesian wells. It's this perfectly pure water that's used by **Abita Brewery** (800-737-2311, ext. 2, www.abita.com) to craft such classic Louisiana elixirs as Abita Amber, Turbodog, and the seasonally popular Mardi Gras Bock. Tours of the brewery are available Saturdays at 1 P.M. and 2:30 P.M. and Sundays at 1 P.M. only; no reservations are required.

Blue Plate Mayonnaise: Made by Luzianne, which is based right in the heart of the CBD on Magazine Street, Blue Plate mayo is made with local cottonseed oil and has been a favorite condiment in these parts since the late 1920s. Luzianne is also the second-largest independent coffee manufacturer in the United States.

Camellia Beans: The magic ingredient in rich and delicious red beans and rice, Camellia-brand dried kidney beans are manufactured in the New Orleans suburb of Harahan and sold throughout the state. Although red kidney beans are the big seller, Camellia also sells black, navy, split pea, lentil, lima, field pea, and crowder pea varieties.

Community Coffee and Tea: Better known these days in Louisiana for its string of festive coffeehouses, Community Coffee and Tea is, first and foremost, a coffee and tea producer. Their packaged ground coffee and bagged and iced teas have a deeply loyal following. You can pick these products up at any Community Coffee (a.k.a. "CC's") espresso café or at most specialty food and gift shops.

Crystal Hot Sauce: Tabasco isn't the only game in town when it comes to pepper sauces. The slightly milder Crystal-brand hot sauce has its diehard fans. It's made right in New Orleans by the Baumer Foods plant, which also produces fruit preserves, Creole mustards, marinades, and many other foods.

Dixie Beer: Made inside a rambling brewery building on New Orleans's Tulane Ave., this rich and tasty beer sold in longneck bottles is arguably the most popular beer of the Deep South. The Jazz Amber Lite and Blackened Voodoo lager are distributed nationally. Sipping a Dixie Beer while slurping down raw oysters is a classic Louisiana tradition.

French Market Coffee: Chicory, a faintly bitter herb root grown mostly in northern Europe, is dried, ground-roasted and then blended with French Market coffee beans to create the inimitable flavor that so many java drinkers cherish. Once you've had French Market Coffee, which is sold all around town and especially in the French Market's Cafe Du Monde, you may never be able to go back to your usual beans.

Melinda's Original Habanero Pepper Sauce: Louisianans love their hot sauces, and Melinda's—based in Metairie—manufactures a blend that differs a bit from the usual suspects. Here the fiery flavors of habanero peppers are blended with lime, onions, carrots, and garlic to create a kicky but complex condiment. Melinda's Mango-Habanero version is terrific for barbecuing.

Pralines: These exquisite melt-in-your-mouth, disc-shaped candies are made with cream, butter, caramelized brown sugar, and pecans. They're sold at virtually every food-related gift shop in southern Louisiana, but one of the best sources of authentic pralines is **Evans Creole Candy Factory** (848 Decatur St., 504/522-7111 or 800/637-6675), in the French Quarter.

Steen's Syrup: This sugarcane syrup–processing plant in the small town of Abbeville, near Lafayette, has been going strong since 1910. Buy a bottle of this thick sweetener to pour over pancakes or bake into cakes and cookies. It's also a key ingredient in K.C. Masterpiece–brand barbecue sauces.

Tabasco Sauce: The mother of all U.S. hot sauces, Tabasco hardly needs a description here. Louisiana families are known to go through a decent-size bottle of the stuff every week or two, and the Tabasco company—based on Avery Island in the heart of the Cajun Wetlands—also makes a number of related sauces, mustards, jerkies, and snacks. Free tours of the **Tabasco factory** are also available (337/365-8173 or 800/634-9599, www.tabasco.com, 9 A.M.–4 P.M. daily).

Tony Chachere's: One of the leading two Cajun and Creole prepared-foods companies in Louisiana, Tony Chachere's is based in the Cajun town of Opelousas and known for a vast array of sauces, boxed products, and the like. The carefully blended food mixes, such as Creole butter beans and rice, are especially good, but also check out the tasty seasoning blends.

Zapp's Potato Chips: There's nothing that complements a muffaletta sandwich from Central Grocery better than a bag of Zapp's Potato Chips (well, that and a can of Barq's Root Beer or Cream Soda). These super-crunchy and shockingly fattening chips truly zip with flavor. Popular types include Cajun Crawtator (made with the same seasonings commonly found in crawfish boil), Hotter 'n Hot Jalapeno, Cajun Dill, Sour Cream & Creole Onion, Bee-Licious (made with honey-mustard), and Sweet Cinnamon Sweet Potato.

Zatarain's: A notable spicemaker based in the West Bank suburb of Gretna, Zatarain's has been turning out tasty food mixes and spices since 1889. The jambalaya mix is particularly good, as are the crab and crawfish boils, but don't overlook such noble and notable delicacies as root beer–extract, frozen sausage-and-chicken gumbo, and cornbread-stuffing mix.

color of the rainbow (and then some), plus body glitter, Tony & Tina cosmetics, wild hair-care products, and offbeat handbags. The environmentally sensitive **Earthsavers** (434 Chartres St., 504/581-4999; 5501 Magazine St., 504/899-8555; 3256 Severn Ave., Metairie, 504/885-5152) has earned a loyal following for its all-natural exfoliants, skin moisturizers, and other skin-care products. The shop also offers spa services and aromatherapy.

ONLY IN NEW ORLEANS

Mardi Gras masks are a big business in New Orleans year-round, and **Little Shop of Fantasy** (517 St. Louis St., 504/529-4243) offers one of the better selections. Many of the masks and Mardi Gras costumes and accessories are made locally, others by artists from all over the world. Some of these items are strictly for collecting, not wearing, unless you're willing to risk getting beer splashed across a $1,200 mask during a crazy Carnival party.

Well, you're in New Orleans, and there are few cities with a sexier vibe, so why not drop by the Quarter's premier sex boutique, **Chartres Street Conxxxioin** (107 Chartres St., 504/586-8006), a 24-hour emporium of movies, books, lingerie, oils, equipment, and assorted playthings. It's popular with straights, gays, and everybody who identifies somewhere in between.

Many of the masks and Mardi Gras costumes and accessories are made locally, others by artists from all over the world. Some of these items are strictly for collecting, not wearing—unless you're willing to risk getting beer splashed across a $1,200 mask during a crazy Carnival party.

The outpost of **Laura's Candies** (938 Royal St., 504/524-9259; 331 Chartres St., 504/525-3880) on Chartres Street is New Orleans's oldest candy store. Great food and a lovely place, with a bigger variety of sweets than some of the other local shops. **Three Dog Bakery** (827 Royal St., 504/525-2253) is the place to pick up a treat, maybe a "pawline" or "snickerpoodle," for Fido. You'll also find humorous toys, accessories, and other goodies. Stogie aficionados can stop by **Cafe Havana** (842 Royal St., 504/569-9006), a laid-back Cuban-inspired coffeehouse with a tropical ambience. Here you can choose from a wide selection of pipes, cigars, and other tobacco products, plus crafts from South and Latin America. You can watch cigars being made at the **New Orleans Cigar Factory** (415 Decatur St., 504/568-1003), which sells many styles and has a walk-in humidor.

Rhonda and Walt Rose, owners of **Louisiana Loom Works** (616 Chartres St., 504/566-7788), hand-weave all of the colorful rag rugs at this shop where you can examine the wares and watch the production process. They also take custom orders and will ship your rug within about a month. **Quilt Cottage** (801 Nashville Ave., 504/895-3791) not only sells finished quilts but also carries an astounding array of fabrics and supplies for making your own quilts; classes are also offered.

Central Business and Warehouse Districts

Most of the CBD is dominated by high-rise hotels and office towers and has few shops of note, although the riverside of the neighborhood, known as the Warehouse District, does contain a handful of art galleries and other fine shops. There are also two large shopping malls at opposite ends of the neighborhood, the Riverwalk, down by the river, and the New Orleans Centre, up by the Superdome.

MALLS AND SHOPPING CENTERS

The **Riverwalk Marketplace** (1 Poydras St., 504/522-1555, www.riverwalkmarketplace.com) is, shop-wise, like many other midscale shopping malls; it's notable for its sweeping river views and especially good food court. It has a number of stalls proffering local or at least local-feeling goods, souvenirs, and crafts, although it's a less atmospheric locale for souvenir shopping than the French Market in the Quarter. Among the many chain shops you'll find are Abercrombie & Fitch, Gap, The Limited, Victoria's Secret, Body Shop, Brookstone, Godiva, and so on. There are 140 shops, plus many restaurants. The **New Orleans Centre** (by the Superdome, 1400 Poydras St., 504/568-0000) is downtown's favorite mid- to upscale retail center, anchored by Macy's and Lord & Taylor and containing some 60 additional, mostly chain shops, including Ann Taylor, Bath and Body Works, and Gap. There's also an outpost of the French Quarter's famous Cafe du Monde.

ART AND ANTIQUES

The Warehouse District has some of the South's most important fine arts galleries, among them **Arthur Roger** (432 Julia St., 504/522-1999), which specializes in modern works and presents highly popular openings and shows, and Galerie **Simonne Stern** (518 Julia St., 504/529-1118), a longtime community fixture that shows the works of both established and emerging tal-

ents from the contemporary art world. A bit north, in the CBD, **Stella Jones Gallery** (201 St. Charles Ave., 504/568-9050) is the city's top arts exhibit space for the works of African-American artists. **Blackamoor Antiques** (600 Julia St., 504/523-7786) focuses on high-quality and often quite rare Asian art and antiques, including Chinese funerary sculpture dating back to 200 B.C. There's also extensive furniture and paintings, especially Taoist and Buddhist artworks, from the 18th and 19th centuries. At the **New Orleans School of Glassworks and Printmaking Studio** (727 Magazine St., 504/529-7277, www.neworleansglassworks.com), you can watch highly skilled glassblowing and printmaking artisans at work and then browse their wares.

DESIGNER

A designers' favorite in the Warehouse District, **Ray Langley Interiors** (434 Julia St., 504/522-2284) has a massive showroom of modern, functional furniture—the sort of stuff you might see in some of the CBD's stylish boutique hotels. Picked up so many goodies that you can't fit everything in your suitcase? Just drop by **Pursestrings** (Riverwalk Marketplace, 1 Poydras St., 504/588-9097) to browse the many colorful and stylish travel bags and totes, plus a wide selection of briefcases, luggage, and handbags. Among New Orleans's many very good jewelry shops, **Adler's** (722 Canal St., 504/523-5292; Lakeside Shopping Center, 3301 Veterans Memorial Blvd., Metairie, 504/523-1952; Oakwood Shopping Center, 197-1085 Westbank Expressway, Gretna, 504/362-5969) has the most loyal following—it's been serving the Crescent City since 1898. Fine watches, crystal, china, and silver are among the fine offerings.

If you need a jacket for your dinner at Galatoire's, consider **Rubenstein Brothers** (102 St. Charles Ave., 504/581-6666), a classic outfitter carrying such exclusive lines as Dolce & Gabbana, Armani, and Kenneth Cole.

Magazine Street and Uptown

Few American streets offer the astonishing variety of shops and boutiques that you'll discover along Magazine Street, which follows the curve of the mighty Mississippi River for some 6 miles from the city's Central Business District out to Audubon Park. Sassy secondhand clothiers, colorful oyster bars, jamming music clubs, and convivial java joints line the way, but it's the lower stretch of Magazine—from about Canal to Jackson Streets—that possesses the city's most fascinating and offbeat antiques district. Magazine Street's prime antiquing row begins around Felicity Street and wends its way upriver to about Jackson Avenue, but there are plenty more pockets of antiques shops farther up.

Commercial activity along Magazine Street slows, intensifies, softens, regains strength, and then seems to disappear suddenly, like so many stages of a passing storm. Magazine Street is broken into little chunks of commerce interrupted by equally interesting rows of historic cottages and houses, in some cases grand and in others quite modest. The greatest thing about this street, apart from its sheer abundance of retail (and dining), is its quirky variety. The customer base along Magazine spans all economic brackets, all ages, and all styles.

The presence of a Starbucks at the corner of Washington and Magazine signals that even this fiercely independent shopping street is not immune to change, for better or for worse. A massive branch of the gourmet health-food grocery chain Whole Foods opened in 2001 near Audubon Park, but otherwise major chain development has been pretty minimal. That may change, as presently there's talk of Wal-Mart opening a branch just a couple of blocks off Magazine, in the Lower Garden District. It would be located where housing projects once stood, and, interestingly, the developer pushing for the Wal-Mart is a longtime proponent of historic preservation who has argued that the benefits of bringing such a store into the neighborhood outweigh the negatives. As charming as Magazine Street is, for example, it has relatively few shops carrying everyday goods at low prices, and in general, Uptown lacks the discount shopping that many of its lower-income residents would benefit from.

Whether or not the Wal-Mart opens, you won't be able to see it, or probably even sense its presence, as you stroll up curious Magazine Street, where you can find an auto repair shop sitting across the street from an Oriental rug shop, or the prestigious Neal Heaton Auction House across from a Popeyes. This is a real urban street, not just a place for tourists to spend money, and so the scenery and the people-watching are happily varied and unpredictable.

ART AND ANTIQUES

Those in the know come to **Collections II and Rousset Antiques and Textiles** (2104 Magazine St., 504/523-2000) in search of museum-quality 18th-century French tables and chairs, especially Louis XVI style, plus delicate embroideries, silks, paisleys, and toiles. Additionally, and at significantly lower prices, the stores features an array of beautiful dinnerware and dining accessories, from reproduction pieces to antiques, all hand-chosen during the owners' regular forays into Paris, Provence, and Normandy. Come to quirky **Antiques-Magazine** (2028 Magazine St., 504/522-2043) to admire the astounding variety of hanging chandeliers and light fixtures and sconces, tending toward the frilly and decadent sorts that can make or break a room—most of them date from the mid-19th century into the middle of the 20th, with an especially strong art deco and Victorian presence. Antiques-Magazine sells mostly smaller items and collectibles, including costume jewelry, cut-glass decorative arts, and art glass.

There are a few more venerable emporia along Magazine than the 14-showroom **Charbonnet & Charbonnet** (2728 Magazine St., 504/891-9948), famed for its exceptional country antiques and accessories, many of them antebellum Southern, with others brought over from England and Ireland. An in-house cabinetmaker custom-designs and ships sturdy yet elegant furnishings of Louisiana cypress and pine. **Bush Antiques & Beds au Beau Rev** (2109 Magazine St., 504/581-3518) is one store where you may want to sleep on your purchase—the dozens of beds sold here are quite spectacular and come from all over Europe and North America, from a mid-19th-century iron-and-brass four-poster to a whimsical cast-iron, green-painted sleigh bed. Other specialties include religious art (even some altars and ecclesiastical chandeliers) and decorative French ironwork that will remind you of the intricate grills and balustrades found on the exteriors of so many New Orleans homes. Head out back to the rear patio and browse the extensive collection of folk art.

Magazine Arcade Antiques (3017 Magazine St., 504/895-5451) is an expansive multi-dealer store that contains just about every kind of antique imaginable, representing every budget, taste, and period. Dolls and dollhouses abound at one stall, while another carries precious Asian porcelains and tables; around the corner you might stumble upon a collection of vintage wind-up music boxes, and beyond that a fabulous display of Delftware, cloisonné, or old-fashioned tin toys. The **Shop of the Two Sisters** (1800 Magazine St., 504/525-2747) is a large corner shop, set inside a handsome Greek Revival townhouse, packed to the rafters with eclectic regional furnishings, mirrors, lighting fixtures, and objets d'art—many of them from faraway lands.

The **Thomas Mann Gallery** (1812 Magazine St., 504/581-2113) is filled with whimsical contemporary art, glassware, jewelry, colorful stemware, and other works in different media. Mann's works are sold in galleries throughout the country, but this is the local flagship. **Eclectique Antiques and Shades of Light** (2116 Magazine St., 504/524-6500) is a very large and impres-

> *Few American streets offer the astonishing variety of shops and boutiques that you'll discover along Magazine Street: Sassy secondhand clothiers, colorful oyster bars, jamming music clubs, and convivial java joints line the way to the lower stretch of Magazine, the city's most fascinating and offbeat antiques district.*

sively stocked emporium carrying a great variety of lamps, shades, and lights. The selection crosses many styles and periods. **Dunn & Sonnier** (2138-40 Magazine St., 504/524-3235) specializes in flower bulbs, iron garden furniture, and eclectic, mostly American-looking antiques. It's a bright and happy shop that's somewhat unusual for the neighborhood.

One of a few excellent resources for treasures rescued from classic Louisiana estates and buildings, **Architectural Salvage & Objects of Desire** (3965 Tchoupitoulas St., 504/891-6080) overflows with vintage doors, window frames, statuary, fountains, garden accessories, and the like. With more than 7,000 square feet of showroom space, **Top Drawer Antiques** (4310 Magazine St., 504/832-9080) is one of largest antiques shops Uptown, with original and reproduction pieces, plus paintings and accessories.

You'll often see potters working inside the estimable **dk Clay Studio and Gallery** (1943 Sophie Wright Pl., 504/581-4700), in a dramatic old building just off Magazine Street, with a large showroom. Blown glass and some great vintage furniture are also sold here. **Casey Williams Pottery** (3919 Magazine St., 504/899-1174) is an especially inviting little shop with pickled-wood floors and neat shelves lined with bowls, plates, and other fine works, most of it in gentle earth tones. Owner and artist Williams works with several prominent New Orleans potters here.

In the quaint Riverbend neighborhood, **Nuance** (728 Dublin St., 504/865-8463) carries a vast range of fine-arts and hand-crafted decorative piece, all made by Louisiana artists. Blown glass, textiles, pottery, and jewelry are among the wares assembled in this Victorian bungalow.

SOUVENIRS AND GIFTS

Orient Expressed Imports (3905 Magazine St., 504/899-3060) is a funny little gift shop with amusing tchotchkes, hand-smocked children's clothing, carved *santos,* and fine linens. A favorite stop for novelty items, curious gifts, and generally irreverent and teen- to adult-oriented oddities, **Big Life Toys** (3117 Magazine St., 504/895-8695; 3923 Cleveland Ave., 504/899-8697) is a good place to find that boxing-nun action figure you've been searching for. The **Bead Shop** (4612 Magazine St., 504/895-3909) occupies a quirky little Creole cottage—it's the perfect crafts boutique for a city that celebrates Mardi Gras with such enthusiasm.

Cameron Jones (2127 Magazine St., 504/524-3119) sells kinetic, colorful, and contemporary housewares, plant stands, wine racks, and other cool fixtures and elements for the home. Check out the funky housewares and locally created arts and crafts at **Two Chicks** (2917 Magazine St., 504/896-8855), where you'll also find pillows and linens, frames, and so on.

Mignon Faget (3801 Magazine St., 504/891-2005; 710 Dublin St., 504/865-7361; the Shops at Canal Place, 333 Canal St., 504/524-2973; Lakeside Shopping Center, 3301 Veterans Memorial Blvd., Metairie, 504/835-2244) has an almost cult following among New Orleans's devotees of fine jewelry. Faget has won countless awards for her creations, many of which incorporate icons and images familiar to Louisiana, such as oyster pendants, red bean charm necklaces, and fleur de lis cufflinks.

Yes, the inevitable **Anne Rice Collection** (across from Lafayette Cemetery No. 1, 504/899-5996) carries the inevitable Anne Rice memorabilia and gear, from Lestat dolls to vampish clothing from the author's own line.

Jim Russell Records (1837 Magazine St., 504/522-2602) is a local institution, known for its more than half-million LPs, 45s, and 78s in all music genres. It's where ardent record collectors go to find the rarest and most obscure vinyl.

If you're looking for an *indelible* souvenir of New Orleans, there's always **Crescent City Tattoo** (4800 Magazine St., 504/269-8282). This safe and reputable piercing parlor is a fixture along funky upper Magazine Street. It offers a full range of designs, from traditional to edgy.

CLOTHING

House of Lounge (2044 Magazine St., 504/671-8300) sells vintage gowns and dresses—it's a fabulous collection of pieces that would make for quite an entrance. Bedroom smoking jackets, feather boas, and colorful corsets may be just what you're looking for to spice up your love life. On the edge of the Riverbend area, **Banbury Cross** (732 Dublin St., 504/866-0449) carries a wide selection of embroidered and smocked children's clothing. A stylish plus-size boutique, **Mrs. Spratt's** (4537 Magazine St., 504/891-0063) carries sizes 1X to 5X, including pieces from some top labels.

At **Ballin's** (721 Dante St., 504/866-4367) fashion-forward shoppers pick up the latest sportswear and evening attire from Vera Wang, Marisa Bartelli, and other top designers. **Magnifeet** (3645 Magazine St., 504/897-3338) has a wonderful selection of top-name shoes, such as Joan & David, Anne Klein, Cole-Haan, and Via Spiga. **Pippen Lane** (2929 Magazine St., Uptown, 504/269-0106) sells all sorts of cute and fun kids' apparel, including linens and shoes. There's also fanciful hand-painted furniture and thought-provoking, educational toys.

Quirky **Aidan Gill for Men** (2026 Magazine St., 504/587-9090) is an unusual spot with old-fashioned barbershop memorabilia, upscale bath products, and ties and other accessories for men.

The North Shore

Separated from the South Shore by enormous Lake Pontchartrain, the North Shore comprises a string of fast-growing middle- to upper-middle-income suburbs, north of which lies a patchwork of rural, wooded towns extending some 40 miles to the Mississippi border. The region is a hidden gem, less famous than the Cajun Country, the plantation towns along the Mississippi River, and, of course, New Orleans. But Louisianans themselves, as well as many who live in other nearby Southern states, have long known of the North Shore's charms—chief among them being that it's simply less touristy than other parts of the state.

It's misleading and perhaps unfair to call the North Shore's most prominent communities—

Slidell, Mandeville, Covington, Ponchatoula, and Hammond—suburbs. Although these towns contain their share of gated communities and strip shopping malls, they're also a trove of nature preserves, forests dense with towering pine and hardwood trees, and funky historic districts abundant with independent shops and eateries. The architecture, topography, and even climate are distinct from the rest of southern Louisiana, bearing a closer resemblance to the charming vintage towns of Mississippi, Alabama, and Georgia.

You'll find relatively few formal attractions in this region, although the Global Wildlife Center in Folsom ranks among the must-sees in the entire state, and Honey Island Swamp near Slidell is de rigueur among enthusiasts of swamp touring. This is also one of Louisiana's top areas for golfing, bird-watching, biking, canoeing and kayaking, and fishing. Fans

downtown
Covington

of indoor recreation shouldn't feel left out, either—there are few parts of the state with a better variety of antiques shops, and the North Shore outranks every other part of the state except New Orleans when it comes to upscale dining.

Spring and fall are probably the biggest months for visiting the North Shore, although many New Orleanians come up here in summer, because it's slightly cooler and the towering pine trees provide plenty of shade. If you're visiting Louisiana for the first time and using New Orleans as your base, consider making at least a day trip to the North Shore, and perhaps spending a night or two—this strategy is especially recommended if you tire quickly of city life. Because the area is relatively affordable and within a 90-minute drive of many of southern Louisiana's and coastal Mississippi's key towns and attractions, it's also convenient to use the North Shore as a base for further exploring.

St. Tammany Parish

The state's fastest-growing parish mirrors other upscale suburbs in the South, such as the boomtown north of Atlanta and Houston, but on a smaller scale. You'll hear the same discussions here about traffic problems, growth management, and community planning, but the growing pains have—to this point—been less dramatic here. One reason is that Lake Pontchartrain provides a massive natural barrier between metro New Orleans and the North Shore. This side of the lake is also the site of some enormous tracts of protected wetlands, so the areas along the east and west branches of the Pearl River, along the lakefront in Lacombe and eastern Mandeville, and in several other parts of the parish will never be developed commercially.

Early visitors to St. Tammany Parish, which took its name in 1812 from the esteemed Delaware Indian chief Tamanend, were drawn here by the lush pine forests and primeval swamps harboring abundant wildlife. Curative artesian water in Abita Springs and cooler temperatures tempted many well-to-do urban dwellers in search of a healthful escape—throughout the 19th century, first steam ships and then trains brought hundreds of New Orleanians to the *autre cote du lac* (other side of the lake), primarily during the sultry summer months. Inns and restaurants catering to city folk popped up, especially in Mandeville and Abita Springs.

The land had been occupied by Choctaw Indians, who are said to have named the area's rivers, and it was the French among the Europeans who investigated the region during the early explorations of New Orleans. Permanent European settlements began to take route throughout the 1800s, and in addition to the parish's early development as a summer resort, timber, agricultural, and boat-building industries thrived here.

The 23-plus-mile Causeway bridge, the longest in the world, first connected Mandeville to the town of Metairie (and the adjacent city of New Orleans) in 1959, which greatly spurred the parish's growth. But St. Tammany really boomed during the 1990s, as a number of businesses moved out here, and many more residents with jobs in New Orleans, Metairie, and other South Shore towns chose to live here, tempted by the natural beauty, excellent schools, low crime, and generally high quality of life.

A number of artists and writers have lived in St. Tammany Parish, including novelist Walker Percy, who lived in Covington (the library there holds a symposium on Percy every April). Actor John Goodman has a home in Mandeville.

SLIDELL

The largest town in the parish, Slidell (population 32,000) is also the closest to New Orleans. The commuter suburb, well known for its excellent public-school system, is home to many workers who drive each day across the bridge to the South Shore or across the state line into Mississippi. The town is most often visited because of Honey Island Swamp, on the eastern edge of the community, which is fed by the West Branch of the

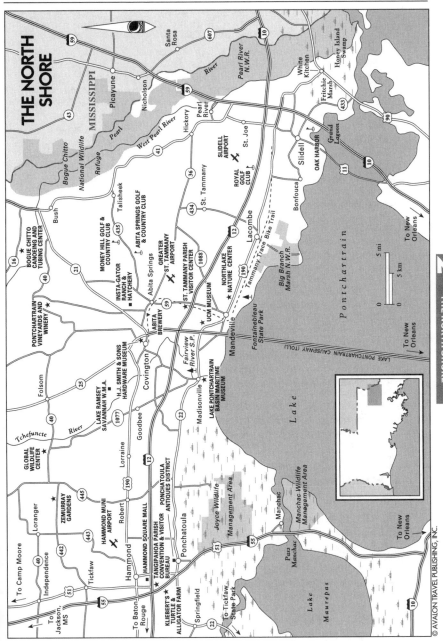

THE NORTH SHORE

SWAMP TOURS

Swamp tours are big business all through southern Louisiana, and of all the tours you can take while visiting New Orleans, these boat rides through some of North America's most pristine and spectacular swamps might be the most memorable. The top destinations for swamp tours are Slidell, Houma, and towns along the Atchafalaya Swamp basin east and south of Lafayette, but you can also find swamp tour operators along the River Road south of Baton Rouge and throughout metro New Orleans.

There are several types of tours, some of them using airboats, some using quieter excursion vessels. The airboats travel at amazing speeds, but they do tend to scare away wildlife.

The narrative accompanying the tour can vary from highly educational to corny, with tall tales about swamp creatures and Cajun folklore. But on a good swamp tour, you'll come away not only having observed a wide variety of wildlife firsthand, but also with a new understanding of the topography and ecology that has shaped New Orleans and southern Louisiana. After all, at one time, all of New Orleans looked more or less like Honey Swamp and the Atchafalaya Basin.

Logistics

Rates for swamp tours vary depending on duration, the boat, and the number of passengers. You can expect to pay about $15 to $25 per adult for a two-hour tour, and kids under 12 are often discounted. Most swamp-tour outfitters give tours year-round, but the best time to go is spring (April and May, especially) and fall (September and October). In winter, animals are less active (alligators are dormant) and the swamps not nearly as lush and vibrant. In summer, it can be awfully hot riding around a swamp in a metal boat for a couple of hours, and the river flow is sometimes low, but you should have ample opportunity to sight wild animals and enjoy verdant foliage.

Although many tour companies offer several tours throughout the day, it's important always to make a reservation, even if only a few hours ahead; tours do book up at busy times. There's a chance, with some outfitters, that you'll be able to show up and get on a tour, but most prefer that you call ahead, and sometimes you won't even be able to find where a tour starts without calling for directions.

Many swamp-tour operators can, for a fee, drive you between New Orleans and the debarkation point. Dr. Wagner's Honey Island Swamp Tours, out of Slidell, charges $45 per adult for a swamp tour that includes van transportation back and forth to New Orleans; the price for a tour where you show up yourself is $20 per adult. Many other companies giving tours on the North Shore, down near Houma, and in the eastern end of the Atchafalaya Swamp basin offer similar deals.

Dr. Wagner's Honey Island Swamp Tours

One of the most respected operators in the state, Dr. Wagner's Honey Island Swamp Tours (985/641-1769, www.honeyislandswamp.com) are led by Dr. Paul Wagner, an environmental consultant with a Ph.D. in wetland ecology. The company can handle nearly 150 guests per trip, using up to seven boats, and guides are all trained by the charming and knowledgeable Dr. Wagner.

Dr. Wagner's tours are geared toward the thinking traveler, and they pass through some of the most primeval terrain in region. One nice thing about the swamps on the North Shore, as opposed to those down in the Atchafalaya Basin or south of New Orleans, is that you see dense groves of very tall trees all through Honey Island—it gives the swamp a lush and dramatic appearance. Honey Island is the second-largest swamp in Louisiana; while Atchafalaya is larger, it's been significantly altered by pipelines, canals, and levees. The Pearl is one of the only rivers in the state that does not have a levee system and is encouraged to flood, which nourishes the wetland and keeps the swamp healthy. About the only evidence of human alteration as you float down the Pearl and into Honey Island Swamp is the I-10 highway bridge that crosses the river, and the rows of fishing camps built on stilts along several stretches of the river.

Honey Island Swamp is an estuary, and a very different ecosystem from the other swamps in the state. It's called an overflow river swamp, and it looks more like a miniature Amazon than like another Gulf Coast swamp. It's very quiet and peaceful, and you'll see lots of turtles out sunning (usually red-eared sliders, though some of the snapping turtles here live to be 150 to 200), along with grey herons, ibis, egrets, hawks, kingfishers, and the occasional owl. Cypress and tupelo are among the most common trees in this and other Louisiana swamps, but you'll also see plenty of green ash, river birch, and red gum trees.

Wood duck is the most common waterfowl. A furry beaverlike creature called nutria, which was introduced to Louisiana from Argentina by the McIlhenny family of Avery Island, is common in Honey Island as well as most of the other swamps in Louisiana. They're cute to look at, but nutria have unfortunately become a nuisance.

Dr. Wagner, who lives in a house on the swamp, covers about 7 or 8 miles during his tours, and although he never promises passengers that he'll show them alligators, the odds of seeing them are strong, as long as it's not winter.

Swamp Tour Operators Elsewhere in Louisiana

Also on the North Shore, **Mockingbird Swamp Tours** (985/386-7902 or 800/572-3046) runs excursions along Bayou Manchac and the swamplands between Lake Pontchartrain and Lake Maurepas.

Many of the best swamp tours are given outside Slidell on the North Shore, or near Houma in the southern heart of Cajun Country, but there are some reliable operators in the metro New Orleans region. At the famous Evergreen Plantation on the Great River Road, **Airboat Adventures** (Hwy. 18, Edgard, 504/454-3882 or 866/467-8438, www.evergreenplantation.com) gives swamp/plantation combo tours.

For a more intimate experience, try **The Last Wilderness** (225/659-2499, www.lastwildernesstours.com), which uses a small Cajun fishing boat to give tours of the Atchafalaya Basin, departing from Bayou Sorrel, not far from Nottoway on the River Road. Guide Dean Wilson takes passengers well off the beaten path, even by swamp standards, and into tight and shallow bodies of water that larger craft can't reach. Last Wilderness also rents canoes and offers canoe tours.

A favorite in Houma is **A Cajun Man's Swamp Cruise** (985/868-4625, www.cajunman.com), conducted by Ron "Black" Guidry, who leads passengers on an entertaining tour through Black Bayou. Guidry is fluent in French and English, and he plays guitar and accordion and sings Cajun ditties while maneuvering his boat through the swamps.

Between Vacherie and Thibodaux, **Torres' Cajun Swamp Tours** (985/633-7739) is a popular operator.

Pure Cajun Boardwalk Swamp Tours (3358 Hwy. 307, Thibodaux, 985/633-9306) offers an entirely different experience. Here you don't have to take a boat ride to enjoy the tour; instead, explore a 1,000-foot (wheelchair-accessible) boardwalk through the swamp. Guided tours are offered, and there's also a large picnic area.

In the heart of Cajun Country, **Champagne's Swamp Tours** (1008 Roxy Dr., St. Martinville, 337/845-5567, www.champagnesswamptours.com) takes passengers out in a 20-foot aluminum crawfish skiff with a very quiet engine. The tour leaves from Lake Martin Landing and passes through a dramatic flooded cypress and tupelo forest, as well as the largest nesting area of wading birds in the state. Another highly recommended company, in nearby Breaux Bridge, is **McGee's Landing** (337/228-2384, www.mcgeeslanding.com).

alligator in Honey Island Swamp

Pearl River (the East Branch forms the border between Louisiana and Mississippi).

The city was established in 1882 as a base camp for construction of the New Orleans and Northeastern Railroad, which ran to Meridian, Mississippi, and connected rail travelers ultimately to New York City and other Northeastern cities. The site was chosen by virtue of its being the nearest high ground to New Orleans on the other side of Lake Pontchartrain. Early industries included brick and creosote manufacturing, lumber milling, and shipbuilding—in fact, Slidell shipyards built a number of military vessels used in World Wars I and II.

It's easy to reach Slidell from New Orleans via I-10, which cuts across the eastern edge of Lake Pontchartrain, but it's more interesting and not all that much longer to take U.S. 90 East, which is Exit 240 from I-10 just a bit northeast of the French Quarter. U.S. 90 winds through the swampland that predominates in eastern New Orleans and, after crossing a short channel that connects Lake Pontchartrain to Lake Borge (which feeds into the Gulf of Mexico), intersects with U.S. 190, which will run you right into downtown Slidell.

Slidell has a modest but engaging Olde Town district, mostly a jumble of 19th-century Victorian clapboard and brick buildings, some newer '50s and '60s cottages. It's not overly trendy, but it's real, and feels like a genuine slice of Louisiana. The anchor in Olde Town is the **Slidell Cultural Center** (444 Erlanger St., 985/646-4375, www.slidell.la.us/arts_center.htm, open 9 A.M.–4 P.M. Mon.–Fri., 10 A.M.–2 P.M. Sat., admission free), which exhibits traveling national and regional art exhibitions in a handsome gallery space.

The town's other attraction is the **Slidell Museum** (2020 1st St., 985/646-4380), a modest history museum with artifacts and documents, some dating as far back as the 1600s, that trace the region's history. It's set in Slidell's old town hall.

From the Olde Town area, turn south onto U.S. 11 and follow it to the next major intersection, which is Hwy. 433, onto which you should make a right turn. If you feel like checking out one of the several interesting residential neighborhoods that fringe Slidell's extensive canal system, make an immediate left onto Palm Drive and follow this road as it wends by waterside homes and skirts the bank of Bayou Bonfouca. You'll eventually hit Canulette Road, which brings you back onto Hwy. 433, where a left turn sets you back in the same direction you were going before the detour onto Palm Drive. Hwy. 433 winds beneath towering pine trees and over a wonderful old pontoon bridge that was featured in the early-1970s James Bond thriller *Live and Let Die* before eventually joining with U.S. 190; a left turn here leads you toward Mandeville by way of the small town of Lacombe.

Lacombe

The ancestral home of both Choctaw and Colapissa Native Americans, Lacombe is set along a picturesque bayou. Much of the southern portion of town is occupied by **Big Branch Marsh National Wildlife Preserve.** Lacombe is less built up than either Slidell to the east or Mandeville to the west, and it's also home to a few of the parish's better restaurants. U.S. 190 is the main drag through Lacombe, and if you continue on it in a westerly direction, you'll soon enter Mandeville.

MANDEVILLE

Considered by many to be greater New Orleans's most exclusive suburb, Mandeville is popular with visitors for its high-end shopping and many great restaurants, but the most distinctive draw is quirky Old Mandeville, a district of restored cottages, eateries, and shops down along Lake Pontchartrain, just east of where the Lake Pontchartrain Causeway connects the town with the South Shore.

From Lacombe via U.S. 190, you'll first pass through the heavily wooded Fontainebleau State Park; the turnoff into the park is on your left a short while after crossing the town line. Beyond the park, continue on U.S. 190 as it passes through a more residential area, and make a left turn onto Jackson Street, which leads south a few blocks until it ends at Lakeshore Drive, onto which you make a right turn. Lakeshore Drive, which runs directly along the Lake Pontchartrain shoreline, offers a wonderful architectural tour of some of Mandeville's most beautiful and—in many cases—historic homes.

Lakeshore runs for several blocks, but at Gerard Street, turn right and perhaps park your car along the street, as this puts you in the heart of historic Old Mandeville, a perfect spot for a stroll. This charming community of generally modest but frilly wood-frame bungalows thrived

THE NORTH SHORE

mansion in Old Mandeville

in the early part of the 20th century as a summer resort for well-to-do New Orleans families who arrived here by train via either Slidell or Hammond, or by ferry across Lake Pontchartrain (this was long before the construction of the Causeway). At the little rail station in Old Mandeville, now a trailhead for the Tammany Trace bike path, hundreds of visitors would debark each weekend. Mandeville Trailhead has a farmer's market on weekends, and there's an amphitheater that hosts concerts and activities. Most of the houses in Old Mandeville date to the first two or three decades of the 20th century. Ferries docked at long piers jutting out from the intersection of Gerard and Coffee Streets. There was a massive wooden waterslide and a number of bathhouses along the shore, where summer visitors splashed about in Lake Pontchartrain. Today, housing prices in Old Mandeville have risen steadily—these little cottages fetch a goodly sum, even the ones that need quite a lot of work.

The best walking route is up Gerard Street for several blocks before making a left turn onto Monroe Street for one block; at Lafitte Street, head back down south toward the lake. Any of these short blocks in Old Mandeville are great for walking, and all are lined with handsome old cottages and homes.

Hop back in your car and backtrack to Lakeshore Drive, turning right and continuing to West Beach Parkway, onto which you turn right. Follow the road a few blocks north and then turn left onto Monroe Street, which runs across Causeway Boulevard, which leads onto the Lake Pontchartrain Causeway to the town of Metairie on the South Shore. The first span of the Causeway opened in 1956, and it was doubled into two spans in 1969. *The Guinness Book of Records* names the 1969 span as the longest bridge in the world, at 23 miles, 1,538 yards. The two spans run parallel to each other, about 80 feet apart and in most places not too high over the water; the entire bridge sits atop 9,000 pilings. For first-timers, a drive across this very, very long bridge can be intriguing, but any local who commutes this way can tell you that the novelty wears off quickly. About 30,000 cars cross over the bridge each day.

Monroe Street continues west of Causeway Boulevard a short distance, and you then make a left turn onto Live Oak Street, a right onto Copal Street, and a left onto Fountain Street, which leads to prodigious **Seven Sisters Oak** (200 Fountain St., admission free). This enormous tree is said to be more than 1,000 years old; it's more than 37 feet in circumference. The oak sits in the front yard of a private home whose owners have very graciously made it accessible to the public—do keep in mind that you're on private property. You can park right in the home's driveway, beside the tree, and there are no formal hours, but visiting from late morning to late afternoon would seem to be the most considerate time to take a look. If you think those handsome live oak trees at Oak Alley Plantation or in New Orleans's Audubon Park are impressive, you'll be awed by this massive tree. You can follow Copal or any of the cross streets for a bit, if you're in the mood to admire some more of Mandeville's fine homes. Retrace your steps to Live Oak Street and head north, making a left turn on West Causeway Boulevard, which cuts in a northwesterly direction to Hwy. 22, onto which a left turn will take you into the mostly residential community of Madisonville.

Madisonville

Named for President James Madison, this growing town of both full-time residences and summer and weekend cottages and houseboats, many of them on or near the Tchefuncte River (meaning "Three Forks" and pronounced chuh-funk-tuh), has a cute downtown along the water. Shortly after Hwy. 22 crosses the river (coming from Mandeville), make a left turn onto Main Street, and follow this winding riverside road to where it dead-ends, at a parking area and boat launch. You can see the circa-1900 Madisonville lighthouse, which sits on an island just off from the shoreline, from the parking area, and you may occasionally see river wildlife along this largely untraveled road. On your way down Main Street you'll also pass the still-nascent **Lake Pontchartrain Basin Maritime Museum** (Main Street, 985/845-9200, www.lpbmaritimemuseum.org, open 10 A.M.–4 P.M. Mon.–Sat.), which occupies a beautiful building that doubles as a banquet hall but for now contains few exhibits. Presently, there's a diorama on rural life on a Cajun bayou, a video on the origins of local watercraft, a re-created blacksmith shop that would have produced Civil War ships, and some other interesting displays. In time, the museum is expected to add many more artifacts—it first has to find ways to raise money.

The town's main attraction is the historic **Otis House,** which is set inside lush 99-acre **Fairview-Riverside State Park** (985/845-3318 or 888/677-3247, www.lastateparks.com, parking $2 per car), just off Hwy. 22, on the east bank of the Tchefuncte. The lovely green park sits at a sharp S-bend of the river and is shaded by dozens of massive live oak trees. Facilities include campsites for tent and RV camping, a playground, and a picnic area. Fishing, boating, and waterskiing are popular along the river. The Otis House dates to 1880, and was the family home for a wealthy sawmill owner. It contains period furnishings, artwork, and fine original architectural detailing, and it's open for tours 9 A.M.– 5 P.M. Wed.–Sun.; admission is $2.

COVINGTON

From downtown Madisonville, follow Hwy. 21 north across I-12 and into the dapper downtown of Covington, which though smaller than Slidell and Mandeville has grown to become one of the North Shore's most popular suburbs. Founded in 1813 as the town of Wharton but soon renamed for War of 1812 hero General Leonard Covington, this bustling community is the seat of St. Tammany Parish and contains one of the liveliest little downtowns in the state. Downtown is situated where the Bogue Falaya and Tchefuncte Rivers meet—it's an utterly charming little town with an artsy personality.

Downtown Covington is also the site of the **H.J. Smith & Sons Hardware Museum** (308 N. Columbia St., 985/892-0460, open store hours, admission free), a small exhibit space inside the H.J. Smith store, which has been up and running since 1876. It includes local artifacts, vintage hardware, and exhibits relevant to both the store's and the town's history. You'll see a 1920s gas pump, a hand-operated washing machine, and a 20-foot-long cypress dugout canoe.

THE NORTH SHORE

Covington

Despite the rather morbid slogan "From Hatchling to Handbag," the **Insta-gator Ranch & Hatchery** (23440 Lowe Davis Rd., 985/892-3669 or 888/892-1560, open by reservation Tues.–Sun., admission $8) makes for an interesting little side trip. It's home at any given time to some 2,000 alligators, most of them intended to be harvested (i.e., killed) and used for handbags, boots, purses, and food. Sound awful? In fact, this ranch and other licensed farms greatly help the wild-alligator population in Louisiana, and the ranching program was developed by the U.S. Fish and Wildlife Service in conjunction with the Louisiana Wildlife and Fisheries. Ranches and farms like this one are required to return a number of their young to the wild. As long as there's a market for alligator goods, there will be alligator harvesting; by licensing qualified establishments to raise and farm alligators, the state is able to forbid alligator hunting in the wild, thereby ensuring the propagation of the species in Louisiana.

Abita Springs

It's just a short drive east from Covington, via Hwy. 36, to the small and funky community of Abita Springs. Acclaimed during the late 19th century for its curative waters, Abita Springs began as a health resort favored by wealthy New Orleanians looking to escape from the sultry and overcrowded city. As a laid-back country town that's more countrified in character than neighboring towns along the shore but still within commuting distance of the Big Easy, Abita Springs might be the perfect healthful escape. Spring water is still bottled here, but the town's most famous elixir nowadays is Abita Beer, which is brewed right in town and distributed all around the state and has developed a following nationwide.

The touch-friendly **UCM Museum** (22275 Hwy. 36, 985/892-2624 or 888/211-5731, http://ucmmuseum.com, open 10 A.M.–5 P.M. daily, admission $3) is a leading oddity of the area—a museum of very curious curiosities, with the facade of an old gas station but comprising several quirky (and rather musty) buildings. This truly bizarre attraction is the brainchild of local artist John Preble, who has painstakingly assembled the quirky and often comical exhibits within. His creations mix folk art, recycled goods, and an array of collectibles to remarkable effect. Among the displays are a stuffed 24-foot-long "bassigator" who would answer to the name Buford, were he an actual living thing. The House of Shards has been built largely with scraps of bottle, license plate, machine parts, and pottery. You'll also find strangely fascinating dioramas constructed largely from discarded parts and pieces that depict everything from voodoo worship to alligator wrestling. The letters "UCM" don't appear to stand for anything, by the way—it's named this way so that you'll pronounce it the "you-see-em mu-se-um." Less out there is an early-20th-century Creole cottage, fully restored, and now the site of arts workshops and classes. The museum sits along pine- and oak-shaded grounds, and is adjacent to a leafy park with a footbridge across a rushing stream and an elegant 1884 picnic pavilion. This is one of the North Shore's best attractions for kids.

Nearby on Hwy. 36, **Abita Brewery** (21084 Hwy. 36, 985/893-3143, www.abita.com), offers free tours and tastings on Saturdays at 1 and 2:30 P.M. and Sundays at 1 P.M. Abita Brewing Company opened in 1986, taking full advantage of Abita Springs' famed water. These tours are low-key and fun, a good opportunity to learn about the brewing process—it's the sort of place where the staff generally takes time to chat with visitors. Abita produces five kinds of beer, ranging from the dark and rich Turbo Dog to the light and bubbly Abita Amber; there are also several seasonal beers.

Folsom

Folsom is a small, rural town north of Covington, reached via Hwy. 25. The town feels a world away from the towns along Lake Pontchartrain, and a few worlds away from the South Shore. Here the gentle, rolling countryside is known for its stables—many horse enthusiasts come to Folsom, and there are riding shows throughout the year. The town is partly in Tangipahoa Parish, where you'll find its most famous attraction, the Global Wildlife Center, which you can reach by

the UCM Museum in Abita Springs

heading west on Hwy. 40 from Folsom's village center. (See the *Tangipahoa Parish* section, below, for a full description of Global Wildlife.)

Bush

From Folsom, follow Hwy. 40 east as it rolls through the rural, northern end of the parish to reach **Pontchartrain Vineyards and Winery** (81250 Old Military Rd./Hwy. 1082, 985/892-9742, www.pontchartrainvineyards.com, open for tours and tastings Wed.–Sun.). It's quite a beautiful place, set amid the horse farms of Bush and eastern Folsom. Begun in 1997, the winery has already won some major awards. It's the only serious winery in the state, and its food-friendly wines are served at some of the major restaurants in the area. Depending on when you go, you might end up participating in the harvest or catching one of the many concerts held there during the summer. Tasting is held in a French Provincial–style brick building and visitor center, which overlooks the gentle hillside planted with grapes. The short but informative tours are more personable than most of those you'll find in major wine-producing areas such as Napa and Sonoma.

ENTERTAINMENT AND NIGHTLIFE

Covington, Slidell, and Mandeville all have a handful of popular bars and music clubs, and Old Mandeville is home to one of the state's only professional theaters. It's pretty easy to find live music just about any night of the week, and St. Tammany Parish's relatively young and professional population accounts for a high "hip" factor at many bars and clubs.

The must-attend for live-music lovers is downtown Covington's **Columbia Tap Room** (434 N. Columbia St., 985/898-0899, www.columbiastreettaproom.com), which presents first-rate rock, folk, and blues bands throughout the week. This is a cool corner bar with big plate-glass windows, through which you'll almost always see a rollicking, happy crowd. The tin-roofed, decidedly rustic-looking **Red Barn Pub** (501 Lafitte St., Old Mandeville, 985/626-3002) looks like a dive but draws an eclectic mix of folks. It's a good place to mix with the locals. There's sometimes acoustic or other light tunes. More downhome and happily ungentrified—depending on which band is playing that night—is **Ruby's**

Roadhouse (840 Lamarque St., Mandeville, 985/626-9748), which presents everything from rock to Cajun. In Olde Mandeville, **Donz Cocktails on the Lake** (1951 Lakeshore Dr., Mandeville, 985/626-9945) is, well, a fun place to drink cocktails on the lake. During a hurricane a few years back, Donz stayed open despite the rising storm surge of Lake Pontchartrain—if you phoned that day, you'd have heard the bartender answer the phone "Donz *in* the Lake." The two local branches of **Daiquiris and Creams** (1729 Gause Blvd., Slidell, 985/641-4656; 1737 U.S. 190, Mandeville, 985/624-3030) present live music many nights and are a popular spot for cocktails and schmoozing.

In Covington, the **Star Theatre** (332 N. New Hampshire St., 985/875-7880, www.skyfire.tv) shows everything from live theater to midnight movies to top Hollywood films; there's a wine bar on premises.

FESTIVALS AND EVENTS

Some of the state's best-attended festivals are held in St. Tammany Parish. The North Shore's reputation as a bird-lover's paradise is capitalized on each spring with the **Great Louisiana Bird Fest,** which is built around a series of naturalist-led "field trips" to St. Tammany Parish's top birding venues—you'll see countless local and migrating species and *might* just spy the extremely rare red-cockaded woodpecker, or even an American bald eagle.

No matter where you are in Louisiana (or in several neighboring states), you can listen to or watch the North Shore's most acclaimed musical event, the **Piney Wood Opry,** which is broadcast on radio and TV stations throughout the Deep South. It's held once a month during the spring and again during the fall, and you can catch the performance live at the Opry's broadcasting headquarters, the Abita Springs Town Hall. You'll hear country, bluegrass, and gospel bands and musicians strum and hum the night away. This event is quite distinct from the many Cajun and zydeco concerts held elsewhere in the state—the Opry's mission is to preserve and celebrate the folk music of the

Columbia Tap Room, Covington

piney woods regions of Louisiana, Mississippi, and Alabama.

From March through October, the last Friday of each month, downtown Covington has the **Columbia Street Block Party,** complete with music, food, and family-oriented activities. Anybody with a green thumb should check out the **Spring Garden Tour,** a self-guided trail through several of downtown Covington's most beautiful gardens during April. Slidell's Olde Town is site of the **Antique District Street Fair,** held once in the spring and once in the fall. The several antiques shops here are joined by hundreds of antiques and home-furnishings dealers from all over the country for a massive street fair that's de rigueur for both serious collectors and casual antiquing hobbyists.

Bogue Falaya Park on the edge of downtown Covington is the site of **Old Fashioned Family Fourth,** with live music, food, and fireworks. Yet another of Louisiana's excellent food festivals, the **Bayou Lacombe Crab Festival** kicks off each June beneath the moss-festooned live oaks of Lacombe Park. Here you can try crab prepared umpteen different ways, enjoy the verdant setting, and listen to live music. In September, boating enthusiasts should not miss the **Madisonville Wooden Boat Festival,** during which hundreds of beautiful, mostly handcrafted wooden boats sail, motor, or row along Madisonville's Tchefuncte River. These craft include both antiques and newer models, ranging in size from 10 to 70 feet. There's live music; a marine flea market with nautical art, boating supplies, and foods; a boat-building workshop for kids, and a boat-building contest and race.

The second weekend in November is the **Covington Three Rivers Art Festival,** a juried arts and crafts show. Slidell's **Christmas Under the Stars** (985/646-4375) has become a North Shore tradition. It kicks off in Olde Town's Griffith Park in early December with the lighting of the neighborhood's many old trees and some music concerts, and it continues with storytelling, theater, choral performances, and other events for about 10 days leading up to shortly before Christmas. All events are free, and virtually all are geared heavily toward families.

Mardi Gras

Covington has two parades through downtown and a picnic and festival on Fat Tuesday in Bogue Falaya Park. But in these towns noted for boating, it's only appropriate that the most popular Mardi Gras events are boat parades. In Slidell, the **Krewe of Bilge** is a colorful procession of boats along the town's canals near Lake Pontchartrain, and in Madisonville, the **Krewe of Tchefuncte** passes along the Tchefuncte River. As at land-based Mardi Gras parades, spectators line the road (or river or canal) and beg costumed revelers riding on what you could literally call "floats" to toss them beads and trinkets.

SHOPPING

St. Tammany Parish is notable for shopping, both for its one-of-a-kind independent boutiques and stores and its abundance of chains and superstores along the main roads in Slidell, Mandeville, and Covington. Fans of art galleries and boutiques will want to focus on downtown Cov-

ington, an artsy retail mecca, as well as on the old sections of Mandeville and Slidell.

Covington

Great little galleries and design shops line Covington's Main Street, which is one of the most charming little downtowns in the state of Louisiana. It's small-town friendly but rather hip. Connecting Covington to Mandeville is U.S. 190, a band of strip malls that's handy if you're looking for fast-food restaurants, big-box stores, and movie theaters.

Some of the more interesting downtown shops include **Petite Pence Antiques** (503 N. Columbia St., 985/892-1897), which carries beautiful mirrors, clocks, and furnishings primarily with origins in Paris and Normandy. **Claiborne House** (320 N. Columbia St., 985/893-0766) contains beautiful furnishings, watercolors, and hulking tables and armoires—it's an excellent

shopping directory in downtown Covington

design space. **Art on Columbia** (501 Columbia St.) is a little gallery containing several shops, among them Purple Llama, Beaulab Baubles, and Garden Mosaics. And the **Brunner Gallery** (215 N. Columbia St., 985/893-0444) is a very important art center in downtown Covington; it's a spectacular space with high ceilings and great natural light. Works by regional and national artists of great acclaim are shown here.

A few blocks from Columbia Street is a smaller pocket of cool boutiques, set along Lee Lane. These include the **Linen Closet** (315 Lee Ln., 985/893-2347), which carries fine bedding, pillows, duvets, and the like. **Eastco Trading** (228 N. Columbia St., Covington, 985/875-0739) imports magnificent teak, mahogany, and bamboo sleigh beds, armoires, planter's chairs, and garden benches from its own custom-furniture factory in Indonesia. Also in downtown Covington, **Boston House** (708 E. Boston St., 985/898-3526) is an eclectic home-furnishings and gift shop with offerings ranging from wooden birdhouses with mosaic roofs and white-porcelain teapot lamps to French cheese plates and Mistral soaps imported from Provence.

Slidell

Not quite as well-known as the North Shore's antiquing mecca, Ponchatoula, Olde Town Slidell does have a few impressive antiques shops, most of them tucked into a quadrant bounded by Front, 1st, 2nd, and Erlanger Streets. It's best just to park the car and stroll about this neighborhood.

RECREATION

In addition to shopping and dining, enjoying the outdoors is the key draw for visitors to St. Tammany Parish, which is noted for its swamps and wildlife preserves, an exceptional bike trail, a few fine golf courses, and excellent fishing and boating both along several bayous and immense Lake Pontchartrain.

Bicycling

St. Tammany Parish has one of the best biking resources in the South, the **Tammany Trace** (985/867-9490), a 31-mile rails-to-trails bikeway

interpretive signs at Mandeville Trailhead, on the Tammany Trace bike path

that runs from Slidell west to Mandeville and then north to Abita Springs before curving west again into downtown Covington. The path—which is paved and also serves the interests of joggers, strollers, inline skaters, wheelchair users, and horseback riders—is the first rails-to-trails conversion in Louisiana; it follows the path of the old Illinois Central Railroad, winding beneath boughs of pine, oak, and magnolia trees and across some 31 bridges and through some of the state's verdant wetlands. The trail cuts right through or near all of the downtown retail and dining districts in the area.

The key trailheads have public rest rooms, parking, and interpretive signs and displays about the region. These are found in Slidell on the west side of town, where Thompson Road extends south from U.S. 190; in the heart of Old Mandeville, where you'll also find an amphitheater and a small interpretive center (and several eateries within walking distance), and farther north in Mandeville just off Hwy. 59 by Exit 65 off I-12 (just beyond the St. Tammany Parish visitor information center, off Koop

Drive). You can also pick up the trail and find parking in downtown Abita Springs, right around where Highways 59 and 36 intersect, and in downtown Covington.

Motorized vehicles are not permitted on the trail, and inline skaters should yield to cyclists, who should yield to joggers, who should yield to walkers, who should yield to horses; pedestrians should stay to the right, as should any slower traffic. The trail may be used from 7 A.M. until sunset

You can rent bikes at the **UCM Museum** (22275 Hwy. 36, 985/892-2624 or 888/211-5731) and at **Kickstand Bike Rental** (690 Lafitte St., across from Old Mandeville trailhead, Old Mandeville, 985/626-9300). Rates are usually around $5 or $6 per hour for a standard mountain bike, or about $15 per day.

Fishing

There's plenty of great catfish and other freshwater fishing in the muddy bayous of St. Tammany Parish, especially in the preserves and state parks mentioned below. There are also charter-fishing operations that take travelers out through Lake Pontchartrain into the Gulf of Mexico. One excellent one, based in Slidell, is **Captain Vinnie's** and **Angling Adventures of Louisiana** (53105 Hwy. 433, 985/781-7811 or 877/4AA-OFLA). Charters angle chiefly for redfish, speckled trout, and flounder; all fishing tackle is provided, and the tours cost about $250 for one or two people and around $400 for four.

In Madisonville, **Fairview-Riverside State Park** (Hwy. 22, 985/845-3318 or 888/677-3247, parking $2 per car) offers great river fishing and crabbing from its banks along the Tchefuncte River; you can also put in a boat here or at one of the other launches in Madisonville. Upriver you're likely to encounter bass, white perch, bluegill, and bream, while down closer to where the river joins Lake Pontchartrain, you can catch channel catfish, redfish, and speckled trout.

There's plenty of great catfish and other freshwater fishing in the muddy bayous of St. Tammany Parish. There are also charter-fishing operations that take travelers out through Lake Pontchartrain into the Gulf of Mexico.

Golf

St. Tammany Parish has some of the best golf courses in the whole state, beginning with the private **Money Hill Golf & Country Club** (100 Country Club Dr., Abita Springs, 985/875-0010, www.moneyhill.com), which hosted the 1999 U.S. Open qualifier and has received numerous awards from major golf publications. Nonmembers can play this course by prior arrangement. **Oak Harbor** (201 Harbor Blvd., Slidell, 985/646-0110, www.oakharborgolf.com) is one of the best public golf courses in the South.

Other reputable public or semi-private courses in the parish include **Abita Springs Golf & Country Club** (73433 Oliver St., Abita Springs, 985/893-2463, www.abitagolf.com) and **Royal Golf Club** (201 Royal Dr., Slidell, 985/643-3000).

Hiking and the Outdoors

One of the most impressive outdoor sanctuaries in southeastern Louisiana is **Big Branch Marsh National Wildlife Refuge** (headquarters at 1010 Gause Blvd., Bldg. 936, Slidell, 985/646-7555, http://southeastlouisiana.fws.gov). There are several access points for the refuge along the northeastern shore of Lake Pontchartrain. Off U.S. 11, just as you cross the lake and enter Slidell, there's a boat launch; a second launch is located off Highway 434, which runs due south from the village of Lacombe down through the refuge and right to the shore of Lake Pontchartrain.

There are several boat ramps and parking areas through Slidell and Lacombe, most of them along bayous that snake inland from the lake and through the refuge. Bayou Liberty Road, which runs west from U.S. 11 in Slidell, and Bayou Paquet Road, which continues west into Lacombe, are good roads for accessing the refuge; on the western border of Big Branch, you'll find parking areas right off U.S. 190, near Cane Bayou on Lamieux Boulevard. The refuge ends at Cane Bayou, which is the Lacombe/Mandeville town border, but you then enter Fontainebleau State Park, through which U.S. 190 runs.

Keep in mind that much of Big Branch is open to hunting (for deer and wildfowl), so be alert and dress accordingly during hunting season. Permits are required for all hunting and fishing, and there are a number of regulations, including the prohibition of several kinds of boats (including motorized craft). Fishing here is restricted to recreational casting and crabbing—no nets, traps, or trotlines are allowed.

Fontainebleau State Park (U.S. 190, Mandeville, 985/624-4443 or 888/677-3668) is—at 2,800 acres—the region's largest recreation area, with facilities such as both primitive and improved campsites, swimming, a playground, and a fishing pier. It's a great park for birdwatchers and hikers, as trails meander through the pine-shaded forest, passing through an ancient grove of live oaks and the crumbling brick ruins of an 1830 sugar mill that was opened by Mandeville's founder, Bernard de Marigny de Mandeville, who operated a sugar plantation here for several decades during the 19th century. He named the plantation Fontainebleau, after the regal French forest hunting ground used by royalty.

The park has direct access onto Lake Pontchartrain, and it's a popular spot for windsurfers and other water-sports enthusiasts. There's a beach along the lake, but swimming is best conducted in the nearby swimming pool, which has full changing facilities. The Tammany Trace bike trail runs through the park, drawing bikers, walkers, and inline skaters. A signed park nature trail identifies some of the many types of trees you'll find here, and visitors can also sometimes observe turkeys, opossums, and rare red-cockaded woodpeckers. A guide to bird-watching inside the park is available at the park's visitor center, and park naturalists conduct guided hikes and nature programs year-round. Entrance fees at all state parks are $2 per vehicle (carrying up to four people), plus 50 cents for each additional person.

Near the park, the **Northlake Nature Center** (U.S. 190, just east of Bayou Castine, 985/626-1238, www.northlakenature.org) is a 400-acre nature preserve with trails that cut through stands of massive pine and hardwood trees. It's yet another great spot for bird-watching.

Sailing and Boating

You can take canoe and tubing trips along the Bogue Chitto, which runs primarily through Washington Parish (between the North Shore and the Mississippi border) and just a bit into the northeastern corner of St. Tammany Parish. In the town of Bogalusa, **Bogue Chitto Canoeing and Tubing Center** (10237 Choctaw River Rd., 985/735-1173) rents tubes and canoes and gives river tours from spring through fall. These are lazy and relaxed river trips that are great fun for kids or adults, and there's no worry of dangerous rapids.

ACCOMMODATIONS

The parish has quite a few enchanting B&Bs, most with one to three guest rooms—they occupy just about every setting in the parish, from the rural piney woods communities in the north to the historic downtowns of Covington and Mandeville. You'll also find a nice selection of modern chain hotels just off the interstate in Slidell and Covington.

Hotels and Motels

$50–100: Hampton Inn (56460 Frank Pichon Rd., Slidell, 985/726-9777 or 800/426-7866, www.hamptoninn.com) is a three-story, 80-room property in tip-top condition and with reasonable rates. About a quarter of the units have refrigerators and microwaves. Another very nice Slidell property is the **Holiday Inn Hotel and Suites** (372 Voter's Rd., 985/639-0890, Slidell, www.holiday-inn.com), which has 57 rooms and 34 suites, and a restaurant, indoor pool, fitness center, and business center. The **Best Western** (625 N. U.S. 190, Covington, 985/892-2681 or 877/766-6700) is a pleasant 75-room property beside the wonderful Dakota restaurant and just a short way north of I-12. Many rooms have microwaves and refrigerators.

$100–150: Courtyard by Marriott (101 Northpark Blvd., just off N. U.S. 190, Covington, 985/871-0244, www.courtyard.com) is perhaps the best chain property in St. Tammany Parish, constantly renovating and offering a DSL Internet connection. It's on the edge of an office park, overlooking a pond and shaded by towering pine trees.

Inns and Bed-and-Breakfasts

$50–100: About a block from Old Mandeville's handsome lakefront, **Pollyana** (212 Lafitte St., Mandeville, 985/626-4053, www.bandbbeside-thelake.com) occupies a sweet pale-blue cottage with a pair of cheerfully decorated rooms with pitched ceilings, floral-print fabrics, and a smattering of antiques. Each unit opens onto a main lounge with a complimentary minibar. Continental breakfast is served on weekdays, a full English-style breakfast on weekends. Just around the corner, **Mar Villa Guest House** (2013 Claiborne St., Mandeville, 985/626-5975 or 877/650-3920, www.marvilla.com) is a wonderfully charming renovated cottage next to the similarly wonderful Broken Egg restaurant. This pink 1870s Victorian with gingerbread trim contains original heart-pine floors, beaded-wood ceilings, and hand-crafted cabinetry. There are three simple but charming units with phones, cable TV, and tile bathrooms with large clawfoot tub/showers. A veranda overlooks the shaded backyard. Several restaurants are within walking distance, as well as the trailhead for the Tammany Trace bike and walking path.

The **Woods Hole Inn** (78253 Woods Hole Ln., Folsom, 985/796-9077, www.woodshole inn.com), just north of Covington in Folsom, was first opened by the aunt and uncle of jazzy crooner Harry Connick Jr. Current owners Marsha and Sam Smalley continue to provide first-class accommodations to travelers seeking a restful retreat in the woods. There are three romantic units, an 1850s cabin with a full kitchen and two suites with refrigerators; all have snacks, fireplaces, TV (no cable) with VCRs, but no phones. The two suites connect through a hallway and are ideal for couples traveling together. The luxurious yet rustic cabin offers the greatest privacy.

For a night in the heart of Big Branch Wildlife Refuge, stay at the **Mildred Fishe Guest Cabin** (26545 Mildred Dr., Lacombe, 800/647-1824, www.bbonline.com/la/mildredfishe), a large two-bedroom cabin with a screened-in porch, outfitted kitchen, central air-conditioning and heating, cable TV, stereo, boat house, dock, and barbecue. There's even a set-up for cleaning any fish you might catch in Bayou Lacombe, on which the cabin is located, or in Lake Pontchartrain, which is 1.5 miles down the bayou. The

Woods Hole Inn, Folsom

cabin lies just 2 miles from Tammany Trace, and it's a favorite stay not only of fishing enthusiasts but also birdwatchers.

An ideal hub for exploring New Orleans, the North Shore, and the nearby Mississippi coastline, the **Garden Guest House** (34514 Bayou Liberty Rd., Slidell, 985/641-0335 or 888/255-0335, www.gardenbb.com) is situated on one of the loveliest properties in the region, shaded by immense pine and live oak trees. Five large guest suites in two separate houses—set down a drive behind the main house of friendly and informative owners Bonnie and Paul Taliancich—look out over 10 acres of lush bayou woodland, dotted with azaleas, camellias, roses, and gardenias; this is a favorite accommodation with nature lovers and birdwatchers. You can also tour the owners' greenhouse, filled with both exotic and indigenous flora. Each suite has a full kitchen, living areas with floor-to-ceiling windows, and comfortable, homey furnishings. A rich and delicious Southern-style breakfast is served in the owner's home each morning. This is a great option for longer stays.

Just north of Slidell, the **Woodridge B&B**

(40149 Crowes Landing Rd., Pearl River, 985/863-9981 or 877/643-7109, www.woodridgebb.com) occupies a grand brick house with elegant columns and grounds dotted with century-old live oak trees. Each of the five large rooms in this building, which once housed a private school, have private baths, air-conditioning, cable TV, and ceiling fans. Antiques—ranging from a pineapple four-poster bed to a sturdy oak chest—fill the rooms. A full country breakfast is included. The inn is just a few minutes' drive off I-59, Exit 3.

$100–150: Just steps from the great shopping in downtown Covington, **Camellia House B&B** (426 E. Rutland St., 985/893-2442, camellia-house@charter.net) contains one gorgeously furnished guest suite with an adjoining sun porch containing a refrigerator, microwave, and dining nook stocked with delicious breakfast food and home-baked cookies. The room, inside a lovely early-20th-century house, is filled with stylish antiques, a plush bed with well-chosen linens, cable TV and a phone with a data port, and a bright and modern bathroom with a shower and pedestal sink; the room has its own exterior entrance, which leads onto the home's wide veranda

Camellia House B&B, Covington

and also has access to a pool and hot tub. The sun porch has its own twin bed and trundle bed, so you can fit a total of four guests in here. Hosts Linda and Don Chambless are friendly and know a great deal about the area.

Almost catty-corner from their house, Maureen and Tom Chambless (Don's brother) own **Blue Willow** (505 E. Rutland St., 985/892-0011, tmchambless@earthlink.net). Here you'll find a pair of suites, each with private exterior entrances through a gated brick courtyard, which has its own hot tub. Both rooms have high ceilings, polished hardwood floors, and decadent four-poster beds and smart furnishings, cable TV and phones with data ports, as well as breakfast setups similar to that of Camellia House. These properties are steps from Tammany Trace bike trail and the Bogue Falaya River and Park.

A secluded getaway in the deep woods of Folsom, **Little River Bluffs** (11030 Garden Ln., 985/796-5257, www.littleriverbluffs.com) anchors a 60-acre wooded property on the artesian-fed Little Tchefuncte River. This is a naturist's dream, with swimming in and kayaking on the river, hiking through the woods, and sunbathing on a sugary-white sandbar. Great blue herons, egrets, otters, and other wildlife inhabit this lush woodland that feels light-years away from New Orleans (which, in fact, is just 55 miles south). There are three accommodations, the A-frame River Chalet, which sits on a bend in the river; the Meadow Cabin, tucked under a canopy of tall pine trees; and the Treehouse, which also overlooks the river. Each has a full kitchen and fireplace; two have whirlpool tubs. These rustic cabins are totally romantic and relaxing. There's a two-night minimum.

Over $250: At the very high end, **Villa Vici Getaways** (985/674-0909, www.villavicigetaways.com) is a pair of luxury cottages a few blocks from each other in downtown Covington. Charropin Beach sleeps two, and St. John Place sleeps four, and both require a two-night minimum. The owners have a rather off-putting payment policy: half is due upon making your reservation (which is nonrefundable), and the balance is due 30 days prior to your arrival—this, too, is nonrefundable. Considering the rates of

$200 to $250 nightly for St. John's and $300 to $350 for Charropin Beach, you better be sure you want to stay at these places before you book. Charropin is set on a 13-acre gated estate with a private beach on the Bogue Falaya River; it also overlooks a swimming pool. It has a private kitchen with top-notch amenities and a full bath with Jacuzzi. St. John Place is an upscale apartment with sleek contemporary furnishings, a full kitchen, laundry, and a living room with a sleeper sofa. The rooms both convey a thoroughly chic aesthetic.

Camping

The entire North Shore is popular for camping, with facilities at both of St. Tammany Parish's state parks as well as a few commercial campgrounds. **Fairview-Riverside State Park** (Hwy. 22, Madisonville, 985/845-3318 or 888/677-3247) has 81 tent and RV sites with water and electric hookups, as well as a separate primitive tent-camping area. It's set along a picturesque bend of the Tchefuncte River. Offering even more sites, and types of sites, is 2,800-acre **Fontainebleau State Park** (U.S. 190, Mandeville, 985/624-4443), where you'll find 126 tent and RV sites with electrical and water hookups, barbecue grills, and picnic tables, plus a bathhouse and waste station. There are also some primitive tent-camping areas and numerous undesignated campsites scattered throughout the park, some near the beach along Lake Pontchartrain. There are also group campsites, as well as a camping lodge that sleeps 10 and has a kitchen and two baths. You can make reservations for the lodge or any of the tent sites at Fairview and Fontainebleau State Parks by calling 877/CAMP-N-LA (877/226-7652).

Among commercial campgrounds, Covington's **Land-O-Pines** (17145 Million Dollar Rd., 985/892-6023, www.land-o-pines.com) is the most popular. There are sites for RVs and tents, or you can rent cottages that sleep up to eight guests and have kitchens and cable TV. The park is open to day-use visitors for $5 per person in winter, $6 in summer. Land-O-Pines has a large pool and long, twisting waterslide, plus a kiddie pool, camp shop, playground, game room, Laundromat, volleyball court, horseshoe pits, fishing ponds, river with white sandy beach, softball field, snack bar, minigolf, and basketball court—you won't run out of things to do at this place.

Another good option is **New Orleans East KOA** (56009 Hwy. 433, Slidell, 985/643-3850 or 800/562-2128, www.koa.com), which has a large plot of RV sites and a pool, minigolf, and fishing.

FOOD

The North Shore's definitive draw may very well be its wealth of exceptional restaurants in every price range. The very best dining experiences on this side of the lake compare favorably with the best in New Orleans, only with lower prices. You'll find some first-rate Creole and Cajun eateries, along with excellent contemporary American, French, Italian, and Asian restaurants. Apart from New Orleans, no other part of the state offers such a variety of accomplished dining venues. Most of the better-known spots are in Mandeville and Covington, but you'll find great places to eat in every town in the parish. Although St. Tammany Parish is less touristy than some parts of the state, it is a hub of upwardly mobile professionals, and this accounts not only for the high number of restaurants but also for the dapper crowds that fill these places many nights, especially on weekends. Reservations are a good idea in this part of the state.

Upscale

One of the top dining venues on the culinarily impressive North Shore, **The Dakota** (629 N. U.S. 190, Covington, 985/892-3712, $17–26) may not look dazzling with its location beside a Best Western motel, but the contemporary American cooking here is anything but ordinary. Start with New Orleans–style barbecued snails sautéed with fresh garlic, roasted tomatoes, rosemary, Abita beer, and butter, perhaps moving on to the Mixed Nest, roasted quail with andouille-cornbread stuffing and an herb glaze paired with grilled duck breast with raspberry-pepper sauce. Food like this would set you back a good bit

more in New Orleans. If you're looking to sample a wide range of chef's delights, opt for the tasting menu, which generally runs from about $40 to $45 per person. **Boule's Prime House** (1202 N. U.S. 190, Covington, 985/809-0969, $21–49), is a clubby steak-and-seafood house with a lively and very popular bar. Pretty standard surf-and-turf fare is served, but people love the big portions, thick steaks, and outgoing and extremely professional service. Dig into the juicy hickory-smoked filet mignon with rosemary butter, or the smoked mallard duck with a sweet fig reduction. Portions are huge, but then so are the prices. There's also a long martini menu, wine list, and dessert selection.

Over in Lacombe, chef Constantin Kerageorgiou has made **La Provence** (25020 U.S. 190, 985/626-7662, $18–26) a veritable temple of gastronomy for years. With its stucco facade, red-tile roof, and authentic furnishings, the place really does look as though airlifted to the North Shore from the south of France. And wait until you taste Kerageorgiou's sublime food, such as fricassee of rabbit (a recipe of the chef's mother), domestic lamb marinated and roasted with fresh Provençal herbs, and terrine of foie gras with apricot confit and warm brioche.

In the heart of Abita Springs, **Artesia** (21516 Hwy. 36, Abita Springs, 985/892-1662, $17–25) became famous in the late '90s under the helm of chef John Besh, who now operates the similarly notable Restaurant August in New Orleans. Although the head chef has changed, the kitchen continues to turn out great food. You might start with traditional oyster-and-artichoke soup, a velvety rich delight here. The menu varies a great deal, mixing in French, local, and international ingredients, from steamed mussels in a sweet but spicy red coconut curry to herb-crusted lamb chops with potato gnocchi, wilted spinach, and a dry sherry sauce with cherries. The simple but exquisite vanilla crème brûlée is a wonderful dessert. The restaurant occupies a former hotel, built in the late 1800s to accommodate visitors to the area's curative springs. There's a somewhat less formal and quite cozy space downstairs, and a dressier dining room upstairs that also has several tables on a gracious exterior balcony.

Creative but Casual

Affordable, arty, and hip, **Etoile** (407 N. Columbia St., Covington, 985/893-8873, $8–16) is a wine bar and restaurant that shares its downtown Covington storefront with the esteemed Louisiana Star wine shop. The airy room has bare cement walls, skylights, high ceilings, and striking oil paintings by co-owner James Michalopoulos, who is noted regionally. The menu tends toward the eclectic—seared wasabi-crusted tuna over daikon root and peanuts tossed in a rice-wine parsley vinaigrette makes a great starter. The risotto du jour is always appetizing, but so is the grilled pork chop swimming in a New Orleans rum barbecue sauce over black-eyed pea slaw and mashed potatoes. There's an impressive wine list, as you might guess considering the shop next door.

A romantic, low-key eatery with a pair of small art-filled dining rooms, **Ristorante del Porto** (205 N. New Hampshire St., Covington, 985/875-1006, $9–15) is perhaps the North Shore's best-kept dining secret—and it's an amazing value, considering the high quality of ingredients and their deft preparation. Contemporary international fare with an Italian slant is on offer here, from slow-roasted fennel-spiced pork with cannellini beans and kale to house-made pappardelle pasta with rabbit ragu and butternut squash. There's a wonderful wine list with many under-$25 vintages.

Judice's (421 E. Gibson St., Covington, 985/892-0708, $5–9) is a bustling, art-filled breakfast-and-lunch café with a long copper-topped counter and pewter-colored pressed-tin ceilings, and tables covered with vintage photos and memorabilia. This is a local institution, great on Saturday after the Farmers Market. Dine on shrimp rémoulade with fried green tomatoes, English muffins topped with poached eggs and a cabernet mushroom sauce, and a wide range of pancake, French toast, and egg dishes, plus salad and sandwiches. It's a fun spot for people-watching. Dinner, with an emphasis on light Italian fare, is served on weekend evenings.

A favorite of celebrities and New Orleans foodies, **Sal and Judy's** (U.S. 190, Lacombe, 985/882-9443) is an old-fashioned trattoria serving inexpensive, hearty red-sauce Italian food. Some naysayers claim the service can be indifferent, but

Etoile and Louisiana Star, Covington

others swear this is the best old-world Italian experience in metro New Orleans.

A hugely popular spot inside a creaky but comfy wood-frame house in Old Mandeville, **Shady Brady's** (301 Lafitte St., 985/727-5580, $6–16) serves rich and modern takes on homestyle Southern favorites. The options are not especially healthful, but if you've been waiting to try Southern cooking, this is the place: choose roast beef po'boy deep-fried with gravy, a Texas-style Caesar salad with fried oysters, or crispy chicken-fried chicken. Slow-smoked barbecue chicken is another standout. Generous sides of corn pudding, red beans and rice, smothered cabbage, and mac 'n' cheese are also well worth the calories. In warm weather, the sunny wooden deck is open for dining.

Urbane and sexy **Cypress Bistro** (115 Gerard St., Mandeville, 985/727-9909, $14–19) fills a handsome space in Old Mandeville with more big-city ambience than other eateries in the area. You might just sip wine or cocktails at the bar while observing the well-coiffed locals, or drop by for a full dinner. The contemporary American chow is consistently good. Start out with a bowl of venison chili with black beans, cilantro crème fráiche, and salsa fresca. Reliable main courses include the bouillabaisse with local fish and shellfish, fennel, tomatoes, and a chipotle–roasted garlic rouille; and roasted peach–and–Jack Daniels pork loin served with a butternut squash mash and grilled peaches. Nearly across the street, **Bistro 124** (124 Gerard St., 985/727-7995, $14–23) has a covered flagstone patio that captures the sophisticated yet laid-back style of New Orleans—the rest of the seating is found throughout the warmly furnished dining rooms of this restored 19th-century house. Several creative sandwiches are served at lunch, including shaved smoked-pork tenderloin with red onion marmalade, sliced avocados, and melted brie with a cilantro-herb vinaigrette. At dinner, consider starting with the Louisiana egg roll (filled with sautéed chicken, roasted pecans, diced sweet potatoes, red onion, and Napa cabbage) before moving on to barbecued shrimp with roasted garlic, mushrooms, sweet onions, and a rosemary beurre blanc. The staff is upbeat and helpful.

Seafood, Pizzas, and Pub Grub

Related to the famous Abita Brewery, the **Abita Brew Pub** (72011 Holly St., 985/892-5837, Abita Springs, $8–14) serves tasty comfort food that complements or even incorporates the locally crafted beers. Crab claws are served with a dipping sauce that includes rosemary, barbecue sauce, and Turbo Dog, a richly dark beer. Other good bets include blackened shrimp with avocado and a smoked-tomato rémoulade, barbecue ribs, and very good crawfish cakes. A large mural on one wall depicts the area's Tammany Trace bike path, which plenty of patrons use to reach this down-home hangout in the village of Abita Springs. There are several outdoor tables, plus a tavern inside with pop and alternative tunes piped in and sports on TV—the crowd tends toward the young and hip.

Isabella's Pizzeria (321 N. Columbia St., Covington, 985/875-7620, large pies $10–15) is a spacious restaurant with unfinished concrete floors, high ceilings, and live music some nights. It's got a cosmopolitan feel for a neighborhood pizza parlor. Specialty pies include the shrimp pesto pie, and you can also sample some hearty pasta dishes or sandwiches (the muffalettas here are commendable). **Times Bar and Grill** (1827 Front St., Slidell, 985/639-3335; also 1896 N. Causeway Blvd., Mandeville, 985/626-1161, $6–12) occupies the railroad station on the edge of Olde Town Slidell; it's well-known for its hefty burgers but also serves pastas, soups, salads, and other casual fare.

A loveable dive in downtown Madisonville, **Coffee's Boiling Pot** (305 Hwy. 21, 985/845-2348, $6–13) is a rambling little dining room where you can sample the most delicious boiled crabs au gratin you'll ever find; boiled crawfish and shrimp are other specialties. Celebrity chef Emeril Lagasse supposedly favors this place. **Mike Schaeffer's Seafood** (158 S. Military Rd., Slidell, 985/646-1728, $5–15) is a very good, casual eatery in a renovated country-elegant wood-frame building not too far from Honey Island Swamp. A wide range of po'boys is available, from the familiar meatball or soft-shell crab to the rather strange french fry variety, plus sides of macaroni, stuffed crab, and sweet-potato fries. Entrées include catfish-and-shrimp platters, steaks, barbecued baby-back ribs, and chicken parmesan with spaghetti. Thursday and Sunday are all-you-can-eat catfish nights. There's a full bar, including a large selection of frozen daiquiris.

Ethnic

Trey Yuen (600 N. Causeway, Mandeville, 985/626-4476; also 2100 N. Morrison Blvd., Hammond, 985/345-6789, $8–15) gained enormous fame a few years back when a major national travel magazine declared it one of the top few Asian restaurants in the country. It's no chore living up to this acclaim, and not everybody thinks this restaurant with enormous and attractive branches in both Hammond and Mandeville is quite so amazing, but there's no denying that it's a great option for well-prepared Chinese food. What sets this place apart from other Asian eateries in the area is its use of regional ingredients—you might, for example, try marinated spiced alligator stir-fried with green onions and fresh mushrooms in a light oyster sauce. Other dishes use crawfish, soft-shell crab, and other local delicacies. More conventional but also excellent is the spicy flaming chicken with baby corn, snow peas, water chestnuts, and a piquant garlic sauce. Both Asian-style dining compounds—though enormous in that banquet-hall sort of way—are characterized by stunning Japanese landscaping and fine Asian artwork inside. Look to **Typhoon** (527 N. Causeway Service Rd., 985/951-7951, $6–15), in Mandeville, for very reliable Thai food, while **Osaka** (792 I-10 Service Rd., Slidell, 985/643-9276, $7–14) is the best choice around here for sushi and Japanese food.

Quick Bites

The **Broken Egg Cafe** (200 Gerard St., Mandeville, 985/624-3388; also 500 Theard St., Covington, 985/893-4412, $4–8) is an adorable breakfast and lunch spot right in Old Mandeville, near the lake. The restored 1920s cottage contains a warren of dainty dining rooms with hardwood floors and teapots filled with fresh flowers. Among the delicious breakfast options are bananas Foster waffles sprinkled with pecans and fresh banana slices, and the Grand Isle omelet with fresh shrimp, onions, and tomatoes, topped

Broken Egg Cafe, Old Mandeville

with salsa and guacamole. A number of hefty sandwiches and salads are served at lunch, including a tasty barbecue burger with cheddar and sautéed onions. Order a side of blackberry grits or spicy chorizo sausage.

Take a break from antiques shopping or attending the Christmas lights festival in Slidell with an eggnog milk shake or a banana split at the retro-adorable **Old Town Slidell Soda Shop** (301 Cousin St., Slidell, 985/649-4806), a giddy, old-fashioned soda fountain where you can sample chocolate-covered cherries, delicious ice cream in many flavors, vanilla cokes, sandwiches, and piping-hot chili. Another good bet in this neighborhood is the **Victorian Tea Room** (2228 Carey St., Slidell, 985/643-7881), a quaint, traditional lunch spot with sandwiches, quiche, homemade breads, sweets, and delicious chicken salad.

Roadside short-order restaurants dot the region, including **Char-Lou's** (27470 U.S. 190, Lacombe, 985/882-7575, under $6), an unassuming, squat dining room with a few outdoor picnic tables where you can order barbecue ribs, po'boys, hot boudin, fresh seafood, and other cholesterol-laden, fattening delights. In downtown Madisonville, **Badeaux's** (109 Hwy. 22, 985/845-7221, under $6) offers similarly enticing if not exactly healthful food.

Java Joints
You'll find the usual national (Starbucks) and Louisiana (C.C.'s and P.J.'s) coffeehouse chains in abundance throughout Slidell, Mandeville, and Covington, but for something a little more atmospheric, in downtown Covington, drop by **St. John's Coffeehouse** (535 E. Boston St., 985/893-5553), a spacious yet homey java place on the busiest street corner, with old-fashioned tile floors, reading lamps on many tables, a shelf of books to browse through, and some sidewalk seating. It can't be beat for people-watching. A wide range of iced and hot drinks are served—this is a great place to chat with locals. There's live music many evenings.

Picnic Supplies and Gourmet Goods
Often compared with Martin Wine Cellar in New Orleans and Metairie, **Hugh's Wine Cellar** (4250 Hwy. 22, Pine Tree Plaza, Mandeville, 985/626-0066) is an outstanding wine shop that also carries fine liqueurs, cognacs, and the like, along with artisanal cheeses and other gourmet foods and gifts. Occupying a bright yellow storefront in downtown Covington, **Columbia Street Natural Foods Market** (415 N. Columbia St., 985/893-0355) sells prepared foods, organic produce, cheeses, free-range chicken, and lots of other goodies, along with sandwiches, wraps, and sushi to go. Covington has a small but lovely **Farmers Market** on the grounds of its town hall, held 9 A.M.–1 P.M. Saturdays and 2–6 P.M. Wednesdays—everything fresh, from Creole cream cheese to produce to pies to homemade dog biscuits to jams and jellies, is proffered. It's a friendly market, a good place to chat with and meet locals.

INFORMATION AND SERVICES
Visitor Information
Information on these towns can be obtained from the **St. Tammany Parish Tourist Commission Visitor Center** (68099 Hwy. 59, just

St. John's Coffeehouse, downtown Covington

Farmers Market, Covington

north of I-12, Mandeville, 70471, 985/892-0520 or 800/634-9443, www.neworleansnorthshore.com). This is one visitor center that's worth dropping by in person, as it occupies a cleverly designed wood-frame building in an authentic Louisiana swamp.

Getting Around

There's virtually no public transportation in St. Tammany Parish, and a private car is a must for exploring. Only in downtown Covington and Olde Town Mandeville will you find accommodations within walking distance of a fair number of shops and eateries, and even in these communities your options are limited. Unfortunately, traffic can be torturously slow in some parts of the parish, especially U.S. 190 between Mandeville and Covington and in Slidell, and Hwy. 59 between Mandeville and Abita Springs. However, U.S. 190 from the western edge of Slidell into Mandeville is

relatively less traveled and quite scenic, as are several of the parishes' state highways, such as Hwy. 22 (from Mandeville west through Madisonville and clear to Ponchatoula in Tangipahoa Parish), Hwy. 21 (from Madisonville northeast up through Covington and on through Bush and Bogalusa), and Hwy. 433 (in Slidell from U.S. 90 winding northwest to U.S. 190). For speed, I-12 can be a lifesaver, and it's usually free from major traffic jams—it runs west to east across the parish, connecting the junction of I-59 and I-10 in Slidell with Mandeville and Covington before continuing on to Tangipahoa Parish and I-55. By way of I-10, it's just a 40-minute drive from downtown New Orleans to Slidell, and by way of the Causeway across Lake Pontchartrain, it's a 45-minute drive from New Orleans to Mandeville. Rush hour traffic jams along both these routes are common, so figure an extra 20 to 30 minutes depending on when you make these drives.

Tangipahoa Parish

As opposed to St. Tammany Parish, which runs chiefly east–west around the northeastern perimeter of Lake Pontchartrain, Tangipahoa (pronounced tan-jah-puh-ho) Parish forms a south–north rectangle, extending from the north shore of Lake Pontchartrain up to the Mississippi state border. The towns down nearest to the lake, Ponchatoula and Hammond, are the most popular with visitors and also the most populated. As you travel north, you'll encounter smaller and sleepier communities with a mostly rural feel, except for the presence of I-55, which cuts along the west side of each of these towns.

The smaller towns in Tangipahoa Parish all have wonderful old vintage rail stations, and all of them have found new uses these days, from a police station in Amite to a senior center in Independence to an antiques and gift shop in Ponchatoula.

PONCHATOULA

Ponchatoula is a quiet little town famous for its plethora of antiques shops. It's the oldest incorporated community in Tangipahoa Parish (dating to 1861), and although it's the closest town in the parish to New Orleans, it feels miles from the big city. You can reach the town coming from New Orleans via I-55, or from St. Tammany Parish to the east, via either Hwy. 22 or I-12 from Madisonville.

The big excitement downtown occurs when the *City of New Orleans* Amtrak train from Chicago speeds through, keeping pedestrians and autos momentarily from crossing the track that pierces the heart of the commercial district. Freight trains also cut through downtown rather often. There's been a rail depot here since 1854, when the Jackson and Great Northern Railroad was first begun; the original depot was burned by Union forces in 1863, and the present depot dates to the 1890s.

These days the depot houses the **Country Market** (E. Pine St. and Railroad Ave., 985/386-9580), which sells homemade jams, jellies, breads,

candies, and other gourmet goods, including praline syrup, green-tomato jam, and fig preserves. Antiques and crafts are also available, and on display is a 1912 steam locomotive that was used during the town's heyday. An old mail car has been converted to an art gallery, and flying high above the depot atop a 177-foot pole is a massive U.S. flag, measuring 30 by 60 feet. One final curious sight here is a large caged-in pool of water in which you can observe Ponchatoula's resident alligator.

Manchac

For a quirky detour, drive south from Ponchatoula along I-55, and glance out to your left as you approach Manchac, a tiny fishing village largely accessible only by boat. You'll see numerous cottages dotting the swampland here, each with a small dock, all of them either supported on stilts or situated on the rare piece of high ground. Take the Manchac exit off I-55; follow the road to the right toward the lakeshore to reach Middendorf's Restaurant, one of the North Shore's best seafood restaurants. Follow Old U.S. 51 south over the Manchac Pass, and you'll find a little nest of activity on your left that includes a daiquiri bar and a rollicking little lounge called Gator's, which is also a debarkation point for swamp tours. Manchac is mostly the domain of local fishermen, and it has the feel of utter seclusion. It's hard to believe that New Orleans International Airport lies just 35 miles south.

Tickfaw State Park

Tickfaw State Park (27225 Patterson Rd., Springfield, 225/294-5020 or 888/981-2020, www.lastateparks.com, open 9 A.M.–dusk daily, admission $2 per vehicle) is at the end of a remote and twisting narrow road west of Springfield, in the middle of what seems like nowhere, about 15 miles west of Ponchatoula. This 1,200-acre park sits astride 3 miles of the Tickfaw River, and you can saunter along about a mile of boardwalk through the lush wetlands, which encompass four different ecosystems: cypress/tupelo swamp, bottomland hardwood forest, mixed pine/hardwood forest, and the Tickfaw River itself. You'll sometimes see heron and egrets swooping into the swamp to grab a crawfish snack. Other wildlife commonly seen in the park include turtles, snakes, wild turkeys, opossum, and wildfowl—and, rarely, you might spot a coyote, deer, fox, or beaver. Rent a canoe for the best chance to really dig deep into the swamp and see wildlife. A nature center (open 9 A.M.–5 P.M. daily) contains excellent exhibits on the park's flora and fauna, and park rangers lead interpretive walks through the swamp and present discussions in the park's amphitheater—call ahead for a schedule. Nighttime educational and entertainment programs are geared toward overnights guests; there are 14 air-conditioned cabins (each with two bedrooms and sleeping accommodations for up to eight persons), with fireplace, full kitchen, and bathroom. You'll also find 30 RV campsites and 20 tent sites. Just outside the park gate you'll find a sno-ball and ice cream stand, an eatery selling po'boys and other light fare, and a minigolf place.

Probably the favorite Hammond attraction is Kliebert's Turtle & Alligator Farm, one of the only alligator farms in southern Louisiana open to the public, a place where the animals are both raised and harvested. Louisiana bans hunting and poaching of alligators, so these farms help protect the species.

HAMMOND

The parish's largest community (with 18,000 year-round residents, another 16,000 college students throughout the school year, and thousands more retirees during the wintertime), Hammond lies just north of Ponchatoula and takes its name from an enterprising Swedish immigrant named Peter Hammond, who arrived in the 1820s and came up with a sappy idea upon observing the region's abundance of pine trees: He started a business that processed the resin from pine trees to make tar, pitch, turpentine, and coal. He also chopped down the trees and used the wood to barrels and kegs.

The city's growth didn't begin in earnest until 1854, when the Jackson and Great Northern Railway was run through Hammond—the tracks still extend through the parish, roughly parallel to U.S. 51 and I-55, from the western shoreline of Lake Pontchartrain to the Mississippi border at Kentwood. A slew of small manufacturing concerns grew up around Hammond following the arrival of the railroad. Perhaps the most successful was a shoe factory begun by Charles Emery Cate, which during the early part of the Civil War provided thousands of Confederate troops with footwear. It was likely for this reason that Union troops torched the community during their swing through the area in 1862. Hammond gradually rebounded and prospered following the war and incorporated as a city in 1889.

Today it's the commercial and residential hub of Tangipahoa Parish, home to one of the nation's fastest-growing colleges, Southeastern Louisiana University (SLU), and a burgeoning population of retirees. A virtual caravan of "snowbirds" arrives from the cold Midwestern states late each fall, working its way south down the I-55 corridor. Here the retirees rent houses or mobile homes, or park their own RVs at one of the many campgrounds set throughout the area. The mild climate and relatively low cost of living is a boon, as is being close enough to New Orleans to make frequent daytrips but far enough away to avoid the occasional inconveniences of urban life. Another reason for the popularity of Hammond with not only retirees but all people is that the city has a fast-growing health-care industry.

SLU formed in 1925 as Hammond Junior College and is nationally renowned for its top-notch Collegiate School of Business, as well as strong programs in industrial technology, nursing, and education. The campus dominates the area north and west of downtown, off Oak Street and University Avenue.

Like many North Shore towns, Hammond has worked hard at improving its downtown in

LOUISIANA ON FILM

Louisiana's lush landscape, antebellum plantation houses, and well-preserved urban areas make for breathtaking, often curious, and always memorable backdrops in motion pictures. It's no surprise that theLouisiana Office of Film & Video (www.lafilm.org) is one of the most aggressive in the country when it comes to attracting producers and directors.

One of the first and most colorful Louisiana films was a dramatization of the life of pirate Jean Lafitte, 1938's *The Buccaneer,* which starred Fredric Marsh and was directed by Cecil B. DeMille. Starlet Dolores del Rio starred in the famous Cajun tale *Evangeline* in 1929. Based on the Henry Wadsworth Longfellow poem about two young Acadian lovers separated during their peoples' expulsion from Canada, it was filmed in St. Martinville on the banks of Bayou Teche. Perhaps the most famous early classic filmed in the state is 1938's *Jezebel,* for which star Bette Davis won the Oscar for Best Actress. It was filmed in part around Lake Charles. Marlene Dietrich played a stunning French countess in the 1941 adventure comedy, *The Flame of New Orleans,* which was filmed in the Big Easy.

And in the category of "it's so bad it's good," Lon Chaney Jr. plays a live mummy accidentally dug up in a rural Louisiana bayou in *The Mummy's Curse* (1944). One of the oldest Tarzan movies, 1918's *Tarzan of the Apes* made use of the jungle terrain around Morgan City.

Few James Bond fans will ever forget the hair-raising boat chase through the bayous of Slidell in the 1973 007 thriller *Live and Let Die,* which opens with a traditional jazz funeral in New Orleans. The gripping family drama *Eve's Bayou* (1997), with Samuel L. Jackson and Lynn Whitfield, was shot in Covington, Madisonville, and Napoleonville.

Sometimes a Louisiana locale is stands in for another part of the South. Such was the case with the 1999 Melanie Griffith and Lucas Black comedy, *Crazy in Alabama*—which was actually crazy in Houma. One scene was set at Lafitte's Blacksmith Shop, the wonderful old Bourbon Street bar.

Dozens of other notable movies have been filmed in these parts. Here's a partial list:

- *A Streetcar Named Desire* (1951) with Vivien Leigh, Marlon Brando, Kim Hunter, and Karl Malden; filmed in New Orleans
- *Thunder Bay* (1953) with James Stewart and Joanne Dru; filmed Morgan City
- *King Creole* (1958) with Elvis Presley and Walter Matthau; filmed in New Orleans
- *The Long Hot Summer* (1958) with Paul Newman, Joanne Woodward, and Orson Welles; filmed in Clinton and Jackson
- *The Horse Soldiers* (1959) with John Wayne and William Holden; filmed in Clinton and Natchitoches
- *Hush . . . Hush, Sweet Charlotte* (1964) with Bette Davis and Olivia de Havilland; filmed in Baton Rouge, and at Houmas House Plantation in Burnside
- *The Cincinnati Kid* (1965) with Steve McQueen, Edward G. Robinson, and Ann-Margret; filmed in New Orleans and Covington
- *Nevada Smith* (1966) with Steve McQueen and Karl Malden; filmed in New Orleans, Baton Rouge, and Lafayette
- *Hotel* (1967) with Rod Taylor and Karl Malden; filmed in New Orleans
- *Easy Rider* (1969) with Peter Fonda and Dennis Hopper; filmed in New Orleans, Lafayette, and Morgan City
- *Sounder* (1972) with Teddy Airhart and James Best; filmed in Clinton, St. Helena Parish, and East Feliciana Parish
- *The Autobiography of Miss Jane Pittman* (1974) with Cicely Tyson and Teddy Airhart; filmed in Clinton

- *The Drowning Pool* (1975) with Paul Newman and Joanne Woodward; filmed on Oaklawn Plantation in Franklin, in Lafayette, and Lake Charles
- *Casey's Shadow* (1978) with Walter Matthau and Alexis Smith; filmed in Lafayette
- *Pretty Baby* (1978) with Brooke Shields, Keith Carradine, and Susan Sarandon; filmed in New Orleans
- *Cat People* (1982) with Nastassja Kinski and Malcolm McDowell; filmed in New Orleans and Slidell
- *The Toy* (1982) with Richard Pryor and Jackie Gleason; filmed in Baton Rouge, and Hammond
- *Tightrope* (1984) with Clint Eastwood and Genevieve Bujold; filmed in New Orleans
- *No Mercy* (1986) with Richard Gere and Kim Basinger; filmed in Baton Rouge and New Orleans
- *The Big Easy* (1987) with Dennis Quaid and Ellen Barkin; filmed in New Orleans
- *Blaze* (1989) with Paul Newman and Lolita Davidovich; filmed in Baton Rouge, New Orleans, Winnfield
- *Fletch Lives* (1989) with Chevy Chase and Hal Holbrook; filmed in New Orleans, Burnside, Gonzalez, Thibodaux
- *Sex, Lies, and Videotape* (1989) with James Spader and Andie MacDowell; filmed in Baton Rouge
- *Steel Magnolias* (1989) with Julia Roberts, Sally Field, Dolly Parton, Shirley MacLaine, and Olympia Dukakis; filmed in Natchitoches
- *Miller's Crossing* (1990) with Gabriel Byrne and Marcia Gay Harden; filmed in Hammond and New Orleans
- *Wild at Heart* (1990) with Nicolas Cage and Laura Dern; filmed in New Orleans
- *JFK* (1991) with Kevin Costner, Kevin Bacon, and Tommy Lee Jones; filmed in New Orleans
- *Passion Fish* (1992) with Mary McDonnell and Alfre Woodard; filmed in Elton, Jennings, and Lake Arthur
- *The Pelican Brief* (1993) with Julia Roberts and Denzel Washington; filmed in New Orleans
- *The Client* (1994) with Susan Sarandon and Tommy Lee Jones; filmed in New Orleans
- *Interview with the Vampire* (1994) with Tom Cruise and Brad Pitt; filmed at Lafayette Cemetery No. 1 and elsewhere in New Orleans; at Oak Alley Plantation in Vacherie; and in Shreveport
- *Dead Man Walking* (1995) with Susan Sarandon and Sean Penn; filmed in Angola Prison, Baton Rouge, New Orleans, and Slidell
- *Something to Talk About* (1995) with Julia Roberts and Dennis Quaid; filmed at Oak Alley Plantation in Vacherie
- *The Apostle* (1997) with Robert Duvall and Farrah Fawcett; filmed in Lafayette
- *Lolita* (1997) with Jeremy Irons and Melanie Griffith; filmed in New Orleans
- *Out of Sight* (1998) with George Clooney and Jennifer Lopez; filmed in Angola Prison and at Krotz Springs
- *Primary Colors* (1998) with John Travolta, Emma Thompson, and Larry Hagman; filmed in New Orleans and at Oak Alley Plantation in Vacherie
- *The Waterboy* (1998) with Adam Sandler and Kathy Bates; filmed throughout Louisiana
- *Double Jeopardy* (1999) with Tommy Lee Jones and Ashley Judd; filmed in New Orleans
- *Inspector Gadget* (1999) with Matthew Broderick and Rupert Everett; filmed in Baton Rouge
- *Monster's Ball* (2001) with Billy Bob Thornton and Halle Berry; filmed in Angola Prison, and LaPlace

THE NORTH SHORE

recent years, and today you'll find a good number of thriving independent eateries and shops, as well as an abundance of historic buildings, on either side of the rail tracks that split the district north–south. Art deco, Queen Anne, and Renaissance Revival styles dominate the architectural streetscape. Perhaps most striking is the 1912 Illinois Central Railroad Depot and, across the street, the Grace Memorial Episcopal Church. Also note the Central Rexall Drug Store at 125 Thomas St.; there's been a pharmacy here in this turn-of-the-20th-century building since 1917. Downtown's most famous building is the Columbia Theatre, which dates to the 1920s and was completely renovated and reopened in January 2002. It's a massive redbrick-and-limestone building with Jacobean and Renaissance Revival architectural elements. The very first talkie, *The Jazz Singer,* was screened here during the theater's earliest days.

Probably the favorite Hammond attraction is **Kliebert's Turtle & Alligator Farm** (41067 W. Yellow Water Rd., 985/345-3617 or 800/854-9164, www.klieberttours.com, open Mar.–Oct. noon–dark daily, admission $6). Kliebert (pronounced "klee-bair") is just southwest of town, easily reached by either the Highway 22 exit from I-55 or, if coming from the north, from Exit 28 off I-55; just follow signs from either exit, as it's a short drive from the interstate. It's best to call ahead to confirm hours and let them know you're coming. This is one of the only alligator farms in southern Louisiana open to the public. Louisiana bans hunting and poaching of alligators in the wild, so these farms raised and harvest the animals, helping to protect the wild species. All farms are required to return to the wild a significant percentage of the alligators born here. At Kliebert's you can get a first-hand look at the gators and turtles; there's also a sanctuary where egrets and heron nest in trees over the alligator habitats.

U.S. 51 NORTH

The string of small towns that extend along U.S. 51 north of Hammond offer little in the way of formal attractions, but there are a few worthy B&Bs and eateries. Also, from the town of Tick-faw, just north of Hammond, you can make the drive east on Highway 442 to reach two of the region's top attractions, the Global Wildlife Center and Zemurray Gardens.

Tickfaw

Tickfaw is a little bump of a village, although there's a very nice and affordable B&B in the center of town. From Tickfaw, you can follow Highway 442 and then Highway 40 for a total of about 10 miles to reach the immense **Zemurray Gardens** (23115 Zemurray Garden Dr., 985/878-2284, open six weeks each year, mid-March–mid-April, 10 A.M.–6 P.M. daily, admission $5), which is famous for brilliant stands of azaleas and a nature path that passes through a dense forest of magnolias, cypress and poplar trees, and flowers of all kinds. It also passes by Mirror Lake, and by lovely cast-bronze statues. Anchoring the garden complex is an early-20th-century Arts and Crafts lodge.

From Zemurray Gardens, continue east on Highway 40 for roughly another 4 miles to reach the **Global Wildlife Center** (26389 Hwy. 40, Folsom, 985/624-WILD, www.globalwildlife .com, open daily, admission $10). There are few more engaging and unusual sites in Louisiana, and yet relatively few visitors to greater New Orleans ever learn about, let alone visit, this remarkable facility, which is well worth the trip off the beaten path. The center covers some 900 rural acres, and once you're within the grounds, it's hard to imagine you're in Louisiana or even in North America—giraffes, zebras, antelope, llamas, camels, and some three dozen other species of mostly African wildlife (nearly 3,000 animals all together) roam freely across the property. You see the animals by boarding covered wagons, which are pulled across the grounds by tractors, in tours that last about 90 minutes.

There's really no set routine or path—the safari guides simply go where the animals are, and in many cases you're allowed to come extremely close to the wildlife. It's an excellent opportunity for photographers. Reservations are not required (except for groups), but visitors are asked to call an automated information line (985/796-3585) for the weekly-changing schedule of guided tours.

The center has a huge gift shop selling all manner of wildlife toys, prints, books, stuffed animals, and so on (proceeds benefit the care of the animals here) and a small concession stand; you can also buy little cups of feed, with which you'll have the opportunity to tempt some of the tamer animals close enough for a memorable photo op.

From the Global Wildlife Center, you can continue east on Hwy. 40 to reach the village of Folsom, which is described in more detail in the St. Tammany Parish section of this chapter, or you can return back to Tickfaw.

Amite

Amite (pronounced *ay*-meet) occupies the site of an important Choctaw Indian settlement along the Tangipahoa River—in fact, the last of the great Choctaw leaders of this area, Chief Baptiste, is said to have welcomed the earliest French settlers here. The derivation of the town's name has two theories: either it's the Choctaw name for "red ant" or it comes from the French for "friendship."

Amite grew to greater significance as settlers from the United States began visiting the region in the 1810s, and it became one of the railroad towns in the 1850s with the construction of the New Orleans, Jackson, and Great Northern Railroad. It grew popular during the summer with prosperous New Orleanians seeking cooler climes and fresh air, especially during the frequent plagues of yellow fever that swept through New Orleans. Most of the impressive summer retreats built here before the Civil War have burned or been torn down, but a few still stand. During the war, Union troops entered Amite and burned the rail depot and destroyed the tracks that led from the depot 10 miles north to Camp Moore. Amite served as a base for Union occupation during Reconstruction, following the war.

Amite became the seat of Tangipahoa Parish in 1869. The original courthouse still stands (it currently houses Cabby's Restaurant). The city boomed as a supply and trade center for southeastern Louisiana's cotton farmers, but it also became notorious through Reconstruction as the site of frequent political and economic unrest, fights, and assaults. By the middle of the 20th century, cotton farming gave way chiefly to dairy farms—Tangipahoa Parish leads Louisiana in milk production, as well as strawberry farming. One of the biggest industries in Amite today is oyster processing; the town hosts the popular Oyster Festival each March. It's also the home of an immense 24-acre foundry and machine shop that produces sugar mills, dock fittings, and marine decks.

You'll find a smattering of handsome early-20th-century buildings in the small downtown, which runs mostly along the rail tracks.

Tangipahoa

Right in the small village of Tangipahoa is **Camp Moore Confederate Museum & Cemetery** (U.S. 51, half a mile north of town, 985/229-2438, www.campmoore.com, open 10 A.M.–3 P.M. Tues.–Sat., admission $2), which was established in 1861 as the largest Confederate training camp in Louisiana during the Civil War (called the War Between the States in these parts). The camp trained some 6,000 to 8,000 soldiers at any given time, a total of at least 25,000. The cemetery here contains the graves of the nearly 1,000 soldiers who died of disease at the camp—two measles epidemics spread through the camp during its tenure. The camp was taken over by Union forces and shut down in fall 1864.

SHOPPING

Ponchatoula is Tangipahoa Parish's mecca for shopping, noted for its antiques shops set around the center of town. It's a great source of bargain-hunting—plenty of the high-end dealers on Magazine and Royal Streets in New Orleans are said to make trips up to Ponchatoula, buy goods here, and then resell them at higher prices in the French Quarter. Nearly 20 antiques shops make up Ponchatoula's impressive little downtown shopping district, all of them within a compact several-square-block area. The best strategy is to park your car in one of the spaces along Pine Street or Railroad Avenue and walk around. Most shops are along Pine Street, between about 8th and 3rd Streets, and most are open from about 10 A.M. till 5 P.M. Mon.–Sat. and from noon until 5 P.M. on Sundays.

Hammond Square Mall (off I-12, Exit 40, 985/542-1660) is the region's largest retail establishment, with about 50 mostly chain shops and Dillard's, Sears, and JCPenney anchor shops.

ACCOMMODATIONS

Situated at one of the South's pivotal interstate junctions, the meeting of I-55 and I-12, Hammond has dozens of chain motels, including a number of properties opened since the late '90s. With New Orleans just 60 miles south and Baton Rouge 50 miles west, and strong motel competition responsible for very competitive rates, this can be an ideal base for visitors to southeastern Louisiana. You'll also find a number of mostly reasonably priced B&Bs spread throughout the parish.

Hotels and Motels
Under $50: The **Econolodge** (2000 S. Morrison Blvd., Hammond, 985/542-9425 or 877/424-6423, www.econolodge.com) has the least expensive rooms of any of the reliable motels in the area. It's close to the junction of I-55 and I-12 and offers free continental breakfast; some rooms have refrigerators.

$50–100: Well-managed and with spacious rooms, the **Comfort Inn in Amite** (1117 W. Oak St., Amite, 985/748-5550 or 800/228-5150, www.comfortinnofamite.com) opened in 2001 and is the best chain lodging option in the northern half of the parish. It has a pool, fitness room, guest laundry, and complimentary hot breakfast.

Opened in 2002, the top-notch **Hampton Inn** (401 Westin Oaks Dr., Hammond, 985/419-2188 or 800/HAMPTON, www.hamptoninn.com) is just west of downtown off I-55 at U.S. 190. The three-story, interior-corridor property has 78 rooms, all with microwaves, refrigerators, irons/boards, and coffeemakers. There's also a coin laundry, business center, fitness room, and pool. The **Super 8 Hammond** (200 Westin Oaks Dr., Hammond, 985/429-8088 or 800/800-8000, www.super8.com) is an economically priced option right off I-55 and U.S. 190. The hotel opened in 2000 and has large, by budget-motel standards, rooms, some with refrigerators

and microwaves; there are several fast-food restaurants within walking distance.

Inns and Bed-and-Breakfasts
$50–100: In Tickfaw, the **G. W. Nesom House** (U.S. 51 at Hwy. 442, 985/542-7159, www.gwnesom.com) is a dramatic Eastlake-style Queen Anne Victorian with a hipped roof and a turret wing. Antiques fill the common areas, three guest rooms, and lavish Bridal Suite of this 1903 house, with sweeping first- and second-floor verandas. A full breakfast is included.

Built in the late 1930s, **Country Lane** (62058 Simpson Ln., Roseland, 985/748-9062, www.bbonline.com/la/countrylane) feels completely rural and secluded, yet it's just a couple of miles from I-55 and downtown Amite. The key draw is the stable with eight stalls and two grassy paddocks and access to some 500 acres of rolling country ideal for horseback riding. It's an easygoing B&B with four guest rooms and two suites, each done with country furnishings, quilts, and rather frilly curtains and fabrics. Some pets are permitted by arrangement.

In downtown Ponchatoula, steps from the antiques district, the **Guest House B&B** (248 W. Hickory St., 985/386-6275) offers a simple and comfortable accommodation. There's just one lovingly maintained cottage, complete with its own kitchen; it's filled with local antiques and is very private, making it ideal for a longer stay, or even to use as a base to explore New Orleans.

$100–150: Michabelle (1106 S. Holly St., 504/419-0550, www.michabelle.com) is a wonderfully decadent B&B on the south side of Hammond's historic downtown, on a tree-shaded street. This imposing white Greek Revival mansion adroitly blends classic French style with Old South charm. The four rooms are rife with late-Victorian antiques, oriental rugs, and gilt-framed paintings. There's an excellent restaurant, whose dining room has a trompe l'oeil ceiling of floating cherubs against a cerulean sky. The grounds are marked by lush gardens, and a three-tier fountain gurgles out front.

Camping
There are six campgrounds in Tangipahoa Parish.

Reliable options include **Hidden Oaks Family Campground** (21544 U.S. 190 E, Hammond, 985/345-9244 or 800/359-0940), which rents canoes and innertubes for use on its lake. Secluded **Tchefuncte Family Campground** (54492 Campground Rd., Folsom, 985/796-3654 or 888/280-1953, www.tchefunctecampground.com) sits along the serene Tchefuncte River; it's an ideal spot if you love swimming.

Indian Creek Campground & RV Park (53013 W. Fontana Rd., Independence, 985/878-6567) also rents cabins. The **New Orleans/Hammond KOA** (14154 Club Deluxe Rd., near I-55 at I-12, Hammond, 985/542-8094 or 800/562-9394) overlooks a small lake and offers a wide range of recreational activities, including a pool, minigolf, fishing, and volleyball.

FOOD

Tangipahoa Parish has fewer high-profile and high-end restaurants than St. Tammany Parish, but great dining is still very much a hallmark of the region, from down-home lunchrooms to family-style seafood and steak restaurants to a handful of trendier spots, found mostly in Ponchatoula and Hammond.

Upscale

Michabelle (1106 S. Holly St., Hammond, 504/419-0550, $16–22), a classy inn, also has a first-rate restaurant with both prix-fixe and á la carte menus. The dining options change often but might include rainbow trout with crabmeat served with a smoked-mussel cream sauce, followed by roast breast of turkey marinated with wild herbs and served with dried cherries and raisins. Chocolate pecan pie is a favorite way to finish things. Tucked inside a cozy 1880 cottage a few blocks east of the rail tracks in Hammond, the **Jacmel Inn** (903 E. Morris St., 985/542-0043, $13–20) is a romantic place for a special yet not necessarily super-expensive dinner. The kitchen turns out a mix of contemporary Creole, Cajun, and loosely Italian fare, including an exquisite starter of escargot served with mushrooms, brandy, ginger, and garlic butter. The bouillabaisse is a classically prepared main dish bursting with local seafood. Several pasta dishes and steaks are also offered.

Creative but Casual

C'est Bon (131 S.W. Railroad Ave., 985/386-4077, $6–12) is a great restaurant in Ponchatoula's downtown antiques district. Try the raspberry-baked brie or the stuffed quail; you can also get burgers and sandwiches, several pasta dishes (like crawfish lasagna), and a tasty bourbon-pecan chicken. The dining room is intimate and clubby, with dark-red wood paneling and exposed brick; it overlooks the rail tracks.

Wonderfully prepared, completely authentic regional Italian fare is served at **Ristorante da Piero** (116 W. Pine St., Ponchatoula, 985/370-6221, $11–22). The grilled *scamoza* cheese appetizer is exceptionally good, served with capers, anchovies, olive oil, and Tuscan bread. But save room for one of the main dishes, such as tender homemade gnocchi with gorgonzola, pancetta, and Roma tomatoes, or sea bass baked in a crust of sea salt. Da Piero favors the cuisine of Italy's Romagna region, and everything is rendered perfectly. On a typical night, Italian opera music is piped in softly through the inviting dining room filled with the owners' family photos and bits of memorabilia—the restaurant feels a bit like a sophisticated salon in a fine Italian home. There's also seating in a cozy loft overlooking the main room.

Tope lä (104 N. Cate St., Hammond, 985/542-7600, $12–28) is a glamorous little restaurant with an attractive young staff and an inviting bar, too, that's nice if you're dining alone. Deft preparation and fresh ingredients account for the success of kitchen. You might start with blackened alligator or potato hushpuppies with hot-pepper jelly, followed by Cajun-marinated duck breast tossed with artichoke hearts, sun-dried tomatoes, mushrooms, and penne in a light marinara sauce, or soft-shell crawfish Atchafalaya stuffed with crawfish and topped with hollandaise sauce. It's a popular lunch spot, too.

Seafood, Pizzas, and Pub Grub

In Independence, a small town between Tickfaw and Amite that's known for its tight-knit population of Italian immigrants, **Gina's** (319

M

THE NORTH SHORE

4th St., 985/878-9479, $4–8) is a tiny lunch spot that serves hearty, home-style fare, such as spaghetti, lasagna, and meatballs. It's only open for lunch, and it's a great place to observe the local color.

The **Country Village** (13101 Hwy. 442, Tickfaw, 985/542-7020, $6–10) works on an unusual concept. It's open only open Friday through Sunday nights, and there's one seating (make reservations); the table is yours for the entire evening. Dinner consists of a long buffet piled high with old-fashioned Southern favorites like fried chicken, ribs, country catfish, and sides of salad and vegetables. On a stage at the front of the dining room, a band plays country, Southern, or bluegrass gospel music while you enjoy your meal. It's a one-of-a-kind Louisiana experience. Out in the country near Folsom and the Global Wildlife Center, you'll find yet another unusual Louisiana culinary experience, **White's Steak & Fish House** (56034 Virgil White Ln., Husser, 985/748-3710, $6–12), a long, low, and rather drab bunkerlike building in a blip of a village called Husser. It's about a 30-minute drive northeast of Hammond, and it's only open Thursday through Saturday evenings. But people come from miles around to sample the steak and seafood, served from a buffet. There's no alcohol.

In downtown Ponchatoula, **Paul's** (100 E. Pine St., 985/386-9581, $3–9) is a bare-bones lunchroom with paneled walls, Formica tables, and a few stools at the counter. The place is known for strawberry daiquiris (a favorite potable in this parish known for strawberry farms), great breakfasts, and rather ordinary diner cooking, such as barbecued chicken, red beans and rice, or stuffed crab. It's nothing fancy, but you can count on honest home cooking and friendly service. In the tiny fishing village of Manchac, south of Ponchatoula off I-55, **Middendorf's Seafood** (30160 U.S. 51, 985/386-6666, $6–14) serves perhaps the freshest seafood in the state, from platters topped with fried oysters, shrimp, and crab to po'boys. The modest dining room has varnished wooden walls and a sprinkling of nautical photos and prints.

Ethnic

La Carreta (108 N.W. Railroad Ave., Hammond, 985/419-9990, $7–14) is a very attractive and hip Mexican eatery by the rail tracks in Hammond, a favorite of college students and yuppies. There's a big redbrick patio with a fountain, and inside, the high-ceilinged space is decked with colorful serapes. This is a great alternative to the cookie-cutter eateries out near the interstate. Steak burritos with green salsa, shrimp fajitas, chiles rellenos, and carnitas are among the kicky offerings. There's live music on Wednesdays.

The most distinguished Asian restaurant in the parish is **Trey Yuen** (2100 N. Morrison Blvd., Hammond, 985/345-6789, $8–15), offering well-prepared Chinese food that has garnered some national attention. It also has a branch in the St. Tammany Parish town of Mandeville.

Quick Bites

Lee's Grill (401 W. Thomas St., 985/345-3091, $4–10) is a slice of retro Louisiana. This great old building with a stainless-steel facade was a real drive-in way back when; now you can eat inside (although there's still a take-out window and lots of parking). Specialties include banana splits, seafood platters, po'boys, half-pound burgers, and very good salads.

Java Joints

The popular New Orleans chain **P.J.'s Coffee & Tea** (224 W. Thomas St., 985/345-1533) has a bright and upbeat location in downtown Hammond, a short drive from the university (and, as you'd expect, it draws plenty of student types). You can get the usual coffees and teas, plus already-prepared Greek and chef's salads, cookies, bagels, and sandwiches.

Picnic Supplies and Gourmet Goods

Independence's rich Italian heritage is evident when you stop by **Blaise's A Taste of Italy** (315 4th St., 985/878-1951), which specializes in homemade ricotta, anise, and almond Italian cookies, and delicious liqueur cakes made with run, amaretto, or hazelnut or peach brandy.

ENTERTAINMENT AND NIGHTLIFE

The college town of Hammond contains the lion's share of area bars and nightspots—this part of the North Shore isn't a major nightlife hub, but there are a few engaging hangouts, including **Chevy's** (1905 Nashville Ave., 985/542-2745), a popular dance club, and **Wall Street Grill and Bar** (216 W. Thomas St., 985/543-0682), a dark and cozy hangout with live folk and rock music.

Hammond is also home to the beautifully restored 900-seat **Columbia Theatre** (220 E. Thomas St., 985/543-4366, www.selu.edu/newsevents/columbia), an elegant 1928 building that now serves as the city's and Southeastern Louisiana University's premier performing arts center. Events here include pop concerts, performances by the Louisiana Philharmonic, and both touring and local plays and musicals.

FESTIVALS AND EVENTS

Tangipahoa Parish hosts several of the state's better-attended events, and if you don't mind the occasionally intense crowds, these can be an excellent time for a visit.

The **Strawberry Festival** (www.lastrawberryfestival.com) constitutes a number of events that take place in and around Hammond from February through mid-April, but the main celebration occurs that final weekend and includes a car show, parade, road race, history exhibits, crafts, food, and so on. Strawberry Festival events leading up to the big weekend include talent shows, dances, a jambalaya cook-off, and other family-oriented fun. This is considered to be one of the nation's largest three-day festivals.

The **Amite Oyster Festival** (985/748-5161) takes place in mid-March at the Tangipahoa Parish Fairgrounds; the bivalve is celebrated and sampled over this weekend-long event. In late April, the town of Independence celebrates its immigrant heritage with the **Italian Festival** (985/878-1902), a great opportunity to sample tasty foods and enjoy music and crafts demonstrations.

Major **Fourth of July** fireworks celebrations are held in Hammond and Ponchatoula.

Oktoberfest (Le Fleur de Lis Complex, Ponchatoula, www.oktoberfestponchatoula.com) is a big event in Tangipahoa Parish; it's one of the largest such celebrations in the state. The **Tangipahoa Parish Free Fair** (Tangipahoa Fairgrounds, Amite, 985/878-3890) draws crowds in early October for games, food, and music. And Hammond hosts the popular **Louisiana Renaissance Festival** (985/429-9992, www.larf.org) each November.

INFORMATION AND SERVICES

Visitor Information

The towns in this region are served by the **Tangipahoa Parish Convention & Visitor Bureau** (42271 S. Morrison Blvd., Hammond, 985/542-7520 or 800/542-7520, www.tangi-cvb.org).

Getting Around

Tangipahoa Parish sits at the crossroads of I-12, connecting Baton Rouge to Slidell, and I-55, which connects New Orleans to Mississippi. As with St. Tammany Parish, a private car is indispensable for exploring the area. Very few accommodations are within walking distance of sights and restaurants, and there are no practical public transportation options.

Practicalities

MEDIA

Tambalaya Magazine (985/892-8768, www.tambalaya.net) is a free monthly with the scoop on live music and entertainment on the North Shore, chiefly in St. Tammany Parish. As for conventional newspapers, most people in these parts rely on New Orleans's **Times-Picayune** (www.nola.com), although Hammond also has a daily newspaper, **The Daily Star** (www.hammondstar.com). Nondaily papers on the North Shore include **The News Banner** (www.tamnet.com), in Covington; the **Ponchatoula Times** (www.ponchatoula.com), in Ponchatoula; and the **Sentry-News** (www.tamnet.com), in Slidell. New Orleans's jam-packed alternative newsweekly **Gambit Weekly** (www.bestofneworleans.com) also has plenty of coverage on dining, nightlife, events, and attractions on the North Shore.

GETTING THERE

The North Shore is at the junction of four interstates: I-10, I-12, I-59, and I-55. This makes driving here from a number of key points—New Orleans, the Gulf Coast, Baton Rouge, Birmingham, and Jackson, Mississippi—extremely easy and direct. From New Orleans you can come either by way of I-10, which deposits you at the east end of the region in Slidell, or by way of the Lake Pontchartrain Causeway, which places you more centrally in the area. Note that there's no toll for crossing this bridge from south to north, toward the North Shore, but you will be charged a toll of $2 for crossing north to south. Driving here is your best bet; you need a car to really explore this region,.

New Orleans International Airport is very close to the Lake Pontchartrain Causeway on the South Shore—the drive from the airport to Mandeville takes about 45 minutes. **St. Tammany Tours** (800/543-6262) runs shuttle buses from the airport to the North Shore, available 24 hours by reservation. The cost is $27 per person, one-way.

Greyhound (800/231-2222, www.greyhound.com) connects several towns along the North Shore to New Orleans and New Orleans International Airport, although transfers are sometimes necessary. Towns on the North Shore served by Greyhound are Amite, Hammond, Mandeville, Ponchatoula, and Slidell. **Amtrak** (800/USA-RAIL, www.amtrak.com) has two trains that pass through the region. The *Crescent* stops in Slidell on its daily run between New Orleans and New York City—it connects the region to Hattiesburg, Mississippi; Birmingham; Atlanta; and Washington, D.C. The *City of New Orleans* stops in Hammond during its daily run between New Orleans and Chicago, with other major stops including Jackson, Mississippi, and Memphis.

The Great River Road

A drive along the Great River Road reveals some of the most striking and curious contrasts between the past and the present, and rural life and industry, that you'll find anywhere in the country. The name Great River Road, in southern Louisiana, does not refer to just one highway but rather a series of roads running along both sides of the Mississippi River, from New Orleans up through the rural plantation country northwest of the city on through the state capital, Baton Rouge, and then up to the charming old-world towns of St. Francisville and New Roads. Just a bit north of here, the east bank runs into the Mississippi state border, and the river continues to function as a state border for about 2,000 miles until it cuts into interior Minnesota.

When most people in these parts refer to the Great River Road, they're speaking most specifically of the stretch that begins west of New Orleans, about where I-310 crosses the Mississippi River, and that ends south of Baton Rouge, around the towns of Plaquemine and Sunshine.

the Alley of the Oaks,
Oak Alley Plantation, Vacherie

The city of Baton Rouge falls squarely between the two sections of river known for Louisiana's most dramatic antebellum plantation houses. North of Baton Rouge, St. Francisville is a delightful and well-preserved southern river town that feels grander and more inviting than any of the towns along the stretch of River Road between New Orleans and Baton Rouge. It's really its own ball of wax, and nearby New Roads, which is situated along a false river (a former bend in the Mississippi that naturally cut itself off over time), is often visited with St. Francisville.

You may have already heard a bit about the striking plantation homes that dot the Great River Road, from relatively modest raised cottages to enormous Greek Revival wedding cakes with dozens of outbuildings and rows of 200-year-old live-oak trees draped with hanging moss. This is no myth. The region is rife with these fabulous homes. And therein lies one of the first notable contrasts. You can leave the big and crowded cities of New Orleans and Baton Rouge and, in less than 30 minutes, find yourself standing on a plantation with more acreage than the French Quarter and fields of sugarcane for as far as the eye can see.

But the Great River Road, even in the sparsely populated areas, is not exactly quaint, or frozen in time. Along considerable stretches of the road, you'll see huge and in places alarming reminders that you're in a state whose economy is more dependent on heavy industry than sugarcane. Oil refineries, chemical plants, and other fortresses of mining and manufacturing line the river, sometimes within a stone's throw of old plantations. The peculiar juxtaposition is fascinating even when it's not very scenic.

Another reminder that the days of paddle-wheel riverboats and quiet agrarian living have long since passed is the high grassy levee that runs virtually uninterrupted along the Mississippi River, all through Louisiana and right up into the states to the north. As you drive along the still narrow, still mostly peaceful River Road, you can't actually see the river. Back in the 1870s, folks could sit out on the veranda at Oak Alley or Nottoway plantations, sipping mint juleps and watching the steamboats chug up and down the

river. No more. On the other hand, in the 1870s, you had to worry about floods wiping out crops, destroying or damaging homes, and otherwise tearing up the landscape.

The levee system effectively bound the Mississippi River, whose course had changed gradually but constantly for thousands of years, into a permanent straitjacket, and it largely eliminated the threat of floods. The levee is an attraction in itself, and in many spots dirt roads lead up over the levee to the batture (pronounced "batch-er," no doubt to the horror of French-speaking persons everywhere), a term that describes the strip of land between the riverbank and the levee. Here on this fertile and regularly flooded area you'll often find populations of deer or, in many areas, cattle grazing. There's a path along the top of the levee in most places, on which you can jog, walk, or ride a bike.

Well into the 19th century, the Mississippi River was the main highway, of sorts, between New Orleans and Baton Rouge, and even with improved roads and then automobile transportation, travelers still had to ride along the twisting, narrow lanes hugging the tight curves of the river well into the 20th century. Governor Huey Long finally pushed through construction of a straight and wide road, the Airline Highway, between New Orleans and Baton Rouge in the 1930s. This diverted traffic, commerce, and people from many of the towns along the River Road.

In the 1950s, the industrial plants began building their hulking structures along the river, and population actually grew rapidly in places, although never nearly to the density found in Baton Rouge or New Orleans. Eventually, an even faster, wider, and more direct highway was built between the two cities, I-10. The River Road was left looking like a rural byway from the Depression era, pockmarked with dozens of huge ships and fringed by massive levees. That's the road you see today. It's not quaint, you can't see the river from your car, but it's still a fascinating place for a roadtrip.

One thing to keep in mind as you visit sites on both sides of the river: The ferry is a charming way to switch back and forth across the Mississippi—it's a short ride, although it doesn't always run as often as people would like. There are several ferry crossings along the Mississippi, as well as several bridges. Fares on ferry boats and tolls on bridges are only collected when crossing westbound.

In addition to the plantations described in this chapter that are open for tours, the River Road passes within view of a number of additional properties not open to the public, but worth taking a look at from the street. You can obtain a detailed driving-tour map and brochure, "Up a Lazy River," which pinpoints many sites and towns along the Great River Road, from any of the offices of tourism in parishes along the river between New Orleans and St. Francisville. You can also see this map online at www.lariverroad.com.

Plantation Country

The most popular part of the Great River Road for most visitors to New Orleans is the stretch from Destrehan, near I-310, to just below Baton Rouge. It's about a 100-mile drive if you travel the roads hugging the curve of the river (whereas, as the crow flies, it's a distance of only about 60 miles).

There aren't a great many attractions along this span, and relatively few places to stay and eat, but you could definitely spend three full days exploring all the plantations open for tours and frequenting some of the better places to stay and eat. As a single-day excursion from New Orleans, you'd be wise to focus your explorations on the west bank communities of Vacherie (home to Laura and Oak Alley Plantations) and Donaldsonville (which has some great places to eat and is close to Nottoway Plantation). If you have just a couple of hours to spare, you can still get a feel for the area by visiting a plantation close to New Orleans, Destrehan.

For a more substantial River Road exploration, consider spending one or two nights at one of the plantations or B&Bs in the area (these are mostly around Vacherie and Donaldsonville). There's also a modern Best Western in Donaldsonville, and a few chain hotels in Gonzales and Sorrento, two suburbs along I-10 between Baton Rouge and New Orleans, an easy drive from most of the plantations.

DESTREHAN

One of the oldest house-museums on the Great River Road, and also one of the nearest to New Orleans, **Destrehan Plantation** (13034 River Rd., Destrehan, 985/764-9315, www.destre-hanplantation.com, open 9 A.M.–4 P.M. daily , admission $10) was built in 1787, although the sweeping Greek Revival mansion you see today, with its eight front columns and double galleries, is the result of a major renovation and expansion in the 1830s. Robin de Logny commissioned the construction of the house, hiring a freed mulatto named Charles (no last name is known) to build it; this process took three years, and de Logny died just two years after moving in. The estate passed into the hands of de Logny's son-in-law. Jean Noel Destrehan, a French aristocrat, bought the house and added the twin wings on either side of the facade in 1810. He and his brother-in-law, Etienne de Boré (the first mayor of New Orleans), earned fame for perfecting a means of granulating sugar, thus helping to turn southern Louisiana into one of the top sugarcane farming regions in North America. De Boré owned a plantation several miles downriver, in what is now the Audubon Park section of New Orleans. Details still visible in this rambling structure include hand-hewn cypress timbers and the distinctive hipped roof typical of West Indies architecture. The house is just 25 miles west of New Orleans, and a mere 10-minute drive from New Orleans International Airport, making it popular with visitors who don't have time to explore the entire River Road but would still like to see a grand Louisiana plantation.

GRAMERCY

San Francisco Plantation (2646 River Rd., Garyville, 985/535-2341 or 888/322-1756,

THE GREAT RIVER ROAD

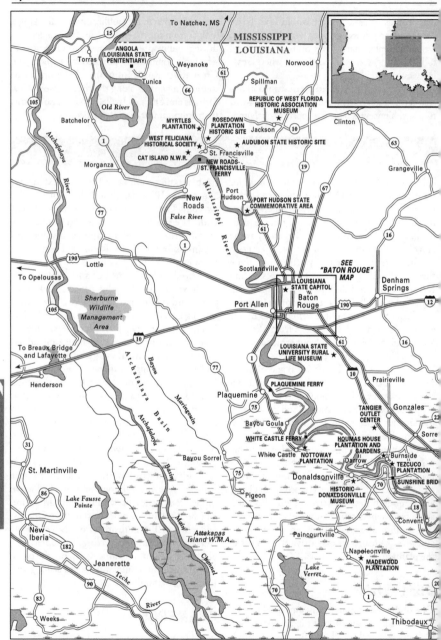

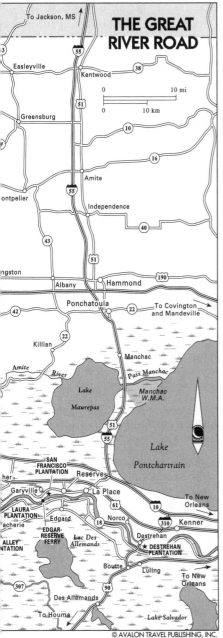

THE GREAT RIVER ROAD

To Jackson, MS

Easleyville

Kentwood

0   10 mi

0   10 km

Greensburg

ontpelier

Amite

Independence

ngston

Albany   Hammond

Ponchatoula   To Covington and Mandeville

Killian

Manchac

Amite   River   Pass Manchac

Lake   Manchac W.M.A.

Maurepas

Lake Pontchartrain

SAN FRANCISCO PLANTATION   Reserves

her

Garyville   La Place   To New Orleans

LAURA PLANTATION   Edgard   Norco   Kenner

acherie

EDGARD RESERVE FERRY   Lac Des Allemands   Destrehan

ALLEY NTATION   DESTREHAN PLANTATION

Boutte

Luling   To New Orleans

Des Allemands

To Houma   Lake Salvador

© AVALON TRAVEL PUBLISHING, INC.

www.sanfranciscoplantation.com, open 9:30 A.M.–5 P.M. daily, admission $10) sits on the east bank of the river, about 25 miles upriver from Destrehan. The house was constructed by Edmond Bozonier Marmillion in 1856, and it's considered the only plantation on River Road that has been authentically restored to its original appearance. The exquisite hand-painted ceilings in five rooms are an important detail, but also note the extensive faux marbling, and the fine antiques made by Mallard and John Henry Belter.

VACHERIE

Oak Alley Plantation (3645 Hwy. 18, Vacherie, 225/265-2151 or 800/44-ALLEY, www.oakalleyplantation.com, open 9 A.M.–5 P.M. daily, admission $10) is about 15 miles upriver, and across the river (take the bridge from Gramercy), from San Francisco Plantation. One of the best photo ops in the South, this incredible alley includes 28 live oak trees, planted in two rows bordering the front walk. Dating back some 300 years, these trees have been here much longer than the present mansion, which is beautiful but certainly wouldn't stand out as it does today without the graceful, arching trees framing it. An early French settler, clearly with some aristocratic aspirations, planted the oaks in the early 1700s, to lead from the river down a path to his rather modest house. More than 100 years later, the property's owner, Jacques Telesphore Roman, used his considerable sugarcane fortune to construct the present Oak Alley mansion. The entire property now comprises about 25 acres; much of the original plantation, which had been well over 1,000 acres, is now undeveloped forest, but about 600 acres is still leased to sugarcane farmers.

As you approach the property, you'll pass the rather modest front gate that marks the beginning of the alley of oaks; you can't enter the property here, as the actual driveway for automobiles lies a short distance farther down the road (just follow the signs). But you can park your car along the dirt driveway leading up and over the Mississippi River levee, and walk up to the gate to snap a picture and admire the trees and the house in the distance. If you walk up the short dirt drive to the top of the levee, you get a very nice view of the river—there's often a tanker or freighter chugging along, contributing to that peculiar contrast between modern industry and 19th-century plantation living that characterizes the whole region. Once you drive onto the grounds, you buy your tickets at a booth and proceed to the Big House, as the mansion is called, for a guided tour. The tours themselves are fairly straightforward and not overly exciting, unless you happen to get an especially colorful guide. But following the tour you can spend as much time as you care to exploring the grounds and relaxing amid the oaks, crape myrtles, and azaleas, or admiring the peacocks and friendly bobtail cats wandering about the property.

One of the best photo ops in the South, this incredible alley includes 28 live oak trees, planted in two rows bordering the front walk. Dating back some 300 years, these trees have been here for much longer than the present mansion.

The plantation has been in several movies, including *Primary Colors,* where it served as the home of Larry Hagman's would-be presidential candidate; at the front gate, before the alley of oaks, the characters of Governor Jack Stanton (John Travolta) and Henry Burton (Adrian Lester) meet with Hagman's Governor Fred Picker. The plantation was also featured prominently in the film of Anne Rice's *Interview with the Vampire* in 1994, starring Tom Cruise and Brad Pitt; in the Julia Roberts vehicle *Something to Talk About;* and in the 1985 made-for-TV adaptation of William Faulkner's *The Long Hot Summer.* Oak Alley has a popular breakfast/lunch café and bed-and-breakfast, and RVs may park on the ground overnight for $10; there are no hookups or campground services and facilities, however, so RVs must be entirely self-contained.

Just downriver from Oak Alley you can embark on one of the most unusual plantation-tour experiences in the country, **Laura: A Creole Plantation** (2247 Hwy. 18, Vacherie, 225/265-7690, www.lauraplantation.com, open 9 A.M.–5 P.M. daily, admission $10) differs from most of the others along River Road in a couple of ways. First, it has a fascinating legacy, as its slave cabins were

where the folktales known as *Br'er Rabbit* were recorded in the late 1870s. A young man named Alcée Fortier, who lived near Laura, took a great interest in the stories recounted by former slaves living on the plantation, and he set about writing down the tales exactly as he heard them here on the plantation. Fortier went on to become a professor at Louisiana State University where he published the collection of stories under the title *Louisiana Folktales.* His friend Joel Chandler Harris then published the considerably more famous *Tales of Uncle Remus,* based on his interviews with slaves in the Carolinas and Georgia. The stories came to be known as the *Br'er Rabbit* tales because one of the two main characters in Fortier's and Harris's collections was Lapin (French for "rabbit").

But maybe the most interesting thing about a visit to Laura is that tour guides base their one-hour talk on the memoirs—which total some 5,000 pages—of the four generations of women who oversaw the compound's inner workings; it's a condensation of the fascinating life of the Creole women who ran the plantation, along with intimate and telling details about their children and extended family and their slaves. The memoirs were compiled in the 1930s by Laura Locoul Gore, who grew up on the plantation and represents the final generation of women at Laura. The tour of Laura offers a provocative and colorful look into the high and low points of Creole life in the early 19th century. At most of the other plantations in this area, tours discuss the original owners, the architecture of the house, and its basic history, but these tours often are based on general second- and third-hand information, and they rarely discuss the lives of the slaves and the day-to-day, firsthand observations of the plantation's occupants.

Another difference at Laura is the plantation house itself, which is not one of the typical glowing white Greek Revival mansions found in this region, but rather a relatively modest though still

Oak Alley Plantation

large raised Creole house that has been, intentionally, only partly restored in order to give guests a more realistic sense of what the house looked and felt like when it was occupied by Laura and her ancestors. As good as this museum is, the quality of your tour varies from guide to guide, as is true at all plantations, but most of the interpreters here do a very nice job.

DONALDSONVILLE

Donaldsonville is a neat little river town with a bustling historic district and many significant commercial and residential structures, both large and small. The town has a handful of good restaurants and places to stay and makes a good base for exploring this whole region, as it's just about 60 miles upriver from New Orleans, 35 miles downriver from Baton Rouge, and within 25 miles of Oak Alley on one side and Nottoway on the other.

The town's latest attraction is the **River Road African-American Museum** (Williams and Lessard Streets, 225/474-5553, www.africanamericanmuseum.org, open 9 A.M.–5 P.M. daily, admission $4), which moved here in September

2003 from a smaller building at Tezcuco Plantation, which was lost in a fire in summer 2002. (Luckily, the African-American Museum itself wasn't lost in this fire, but the grounds at Tezcuco are no longer open to the public.) At this new museum you'll find a wide variety of exhibits and collections related to the River Road's rich African-American heritage. These include a monument to the many black soldiers who fought for the Union during the Civil War at Fort Butler, right in Donaldsonville, on the banks of the Mississippi (another organization plans to restore the site of Fort Butler and turn it into a museum and national historic park). Also on display is a tribute to Leonard Julien, who in 1964 invented the sugarcane planting machine, an innovation that vastly reduced the number of men, wagons, and tractors necessary to plant a field of sugarcane. And you'll learn about Madam C. J. Walker, who became America's first female self-made millionaire by inventing a hair-care product in 1900. The museum pays tribute to the thousands of slaves who were brought to towns along the Great River Road, and displays artwork, African masks, exhibits on musicians, and many other documents and photos.

You can learn more about the general history of the area at the **Historic Donaldsonville Museum** (318 Mississippi St., 225/746-0004, open 10 A.M.–4 P.M. Mon.–Fri., by appointment weekends, donation suggested), which is housed with the stately Italianate Lemann Store Building. A variety of artifacts, including some from the original Lemann department store, are displayed, as well as a replica of the town's old movie theater, a re-created corner grocery store, and a gallery of collectibles and keepsakes donated by local townspeople over the years.

The nearest plantation to Donaldsonville is just across the river and then a few miles downriver. The setting of the Bette Davis film *Hush . . . Hush, Sweet Charlotte*, stunning **Houmas House Plantation and Gardens** (40136 Hwy. 942, River Rd., Burnside, 225/473-7841 or 888/323-8314, www.houmashouse.com, open 10 A.M.–5 P.M. daily—closes an hour earlier Nov.–Jan., admission $10) includes two adjacent grand homes, an 1840 Greek Revival and a 1790s colonial, set on an extensive property of oak-shaded grounds. Each house contains antiques and furnishings from the period. At the plantation's peak, it encompassed some 20,000 acres of sugarcane crops. An Irishman named John Burnside bought it for the princely sum of $1 million in 1858 and promptly declared his immunity during the Civil War, on the grounds that he was a British subject. Union forces honored the declaration and left Burnside and his house alone during their march up the Mississippi River from New Orleans to Baton Rouge. By the end of the century, a new owner, Colonel William Porcher, increased sugarcane production to 20 million pounds per year, more than any other operation in the state. Houmas House fell gradually upon hard times during the early 20th century but the house and remaining grounds (much of the property was subdivided and sold off over time) were bought by George B. Crozat in 1940, and he set about restoring the place. Hollywood came calling in the early 1960s.

A bit farther downriver, one of the Great River Road's most popular plantation homes, **Tezcuco Plantation** (3138 Hwy. 44, Burnside, 225/562-3929), was completely lost in a fire in May 2002.

The outbuildings, which includes some small museums and several bed-and-breakfast accommodations, were spared but were not, as of this writing, open to the public. One museum on the site, the River Road African-American Museum, moved into a bigger and better facility in Donaldsonville in September 2003.

NAPOLEONVILLE

If you're not in a rush, consider making a detour to this small town on Bayou LaFourche, which you reach via either Highway 70 (if you're coming from Vacherie on Highway 18 or from the East Bank by way of the Sunshine Bridge) or down Highway 308 (if coming from downtown Donaldsonville). The draw here is **Madewood Plantation** (4250 Hwy. 308, Napoleonville, 504/369-7151 or 800/375-7151, www.madewood.com, open 10 A.M.–4:30 P.M. daily, admission $6), a 21-room Greek Revival mansion from 1846 that's most famous as a bed-and-breakfast but is also open for tours. The mansion is finely appointed, but tours are relatively simple and it's probably not worth coming all the way here simply to see the house, unless you're considering staying overnight or you happen to be passing through the area, perhaps en route between Thibodaux and Donaldsonville. That being said, tours are less pricey here than at some of the larger plantations.

WHITE CASTLE

Famous because it's the largest plantation home in the South, the 65-room **Nottoway Plantation** (Hwy. 1, Whitecastle, 225/545-2730, www.nottoway.com, open 9 A.M.–5 P.M. daily, admission $10) is one truly immense Greek Revival mansion, with an interior of about 53,000 square feet. John H. Randolph built this wedding cake of a house in 1859, where it acted as the centerpiece of a 7,000-acre sugarcane plantation. A favorite of tour groups, Nottoway is also heavily in the business of events and weddings; it functions as a small hotel, with 13 rooms, and has a popular restaurant. It's a marvel, but you probably won't come away with the same intimate sense of the place as you might at Laura or one of the smaller and lower-key properties in the region. Nottoway lies about 12 miles upriver from Donaldsonville, on the same side of the river.

FESTIVALS AND EVENTS

Aside from its tourist following, this area is strung with villages and towns with low populations, and big gatherings and festivals are few and far between. Some of the plantations have annual events, such Oak Alley's **Spring Arts and Crafts Festival** in late March, and Laura Plantation's **Br'er Rabbit Folk Festival** in October. A few towns have rather modest Mardi Gras parades, including Lutcher and Gramercy. Donaldsonville hosts the **Sunshine Festival** (225/473-4814, www.sunshinefestival.com) each November, a country fair with live bands, local foods, a "kiddie land" with rides, and arts and crafts. Christmas is one of the best times to explore the River Road, as on many evenings towns along the river hold **Christmas Bonfire** parties throughout December, during which participants enjoy food and music as they build huge piles of wood. By Christmas Eve, the more than 100 bonfires constructed along the river are set ablaze. Check the website www.festivalofthe-bonfires.org for details. Oak Alley also joins in the fun with its own Christmas bonfires twice in early December. The bonfires are a longtime Louisiana tradition along the river. Some say the tradition was begun as a way to welcome the Cajun version of Santa Clause, PaPa Noel, while others suggest that the fires were lit to help travelers along the river on Christmas Eve make their way to midnight mass.

SHOPPING

In LaPlace, **Jacob's World-Famous Andouille** (505 W. Airline Hwy., 985/652-9080 or 877/215-7589, www.cajunsausage.com) is the original source for this Louisiana treat. You can stop inside the shop, that's been going strong since the 1920s, or buy smoked meats and other gourmet ingredients via the web or mail-order.

Just off I-10 in Gonzales, a suburb between New Orleans and Baton Rouge that's just 10 miles north of Donaldsonville and close to a cluster of chain hotels and restaurants, **Tanger Outlet Center** (Hwy. 30 at I-10, 225/647-9383 or 800/406-2112, www.tangeroutlet.com) is a favorite diversion for shopaholics. Among the scores of chain outposts here are Bass, Gap, Guess?, Jockey, Jones New York, Levi's, Liz Claiborne, Samsonite, Nine West, Corning Revere, and Mikasa.

ACCOMMODATIONS

There aren't a tremendous number of lodging options along the Plantation Country section of the Great River Road. If you prefer the anonymity and value of a modern hotel, your only centrally located choices are in the towns of Gonzales, just off I-10, and Donaldsonville, a bit farther south. But you can stay on the premises of some of the historic plantations, and at Nottoway and Madewood, you can actually book a room inside the main house.

Hotels and Motels

$50–100: Just on the west bank of the river near the Sunshine Bridge, Donaldsonville's **Best Western Plantation Inn** (2179 Hwy. 70, 225/746-9050 or 800/528-1234, www.bestwestern.com) is a modern and appealing base with clean and attractive rooms with colonial-inspired furnishings. The setting off Highway 70 is unremarkable but inoffensive. The 62 rooms have microwaves, refrigerators, and hair dryers, and continental breakfast is included. There's also a pool and guest laundry.

Convenient to I-10, about midway between Baton Rouge and New Orleans, the **Holiday Inn Gonzales** (1500 Hwy. 30, Gonzales, 225/647-8000 or 800/946-5432, www.holidayinn gonzales.com) is also very accessible to the plantations on River Road—about 20 miles from Oak Alley, and just 10 from Donaldsonville. There are 171 rooms, plus a fitness center and pool; continental breakfast is included. A branch of the excellent local seafood chain Mike Anderson's is on premises.

Inns and Bed-and-Breakfasts

$100–150: There are five comfortable guest units in turn-of-the-20th-century cottages on the grounds of **Oak Alley Plantation** (3645 Hwy. 18, Vacherie, 225/265-2151 or 800/44-ALLEY, www.oakalleyplantation.com). Don't be put off by the simple white exteriors of these attractive but plain cottages; the richly furnished, antiques-filled interiors capture the warmth and history of plantation living on the River Road, and most units have full kitchens. The rooms do not have phones or TVs. A full country breakfast is included.

One of the most charming places to stay in the area, **Lafitte's Landing at Bittersweet Plantation** (404 Claiborne Ave., Donaldsonville, 225/473-1232, www.jfolse.com) offers five luxury suites with such creature comforts as CD players and VCRs; a refrigerator and minibar stocked with complimentary red and white wine, soft drinks, and other goodies; and in some cases working fireplaces and Jacuzzi tubs. Attached is John Folse's famed Lafitte's Landing restaurant.

You can't beat the location of **Bay Tree Plantation B&B** (3785 Hwy. 18, Vacherie, 225/265-2109 or 800/895-2109, www.baytree.net), next to Oak Alley and right on River Road, if it's the Plantation Country you're aiming to see. Rooms are in two buildings and a separate and quite luxurious cottage; all have private baths, some with whirlpool tubs. Fainting couches, lavish carved-wood beds and furnishings are all part of the appeal. All units have cable TV and plush robes. The Roman Suite has a master bedroom and one smaller room with a double bed—it's ideal for couples and families, and it was Brad Pitt's home away from home when he was in the area filming *Interview with the Vampire*. This plantation was built in the 1850s by a relative of Oak Alley owner Jacques Roman. Full breakfast, complete with Louisiana's famous Community Coffee, is included.

$150–250: Nottoway Plantation (Hwy. 1, Whitecastle, 225/545-2730 or 866/LASOUTH, www.nottoway.com), the largest plantation house in the South, has 13 guest rooms, set among the main house, the boys' wing, and the overseer's cottage. If it's a special occasion, you might consider booking the Master Bedroom Suite, which contains the original bedroom furnishings of the house's builder and first owner, John Hampton Randolph. There are two other large and beautiful suites, including the Bridal, which has three rooms, a Jacuzzi, and a private pool; and the Randolph, an airy third-floor room with clear views over the Mississippi. The catch with the Randolph and the Master Bedroom Suite are that they're open during the day for tours, meaning that you must check out by 9 A.M. and can't check in until 5 P.M. Other rooms range from a modest and cozy room with a sleigh bed to one of the huge original bedrooms, with a fireplace and a grand mahogany four-poster double bed. A complimentary guided tour of the house along with full breakfast are included, and overnight guests may also explore the house on their own in the early evening, and enjoy the oak-shaded grounds and large swimming pool.

Over $250: One of the grand plantation homes that also offers overnight accommodations, **Madewood** (Hwy. 308, Napoleonville, 800/375-7151, www.madewood.com) sits along Bayou LaFource, about 20 miles from Donaldsonville and the Mississippi River. It's just 15 miles northwest of Thibodaux, making it a good base if you're planning to explore both the Great River Road and Houma's Cajun wetlands. Madewood stands out among other plantations offering overnight stays for a couple of reasons. Five of the guest rooms are set right in the mansion, and even the three located in the Charlet House, an 1830s Greek Revival raised cottage, feel highly romantic if less ornate. Second, overnight accommodations here include an evening wine-and-cheese reception followed by dinner with your fellow guests at a long oak dining room table. After this you can retreat to the parlor for coffee or a liqueur before sleeping off the huge and elaborate meal in order to make room for breakfast. Staying here is a social experience, insofar as meals are concerned, but also a romantic one, as the rooms are truly spectacular, with high ceilings, tall four-poster beds, long flowing drapes, Oriental rugs, and fine ceiling medallions and plaster moldings. There are no phones or TVs in the rooms of this 1846 mansion.

FOOD

You won't find a vast number of restaurants along the River Road between New Orleans and Baton Rouge, but there are a few nice options, especially around Donaldsonville. It's also a fairly short drive up to the I-10 towns of Gonzales and Sorrento to find a wide variety of chain and fast-food restaurants.

Traditional Creole and Cajun

In White Castle, the grand **Nottoway Plantation** (Hwy. 1, 7 miles south of Plaquemine, 866/LASOUTH, $14–25) presents fine if not especially exciting old-Louisiana cooking in its resplendent and stately dining room, called Randolph Hall. Prime rib of beef au jus, crawfish étouffée, smoked and grilled quail, and blackened crab cakes over eggplant are favorite dishes. The adjacent Randolph Parlor is a civilized place to wind down an evening, perhaps over cordials or cigars.

Cafe LaFourche (817 Bayou Rd., 225/473-7451, $11–20) is an attractive steak and seafood house in downtown Donaldsonville. It's a simple but elegant place with a black-and-white floor, a good bet for authentic and reasonably priced Cajun fare. The 16-ounce "swamp steak" (a rib eye topped with fresh seafood) is a house specialty, but don't overlook the platter of shrimp, scallops, and oysters with spicy marinara sauce over angel hair pasta, or the soft-shell crab smothered with crawfish étouffée. Fried seafood platters, po'boys, and a very good turtle soup are also offered, and sticky pecan cheesecake ranks among the tastiest desserts.

Creative and Contemporary

Lafitte's Landing at Bittersweet Plantation (404 Claiborne Ave., Donaldsonville, 225/473-1232, $16–27) is one of the only restaurants in these parts where you can get a meal that's as complex, imaginative, and expertly rendered as at just about any of the top contemporary restaurants in New Orleans—make this your destination when you're celebrating. Owner and head chef John Folse is one of the state's culinary wizards, having produced books and hosted TV and radio cooking shows. His cooking mixes Cajun, Creole, and Old South traditions with many recipes of today. The menu changes often, but you might consider the starter of pan-seared venison napoleon layered with roasted sweet potatoes and a port demi-glace; or the roast beet and crab salad with tarragon mayonnaise. Typical entrées include mahimahi St. James (a grilled fillet served with chipotle cream over arugula and topped with grilled shrimp) and pan-seared duck breast over white beans and andouille-corn dressing, with a peach glaze. Meals are served in a gracious dining room with period wallpapers, gilt mirrors, a fireplace, and tables set with fine linens and china.

Casual Cooking

The Cabin (Hwys. 22 and 44, Burnside, 225/473-3007, $6–17) is as much a museum of the area's Cajun culture as it is a restaurant. Walls of this former slave cabin (circa 1850), with its original cypress roof, are papered with old newspapers, as was the tradition in the 19th century. The rustic dining room is packed with interesting memorabilia, including vintage farming tools, old paintings, and furniture. There's also dining in an inviting courtyard out back. This is a great place to try blackened redfish, a Louisiana specialty that's prepared to perfection here. Also try the soft-shell crab, shrimp scampi, pork sausage, barbecue beef po'boys, and crawfish omelets.

Nobile's (2082 W. Main St., Lutcher, 225/869-8900, $6–14) offers a nice range of homestyle Louisiana favorites, from country steaks to fresh shrimp—it's not fancy, but the chef uses only the freshest vegetables and ingredients. The restaurant occupies a handsome 1870s building and for years provided sustenance to the many workers employed in the area's cypress industry.

Loyal fans insist that nobody prepares fresher seafood in this part of the world than **Hymel's** (8740 Hwy. 44, Convent, 225/562-9910, $8–20), a zero-ambience roadhouse where you can dive into boiled crawfish and crabs, fried shrimp and oysters, and fresh oysters on the half-shell.

Quick Bites

Right by Laura Plantation, **B&C Cajun Restaurant** (2155 Hwy. 18, Vacherie, 225/265-8356, $5–12) serves some of the tastiest seafood around, including wonderful oyster po'boys, fried alligator, and seafood gumbo. **D.J.'s Pizza** (Hwy. 20, Vacherie, 225/265-7600, $6–14) serves a nice range of pizzas, plus meatball po'boys, pastas, and leafy salads.

It's open only for breakfast and lunch, but the cheery café at **Oak Alley Plantation** (3845 Hwy. 18, Vacherie, 225/265-2487, $5–13) serves top-notch victuals, from chicken fricassee and shrimp Creole to seafood po'boys and a tempting dessert of bread pudding with whiskey sauce. Blue Bell brand ice cream is served in Oak Alley's Plantation Cafe. In Gramercy, **Dimm's Bakery** (Main St., 225/869-8381, $3–8) serves delicious po'boy sandwiches, plus pastries, doughnuts, fresh-baked bread, and other goodies. It's a great snack break between plantation hops.

Java Joints

In LaPlace, a branch of the acclaimed New Orleans–based coffeehouse chain **P.J.'s** (301 Union Ct., 985/651-0072) serves designer drinks, great sandwiches, and excellent pastries and desserts. It's just off Main Street, about 2 miles north of the East Bank of the river, and 2 miles south of Exit 209 off I-10.

INFORMATION AND SERVICES
Visitor Information

For information on Gramercy, Lutcher, Vacherie, and Convent, contact **St. James Parish Tourism**

BONNET CARRÉ SPILLWAY

The only real break along the Great River Road levee south of Baton Rouge occurs about 25 miles upriver from New Orleans, near the small town of Norco. Here the Bonnet Carré Spillway acts as a floodgate protecting New Orleans from a devastating flood. The Mississippi River actually sits at a higher elevation than the land around it, including New Orleans and Lake Pontchartrain. The Bonnet Carré Spillway is situated at a point where the river passes close to Lake Pontchartrain, just under 6 miles from its southwestern shore. The spillway connects to a floodplain of about 8,000 acres, which is crossed by I-10, U.S. 61, and rail tracks, all of which are elevated on stilts. If the river gets too high, the floodgates at the Spillway can be opened to divert water from the river across the floodplain and into Lake Pontchartrain, sparing New Orleans and other cities downriver. Except during times of flooding, when the gates are partially or entirely opened, you can drive across the paved road that runs across the floodplain, parallel to the spillway.

The floodplain over which water is diverted to Lake Pontchartrain is about 8,000 acres, and it was chosen not only because it was a short distance between the lake and the river, but because it had already been compromised four times by major floods along the river. The Bonnet Carré Spillway was built following one of the worst floods in the state's history, a 1927 wash that rendered the levee useless. Work on the $14 million project commenced in 1929 and was completed two and a half years later.

Operated by the Corps of Engineers, the Spillway is opened when either the river flow or the height of the river is severe enough that it stresses the levee system. This can happen even when the floodwaters have not risen very far. If waters rise even to a moderate flood stage for a prolonged period, they can saturate the earthen levees, which may begin to erode away. Thus far, the spillway has been opened nine times, in 1937, 1945, 1950, 1973, 1975, 1979, 1983, and 1997.

Bonnet Carré isn't the only major structure of its kind in Louisiana; well upriver from Baton Rouge, near the town of Morganza, the Morganza Floodway can be opened to divert water across a flood plain and into the Atchafalaya Swamp basin.

(P.O. Box 106, Convent, 225/562-2358 or 800/FOR STJAMES, www.stjamesla.com). The **Ascension Parish Tourist Commission** (6470 Hwy. 22, Suite A, Sorrento, 888/775-7990, www.ascensiontourism.com) handles tourism in the towns of Gonzales, Sorrento, Darrow, and Donaldsonville. Tourism for Destrehan and Luling are handled by the **St. Charles Parish Department of Economic Development and Tourism** (P.O. Box 302, Hahnville, 985/783-5140, www.stcharlesgov.net/tourism). Check in with the **Iberville Parish Tourist Commission** (23405 Church St., Plaquemine, 225/687-5190, www.parish.iberville.la.us) for information on Plaquemine, Sunshine, and White Castle.

Tours

New Orleans Tours (4220 Howard Ave., New Orleans, 504/212-5951 or 866/596-2698, www.notours.com) is one of the leading and most reliable operators for tours from New Orleans out to the plantations. It offers a variety of half- and full-day bus excursions out to Laura, Oak Alley, and other antebellum homes along the River Road.

GETTING AROUND

This is a part of the state with little or no public transportation but a very good network of roads, so plan to visit the area using a car. If you're staying in New Orleans, check with your hotel concierge or bed-and-breakfast for information on companies that offer half- or full-day tours out to some of the plantations.

To access the lower towns along the Great River Road from New Orleans, follow I-10 west to I-310, and exit onto Highway 48 (Exit 6), which puts you right by Destrehan. From here, you can follow Highway 48 northwest along the east bank of the river, or you can cross the I-310 bridge and follow Highway 18 along the west bank. Keep in mind that River Road is not just one road—it's a combination of numbered highways that run alongside both banks of the Mississippi River. So as you drive along, it's best to have a map with you and to stick with the roads that hug the river, not just to a particular route number.

Along the west bank, Highway 18 is the River Road for many miles, as far as Donaldsonville, but north of that, the river's west bank is traced by Highway 405 and Highway 988 up to Port Allen, opposite Baton Rouge. Along the east bank from Destrehan, the river is traced by Highway 48, then Spillway Road across the Bonnet Carré Spillway (which can be closed due to high water and flooding, in which case traffic is detoured along the interior to U.S. 61 Airline Highway), and then along Highways 628, 636, 44, 942, 75, 141, 75 again, and then 991 clear to Baton Rouge. Several bridges and ferries connect roads on either bank of the river between Baton Rouge and New Orleans, making it very easy to get back and forth.

The highlights of the River Road are mostly in St. James and Ascension Parishes, which are about midway between New Orleans and Baton Rouge. If you're planning to spend most of your time in this area, around Donaldsonville and Vacherie, it's quickest to drive up I-10 for 50 miles to Exit 182 (Sorrento), and then follow Highway 22 for 10 miles down to Donaldsonville, or follow Highway 70 (off Hwy. 22) 7 miles over the Sunshine Bridge to Hwy. 18, which leads another 15 miles to Vacherie. From the Hwy. 22 exit off I-10, it's about 30 miles to Baton Rouge, and 85 to Lafayette.

One thing to keep in mind about Highway 22, on the chance that you're also planning to spend time in the New Orleans North Shore area, near Hammond and Mandeville, is that you can take this winding country highway all the way from Donaldsonville through Sorrento (rather than hopping onto I-10) and through the Amite River area up to the antiques mecca of Ponchatoula, and eventually to Mandeville. It's a scenic, twisting drive past bayous and river homes, and it's a nice alternative to the interstates. Total mileage from Donaldsonville to Ponchatoula via Highway 22 is 50 miles, and the drive takes about 90 minutes. You'd save about 15 minutes if you went by way of I-10 to I-55, but that drive is 65 miles and much less interesting.

See the *On the Road* chapter for details on reaching New Orleans and Baton Rouge from other parts of the country by train, plane, and bus.

THE GREAT RIVER ROAD

Baton Rouge and St. Francisville

Technically, it would be fair to describe St. Francisville as being the northernmost community of the Great River Road's Plantation Country, but this leafy, dignified town near the Mississippi border actually looks and feels a bit different from the other communities with plantations along the road. The terrain is hilly and studded with pine and hardwood forest, and the plantation homes here are not set along the levee but rather back a few miles on or near the region's main highway, U.S. 61.

This picturesque town is also separated from the Plantation Country described above by Louisiana's state capital and second-largest city, Baton Rouge, a largely corporate and industrial community that has a handful of excellent museums and attractions in its downtown, which is in the midst of a serious urban makeover. It makes good sense to visit Baton Rouge en route to St. Francisville, which lies about 45 minutes north of it. Baton Rouge has dozens of chain hotels and motels, plus a wide range of restaurants; it's an affordable place to stay, but its accommodations generally lack character. St. Francisville has fewer services, lodgings, and restaurants, but those you will find here tend to be historic or, at the very least, representative of the area's history and architecture.

Two small communities within a short drive of St. Francisville, New Roads and Jackson, also bear exploration. If you only have one or two nights to visit this part of the River Road, focus on St. Francisville if it's Louisiana's antebellum plantations that most interest you. If you're more interested in museums, and especially if you have kids in tow, try to spend at least an afternoon in Baton Rouge.

BATON ROUGE

Unfortunately, there aren't too many back ways to drive from New Orleans to Baton Rouge—you can take the old Airline Highway (U.S. 61), but most of the stretch is commercially robust, with numerous traffic lights and no real sense of the towns you pass through. You can also bypass the I-10/U.S. 61 corridor and slip up along the stretch of the Great River Road described above, but this really only makes sense if you give yourself a full day or even an overnight stop and explore some of the plantations and related diversions. Without stops, the drive from Baton Rouge to New Orleans along the River Road takes several hours—and just imagine that before Huey Long rammed through the Airline Highway, this was the only road between the two cities.

Baton Rouge is more of the typical new Southern city than New Orleans. It sprawls in virtually every direction, not necessarily unpleasantly. Many of the older, outlying residential neighborhoods are quite charming to drive through, and in general, Baton Rouge feels clean, prosperous, but perhaps lacking a distinct identity all its own. It's a political city and a collegiate city, and government and education provide its personality more than the streets, buildings, and topography. But you'll find a few of Louisiana's most enriching and engaging attractions in Baton Rouge: the Capitol, the Rural Life Museum, the Old State Capitol, and U.S.S. *Kidd* are first-rate, well worth planning an overnight here. If you only have time to pass through the city en route elsewhere, it is possible to see these four attractions in a half-day.

Once the seat of the state government, the **Old State Capitol** (100 North Blvd., 225/342-0500 or 800/488-2968, www.sec.state.la.us, open 10 A.M.–4 P.M. Mon.–Sat., noon–4 P.M. Sun., admission $4) was constructed in 1850 and is one of the state's few prominent examples of large-scale Gothic architecture. Inside you'll find a vast and wonderfully presented warren of interactive and multimedia exhibits on a wide variety of topics, including Huey Long's assassination, the history of elections and campaigns in Louisiana, the Louisiana Purchase, citizenship and voting, and state history. It's the sort of museum that's as enjoyable for kids as for adults, and the variety of documents, artifacts, collectibles, and curios displayed here is impressive.

The **U.S.S. *Kidd*** (Government Street and S. River Road, 225/342-1942, www.usskidd.com, open 9 A.M.–5 P.M. daily, admission $6) is the only ship anywhere on exhibit that's still in its wartime camouflage paint. This World War II-era Fletcher-class destroyer was awarded 12 battle stars for serving during World War II and the Korean War; it was struck by a Japanese kamikaze plane during the WWII Battle of Okinawa—an attack that killed 38 members of the *Kidd*'s crew. It has been carefully restored and can now be toured, along with two military aircraft from past wars, an exhibit on *Old Ironsides* that includes a full-size section of the U.S.S. *Constitution*'s gun deck, and the largest model-ship collection in the South.

The **Louisiana State Capitol** (State Capitol Dr., off N. 3rd St., 225/342-7317, www.crt.state .la.us, open 8 A.M.–4:30 P.M. daily (observation deck closes at 4 P.M.), admission free), a nifty 34-story art deco wonder, was completed in January 1932 and took 14 months to build, with a price tag of about $5 million (not exactly chump change

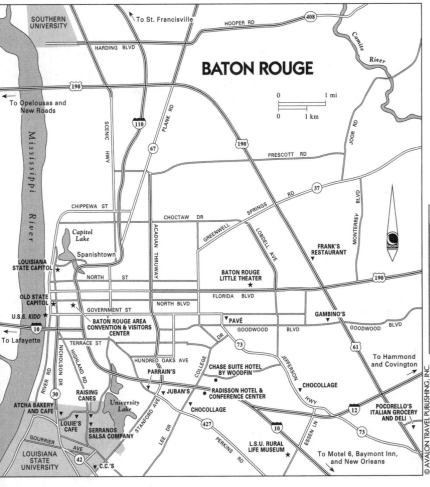

THE GREAT RIVER ROAD

© AVALON TRAVEL PUBLISHING, INC.

the Louisiana State Capitol, Baton Rouge

in those days). It is, at 450 feet, the tallest U.S. capitol building. One of the highlights of a visit here, and a surprising number of visitors seem to overlook it, is touring the 27 acres of spectacularly landscaped gardens. You can also ride the elevator to the 27th-floor observation deck, which affords spectacular views of the countryside, and look around the entrance and the chambers (when the state congress is not in session), and see exactly where flamboyant governor and U.S. Senator Huey P. Long was assassinated.

A historic residential neighborhood just east and south of the Capitol Building, **Spanishtown** is worth a drive or walk through to admire the 19th- and early-20th-century wood-frame houses.

North of the Capitol grounds and downtown, the river is lined with massive oil refineries, their towers lighted like newfangled Christmas trees at night—it's a striking display of lights, and although it's enormously industrial and maybe even unpleasant to look at by day, the nighttime view is almost artful.

A fourth important attraction in Baton Rouge, the **Louisiana State University Rural Life Museum** (4650 Essen Ln., just south of I-10, 225/765-2437, http://rurallife.lsu.edu, open 8:30 A.M.–5 P.M. daily, admission $7) is a shor drive southeast of downtown. This living-history museum is set on the 450-acre **Burden Research Plantation,** and is dedicated to preserving and interpreting the lifestyles and cultures of pre-industria Louisiana. Numerous buildings and exhibits show different aspects of early Louisiana living, including a grist mill, sugarcane house and grinder, church schoolhouse, blacksmith shop, and outdoor oven Inside a large barn you can examine tools and vehicles spanning more than 300 years. There are a few historic houses that reveal Louisiana's rich tradition of folk architecture, which was common in rural areas during the state's earliest years. You can also tour the extensive Windrush Gardens, a 25-acre plot of semiformal gardens abundant with winding paths, ponds, and flora found typically in 19th-century plantation gardens. Special events are held all year round, during which docents offer demonstrations using some of the vintage farming and household equipment.

ST. FRANCISVILLE

St. Francisville is the second-oldest incorporated town in Louisiana, although it was born out of rather inauspicious beginnings. Back in the 1730s, Spanish Capuchin monks developed a small settlement across the Mississippi River in what is now Pointe Coupee Parish (home to the town of New Roads). The monks found, however, that they could not develop a reliable burial ground on this side of the river, because its low elevation left it vulnerable to frequent floods, which washed away the cemetery. The monks began rowing the bodies of the deceased across the Mississippi and burying them on the relatively high bluffs that now form the foundation for downtown St. Francisville.

A permanent settlement was established in 1785 when the King of Spain issued land grants in an effort to settle a large area north and west of New Orleans, which came to be called the Distrito de Nueva Feliciana, part of the colony of Spanish West Florida. The small town of St. Francisville was formally laid out along the very same bluff the Capuchin monks found so useful. Below the proper town of St. Francisville, down

United Methodist Church, St. Francisville Historic District

the hill from the bluffs, a second settlement known as Bayou Sara thrived during the early 19th century, as the small bayou for which it was named provided a safe anchorage for flatboaters transporting goods down the Mississippi. Cotton and other trade made Bayou Sara the most important port on the Mississippi between Natchez and New Orleans by 1860, but the Civil War, a fire, major floods, and the onset of the railroad industry rendered Bayou Sara a virtual ghost town by the end of the 19th century.

St. Francisville was not affected by the misfortunes of its neighbor down the hill; rather, many of the men who earned vast riches in the Mississippi River shipping industry built fancy homes along the bluff and even further inland. Today St. Francisville's lovely historic district contains nearly 150 structures built during the town's shipping heyday, during the 19th century. Some of these houses are quite large, and the district contains a wide range of Victorian residential styles. It's an easy neighborhood for a walk, flat and with little street traffic. Among the buildings preserved here are three of the state's most beautiful churches, the **Our Lady of Mt. Carmel Roman Catholic Church** (on the west end of the district, just off Ferdinand Street), which was completed in 1893 according to a design by Civil War Confederate General P. G. T. Beauregard; the **Grace Episcopal Church** (further east along Ferdinand), which was built in the Gothic style in 1858; and the **United Methodist Church** (Royal and Fidelity Streets), a stately 1899 structure.

Many of the houses in this district have magnolia and other flowering trees lining the sidewalks and perimeters of their yards, or ornate iron fences. These aren't all mansions, as a number of charming smaller cottages are mixed in with the larger homes. It's truly one of the prettiest neighborhoods to stroll through in Louisiana. Down the hill from the district you can see what remains of Bayou Sara, including a handful of modest cottages and shotgun houses and a 19th-century rail station and warehouse that now house a deli and gift shop.

Along the main drag, Ferdinand Street, you'll find a number of antiques shops, as well as the

ANGOLA: THE LOUISIANA STATE PENITENTIARY

About 25 miles northwest of the beauty and gentility of St. Francisville is perhaps the most notorious (at least historically) prison in the United States, Angola, which has been dubbed the "Alcatraz of the South," among many less flattering things. These days, Angola has been reformed, and its notoriety has died down, but it's still the largest state prison in the country—definitely not a place you want to spend time involuntarily.

In its effort to clean up, Angola has created the quite interesting and surprisingly forthcoming **Louisiana State Penitentiary Museum** (follow Hwy. 66 from U.S. 61, 225/655-2592, www.angolamuseum.org, open 8 A.M.–4:30 P.M. Mon.–Fri., 9 A.M.–5 P.M. Sat., and 1–5 P.M. Sun., donation suggested), which examines the facility's history as well as its onetime reputation as the "bloodiest prison in America."

The 18,000-acre prison sits in a bend of the Mississippi River, surrounded on three sides by water and by the gently rising Tunica Hills on the other; it's just a few miles south of the Mississippi border. Much of Angola is farmland, and inmates are required to work the fields five days a week, eight hours a day. Corn and soybeans are the main products grown here, but there are many other crops, plus a herd of cattle numbering about 1,500.

One of the best times to plan a visit is October; every Sunday of that month, the prison hosts the **Angola Rodeo** (225/655-2030, www.angolarodeo.com), which was begun in 1965 and is the longest-running prison rodeo in the country. The event takes place in a 7,500-seat stadium, and professional judges and rodeo stock are brought in—this is no amateur show. In the late '90s, an arts-and-crafts show was added, which takes place beginning at 9 A.M. (the rodeo doesn't start until 2 P.M.) and includes a variety of wares and decorative items produced by inmates. This, like the rodeo itself, has become a phenomenally popular event. In 2001, the rodeo expanded to run on two Sundays each April, as well as on the four Sundays in October. Tickets to the rodeo cost $10, and proceeds go to cover expenses and also into a fund that provides for education and recreational supplies for inmates at Angola.

The museum and the rodeo notwithstanding, Angola's legacy is a grim one. The prison was run privately when it was founded in 1844, then occupied by Union troops during the Civil War, and then run privately again by a Confederate general named Samuel James from 1869 until 1900. Brutality was rampant in these years—it's reported that the average lifespan of inmates at Angola was just five years.

The state took over Angola in 1901, but medical treatment and living conditions remained poor for many years. Music played a vital role for many Angola inmates, the most famous being the blues pioneer Leadbelly, who served time here for brandishing a knife during a fight. Leadbelly's blues music was so well-received that it caught the attention of record makers, who recorded his hit "Good Night Irene" here while the promising talent served his time. Leadbelly was soon freed from prison, and in the late 1930s he developed a tremendous musical reputation in New York City and later Paris.

Amazingly, for some 50 years, Angola operated with no paid guards. Instead it was staffed with so-called "trusty guards," favored inmates who were furnished with weapons and were notorious for ignoring or perpetuating prison violence. In the 1960s and early '70s, stabbings, beatings, and deadly fights were commonplace, occurring once a day on average.

Angola began its most dramatic period of reform in 1973, when it eliminated the "trusty guard" system and began changing many of its policies. It finally obtained accreditation from the American Correctional Association (ACA) in 1993. Angola's most recent claim to fame is that it incarcerated Matthew Poncelet, whose plight inspired the Susan Sarandon and Sean Penn movie *Dead Man Walking*.

West Feliciana Historical Society (11757 Ferdinand St., 225/635-6330), which doubles as the tourist information center for West Feliciana Parish. Inside you can pick up brochures and examine historic photos, documents, and memorabilia that tell the story of St. Francisville and Bayou Sara.

St. Francisville has a handful of plantation homes open to the public for tours, the most famous and prominent being **Rosedown Plantation State Historic Site** (12501 Hwy. 10, 225/635-3332 or 888/376-1867, www.lastateparks.com, open 9 A.M.–5 P.M. daily, admission with house tour $10; gardens and grounds only $5), on the east side of downtown, right off U.S. 61. Built by one of the nation's wealthiest men of his day, Daniel Turnball, this neoclassical columned manor house was constructed in 1834 as the centerpiece of a massive cotton plantation that at one time totaled nearly 3,500 acres and required the labor of some 450 slaves. Turnball furnished his palace with the finest furnishings from Europe, the East Coast, and New Orleans. He also laid out, over time, some 30 acres of formal gardens.

Rosedown remained in the Turnball family for a remarkably long period by Louisiana plantation standards, until 1956, despite the fact that the family lived in near-poverty following the Civil War, leasing much of the land to sharecroppers. Descendants of Turnball lived in the second-floor quarters of the house even after opening the plantation to visitors for touring beginning in the 1930s. The remaining heirs sold the house upon the death of Turnball's last direct descendent, Nina Turnball, in 1956, and the new owner, Catherine Fondren Underwood, set about restoring the home as near to its original appearance as possible. The plantation now encompasses 371 acres and includes the mansion as well as several outbuildings. State park staff and volunteers give guided tours.

One of the more colorful attractions in town is **Myrtles Plantation** (7747 U.S. 61, 225/635-6277 or 800/809-0565, www.myrtlesplanta-tion.com, open 9 A.M.–5 P.M. daily, admission $10), which bills itself among the most haunted houses in the United States. It's also operated as a bed-and-breakfast, so if you're curious about ghosts, here's your chance to spend the night among, as legend has it, several of them. Apart from this considerable lure, the 1796 house is notable for its hand-painted stained glass, Aubusson tapestry, Baccarat crystal chandeliers, Carrara marble mantels, and gilt-leaf French furnishings. Little expense seems to have been spared in its construction. Engaging historical tours that touch on the house and its grounds are given during the day, but the considerably more colorful Mystery tours offered on Friday and Saturday evenings are the real draw.

Many of the houses in this district have magnolia and other flowering trees lining the sidewalks and perimeters of their yards, or ornate iron fences. It's truly one of the prettiest neighborhoods to stroll through in Louisiana.

St. Francisville's leading attractions aren't all manmade. **Cat Island National Wildlife Refuge** (off Ferdinand Street in the Bayou Sara section of town, 225/635-4753, http://southeast.fws.gov /CatIsland, open dawn–dusk daily, admission free), which was established in fall 2000, is a favorite haunt of hikers, wildlife photographers, fishing enthusiasts, and others who appreciate being out in the wilderness. The 10,000-acre expanse of forested wetlands sits along the southernmost unleveed span of the Mississippi River, and most years it floods completely, usually between December and June. Vehicles are prohibited on refuge roads during periods of flood. The refuge's greatest resource is its wildlife, from black bears and white-tailed deer to bobcats and river otters. Fish commonly caught in the preserve's waters include largemouth bass, bream, and catfish.

Technically in Jackson but actually close to downtown St. Francisville, which is about 10 miles north, **Port Hudson State Commemorative Area** (236 U.S. 61, Jackson, 225/654-3775 or 888/677-3400, www.lastateparks.com, open 7 A.M.–9 P.M. daily, admission $2 per car) was built in memory of what's been dubbed the "longest true siege in American military history." During the Civil War, in response to a Union

THE GREAT RIVER ROAD

effort to control the Mississippi River and thereby split the Confederacy into two distinct geographic halves, Confederate forces built a military fortification on the river bluffs at the tiny town of Port Hudson. On May 27, 1863, the Union army, with some 30,000 troops and fresh from victory in Baton Rouge, began a fierce attack on the 4.5-mile string of earthwork fortifications manned by some 6,800 Confederates. The South managed to hold their ground for an amazing 48 bloody and tragic days of fighting that saw casualties in the thousands on both sides. Upriver, however, the city of Vicksburg fell to Union hands, so Confederate commander Franklin Gardner, realizing the defense of Port Hudson was now a moot point, negotiated a surrender, thus ending the siege.

Today at Port Hudson there's an extensive state park preserving the original fortifications and interpreting the battle in a museum. Living-history events and war re-enactments are held throughout the year. Other features include 6 miles of trails.

New Roads

To reach New Roads from St. Francisville, you head west on Ferdinand Street about a mile past Our Lady of Mt. Carmel church to the ferry landing at the end of the road (clearly marked signs point the way). Take the ferry, which runs frequently from early morning until midnight and costs $1 westbound (the direction you travel to get to New Roads); the ride is free eastbound.

New Roads is a small, dapper village that looks like a classic Mississippi River town, except for one thing: it's not on the Mississippi. The long, curving body of water on which the town is situated is the False River, which was formed when a sharp S-shape bend in the Mississippi River, which essentially doubled back on itself, was breached when the river took a more direct course. The remaining 22-mile curve, now cut off from the river, became what's called an oxbow lake. New Roads sits along the False River's west bank, and many stately Creole-style houses and commercial buildings in town overlook the water, which is popular for boating and swimming. Because it's not a flowing industrial river constantly muddied from silt and soil on the river bottom, the False River is an appealing shade of blue.

In New Roads's scenic little downtown you'll find a smattering of shops and eateries, notably some excellent antiques shops, all along a quite walkable little strip on Main Street. There are no formal museums in town, but you can obtain a free self-guided walking/driving tour from the Pointe Coupee Parish Chamber of Commerce.

Jackson

After exploring St. Francisville and New Roads, if you have time, consider making the enjoyable side trip east to Jackson from St. Francisville via Highway 10 (a distance of about 12 miles). There are a few historic sites and antiques shops you can look at in Jackson, a bump of a village that has a frozen-in-time feel and some interesting old buildings (including a town hall crowned by an onion dome).

Up a block from Main Street is the **Republic of West Florida Historic Association Museum** (College and High Streets, Jackson, 225/634-7155, open 10 A.M.–5 P.M. Tues.–Sun., donation suggested), which includes an old cotton gin, a working railroad, military aircraft, scientific and musical artifacts, and several outbuildings containing a variety of history-related exhibits; it flies the several different flags that have flown over this community over the years.

Just up from the museum on the right is the sprawling and quite grand **Centenary State Historic Site and Historic College** (3522 College St., Jackson, 225/634-7925 or 888/677-2364, www.lastateparks.com, open 9 A.M.–5 P.M. daily, admission $2 per car), a pine-shaded campus of what opened in 1826 as the College of Louisiana. It closed 20 years later because of declining enrollment, at which time the Methodist/Episcopal-operated Centenary College of Brandon Springs took over the gracious campus and buildings. During the Civil War, the college closed, and the buildings were used first by Confederate and then by Union troops. Centenary reopened following the war but suffered low enrollment and finally moved to Shreveport, where it remains today, in 1908. Sadly, the Main Academic Building and the East Wing were demolished in the

Republic of West Florida Historic Association Museum, Jackson

1930s, so today all you can visit is the school's redbrick Greek Revival West Wing.

As you leave town, head back on Highway 10, but just a mile out of town, after the road crosses over a bayou, make a left onto Highway 965, at the sign pointing toward Audubon State Historic Site. Follow this road for several miles beneath a dense canopy of oak and pine trees, by a few private plantation homes. You can pause along the way for a visit at **Audubon State Historic Site** (Hwy. 965, Jackson, 225/342-8111 or 888/677-1400, www.lastateparks.com, open 7 A.M.–9 P.M. daily, admission $2 per car), which you reach about 5 miles after you turn onto Highway 965. In this dense, junglelike 100-acre park you'll find good hiking trails through the magnolia and poplar trees, as well as the 1806 Oakley House, a distinctive West Indies–style colonial house where famed wildlife painter James J. Audubon lived briefly in 1821; records indicate that he worked on at least 32 of his wildlife paintings while living in the house. Other facilities include a picnic shelter and several outbuildings from the original plantation. Guided tours of the house are given throughout the day.

About 2 miles west of Audubon State Historic Site, you come to U.S. 61, onto which a right turn takes you back up 1.5 miles to St. Francisville. The entire loop, depending on how long you stop at the museums, can be done in an hour or a few hours.

ENTERTAINMENT AND NIGHTLIFE

The **Baton Rouge Little Theater** (7155 Florida Blvd., 225/924-6496, www.brlt.org) presents musicals throughout the year.

Gino's Restaurant (4542 Bennington Ave., Baton Rouge, 225/927-7170) holds a highly regarded jazz jam on Thursday nights from 8–11 P.M. Downtown, **M's Fine & Mellow Café** (143 3rd St., Baton Rouge, 225/344-5368) has live music—all different kinds, depending on the evening—Wednesday through Saturday. Head to **Phil Brady's Bar** (4848 Government St., Baton Rouge, 225/927-3786) for its well-attended Thursday night blues jams. Another great place to hear live blues, especially on weekends, is **Tabby's Blues Box and Heritage Hall** (1314 North Blvd., Baton Rouge, 225/387-9715).

EXCURSION TO NATCHEZ, MISSISSIPPI

If you can't get enough of those grand antebellum mansions, and are eager to explore further along the Great River Road, consider extending your trip from St. Francisville up along the east bank of the Mississippi River, just 60 miles north up U.S. 61, to Natchez, Mississippi.

This sparkling jewel of the South is the oldest settlement on the lower Mississippi River. It's named for the Natchez Indians, who are believed to have thrived in this region as early as 1200 A.D. A handful of French explorers passed through during expeditions up and down the river during the 16th and 17th centuries, and France formally established a military outpost, Fort Rosalie, on the town banks in 1716. Following a bloody uprising by the Natchez tribe in 1729, French troops retaliated by annihilating the area's indigenous inhabitants in a matter of years.

Natchez passed into British, Spanish, and finally American hands during the second half of the 18th century, and developed into a highly prosperous hub for shipping cotton by riverboat. When Mississippi formally joined the Union in 1817, Natchez was named its first capital (it was later succeeded by Jackson as the permanent capital). During these years, dozens of elaborate and often grandiose mansions were built around town. Concurrently, the riverboat landing area down beneath the bluffs, still known today as Natchez Under-the-Hill, devolved into a den of gambling, prostitution, thievery, and drinking.

By the time of the Civil War, Natchez had become one of the wealthiest communities in the South. The city joined the Confederate cause against the Union with great trepidation, recognizing secession and prolonged military engagement as obvious threats to its prosperity. In 1863, despite valiant resistance, the upriver towns of Vicksburg and Port Gibson succumbed to advances by Union troops who, upon entering Natchez, found a town quite willing to surrender without a fight. Most of the city's lavish mansions were spared, and Natchez remains one of the best-preserved antebellum towns of the South.

The Natchez economy declined precipitously following the Civil War, bottoming out with the decline of steamboat travel and a wretched boll weevil infestation in 1908, which destroyed the region's cotton crop. Simultaneously, however, locals began taking a keen interest in preserving the community, and in 1932 the Natchez Pilgrimage began, affording the opportunity to tour dozens of fine homes.

Natchez remains famous for its mansions, and also has a number of fine old hotels, restaurants, and shops, many of them set around the well-preserved downtown. The most popular times to visit are during the three pilgrimage seasons, which occur in the spring (mid-March–mid-April), fall (three weeks beginning in early October), and at Christmastime (throughout December). A number of companies give tours of the city, from horse-drawn carriage rides to cemetery strolls to trolley rides.

From Natchez, you can easily continue up U.S. 61 to explore two more Mississippi towns rich in Civil War history, Port Gibson and Vicksburg, which are 42 and 72 miles further respectively. Or you can drive northeast on the scenic **Natchez Trace Parkway** (access from U.S. 61, about 10 miles east of town, 601/680-4025 or 800/305-7417, www.nps.gov/natr), a winding, two-lane road that follows ancient Native American trails. The parkway leads through the city of Jackson before continuing on through the northeastern corner of the state, into northwestern Alabama, and up through central Tennessee, where it ends near Nashville.

Sightseeing Highlights

Touring mansions is the big draw here, and although some homes are open only during the pilgrimage season, many others can be visited year-round. Tours of individual houses can be arranged through **Natchez Pilgrimage Tours** (800/647-6742, www.natchezpilgrimage.com);

admission to each house is $6 ($15 for any three houses). If your time is limited, consider focusing on the following highlights.

- An 1818 planter's "cottage" overlooking the river, **The Briars** (31 Irving Ln.) was the site of Confederate President Jefferson Davis's wedding.

- 1856 Greek Revival mansion **Dunleith** (84 Homochitto St.) sits on 40 manicured acres with many outbuildings.

- One of the oldest buildings in town, **Governor Holmes House** (207 S. Wall St.) dates back to 1794.

- Oft-photographed **Longwood** (Lower Woodville Rd.), circa 1860, is the largest octagonal house in America.

- Five-story **Stanton Hall** (401 High St.), built in 1857, contains a priceless collection of art and antiques.

- The **Natchez National Historical Park** (1 Melrose-Montabello Pkwy., 601/442-7047, www.nps.gov/natc) is headquartered at another fine mansion of the time, **Melrose**, which is open for tours.

- The **Natchez Convention & Visitors Bureau/Visitors Reception Center** (640 S. Canal St., just off U.S. 84/65 near the bridge over the Mississippi River, Natchez, MS 39120, 601/446-6345 or 800/647-6724, www.natchez-ms.us) has a fabulous visitors center overlooking the river, where you can book hotel rooms, peruse the extensive bookshop, and watch a movie detailing the town's history.

Accommodations

The jewel among the town's several fine inns is **Monmouth Plantation** (36 Melrose Ave., 601/442-5852 or 800/828-4531, www.monmouthplantation.com), a lavish compound with 31 rooms and suites. Also quite wonderful is **Dunleith** (84 Homochitto St., 601/446-8500 or 800/433-2445, www.natchez-dunleith.com, $150–250), a stately Greek Revival mansion with 22 sumptuous rooms, most with whirlpool tubs. Dunleith has appeared in several films, including *Showboat*.

In the heart of downtown, the handsome 1927 **Natchez Eola Hotel** (110 Pearl St., 601/445-6000 or 866/445-EOLA, www.natchezeola.com, $100–150) has compact but warmly furnished rooms with city or river views; many have fireplaces and balconies. The well-located and moderately priced **Ramada Inn Hilltop** (130 John R. Junkin Dr., 601/446-6311 or 800/256-6311, www.ramada.com, $50–100) ranks among the best chain options in town.

Food

At **Monmouth Plantation** (36 Melrose Ave., 601/442-5852, $40 fixed price), you might sample a starter of smoked-tomato gazpacho with grilled shrimp, followed by Mississippi Quail with apple-smoked bacon and pepper marinade. In the once roguish and now gentrified Under-the-Hill neighborhood, **Magnolia Grill** (49 Silver St., 601/446-7670, $14–28) specializes in traditional Cajun and Creole fare. The **Castle at Dunleith** (84 Homochitto St., 601/446-8500, $17–23) can be counted on for such elaborate contemporary fare as shiitake mushrooms with a mirliton-seafood stuffing and a tasso cream sauce, followed by grilled Norwegian salmon with Dijon dill hollandaise. **Biscuits & Blues** (315 Main St., 601/446-9922, $11–22)

continued on next page

is known for its Sunday brunch. Try the grillades and grits—pork tenderloin pan-seared and smothered with rich gravy and served over garlic-jalapeño cheese grits. It also turns out delicious meals at lunch and dinner; there's live blues music most nights.

Pearl Street Pasta (105 S. Pearl St., 601/442-9284, $9–$22) is a cute spot with a friendly staff and delicious contemporary pasta—shrimp-and-crabmeat pasta with a white cream sauce or pasta jambalaya with olive oil and a cream sauce are notables.

Stop by the **Wharf Master's Restaurant and Bar** (57 Silver St., 601/445-6025, $10–$20), for barbecue chicken with baked beans, shrimp étouffée, and hot Natchitoches-style meat pies. **Edna's Cake Creations and Confections** (483 John R. Junkin Dr., 601/443-9000) is your source for delicious cookies, cakes, candies, and the like. Drop by the no-frills **Malt Shop** (4 Homochitto St., 601/445-4843, under $5) for hearty oyster or roast beef po-boys, burgers, Frito pies, and banana splits.

College students and other music fans pack into the **Cadillac Cafe** (5454 Bluebonnet Rd., Baton Rouge, 225/296-0288) and **The Varsity** (3353 Highland Rd., Baton Rouge, 225/343-JAMS) for hard-driving rock and blues.

The city's favorite gay and lesbian dance club is **Icon** (2183 Highland Rd., 225/242-9491), in an iffy neighborhood near LSU's campus.

FESTIVALS AND EVENTS

In Jackson, the **Pecan Ridge Bluegrass Festival** (225/634-7155) is held in May, July, and September and draws top musicians in this genre. On Saturdays throughout May, St. Francisville hosts **Summerfest** (225/927-2776), a series of outdoor concerts featuring the Baton Rouge Symphony performing alongside guest artists.

ACCOMMODATIONS

Baton Rouge has about two dozen major chain hotels and motels, most of them set just off I-12 and I-10, on the southeast side of town. Up in St. Francisville and New Roads, you'll find a nice range of inns and B&Bs, some quite simple but a number of them luxurious and somewhat pricey.

Hotels and Motels

Under $50: Bargain hunters should go with the nicest of three **Motel 6** (I-10 at Siegen Lane, Baton Rouge, 225/291-4912 or 800/4-MOTEL-

6, www.motel6.com) properties in the Baton Rouge area. This one is within a walk or short drive of several restaurants and shopping centers.

$50–100: In southeastern Baton Rouge, the **Baymont Inn & Suites** (10555 Rieger Rd., at I-10 and Seigen Lane, 225/291-6600 or 877/BAYMONT, www.baymontinns.com) is a reasonably priced hotel with an outdoor pool and nice-size rooms with recliner armchairs and good work spaces.

The **Best Western St. Francisville** (U.S. 61 at Hwy. 10, 225/635-3821 or 800/826-9931, www.bestwestern.com) may be a modern chain hotel, but it's warm and inviting nonetheless. It lies just outside the historic district on U.S. 61, on a large well-manicured property set well off the road and overlooking a 5-acre lake. Amenities include a pool and in-room coffeemakers, irons and boards, and voice mail.

$100–150: An upscale 330-room business-oriented hotel near a cluster of shops, restaurants, and office buildings, the **Radisson Hotel & Conference Center** (4728 Constitution Ave., Baton Rouge, 225/925-2244 or 800/333-3333, www.radisson.com) is well-situated and has extensive amenities and facilities including a full-service restaurant and bar, 24-hour room service, a pool and patio, and in-room coffeemakers, irons and boards, and two phones. The **Chase Suite Hotel by Woodfin** (5522 Corporate Blvd., Baton Rouge, 225/927-5630 or 800/WOODFIN, www.woodfinsuitehotels.com) is an all-suite property in the same compound as a Barnes & Noble superstore and a massive cineplex. Although geared toward long-term stays, the hotel also offers special weekend packages geared toward the leisure trade. Suites have full kitchens, CD players, and TVs with VCRs, and other hotel features include a pool, complimentary continental breakfast, a sports court, and health club privileges.

Inns and Bed-and-Breakfasts

$50–100: St. Francisville Inn & Restaurant (5720 Commerce St., 225/635-6502 or 800/488-6502, www.stfrancisville.com) looks like a cover of *Southern Living,* complete with a front yard shaded by towering moss-draped live oaks. But for its location next to a convenience store and across from a Dollar General discount shop and a Ford dealer, you'd swear it's the late 19th century standing on the grounds. The rambling Victorian house dates to the late 1870s. Next door is Parker Memorial Park, and the gracious homes of the historic district are within walking distance. Rooms are simply furnished but pleasant and well-priced; all have private baths, cable TV, and phones, and one has a Jacuzzi tub. A full buffet breakfast is included. There's also a popular restaurant on-site.

In New Roads, with frontage that includes a boat dock and fishing pier right on the False River, **Mon Reve** (9825 False River Rd., 225/638-7848 or 800/324-2738, www.monreve-my-dream.com) is a splendidly restored 1820 French Creole plantation house with a stately front gallery. There are three rooms, each with its own color scheme (pink, green, or blue). All have high-thread-count linens, polished hardwood floors, and antiques, plus cable TV and private baths. A full country breakfast is included.

$100–150: The **Barrow House Inn** (9779 Royal St., St. Francisville, 225/635-4791, www .topteninn.com) comprises a pair of houses, one from the late 1700s and the other from around 1810. Among the two buildings, which are in the heart of St. Francisville's historic district, are several rooms and suites, each decorated with 1840s to 1870s antiques. Fluffy four-poster canopy beds, darkwood armoires, and Oriental rugs are among the furnishings. In one house, a sun room contains a collection of 21 first-edition Audubon prints. Breakfast is served on fine china with silver flatware—you're given a choice of continental or one of three full New Orleans–style breakfasts.

In Jackson, a short drive east of St. Francisville, the dignified **Old Centenary Inn** (Hwy. 10, Jackson, 225/634-5050, www.oldcentenary inn.com) is a luxurious 1935 Colonial Revival inn with eight antiques-filled rooms, each with phone, TV, and VCR, and a private bath with two-person Jacuzzi tub. A full breakfast is included. It's a great value, in part because Jackson is less touristy than St. Francisville. The same owners operate a smaller four-bedroom Greek Revival inn called **Millbank** (3045 Millbank St., Jackson, 225/634-5901, www.oldcentenary inn.com), which also has a restaurant on-site.

$150–250: For the chance to stay in what many believe to be the most haunted house in Louisiana, book a room at **Myrtles Plantation** (7747 U.S. 61, St. Francisville, 225/635-6277 or 800/809-0565, www.myrtlesplantation.com), one of the most popular touring plantations in the St. Francisville area. The ornately furnished 1796 main house contains six handsome and expansive rooms and suites. The General David Bradford Suite has two adjoining verandas and a huge four-poster bed; it's among the most luxurious of the accommodations. Less pricey is the old caretaker's cottage, which has its own porch, and the four garden rooms, each with an antique Chippendale clawfoot tub, in outbuildings behind the main house. Myrtles Plantations also has a fine full-service restaurant, the OxBow Carriage House.

FOOD

Where there are politicians, there are almost always good restaurants, and Baton Rouge confirms this rule with its wide variety of very nice places to eat. It's also a student town, and you can find several good and relatively affordable spots for a meal around the campus of LSU. Overall, this entire area, including St. Francisville and the other smaller town north of Baton Rouge, is full of good dining. The emphasis is less on Creole and Cajun fare and more on both creative

THE GREAT RIVER ROAD

and traditional Southern and Continental cooking, but you'll find a healthy variety of classic Louisiana ingredients on most of these menus.

Traditional Creole and Cajun

Morel's Restaurant (210 Morrison Pkwy., New Roads, 225/638-4057, $12–22) serves a mix of traditional Creole and Continental dishes, such as grilled catfish *piperade,* served on steamed rice and finished with a Creole sauce and sautéed bell peppers. The shrimp rémoulade on fried eggplant is a typically tantalizing appetizer. Built on the False River as the parish's first automobile dealership in 1917, **Satterfield's Riverwalk** (108 E. Main St., New Roads, 225/638-8062, $8–20) is today one of the region's most reliable and popular places for well-prepared Creole and Italian fare. There's seating on a deck overlooking the river at black wrought-iron chairs and tables, and in an elegant but casual dining room with tall windows affording great views. House specialties include fillet of beef topped with a crawfish-tarragon-cream sauce, grilled catfish with fresh home-grown vegetables, and trout amandine. Lighter salads and sandwiches are also available.

Creative and Contemporary

Perhaps the most stylish restaurant in Baton Rouge, and thus a favorite of politicos and business execs, **Juban's** (3739 Perkins Rd., 225/346-8422, $16–30) has been serving innovative Louisiana-influenced fare since the early 1980s, when owner-chef John Mariani's temple of fine cuisine was named one of America's "Best New Restaurants" in the pages of *Esquire.* The restaurant is known for such signature dishes as crab and angel hair pasta fried crispy over a sauce of beurre blanc, and seafood-stuffed soft-shell crab topped with Creolaise sauce and duck breast pan-seared with Louisiana fig glaze and fried plantains. Pecan-smoked salmon with capers and boursin cheese makes a nice starter.

Another of Baton Rouge's more interesting dining options, **Pavé** (711 Jefferson Hwy., Baton Rouge, 225/248-1381 $15–21) serves delicious sushi rolls (spicy tuna, crab-and-avocado, and so on) along with dazzling contemporary American cooking: whole roasted duck over blueberry risotto, green peppercorn–and–mandarin sauce, and a grilled green onion crepe, or yellowfin tuna tartare with orange tobiko caviar, slivered cu-

Ma Mama's restaurant, New Roads

cumbers, aioli, and baby lettuce. The dining room is trendy and smart, as is the crowd.

Northeast of Baton Rouge, and east of St. Francisville and Jackson, it's worth making the drive to the **Front Porch Restaurant and Bar** (9173 Hwy. 67 South, Clinton, 225/683-3030, $13–22) to sample some of the area's best and creative cooking. Try wood-grilled tuna topped with Key lime butter, roasted chicken with a roast-garlic and mushroom sauce, and broiled mushrooms stuffed with crab and shrimp and topped with buttered rum.

Casual Cooking

Ma Mama's (124 W. Main St., New Roads, 225/618-2424, $8–17) is a great spot for home-style Italy-meets-Louisiana cooking, such as soft-shell crab bites or crawfish balls to start, perhaps followed by parmesan shrimp pasta, baked spinach lasagna, pork chops, or a rib eye steak. The restaurant occupies a dapper historic building in the center of town. Casual **Parrain's** (3225 Perkins Rd., at foot of I-10 exit, Baton Rouge, 225/381-9922, $10–17) serves first-rate seafood such as crab au gratin, catfish perdu (semi-boneless fried catfish topped with crawfish étouffée), whole fried Cornish game hen with slaw and dirty rice, and crawfish po'boys.

As you pull into Jackson on Highway 10 from St. Francisville, note **Bobby's Drive-In Restaurant** (1427 Charter St., 225/634-7190, $4–9), a great place to get your fix of fried chicken, curly fries, oyster po'boys, dirty rice, and barbecued ribs. You can eat in your car or in the very modest dining room with green-and-white-checked plastic tablecloths, linoleum floors, and a few stuffed and mounted animals. It ain't fancy.

In Plaquemine, a town just south of Baton Rouge on the Great River Road, the cheerful **City Cafe** (57945 Main St., Plaquemine, 225/687-7831, $7–21) is a reliable choice for steaks and seafood specialties, from yellowfin tuna to T-bones. Po'boys and sandwich are also served, along with potato skins, cheesesteaks, and more casual fare. There's a long list of desserts, among them praline fudge brownies.

Ethnic

Serranos Salsa Company (North Gates of LSU, 3347 Highland Rd., 225/344-2354, $8–15) presents tasty Latin American and Mexican fare. You might try Cuban-style pork carnitas (smoked orange-and-lime-marinated pork roast with garlic and spices), tequila-marinated lime shrimp, or fish tacos with Serrano-chile cream sauce and pico de gallo.

Quick Bites

A favorite place of students craving sustenance late into the evening, **Louie's Cafe** (209 W. State St., Baton Rouge, 225/346-8221, $5–11) serves delicious home-style greasy-spoon fare 24 hours a day. Breakfast hits include the seafood Louie omelet (with crawfish, veggies, spiced butter, and herbed cream cheese), pecan pancakes, huge cheeseburgers, and po'boys. Louie's has long been famous for its hash browns—try the version with sautéed mushrooms, colby cheese, and sour cream. Simple and casual **Frank's Restaurant** (8353 Airline Hwy., Baton Rouge, 225/928-4575, $4–8) serves tasty breakfast fare, including house-smoked sausages, and also sells stuffed brisket, fried turkey, and other fine meats to go.

Raising Canes (3313 Highland Rd., Baton Rouge, 225/387-2662, $3–7) is a local fast-food chain that's famous for its boneless chicken breast, chicken finger sandwiches, and special sauce. There are a few branches around town, but the one by LSU is the most atmospheric, and it's open late, too. Pick up a barbecue-brisket po'boy, sausage sandwich, plate of boudin bites, or a combo plate at **Road Side BBQ & Grill** (4641 Main St., 225/635-9696, $4–10), in Zachary, which is a bit north of Baton Rouge.

Magnolia Cafe (5687 Commerce St., St. Francisville, 225/635-6528, $6–10) serves a nice mix of sandwiches, Mexican fare, and pizzas—a slightly unlikely trinity of great kinds of food. Seafood enchiladas, French dip po'boys, and burgers are popular items.

Java Joints

There are about a dozen branches of the Louisiana chain **C.C.'s Coffee** (800/525-5583, www.ccscoffee.com) set around Baton Rouge. The one just beyond the South Gates at LSU

THE GREAT RIVER ROAD

(4410 Highland Rd., 225/761-9220) is a favorite of students, has free high-speed Internet, and sometimes has live entertainment.

In New Roads, break for coffee, a light lunch, or snacks at **Espresso Etc.** (110 E. Main St., 225/618-8701), a warm and cozy storefront café right in the center of town. Quiche, sandwiches, salads, and sweets are among the offerings, and you can also browse for jewelry, art, and crafts by local artists.

Picnic Supplies and Gourmet Goods

Gambino's (8646 Goodwood Blvd., Baton Rouge, 225/928-7000) is known for its huge six-layer Doberge cakes, available in chocolate, lemon, and caramel. Cookies, king cakes, biscotti, and sublime pralines are also available.

Many people in Baton Rouge say that **Pocorello's Italian Grocery and Deli** (12240 Coursey Blvd., 225/293-3737) serves the best muffalettas outside New Orleans; you can also pick up meatball-and-eggplant po'boys, stuffed artichokes, and other prepared foods and imported Italian groceries. Middle Eastern snacks, groceries, baked goods, and other fare are served and sold at **Atcha Bakery and Cafe** (3221 Nicholson Dr., Baton Rouge, 225/383-7482).

Maybe the definitive source of gourmet chocolates in the Baton Rouge areas, **Chocollage** (3056 College Dr., Village Square, 225/924-1748; also 7939 Jefferson Hwy., 225/216-2462) sells fine Belgian truffles and candies.

Hodge Podge Wine Shop and Deli (11429 Ferdinand St., St. Francisville, 225/635-2663) occupies part of the old Bayou Sara rail station complex at the bottom of the hill from downtown, close to the ferry. It's a cute place with ample seating on its large porch, and in addition to selling wine and gourmet foods, it serves excellent sandwiches, salads, and light snacks. Next door, also in part of the old rail station, is Bayou Sara Market, an antiques shop.

INFORMATION AND SERVICES

For information on Baton Rouge, contact the **Baton Rouge Area Convention & Visitors Center** (730 North Blvd., Baton Rouge, LA 70802, 800/LA-ROUGE, www.bracvb.com); there's also a tourism information center stocked with brochures on the ground level of the Louisiana State Capitol building. Information on St. Francisville and Jackson can be obtained from the **West Feliciana Parish Tourist Commission** (P.O. Box 1548, St. Francisville, LA 70775, 800/789-4221, www.stfrancisville.us), which has a small visitor center inside the West Feliciana Historical Society. Information on New Roads can be obtained by the **Greater Pointe Coupee Chamber of Commerce** (P.O. Box 555, New Roads, LA 70760, 225/638-3500, www.pcchamber.org), which has a rack of brochures in the lobby of its office at 160 East Main Street. And Jackson's tourism is handled by the **East Feliciana Parish Tourist Commission** (P.O. Box 667, Jackson, LA 70748, 225/634-7155, www.felicianatourism.org).

GETTING AROUND

From New Orleans, it's a straight 80-mile shot up I-10 to reach Baton Rouge; the drive takes an hour and 15 minutes. From here, it's another 30 miles up U.S. 61 to reach St. Francisville. As with the rest of the Great River Road, a car is your best way to get around. Even in Baton Rouge, which has a somewhat compact downtown in which you can walk among a few attractions, the hotels are mostly outside of downtown to the east, off the interstate, making a car handy and public transportation impractical.

See the *On the Road* chapter for details on reaching New Orleans and Baton Rouge from other parts of the country by train, plane, and bus.

Cajun Country

After New Orleans, southern Louisiana's Cajun Country, anchored by the city of Lafayette, attracts the most attention from visitors of any part of the state. There are a few basic commonalities between this area and New Orleans, but all too often outsiders lump the two areas together, as though Cajun culture is simply an extension of New Orleans, and that Creoles and Cajuns are one and the same. In fact, this part of Louisiana was settled for different reasons and by different people than was New Orleans, and everything from the food to the music to the accents in this part of the state are different, not only from the rest of the state but anywhere in the world.

History

The area now known as Acadiana, or Cajun Country, was inhabited by several Indian tribes before European trappers and settlers began establishing outposts here. The Attakapas and Chitimacha, who were bitter enemies, were the principal tribes around what is now Lafayette, St. Martinville, New Iberia, and Morgan City. The earliest Europeans in the area were mostly French trappers and then a handful of cattle ranchers, who began setting up small trading posts and farms in the early 1700s. It was not until around 1760 that the earliest Cajuns moved to the region, arriving by boat and establishing the town of St. Martinville.

Shadows-on-the-Teche,
New Iberia

The word "Cajun" is a corruption of "Acadian," the name for French settlers who had lived in Canada's Maritimes provinces, especially Nova Scotia, during the 17th and 18th centuries. The settlers came mostly from the Vendée region of far western France, and they began arriving during the very early 1600s, well before English colonists had established a foothold in Massachusetts. When Great Britain secured control of the Canadian region in 1713, the thousands of Acadians living in Nova Scotia resisted and in some cases flouted the authority of the British crown. Acadians developed a reputation for being fiercely independent, and they refused to submit to England's authority or learn English. To sign the oath of loyalty to the British Crown would have rendered an Acadian obligated to fight on behalf of the British against the French during the French and Indian Wars.

The Cajun were just one group of refugees or hard-luck immigrants, along with whites and freed blacks from Haiti and residents of the Spanish Canary Islands, who helped to change the territory from a financially dubious backwater into an agricultural and trade powerhouse.

After years of tension between British authorities and Acadian residents, the British colonial government established a ruthless program, which came to be known by the French as the *Grand Dérangement* (literally the "Great Disturbance"), in which they rounded up the region's French settlers and expelled them from Canada. In many instances they told men, women, and children to gather at a local church, where they were to hear an important announcement. On entering the church, the doors were locked and the French families imprisoned and then led to waiting ships bound for Europe, the Caribbean, and the East Coast colonies that would eventually become the United States.

Some colonies turned away the ships carrying refugees, and in other places they were accepted as indentured workers with no rights. Everywhere they were subject to great suspicion and prejudice. In Colonial America at this time, Catholics were severely distrusted and, often, persecuted by the Protestant church-state, although attitudes did begin to shift following the

American Revolution, when French Catholics played a vital role in the colonists' overthrow of British rule.

In two major waves, one in 1764 and the other in 1785, about 3,000 to 4,000 expelled Acadians and their descendants moved to southern Louisiana to start anew. Contrary to popular opinion, very few of the state's Cajuns came here directly from Nova Scotia; most had returned to France to live but failed, for the most part, to assimilate back into French society, having become a distinct people after living in Nova Scotia for several generations. They were truly without a home, and Louisiana welcomed them as much as anything because the young territory was eager to attract settlers, especially in the southwestern part of the region, which was considered to be dangerous frontierland occupied by aggressive Attakapas Indians.

Interestingly, during the two major Cajun arrivals, Louisiana was under Spanish rather than French control. The Cajuns cared little who governed the territory and more that they would be moving someplace where people spoke French and practiced Catholicism. The Spanish government, like the French one before it, was genuinely thrilled to attract any significant mass of settlers, and they were particularly happy that the Cajun refugees were interested in developing and working farms. The Cajuns were just one group of refugees or hard-luck immigrants, along with whites and freed blacks from Haiti and residents of the Spanish Canary Islands, who helped to change the territory from a financially dubious backwater into an agricultural and trade powerhouse by the time America admitted Louisiana into the Union as the country's 18th state, in 1812.

The city of Lafayette, with a population of about 110,000, acts as the capital of the Acadiana, which comprises 22 southern Louisiana parishes, from Calcasieu and Cameron Parishes on the western border with Texas to the parishes around New Orleans in the east—the total population of these 22 parishes is nearly 1.3 million. Cajuns remain a relatively close-knit group—about 400,000 residents of Louisiana identify themselves as primarily Cajun, and of the roughly 700,000 nationally who claim Cajun ancestry, about 75 percent live in Louisiana or neighboring Texas. In Vermilion and Acadia Parishes, which are southwest and west of Lafayette, more than 45 percent of the residents claim to be of Cajun descent. More than a third of the residents in Assumption, Cameron, Evangeline, Iberia, Jefferson Davis, Lafourche, St. Landry, and St. Martin Parishes also claim to be Cajun. Lafayette Parish, despite being the hub of the area, is only about 25 percent Cajun, a figure that's declining each decade as greater numbers of outsiders settle there. By contrast, fewer than 1 percent of all New Orleanians claim to be of Cajun descent.

Orientation and Planning

Acadiana is shaped roughly like a scythe and follows U.S. 90 west to southeast, from Lake Charles to Houma. The long, rectangular handle of the scythe extends from Lake Charles to Lafayette along both U.S. 90 and the parallel U.S. 190 corridor, from Kinder to Opelousas. This part of Acadiana is considered to be the Cajun prairie, where early settlers earned their livelihood farming. The curving blade of the scythe extends southeast along the U.S. 90 corridor from Lafayette down through New Iberia and Morgan City and then about as far east as Houma. This region is considered the Cajun wetlands, where the settlers derived their livelihood chiefly from fishing and trapping. From Houma, it's just a 60-mile drive to New Orleans.

This chapter is broken down into three key regions, Lafayette and Central Acadiana, the Cajun Prairie, and the Cajun Wetlands. Lafayette and Central Acadiana encompass portions of both prairie and wetlands but are, geographically and culturally, more the latter. This area contains a great many attractions, restaurants, accommodations, and charming, historic small towns. If you only have a little time out this way, be sure to spend time in Lafayette and the surrounding area.

The Cajun Prairie includes the towns northwest and west of Lafayette, including Opelousas and Eunice along the U.S. 190 corridor, Rayne and Crowley along the U.S. 90 corridor, and Lake Charles out near the Texas border. Opelousas and Eunice are notable for their musical heritage, as both traditional Cajun and zydeco music have flourished here. Lake Charles is a growing city, and the towns between it and Lafayette have a smattering of things to see and do, but this is part of the Cajun Country need not be your highest priority. It's the farthest section from New Orleans, although it's worth checking out if you're visiting the state by way of Texas, which it borders.

The Cajun Wetlands take in the string of towns between the Atchafalaya River and Houma and contain far fewer attractions than Lafayette and environs. However, this is Action Central for fishing and swamp-touring enthusiasts, and it's also close to the Plantation Country, covered in the Great River Road chapter. If you're seeking just a taste of Cajun culture and would prefer not to stray far from New Orleans, a night or two out near Houma or Thibodaux might suit you perfectly. You can also travel through this part of the region en route from New Orleans to Lafayette—with construction crews gradually improving U.S. 90 in an effort to convert it into the continuation of I-49, this road becomes wider and faster every year.

It's fairly easy to spend four or five days in this part of the state, especially if you hit all the major attractions between Lafayette and Houma. If you have more time, consider a longer exploration of Cajun Country, perhaps spending some nights in Eunice or Lake Charles. If you enjoy the outdoors and the music and food heritage of the area, you're unlikely to run out of things to see and do. But if you came to Louisiana craving the lively pace and big-city buzz of New Orleans, you might be best limiting your time in Cajun Country to a few days or less. Greater New Orleans and Acadiana enjoy more differences than similarities, but therein lies much of the charm of Louisiana's Cajun Country.

CAJUN COUNTRY

Lafayette and the Cajun Wetlands

The heart of Cajun Country, Lafayette and Central Acadiana includes the city of Lafayette and towns in its immediate vicinity, stretching about as far down as the Atchafalaya River—the communities most popular with visitors include, in order of their proximity to Lafayette, Breaux Bridge, St. Martinville, New Iberia, Abbeville, and Franklin.

LAFAYETTE

Lafayette is the most important city in Acadiana, and what many people consider to be its hub. As with the surrounding towns in the region, the cultural makeup is really less purely Cajun than outsiders sometimes imagine. Certainly there are many people here of Cajun descent, and many who speak the local Cajun dialect of French as their preferred first language, but residents of the region are also strongly of African, Spanish, Northern European, and Native American origin.

The city is easily reached from New Orleans, Houston, and the rest of the region—it's just off I-10 and I-49, a little more than two hours west of the Crescent City, and it contains the bulk of the region's chain motels and hotels, fast-food and other restaurants, and shops and services. There's also a decent-size regional airport with direct service to a handful of Southern cities.

This is a thoroughly modern city, not an especially quaint or old-fashioned one. The city sprawls, and much of it feels suburban and overrun with strip malls. However, it's also home to some excellent museums on Cajun culture, and it has some first-rate Cajun music clubs and restaurants. And the formerly depressed downtown area has received a major makeover in recent years, with new museums, clubs, and restaurants.

It's subtropical in climate, owing to its location just 40 miles north of the Gulf of Mexico and 15 miles west of Atchafalaya Swamp. Attakapas Indians inhabited the area for many decades dating as far back as the late 1600s, but their dominance was overturned by a legion of three opposing southern Louisiana tribes who formed an alliance to defeat the notoriously warlike Attakapas; these included the Opelousas, Choctaw, and Alabamons.

Although it's the Cajun capital of the state, it was not actually settled by Acadian exiles until the Spanish government assumed control of the region in the 1760s, by which time a few French trappers and farmers had already put down roots here. The earliest group of Acadians, who had moved from Canada to a hodgepodge of East Coast ports and Caribbean islands, first arrived in nearby St. Martinville in 1765. But when the larger wave of Cajun arrivals hit Louisiana in 1785, with the blessing of the territory's Spanish government, Lafayette truly grew into a center of Cajun life. These many hundreds of Cajuns arrived from France, to which they had returned following their brutal expulsion from the Canadian Maritimes.

The earliest known permanent European settlement in what is now Lafayette was established by the English and known as Petit Manchac; it was a small trading post on the banks of the Vermilion River, approximately where it is crossed today by the Pinhook Avenue bridge (right beside the Hilton hotel). It wasn't until 1821, when an Acadian descendant named Jean Mouton donated land for the construction of a Catholic church, that the settlement really took hold as a major center of Cajun life.

Lafayette Parish was created (from the western edge of what had been St. Martin Parish) by the state legislature in 1823, and the young town, then known as Vermilionville, for the major bayou that passed through it, was named the parish seat. In 1884, the fast-growing settlement was rechristened Lafayette, in honor of the French Marquis de Lafayette, who acted so heroically in the American Revolutionary War.

Today Lafayette is the hub of an eight-parish area with a metro population of about 600,000, some 110,000 of them within city limits. It's one of the state's faster-growing cities, with a blossoming economy to go with it. Per capita

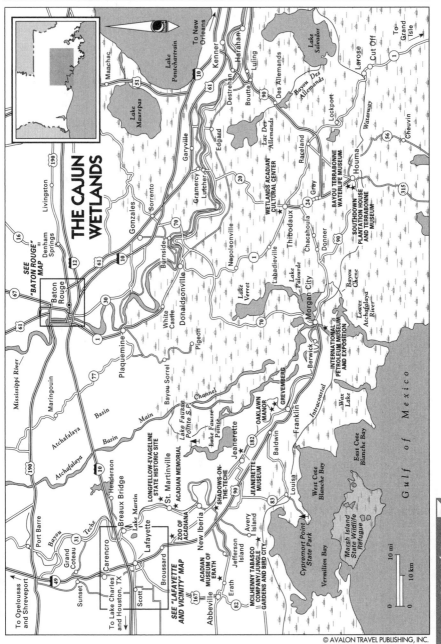

THE CAJUN WETLANDS

SEE "BATON ROUGE" MAP

Gulf of Mexico

WETLANDS ACADIAN CULTURAL CENTER

BAYOU TERREBONNE WATERLIFE MUSEUM

SOUTHDOWN PLANTATION HOUSE AND TERREBONNE MUSEUM

INTERNATIONAL PETROLEUM MUSEUM AND EXPOSITION

LONGFELLOW-EVANGELINE STATE HISTORIC SITE

ACADIAN MEMORIAL

SHADOWS-ON-THE-TECHE

JEANERETTE MUSEUM

OAKLAWN MANOR

ZOO OF ACADIANA

ACADIAN MUSEUM OF ERATH

MCILHENNY TABASCO COMPANY/JUNGLE GARDENS AND BIRD CITY

Cypremort Point State Park

Marsh Island State Wildlife Refuge

SEE "LAFAYETTE AND VICINITY" MAP

To Opelousas and Shreveport

To Lake Charles and Houston, TX

To New Orleans

To Grand Isle

Mississippi River

Atchafalaya Basin

Lower Atchafalaya River

© AVALON TRAVEL PUBLISHING, INC.

CAJUN COUNTRY

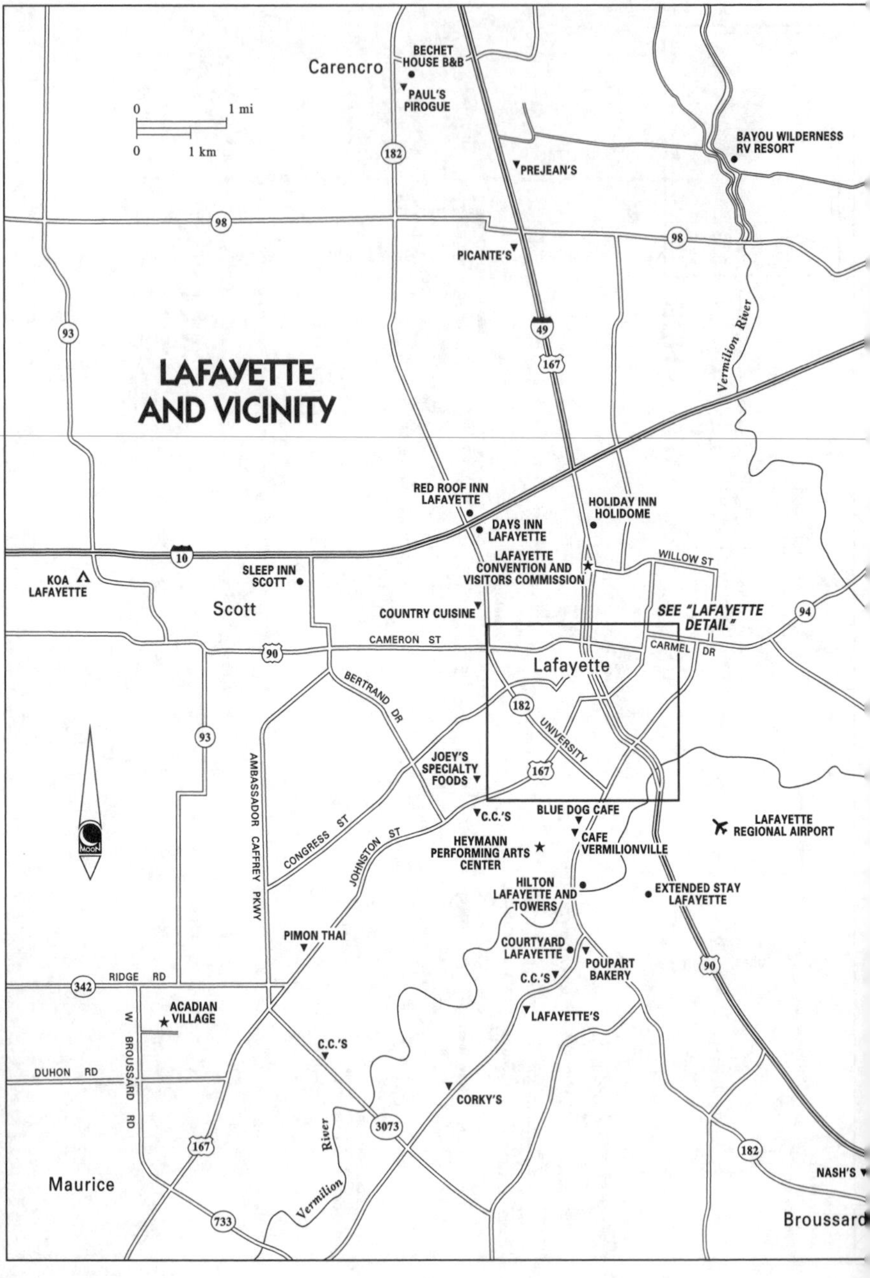

LAFAYETTE AND VICINITY

Carencro

BECHET HOUSE B&B

PAUL'S PIROGUE

BAYOU WILDERNESS RV RESORT

182

PREJEAN'S

98

PICANTE'S

98

49

167

93

Vermilion River

RED ROOF INN LAFAYETTE

HOLIDAY INN HOLIDOME

DAYS INN LAFAYETTE

10

LAFAYETTE CONVENTION AND VISITORS COMMISSION

WILLOW ST

94

KOA LAFAYETTE

SLEEP INN SCOTT

SEE "LAFAYETTE DETAIL"

COUNTRY CUISINE

Scott

CAMERON ST

CARMEL DR

90

Lafayette

BERTRAND DR

182

93

UNIVERSITY

167

AMBASSADOR CAFFREY PKWY

CONGRESS ST

JOHNSTON ST

JOEY'S SPECIALTY FOODS

C.C.'S

BLUE DOG CAFE

LAFAYETTE REGIONAL AIRPORT

HEYMANN PERFORMING ARTS CENTER

CAFE VERMILIONVILLE

HILTON LAFAYETTE AND TOWERS

EXTENDED STAY LAFAYETTE

PIMON THAI

COURTYARD LAFAYETTE

POUPART BAKERY

342

RIDGE RD

C.C.'S

90

W BROUSSARD RD

ACADIAN VILLAGE

C.C.'S

LAFAYETTE'S

DUHON RD

182

167

CORKY'S

River

3073

NASH'S

Maurice

733

Vermilion

Broussard

0   1 mi
0   1 km

MOON

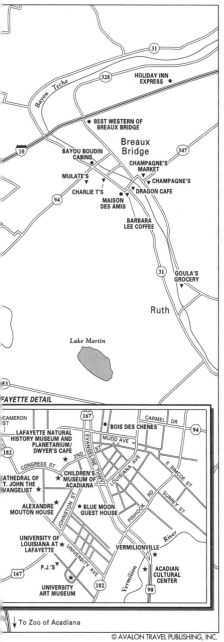

FAYETTE DETAIL

© AVALON TRAVEL PUBLISHING, INC.

income in Lafayette Parish grew by 54 percent between 1990 and 2000, and today Lafayette has the third-highest per capita income in Louisiana. The low cost of living and central location have made it a desirable tech city.

Sights

A great place to begin a tour is the National Park Service's superb **Acadian Cultural Center** (501 Fisher Rd., 337/232-0789, www.nps.gov/jela, open 9 A.M.–5 P.M. daily, admission free), which offers an excellent general overview of Cajun history and culture. It's a short drive southeast of downtown Lafayette, just off U.S. 90 by Lafayette Regional Airport. Well-labeled and often large-scale exhibits, artifacts, and photos are set throughout the museum space in this contemporary building designed to resemble a Cajun cottage. You can easily spend an hour in here absorbing the lore of Cajun music, family life, cooking, language, and fishing, and exploring the serpentine route Acadians journeyed from Nova Scotia to southern Louisiana. In a large theater, the 40-minute movie *The Cajun Way: Echoes of Acadia* is shown hourly until 4 P.M. and is definitely worth making time for; it offers a gut-wrenching but inspirational look at the plight of Cajuns and their astounding resolution balanced with their love of celebration and tradition that has kept them a distinct cultural group to this day. Check for interpretive programs, videos, and performances scheduled regularly throughout the year, and when in New Orleans, be sure to drop in on the headquarters of the Jean Lafitte National Historical Preserve, in the French Quarter at 419 Decatur St. Here you'll find information on all of the park's six sites throughout southern Louisiana, including two centers, on wetland Cajuns and prairie Cajuns, in the towns of Thibodaux and Eunice, respectively.

Within view of the Acadian Cultural Center, **Vermilionville** (300 Fisher Rd., 337/233-4077 or 866/99-BAYOU, www.vermilionville.org, open 10 A.M.–4 P.M. Tues.–Sun., admission $8) is another must-see for understanding Cajun culture. This 23-acre living-history compound comprises five restored historic houses, 12 reproduction period buildings, and exhibits on

house at Vermilionville

indigenous persons, the areas wetlands, and Cajun and zydeco music (which is performed live here regularly). You can attend cooking demonstrations, eat in the casual restaurant and bakery, and walk through a nature trail identifying Louisiana plant life. This setup differs a bit from the smaller Acadian Village, another Lafayette living-history center in a different part of town, which has fewer staff and holds fewer demonstrations. Vermilionville is, rather oddly, set near the airport and several modern warehouses, but once you enter the re-created village, it feels quite authentic; there's even a lazy bayou running through the property. Different buildings, some authentic from the period and others exact replicas, include a chapel and presbytére (where a clergyman would have lived), an Acadian barn where volunteers engage in boat building and net and trap making, and several residences, the oldest dating from 1790. Every element of Vermilionville sheds light onto the culture of the area's original Cajuns, from the homestyle cooking of La Cuisine de Maman restaurant to live music-and-dance programs. The guides here are knowledgeable and enthusiastic, too.

Similar in approach but a bit smaller in scope

is **Acadian Village** (200 Greenleaf Dr., 337/981-2364, www.acadianvillage.org, open 10 A.M.–5 P.M. daily, admission $6), which is on the southwest side of town, easily accessed as you head down U.S. 167 toward Abbeville. This complex is a replicated Cajun village from the late 1800s, with several buildings moved here from their original sites throughout the region. These include a general store, a circa-1800 cottage brought over from St. Martinville, a blacksmith shop, a replica of an 1850 chapel, and several period houses. The layout and setting is somewhat more picturesque than Vermilionville, and the experience here offers an excellent and highly entertaining sense of what an actual bayou village might have looked like 150 years ago. At Acadian Village, you mostly explore on your own, at your own pace, rather than being led by docents, which can make for a refreshing change of pace if you're a bit tired of being led in groups through plantations and museums. The buildings here are packed with old artifacts, metalworking tools, everyday tools, household goods and textiles—you could spend a while here just poking around. The disturbingly realistic re-created doctor's office may leave you thankful for the advances that have been made since the 19th century in medical diagnostics and procedures.

There's a large picnic pavilion, which sometimes hosts special events and demonstrations. Alongside the narrow bayou that cuts through the village, you're likely to see turtles sunning themselves on logs, and guinea hens and rather aggressive geese wandering about. An interesting side attraction is the Mississippi River Museum, set in a modern building on the edge of the village; it contains murals depicting Indian life and European settlement throughout the Mississippi River Valley, plus 200- and 400-year-old canoes fashioned of cypress wood, which virtually never rots and so last for eons. The museum, which is free with admission to Acadian Village, also contains taxidermic wildlife and old maps and charts of the area.

Downtown Lafayette, which is contained roughly within a triangle bound by West University Avenue (Hwy. 182), Johnson Street (U.S. 167), and Congress Street, has gradually been revitalized since the mid-'90s and has a handful of attractions, plus a growing number of places to eat and shop. This business district is where banks and oil companies built offices throughout the 20th century, making it Acadiana's commercial center.

The **Alexandre Mouton House/Lafayette Museum** (1122 Lafayette St., 337/234-2208, open 9 A.M.–4:30 P.M. Tues.–Sat., 1–4 P.M. Sun., admission $3), the 19th-century home of Louisiana's first Democrat governor, occupies one of the most striking buildings downtown. Furnishings from different generations of the Mouton family fill the house.

A couple of blocks north and west, near the third-oldest oak tree recognized by Louisiana's Live Oak Society, the **Cathedral of St. John the Evangelist** (914 St. John St., 337/232-1322, 9 A.M.–noon and 1–4 P.M. Mon.–, admission free) is a striking Dutch Romanesque church of considerable proportion. It dates to 1916 and has an above-ground cemetery dating to a century before that. Tours are available by appointment, but you're also welcome to drop by and look around on your own. There's a gift shop selling inspirational jewelry, crafts, and cards.

On the northeast side of downtown, an easy walk from the cathedral, you'll find one of the city's newest attractions, opened in 2003, the **Lafayette Natural History Museum and Planetarium** (433 Jefferson St., 337/291-5544,

Acadian Village, Lafayette

© ANDREW COLLINS

chapel at Acadian Village

www.lnhm.org, open 1–9:30 P.M. Tues., 1–5 P.M. Wed.–Fri., 10 A.M.–6 P.M. Sat., and 1–6 P.M. Sun., admission $5), which is housed within a stunning many-windowed three-story building in the city's up-and-coming downtown; the 72,000-square-foot space had housed an old department store. It's a classic hands-on place where kids and adults can poke, prod, handle, and experiment with scientific objects, and examine collections of Native American crafts, paintings and pottery of Louisiana artists, rare books, photographs, meteorites and tektites, and other curious artifacts. The planetarium, with its 40-foot dome, presents a wide range of astronomy programs. The museum also sponsors a series of lunchtime concerts in downtown's Parc Sans Souci (at 201 E. Vermillion St.), which include live blues, folk, and percussion music.

Also popular with younger visitors is the nearby **Children's Museum of Acadiana** (201 E. Congress St., 337/232-8500, open 10 A.M.–5 P.M. Tues.–Sat., admission $5), whose many fanciful exhibits touch on Acadian history as well as natural science, space, nutrition, and the arts. Kids can explore a mock grocery store or bank or a real ambulance, stage their own shows in a kid-size TV station, and admire art in a gallery with rotating exhibits.

Currently under construction, the **Acadiana Center for the Arts** (www.acadianaartscouncil.org) is slated for completion in 2005 and will include a museum exhibition space, a performing arts center, and educational facilities. Opening at the corner of Jefferson and Vermilion Streets, it will be yet another piece in the downtown renaissance. The first phase of construction, which includes some of the exhibition space, opened in September 2003.

After New Orleans and Baton Rouge, Lafayette has the third-largest presence of college students of any community in southwestern Louisiana, with the **University of Louisiana at Lafayette** (104 University Circle, Hwy. 182 and U.S. 167, 337/482-1000, www.ull.edu), which enrolls some 16,000 students. The campus is just south of downtown. Cypress and oak trees dot the attractive campus, which has a mix of older and newer buildings. Visitors should be sure to check out the **University Art Museum** (710 E. St. Mary Blvd., 337/482-5326, www.louisiana.edu/uam), which moved into a large and new 40,000-square-foot space in fall 2003. This move is helping to turn what had been a fairly modest facility into the premier art museum in the Gulf Coast region between Houston and New Orleans. UAM mounts important traveling exhibitions throughout the year and has a diverse and growing permanent collection with notable works by regional, national, and international artists dating over the past four centuries.

Broussard

Broussard is a small community just south of Lafayette via U.S. 90. The main attraction here is the **Zoo of Acadiana** (116 Lakeview Dr., 337/837-4325, www.zoo-of-acadiana.com, open 9 A.M.–5 P.M. daily, admission $8), which opened in 1992 and is home to some 800 animals representing more than 50 species. You walk through the jungle-like park along tree-shaded boardwalks and paths, observing the animals in realistic enclosures that replicate nature as much as possible. There's also a petting zoo and a train. Favorite activities include the feedings of Australian parrots, playful otters, black bears, and alligators. Monkeys, llamas, and giraffes are among the most popular animals to watch. Between November 24 and December 30 (excluding Thanksgiving and Christmas, when the zoo is closed), the zoo stays open until

9 P.M. for the Safari of Lights, when the entire zoo is decorated for the holidays.

BREAUX BRIDGE

It's a 15-minute drive east of Lafayette, via either I-10 or the more scenic but slower Highway 94, to reach Breaux Bridge, which is also the first major Cajun community you'll come to if you approach the region from New Orleans and Baton Rouge, via I-10. Breaux Bridge is a low-key country Cajun town with a small but vibrant downtown district that makes for a pleasant stroll and offers some interesting window-browsing. There are a couple of small parks downtown, one of them with plaques discussing the many bridges that have crossed Bayou Teche at this point, hence the name of the town. It was in 1799 that an Acadian immigrant named Firmin Breaux constructed the first crossing in town, a modest footbridge. The town was not officially laid out until a descendant of Breaux, a woman named Scholastique Picou Breaux, drew up plans and began subdividing her farmland into smaller lots and selling them to other settlers.

Apart from a couple of excellent places to eat and some charming B&Bs, the town's main claim to fame is **Lake Martin** (off Hwy. 170, reached via Hwy. 31), 3 miles south of downtown, and the largest nesting area for wading birds in the state. You can walk along a nature trail by the water, watch for the many varieties of bird (as well as nutria, snakes, turtles, and alligators), or take one of the excursions here offered by **Champagnes' Swamp Tours** (337/845-5567, www.champagnesswamptours.com).

ST. MARTINVILLE

About 15 miles south of Breaux Bridge via Highway 31 or south of Lafayette via U.S. 90 to Highway 96, small but bustling St. Martinville (population 7,200) is the quintessential Cajun town, set on Bayou Teche and abundant with historic houses and sites that relate to the region's establishment as an Acadian stronghold. The earliest Acadians arrived at this spot in 1765, making their way here up Bayou Teche from the Gulf of

---

BAYOU TECHE

Bayou Teche runs through the Cajun towns of Breaux Bridge, St. Martinville, and New Iberia, forming the natural western levee of the basin. "Teche" is an old Attakapas Indian name for "snake." Native American legends offer different origins for the name, including one that suggests that a snake actually created the river: Chitimacha warriors destroyed a massive venomous serpent many miles in length, and as the beast died from its wounds, it writhed and deepened a twisting track in the mud that became the riverbed of Bayou Teche.

The Teche begins just east of Opelousas in the town of Port Barrie, where it flows from Bayou Courtableau. Roughly paralleling I-49, it meanders through the towns of Arnaudville and Cecilia before cutting beneath I-10 and entering Breaux Bridge. It's along this stretch, from Arnaudville to Breaux Bridge, that the banks of the river are shaded by tall oak trees, dramatically draped with moss. A couple of miles downstream from St. Martinville, the Teche passes through Keystone Locks and Control Structure, constructed by the U.S. Army Corps of Engineers to increase the bayou's water level, making it navigable for boats heading upstream to Port Barrie.

You can drive alongside much of the Teche along several state highways, especially from New Iberia south through Jeanerette and Franklin. It eventually passes through yet another flood control facility before finally emptying into the Lower Atchafalaya River.

Mexico. The region was already home to Attakapas Indians, long rumored to practice cannibalism, and it was with some trepidation that a handful of trappers set up a frontier trading post here in the mid-1750s. They were followed by cattle farmers, encouraged to settle by the authorities in New Orleans, who sought a source of beef with which to feed the city's growing population.

The earliest Acadian refugees, having been first exiled to colonies along the East Coast, came to Louisiana hoping, correctly, to find a relatively welcome environment—at the very least, a population that was mostly French and Catholic. They first piled into New Orleans, poor and without a concrete plan. The local government furnished the Acadians with basic food, provisions, and farming tools and granted them a parcel of land in the Attakapas District, the name at that time for what is now St. Martin, St. Mary, Iberia, Vermilion, and Lafayette Parishes.

During this first year of Cajun settlement, France ceded Louisiana to the Spaniards, but the new government welcomed the Cajuns with great enthusiasm. For military reasons, they wanted to see the Attakapas District grow into a self-sustaining part of Louisiana, and during the Spanish reign, St. Martinville and the many neighboring towns grew with new arrivals of Cajuns as well as refugees from the revolution in France, Spaniards from the Canary Islands, enterprising Creole families from New Orleans and Mobile, and slaves from West Africa.

Over time, Attakapas became a formal parish, whose name was changed to St. Martin Parish in 1807, the town of St. Martinville having been christened by a Catholic priest. The community grew from a loose collection of farms and a few larger plantations into a proper town, the urban core of which formed along the streets emanating from Church Square, still today downtown's charming focal point. In 1817, St. Martinville, now a prominent trading center in the new U.S. state of Louisiana, became the sixth city in the state to incorporate. Growing contingents of Italians, Germans, and Creoles who had fled from Haiti joined the chiefly French and Cajun inhabitants. Around this time, steamboat travel made it relatively easy for visitors to travel to

and from St. Martinville on the Bayou Teche, which until well into the 19th century served as the principal "highway" in and out of the region. By the mid-1850s, St. Martinville had earned the nickname Petit Paris for its bounty of fine hotels and cultural venues, including an impressive theater.

Although this small, bustling city remains a center of cultural and social life in the Cajun Country, it has never really grown to become much more substantial or populous than it was during the 19th century—this is a big reason the town feels so warm and inviting today. It's bypassed by major highways, and it never grew into a center for southern Louisiana's oil refining and banking the way nearby Lafayette did. Walking through town today, you might not think to call it a city, even though, governmentally, St. Martinville is just that. These days St. Martinville is, in addition to being a significant tourism center, a hub of sugarcane and crawfish harvesting, as well as a factory base for the undergarment manufacturer Fruit of the Loom—it's St. Martinville's largest employer, with nearly 3,000 workers. The town is also known for Louisiana Hot Sauce, a Tabasco rival found on many kitchen and restaurant tables throughout the South.

To explore St. Martinville, start by parking anywhere near Church Square, which anchors downtown at Bridge and Main Streets. Presiding over Church Square is the house of worship for which the town and parish are named, **St. Martin de Tours Catholic Church** (Bridge and Main Streets), which dates to 1765 and is one of the oldest churches in the Gulf South. It contains a replica of the Grotto of Lourdes, which was added in 1870.

A centerpiece of the town is the restored **Duchamp Opera House** (200 S. Main St., 337/394-6604), the very building that, when built in the 1830s, helped to establish the town's reputation as a cultural hub; throughout the 19th century, it was the site of traveling shows, operas from New Orleans, and local theatrical performances. Throughout most of the 20th century it functioned as a department store but has been refurbished to its original purpose and now is home of the Evangeline Players theater group as

© ANDREW COLLINS

St. Martin de Tours Catholic Church, St. Martinville

well as a venue for other shows. Also here is a multidealer antiques shop.

A couple of blocks behind Church Square, at the corner of Evangeline Boulevard and South New Market Street, you can see one of the most visited and photographed icons of Cajun history, the Evangeline Oak, a massive tree named for the protagonist of Henry Wadsworth Longfellow's tragic epic poem of Cajun heartbreak, *Evangeline.* The tree sits overlooking Bayou Teche, marking the apocryphal site where lovers Evangeline and Gabriel, separated during the ruthless Cajun exile from Canada, eventually reunited.

Right beside the park with Evangeline Oak is the **Acadian Memorial** (New Market Street, www.acadianmemorial.org, 337/394-2258, open 10 A.M.–4 P.M. daily), a tribute to the Acadians who settled here. Features include a 12-by-30-foot mural Robert Dafford that depicts the arrival of Acadians between 1765 and 1788; the mural has a twin in Nantes, France, that shows the Louisiana-bound refugees boarding a ship from

France in 1785. There's also a granite-and-bronze Wall of Names, which lists some 3,000 persons who were identified in early state records as having been Acadian refugees. In the Acadian Memorial garden, an eternal flame burns from the center of a polished granite oval. Next door, in the **St. Martinville Cultural Heritage Center** (121 New Market St., open 8 A.M.–4 P.M. Mon.–Fri.), you can use the memorial's multimedia center to research genealogy and history on Acadians, and you can tour a small but nicely done museum on the history of Cajuns in southwestern Louisiana. Donation suggested.

Inside the St. Martinville Cultural Center, the **African American Museum** (121 New Market St., 337/394-2273, open 10 A.M.–4 P.M. daily, donation suggested), which opened in 2001, uses clever multimedia exhibits and illustrated displays to interpret the history and heritage of the West African slaves who were brought to Louisiana, sold, and moved to this part of the state. The focus is especially on the Wolof, Bambara, and Mandiga tribes of Senegal. Many slaves bound for Louisiana were shipped out of Africa by way of Goree Island, about 2 miles off the shore from Dakar, Senegal. Documents discuss the plight of the hundreds of thousands of Africans and their descendents who lived as slaves in Louisiana from 1699 until 1862, when Union forces occupied the state. It's explained that slaves brought to the New World on French ships generally endured less harsh and brutal conditions than on British ships, because the French traders were paid bonuses if they kept their captives alive—even so, the mortality rates on slave ships was extremely high, and it was not uncommon for half of the women and men forced onto ships in Africa to perish on the journey. Exhibits also explain the origin of the term Creole and *gens de couleur libres* (free people of color).

About a mile north of Church Square is the historic Maison Olivier plantation house, which can be visited by guided tour and anchors the first state park established in Louisiana, **Longfellow-Evangeline State Historic Site** (1200 N. Main St., St. Martinville, 337/394-3754 or 888/677-2900, www.lastateparks.com, open 9 A.M.–5 P.M. daily, admission $2). In addition to

CAJUN COUNTRY

the plantation house, the park contains a farmstead (also open for tours) and a small historical museum. All are set along a lovely meadow with paths leading beside Bayou Teche. Originally a *vacherie* (cattle ranch), the plantation was turned into an indigo farm and eventually a highly profitable sugar plantation on which Maison Olivier was built around 1815. The house is a classic raised Creole cottage, a style of architecture unique to Louisiana that incorporates French, Caribbean, and Creole influences. Mostly mid-1800s antiques fill the house. A small footbridge crosses a narrow bayou to the Acadian Farmstead, which illustrates how a typical Cajun farmhouse might have been furnished in the early 1800s. The small Cajun history museum is not especially thrilling, with static, rather dated exhibits, but it does provide some insights into the region's heritage, and it's also where you check in to sign up for a tour of the plantation house or farmstead. Near the museum is a small and very rustic Cajun cabin that gives a nice sense of the difference between the lifestyles of wealthy Creoles and the lower-income Cajuns—the cabin is furnished with original Louisiana cypress pieces, and a small garden in back is planted with medical and culinary herbs popular in this part of the state for many decades.

The second state-operated attraction in town is geared more toward the many outdoors enthusiasts drawn to the Atchafalaya Swamp basin. **Lake Fausse Pointe State Park** (5400 Levee Rd., 337/229-4764 or 888/677-7200, www.crt .state.la.us, day-use admission $2 per vehicle for up to four persons, and 50 cents for each additional person) sits about 18 miles southeast of downtown St. Martinville, just off West Atchafalaya Levee Road. From town you head east on Highway 96, then right onto Highway 679, left onto Highway 3083, and then right onto the levee road; continue along here for 7 miles to reach the park, which sits on the east side of Lake Fausse and fringes Atchafalaya Swamp—it may take a little effort to get here, but the drive is through beautiful wetlands. Before massive levees were built on the eastern and western sides of Atchafalaya Swamp, the entire occupied by this park was part of the swamp, whose boundary extended from Bayou Teche clear to the Mississippi River. Chitimacha Indians lived in this area first, followed by French trappers, Acadian farmers, and then settlers from mainland Spain and the Spanish Canary Islands.

Although Lake Fausse is popular for boating and fishing, it's generally a tranquil place that has for decades been a favorite haunt of wildlife photographers and bird-watchers—there are many areas within the park that seem almost primeval in their serenity and lush foliage. Facilities include a boat launch, a boat dock with rentals, picnic pavilions, a camp store, 18 overnight camping cabins (with screened-in porches, air-conditioning, and piers out over water) and numerous primitive tent sites, an RV camping area (with water and electricity hookups), a conference center, and an extensive network of hiking trails.

NEW IBERIA

Although much smaller than Lafayette and 30 minutes farther south, New Iberia is another excellent base for exploring the Acadiana. It's very close to Avery Island, Abbeville, and St. Martinville (which is 9 miles north, via Hwy. 31), and New Iberia is less dominated by retail chain sprawl than Lafayette. It has a few key attractions in its own right, and a gentrifying downtown commercial district with a handful of noteworthy shops and cafés.

The seat of Iberia Parish, New Iberia—along with the several surrounding villages—was land occupied by the Attakapa Indians before Acadians began trickling in during the 1760s, following their landing at St. Martinville. The same decade, Spain took possession of Louisiana, and in 1779 a group of immigrants from the Spanish city of Málaga settled the town, attempting to farm flax and hemp. Their agrarian endeavors failed, but settlers remained, and the town—today the only permanent settlement in the state established by Spaniards—took the name New Iberia, after Spain's Iberian Peninsula.

Farming did eventually flourish here, with sugarcane becoming the dominant crop as it did elsewhere in Acadiana—still today, Iberia Parish

boating on Bayou Teche, New Iberia

produces more sugarcane (much of it in nearby Jeanerette) than any other parish in Louisiana. New Iberia's most prominent attraction, Shadows-on-the-Teche plantation, was built as the administrative center in 1834 of a prolific network of sugarcane-farming operations. Cattle farming grew into an important industry through about the 1860s, and the area's several salt domes, the most famous being Avery Island, also become important to the economy. The town is home to the oldest extant rice mill in the United States, Conrad Rice Mill. This is a bit odd, as the state's major rice-producing area is well northwest of New Iberia, along the U.S. 90/I-10 corridor between Lafayette and Lake Charles.

The best way to get a feel for downtown New Iberia is to park along the main drag, West Main Street, and wander its blocks. This is a one-way street, the northbound portion of Highway 182, so if you're approaching New Iberia by way of Highway 14 from U.S. 90, which you likely would if coming from Lafayette or Houma, turn right onto St. Peter Street (the southbound portion of Highway 182) as you enter downtown, and continue for several blocks to Lewis Street (there's a Pizza Hut on the corner); make a left

turn, and then a quick left again onto Main Street (Hwy. 182 northbound). The first several blocks of this drive pass by a dazzling array of finely preserved mostly 19th-century homes in several styles, from the classic Greek Revival to painted-lady gingerbread cottages.

Right about at Center Street (Hwy. 14), you'll come to the city's leading attraction, and one of the true must-see museums of Acadiana, **Shadows-on-the-Teche** (317 E. Main St., 337/369-6446, www.shadowsontheteche.org, open 9 A.M.–4:30 P.M. daily, admission $7, free to members of National Trust for Historic Preservation), a dignified white-columned brick house built by sugarcane farmer David Weeks in 1834. Weeks died of an unknown malady during a trip to New Haven before ever living in the house. His wife, Mary C. Weeks, ran the house and oversaw the plantation for years afterward. The house is much smaller than some of the leviathan plantation houses along the Great River Road, and that's one reason it makes for a better tour—you aren't treated to an endless march through rooms and outbuildings. But the best things about Shadows is that the National Trust for Historic Preservation, which owns the house, also has a collection of

© ANDREW COLLINS

Evangeline Theater, downtown New Iberia

some 17,000 paper documents relevant to the lives of the plantation's inhabitants and its day-to-day inner workings. Guides at Shadows draw on these records to help paint a vivid picture of life here, and often the most fascinating bits of information to modern visitors revolve around seeming minutiae, such as inventories of the kitchen pantry, rather than the grandest or fanciest antiques. Some of the volunteer guides who give house tours are actual descendents of David and Mary C. Weeks. In addition to having a well-documented history, Shadows-on-the-Teche is one of the better-furnished plantation homes around. Other details inside the Classical Revival house include a lavish Italian marble floor in the formal dining room and the wide galleries at the exterior facade.

The home's last private owner, David Weeks Hall, worked hard to find a way to have the house saved as a museum; as fate would have it, he passed away in 1958 exactly one day after the National Trust for Historic Preservation agreed to take the house. Hall was something of a renaissance man and a well-known figure among the assorted literati who passed through New Iberia during the first half of the 20th century. You can

still see the autographs of many of his distinguished guests on a door in his ground-floor studio—among the signatures are those of Elia Kazan, Walt Disney, Cecil B. DeMille, and Henry Miller.

Center Street in New Iberia is so named because it was the center of the vast Weeks plantation, which once extended many miles south from this building, clear out to Weeks Island (a.k.a. Grand Cote), the actual sugarcane-farming operation that so enriched the Weeks family. One of the many interesting details that comes out during the tour is that the Weeks family actually had to pay dearly for processed sugar. Sugarcane was harvested here in southwestern Louisiana but refined in factories on the East Coast, so Louisiana families had to buy it back at a considerable cost in its refined form (ironic when you consider that unrefined "sugar in the raw" today now commands high prices in supermarkets and gourmet-food shops). Like many others in Louisiana, the plantation was occupied by Union troops during the Civil War. Soldier camped around the grounds, and officers lived on the ground floor. It was an uneasy time for the Weeks family, and the matron of the family,

Mary C. Weeks, died in the house during the Union occupation. The house's verdant grounds sweep right back to the muddy Bayou Teche, and you can stroll through the beautiful, somewhat formal gardens, which feature some 25 varieties of trees.

From Shadows-on-the-Teche, continue your stroll up Main Street, where you'll transition from the more residential section of town into the commercial district. Note the ornate art deco Evangeline Theatre on your right; it opened in 1930 as a motion-picture house and closed in 1960, sitting dormant until 1994, when it underwent a full restoration. To get a good look at Bayou Teche, cross the waterway at Bridge Street—on a warm day you'll often see boaters speeding along the murky brown water, which is not polluted but rather brown from the sediments constantly being stirred up on the river bottom. As a tour guide at Shadows-on-the-Teche noted, "you know your gumbo roux is just right when it's the color and consistency of Bayou Teche."

On the south side of downtown, you can tour the Konriko company's **Conrad Rice Mill** (307 Ann St., 337/367-6163 or 800/551-3245, www.conradricemill.com, open 9 A.M.–5 P.M. Mon.–Sat., admission free), America's oldest rice operation, having been founded in 1912. This factory museum has exhibits on the region's Cajun culture and specifically on how rice proved to be a key crop in the southwestern Louisiana economy. Parts of the mill building date to 1914, although it has received several additions over the years. During the factory tour through this rambling old mill, you get to see how rice is packaged, formed into rice cakes, and processed today. There's also the inevitable company store, where you can buy a broad assortment of rice products, along with T-shirts and related souvenirs.

Avery Island

Perhaps the most visited section of New Iberia, the community of Avery Island is home to a pair of seminal Cajun Country attractions, Jungle Gardens and the Tabasco Factory. Avery Island is not an island in the sense that most people think of one—namely, it is not surrounded by water. It is, in fact, a salt dome, which rises rather gently above the surrounding wetlands and has been a

Tabasco Factory at Avery Island, near New Iberia

source of commercial salt since the 1860s. The earliest salt works on the island were short-lived but important for Confederate troops during the Civil War. It was in 1862 that a significant cache of rock salt was discovered here—the first such deposit in all of North America. Union troops, upon securing the area, immediately destroyed the salt mines, which were not reopened until 1880. Avery Island continues to be a source of commercial salt. But salt is not Avery Island's claim to fame; rather, it's another savory condiment, Tabasco Sauce, which Edward McIlhenny first bottled on Avery Island in 1868.

To reach Avery Island, follow Highway 329 about 6 miles southwest from U.S. 90 in New Iberia. You'll come to a small guardhouse where a nominal toll of 50 cents is collected, the money going toward the maintenance of the community roads, and then you proceed to the driveways for the Tabasco factory (on your left) and, beyond that, for Jungle Gardens.

The tour of the **McIlhenny Tabasco Company** (Avery Island, 337/365-8173 or 800/634-9599, www.tabasco.com, open 9 A.M.–4 P.M. daily, admission free) is actually pretty underwhelming, but then again, it's free. The tour begins with a shamelessly promotional video expounding on the virtues of Tabasco Sauce, suggesting that you simply cannot eat enough of the stuff. You'll see images of happy and hungry folks gleefully squirting gobs of Tabasco onto just about every food but ice cream. You're then given a small souvenir bottle of the vaunted condiment before proceeding along wall of windows through which you can observe the inner workings of the factory, where a jumble of machines and conveyor belts bottles, caps, and labels the sauces. You walk through a small museum of Tabasco memorabilia at the end of your tour, and can then wander across the parking lot to the faux-old-fashioned Country Store. Here you can buy Tabasco neckties, golf balls, sweat pants, boxer shorts, plus various food products made with the sauce. It's all good, clean, hot fun, and the experience is especially nice for kids who may be getting a little tired of touring historic house-museums. And now for the obligatory Tabasco trivia tidbit: The company holds the second-oldest food trademark in the country (issued in 1870), according to the U.S. Patent Office (Tabasco is mum on who holds the oldest).

turtle at Jungle Gardens and Bird City, Avery Island

Slightly less famous but of arguably much greater interest on Avery Island is the McIlhenny family's 250-acre **Jungle Gardens and Bird City** (Avery Island, 337/365-8173 or 800/634-9599, www.tabasco.com, open 9 A.M.–5 P.M. daily, admission $6). A narrow 4-mile country lane winds through this garden complex, which you can do in less than an hour by car or over the course of a few hours if you decide to hoof it. You can also park in several spots along the drive and get out to walk around. Thousands of subtropical plants and trees, including massive moss-draped live oaks (in case you haven't tired of these yet), grow throughout these wild gardens, which are home to deer, turtles, nutria, raccoons, black bear, and alligators (during the warmer months, it's fairly easy to spot the gators, and you can often get close enough for a picture, although—as common sense dictates—you should absolutely not approach these animals directly).

But the big draw at Jungle Gardens is Bird City, a massive nesting ground for graceful (and big) great white egrets. You reach this area by parking at the designated spot (you will receive a trail map when you pay your admission at the Jungle Gardens gift shop on entering the park). Long platforms are set on stilts rising out of a large marshy pond, and the egrets build nests here—they're most prolific from December through July, when you may see many hundreds of these creatures squawking, gathering branches, mating and courting, flying overhead, and putting on a spectacular show. A three-story observation deck sits opposite the nesting platforms, close enough—especially if you have a decent zoom lens—to snap some wonderful pictures. The gardens also include the most complete collection of camellias in the world and a Buddhist temple containing a statue dating back to the 12th century. Although the gardens are open year-round, they're less thrilling in winter, from November through February, when much of the plant life is dormant, not to mention the hibernating alligators.

Jeanerette

About 12 miles southeast of New Iberia via Highway 182, Jeanerette is the capital of the state's sugarcane industry, and you can learn a bit about this legacy at the small but informative **Jeanerette Museum** (500 E. Main St., 337/276-4408, open 10 A.M.–noon and 1–4 P.M. Mon.–Fri., donation suggested), which contains photos and illustrated exhibits as well as artifacts and memorabilia related to this livelihood. There are also exhibits on African-American history, Mardi Gras, and the cypress-logging industry.

There's a huge sugarcane-processing plant right on Bayou Teche along Highway 182. You can't go inside, but on winter days during the processing season, you can watch some of the harvesting process from the road.

For as watery a place as the Cajun Wetlands are, it's actually not all that easy to find direct access to the open gulf waters. One of the best opportunities for this sort of exploration is to head down to **Cypremort Point State Park** (Beach Lane, off Hwy. 319, Cypremore Point, 337/867-4510 or 888/867-4510, www.crt.state.la.us, Sun.–Thurs. 6A.M.–9P.M., Fri.–Sat. until 10P.M., $2 per vehicle), which fronts a cove on Vermilion Bay, an arm of the Gulf of Mexico. To access the park from U.S. 90 in Jeanerette, make a right turn onto Highway 318, following this until it joins with Highway 83; continue south on 83 into the village of Cypremort, making a left turn onto Highway 319, which leads another 5 miles or so to the park entrance; the whole drive takes about 30 to 40 minutes from downtown Jeanerette.

Within the 185-acre park you'll find a half-mile stretch of man-made beach, one of the only ones in the region, along with a motorized-boat launch (actually just outside the park entrance), a sailboat launch, and picnic pavilions. There's also a fishing pier, from which you can cast a line for flounder and redfish. Swimming and beach-bumming are favorite activities here, but it's also a hot spot for windsurfing, sailing, and most any other type of recreational seafaring. This is a remote park, and wildlife sightings are not uncommon, from muskrats, deer, and gators to even the occasional rare Louisiana black bear.

FRANKLIN

Franklin, about 16 miles southeast of Jeanerette via U.S. 90, has long been one of the most pros-

LOUISIANA'S SUGARCANE INDUSTRY

Based chiefly in Acadiana, the state's sugarcane industry extends across 25 Louisiana parishes and encompasses some 450,000 acres of farmland (an area roughly two-thirds the size of Rhode Island). Revenue for Louisiana in a typical year exceeds $1.5 billion, the result of harvesting some 15 million tons of sugarcane, which represents about 20 percent of the sugar planted in the United States. There are about 700 sugarcane farms throughout southern Louisiana today, employing about 11,000 workers, another 16,000 people work in other capacities in the state's sugarcane industry.

The earliest Louisianans engaged in this industry were Jesuit priests who planted crops along what is now Baronne Street, in New Orleans's Central Business District. This was in 1751, nearly a half-century before the city's earliest mayor, a sugar planter named Etienne de Boré, developed the first method of granulating sugar commercially, at his plantation that stood where Audubon Park is today. The industry has suffered setbacks in the form of floods, occasional disease epidemics, and some prolonged deep-winter freezes, but has for the most part been a steady crop for Louisiana over the past 200 years.

Growing sugarcane is a time-consuming and labor-intensive process. The rows of stalks are planted each fall, and the buds produce shoots of cane the following spring. By late summer, the fresh cane shoots have grown to a size conducive to sugar production, and over the fall through early winter months they are harvested. The good news is that the stalks will regenerate two to four more times before the field must be allowed to lie fallow for a year and then replanted. This means that one field planted with sugarcane can be harvested annually for three to five years.

The cane is then cut and loaded onto wagons, where it's brought to one of the many sugar refineries throughout southern Louisiana; there the raw cane is washed and crushed, the juice collected and reduced over boiling heat until it becomes a thick liquid, which is then separated into crystals (raw sugar) and molasses (used to produce livestock feed). Raw sugar is then sold to refineries, where the crystals are melted and the impurities removed. A byproduct of the cane refining is bagasse, a fuel that is used to power cane processing factories.

---

perous sugarcaning communities anywhere, and the success of this industry during the 19th century is reflected by the some 400 homes and other notable structures in the city's beautiful historic district. The neighborhood, set along the main thoroughfare, Highway 182, makes for a pleasant afternoon or early evening stroll, the sidewalks lighted with old-fashioned street lamps. With all the wealthy plantations and prominent families in Franklin over the years, it's little wonder that the town has produced five Louisiana governors (most recently Mike Foster, as well as his grandfather Murphy Foster, who served in the 1890s), three U.S. Senators, a Chief Justice of the Louisiana Supreme Court, and several other prominent figures.

Franklin is still a big sugar producer, and it also has three plants producing carbon black, a pe-troleum-based compound essential to the production of tires and many mechanical rubber goods as well as plastics, paints, and printing inks.

The leading attraction in town is **Grevemberg** (407 Sterling Rd., 337/828-2092, www .grevemberghouse.com, open 10 A.M.–4 P.M. daily, admission $4), a Greek Revival mansion built in 1851, its four fluted Corinthian columns and gracious second- and ground-floor galleries striking a regal pose over the flowering grounds. Inside you can view an estimable collection of mostly 19th-century antiques, plus antique toys, Civil War memorabilia, reproduction period wallpapers, and numerous decorative pieces.

Franklin's other leading house-museum is owned by politician Mike Foster, who served as Louisiana's governor from 1995 through January

2004, when he was prevented from running again by term-limit laws. **Oaklawn Manor** (Irish Bend Road, off Hwy. 182, 337/828-0434, open 10 A.M.–4 P.M. daily, admission $6) is a brick fortress with 20-inch-thick walls built in 1837 in the Greek Revival style. It stood as the heart of a massive sugarcane plantation during its heyday and is today known for its formal gardens, which bear a resemblance to those of Versailles. You'll also see a number of aviary houses set along the ground, which contain both domestic and tropical birds. The house was featured in the 1975 crime flick *The Drowning Pool*, which starred Paul Newman, Joanne Woodward, and Melanie Griffith. It was the producers at Warner Bros. Studios who had the aviary built for the film, but it fits in perfectly with Oaklawn today. Inside you'll find antique bird prints by Audubon, John Gould, and Prideaux John Selby, along with a collection of priceless antiques.

ABBEVILLE

Although it's not a large city, Abbeville feels more urbane and bustling than some of the other towns around Acadiana. It was founded in 1843, and the downtown area now comprises a large historic district with a mix of attractive commercial and residential architecture. It's also home to **Steen's Syrup Mill** (800/725-1654, www.steensyrup.com), the world's largest sugarcane-syrup plant. There are several engaging shops and eateries downtown, which sits along Bayou Vermilion on its course from Lafayette down to Vermilion Bay. Anchoring the town center is one of Acadiana's most picturesque places of worship, **St. Mary Magdalen Catholic Church,** a redbrick Romanesque structure built in 1911 and possessing a high steeple and an ornate interior. It sits at the corner of Pere Magret Street and Quia des Beaux Arts.

Abbeville can be reached either from Lafayette south via U.S. 167 (20 miles) or from New Iberia west via Highway 675 to Highway 14 (20 miles). A great way to take in Abbeville is to head down in the late afternoon, stop in one of the two excellent oyster bars in the center of town for an inexpensive and delicious meal, then catch a theatrical performance at the **Abbey Players**

St. Mary Magdalen Catholic Church in downtown Abbeville

Theatre (State and Lafayette Streets), which was built in 1908 and originally housed a bar.

Erath

East of Abbeville, roughly midway between it and U.S. 90 in New Iberia, is the small town of Erath, worth a look to check out the small but informative **Acadian Museum of Erath** (203 Broadway, 337/937-5468, www.acadianmuseum.com, open 1–4 P.M. Mon.–Fri., donation suggested), set inside a small complex of early-20th-century storefronts right off Highway 14. The museum contains three rooms with exhibits on the area's history. The first traces the founding of Canadian Acadia in 1604; the second tackles the Grand Dérangement, or deportation of Acadians from Canada; and the last one explores the rebirth of Acadiana in southwestern Louisiana.

HOUMA

Houma is the base for exploring the eastern end of the Cajun Wetlands—it's also the only incorporated town in all of Terrebonne Parish, an enormous but sparsely populated parish that includes many of the fishing and oil-rigging outposts down along the Gulf. There's a wide variety of dining options here, plus a handful of chain hotels and B&Bs, and from here you're within striking distance of numerous swamp-tour and fishing excursions. Houma doesn't have a great many attractions, although downtown, bounded roughly by Park Avenue and Verrett Street, and by Canal Street and Barrow Street, does have a good many historic buildings of architectural significance, including churches, Victorian storefronts, and houses—many of these buildings date to the late 19th century, which is when the city was established. You can get a free copy of the illustrated Houma Downtown Walking Tour from the Houma Convention and Visitors Bureau.

Bayou Terrebonne runs through the heart of Houma, fringing the northern end of downtown and intersecting with the Intercoastal Waterway, which snakes through a good bit of Terrebonne Parish. It's the main bayou in a vast network of waterways that converge in Houma.

Probably the best way to get a sense of the various industries and livelihoods that have formed the foundation for life in the Cajun Wetlands is to tour the **Bayou Terrebonne Waterlife Museum** (7910 W. Park Ave., 985/580-7200, www.houmaterrebonne.org/waterlife.asp, open 10 A.M.–5 P.M. Mon.–Fri. and noon–4 P.M. Sat., admission $3), where interactive and well-laid-out exhibits discuss fishing (both occupational and recreational), shellfish harvesting, oil and natural gas mining, and hunting and trapping. You'll see a mounted 13.5-foot alligator, an exhibit and documents on hurricanes, a shrimp boat, and a display on Louisiana cypress trees. It's housed inside a former barge and freight warehouse, built in the 1880s, on Bayou Terrebonne.

Make time to visit **Southdown Plantation House and Terrebonne Museum** (1208 Museum Dr., off Hwy. 311, 985/851-0154, www.southdownmuseum.org, open 10 A.M.–4 P.M. (last tour an hour before closing) Tues.–Sat., admission $5), a 19th-century manor house that once anchored a large sugar plantation. The eclectic exhibits inside trace local history, including a large collection of Boehm and Doughty porcelain birds and flowers and the re-created Washington, D.C., office of Allen J. Ellender, a U.S. Senator from 1937 through 1972. The house also contains original 19th-century furnishings of the Minor family, who lived here during the plantation years.

MORGAN CITY

Originally part of the territory inhabited by both the Attakapas and Chitimacha Indians, who first named the Atchafalaya River (meaning simply "long river"), Morgan City has been famous over the past two centuries for shrimp fishing, and over the past century as a base for workers on the many offshore oil rigs in the Gulf. This town on the east side of the Atchafalaya River, about 20 miles from where it empties into the Gulf, was first settled as a sugarcane plantation operated by a noted Kentucky surgeon and planter named Walter Brashear. The town took his name and became important during the Civil War, when Union troops occupied it, treasuring its strategic location as a gateway to the Atchafalaya Swamp and a means to cut off Confederate supply lines from Texas.

The town really took off in the 1870s, however, when entrepreneur Charles Morgan dredged the Atchafalaya Bay Channel deep enough for large ships, instantly turning the town into a major trade center for animal fur, shrimp and other seafood, and timber from cypress trees. Brashear was renamed in his honor in 1876. Morgan City was truly immortalized, however, by Hollywood, when it chose this subtropical land with lush swamps as the locale for the first *Tarzan* movie in 1917, starring Elmo Lincoln. The city's boom period began in the 1930s, when its shrimp-fishing industry developed into one of the most prolific in the world. Shortly after World War II, Kerr-McGee Industries drilled Louisiana's first offshore oil well, far out into the Gulf, and Morgan City became the point from which workers and equipment were moved out to this and the many rigs that followed. Today the city

© ANDREW COLLINS

the Atchafalaya River, Morgan City

possesses the largest commercial marine fleet in the world (Tidewater Inc.) and also the world's largest helipad (operated by Petroleum helicopters), which is used for transporting workers and supplies back and forth between Morgan City and the offshore oil rigs in the Gulf. The importance of these two industries continues to be celebrated every Labor Day weekend during the Louisiana Shrimp and Petroleum Festival.

Morgan City is oil country, a hard-working place. The most interesting area is the old downtown, which is set just back from the river below the massive Hwy. 182 and U.S. 90 bridges over the Atchafalaya River. A striking thing about this downtown area is that all along Front Street, a 22-foot-tall concrete retaining wall runs between town and the river; it was built in 1985, replacing a 13-foot wall that was easily overcome during major floods in 1973. On the riverside of the wall are some warehouses and docks, with a number of shrimp boats tied up along the pier. Doors in the wall allow traffic to flow between the river and the town. During bad storms, the doors are shut, and Morgan City is cut off from the rising tide, as is the Berwick area on the other side of the river. The flood wall is much uglier than a levee,

although it's certainly a more efficient use of space, since the wall is just a couple of feet thick, whereas levees take up a considerable swath of land along the riverbank.

Morgan City couldn't exactly be called bustling, and many of its downtown storefronts sit vacant today, but it's an interesting old town. To connect with the other side, take the older and smaller of the two bridges across the river, over which Hwy. 182 runs—this puts you squarely in Berwick, a town with several seafood-processing plants and marine businesses. The downtown historic district runs about four blocks deep from the Atchafalaya River, between the U.S. 90 bridge and Railroad Avenue. You can obtain a free self-guided walking tour map from the Cajun Coast tourism office.

One attraction that's definitely worth a look is the fascinating **International Petroleum Museum and Exposition** (111 1st St., 985/384-3744, www.rigmuseum.com, tours 10 A.M. and 2 P.M. Mon.–Sat., admission $5), a.k.a. "Mr. Charlie Rig," built as the first submersible oil drilling rig in 1952. The museum's claim to fame is that it's the only place in the world where visitors can walk along an authentic oil rig. Mr.

THE ATCHAFALAYA BASIN SWAMP

The Atchafalaya (pronounced UH-cha-fuh-lye-uh) is the main distributary of the Mississippi River, and an active, living delta through which flows the 135-mile-long Atchafalaya River. At about 15 miles in width, the basin is the largest overflow swamp in the United States, and covers some 850,000 acres, about a third of the total land mass of Louisiana.

A swamp is any low ground overrun with water but punctuated by trees; marshes are similar but have few or no trees. This swamp began forming around 900 A.D., when the Mississippi River began to change its course, which had favored an easterly shift once it reached southern Louisiana. For many centuries the river then flowed through the present-day Bayou Lafourche, which passes through the city of Houma and eventually empties into the gulf.

Annual flooding forced heavy waters into the low-lying and dense forest on either side of the Mississippi River. Eventually natural levees formed and contained the water permanently. In recent centuries, the Mississippi River has shifted still farther back toward the southeastern section of the state.

Historically, this swamp cultivated some of the richest and most fertile soil in the South, not to mention prolific fishing grounds, making it the perfect place for the exiled Acadian refugees who arrived in the mid- to late-18th-century and established roots all through the basin. The geography of the swamp effectively cut the early Cajun settlements off from the rest of the state, helping them to preserve their distinct heritage and language. They remain a remarkably close-knit society to this day.

Atchafalaya swamp's appearance and character have both changed dramatically throughout the 20th century. Discoveries in the 1920s of vast oil and natural-gas reserves brought prosperity to the region, as well as large numbers of newcomers. Major floods, most notably in 1927, have at different times forced small communities within the basin to abandon their homes and settle on higher land. And in 1973 the federal government constructed an 18-mile-long bridge through the swamp, extending I-10 from New Orleans and Baton Rouge to Lafayette. The work of the Corps of Engineers, which involved erecting massive flood gates at the intersection of the Mississippi and Atchafalaya rivers, is what prevented the Mississippi from seeking a permanent shortcut through the swamp to the Gulf.

The construction of these flood-control systems and levees, as well as oil-pipelines and other man-made structures, has not only forever altered the swamp but has at times threatened its well-being. The largest bottomland hardwood forest in the country, Atchafalaya is still home to fertile and productive fish and wildlife habitats. More than 50,000 egrets, ibises, and herons nest in the region, with some 300 additional bird species represented. The basin claims about 65 species of reptile and 90 types of fish. Other inhabitants include deer, alligators, bobcats, turtles, alligator gar fish, bald eagles, bears, nutria, wood ducks, cranes, raccoons, possums, osprey, and coyotes.

Charlie himself was used from the early '50s until 1986. Here's how it worked: the 220-foot-long mobile oil barge, which could accommodate 58 workers, would be towed to a shallow-water location (no deeper than 40 feet), where massive tanks inside the barge would be filled with water. The barge would sink to the gulf floor, and drilling would commence. At the end of the drilling cycle, the water tanks would be pumped out and filled again with air, whereupon the rig would float to the surface and be towed to its next location. It's often said that this very rig revolutionized the oil-drilling industry, allowing greater flexibility and maneuverability for drilling off-shore—unquestionably, it changed the nature and the fortunes of life in southwestern Louisiana. These days, you can tour the entire rig, which rests above water. On the 90-minute tour you get a real sense of what it's like to live and work on one of these self-contained industrial islands in the gulf.

Other exhibits at the museum discuss how crude oil is mined and refined, and a history of how mankind began tapping into the earth's vast oil reserves in the 19th century. The museum sits in the Atchafalaya River, right at the junction with the Intercoastal Waterway.

Across the river from Morgan City is the smaller fishing and industrial town of Berwick, and beyond that on U.S. 90 is Patterson. Neither place has much in the way of attractions or interest to travelers, but together these communities were a major source of commercial cypress for many years. At one time, Patterson had the largest cypress sawmill in America.

THIBODAUX

The **Wetlands Acadian Cultural Center** (314 St. Mary St., 985/448-1375, www.nps.gov/jela, open 9 A.M.–6 P.M. Tues.–Thurs., 9 A.M.–5 P.M. Fri.–Sun., and 9 A.M.–7 P.M. Mon., admission free), yet another facility of the outstanding Jean Lafitte National Historical Park and Preserve, touches on the plight of those Cajuns who settled in swamps and marshes and along bayous throughout the southeastern side of the Atchafalaya Basin. Most of the Cajun refugees who put down roots in this region, which includes the swamps and marshes around Thibodaux and Houma, earned their living as trappers, hunters, and fishermen, as opposed to the Cajuns who moved to the prairies to farm.

Inside the center you'll find a wide variety of well-displayed artifacts that tell the story of the Acadian settlement, along with diagrams, charts, photography displays, and similarly useful and easy-to-follow documents. As with all of the Jean Lafitte sites, a great effort has been made to illustrate what everyday life was like for early Cajuns and subsequent generations right through the present day. Other facilities include a 200-seat theater that mounts a variety of programs and lectures on Acadian culture, as well as plays performed by the Thibodaux Playhouse, a local theatrical group. In a crafts demonstration room

you can watch local artisans build boats, carve out duck decoys, make fishing nets, and create local household and decorative items. The center has an excellent bookshop stocked with books on Cajun history (including many titles appropriate for children) and local music CDs. Check for interpretive programs, videos, and performances, scheduled regularly throughout the year, and when in New Orleans, be sure to drop in on the headquarters of the Jean Lafitte National Historical Preserve, in the French Quarter at 419 Decatur St. Here you'll find information on all of the park's six sites throughout southern Louisiana.

SHOPPING

Shops selling Cajun-related gifts, books, arts and crafts, music tapes and CDs, and book are easy to find throughout Acadiana, especially attached to the museums described above. One of the best sources of these types of goods is the **farmers market** held in downtown New Iberia's Bouligny Plaza (off Main Street); it's held 4–7 P.M. Tuesdays and 8–11 A.M. Saturdays. You'll find baked goods, produce, candies, blacksmith wares, herbs, hand-dipped candles, crafts, and local art. (Bayou Teche Farmer's Market takes place across from Victor's.)

New Iberia is one of the best towns for shopping in the area, as it's home to a handful of very nice independent shops and boutiques, including several antiques shops. Stroll along Main Street and the blocks just off it. Be sure to check out **Books Along the Teche** (110 E. Main St., 337/367-7621), a small but first-rate independent bookstore that specializes in the books of James Lee Burke, author of the Dave Robicheaux detective novels.

In downtown Lafayette, **Jefferson Street Market** (538 Jefferson St., 337/233-2589) is a collection of shops and designers selling imported textiles, custom-crafted cypress furnishings, folk art, decorative items, local art, antiques, and similar items—it's a must if you're looking to pick up authentic southwest Louisiana items for the home. There's a small cafe on site, Keller's Bakery, where you can pick up gourmet sandwiches and snacks. Another important shopping stop downtown is **Sans Souci** (219 E. Vermilion St., 337/266-7999), a gallery featuring the works of members of the Louisiana Crafts Guild—you'll find clothing and textiles, small furniture, pottery, ceramics, glass, wood, and many other types of decorative items.

In the heart of downtown Breaux Bridge you'll find a handful of boutiques, among them **Breaux Bridge Trading Co.** (202 Guilbeau St., 337/332-5381), a multidealer complex of antiques shops.

ACCOMMODATIONS

This part of the Cajun Country has dozens of B&Bs, ranging from small and rustic cabins overlooking swamps and bayous to regal Greek Revival manor houses filled with museum-quality antiques. The greatest number and variety of such properties are in Lafayette, Breaux Bridge, New Iberia, and St. Martinville. Lafayette also has dozens of chain motels and hotels, many of them along U.S. 90 just south of I-10 or along the city's main commercial drags, such as Pinhook and Kaliste Saloom Roads. There's also a small cluster of chain hotels off U.S. 90 at Highway 14 in New Iberia.

Lodging costs are much lower in Acadiana than in New Orleans, with most mid- to u[...] scale chain hotels charging nearly but still l[...] than $100, except during very busy times, a[...] many perfectly decent lower-end propert[...] charging under $50. B&B prices vary more, b[...] even the most luxurious properties in the a[...] generally keep their rates under $150, while in[...] that cost between $50 and $100 nightly make[...] the majority.

Hotels and Motels

Under $50: Although it's a chain with an u[...] even track record, the **Days Inn Lafaye[...]** (1620 N. University Ave., 337/237-8880[...] 800/329-7466, www.daysinn.com), just off[...] 10 north of downtown, offers among the b[...] values in the region. The place was complet[...] revamped in 2000 and has clean, attracti[...] rooms whose fox-print-covered walls may n[...] have you believing you're at a Ritz-Carlton b[...] do at least brighten things up. Amenities i[...] clude a pool; in-room writing desks, m[...] crowaves, and refrigerators; and a courtec[...] staff. Another very inexpensive option alo[...] the same strip is the **Red Roof Inn Lafaye[...]**

view from the Hilton Lafayette of Bayou Vermilion

(1718 N. University Ave., 337/233-3339 or 800/RED-ROOF, www.redroof.com), a generic but reliable budget property.

$50–100: The fanciest chain property in the area, the **Hilton Lafayette and Towers** (1521 W. Pinhook Rd., 337/235-6111 or 800/774-1500, www.hilton.com) sits on the banks of Bayou Vermilion and has 330 warmly furnished rooms with French Provincial–inspired furnishings. The 15-floor hotel offers nice views of the countryside and is centrally located, close to the airport and downtown. There's a pretty good full-service restaurant and a hotel bar that's popular with locals and has live bands fairly often. Other pluses include a 24-hour business center, a fitness center, in-room high-speed Internet, room service, and a full laundry service. The Hilton's main competitor, the **Holiday Inn Holidome** (2032 N.E. Evangeline Thruway, 337/233-6815 or 800/465-4329, www.holiday-inn.com), differs markedly in location and ambience. It's a low-rise property just off I-10 and the junction with I-49, and it sits on 17 landscaped acres with picnic areas, playgrounds, and a large game room—the setting and activities make it a favorite with families. Other features include a large health center, an indoor pool, and a full restaurant.

The **Sleep Inn Scott** (2140 W. Willow St., Scott, 337/264-0408 or 877/424-6423, www.sleepinn.com) is a midpriced chain just off I-10 a few miles northwest of Lafayette, a good choice to be closer to Lake Charles and away from the heavily trafficked I-10 exits north of downtown. Rooms are compact, but some suites have whirlpools, and perks include a free morning paper and continental breakfast; all units have built-in work areas. A terrific all-around option with a quiet location on the southwest side of town, an area less overrun with strip malls than out by the interstate, the **Courtyard Lafayette** (214 Kaliste Saloom Rd., 337/232-5005 or 800/321-2211, www.marriott.com) has pleasantly landscaped grounds, a friendly staff, warm and inviting public areas, and 90 spacious and well-lighted rooms with work desks, voice mail, in-room movies, and irons and ironing boards.

Extended Stay Lafayette–Oil Center (807 S. Hugh Wallis Rd., Lafayette, 337/232-8313 or 800/EXT-STAY), part of a chain of economical properties designed for guests staying several days or more, is just across U.S. 90 from Lafayette Regional Airport, on the south side of town, which puts you a bit closer to New Iberia and St. Martinville than most of the city's hotels. The other big advantage to this hotel is that its amenities work well if you're traveling with friends or family or staying a while: Rooms are 300 square feet, with recliner chairs, kitchens equipped with dishes and silverware, and ample space for up to four guests.

Built in the late '90s, the **Comfort Suites New Iberia** (2817 Hwy. 14, 337/367-0855 or 877/424-6423, www.comfortsuites.com) is one of the best values in town. Rooms are bright and large with both beds and sleeper sofas, and there's an indoor pool and exercise room. The big, pink, vaguely Carribean-style building, with 50 guest rooms, is just off U.S. 90, a short drive from downtown New Iberia and Avery Island. Practically next door is the **Best Western Inn & Suites of New Iberia** (2714 Hwy. 14, 337/364-3030 or 800/780-7234, www.bestwestern.com), a 150-room low-rise built in the early 1980s but completely overhauled in 1999. Amenities include a restaurant and lounge and outdoor pool.

Outside of Lafayette and New Iberia, chain hotels are limited to a handful of spots, including the **Best Western of Breaux Bridge** (2088-B Rees St., Breaux Bridge, 337/332-1114 or 888/783-0007, www.bestwestern.com), a run-of-the-mill 50-room property just off I-10, a short drive north of town, and the **Best Western Forest Motor Inn** (1909 Main St., Franklin, 337/828-1810 or 800/828-1812, www.bestwestern.com), a qualitatively similar motor court with 88 rooms, an Olympic-size outdoor pool, a restaurant, business services, and a convenient location just outside Franklin's historic district. There's also a very nicely maintained **Holiday Inn Express** (2942 Grand Point Hwy., Breaux Bridge, 337/667-8913 or 800/465-4329, www.hiexpress.com), just off I-10 near the Henderson. It's the closest hotel in Acadiana to Baton Rouge via I-10.

A nice, inexpensive, and well-kept motel with a large pool in back, the **Ramada Houma** (1400 W. Tunnel Blvd., Houma, 985/879-4871 or

888/989-8367, www.bayoucountryinns.com) is within walking distance of several restaurants and has its own decent place to eat on-site. The 153-room property has a lounge, an outdoor pool, a hot tub, and pleasantly landscaped grounds. The same owners also operate the **Plantation Inn** (1381 W. Tunnel Blvd., 985/868-0500 or 800/373-0072, www.bayoucountry inns.com), a somewhat more upscale modern hotel with a lounge and restaurant.

An affordable option in downtown Houma, the **Fairfield Inn** (1530 Martin Luther King Blvd., 985/580-1050 or 800/228-2800, www .fairfieldinn.com) has three stories of airy, clean rooms with free local calls, work desks, and very good lighting. There's continental breakfast, same-day dry-cleaning, an indoor pool and hot tub, and an exercise room.

Inns and Bed-and-Breakfasts

Under $50: A quasi-hostel, the affordable **Blue Moon Guest House** (215 E. Convent St., Lafayette, 337/234-2422, www.bluemoonhos-tel.com) is a great choice for budget travelers—it's a clean, centrally located Acadian-style wood-frame house with five larger rooms that can accommodate up to 30 persons. The dorm-style units are first-come, first-served and can be converted into private rooms if there's availability; if you're seeking one of the private rooms, it's best to email ahead and make a reservation. The late 1890s house, with hardwood floors and sunny rooms with both double and single-size bunk beds and in some cases private beds, is open to guests of all ages, including families. The owners, who speak English and French, run a laid-back and friendly place where guests tend to mingle and get to know each others. There's Internet access and a self-service kitchen, and local bands perform on the expansive back deck many evenings and also on Sunday afternoons.

$50–100: Steps from St. Martinville's Evangeline Oak, the **Old Castillo B&B** (220 Evangeline Blvd., 337/394-4010 or 800/621-3017) is a stately redbrick Greek Revival inn that was built in the 1800s as a private home but was soon converted into a hotel. During most of the 20th century, the building served as the city's only high school for girls, run by the Mercy nuns. There are five rooms with high ceilings, hardwood floors, and fine antiques, and the ground floor houses La Place d'Evangeline Restaurant.

You can't get much closer to the swamp country than by staying at the **Riverside Cottage B&B** (2091 Atchafalaya River Hwy., Breaux Bridge, 337/228-2066, www.theriversidecot-tage.com), a tranquil country house with three spacious suites, each with a private balcony overlooking the gentle Atchafalaya River. Rooms have sleeper sofas and can accommodate up to four guests, and each also has private, cable TV, phone, refrigerator, microwave, and coffeemaker. Two of the rooms are floral-themed, and the Country Suite has rich hardwood floor and wood paneling. Furnishings are simple, warm, and un-fussy, and guests enjoy plenty of privacy here, making it a favorite spot with couples seeking a secluded retreat from civilization.

With rates lower than most of the cookie-cutter motels around the area, **Bayou Boudin Cabins** (100 W. Mills Ave., Breaux Bridge, 337/332-6158, www.bayoucabins.com) makes a fun and funky alternative. There are eight cozy cabins right by Bayou Teche, close to downtown and within walking distance of famous Mulate Restaurant; and there's a home-style café right on the premises, serving seafood boudin, crack-lins, andouille gumbo, and the like. The cabins are rustic but endearingly furnished—one has old newspaper for wallpaper, another contains a handmade pencil-post queen-size bed. Some have screened porches, another is decked in '50s-style furnishings, and they all have cable TVs. A full breakfast is included.

A charming cottage on the banks of the Intercoastal Waterway, **Honduras House B&B** (1023 Saadi St., Houma, 504/868-1520) offers three simply furnished rooms with Victorian antiques and private baths (one is handicapped accessible). The largest accommodation has a full sitting room and a porch overlooking the water. Also onsite is Melvin's Restaurant, which serves casual regional fare.

$100–150: Stay at the stately **Hanson House** (114 E. Main St., Franklin, 337/828-3217 or 877/928-3271, www.bigdogz.com/hh) for t chance to experience the high-style romance of an antebellum mansion—there aren't many buildings like this in Cajun Country. The Greek Revival home, built by an evidently quite successful British ship's captain in 1849, sits along Franklin's main drag, in the heart of the town's historic district—it's between Lafayette and Houma, making it a good choice for exploring the length of the Cajun wetlands. Furnishings are eclectic, ranging from ornate Victorian carved-wood beds and dressers to more modern pieces from the 1940 and '50s; both private and shared baths are available. An extensive and filling Southern breakfast is included.

One of St. Martinville's architectural gems, **Bienvenue House** (421 N. Main St., 337/394-9100 or 888/394-9100, www.bienvenuehouse.com) was built in 1830 and today contains four lovely rooms with a mix of country-inspired and more formal antiques. Breakfasts here are a lavish affair, and many of the town's restaurants and shops are within a short walk. Upscale **Maison Des Amis and Chez Des Amis** (140 Bridge St., Breaux Bridge, 337/507-3399, www.cafedesamis.com) comprises a pair of the most elegantly furnished homes in Cajun Country. Maison Des Amis has a two-bedroom suite and a standard room, while Chez Des Amis is a smaller cottage with a pair of standard guest rooms. Furnishings are well-chosen and stylish, from plush linens and pillows to fine darkwood Victorian antiques. Each cottage is filled with the artwork (for sale) of prominent Louisiana artists and has a sitting area, and guests enjoy a full breakfast in the acclaimed Cafe Des Amis. The inns are along Bayou Teche, a short drive from the nature preserve at Lake Martin.

With a convenient downtown location in New Iberia, just across the street from Shadows-on-the-Teche, **Le Rosier** (314 E. Main St., New Iberia, 337/367-5306 or 888/804-ROSE, www. lerosier.com) contains six romantically furnished rooms. The hosts are friendly, and there's an equally convivial Dalmatian doggy on hand to greet guests. Rooms have DSL lines and desks. It's a very charming house with a spacious breakfast area. The six very secluded units are inside an outbuilding in back of the main house. It's a first-class operation all around.

In Lafayette, **Bois des Chenes** (338 N. Sterling St., 337/233-7816) occupies an 1820s plantation on the edge of downtown. Three of the suites, each with private bath, cable TV, and minirefrigerators, are inside an 1890s carriage house, behind the main home. The upstairs unit can accommodate five guests, the other two suites—on the ground floor—are each double-occupancy. Each is decorated elegantly in a different regional style: country Acadian, Louisiana Empire, and classic Victorian. In the main home, there are two full suites with the same amenities; one has a working wood fireplace (and it does come in handy on those chilly winter evenings).

A relaxing and informal getaway about a 10-minute drive north of Lafayette, **Bechet House B&B** (313 N. Church St., Carencro, 337/896-3213 or 866/896-3211), pronounced "bay-shay," sits in the heart of downtown Carencro—close to Prejean's, Paul's Pirogue, and several other great restaurants. The 1890s Victorian house, built of fine red cypress, contains six airy rooms, each with a slightly different theme but similarly exquisite antiques, some built by prominent Louisiana craftsmen. The Hydrangea Room is known for its collection of teddy bears, the Iris Room enchants romantics with its deep cast-iron soaking tub (it also has a separate shower), and the spacious Monkey Room has whimsical designs, fabrics, and colors. Small pets are welcome, as are children. This is a great base if you plan on exploring some of the northern Cajun prairie towns, such as Opelousas and Eunice, which are 20 and 45 minutes away respectively.

Grand Bayou Noir (1143 Bayou Black Dr., Houma, 985/873-5849, www.grandbayou noir.com) sits on 4 acres studded with gracious oak and fruit trees, fronting the peaceful Bayou Black. Guest rooms in this imposing 1930s Colonial Revival house have private baths and elegant antiques, plus cable TV; one suite has a private balcony and sitting area.

Over $250: The Gougenheim (101 W. Main St., New Iberia, 337/364-3949, www.gougen heim.com) is an impressive, elegant 1894 building on Main Street, very near Victor's Cafeteria. It was constructed as the Washington Ballroom, where it hosted many wedding receptions and important social functions, and it was beautifully restored by its current owners and converted into a B&B in 2001. There's a large veranda that wraps around the second floor, and four large guest apartments: a one-bedroom, a two-bedroom, and two with three bedrooms. Hardwood floors, detailed woodwork, exposed brick, and posh furnishings give this the feel of a small luxury hotel; some units have spiral staircases leading up to sleeping lofts. Amenities include large TVs with VCRs, designer kitchens with granite counters and stainless-steel appliances, and private balconies overlooking downtown New Iberia's historic district.

Camping

In quiet Carencro, **Bayou Wilderness R.V. Resort** (201 St. Clair Rd., 337/896-0598, www.bayouwildernessrvresort.com) is north and east of Lafayette and has 120 full pull-through RV sites set on 50 acres of wooded grounds. The resort has oodles of activities and recreational diversions, including a pool with slides, a Jacuzzi, a tennis court, shuffleboard, a playground and video arcade, and trails through cypress groves and by natural fishing ponds. There's also a well-stocked camp store. The property is right by Bayou Vermilion.

Right in the center of things (well, just west of town), **KOA Lafayette** (537 Apollo Rd., Scott, 337/235-2739 or 800/562-0809, www.koa.com) is right off I-10 and has a wealth of facilities, including two pools, minigolf, Cajun driving tour cassettes that you're free to borrow, and fishing in a 10-acre stocked lake. In addition to the 175 level concrete sites, you can stay in one of the 20 camp cabins.

Another popular camping area in the region is **Maxie's Campground** (U.S. 90, Broussard, 337/837-6200, www.maxiescampground.com), which is southwest of Lafayette, within easy striking distance of Avery Island, New Iberia, and St. Martinville—it's very near the Zoo of Acadiana. There are 70 RV sites with full hookups, plus laundry facilities and restrooms with showers. This is less a resort and more a picturesque, tree-shaded meadow where you can safely and comfortably park your RV.

FOOD

To somebody visiting from another part of the country or even a differently country entirely, the food served at most restaurants in Acadiana might not seem like a significant departure from that served in New Orleans. The Cajuns use a lot of local fish—oysters, soft-shell crabs, crawfish, shrimp, redfish, catfish. And you'll find gumbo, bread pudding with rum sauce, red beans and rice, étouffée, jambalaya, and plenty of other foods common to New Orleans on menus in Lafayette, New Iberia, and elsewhere. The difference, really, is that while it's not hard to find the main dishes of Cajun cooking on menus all throughout New Orleans, you don't often find the full range of New Orleans cuisine on Cajun menus—although alligator fritters, cracklins, and boudin are far easier to find in Breaux Bridge or Abbeville than in the French Quarter. The true Creole classics of the Big Easy, such as oysters Rockefeller, bananas Foster, shrimp remoulade, turtle soup, and fish slathered in rich cream sauces are less common out this way, found only at a handful of upscale places that specialize in a more urbanized form of Louisiana fare.

This is not to say that the food served in Cajun restaurants is any less fresh, authentic, or tasty—only that preparations tend to be simpler and more straightforward, even if portions at Acadiana restaurants are consistently every bit as overwhelming as in New Orleans. Happily, prices at Cajun Country restaurants are much lower than at comparable places in New Orleans—even at the most sophisticated eateries in Lafayette, it's rare to see entrées on menus costing much more than $20. Similarly, dress is more casual, and the ambience of restaurants less formal—in fact, some of the most respected eateries in Acadiana for food have almost depressingly drab dining rooms. It's as though Cajuns are a bit suspicious of a restaurateur who would go to great lengths to gussy up a place, as though maybe it's an attempt to mask substandard food.

That all being said, the dining scene in Acadiana, especially in fast-growing Lafayette and sophisticated New Iberia, is changing, just as it is everywhere. A number of places serving innovative, impressionistic versions of traditional Cajun cooking have opened in these parts in recent decades, and their legions will no doubt multiply in the coming years.

Traditional Creole and Cajun

Lafayette's (1025 Kaliste Saloom Rd., Lafayette, 337/216-9024, $11–26) is a fairly standard-issue steak-and-seafood place doling out huge portions of extremely fresh seafood. The fare served here is generally rich and heavy, in many cases deep-fried—just the way plenty of people in these parts like it. Sample coconut shrimp; crawfish-and-artichoke bisque; mahimahi Creole-style with a sauce of crawfish, shrimp, wild mushrooms, parsnips, and hollandaise sauce; tandoori-style tilapia; and whole semi-boneless applewood-smoked-bacon-wrapped quail with a stuffing of crawfish, crab, and shrimp. Lafayette's is set in a sprawling, modern building made to look like a plantation house, with dining rooms set around a central bar. Prices are reasonable, and servers are young and friendly.

A longtime favorite for Cajun music and authentic food, **Mulate's** (325 Mills Ave., Breaux Bridge, 337/332-4648 or 800/422-2586, $13–19) is a cavernous, noisy, and happy place built with cypress logs brought over from nearby Henderson Swamp—it's on busy Highway 94, on the northwest side of town, an easy drive from Lafayette or Exit 109 off I-10. Specialties from the long, long menu include catfish Mulate (topped with crawfish étouffée), crabmeat au gratin, and—when you just can't make up your mind— Mulate's Cajun Seafood Platter, which includes stuffed crab, fried crawfish tails, butterflied shrimp, fried catfish, fried oysters, jambalaya, corn macque choux, and home-style fries. It's tourist central at this place, but it's hard not to enjoy yourself here, even if you don't love crowds—the music is infectious.

Overlooking Evangeline Oak and occupying the ground-floor of the Old Castillo Hotel, **La Place d'Evangeline Restaurant** (220 Evangeline Blvd., 337/394-4010, $9–18) serves an eclectic mix of steak and seafood dishes, from filet mignon to blackened snapper. The high-ceilinged dining room has hardwood floors and tall win-dows looking out over this charming neighborhood in the town's historic center.

Clementine's (113 E. Main St., 337/560-1007, $13–23) is New Iberia's classiest restaurant, a white-linen and fine-flatware sort of place, but the dress and mood are still casual. The walls are lined with the paintings of locally prominent artists—the restaurant is named for painter Clementine Hunter. The cooking tends toward traditional Cajun and Creole, with a few nods to today's contemporary styles, such as crawfish cakes with a kicky Creole-style sauce, corn-and-crab bisque, and tender black Angus steaks. Still, it's the straightforward chicken-and-andouille gumbo that really stands out. There's a well-thought-out wine list. You'll find this homey restaurant right on Main in the heart of the historic district. There's live music on weekend evenings.

In downtown Broussard, **Nash's** (101 E. 2nd St., 337/839-9333, $10–20) occupies a stately 1908 house surrounded by mature oak and cedar trees. The kitchen specializes in both traditional upscale Creole and Italian fare, a breed of cooking that's relatively common in New Orleans but unusual in Acadiana. You might start with crab cakes topped with a Creole horse-radish cream or Italian sausage served over caramelized onions with roasted peppers and Italian red gravy. Worthy entrées include shrimp-and-eggplant parmigiana over angel hair pasta, cornmeal-dusted oysters, filet mignon, or grilled amberjack with a lemon-butter sauce served over shrimp fettuccine.

Prejean's (3480 I-49 Access Rd., 337/896-3247, $15–25), directly south of Evangeline Downs, is as popular for its live Cajun music as for the very good food. The rambling dining room is presided over by a friendly and efficient staff. Of the big Cajun dance hall–slash–dining rooms in the region, Prejean's serves the best, and most inventive, Cajun and Creole food, including such specialties as mesquite-grilled yellowfin tuna Rockefeller with lobster sauce; skillet-cooked shrimp, crab, and crawfish in crab-butter cream topped with jack cheese; catfish Catahoula (stuffed with shrimp, crawfish, and crab); alligator Grand Chenier (white tailmeat with a crab-shrimp stuffing), and a mixed grill of mesquite-grilled elk chop, blackened venison chop, and buffalo tenderloin, each with its own sauce. Chocolate crème brûlée ranks among the favorite desserts. The whole time you're enjoying the dinner, you can enjoy live music and dancing at the front of the dining room. Lunch and breakfast are also available—the crawfish-and-andouille eggs scramble is notable.

Don't be put off by the location amid fast-food restaurants, **Savoie's** (1377 Tunnel Blvd., Houma, 504/872-9819, $5–24) is the real thing—a first-rate, down-home Cajun seafood restaurant that's also acclaimed for its steaks and Continental-style dishes, like veal Monica (topped with crayfish). Po'boys and the fried speckled trout platter are additional favorites at this rustically decorated spot with a young, friendly waitstaff. The restaurant is pronounced "**sav**-wahs." Another great standby for Cajun fare, **A-Bear's Cafe** (809 Bayou Black Dr., Houma, 985/872-6306, $7–17) has been serving good, no-nonsense food (red beans and rice, catfish, boiled shrimp) since the early 1960s in an atmospheric 1920s building. On Friday nights there's live Cajun music.

Arguably the best fish house in an area known for them, **Eastway Seafood West Cajun Restaurant** (1029 W. Tunnel Blvd., Houma, 985/876-2121, $8–20) serves a vast range of creatures from the sea, in both traditional Cajun and somewhat more contemporary preparations. There's rare grilled tuna, red snapper, frogs' legs, oysters on the half shell, and some toothsome desserts, including traditional bread pudding with rum sauce and homemade peanut-butter or chocolate fudge. The Cajun mudbug-and-corn soup is a house specialty.

Creative and Contemporary

If you only have a chance for one dinner in the Cajun Country, give strong consideration to **Cafe Vermilionville** (1304 W. Pinhook Rd., Lafayette, 337/237-0100, $18–28), a snazzy yet friendly restaurant set inside a stunning 1810s raised Creole cottage that brightens up an otherwise dull road clogged with strip malls. During its early years, it served as Lafayette's only inn; now chef Ken Veron serves his innovative style fine Cajun cooking within its historic walls. T menu changes often, but here are a few recent vorites to whet your appetite: there are the start of smoked duck and figs au poivre, or the cra fish beignets with a spicy Creole dipping sau The salad with bronzed shrimp, artichokes, a Montrachet goat cheese is a knockout. Amo the entrées, consider Louisiana speckled tr dusted with sweet-potato flour and finished w jumbo lump crabmeat and lemon-and-thy beurre blanc; or marinated chicken breast broi over an open flame and topped with crawf tails and French mushrooms and then serv with a roasted garlic-and-chive butter. Cafe V milionville has one of the most respected w lists in the area.

Gabrielle's (100 N. Main St., St. Martinvi 337/394-4446, $11–23) is one of the fanc eateries around, set inside a pale yellow hou with an attractive balcony; the dining room h tall windows overlooking Church Square in h toric St. Martinville, a charming place in t charming town with very good Creole and Caj food, tending toward the sophisticated (for ample, the fried seafood items are all availa grilled, which is quite uncommon in this p of the world). There's a great crab bisque, or y might start with Gabriel's sampler appetizer pl ter, with shrimp, oysters, catfish, crab finge and alligator. A specialty is the grilled tuna A dian, topped with lump crabmeat and serv with jambalaya. It's a noisy place that can busy, but it's also casually elegant.

In Lafayette, whence famous "blue dog" ar George Rodrigue hails, the **Blue Dog Cafe** (12 W. Pinhook Rd., 337/237-0005, $13–22) filled with the canine art so beloved by so ma people. But the real reason to dine inside t cheery house along a busy road on the south s of town is to sample the creatively rende Louisiana cuisine, from velvety corn-and-cr bisque to tender seafood wontons—and th are just the starters. Dig in to honey-glazed du and some of the best crawfish étouffée in to when you're truly hungry.

Some of the most creative cooking in the a is served at **Cafe Des Amis** (140 E. Bridge S

Breaux Bridge, 337/332-5273, $12–20), a snazzy yet laid-back storefront eatery set in a 19th-century building. Oven-glazed duckling glazed with cane syrup and pepper jelly, and sesame-encrusted drum topped with shrimp and sautéed in fresh chopped tomatoes and lime juice are house specialties, but don't overlook sushi-grade tuna served rare with a black peppercorn crust. The restaurant serves breakfast and lunch, too, including Saturday morning zydeco concerts; there's also live acoustic music on Wednesday evenings.

It's worth the short drive north to **Catahoula's** (234 Martin Luther King Dr./Hwy. 93, Exit 11 from I-49, Grand Coteau, 337/662-2275 or 888/547-2275, $14–24), which is named for the state dog of Louisiana, a special blue-eyed dog descended from the dogs used by explorer Hernando de Soto during his journey through southern Louisiana in the 1530s—the walls of the restaurant, which occupies an old hardware-and-feed store, are lined with photos of these majestic dogs. Exceptional regional fare is served, including raspberry roast duckling, seared ahi tuna on skewers, crabmeat cheesecake, and seafood Napoleon.

Casual Cooking

Not surprisingly, you'll see an actual varnished pirogue hanging from the ceiling at **Paul's Pirogue** (209 E. St. Peter St., Carencro, 337/896-3788, $5–18), a wood-paneled, rustic dining room in downtown Carencro. You'll find both communal and individual tables at this storefront spot with friendly, low-key service. The special combo dinners are the big draw here—with the crawfish version you get crawfish salad, bisque, étouffée, boulettes (fried dumplings), and a generous pile of boiled crawfish, along with fried or stuffed potatoes and dessert. It's a delicious, messy affair. Less overwhelming but equally tasty are the simpler dishes, such as shrimp-and-crab étouffée, Paul's pepper (a bell pepper stuffed with crabmeat), snapper Kori (served under a mound of sautéed crabmeat), and fried frogs' legs.

Soul food doesn't get much better than what you'll taste at **Country Cuisine** (709 N. University Ave., 337/269-1653, $5–13), a simple low-frills restaurant that has a set menu but also comes up with a nice mix of daily specials. Favorites include barbecued ribs and chicken, shrimp and okra, meatball stew, stuffed pork chops, and a wide range of sides—black-eyed peas, smothered potatoes, cabbage, mac-and-cheese, baked beans.

Lagniappe, Too (204 E. Main St., New Iberia, 337/365-9419, $7–14) is a cute art-filled sunny café just a block or two from Shadows-on-the-Teche. It's very casual, with red-and-white-checked plastic tablecloths, and large windows overlooking busy Main Street. You'll find a classic menu of Cajun gumbos, bisques, po'boys, salads, seafoods, and grills. Have a slice of banana-mango cake to finish off your meal. Everything on the menu is prepared fresh from scratch. It's mostly a lunch place, but dinner is served on Friday and Saturday nights.

Black's (319 Pere Megret, 337/893-4266, $4–11) is arguably the most atmospheric of Abbeville's handful of outstanding oyster bars—it's a large tavern with high ceilings and tall brick walls and plain wood tables. Fresh oysters on the half shell cost just $4.50 a dozen, but you can also get alligator bits, soft-shell crab loaves, and delicious grilled chicken salad with homemade ranch dressing. The dining area and bar are filled with mounted fish and posters of local scenes. **Foti's Oyster Bar** (108 S. Main St., St. Martinville, 337/394-3058, $5–13) in St. Martinsville is a funky little oyster bar with a few picnic benches on the sidewalk facing the Catholic church and historic square in St. Martinville. In addition to raw bivalves, you can also order plates of boiled crab, shrimp, and other seafood. There are just a handful of wooden tables inside.

The **Seafood Connection** (999 Parkview Dr., New Iberia $5–11) may occupy a humble cinderblock building with no windows and long rows of plain tables bathed in fluorescent light, but this phenomenally popular restaurant is staffed by super-nice servers and excellent fry cooks who turn out some of the tastiest fish and shellfish around. Here you can order fresh platters of boiled crab and crawfish, stuffed shrimp or crab, and fried soft-shell crab, oysters, and frog's legs. It's open daily and quite late by New Iberia standards, and it's a great value. Just keep in mind that virtually everything on the menu once swam in the sea, so landlubbers should look elsewhere.

A favorite spot for casual American fare, **Rick's** (1023 Tunnel Blvd., Houma, 985/879-4386, $7–20) is popular for its large patio set around a fountain and century-old oak tree. The dining room is festive and informal, usually abuzz with laughter and conversation. Rick's serves a very good corn-and-crab chowder, plus popcorn-shrimp salad, a rib eye–and–lobster combo platter, blackened chicken, and crawfish étouffée. Hot French bread and strawberry butter are served with each meal. **Red Fish Pizza** (224 S. Hollywood Ave., Houma, 985/872-1400, $6–14) serves some of the tastiest gourmet pies around, along with bounteous salads and fresh pasta dishes.

Ethnic

Rather close to the famous Cajun restaurant Prejean's (but on the opposite side of I-49), **Picante's** (3235 N.W. Evangeline Thruway, 337/896-1200, $4–13) is a stellar Mexican restaurant with a youthful, friendly staff and spicy fare ranging from fairly typical Tex-Mex dishes to a few items with distinctly local flair: huge Cajun chimichangas are packed with crawfish étouffée and Mexican rice, and topped with avocados, sour cream, and a corn cake. Another fine offering is the chile-and-cheese-stuffed steak. The decor is fairly standard for the genre, with colorful Mexican art—a high point for many regulars is karaoke and live music, offered several nights a week.

Pimon Thai (3904 Johnson St., Lafayette, 337/993-8424, $7–16) is one of a handful of good Asian restaurants in Acadiana. Traditional coconut-lemongrass-chicken soups, chicken satays, and green and red curries with shrimp, chicken, or beef are among the offerings.

On weekends, you can listen to live zydeco and Cajun music while brunching on tasty and relatively authentic Chinese and Japanese fare at **Dragon Cafe** (107 S. Main St., Breaux Bridge, 337/507-3320, $6–18), a colorful place in the heart of Breaux Bridge's historic downtown, which is also open for lunch and dinner most days. There's a sushi bar, too. The place is especially renowned for its elaborate flaming desserts.

Quick Bites

Hungry Lafayette diners have been enjoying home-style breakfast and lunch fare of **Dwye Cafe** (323 Jefferson St., 337/235-9364, $4– since 1927. The low-key downtown restaur opens at 5 each morning and features a fre daily plate lunch that includes a mix of entr and vegetables, plus great burgers, biscuits a gravy, eggs, and other hearty, honest fare. Drop **Corky's** (2208 Kaliste Saloom Rd., Lafayet 337/989-9020, $5–12) for authentic Memph style barbecue, including ribs, chicken, smok sausage, and pulled pork.

Charlie T's (530 Berard St., Breaux Brid 337/332-2426, under $6) is a wonderful d serving smoked and specialty meats, boud cracklins, and other Cajun delicacies. In dow town New Iberia, a sign outside **Victor's Ca teria** (109 W. Main St., 337/369-9924, $5–8) plain, almost dowdy lunch and breakfast roo proudly announces "Dave Robicheaux eats he But even if you're not an ardent fan of the tional Cajun detective made famous by nov ist James Lee Burke, you should drop to sam the hearty, home-style cooking, including a f ulous crawfish pie and an ever-changing roster fresh-baked pies and cakes. Breakfast is serv daily from 6 to 10 A.M. and lunch every day Saturday. There's often a line to get in, bu moves quickly.

With a '50s theme and staff dressed acco ingly, **Duffy's Diner** (1106 Center St., N Iberia, 337/365-2326, $4–12) is a fun place take kids—the ice-cream treats and malts luscious and largely portioned. In addition the usual diner favorites, Duffy's serves co mendable fried seafood, oyster po'boys, and ot Cajun fare.

A Houma institution, **Boudreau & T bodeau's Cajun Cookin** (5602 W. Main 985/872-4711, $5–17) serves some of the tas est home-style local fare in the area, fro po'boys to crawfish boils to massive (and f tening and delicious) breakfasts. You won't home hungry after a platter of country-fr steaks or the soft-shell crab and stuffed-cr combo. The place is festive and borderline si with goofy Cajun jokes printed on both t walls and the menu (" . . . you know you're Cajun if there's more furniture on your porch than in your living room"). Perhaps the best thing about this place is that it's open 24 hours, a rarity in these parts. A multitude of home-made ice creams are served at **Scarlet Scoop** (300 Barrow St., Houma, 985/872-5114), a local parlor that's a favorite place for a break before or after exploring the area.

Stop by down-home **Rita Mae's Kitchen** (711 Federal Ave., Morgan City, 985/384-3550, $4–10) for short-order fried seafood, gumbos, plate lunches, and other soul-cooking specialties. It's nothing fancy, but the food is consistently tasty and the small dining room in this tin-roofed cottage is bright and cheerfully decorated, with black-and-white tile floors and both counter and table seating. It's in the heart of Morgan City's historic downtown, a few blocks from the river, and the kitchen turns out three meals a day.

Java Joints

A branch of the popular New Orleans coffee-house, **P.J.'s Lafayette**(200 E. St. Mary St., 337/572-9555) sits adjacent to the bustling campus of University of Louisiana Lafayette. The spacious café with a sunny upstairs terrace and ample seating beneath the shade trees along St. Mary Street is often packed with students and professors. In addition to coffees and teas, you can get very good sandwiches and desserts here, too. P.J.'s formidable rival, also based in New Orleans, **C.C.'s** (3810 Ambassador Caffrey Pkwy., Suite 100, 337/981-4343; 2668 Johnson St., Suite C-4, 337/269-9281; 340 Kaliste Saloom Rd., Suite D, 337/233-0429), has three locations in Lafayette, all of them providing free high-speed Internet service, not to mention excellent coffee and light food. In Breaux Bridge, **Barbara Lee Coffee & Tea** (110A Bridge St., 337/332-3594) is a cute and friendly downtown café where you can grab a quick bite, perhaps a cup of gumbo or a fresh salad. Pastries and cakes are also served.

Picnic Supplies and Gourmet Goods

Champagne's Breaux Bridge Bakery (105 S. Poydras St., 337/332-1117) has been a snacking institution in Breaux Bridge since 1888—the wonderful cakes, breads, cookies, and other baked goods are worth stocking up on before an outing or on your way to your inn or hotel. Also useful for salads, boudin, and Cajun groceries and food products is **Champagne's Market** (241 Rees St., Breaux Bridge, 337/332-2243). **Goula's Grocery** (1014 Ruth Bridge Hwy., Breaux Bridge, 337/332-6006) is famous for its hot boudin and hot cracklins, along with other fine meats and Cajun delicacies—they ship all over the country.

Louisiana School of Cooking (112 S. Main St., St. Martinville, 337/394-1710, www.lacooks.com) sits right on Church Square and offers an impressive range of gourmet and local foods and cooking items, including cookbooks by some of Cajun Country's most distinguished chefs—Emeril Lagasse, Marcelle Bienvenue, and Patrick Mould. In fact, the school is operated by Patrick Mould, an experienced kitchen wizard who has taught Cajun and Creole cooking on television and in books. He's also helmed several important area restaurants. Classes cover different Cajun meals and are geared toward both groups and individuals. In the shop you can pick up hot sauces, local seasonings and spices, james and jellies, coffees, packed foods, and so on.

In Lafayette, **Joey's Specialty Foods** (503 Bertrand Dr., 337/237-3661 or 877/466-8873, www.cajun-joeys.com) is another great source of local packaged and prepared foods—they do a brisk mail-order business from their website. Game and meats, box and picnic lunches, hot sauces, candies, deli fare, and all kinds of seafood are available. **Poupart Bakery** (1902 W. Pinhook Rd., Lafayette, 337/232-7921; also 207 E. Bridge St., St. Martinville, 337/394-5366) is a favorite spot for breakfast Danishes and pastries. This bakery serves delectable cream cheese croissants, French bread, cheesecakes, dobash cakes, and coffees.

ENTERTAINMENT AND NIGHTLIFE

In this part of the world, it's the restaurant that doesn't have live music, at least on weekends, that's the exception. You can catch Cajun song

CAJUN AND ZYDECO MUSIC

Cajun and zydeco are terms often confused with one another or used to describe the same music, but they have distinct origins and subtle but important differences. Both have their origins in southwest Louisiana's Cajun Country, and they have each enjoyed a huge surge in worldwide popularity since the 1980s. They're also sometimes credited with being the progenitors of modern country-western music, which is a relatively new phenomenon when compared with Cajun and zydeco.

Cajun music derives, as one would guess, from the French culture of Cajun settlers who came to southwestern Louisiana primarily during the 18th and early 19th centuries—it's nearly always sung in French—but this upbeat, danceable music form also has German, Anglo-American, and African influences. Originally Cajun tunes revolved around fiddles, but the influence of German settlers led to the use of push-button accordions during the late 1800s, and now both these instruments are the keystones of any good Cajun band. Nowadays Cajun bands typically include a bass and drums. A *tit fer* is another instrument common to the genre—this iron triangle struck with a spike is used to add rhythm.

When live Cajun is performed, you'll generally see folks dancing either waltzes or two-steps. Like many of the country tunes that have been inspired by it, Cajun music often tells the tale of something tragic or unhappy, such as failed romances, early deaths, or other hardships common to life among the Acadian immigrants of early southern Louisiana.

But many songs are funny and self-effacing, playing on an often unfortunate circumstance for laughs. Many of today's Cajun tunes have their origins in the Acadian folk music of Canada, and also in the traditional fiddling tunes of France. It is truly folk music, and the early traditions were never written down but passed along from generation to generation, just as many old Cajun tales were. The earliest recordings of Cajun music date to the late 1920s. Top venues for Cajun today include Randol's and Prejean's restaurants in Lafayette and Mulate's in Breaux Bridge, and also in its satellite restaurants in Baton Rouge and New Orleans.

One of the most famous and distinguished Cajun-Western bands is the Hackberry Ramblers, whose albums have been nominated for Grammies in recent years. Back in 1933, fiddler Luderin Darbone and accordionist Edwin Duhon formed the band, mixing the toe-tapping sounds of traditional Cajun music with western swing and folky hillbilly influences. They used to power the electric sound system at local dance halls by hooking up to Darbone's Model-T Ford. They released their first album with RCA Bluebird in 1935, and they continued to perform and record for decades following. In the early 1980s, a renewed interest in Cajun music was born, and the Ramblers, based in Lake Charles, enjoyed a popular resurgence.

and dance and zydeco at a number of places all through the area, but Lafayette and the neighboring towns seem to support any kind of music that you can tap your toes to.

Much of the action is centered in Lafayette, which is also home to the stately **Heymann Performing Arts Center** (1373 S. College Rd.), which hosts a variety of entertainment mounted by the **Performing Arts Society of Acadiana** (337/237-2787, www.pasa-online), including pop concerts, dance troupes, theater, and opera. Also calling the arts center home is the esteemed

Acadiana Symphony Orchestra (337/232-4277, www.acadianasymphony.org), whose season includes about a dozen concerts and runs from September through July.

As for nightlife, **Hamilton Club** (1716 Verot School Rd., 337/984-5931) in Lafayette is a great place to catch zydeco, and El Sido's Zydeco and Blues Club (803 Martin Luther King Dr., Lafayette, 337/235-0647) has some of the best live music anywhere in Acadiana. Opened in 2003, **307 Jazz & Blues Club** (307 Jefferson St., 337/262-0307) has quickly become a favorite for

The music now tends toward a faster-paced, rollicking honky-tonk vibe. In 2003, the Ramblers were filmed performing at Eunice's weekly *Rendez-vous des Cajuns* on NBC's *Today* show to celebrate the band's 70th anniversary. Leading the performance were fiddler Darbone and accordionist Duhon, still going strong at ages 90 and 92 respectively.

While Cajun is a predominantly Anglo music form, its cousin zydeco has its roots with the African-American sharecroppers and farmers of the same region. The two music styles clearly influenced each other, with zydeco evolving from a tradition called "La La," a term for an early style of music played among African-Americans in homes and at some clubs that used only an accordion and a washboard for instruments. Zydeco is much more closely linked to blues and R&B music. It's a younger music genre than Cajun; it utilizes either an accordion or push-button piano and also incorporates a *frottoir* (literally "rub board," or washboard), as opposed to the *tit fer* (triangle) used in Cajun music.

Many of the Creole African-Americans in southern Louisiana came from the Caribbean, which also helped to shape this music style. In Afro-Caribbean culture, there's a syncopated style of a cappella music called *juré* that is sometimes cited as zydeco's true predecessor.

In the middle of the 20th century, zydeco came to be influenced by the burgeoning R&B and blues music of the South, and it continues to evolve and change as zydeco musicians borrow from rock, jazz, soul, and even rap and hip hop. Clifton Chenier, of Opelousas, is often considered the father of modern zydeco—he toured throughout the United States and Europe in the 1960s, helping to spread the popularity of this inimitable style.

The name zydeco is said to derive from the French phrase "les haricots sont pas salés," meaning "the snapbeans are not salty." The first two words, "les haricots," are pronounced "lay-ZAH-ree-coh", which has been shortened over the years to zydeco, pronounced "ZAH-dee-coh." The phrase in question referred to a period of such financial hardship that one could not afford to so much as season basic foods—and so, as with Cajun music, zydeco often touches on themes of struggling to persevere and make do during difficult times.

Both zydeco and Cajun music are best appreciated live, ideally someplace where you can get out on the dance floor and cut loose, or at the very least—if you're shy—tap your toes a bit. Both forms go hand-and-hand with eating, and you'll find that many of the best Cajun and soul restaurants of southern Louisiana, especially near Lafayette, have live zydeco and Cajun music many nights of the week. The little town of Eunice, about 45 miles northwest of Lafayette, is one of the best places to catch live performances—here the Liberty Theatre hosts live Cajun and zydeco music on Saturday nights.

top-notch live entertainment. The **Grant Street Dance Hall** (113 W. Grant St., 337/237-8513) is another great place to catch live music, from swamp pop and Cajun to hip-hop dance music and modern rock. Downtown Lafayette is the region's hub of gay nightlife, with **Sound Factory** (209 Jefferson St., 337/269-6011) and **Jules** (533 Jefferson St., 337/264-8000).

In downtown New Iberia, **Napoleon's** (129 W. Main St., 337/364-6925) is a swanky little cocktail bar with armchairs, paintings of the "Little Corporal" himself, and jazz and folk bands

regularly. **Landry's Restaurant** (2138 U.S. 90W, New Iberia, 337/369-3772) presents live Cajun bands on weekend evenings.

Houma's **A-Bear's Cafe** (809 Bayou Black Dr., Houma, 985/872-6306) is a great place to catch live Cajun and old-time rockabilly music. **Bayou Delight** (4038 Bayou Black Dr., Houma, 985/876-4879) also features Cajun and rockin' oldies. At **Bayou Vue Cafe** (7913 Main St., Houma, 985/872-6292) there's live Cajun, country, zydeco, and other local tunes many nights. **Smokey Row** (7834 Main St., Houma,

985/857-9003) is a great place to catch live R&B tunes most nights of the week. **Club Neptune** (131 Neptune Ct., Houma, 985/580-4921) books both locally and, occasionally, national known pop and rock bands.

FESTIVALS AND EVENTS

Outside New Orleans, no part of the state enjoys a good festival more than Lafayette and Central Acadiana. Scores of engaging events are held in towns all through the region, and virtually year-round. Sultry summer is the one time when there seems to be fewer things going on, but it's always worth checking with the local tourist boards to find out whether there's a party or gathering scheduled during the time of your visit. Lafayette also stages the second-largest Mardi Gras celebration in the state.

Mardi Gras

There are Mardi Gras events all through the region in the weeks leading up to Fat Tuesday, with an especially high concentration of them occurring in Lafayette. You can attend everything from the **Krewe des Chiens Mardi Gras Ball** (337/984-7611, www.paradefordogs.com), a procession of pooches that includes music, food, and a silent auction (to raise money for homeless dogs), to the **Krewe of Vermilion Children's Parade** (337/893-8121) in the town of Erath, to **Mardi Gras Parade and Fais-Do-Do** (337/232-7667, www.cityofscottla.com) in the small town of Scott. In Lafayette, you can attend the carnivalesque **Le Festival de Mardi Gras á Lafayette,** which takes place adjacent to Cajundome and the Cajunfield. There are live bands, rides, a games midway, and other festivities. Sometimes it's the smaller and less formal Mardi Gras events that are the most enjoyable, and that can afford outsiders the best chance to meet and talk with locals and learn about the different Mardi Gras customs.

Spring and Summer

In April, bicycle riders flock to the area for **Cycle Zydeco: Louisiana's Cajun/Creole Food and Music Cycling Festival** (www.cyclezydeco.com). This four-day bike tour moves at a leisurely pace through the city and surrounding countryside participants can enjoy live music and food a number of venues. Musical performers from over the French-speaking world descend Lafayette each April for **Festival International Louisiane** (337/232-8086, www.festivalin national.com), a massive party that showca all kinds of local and French music, plays French, and other Francophone fun.

Things really heat up in early April at N Iberia's **Hot Sauce Festival** (337/365-7539) SugArena on Highway 3212. A big part of fu attending the Sauce Piquante Cook Off, wh participants compete in three categories: seafo non-seafood, and most festively decorated boo Other activities include a petting zoo, an a and crafts show, live music, and a hot-air b loon rally. Also in April, head to Abbeville the **Carousel of Arts** (337/898-4114, www.v milion.org), a music, fine-arts, and theater fe val with an arts-and-crafts show and a spiri gumbo cookoff.

Fans of mudbugs gather at the **Breaux Brie Crawfish Festival** (337/332-6655, www.bbc fest.com) in early May to sample the tasty tre and listen to live Cajun and zydeco music. one of the most popular events in the regi In late May, the family-oriented **Cajun Hea land State Fair** (337/265-2100, www.caju dome.com) is a lively indoor celebration w carnival rides, a petting zoo, and live enterta ment and food.

Of all places, the little town of Erath throws c of the biggest and most festive **Fourth of J celebrations** (337/937-5861, www.erath4.co in the area, with pageants, carnival rides, and f works. It takes place over several days leading to the Fourth. Lafayette's **Le Cajun French Mu Festival and Awards Show** (337/233-96 www.cajunfrenchmusic.org) is a three-day ea August event dedicated to the promotion a preservation of Cajun song and dance as wel French heritage. There's music, an awards sho food, and demonstrations.

It may sounds like an odd mix, but **Louisiana Shrimp and Petroleum Festi** (800/256-2931, www.shrimp-petrofest.org) Morgan City is quite a hoot, with fireworks, mu seafood, a children's village, and a blessing of the fleet. It's held in late August or early September.

Fall and Winter

The third weekend of September, just as the hot weather begins to break (usually), Lafayette holds its rollicking **Festivals Acadiens,** a chance for visitors to learn about Cajun culture through its rich musical traditions. You can learn the Cajun waltz or two-step, and how accordions, tit fers, and fiddles figure into the sounds of Cajun song and dance. Outside Mardi Gras, this is one of the most well-attended and popular festivals in the region. The event comprises several smaller ones throughout the area, including the Festival de Musique Acadienne, the Bayou Food Festival, the Louisiana Native American & Contemporary Crafts Festival, Downtown Alive!, Kids Alive!, and La Vie Cadienne Wetlands & Folklife Festival. Events are held all through the area, from downtown to lovely Girard Park near the University of Louisiana at Lafayette to the ground of the Lafayette Natural History Museum.

Come October, Abbeville celebrates its **Louisiana Cattle Festival** (337/893-9712, www.louisianacattlefestival.org), which is dedicated to the area's legacy as a cattle-ranching hub in the late 1700s. There's food, music, a street fair, and a queen's pageant. November's **Broussard Community Fair** (337/837-6363, www.beausoleil-broussard.com) is a great time to visit this small and charming town southwest of Lafayette.

Breaux Bridge kicks off the holiday season with a **Cajun Christmas Bayou Parade** (337/332-8500, www.bayouparade.com) in late November—a long parade of lights stretches down along Bayou Teche, and there's a fireworks display.

In mid-October, head down to Houma for the **Downtown on the Bayou Festival,** which features four stages of Cajun, zydeco, jazz, country, rock, and gospel music. Drawing more than 90,000 visitors each year, it's one of the region's top draws.

All through December, many of New Iberia's grandest homes are trimmed with lights and decorations for **Christmas on the Bayou** (888/9-IBERIA, www.iberiaparish.com), which includes

holiday concerts downtown, parades, and celebration. Lafayette offers similar activities at its **Cajun and Creole Christmas** (800/346-1958, www.lafayettetravel.com), which runs through the month at a variety of venues.

INFORMATION AND SERVICES

The **Lafayette Convention and Visitors Commission** (Box 52066, Lafayette, 70505, 337/232-3737 or 800/346-1958, www.lafayettetravel.com) serves as an umbrella tourism organization for most of the Acadiana towns between Opelousas and Morgan City, and between Jennings and Henderson. The LCVC has a large visitor center on the median of U.S. 90, just a bit south of I-10, where you can ask for advice on where to stay and pick up hundreds of brochures, walking-tour maps, and visitor guides. Most of the other nearby parishes also have tourism organizations, the most prominent being the **Iberia Parish Convention and Visitors Bureau** (2704 Hwy. 14, New Iberia, 70560, 888/9-IBERIA, www.iberiaparish.com). Also, for more detailed information on Franklin, contact the **Cajun Coast Visitors & Convention Bureau** (Box 2332, Morgan City, LA 70381, 985/395-4905 or 800/256-2931, www.cajuncoast.com). You can also stop by either of the Cajun Coast tourism office visitor centers, one in Patterson (a few miles west of Morgan City) at 112 Main St. (985/395-4905 or 800/256-2931), and the other in Franklin at 15307 U.S. 90 (337/828-2555). The free *Times of Acadiana* (337/237-3560, www.acadiananow.com) serves Lafayette and environs with scads of listings and entertainment coverage.

The **Houma Area Convention and Visitors Bureau** (114 Tourist Dr., off U.S. 90, Gray, 985/868-2732 or 800/688-2732, www.houmatourism.com) has a visitor center with brochures and information on Houma and surrounding towns.

For information on Morgan City and Berwick, contact the **Cajun Coast Visitors & Convention Bureau** (P.O. Box 2332, Morgan City, 70381, 985/395-4905 or 800/256-2931, www.cajuncoast.com). You can also stop by either of the Cajun Coast tourism office visitor centers, one in

Patterson (a few miles west of Morgan City) at 112 Main St. (985/395-4905 or 800/256-2931), and the other in Franklin at 15307 U.S. 90 (337/828-2555). Free and found at many hotels and restaurants, Houma's *Gumbo Entertainment Guide* (985/876-3008) is a monthly paper filled with event and nightlife listings, and other lively goings-on.

GETTING AROUND

Within the area, you really need a car to maximize your flexibility and maneuverability. **Lafayette Transit System (LTS)** (337/291-8570, www.lafayettelinc.net/lts) does provide bus service around that city, but since many of the area's main attractions are in outlying towns not served by LTS, this is an impractical option.

From New Orleans, there are two main routes to Lafayette and environs. You can either take the straight, easy 135-mile shot across I-10 through Baton Rouge, which takes a little over two hours. Or you can opt for the more circuitous 160-mile route via U.S. 90, which takes around three hours. Most people who drive the latter route take their time and stop for a bit in some of the Cajun wetlands communities, such as Houma or Thibodaux. U.S. 90 will eventually become an extension of I-49, which presently runs from Shreveport southeast to Lafayette, and already many improvements have been made to this road—in many places it's now a limited-access highway with a 70 mph speed limit.

See the *On the Road* chapter for details on reaching New Orleans and Lafayette from other parts of the country by train, plane, and bus.

The Cajun Prairie

Although Cajuns are more commonly associated with swamplands and rivers, and with the communities between Lafayette and Houma, a considerable number of these early refugees moved north and west of this area in search of arable land suitable for farming. These Cajuns settled chiefly between Lafayette and Lake Charles, and between Opelousas and Kinder, or as far west as De Quincy. Here they raised cattle and grew a variety of crops, including sugarcane, cotton, and vegetables. Without the mysterious lure of the swamps in or near the Atchafalaya Basin, the Cajun Prairie lacks the tourist cachet of the wetlands, and because these towns were settled later than St. Martinville, Breaux Bridge, and some of the other historic communities near Lafayette, the region is decidedly less quaint and cutesy.

However, the area between Eunice and Opelousas has long been famous for cultivating the Cajun and zydeco music that's such an integral part of Cajun life today, and in all the towns and cities in the Prairie region, you'll find a wealth of great restaurants serving authentic Cajun chow. There are fewer key museums and attractions in this part of Cajun Country, but it's definitely a region that bears exploring, and its largest city, Lake

Charles, has quite a lot to see and do, including some of the state's most popular casinos.

Lake Charles is quite distinct from most of Cajun Country—many comment that it feels more like southeast Texas, which it borders, than Lafayette or even the Cajun towns relatively close to it, such as Crowley and Jennings. However, more than a few Cajuns settled in Lake Charles and the towns around it, and because this city of 72,000 lies just 75 minutes west of Lafayette via I-10, it makes for an easy visit as part of a longer excursion through Acadiana. Lake Charles is best known for its casinos, which attract Texans by the bus- and carload (gambling is not legalized in Texas), but the city also has some engaging museums as well as some downtown historic districts with wonderfully ornate and well-preserved Victorian architecture. Not a whole lot smaller than Lafayette, the city also has a bounty of chain motels and hotels (plus some casino accommodations), as well as the usual slew of fast-food restaurants, colorful seafood eateries, and Cajun hangouts.

Although you can easily reach Lake Charles via I-10, it's a far more interesting and culturally enriching drive if you take I-49 north from

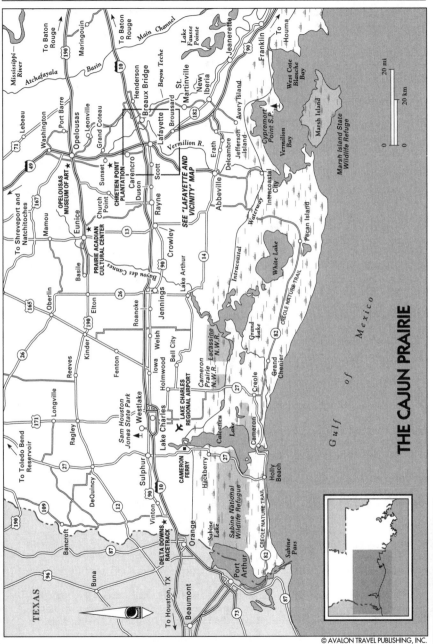

THE CAJUN PRAIRIE

CAJUN COUNTRY

EXCURSION TO NATCHITOCHES

Visitors to Louisiana are sometimes surprised to learn that the state's earliest permanent European settlement is not New Orleans, nor any community on or near the Gulf. Intimate and relentlessly charming Natchitoches was founded as a Red River trade outpost in 1714 by the French. It is, in fact, the oldest community in the central third of the United States. Today it's perhaps the most charming and popular weekend getaway in northern Louisiana.

This town of 40,000, also home to Northwestern State University, sits along the sleepy Cane River in northwestern Louisiana, just 70 miles southeast of Shreveport. The settlement was established here in the early 1700s because this was the northernmost navigable point along the Red River at the time. (A massive logjam was later cleared, allowing river travel to continue on to Shreveport.) The town's convenience to I-49 makes it a popular overnight stop for visitors to southern Louisiana driving from the Dallas–Fort Worth area, about four hours away. In the other direction, Lafayette is a little more than two hours' drive southeast. New Orleans is just 4.5 hours' drive.

Of all the Louisiana place names with unusual pronunciations, Natchitoches probably confounds the most people. The prevalent pronunciation is "NACK-ih-tish," but sometimes you'll here it with a "tush" or "tosh" as the final syllable. The name comes from the Natchitoches Indians, members of the Caddo tribe, who originally inhabited the region.

Downtown Natchitoches comprises a 33-block national historic district. It may seem familiar from and the 1989 tearjerker *Steel Magnolias,* based on a play written by local son Robert Harling, Jr. Julia Roberts' character, Shelby Eatenton Latcherie was based on Harling's own sister. The success of the film spurred interest in this relatively quiet college town. Today you tour compnaies offer guided walking and bus tours of Natchitoches that point out houses and other locales featured in the movie. **Natchitoches Transit Company** (318/356-8687, www.natchitoches.net/transit) is one of the best; it gives guided tours on historic streetcars.

Natchitoches celebrates its festivals with great fanfare, including lively **Mardi Gras** events in late winter; the **Natchitoches Historic Pilgrimage** in October; during which visitors can tour many of the town's historic homes; and **Christmas in Natchitoches.** This six-week-long event draws thousands of visitors (meaning that hotels fill up early) and includes fantastic displays of holiday lights, fireworks shows, parades, food tastings, and tours of historic homes rife with decoration.

Sightseeing Highlights

Wandering through the impressive historic district, with its several antiques shops, is a great way to spend an afternoon. Be sure stop by **Kaffie-Frederick Mercantile** (758 Front St., 318/352-2525) a rambling dry-goods store established in 1863 by Prussian Jewish immigrants and packed with quirky gifts and household items. Stately cobblestone **Front Street,** which overlooks the river, is ideal for a stroll. You'll find delicate wrought-iron benches along the sidewalks.

Natchitoches has a number of historic homes open to the public, several of which also double as bed-and-breakfasts; the best way to see most of these is on a guided tour or during the October pilgrimage season. Other key draws include the Richardsonian Romanesque **Old Courthouse State Museum** (2nd and Church Sts., 318/357-2270), which was built in 1896 and now contains exhibits and artifacts related to the town's founding and growth, as well as rotating history and art shows.

The town is part of the **Cane River National Heritage Area** (318/352-0383, www.nps.gov/cari), which comprises five historic Creole plantations open for tours, the most famous being **Melrose Plantation** (Hwys. 119 and 493, 318/379-0055), a nine-building compound dating from 1796. It was the home of several celebrated artists and writers, including "primitive" painter Clementine Hunter, and writers Lyle Saxon and Erskine Caldwell. Farther south you can visit the **Kate Chopin House** (Hwy. 1, Cloutierville, 318/379-2233), home of the early feminist and author of *The Awakening*. The house also contains the Bayou Folk Museum.

Fort St. Jean Baptiste State Commemorative Area (130 Moreau St., 318/357-3101 or 888/677-7853, www.crt.state.la.us), offers tours of a full-scale replica of the first permanent European settlement in this part of the country.

Nearby, in the small town of Natchez (Louisiana—not to be confused with better-known Natchez, Mississippi), **Magnolia Plantation** (5487 Hwy. 119, 318/379-2221), contains the only wooden cotton press still in its original locale. It's been in the same family since 1753. Also in Natchez, **Oakland Plantation** (4386 Hwy. 494, 318/352-0383) is a classic raised Creole cottage where the focus is on farming and social customs of antebellum Louisiana.

The **Natchitoches Parish Visitors Bureau** (781 Front St., 800-259-1714, www.historic-natchitoches.com) is a good resource for planning your visit.

Accommodations

Run by the same owners, the **Good House B&B** (314 rue Poete St., 318/352-9206 or 800/441-8343, www.goodhousebandb.com) and the **Judge Porter House** (321 2nd St., 318/352-9206 or 800/441-8343, www.judgeporterhouse.com) are around the corner from each other on the edge of downtown. A 1930s English country-style cottage covered with ivy and set under the boughs of pecan trees, the Good House offers a pair of guest rooms, one with chintz fabrics and wicker furniture, and the other with a large four-poster brass bed and English antiques. Larger and more imposing, the five-guest-room Judge Porter House is a grand Queen Anne–style home with a two-story wraparound gallery porch and tall windows facing out on lushly landscaped grounds. An elaborate breakfast, served by candlelight, is included each morning.

The **Queen Anne** (125 Pine St., 318/352-0989 or 888/685-1585, www.queenannebandb.com) has French, English, and American antiques. Each of the sunny rooms has tall windows, phones, and cable TV. This lovely yellow house was built in 1905, and the owners have restored it impeccably. One of the first B&Bs to open in town, **Fleur de Lis B&B** (336 2nd St., 318/352-6621 or 800/489-6621, www.virtualcities.com/ons/la/z/laz4501.htm, $50–100) dates to 1903 and is one of the town's most striking Queen Anne–style buildings. It has five charming rooms. Breakfast is served at a 12-foot-long antique table made of Louisiana cypress.

There are also several chain properties in and around Natchitoches, including a very nice **Hampton Inn** (5300 University Pkwy., 318/354-0010 or 800/HAMPTON, www.hamptoninn.com, $50–100) and the affordable **Super 8** (801 Hwy. 1 Bypass, 318/352-1700 or 800/800-8000, www.super8.com, under $50).

Food

A relaxing but elegant restaurant along charming Front Street, **The Landing** (530 Front St., 318/352-1579, $12–22) serves exceptional Creole fare, such as crawfish and oyster platters, grilled red snapper, filet mignon, and the best fried green tomatoes in town. **Mariner's Restaurant** (N. Hwy. 1 Bypass, 318/357-1220, $12–32), overlooking nearby Sibley Lake, serves prodigious portions, from stuffed crab to barbecued shrimp to steak Oscar (topped with crabmeat). There's live music and dancing many evenings. **Pioneer Pub** (812 Washington St., 318/352-4884), in a rustic building across from the town's visitors center, offers a nice selection

continued on next page

of draft beers from around the world, plus burgers and light cooking. It's another fun place to listen to music and chat with locals.

Good Italian fare is available at **Dominic's** (805 Washington St., 318/354-7767, $9–21). Try fettuccini Alfredo with crawfish, shrimp-and-crabmeat au gratin, or eggplant parmigiana with linguini. Save room for Amaretto cheesecake.

Lasyone's Meat Pie Kitchen (622 2nd St., 318/352-3353, $4–9) is famous for its namesake meat pies, which consist of ground pork and beef with vegetables, Worcestershire sauce, and Cajun spices baked in a pie crust. Other goodies include shrimp po-boys, chicken-fried steak, and catfish platters. The Cane River cream pie makes for a memorable sweet ending; it's also a great option for breakfast. **Merci Beaucoup** (127 Church St., 318/352-6634, under $7) is a charming spot for a late breakfast or lunch. Creative Cajun and American fare is served, as well as gourmet coffees and sweets.

Lafayette to Opelousas and head west from there on U.S. 190 through Eunice, Basile, and Kinder to U.S. 165, which leads southwest down to I-10, from which you have to drive just 15 miles more to reach Lake Charles. These modest, agrarian towns along U.S. 190 form something of a Cajun and zydeco music trail. You'll find only a handful of places to stay and eat in each town, but the live-music clubs in these parts play some of the best music in the region, and on Saturday mornings you can show up at the Savoy Music Center and Accordion Factory and have a wonderful time listening to local musicians jamming together.

OPELOUSAS

Named for the Opelousas Indians, this city of 22,000 at the junction of U.S. 190 and I-49 was established by the French as the administrative capital of Le Poste des Opelousas in 1720, just a couple of years after the founding of New Orleans. Little came of the area during the first century, as it shifted from French to Spanish governance, but by the time of the Louisiana Purchase, a mix of Cajuns, English, Scotch-Irish, and German settlers had established farmsteads here, taking advantage of the richly fertile lands. The area surrounding Opelousas was named St. Landry Parish in 1804, after a particularly beloved bishop.

As a farming region, Opelousas and the rest of the towns along U.S. 190 became heavily popu-

lated with African slaves, who were needed more here than in the wetland areas of Cajun Country, where trapping and fishing were central to the economy. Today's Opelousas is a rich mix of Cajun, African-American, and Northern European traditions, with a healthy celebration of the area's Native American heritage thrown in. The big stops here are local music clubs specializing in zydeco and Cajun song and dance.

Also be sure to check out what's on display at the **Opelousas Museum of Art** (100 N. Union St., 337/942-4991, open 1 –5 P.M. Tues.–Fri., 9 A.M.–5 P.M. Sat., $3 donation requested), which presents rotating exhibits lent from major museums around the region, as well as private collections. It's worth dropping by just to get a look at the striking Federal-style building, constructed of brick in the early 1800s as a tavern.

Grand Coteau

This historic village can be visited as a quick stop en route from Lafayette up I-49 to Opelousas. Grand Coteau's main attraction, just west of town, on the other side of I-49, is **Chretien Point Plantation** (665 Chretien Point Rd., Sunset, 337/662-7050 or 800/880-7050, www.chretienpoint.com, open April–Sept. 11 A.M.–5 P.M. daily, Oct.,–March, 1–5 P.M. daily, admission $7), a gracious 1831 plantation house set on 20 acres of lush grounds; it's one of the most stately such homes away from the Great River Road. The plantation's dramatic staircase served as the model for Tara in the film adaptation of *Gone with the Wind,* and designers of the mansion drew their own inspiration from another famous structure, the Palace of Versailles in France—this is evident in the arched Palladian lunette windows above the exterior doors and windows. Dignified Tuscan columns are set around the home's brick exterior—one of the columns was torn off by a Union cannonball in the heat of Civil War battle, and the front door still has a number of bullet holes. In addition to touring the house, you can also book a room here.

EUNICE

A farming community about 20 miles west of Opelousas, Eunice is the musical heart and soul of Acadiana, an important stop for any traveler interested in the heritage of zydeco and Cajun music. It's also home to the westernmost unit of Jean Lafitte National Historical Park and Preserve, the **Prairie Acadian Cultural Center** (250 W. Park Ave., 337/262-2862, www.nps.gov/jela, open 8 A.M.–6 P.M. Tues.–Fri. and 8 A.M.–6 P.M. Sat., admission free). The center tells the story of the Cajuns who settled north and west of the Atchafalaya Swamp, in the southern Louisiana prairie communities along the present-day U.S. 190 and I-10 corridors, from Opelousas and Lafayette west to Kinder and Lake Charles. Here they raised cattle and other livestock; cultivated rice, cotton, and sugarcane; and led lives quite different from their wetland relatives. The exhibits at this interpretive center bear some resemblance to those at the Acadian Cultural Center in Lafayette, and the Wetlands Acadian Cultural Center in Thibodaux, but here there's more focus on the region's dependence on agriculture and on its musical roots. The center's theater hosts frequent Cajun and zydeco concerts as well as lectures, videos, and other programs on the area's heritage. Weaving, spinning, musical instrument making, and other crafts demonstrations are given regularly, and you can watch local cooks prepare authentic Cajun, soul, and Creole meals in an exhibition kitchen. The bookshop here has an outstanding selecting of Cajun and zydeco CDs and tapes. Check for interpretive programs,

videos, and performances, scheduled regularly throughout the year, and when in New Orleans, be sure to drop in on the headquarters of the Jean Lafitte National Historical Preserve, in the French Quarter at 419 Decatur St. Here you'll find information on all of the park's six sites throughout southern Louisiana.

Next to the center is the famous **Liberty Theater** (S. 2nd St. and Park Ave., 337/457-7389), an old movie house built in 1924 that was restored after having fallen into a state of neglect in 1986, when local citizens banded together to revive it. Today it's the site on Saturday nights (at 6 P.M.) of *Rendezvous des Cajuns,* a two-hour live radio variety show with Cajun and zydeco music, along with storytelling, jokes, recipes, and other tidbits of Cajun lore. It's a memorable way to become acquainted with the region and its rich musical history. Admission to the radio variety show is $5, and you can buy tickets at the theater that day, beginning at 4 P.M.

Along the same block is the **Eunice Museum** (220 S. C. C. Duson Dr., 337/457-6540), which marks the site where town founder C. C. Duson sold the community's first lots in 1893. The museum occupies Eunice's original rail depot, and it's filled with artifacts, toys, displays, a loom and spinning wheel, and rotating exhibits relevant to the town's and region's growth. Continue on to the **Cajun Music Hall of Fame and Museum** (240 S. C.C. Duson Dr., 337/457-6534, www .cfma.org, open summer 9 A.M.–5 P.M. Tues.–Sat. and winter 8:30 A.M.–4:30 P.M. Tues.–Sun., admission free), which honors more than 30 prominent Cajun musicians and their contributions to the genre. The exhibit space is filled with photos, old musical instruments, and other displays tracing the heritage and development of Cajun music.

LAKE CHARLES

From Eunice, it's a 60-mile one-hour drive to reach Lake Charles, a city of 75,000 that's the hub for western Acadiana and the seat of Calcasieu (pronounced **cal**-kuh-shoo) Parish. The city's strongest draw is with gamblers, who flock to Delta Downs horseracing park just west of town, in Vinton, and a pair of riverboat casinos,

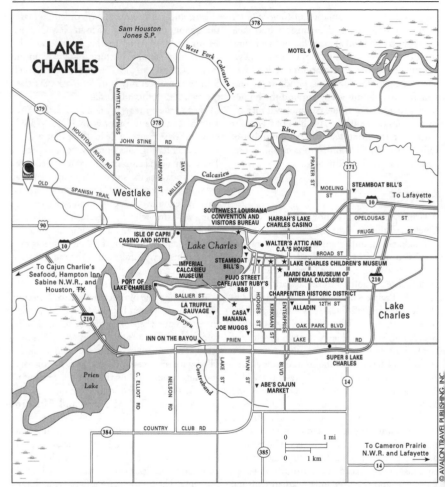

LAKE CHARLES

Sam Houston Jones S.P.

MOTEL 6

West Fork Calcasieu R.

River

Calcasieu

Westlake

STEAMBOAT BILL'S
To Lafayette

SOUTHWEST LOUISIANA
CONVENTION AND
VISITORS BUREAU

HARRAH'S LAKE
CHARLES CASINO

ISLE OF CAPRI
CASINO AND HOTEL

Lake Charles

WALTER'S ATTIC AND
C.A.'S HOUSE

To Cajun Charlie's
Seafood, Hampton Inn,
Sabine N.W.R., and
Houston, TX

IMPERIAL
CALCASIEU
MUSEUM

STEAMBOAT
BILL'S

LAKE CHARLES CHILDREN'S MUSEUM

PORT OF
LAKE CHARLES

PUJO STREET
CAFE/AUNT RUBY'S
B&B

MARDI GRAS MUSEUM OF
IMPERIAL CALCASIEU

CHARPENTIER HISTORIC DISTRICT

Lake
Charles

LA TRUFFLE
SAUVAGE

CASA
MANANA

ALLADIN

JOE MUGGS

INN ON THE BAYOU

Prien
Lake

SUPER 8 LAKE
CHARLES

ABE'S CAJUN
MARKET

0   1 mi
0   1 km

To Cameron Prairie
N.W.R. and Lafayette

© AVALON TRAVEL PUBLISHING, INC.

one on the northeast shore of Lake Charles, and the other on the northwest shore.

But Lake Charles is also a base for outdoors enthusiasts, who enjoy the lake and its nearby wildlife preserves. The actual body of water known as Lake Charles is a rippling blue lake where on warm days you're apt to see sailboats and windsurfers riding the waves, and sunbathers enjoying the only inland white-sand beach on the Gulf Coast. South of the city, bird-watchers, fishers, and hikers flock to Sabine National Wildlife Refuge (the Gulf of Mexico's largest refuge for wildfowl) and Cameron Prairie National Wildlife Refuge.

As in Lafayette, Attakapas Indians originally lived on the land where Lake Charles and its neighboring towns are situated; the region's original name (still the name of the parish) Calcasieu, was a war cry of the Attakapas, and meant roughly "screaming eagle." The earliest settlers were Frenchmen attracted not only to the area's fishing and trapping but to the vast stands of virgin forest. French settler Martin LeBleu built a permanent homestead about 6 miles west of

Lake Charles in 1780, and soon after, an Italian named Carlos Salia (who changed his name to the Gallic version, Charles Sallier) also set up a home here. It's said that Sallier befriended the infamous pirate Jean Lafitte, who came to rely on the large lake near Sallier's homestead as a great place to store stolen treasures, as it was just 30 miles from the Gulf of Mexico via the Calcasieu River yet well out of sight of authorities. Lafitte began referring to this body of water as "Charlie's Lake," and over time the town grew to be officially named Lake Charles.

Officially, however, Lake Charles' status as town sat in limbo for some time. Following the Louisiana Purchase of 1803, this greater area, known as Rio Hondo Territory, existed without a clear government, as neither the Spanish nor the new U.S. government claimed the area. The Admas-Onis Treaty of 1819 finally resolved the issue, naming the Sabine River, about 30 miles west of Lake Charles, as the official border between the state of Louisiana and the Spanish territory of Texas.

Lake Charles progressed as a center of cattle farming and lumber, settled early on by hundreds of Cajuns who came by way of Lafayette and the wetlands of the Atchafalaya Basin. The introduction of rail service in 1880 further popularized Lake Charles, and helped to make it an important way station between New Orleans and Houston. Around the turn of the 20th century, considerable reserves of sulfur were discovered in the area west

THE CREOLE NATURE TRAIL

From Lake Charles, the best way to get a feel for the region's scenic beauty and natural resources is to make the loop drive along the **Creole Nature Trail** (www.creolenaturetrail.org), which leads you down Highway 27, beginning west of Lake Charles, following the road down to Holly Beach, continuing east and taking the ferry across the Calcasieu ship channel, and following Highway 27 back up along the east side of Lake Calcasieu, to where it joins with Highway 14, which leads you back into the east side of Lake Charles. The entire loop is about 109 miles, and without stops it takes about 3 hours. Add an extra hour or a few if you plan on stopping for a while at Sabine National Wildlife Refuge, or to relax along the water at Holly Beach.

A side excursion is to take Highway 82 west once you reach Holly Beach, all the way to Sabine Pass, the mouth of the Sabine River and the border between Louisiana and Texas. There's a small lighthouse, Sabine Light, overlooking Sabine Pass, and the dirt road leading out to this building is one of the only spots in Louisiana where you can see cacti growing naturally. This adds another 55 miles round-trip to the drive described above.

The largely flat drive, which is one of the nation's National Scenic Byways, mostly fringes marshland or the Gulf of Mexico. The most popular stop is **Sabine National Wildlife Refuge** (3000 Holly Beach Hwy., Hackberry, 337/762-3816, http://sabine.fws.gov, open dawn–dusk, admission free), a 125,000-acre preserve that can be accessed from Highway 27, about 8 miles south of the small village of Hackberry (famous as the home of the seminal Louisiana Cajun band the Hackberry Ramblers). The refuge has several dirt and boardwalk trails out into the marsh, where you can look for birds and the occasional alligator (do not bring dogs along on these hikes, as they're a common target of gators). There's a small natural history museum that gives a run-down on local flora and fauna; mounted displays show the types of wildlife, fish, and birds common to this refuge. There are designated areas for freshwater boating through the marshes.

The other notable stop along here is **Cameron Prairie National Wildlife Refuge** (1428 Hwy. 27, Bell City, 337/598-2216, http://cameronprairie.fws.gov), which is right on Highway 27 about 25 miles southeast of Lake Charles and 25 miles northeast of Cameron. Here you'll find a visitor center with interpretive exhibits on the flora and fauna, plus a wildlife driving tour, boat launches, and fishing areas.

of Lake Charles, and thus the mining town of Sulphur was born. The market for sulfur dried up by the mid-1920s, but by now Lake Charles had grown into one of the state's most important cities.

In 1926 Calcasieu channel was dredged, making it possible for large ships to make their way from the Gulf of Mexico to Lake Charles, and this helped spur the development of the petrochemical industry that's still so important in Lake Charles today.

The **Isle of Capri Casino and Hotel** (100 Westlake Ave., 800/THE-ISLE, www.isleofcapricasino.com) sits along the northwestern shore of the lake and has an all-suite hotel (opened in 2001), three restaurants (including the popular Calypso's Seafood Buffet), and 50,000 square feet of gaming, plus lounges and a theater that books live, mostly Louisiana-based musicians and bands. On the northeast side of the lake, **Harrah's Lake Charles Casino** (505 N. Lakeshore Dr., 800/HARRAHS, www.harrahs.com) offers similar but in some cases more extensive facilities: a massive hotel, six restaurants (including a buffet, Asian, steak-and-seafood, sandwich, and two Cajun eateries), a multitude of slots and gaming tables, and a theater. Each 24-hour casino is actually made up of a pair of riverboats, which have been built to resemble the old paddle-wheelers of the 19th century, which used to ply the Mississippi River. One of the boats is always docked, while the other is out cruising around the lake. As gambling casinos are not legal in Texas, Lake Charles is especially popular with travelers from Houston, San Antonio, and other southern Texas towns (northern Texas gamblers tend to frequent the casinos in Shreveport, in northwest Louisiana).

Downtown Lake Charles has a handful of attractions, including the **Lake Charles Children's Museum** (925 Enterprise Blvd., 337/433-9420, open 10 A.M.–5 P.M. Tues.–Sat., admission $3.50); and the **Mardi Gras Museum of Imperial Calcasieu** (809 Kirby St., 2nd floor, 337/430-0043, open 1–5 P.M. Tues.–Sat., admission $3.50), which has the largest collection of Mardi Gras costumes anywhere. You can learn about the city's history at the **Imperial Calcasieu Museum** (204 W. Sallier St., 337/439-3797, open 10 A.M.–5 P.M. Tues.–Sat., admission $2), which contains an art gallery and extensive collection of early Louisiana Colonial furniture, a re-created late-19th-century barbershop, and a collection of original Audubon prints. On the grounds, the enormous **Sallier Oak**, which dates to the late 1600s, stands guard over the museum and is a member of the Live Oak Society.

In a city that developed into a major lumber center during the 19th century, it's hardly surprising that Lake Charles is rife with fine Victorian wood-frame homes, many of them in the **Charpentier Historic District,** which is bound roughly by Belden Street to the north, Louisiana Avenue to the east, Kirby and 7th Streets to the south, and Ryan Street to the west. Many of the people who came to Lake Charles in the 1880s to work in the timber industry hailed from the Midwest, and the architectural style that grew up in this district is more typical of the gingerbread, Gothic, Eastlake, and Queen Anne houses found in Michigan and Indiana than elsewhere in Louisiana. Excellent self-guided walking/driving tours of this neighborhood are available from the Southwest Louisiana Convention and Visitors Bureau.

Northwest of downtown, 1,100-acre **Sam Houston Jones State Park** (107 Sutherland Rd., 337/855-2665 or 888/677-7264, www.crt.state.la.us, open 9 A.M.–dusk daily, admission $2 per car) is set around a rich pine forest with a fenced-in 10-acre deer habitat, many hiking trails, two boat launches, fishing areas, a picnic grove, and a small but nicely done nature center (open 9:30 A.M.–3:30 P.M. Wed.–Sun.). There's also a campground with 12 vacation cabins, 62 RV sites, and 19 tent sites. The nature center has three rooms, each focusing on a different habitat. Inside you'll find many kinds of animals, including snakes both venomous and nonvenomous (which you can sometimes hold). Wildlife sometimes seen around the park includes alligators (which are less common here than around central Acadiana), red foxes, flying squirrels, mink, coyotes, skunks, raccoons, red-eared slider turtles, and plenty of snakes. Fishing enthusiasts will find catfish, bluegills, largemouth bass, and spotted gar.

Vinton

On I-10 at the Texas/Louisiana border, Vinton is best known as the home of **Delta Downs Racetrack** (2717 Hwy. 3063, 800/589-7441, www.deltadowns.com), which has racing year-round, plus an off-track-betting parlor and slot machines.

SHOPPING

Downtown Lake Charles has quite a number of antiques shops, many of them on or near Ryan Street, both at Broad and 12th Streets. A full brochure listing local shops is available from the Southwest Louisiana Convention & Visitors Bureau.

ACCOMMODATIONS

Lake Charles is your main base for exploring the western part of the area, and Lafayette and Opelousas the eastern part. You'll find dozens of chain properties and a handful of inns in Lake Charles, and a few places to stay in Opelousas. There are also a few motels off I-10 between Lafayette and Lake Charles.

Hotels and Motels

Under $50: You'll find the lowest rates in town at the clean and simple **Motel 6** (335 U.S. 171, 337/433-1773 or 800/466-8356, www.motel6 .com), which is about 8 miles north of downtown Lake Charles.

$50–100: In Lake Charles, whether or not you're in town to partake of the considerable gaming facilities, the **Harrah's Lake Charles Casino Hotel** (505 N. Lakeshore Dr., 337/437-1500 or 800/HARRAHS, www.harrahs.com) makes an excellent choice, as it has six restaurants on site, a central location at the northeast side of the lake, and 330 tastefully furnished rooms. There's also an outdoor pool. Because it's a gaming facility that generates more revenue from casinos than hotel rooms, the rates here are relatively low considering the high quality of the rooms.

One of the most interesting lodging options in Lake Charles, because of its location, is **Inn on the Bayou** (1101 W. Prien Lake Rd., 337/474-5151 or 800/OH-BAYOU, www.innonthe-

bayou.com), which sits right on Bayou Contraband, so named because Jean Lafitte allegedly hid his spoils along here. This modern motel has a 550-foot boat dock with deep-water access, fishing, and a large pool and sundeck. Rooms are typical of what you'd find at a midprice chain hotel, but they do all have large work desks and plenty of room, and all are equipped with free high-speed Internet.

Superior to the typical properties that are represented by this chain, the **Super 8 Lake Charles** (1350 E. Prien Lake Rd., 337/477-1606 or 800/800-8000, www.super8.com) was built in 2000 and has large rooms, interior corridors, and in-room coffeemakers, microwaves, refrigerators, irons, and hair dryers. The hotel is on the south side of town, just off I-210, which bypasses Lake Charles from I-10.

In Sulphur, just west of Lake Charles but right at the beginning of the Creole Nature Trail, the **Hampton Inn** (210 Henning Dr., 337/527-0000 or 800/HAMPTON, www.hampton-inn.com) is a reliable bet, with a pool, fitness center, and business services. The outstanding seafood restaurant Cajun Charlie's is next door.

About midway between Lafayette and Lake Charles, just off I-10, the **Comfort Inn Jennings** (607 Holiday Dr., Jennings, 337/824-8589 or 877/424-6423, www.comfortinn.com) makes for a safe and comfortable base.

Eunice doesn't have many accommodations, but the **Best Western Eunice** (1531 W. Laurel Ave., 337/457-2800 or 800/962-8423, www.best western.com), an attractive two-story hotel built in 1995, is a reliable option. There are 35 rooms along with an outdoor pool and hot tub. In Opelousas, your best bet is the **Holiday Inn** (5696 I-49 N. Service Rd., 337/948-3300 or 800/HOLIDAY, www.holiday-inn.com), a 75-room midrise hotel with an indoor pool, Jacuzzi, business center, and on-site restaurant. All rooms in this 2001 property have coffeemakers and two-line phones, and some have Jacuzzi tubs. It's right off the interstate.

Inns and Bed-and-Breakfasts

$50–100: In Lake Charles's lovely Garden District, **Walter's Attic and C.A.'s House** (618 and

624 Ford St., 337/439-6672 or 866/439-6672, www.cas-house.com) together comprise one of the most distinctive—and distinguished—accommodations in this area dominated by chain hotels. There are four opulently furnished rooms in C.A.'s House, a 1900 white Colonial Revival mansion with four columns running along the grand facade and lushly landscaped grounds. Walter's Attic has just one room, set in the attic of an 1893 house, but it's nearly 1,200 square feet and feels completely private and charming, with its pitched 16-foot ceilings, sleigh bed, and exterior private entrance. Guests at either place have access to each property's hot tub and to the heated pool at Walter's Attic—that is, until 7 each evening, when access to the tub and pool at Walter's Attic is restricted to the guests staying in that unit (as you might guess, it's a popular one with honeymooners and others celebrating a special occasion).

The same folks who own Pujo St. Cafe and Market run one of western Acadiana's most inviting inns, **Aunt Ruby's B&B** (504 Pujo St., Lake Charles, 337/430-0603, www.auntrubys.com), a reasonably priced spot with six upscale rooms, all with private baths, cable TV, and phones. Opened originally as the city's first boarding house, this 1911 home in the Charpentier Historic District has a garden-filled front yard and a relaxing veranda. The lake, and the casinos, are just a few blocks west. Full breakfast is included.

$100–150: One of the more unusual lodgings in the region, **Potier's Prairie Cajun Inn** (110 W. Park Ave., Eunice, 337/457-0440, http://potiers.net) occupies a small, restored 1920s hospital. The inn also sells Cajun gifts and crafts, and many of the 10 suites are filled with these items, along with handcrafted furniture; each also has a living room, kitchen (stocked with breakfast supplies), and bathroom. Public areas include a courtyard (with, oddly, an original—but decommissioned—outhouse) with a hot tub.

$150–250: In Sunset, near Grand Coteau and just a short way west of I-49 en route from Lafayette to Opelousas, you'll find one of the South's most elegant inns, **Chretien Point Plantation** (665 Chretien Point Rd., Sunset, 337/662-7050 or 800/880-7050, www.chretien-point.com), which is also one of the top touring house-museums in Acadiana. Guests can choose from among five richly furnished rooms and also received a full and hearty breakfast, a guided tour of the plantation house and grounds, complimentary hors d'oeuvres and cocktails each evening, and use of the large swimming pool. Hand-carved antique beds—some of them fourposters, all with plush bedding and pillows—Oriental rugs and hardwood or brick floors, and garden or pool views enchant guests, many of them here to celebrate a special occasion.

FOOD

With few exceptions, restaurants in western Acadiana are even less formal than those in Lafayette, although you will find a few slightly more upscale and urbane places to eat in Lake Charles. What there's no lack of are great eateries serving homestyle Cajun and soul food, including quite a few places that have live jazz, Cajun, and zydeco tunes. In Lake Charles, you'll also find several restaurants (including inexpensive all-you-can-eat buffets) at the two casinos.

Traditional Creole and Cajun

It's worth the short trip from Lake Charles to Sulphur to sample the spicy and filling Louisiana cooking at **Cajun Charlie's Seafood** (202 Henning Dr., Sulphur, 337/527-9044, $7–18), which is especially famous for its extensive lunch buffet, during which you can scarf down as much as you want of fried seafood, sweet potatoes, bread pudding with rum, whitefish, catfish, hushpuppies, jambalaya, and the list goes on and on. Dinner is no less of an event, with many of the same foods available in larger portions á la carte. The dining room is packed to the rafters with fun bric-a-brac—old farm tools, vintage advertising signs, mounted wildlife, fishing nets, and even an old pirogue hanging from one rafter. In the adjoining gift shop you can browse for books, dolls, gift boxes of boudin, and cards.

In Jennings, **Boudin King** (906 W. Division St., 337/824-6593, $6–16) specializes in its namesake, prepared daily using pork, long-grain rice, and spicy seasonings, but it's also a handy stop for crispy fried chicken, filé-crawfish gumbo, red beans and rice with smoked sausage, and other regional delights. The same owners offers similarly good food at **Cajun Way Family Restaurant** (1805 Parkers Ave., Crowley, 337/788-2929, $6–16), another great stop on the way between Lafayette and Lake Charles.

Just off I-10, between Lafayette and Lake Charles, quirky Rayne is home to the even quirkier **Chef Roy's Frog City Cafe** (1131 Church Point Hwy., 337/334-7913, $9–15), a rambling barn-red restaurant by the Days Inn, serving superb seafood and Cajun fare—not too mention fried frogs' legs, a popular dish here in the frog capital of Louisiana. Some top picks here include fried coconut-beer shrimp served with a tangy orange sauce, shrimp fettuccine, crawfish au gratin, crab White Lake (eggplant fried and topped with crab stuffing). There's also a drive-thru window, where you can order margaritas and daiquiris, shakes and ice cream, and fresh-boiled seafood (when in season).

In Eunice, you can catch live Cajun and zydeco tunes on Tuesday evenings at **Nick's** (123 S. 2nd St., 337/457-4921, $6–14), an elegantly restored downtown bar and grill from the 1930s, close to the museums and Liberty Theatre. In season, treat yourself to a massive platter of boiled crawfish. Any time of year, this is a great choice for traditional Cajun cooking, and the service is friendly and helpful.

Creative and Contemporary
Pujo Street Cafe & Market (901 Ryan St., Lake Charles, 337/439-2054, $10–22) is a beautiful space with high pressed-tin ceilings and exposed brick walls, black-and-white photos, French doors, and crisp white napery. It feels like something out of New Orleans's Warehouse District. The large central bar makes for a nice gathering point. The food is fresh and innovative: try the crawfish salad with spinach, roma tomatoes, red onion, and honey Dijon dressing, or the Caribbean-style sea bass with mango salsa and scallion rice.

Sublime Northern Italian and Southern French cuisine is served at **La Truffle Sauvage** (815 Bayou Pines W., Lake Charles, 337/439-8364, $26–34),

which occupies a romantic cottage on the west side of downtown, just a few blocks below the lake. The white-glove restaurant with live piano on Tuesday evenings is the setting for some of the state's finest cooking outside New Orleans. Start with the yellowfin tuna carpaccio with extra-virgin olive oil, fresh lemon, avocado relish, and Parmigiana-Reggiano cheese, or the duck consommé with crab-and-mushrooms ravioli. Main courses include braised lamb shank with risotto Milanese, natural jus, and horseradish gremolata, and the signature dish: pan-roasted scallops and duck foie gras with green lentils, white truffle oil, and 50-year-aged balsamic vinegar.

Casual Cooking
Break up your trip on the Creole Nature Trail with a light meal at **Pat's Restaurant** (513 Marshall St., Cameron, 337/775-5959, $4–11), a casual locals hangout known for delicious fried chicken, shrimp étouffée, and fried seafood platters and po'boys. For well-prepared, traditional seafood, head to **Steamboat Bill's** (1004 Lakeshore Dr., Lake Charles, 337/474-1070; also 732 N. Martin Luther King, Lake Charles, 337/494-1700, $12–22), a waterfront restaurant that's usually packed with hungry diners.

Ray's Diner (2979 S. Union St., Opelousas, 337/942-9044, $5–13) has won numerous awards for serving the best crawfish étouffée in the area, plus steaks, boiled crawfish and crabs, and hearty breakfast fare. Since the late 1920s, the **Palace Cafe** (135 W. Landry St., Opelousas, 337/942-2142, $4–11) has been doling out honest home-style fare, including daily blue-plate specials and wonderfully crispy and juicy fried chicken.

In Eunice, **Mama's Fried Chicken** (1640 W. Laurel Ave., 337/457-9978, $5–13) really does serve the best fried chicken in town, but you can also get tasty crawfish étouffée, plate lunches with plenty of vegetable sides, and red beans and rice.

Ethnic
In the south side of downtown Lake Charles, **Casa Manana** (2510 Ryan St., 337/433-4112, $7–15) serves commendable Tex-Mex food, which is saying a lot in a city just 30 miles from

the Lone Star State—if you don't serve decent Mexican fare in these parts, you don't survive. The chow here is Americanized but spicy and well portioned. Consider the tamale combo, portobello mushroom fajitas, baby back ribs, and eggplant San Miguel (breaded and topped with shrimp and a pico de gallo–cheese sauce). With very good sushi and a wide range of hibachi-grill specialties, **Miyako** (915 E. Prien Lake Rd., 337/478-1600, $8–18) is Lake Charles's top pick for Japanese food.

One of the state's better sources of authentic Middle Eastern fare, **Alladin** (2009 Enterprise Blvd., Lake Charles, 337/449-0062, $5–12) serves chicken shawarma, kibbe, falafel platters, and other Lebanese specialties in a simple but warmly decorated space in downtown Lake Charles.

Quick Bites

East of Opelousas, **Bourque's Supermarket** (581 Saizon St., Port Barre, 337/585-6261, under $6) is noted for its delicious stuffed bread filled with jalapeño peppers and gooey cheese and sausage. Boudin and cracklins are also served in this low-key roadside shop. A quaint lunchroom that also sells antiques and collectibles, cozy **Back in Time** (123 W. Landry St., Opelousas, 337/942-2413, $4–8) serves a wide range of soups, salads, and sandwiches, plus desserts made on premises and flavored coffees.

Smoky southwest Louisiana barbecue is the draw at **Allison's Hickory Pit** (501 W. Laurel Ave., Eunice, 337/457-9218, $3–7), a tiny place that's open only for lunch Friday through Sunday.

Java Joints

Inside the Books-A-Million bookstore south of downtown, **Joe Muggs** (2934 Ryan St., 337/436-3577) is a pleasant stop for cappuccinos, espressos, flavored coffees, chai teas, sweets, and sandwiches.

Picnic Supplies and Gourmet Goods

If you find yourself craving the flavors of Acadiana at home, give **Abe's Cajun Market** (3935 Ryan St., Lake Charles, 337/474-3816) a call, or just drop by the market before you leave town. Abe's is famous for the *turducken,* a true Louisiana specialty, not to mention an exercise in excess.

This fowl conglomerate consists of a deboned turkey, which is stuffed with a deboned duck, which is stuffed with a deboned chicken, which is stuffed with your choice of cornbread or crawfish. The massive platter serves 15 to 20 people and can be shipped to you anywhere in the United States for about $90, including shipping. Other delicacies available at Abe's include étouffée, gumbo, Cajun sausage, Cajun-stuffed pork chops, beef jerky, and jambalaya.

The famous purveyor of Louisiana prepared foods and spices, **Tony Chachere's Creole Foods** (519 N. Lombard St., 337/948-4691 or 800/551-9066, www.tonychacheres.com) is right in downtown Opelousas and is open for free tours a few times a day; call ahead for times. You can also shop here for Chachere's mixes (like Creole butter beans and rice), hush puppy batter, and seasoning blends.

ENTERTAINMENT AND NIGHTLIFE

All through the U.S. 190 corridor and the towns north and south of this stretch, you can find bars and clubs playing rollicking, bone-shaking music, from swamp pop to traditional Cajun to zydeco—it's one of the premier live-music regions in the country, which is remarkable when you consider that most places with notable music scenes are in highly populated urban centers, where clubs can pack in large audiences. In the Cajun Prairie, people play music because they love to, not with the expectation that they'll get rich.

Here's a quick roundup of some of the top places to hear live music in the region. Eunice is the hub of all this activity. **Allen's Lakeview Cajun Dance Hall** (N. Hwy. 13, Eunice, 337/546-0502) gets busy on Saturday nights from 8 P.M. until midnight. The **Purple Peacock** (U.S. 190, Eunice, 337/546-0975) is a favorite place to catch live rock and roll. The **Liberty Theatre** (2nd St. and Park Ave., Eunice, 337/457-6575) hosts *Rendezvous des Cajuns,* on Saturdays from 6 to 8 P.M.; see Exploring, above, for details. Another big draw is the **Savoy Music Center and Accordion Factory** (U.S. 190 East, 3 miles east of town, 337/457-9563), which holds informal jam sessions on Saturday morning from 9 A.M. until noon. **Acadiana Sounds Recording Studio** (203 S. 2nd St., Eunice, 337/457-1786) also contains Dee's Cajun Gifts—it's a great place to pick up CDs and tapes of zydeco and Cajun music.

Slim's Y-Ki-Ki (8383 Hwy. 182, Opelousas, 337/942-6242) has been one of the area's favorite zydeco dance halls since shortly after World War II; it's open mostly on weekend evenings and brings in some of the top bands in Louisiana. In Basile, about 10 miles west of Eunice via U.S. 190, **D.I.'s Restaurant** (6533 Evangeline Hwy., 337/432-5141) is famous for its live Cajun performances, which include prominent local bands most evenings and renowned jam sessions on Wednesday nights. Northwest of Lafayette and southwest of Opelousas, the little hamlet of Church Point, 15 miles southwest of Opelousas, is home to **Le Vieux Moulin** (the Old Mill) (402 Canal St., 337/684-1200), which has live music on Saturday mornings and sells handmade Cajun instruments. West of Opelousas in tiny Lawtell, the **Offshore Lounge** (227 Perry Dr., 337/543-7180) presents zydeco bands on weekend evenings. Another great club in Lawtell is **Richard's** (11178 U.S. 190, 337/948-8646), which has been dubbed the "Grand Ole Opry of Zydeco" by devotees; it's been around since the early 1950s.

In Lake Charles, **Lloyd's Lounge** (4101 U.S. 90 E, 337/436-9160) is a lively place to listen to live Cajun bands.

> *All through the U.S. 190 corridor and the towns north and south of this stretch, you can find bars and clubs playing rollicking, bone-shaking music, from swamp pop to traditional Cajun to zydeco. In the Cajun Prairie, people play music because they love to, not with the expectation that they'll get rich.*

FESTIVALS AND EVENTS
Spring and Summer

In Opelousas, **Main Street Revived** is an evening R&B concert held at the corner of Bellevue and Main on Friday nights from late March through late May. Up in Ville Platte, get your taste buds geared up in late June for the **Festival de la Viande**

Boucanée (Smoked Meat Festival) (337/363-6700), which includes military demonstrations, a jet fly-by, an arts and crafts show, and the World Championship Smoked Meat Cook-off.

In Lake Charles in mid-July, music lovers attend the **Cajun French Music Association Annual Food/Music Festival** (800/456-7952), a two-day event held at the Burton Coliseum that showcases plenty of great Cajun music plus great food, from boudin balls to cracklins.

Fall and Winter

Rayne holds the not-to-be-missed **Frog Festival** (337/334-2332, www.rayne.org/chamber.html) each September, which features live Cajun bands, rides, an accordion contest, and frog racing and jumping. Labor Day weekend in Opelousas is the time for the **Southwest Louisiana Zydeco Music Festival** (337/942-2392, www.zydeco.org), three days of great concerts, plus foods and arts and crafts.

Music lovers should not miss the **Eunice Folklife Festival** (337/457-7389, www.eunice-la.com) in late October, which includes two long days of great Cajun, zydeco, country-western, bluegrass, and gospel acts. Also in mid- to late October, you can wander over to Crowley for the **International Rice Festival** (337/788-4100, www.crowley-la.com) or to Opelousas for the **Annual Louisiana Yambilee Festival** (337/948-8848, www.cajuntravel.com), a country fair with rides, music, a parade, and pageants.

Mid-November in Port Barre, about 10 miles east of Opelousas on U.S. 190, you can attend the **Cracklin Festival** (877/948-8004, www.cajuntravel.com), which features a cracklin cook-off, music, rides, and more food.

In March, African-American culture is celebrated at the **Black Heritage Festival** (337/777-9311, www.bhflc.com), at the Lake Charles Civic Center. Featured are impressive gospel concerts, heritage displays, and conferences and gatherings.

Mardi Gras

Courir de Mardi Gras is a style of Mardi Gras celebration that's particular to some of the more rural towns in the parish, such as Eunice, and it's also celebrated at the Vermilionville living history museum in Lafayette. During this Mardi Gras Run, participants set out through a town on horseback, in wagons, and even in pickup trucks on a mad dash to obtain ingredients for a massive pot of gumbo. Probably the most famous and fun version of Courir de Mardi Gras is the one held in Church Point, a small town about 25 miles northwest of Lafayette. For details on this event, call 337/684-2739 or visit www.church-pointcourirdemardigras.com.

INFORMATION AND SERVICES
Visitor Information

For information on the towns of Opelousas, Eunice, Grand Coteau, and Washington, contact the **St. Landry Parish Tourist Commission** (Box 1415, Opelousas, 70571, 877/948-8004, www.cajuntravel.com). Pick up information on Lake Charles and surrounding towns at the **Southwest Louisiana Convention and Visitors Bureau** (1205 N. Lakeshore Dr., 337/436-9588 or 800/456-SWLA, www.visitlakecharles.org).

Getting Around

The entire region is best explored by car. I-10, which leads from Lafayette to Lake Charles, is a wide interstate highway with a 70 mph speed limit, as is I-49, which leads north from Lafayette to Opelousas. U.S. 190 is a slower road, especially where it passes through the downtowns of Eunice, Basile, and several other towns in the area, but it offers a more scenic view of the region.

See the *On the Road* chapter for details on reaching New Orleans, Lafayette, and Lake Charles from other parts of the country by train, plane, and bus.

Resources

Suggested Reading

As many books have been written about New Orleans and the Cajun Country as just about any part of the country, but there are several, both fiction and nonfiction, that can especially enhance your trip to the region. Most of those listed below focus exclusively on New Orleans, but you'll also find several that cover other parts of southern Louisiana.

You may recognize the "Images of America" series, by **Arcadia Publishing** (888/313-BOOK, www.arcadiapublishing.com), from the trademark sepia covers of its hundreds of small soft-cover historic-photo essays on more than 1,000 communities across the country. These fascinating books are produced by a small firm in Charleston, South Carolina, and each title typically contains from 200 to 250 early black-and-white photos of a particular region, along with running commentary that is usually authored by a local historian, librarian, or archivist. The books cost from $15–25, and presently there are 22 titles on Louisiana, three of them dealing specifically with New Orleans.

Description and Travel

Douglas, Lake, and Jeannette Hardy. *Gardens of New Orleans: Exquisite Excess.* Chronicle Books, 2001. A companion photo book to *New Orleans: Elegance and Decadence,,* this elegant tome takes readers into the many secrete and sensuous gardens of the Big Easy.

Fry, Macon, and Julie Posner. *Cajun Country Guide.* Pelican Publishing Co., 1998. An in-depth tour guide on the Cajun Country, with extensive anecdotes and histories on just about every town in the region, large or small.

Sexton, Richard, and Randolph Delehanty. *New Orleans: Elegance and Decadence.* Chronicle Books, 1993. A handsome photo essay that distills the essence of New Orleans's architecture, art, landscape, and culture.

Sternberg, Mary Ann. *Along the River Road.* Louisiana State University Press, 2001. An excellent and amazingly thorough history and description, mile by mile, of the towns and plantation homes strung along the Great River Road.

Sullivan, Lester. *New Orleans Then and Now.* Thunder Bay Press, 2003. This photography collection takes vintage black-and-white photos of city landmarks and streets and contrasts them with contemporary shots of the same scenes. The book offers a wonderful look at how the city has changed, and more important, how in so many places it hasn't.

Workers of the Federal Writers' Project of the Works Progress Administration for the city of New Orleans. *New Orleans City Guide.* Riverside Press Cambridge, 1938 (out of print). Arguably the best treatment of the city ever written is this dense and fascinating work compiled by the Works Progress Administration (WPA) Workers of the Federal Writers' Project. Part of the amazingly well-executed and thoroughly researched American Guide Series, the book is long since out of print (many titles within this series have been picked up in recent years and reprinted, but not yet New Orleans, alas). Your best hope of finding a copy of this wonderful tome is by scouring the racks of used bookstores or websites such as eBay. Depending on its condition and age (and whether it has its original cover and map), this guide should sell for anywhere from $10 to $40. Or try your local library.

Workers of the Federal Writers' Project of the Works Progress Administration for the state of Louisiana. *Louisiana State Guide.* Hastings House, 1941 (out of print). The same idea as the aforementioned New Orleans city guide, this 746-page book has complete and in-depth coverage of the entire state. Used copies usually sell for between $25 and $75.

An additional work on Louisiana sponsored by the WPA in 1945, and written by one of the state's most talented and colorful writers, Lyle Saxon, is *Gumbo Ya-Ya: A Collection of Louisiana Folk Tales*. First editions of this title can be found used for anywhere from $25 to $75, or you can buy a relatively recent printing of this title at many bookstores. The edition currently in print was reissued by Pelican Publishing Co. in 1987.

Maps and Orientation

There are a number of decent folding maps of New Orleans, Baton Rouge, Lafayette, and Louisiana. The **Louisiana Office of Tourism** (1051 N. 3rd St., Room 327, Baton Rouge, LA 70802, 225/346-1857 or 888/225-4003, www.louisianatravel.com) can send you a very good general state map.

DeLorme. *Louisiana Atlas and Gazetteer.* DeLorme Publishing, 2001. DeLorme publishes a state atlas that's part of its Gazetteer series. While this series shows much greater detail than your run-of-the-mill atlas, it's not very trustworthy as a serious navigational aid. A disturbing number of errors appear on these pages—in particular, the DeLorme atlas has a tendency to show dirt roads and even trails as primary paved thoroughfares, creating the potential for all sorts of frustrating wild goose chases.

Microsoft. *Microsoft Streets and Trips.* Microsoft, 2003. A very useful digital tool, Microsoft Expedia Streets covers the entire United States (and Canada). With this disc, you can type in virtually any street address in Louisiana (or any other state, for that matter) and instantly have it pinpointed on a full-color detailed map on your computer screen.

Rand McNally. *Rand McNally StreetFinder: New Orleans and Vicinity.* Rand McNally &

Co., 2003. Very precise maps on the city are published by Rand McNally. The easy-to-read and well-labeled *Rand McNally StreetFinder: New Orleans* is an excellent atlas with great detail, including city coverage. Rand McNally produces a similar atlas on Baton Rouge, and fold-out maps on New Orleans, Baton Rouge, Lafayette, Lake Charles, Houma/Thibodaux/Morgan City, and the entire state.

Shearer. *The Roads of Louisiana.* Shearer Publishing, 1998. Similar in scale to the DeLorme atlas described above, and quite reliable.

Biography and History

Asbury, Herbert. *The French Quarter: An Informal History of the New Orleans Underworld.* Thunder's Mouth Press, 2003. An unconventional look at the city's seamy side, Asbury's colorful account looks at the city's infamous red-light districts, illegal gaming, and other not-so-legitimate activities.

Benfey, Christopher E. G. *Degas in New Orleans: Encounters in the Creole World of Kate Chopin and George Washington Cable.* Benfey uses the brief visit by Degas to New Orleans in the early 1870s to examine the city and its Creole society during the late 19th century.

Cable, George Washington. *Old Creole Days: A Story of Creole Life.* Pelican Publishing Co., 1991 (reprint). Victorian novelist and essayist Cable captures life in old Creole New Orleans during the 19th century. Cable wrote many other popular books about the city.

Campanella, Richard. *Time and Place in New Orleans: Past Geographies in the Present Day.* Pelican Publishing Co., 2002. An eye-opening study of the unlikely establishment of New Orleans in the middle of a malaria-ridden swamp—it's filled with historic and contemporary maps and photos that trace the evolution of New Orleans.

Cowan, Walter, and John C. Chase, Charles L. Dufour, O. K. LeBlanc, John Wilds. *New Orleans Yesterday and Today: A Guide to the City.* Louisiana State University Press, 2001. A wonderful collection of historical essays that trace the city's history by offering concise glimpses into areas such as food, music, and race. Several of the same authors penned a broader history on the state, *Louisiana Yesterday and Today: A Guide to the State,* which was published in 1996 by Louisiana State University Press.

Garvey, Joan B. *Beautiful Crescent: A History of New Orleans.* Garmer Press, 1997. A nice and comprehensive general overview of the city, from its geology to its people.

Williams, Harry T. *Huey Long.* Random House, 1981. A superb and gripping biography of the "Kingfish," the man who shaped Louisiana politics for many years after his death.

Johnson, Walter. *Soul by Soul: Life Inside the Antebellum Slave Market.* Harvard University Press, 2001. This is a gripping and raw account of North America's largest and most notorious slave market, which was centered right in New Orleans. Narratives, court records, bills of sale, and other documents are used to trace harrowing legacy of slavery.

Remini, Robert Vincent. *The Battle of New Orleans: Andrew Jackson and America's First Military Victory.* Penguin USA, 2001. Remini examines the great battle that secured a young America's victory against the British during the War of 1812.

Special Interest

Florence, Robert. *New Orleans Cemeteries: Life in the Cities of the Dead.* Batture Press, 1997. An insider's history and tour of the city's famous above-ground cemeteries.

Huber, Leonard V. *Mardi Gras: A Pictorial History of Carnival in New Orleans.* Pelican Publishing Co., 1989. A nice overview of the history of the city's most famous celebration.

Tallant, Robert. *Voodoo in New Orleans.* Pelican Publishing Co., 1983 (reprint). A classic compendium and history about one of New Orleans's most fascinating topics. Tallant is also author of the similarly informative *Voodoo Queen.*

Music

Armstrong, Louis. *Satchmo: My Life in New Orleans.* DaCapo Press, 1986. The definitive autobiography by the definitive New Orleans jazz icon.

Berry, Jason. *Up from the Cradle of Jazz: New Orleans Music Since World War II.* DaCapo Press, 1992. A terrific survey tracing the history of music in the Big Easy.

Lomax, Alan. *Mister Jelly Roll: The Fortunes of Jelly Roll Morton, New Orleans Creole and Inventor of Jazz.* University of California Press, 2001. This is a fascinating examination of not only one New Orleans jazz luminary, but the development of the city's music scene.

Ondaatje, Michael. *Coming Through Slaughter.* Vintage Books, 1996. A colorful tale of Buddy Bolden, one of the earliest New Orleans jazz greats. Ondaatje is most famous for *The English Patient.*

Food

Brennan, Dick, and Ella Brennan. *The Commander's Palace New Orleans Cookbook.* Crown Publishing, 1984. It's been around for a while, but this remains one of the seminal recipe collections for classic Creole cuisine, culled from one of the greatest restaurants in the world.

Guste, Roy F. *The 100 Greatest New Orleans Creole Recipes.* Pelican Publishing Co., 1994.

Guste may not be a household name like Emeril or Prudhomme, but his collection is uncompromisingly authentic and filled with colorful flavors.

Johnson, Pableax. *Lonely Planet World Food New Orleans.* Lonely Planet, 2000. A culinary take on traveling through New Orleans and the Cajun Country.

Lagasse, Emeril. *Emeril's TV Dinners.* William Morrow, 1998. Nouvelle Creole recipes from the schmaltzy celebrity chef's cooking shows.

Litwin, Sharon (editor). *Zagat 2003 New Orleans Nightlife.* Zagat Survey, 2003. The definitive round-up of New Orleans nightlife, complete with the sometimes witty, sometimes mean comments from hundreds of readers surveyed.

Prudhomme, Paul. *Chef Prudhomme's Louisiana Kitchen.* Morrow Cookbooks, 1984. A compendium of classic recipes by the New Orleans master of Cajun cooking.

Zagat. *Zagat 2002 New Orleans Restaurants.* Zagat Survey, 2002. Great reader tips and suggestions on where to eat in New Orleans and the metro area; an indispensable guide for food lovers in the Big Easy.

Memoir, Fiction, and Literature

Burke, James Lee. *Neon Rain: A Dave Robicheaux Novel.* This is one of the more popular books in a series of gripping crime stories featuring Dave Robicheaux, a New Orleans homicide cop. In later books Robicheaux has left New Orleans and lives in the Cajun Country town of New Iberia. The tourism offices and visitor centers around New Iberia and Lafayette distribute a free brochure, "James Lee Burke's Acadiana," which lists more than a dozen real places around New Iberia that figure prominently in the Dave Robicheaux novels.

Chopin, Kate. *The Awakening.* Dover Publications, 1993 Reissue. One of the great literary classics of the South, Chopin's 1899 novel about a woman who flouts New Orleans Creole society by leaving her husband and family and children caused a huge scandal. The circumstances may seem tame today, but this remains an emotionally powerful work.

Long, Judith. *Literary New Orleans.* Hill Street Press, 1999. A delightful anthology of works by some of the city's most notable authors, from Truman Capote to James Lee Burke to Sheila Bosworth to Zora Neal Hurston.

Percy, Walker. *The Moviegoer.* Vintage Books, 1998 Reissue. Percy, who died in 1990, was one of Louisiana's most talented writers, and this somewhat underrated existential story about a New Orleans stockbroker is one of his finest.

Rice, Anne. *Witching Hour.* Knopf, 1990. The Garden District's most famous resident, Anne Rice has written a number of tales of witchcraft and vampires set throughout New Orleans. This is one of her most mesmerizing works, but also look out for the four works that make up the *Vampire Chronicles: Interview with the Vampire, The Vampire Lestat, The Queen of the Damned,* and *The Tale of the Body Thief.*

Rice, Christopher. *A Density of Souls.* Miramax, 2000. Rice's auspicious debut novel depicts the lives of four high school students grappling with coming of age and sexual identity in New Orleans. Rice is the son of novelist Anne.

Smith, Julie. *New Orleans Mourning.* Ivy Books, 1991 (reissue). Part of a series of popular mystery books revolving around policeman Skip Langdon. Other engrossing books in the collection include *Mean Women Blues* and *Louisiana Bigshot.*

Toole, John Kennedy. *A Confederacy of Dunces.* Grove Press, 1987 (reissue). A critically acclaimed tragicomic novel published seven years after the suicide of its young author, this peculiar tale hosts an even stranger cast of Louisiana characters.

Tyree, Omar. *Leslie.* Simon & Schuster, 2002. Drugs, voodoo, and murder figure into this edgy story with compelling characters.

Warren, Robert Penn. *All the King's Men.* Harvest Books, 1996 (reissue). A thinly veiled fictional look at the controversial life of Huey Long, Warren's work goes beyond mere political rehashing to become a gripping and compelling study of one of 20th-century America's most controversial figures.

Williams, Tennessee. *A Streetcar Named Desire.* Signet, 1989 (reissue). The seminal Williams play set in New Orleans. Less famous but more directly about life in the French Quarter is *Vieux Carré,* which Williams wrote based on notes from journals he wrote while living in New Orleans.

Internet Resources

New Orleans has dozens of regional websites and several useful sites that are either statewide or focused on the southern portion of Louisiana. Furthermore, a number of national sites covering everything from transportation to the outdoors have specific web pages on just Louisiana.

Tourism and General Information

Citysearch
www.neworleans.citysearch.com
This internationally known site contains listings and limited editorial information on new restaurants, museum exhibitions, which movies are playing where, and where to find hotels. While the coverage is chiefly about New Orleans, you'll also find listings for the other towns and cities throughout the state. Unfortunately, outdated information appears routinely on this site.

Digital City
www.digitalcity.com/neworleans
The competing web company of Citysearch, Digital City has comparable coverage to New Orleans, and better coverage of other parts of the state. Both sites also include ratings by site users, which can be very useful and extremely entertaining.

New Orleans Magazine
www.neworleansmagazine.com
Very useful and well-produced monthly with excellent dining, arts, and events coverage.

The Official State of Louisiana Home Page
www.state.la.us
The official state website comes in handy when you're looking for detailed information on state and local politics, regional demographics, the state library, and local laws.

The Official State of Louisiana Tourism Home Page
www.louisianatravel.com
The mother of all Louisiana travel and tourism websites, with links to the state's dozens of regional tourism sites. Some of those that promote tourism in areas covered in this book include:

New Orleans
www.neworleanscvb.com

St. Tammany Parish Tourist & Convention Commission
www.neworleansnorthshore.com

Tangipahoa Parish Convention & Visitors Bureau
www.tangi-cvb.org

Baton Rouge Area Convention & Visitors Bureau
www.visitbatonrouge.com

St. James Parish Welcome Center
www.stjamesla.com

Houma Area Convention and Visitors Bureau
www.houmatourism.com

Lafayette Convention & Visitors Commission
www.lafayettetravel.com

Southwest Louisiana/Lake Charles Convention & Visitors Bureau
www.visitlakecharles.org

Within each site you'll find a trove of links to regional attractions, dining, lodging, events, transportation, and other valuable information.

New Orleans *Times-Picayune*
www.nola.com
This website produced by the state's most widely read paper ranks among the most comprehensive and informative online resources in Louisiana.

Transportation

Louis Armstrong New Orleans International Airport
www.flymsy.com

Find out about parking, airlines, check-in information, and arrivals and departures at the state's main airport.

Amtrak
www.amtrak.com

Home page for the national rail service with several stops in Louisiana.

Greyhound
www.greyhound.com

The nation's leading bus line makes a number of stops in Louisiana.

Louisiana Department of Transportation and Development
www.dotd.state.la.us

Site providing extensive information on traveler resources and road conditions, licenses and permits, upcoming roadwork and projects, and construction bid notices.

Louisiana Department of Transportation Ferryboat site
www.dotd.state.la.us/operations/ferry.shtml

Find out about rates and scheduling for the many ferries that cross the Mississippi River and several other bodies of water around the state.

Sporting and the Outdoors

Louisiana Department of Natural Resources
www.dnr.state.la.us

Among Louisiana's top internet resources for outdoors enthusiasts, the DNR home page provides information and policies pertaining to boating, hiking, hunting, fishing, beachgoing, and many other activities.

Louisiana Office of State Parks
www.crt.state.la.us/crt/parks

This site provides links to every property in the state park system. Also has information on primitive camping at state parks.

Louisiana chapter of the Nature Conservancy
http://nature.org/wherewework/northamerica/states/louisiana

Hikers might want to visit this site, which contains information about the Conservancy's Lousisana refuges and preserves.

Orleans Audubon Society
www.jjaudubon.net/ppdoas.htm

Great site for birding, with specifics on the society's New Orleans chapter.

Louisiana Golf Association
www.lgagolf.org

Here golfers can learn all about the state's many public courses.In

Index

M Index

Plantations

Acknowledgments

It would have been impossible to research and write this book without the assistance and support of several employees of Louisiana's travel and tourism industry. To the following individuals I'm ever grateful: Christine DeCuir and Beverly Gianna in New Orleans, Bruce Morgan and Jeff Richard (with the Louisiana Office of Tourism) in Baton Rouge, Donna O'Daniels in Covington, Betty Stewart in Hammond, Kelly Strenge in Lafayette, and Lisa Chmiola in Lake Charles.

I'd also like to thank several other friends in Louisiana who contributed recommendations, advice, and assistance, among them Cary Alden, Dolly Barrios, Vicky Bayley, Rob Boyd and Kevin Wu, Eddie Breaux, Shawn Broussard, Simone Rathle, and—the person who has most inspired me to travel regularly to Louisiana—Forrest H. "Woody" Bennett.

I'm very grateful to the staff at Avalon Travel Publishing, especially my very patient and thorough editor, Kevin McLain, and my insightful copy editor, Emily McManus.

And, finally, I'd to thank Michael Garcia for being unconditionally supportive during the many weeks I spent away in Louisiana researching this book, and back at home glued to my laptop writing it. To my furry research assistants, Mary and Mister Grant, I am also deeply indebted.

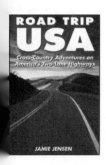

U.S.~Metric Conversion

1 inch	=	2.54 centimeters (cm)
1 foot	=	.304 meters (m)
1 yard	=	0.914 meters
1 mile	=	1.6093 kilometers (km)
1 km	=	.6214 miles
1 fathom	=	1.8288 m
1 chain	=	20.1168 m
1 furlong	=	201.168 m
1 acre	=	.4047 hectares
1 sq km	=	100 hectares
1 sq mile	=	2.59 square km
1 ounce	=	28.35 grams
1 pound	=	.4536 kilograms
1 short ton	=	.90718 metric ton
1 short ton	=	2000 pounds
1 long ton	=	1.016 metric tons
1 long ton	=	2240 pounds
1 metric ton	=	1000 kilograms
1 quart	=	.94635 liters
1 US gallon	=	3.7854 liters
1 Imperial gallon	=	4.5459 liters
1 nautical mile	=	1.852 km

To compute Celsius temperatures, subtract 32 from Fahrenheit and divide by 1.8. To go the other way, multiply Celsius by 1.8 and add 32.

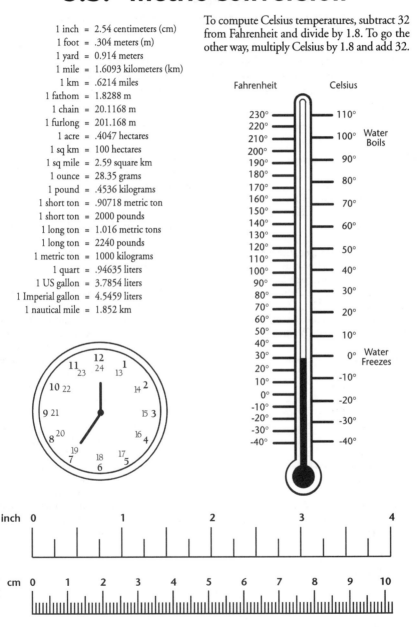

Keeping Current

Although we strive to produce the most up-to-date guidebook humanly possible, change is unavoidable. Between the time this book goes to print and the moment you read it, a handful of the businesses noted in these pages will undoubtedly change prices, move, or even close their doors forever. Other worthy attractions will open for the first time. If you have a favorite gem you'd like to see included in the next edition, or see anything that needs updating, clarification, or correction, please drop us a line. Send your comments via email to atpfeedback@avalonpub.com, or use the address below.

Moon Handbooks New Orleans

Avalon Travel Publishing
1400 65th Street, Suite 250
Emeryville, CA 94608, USA
www.moon.com

Editor and Series Manager: Kevin McLain
Copy Editor: Emily McManus
Graphics Coordinator: Susan Snyder
Production Coordinator: Darren Alessi
Cover Designer: Kari Gim
Interior Designers: Amber Pirker,
Alvaro Villanueva, Kelly Pendragon
Map Editor: Olivia Solís
Cartographers: Kat Kalamaras,
  Mike Morgenfeld
Indexer: Greg Jewett

ISBN: 1-56691-550-3
ISSN: 1546-4237

Printing History
1st Edition—April 2004
5 4 3 2 1

Text © 2004 by Andrew Collins.
Maps © 2004 by Avalon Travel Publishing, Inc.
All rights reserved.

Avalon Travel Publishing is a division of
Avalon Publishing Group, Inc.

Some photos and illustrations are used by permission and are the property of the original copyright owners.

Front cover photo: © John Elk III
Table of contents photos: © Andrew Collins

Printed in the United States by
Malloy Lithography